CONTENTS.

PART I.

THE EVOLUTION OF INTERNATIONAL COPYRIGHT.

CHAPTER I.

THE NATURE AND ORIGIN OF COPYRIGHT.

CHAPTER II.

INTERNATIONAL INFRINGEMENT.

CHAPTER III.

NATIONAL PROGRESS TOWARDS PROTECTION OF FOREIGN WORKS.

PART II.

THE THEORY OF INTERNATIONAL COPYRIGHT.

CHAPTER I.

THE POLITICAL ECONOMY OF COPYRIGHT.

CHAPTER II.

INTERNATIONAL PROTECTION BY MEANS OF TREATIES.

CHAPTER III.

PROSPECT OF A UNIVERSAL LAW OF COPYRIGHT.

CHAPTER IV.

ALIEN AUTHORS AND ALIEN LAWS.

PART III.

THE BERNE CONVENTION.

Acceded to by Great Britain under the International Copyright Act, 1886.
(With a Chapter on the Montevideo Convention.)

CHAPTER I.

THE INTERNATIONAL COPYRIGHT UNION.

CHAPTER II.

GENERAL PRINCIPLES OF THE BERNE CONVENTION.

CHAPTER III.

THE PROTECTION GIVEN BY THE BERNE CONVENTION.

CHAPTER IV.

WORKS PROTECTED BY THE BERNE CONVENTION.

CHAPTER V.

INFRINGEMENTS, REMEDIES, AND PROCEDURE UNDER THE BERNE CONVENTION.

CHAPTER VI.

THE REVISION OF THE BERNE CONVENTION.

CHAPTER VII.

THE MONTEVIDEO CONVENTION, 1889, AND OTHER AMERICAN CONVENTIONS.

PART IV.

INTERNATIONAL COPYRIGHT IN THE BRITISH DOMINIONS. COLONIAL COPYRIGHT.

CHAPTER I.

THE PROTECTION ACCORDED TO FOREIGN AUTHORS IN GREAT BRITAIN.

CHAPTER II.

COLONIAL COPYRIGHT.

PART V.

THE PROTECTION OF FOREIGN AUTHORS IN THE UNITED STATES.

APPENDIX.

SYNOPSES AND TABLES.

BIBLIOGRAPHY.

Acollas . . La Propriété Littéraire et Artistique. 1888.

Bar . . . . The Theory and Practice of Private International Law. (Translated by G. R. Gillespie.) 1892.

Burke . . . The Law of International Copyright between England and France. 1852.

Chamier . . Law Relating to Literary Copyright. 1895.

Cohen . . . The Law of Copyright. 1896.

Copinger . . The Law of Copyright in Works of Literature and Art. 1893.

Cutler, Smith, and Weatherly The Law of Musical and Dramatic Copyright. 1892.

Darras . . Du Droit des Auteurs et des Artistes dans les rapports internationaux. 1887.

Drone . . . The Law of Copyright in Intellectual Productions in Great Britain and the United States. Boston, 1879.

Godson . . Treatise on the Law of Patents and of Copyright, with a Supplement by Peter Burke. 1851.

Hall . . . International Law. 1895.

Hamlin . . Copyright Cases and Decisions. New York, 1904.

Holland . . The Elements of Jurisprudence. 1896.

Hotten . . . Literary Copyright. Seven Letters. 1871.

Jerrold . . A Handbook of English and Foreign Copyright. 1881.

Lancefield . . Notes on Copyright: Canadian Literary Bureau, Hamilton, Canada, 1896.

Lieber . . . Manual of Political Ethics. 1839.

Lowndes . . An Historical Sketch of the Law of Copyright, with Remarks on Serjeant Talfourd's Bill. 1840.

Lyon-Caen and Delalain Lois françaises et étrangères sur la Propriété Littéraire et Artistique. 2 vols. 1889. Supplement. 1896.

Macgillivray . The Law of Copyright. 1902.

Maugham . . The Laws of Literary Property. 1828.

Morgan . . The Law of Literature. 2 vols. New York, 1878.

Nicolau . . La Propriété Littéraire et Artistique au point de vue international. 1895.

Phillips . . The Law of Copyright. 1863.

Pouillet . . Traité théorique et pratique de la Propriété Littéraire et Artistique. 1894.

Pouillet . . Dictionnaire de la Propriété Industrielle, etc. 2 vols. 1887.

Purday . . Copyright. A Sketch of its Rise and Progress. 1877.

Putnam . . The Question of Copyright. New York, 1896.

Rattigan . . Private International Law. 1895.

Renouard . . Traité des Droits d'Auteurs. 2 vols. 1838.

Scrutton . . The Law of Copyright. 1903.

Shortt . . . The Law relating to Works of Literature and Art. 1884.

Talfourd . . Three Speeches in favour of a Measure for an Extension of Copyright. 1840.

Westlake . . A Treatise on Private International Law. 1890.

Westlake . . Chapters on the Principles of International Law. 1894.

Winslow . . The Law of Artistic Copyright. 1889.

Papers, Periodicals, etc.

English International Acts, 1838, 1844, 1852, 1875, and 1886.

English Colonial Acts, 1847, 1875.

British North America Act, 1867.

Customs Laws Consolidation Act, 1876.

Revenue Act, 1889.

Lord Monkswell's Copyright Bills (H.L.), 1897, 1899, 1900.

Lord Herschell's Copyright Bill (H.L.), 1898.

Le texte de la Convention de 1886, avec l'Acte Additionnel de 1896. Berne, Bureau International de l'Union.

Orders in Council bringing the above into effect.

Copy of Correspondence relating to a Convention between Great Britain and the United States. 1881.

Copy of Correspondence relating to a Copyright Conference at Paris (1896). 1897.

Copy of Correspondence on the subject of the Law of Copyright in Canada. 1895.

Papers, Periodicals, etc.—continued.

Report of the Royal Commission, 1878.

Report of the Select Committee (H.L.) on the Copyright Bill (H.L.), 1898.

Report of the Select Committee (H.L.) on the Copyright Bill (H.L.), 1899.

Report of the Select Committee (H.L.) on the Copyright Bill (H.L.), 1900.

Actes des Conférences à Berne, 1884, 1885, and 1886 (3 vols.). Berne, Bureau International de l'Union.

Actes de la Conférence de Paris, 1896. Berne, Bureau International de l'Union.

Le Droit d'Auteur, Organe Mensuel du Bureau International. Berne, Bureau International de l'Union, January 15, 1888 to May 15, 1905.

Comptes Rendus des Congrès Internationaux et Bulletins de l'Association Littéraire et Artistique Internationale.

The Law of Copyright in Germany. Longmans, 1902 (translation of Acts of June 19th, 1901).

Recueil des Conventions et Traités concernant la Propriété Littéraire et Artistique. Berne, Bureau International de l'Union, 1904.

Index to Le Droit d'Auteur (Tables générales des matières). Berne, Bureau International de l'Union, 1903.

Circular of the Department of Agriculture containing the Copyright Act, 1886. Ottawa, Canada.

U. S. Copyright Enactments, 1783-1900. Library of Congress Copyright Office, Bulletin No. 3.

U. S. Act approved March 3rd, 1905. Library of Congress Copyright Office, Information Circular No. 33.

TABLE OF CASES CITED.

The initials D.A. are used throughout this table to indicate that a report of the case in question is given in *Le Droit d'Auteur*, the official organ of the International Union.

xix

PART I.

THE EVOLUTION OF INTERNATIONAL COPYRIGHT.

CHAPTER I.

THE NATURE AND ORIGIN OF COPYRIGHT.

§ 1. The Author's Moral Right in his Work.
§ 2. The Creation of Property.
§ 3. Property Features of Copyright.
§ 4. Evolution of the Legal Right.

CHAPTER II.

INTERNATIONAL INFRINGEMENT.

§ 1. Copyright as a National Right.
§ 2. The Ethics of Unauthorised Reprinting of Foreign Works.
§ 3. Former Importance of the Trade in Foreign Reprints.
§ 4. Early Piracy of English Works.
§ 5. Early Piracy of French Works.
§ 6. Early Piracy of German Works.

CHAPTER III.

NATIONAL PROGRESS TOWARDS PROTECTION OF FOREIGN WORKS.

§ 1. Progress in Great Britain.   § 2. Progress in France.
§ 3. Progress in Germany, Austria, and Hungary.
§ 4. Progress in Italy.   § 5. Progress in Spain.
§ 6. Progress in Belgium.   § 7. Progress in Switzerland.
§ 8. Progress in various other Countries.

CHAPTER I.

THE NATURE AND ORIGIN
OF
COPYRIGHT.

SECTION I.

THE AUTHOR'S MORAL RIGHT IN HIS WORK.

Distinction between moral and legal right—Might and right—Elements included in the author's right—Legal right—Relation of legal and moral rights.

Distinction between Moral and Legal Right.—Of the *legal* right of an author over his production there is now no doubt in civilised countries. But his *moral* or ethical right, which is hall-marked as a right by its development into a *legal* right, has given rise to much learned discussion. A study of the old opinions is mainly of antiquarian interest; nevertheless such a study frequently throws light upon the cases which form our precedents at the present time, and assists in the decision of the new problems which so frequently arise in this subject, where decided cases cover only a small portion of the possible field.

A good deal of confusion arose, and still arises, in matters of jurisprudence—the science and philosophy of law—on account of the equivocal nature of the terms used. Great thinkers frequently differ on a question because the terms employed convey different meanings to their minds, when, as a matter of fact, their mental views are substantially the same. For this reason, the relation of the terms 'right,' 'moral right,'[1] and 'legal right,' should be clearly distinguished and defined.

At the present time the question: *Has the author a right to copyright?*[2] would be, if the word 'right' were used in a strict legal sense, on a par with the question, *Is coined gold money?* But the problem *whether the author has a moral right in his production* calls for an examination into the relations between an author's right in his work and a moral right, the latter term being a genus of which the former claims to be a species.

Might and Right.—Without dwelling at length on the so-called 'rights' of primitive times, it is easy to conceive that each man's *might*, the power of his arm, would avail to prevent others from using or abusing his property and to make others render him any particular service which that might could enforce, without regard to the approval or reprobation of his neighbours. Indeed the researches of historical jurists have discovered a state of society when might was synonymous with right.

---

[1] This term 'moral right' is used throughout this book in preference to 'natural right.' For 'natural right' is often employed not only in the sense of 'moral right,' but with at least two other important meanings. In one of these it is synonymous with 'might,' and in the other it denotes those original or innate rights and capacities on which a man enters when he is born. Such primordial rights are 'the right to his life, his body, not to be capriciously or maliciously touched, pushed or struck, and the right to personal freedom.' Plainly copyright has nothing in common with these; for no man is an author at the time of his birth.

[2] According to the English Act of 1842 copyright is 'the sole and exclusive liberty of printing or otherwise multiplying copies.'

Definition of a Right.—Yet even in those early times of 'might' most of the fundamental elements included in the conception of 'right' were to be found, to wit:—

  (i) The person entitled.

 (ii) The person obligated.

(iii) The object claimed, which becomes the *subject* of the right.

(iv) The act or forbearance with regard to the object.

But the essential difference between might and right lies in the power which enforces the right, for now the force of *public opinion* or of the *law* takes the place of the strong arm of primitive times.

Keeping in view the fact that it must reside in some definite person or persons, a right may now be defined as that which commands

  (i) The approval or at least the acquiescence of public opinion with regard to its exercise;

 (ii) The reprobation of public opinion against the conduct of another in preventing its exercise.[1]

Elements included in the Author's Right.—If the right be over some thing, the thing, which is the *subject* of the right, must itself be considered. Examining the author's relation to his production with the view of finding there the series of elements comprehended in a 'right,' it is easy to discover the person entitled, an act and forbearance claimed, and the person (in this case the public) bound. To complete the

---

[1] Professor Holland's definition is: 'When a man is said to have a right to do anything, or over anything, or to be treated in a particular manner, public opinion would see him do the act, or make use of the thing, or be treated in that particular way, with approbation, or at least with acquiescence; but would reprobate the conduct of any one who should prevent him from doing the act, or making use of the thing, or should fail to treat him in that particular way.'— Holland, *Elements of Jurisprudence*, 8th Edition, p. 71.

series, it remains to show that the work of an author generally is a fitting subject of a right, that is, such that public opinion would see him make use of his production with approbation and would reprobate the conduct of any one who should prevent him making use of it.   This brings us to the distinction between 'moral right' and 'legal right.'

Legal Right.—A 'legal right' is defined as a capacity residing in one man of controlling, with the assent and assistance of the State, the actions of others.[1]   That which gives validity to a legal right in every case is the force which is lent to it by the State.

It will be seen that 'moral right' takes a middle position between 'might' and 'legal right';[2] for as the definition of a moral 'right' can be built up from the terms embraced in the definition of 'might' by substituting the wider term 'force of society' for the term 'brute force,' so it can be deduced from the definition of 'legal right' by substituting the indefinite 'force of society' for the more definite 'force of the State.'

The Relation of Legal and Moral Right.—Law exists for the creation, definition, and protection of *legal* rights.   The moral right of the author is therefore clearly outside the domain of the Law of Copyright, which gives him the sole and exclusive liberty of multiplying copies, and includes also the protection of this right.   But in the creation of legal

---

[1] Holland, *Elements of Jurisprudence*, p. 72.

[2] In addition to its use in the 'right of might,' 'natural right,' 'moral right,' and 'legal right,' the term 'right' is often employed to denote that which is just.   This meaning, as contrasted with 'legal right,' is well illustrated by Austin. 'If, for example, I owe you £100, you have a "right" to the payment of the money ; the right importing an obligation to pay the money which is incumbent upon me.   Now, in case I make the payment to which you have "a right," I do that which is "right" or just, or I do that which consists with "right" or justice.'—Austin, *Jurisprudence*, p. 285.

rights, the law looks mainly to the subjects of moral rights.[1] The recognition therefore of a moral right over a thing is a great step towards the attainment of a legal right.

It is therefore necessary to enquire whether the author has such a right over his production that public opinion will see him use and enjoy it with approval, and regard any disturbance of this use with disapproval; and if this right exists to ask what is its nature.

To answer these questions is the object of the next chapters, in which it will be shown that copyright is a right, and that this right is a right of property. The traditional methods of acquisition as well as the features and attributes of property will be surveyed, and the degree to which the author's production and his right over it correspond with these will be measured.

---

[1] Legal rights are normally developments of corresponding moral rights, but in particular cases the two may be opposed; *e.g.* the eviction of a sick tenant for non-payment of rent.

SECTION II.

THE CREATION OF PROPERTY.

Property in its strict sense a right, not a thing—Acquisition by Preoccupancy—Labour as a title to property—The Public Domain of intellectual works—Locke on labour as a title to property—Copyright based on labour—Copyright a tenure by creation—Foreign opinions on the nature of Copyright.

Property in its strict sense a Right, not a Thing.— Property strictly speaking is a *right*, not a *thing ;* or as it has been put, ' Property is a metaphysical thing.' It is often convenient, however, to use the word for the thing over which the right can be exercised, *e.g.* a house, a horse, a tool; but in so doing it should always be remembered that it is the *right* over the thing which is the property ; the thing without the right is useless.

In everyday life property is, for the most part, derivatively acquired, by sale, gift, bequest, or other act of party, or judgment or other operation of law. But it may also be originally acquired ; indeed, original acquisition must perforce have taken place before ever it became derivative property.

Acquisition by Preoccupancy.—According to what Maine calls 'the popular theory of the origin of property,' the original method of acquiring property, whether in lands or in movables, was that of preoccupancy—first occupancy— which the Romans designated *occupatio.* For this the term ' occupancy ' has been used as the English equivalent by Blackstone and others ;[1] but to avoid ambiguity ' preoccupancy ' seems preferable to make it clear that the acquirement in question is original and not derivative.

---

[1] According to Blackstone the claim of an author to property in his work is reducible to preoccupancy, a new thing having been created by labour and skill.

'Preoccupancy' may be defined as taking and retaining as one's own what previously belonged to no one, i.e. *res nullius.* Such things are potentially *res omnium*—the property of everybody—and become the property of an individual by *occupatio.* Labour spent on the property strengthens and confirms the right ; indeed without labour preoccupancy gives but a comparatively barren title at all times.

In primitive communities the value of movable property was not great ; the bare necessaries of life, food and shelter, and the implements required for obtaining these, sufficed while the land was held in common. Later, when the land was allowed to pass from father to son,[1] it became a property compared with which personal effects, though vastly increased in variety and quality, were relatively of small value ; and up to comparatively modern times land continued to be the most important kind of property.

Labour as a Title to Property.—The bare preoccupancy of land necessitates no labour beyond the coming on it, and even that might be merely 'for rest and shade' ; but in order to turn the occupancy to account, and to take the profits of the land, its crops and fruits, labour is essential. So too with the preoccupancy of animals *ferae naturae ;*[2] although its essence lies in the *first taking* rather than in the labour attendant on it, the latter also is plainly essential.

The domain of Nature still offers certain kinds of property to those who fulfil the necessary conditions. Even to-day fishing, hunting, and other time-honoured means of preoccupancy will enable property to be gained in animals *ferae naturae,*

---

[1] Under the feudal system the land was originally given by the lord as a reward in consideration of services, and generally devolved to the son with the same retainer of services as the consideration for his tenure. Alienation of land was for a long time not allowed ; it invariably passed to the heir or reverted to the lord.

[2] Wild animals and birds, and fish in the open sea.

which with certain reservations, made by municipal law, are in the common stock—*res omnium*—and are potential property. Land, however, is now seldom acquired by preoccupancy. The process has long ago exhausted the most desirable, for land cannot be multiplied like beasts and fowl; still, new districts are from time to time opened out, and in them not only is the labour attendant on preoccupancy required, but also it is generally made a condition of property that additional labour be spent upon the land which is the subject of a grant.[1]

The Public Domain of Intellectual Works.—At the present time perhaps the most fruitful source of property is not the domain of nature, but incorporeal ideas, on which the intellect may be exercised in much the same way as manual labour is expended in the occupation of corporeal *res nullius*. A vast accumulation of ideas, the product of centuries, has through the medium of books become the common property of mankind;[2] and these free ideas are said to be in 'the public domain,' a sort of common field which anyone may use at will. From this public domain it is open to anyone to appropriate what he likes; and by turning the old ideas over in his mind and reproducing them in an original form the appropriator is able to acquire property—grounded on labour—in his new work. Such takings do not exhaust the public domain, for the same ideas may be recast and developed in a million different ways. It will be seen too that even with the most modern kinds of property labour is an integral part of the process by which a right based on preoccupancy is required.

---

[1] The Dominion Laws of Canada, following the regulations generally adopted in mining centres, require in the Klondyke district not only that a claim for which a title is granted should be staked out personally by the claimant, but that a certain amount of work should be expended upon it in each year.

[2] A copyright work may become common property either by the expiration of the statutory term of copyright or, which rarely happens, by the abandonment of the copyright on the part of the author while some part of the statutory term has yet to run.

Indeed subjects such as inventions and copyrights, which are the results of intellectual labour, need much more for their acquisition than the mere physical taking which sufficed for the bare necessities of primitive times, and have in consequence a higher claim to be treated as property.

Locke on Labour as a Title to Property.—John Locke, the champion of labour, wrote in 1689 his famous work on *Civil Government*, which contains an able essay on property. He claims for labour a place in the acquisition of property far superior to that of preoccupancy pure and simple. He regards the first-coming to a subject of property as an essential of its acquirement, but he considers the labour spent upon it as that which really annexes it or brings it into being as property.[1]

Another argument upon which Locke lays much stress is that when followed by labour appropriation from the common stock not only does not impoverish it, but actually adds to it. It has already been pointed out that, at one time, land bore a far higher value than all other kinds of property. Locke holds that it is labour which has altered this state of things.[2]

---

[1] 'The labour of his body and the work of his hands we may say are properly his. Whatsoever, then, he removes out of the state that Nature hath provided and left it in, he hath mixed his labour with, and joined to it something that is his own, and thereby makes it his property. It being by him removed from the common state Nature hath placed it in, it hath by this labour something annexed to it that excludes the common right of other men. For this labour, being the unquestionable property of the labourer, no man but he can have a right to what that is once joined to, at least where there is enough and as good left in common for others.'—*Civil Government*, § 27.

[2] 'For it is labour, indeed, that puts the difference of value on everything . . . I think it will be but a very modest computation to say that of the products of the earth useful to the life of man nine-tenths are the effects of labour; nay, if we will rightly estimate things as they come to our use, and cast up the several expenses about them,—what in them is purely owing to Nature, and what to labour,—we shall find that in most of them ninety-nine hundredths are wholly to be put on the account of labour.'

'For whatever bread is more worth than acorns, wine than water, and cloth or

Copyright based on Labour.—Copyright is considered by Blackstone as a species of property grounded on labour and invention, and more directly reducible to the head of occupancy—*i.e.* preoccupancy—than any other. Blackstone thus approves Locke's view that the right of occupancy depends mainly upon the personal labour of the occupant. 'When a man,' says the learned commentator, 'by the exertion of his rational powers, has produced an original work, he seems to have clearly a right to dispose of that identical work as he pleases.'[1]

To this may well be added the opinion of Francis Lieber, in his *Political Ethics :*—'Because there was no copyright in early times,—because there were no books, or books did not yield any profit to make copyright worth anything,—it is believed by many to this day that copyright is an invented thing, and held as a grant bestowed by the mere grace and pleasure of society ; while, on the contrary, the right of copyright in a book seems to be clearer and more easily deduced from absolute principle than any other. It is the title of actual production and of preoccupancy. If a canoe is mine because I made it, shall not that be mine which I actually created, a composition ? '

Copyright a Tenure by Creation.—But there are many who put the claim of a work created by an author through intellectual labour on even a higher plane than Locke placed that of property gained by manual labour. Thus Benjamin

silk than leaves, skins, or moss, that is wholly owing to labour and industry : the one of these being the food and raiment which unassisted Nature furnishes us with ; the other, provisions which our industry and pains prepare for us ; which how much they exceed the other in value when anyone hath computed, he will then see how much labour makes the far greatest part of the value of things we enjoy in this world.'—*Civil Government*, §§ 40, 42.

[1] Kerr's *Blackstone*, II., p. 359.

Disraeli, addressing the House of Commons in April 1838, on behalf of Talfourd's Copyright Bill, said :—

' The tenure by which they—works requiring great learning, great industry, great labour, great capital in their preparation—are held is, in my opinion, superior to that of all other property : for it is original.   It is tenure which does not exist in a doubtful title, which does not spring from any adventitious circumstances.   It is not found ; it is not purchased ; it is not prescriptive.   It is original.   So it is the most natural of all titles, because it is the most simple and least artificial.   It is paramount and sovereign, because it is a tenure by creation.'

In *Jefferys v. Boosey*, 1854, Justice Erle expressed himself as follows :—

' The origin of the property is in production.   As to works of imagination and reasoning, if not of memory, the author may be said to create ; and in all departments of mind new books are the product of the labour, skill, and capital of the author.'

Foreign Opinions on the Nature of Copyright.—Nor is this view confined to English jurists ; it is shared by other nations, including the French, who have set a pattern to the world in liberal recognition of the rights of authors generally, and the Americans, who still maintain a narrow-minded disregard of the rights of foreign authors.   Justice Thompson, an eminent American judge, held in the great case of *Wheaton v. Peters*, that ' the great principle on which the author's right rests is that it is the fruit or production of his labour, and that labour by the faculties of the mind may establish a right of property as well as by the faculties of the body. . . . Every principle of justice, equity, morality, fitness, and sound policy concurs in protecting the literary labours of men to the same extent that property acquired by manual labour is protected.'

The French opinion, which is well represented by Pouillet and Darras, the leading writers in France on the rights of authors, may be summarised thus :—

The author's right is not established by any title deed ; it comes into existence *pari passu* with the work.

From its origin *labour*, the production of the author, being the result of creation, has even a more undeniable right to be considered property than that which was not formed by its owner ; and this creative origin more than answers any old objections that copyright does not fall in with the formulated ideas of what constitutes property.

The sound theory which assigns the origin of property to work gives a truer right than mere possession. The author's claim to copyright is based on labour first hand.

'The author of a book,' said Marion before the Parliament of Paris in 1586, 'is absolute owner of it, and as such can deal with it freely.' 'He creates,' ran d'Héricourt's Petition in 1725, 'therefore his creation belongs to him, to enjoy and to do with as he pleases.'

Copyright protection is the just price of the author's labour. This opinion was expressed by Louis XVI. of France in a letter of 6th September, 1776, written with reference to the decrees of 1777 :—'I have discussed this question,' he says, 'with many literary men ; and it appears to me that it is one about which learned men feel keenly. It concerns a very large number of my subjects who are in all respects worthy of my protection. The exclusive privilege of printing books, as we have recognised, is a concession founded on justice. For an author it is the price of his labour ; for a publisher it is a guarantee for the capital laid out.'

SECTION III.

PROPERTY FEATURES OF COPYRIGHT.

Attributes of property—Possession and detention—Development of property in England—Tangibility is not now essential—Distinguishability and value—Definitions alter with progress—The buyer's right—Copyright as a reward—The author's work and the public benefit—To what class of rights does copyright belong.

Attributes of Property.—We have examined some of the modes of acquisition of property ; but to establish our position completely we must prove that copyright possesses the necessary features of a subject of property, as without these it is incapable of ownership.   On examining the various modes of property and the claims of its subjects it will be found that they possess certain fundamental attributes which must be considered as the essentials of 'property.'   We shall now show that these attributes are to be found in the author's production.

Possession and Detention.—'Possession is only incipient property,' says Gans.   Animals *ferae naturae* are no man's property till taken, and even then property in them depends upon their detention.   In the words of Von Savigny,[1] 'by the possession of a thing we always conceive the condition in which not only one's own dealing with a thing is physically possible, but every other person's dealing with it is excluded. . . . This condition is called detention.'   The most elementary method of detention is to enclose, to imprison, or in some way to 'fasten on.'   In course of time however, in addition to actual enclosure, various modes of constructive detention were accepted as giving rise to property.

[1] Von Savigny's *Treatise on Possession*, translated by Sir Erskine Perry, 1848.

So that at length not only was the right of excluding others recognised when the subject of property was in the actual possession of the owner, but where distinguishing marks were put upon it possession was allowed to be constructively retained ; *e.g.* in the case of animals which, if earmarked, could be let loose without falling back into the common domain. And, later, where a manifest and reasonable intention to preserve possession was shown, constructive possession was admitted on account of the *intentio possidendi* even where contact was interrupted and there were no marks denoting proprietorship, as in the case of the hawk in falconry, or of doves and bees flying about the dove-cote and hive.

Development of Property in England.—The phases of the development of the idea of property are well illustrated by the history of the early acquisition of land in England. At first actual presence on the land, the *treading* of it, was absolutely necessary for its acquisition, just as personal contact was necessary for original possession by preoccupancy. Perception by the sense of sight from a tower or hill which might be miles away next took the place of the actual presence on the land. Then the intention to possess coupled with the ability to do so gave to anyone who came sufficiently near just as much power over it as if he had made actual entry. Eventually the view was accepted that 'prehension may be done by attorney with the same force as if done by one's self'; and at the present day no physical delivery whatever is requisite for the transfer of property in land.

Tangibility is not now essential.—In every mode of original acquirement of property already mentioned it will be seen that there is one important factor essential, *i.e.* the primary physical act known as prehension. The grasping of abstract conceptions was difficult in uneducated times, and according to old ideas immediate bodily contact, the treading by the feet with respect to land, and the 'taking in the hand with respect to movables,' was essential to the acquisition of possession. Tangibility, which appeals to the lowest of the animal senses, was at one time a necessary attribute of every subject of property ; everything with embodiment or substance, on which distinguishing proprietary marks could be placed to show its ownership when not in actual possession, was regarded as fit for property, while all that was not plainly 'palpable to sense or feeling' was denied that character. Thus no property could be gained in any merely abstract thing. But in time the strict requirement of bodily contact as an essential condition of property was relaxed, first, with regard to the *factum* of possession, by allowing the possession of tangible objects to be gained without actual prehension where the ability to take up was indisputable, and, secondly, by the admission of valuable intangibles as subjects of property on the analogy of tangibles ; though for a long time such incorporeal property was closely connected with, indeed often appurtenant to, corporeal property.

In the year 1769 Justice Yates, in the famous case of *Millar v. Taylor*,[1] made the astounding statement that 'it is a well-known and established maxim (which, I apprehend, holds as true now as it did two thousand years ago) that nothing can be an object of property which has not a corporeal substance.' It is not, therefore, surprising that he refused to recognise copyright as a subject of property. All the old objections were brought forward by him : property, he maintained, must have a corporeal substance, it must be capable of occupancy, it must be tangible and bear distinguishing proprietary marks.

---

[1] *Millar v. Taylor*, 4 Burr. 2303.   In this great case the claim of the author to property in his literary works was for the first time exhaustively discussed. The case occupies over one hundred pages of Burrows's *Reports*.

'I have before observed,' said he, 'the dangerous snares which this *ideal property* will lay, as it carries *no proprietary marks* in itself, and is not bound down to any formal *stipulations*. So *obscure* a property (especially after the work has been a long while published) might lead many booksellers into many *litigations*.'

But, as Justice Aston said, 'Great men, ruminating back to the *origin* of things, lose sight of the *present* state of the world, and *end* their inquiries at that point where they should *begin our* improvements'; while, according to Lord Mansfield, 'the single opinion of such a man as Milton, speaking, after much consideration, upon the very point, is stronger than any inferences from gathering acorns and seizing a vacant piece of ground; when the writers, so far from thinking of the very point, speak of an imaginary state of nature before the invention of letters.'

The definitions of Justice Yates will be found, in the words of Justice Aston, 'principally to apply to the necessaries of life, and the grosser objects of dominion, which the immediate natural occasions of men called for: and for that reason, the property, so acquired by occupancy, was required to be an object useful to men, and capable of being fastened on.'

Distinguishability and Value.—Yet copyright is not utterly lacking in the *indicia certa* which the old rule required; true, the author's production has primarily no corporeal existence, but it is communicated by ink and paper, materials which are themselves tangible, while an intellectual production can be distinguished quite as well as property on which the old earmarks were placed.

'A distinguishable existence in the thing claimed as property, an actual value in that thing to the true owner, are its essentials. . . . For the capacity to fasten on, as a thing

C

of a corporeal nature, being a requisite in every object of property, plainly partakes of the narrow and confined sense in which property has been defined by authors in the original state of things. A capacity to be distinguished answers every end of reason and certainty; which is the great favourite of the law, and is all that wisdom requires to secure their possessions and profits to men, and to preserve the peace.'[1]

'The order of a man's words is as singular as his countenance,' said Justice Erle in *Jefferys v. Boosey*; and indisputably an author's work is as definite and permanent as many objects to which the right of property has not been denied.[2]

Definitions alter with Progress.—'Distinct properties,' says Puffendorf, 'were not settled at the same time nor by one single Act, but by successive degrees; nor in all places alike: but property was gradually introduced, according as either the condition of things, the number and genius of men required; or as it appeared requisite to the common peace.' The rules relating to property must keep pace with its increase and improvement. Where the advance of civilisation and the progress of science offer new material for the domain of property the scope of that term must be altered[3]

---

[1] Aston, J., in *Millar v. Taylor*, 4 Burr. 2303 at p. 2340.

[2] The poems of Homer, though not originally even written, were handed down in a recognisable form from generation to generation; while slaves and horses, undisputed subjects of property, disappeared by the law of mortality, and valuable vases and statues were always liable to destruction on account of their perishable nature.

[3] *E.g.* Previous to the exploration of Australia, it was considered that whiteness was a necessary attribute of all swans. No swans were known which were not white. But in the new country birds were discovered which possessed all the zoological requirements necessary for inclusion in the class of swans, but were nevertheless black. Since then the quality of whiteness has been excluded from the necessary characteristics of swans. The class has been enlarged to admit the newcomers.

accordingly. When subjects are discovered or created which are recognised as capable of ownership, and a legal and determinate owner can be assigned to them, any appeal to antiquated metaphysical definitions should be dismissed.

The Buyer's Right.—Even granting that the author's right of property in his work has been validly established, it is obvious that such a right would be of little use to its owner if by selling copies he was held to part with it. Hence it is necessary to consider whether the sale of a work in book form should be held to imply a surrender on the part of the author of his right to multiply copies.

According to Justice Yates in *Millar v. Taylor,* ' the act of publication when voluntarily done by the author himself is, virtually and necessarily, a gift to the public. For when an author throws his work into so public a state that it must immediately and unavoidably become common, it is the same as expressly giving it to the public. He knows before he publishes that this will be the necessary consequence of the publication; therefore he must be deemed to intend it. For whoever does an act of any kind whatever, designedly and knowingly, must of course intend every necessary consequence of that act. To this I might add that in every language the words which express the publication of a book express it as giving it to the public. . . . . Ideas are free ; but while the author confines them to his study they are like birds in a cage, which none but he can have a right to let fly ; for, till he thinks proper to emancipate them, they are under his own dominion.'

But to constitute abandonment of property surely there must be intention, actual or presumed. Literary property is subject to this principle as much as material property. And as on publication the author has no intention to abandon his

property—for even Justice Yates admitted the author's right
before publication—there must be some agreement to abandon,
express or implied, and certainly the author is no party to
such an agreement.

'What! is there no difference,' said Justice Aston,
'betwixt selling the property in the work and only one of
the copies? To say "selling the book conveys all the
right" begs the question. For, if the law protect the book,
the sale does not convey away the right, from the nature
of the thing, any more than the sale conveys it where the
statute protects the book.

'The proprietor's consent is not to be carried beyond his
manifest intent. Would not such a construction extend the
partial disposition of the true owner beyond his plain intent
and meaning? Which, from the principles I have before laid
down, is no more to be done in this compact, than in the case
of borrowing or hiring.'

Justice Aston went on to ask 'can it be conceived that,
in purchasing a literary composition at a shop, the purchaser
ever thought he had bought the right to be the printer and
seller of that specific work?'—a question which it seems idle
to discuss. The right of the purchaser in a book may be
likened to that of a householder in the supply of water from a
water company to his house. The payment of his rate entitles
him to make all proper use of the water, but he cannot sell it
to others; and so the buyer may read a book and have the
individual enjoyment of it, but nothing more. He has bought
one copy, not the right of multiplying.

The buyer's right as against the author should of course,
like all other matters of contract, be regulated by the intention
of the parties. But, in the absence of express statement, it
becomes necessary to infer intention from the nature and
objects of the sale. As soon as the conception of copy-

right was clearly realised, it was easy to see that neither the author nor the purchaser intended that this right should be affected by the sale of individual copies of the work. It was advisable to establish a presumption to this effect ; and, accordingly, by the middle of the nineteenth century, the majority of civilised countries had passed statutes securing the author in the possession of his copyright after publication for a certain fixed term of years.

Copyright as a 'Reward.'—The limitation to term has led many writers to suppose that, instead of being the legal recognition of a right of property which in theory always resided with the author, copyright partakes of the nature of a reward. This view has given rise to much learned discussion.

'Reward is either of gift or by contract.'[1] But the nature, quantity, quality, permanency, and duration of the gift or wage, must be taken into account before the value of the reward can be assessed. A reward may be almost anything which can be enjoyed in either the legal or the ordinary sense. It may be an estate or a mere toy or even so abstract as a holiday or the hope of future happiness.

A reward, as generally understood, may be discontinued at pleasure. It is as a rule offered as an inducement to do some particular act, under certain prescribed conditions ; but in practice it continues to be offered only until the general purpose for which it is brought into existence is accomplished, and is then withdrawn. The offer may be revoked at the pleasure of the offeror.

In England as far back as 1643 an Ordinance recognised the 'owner or owners' of literary property. This was re-enacted by the Licensing Act of 1662, and ownership in literary

---

[1] *Hobbes' Works*, collected by Molesworth, vol. iii., p. 305.

property has been admitted ever since. During the last century there has been considerable moral progress in the recognition of the author's rights. A *reward* which, offered as an act of grace, is made terminable at pleasure, or which cannot be claimed by *all* who fulfil the conditions, is plainly no adequate return for the author's work.

Looking at the matter as it stands at the present day, without regard to the origin of the right, the truth of the following proposition seems self-evident. Copyright, which defines the right of an author with regard to his production, is undoubtedly given to him as a recompense for his creative work; this recompense is accorded by the State as a matter of moral obligation, and, therefore, unless the term reward can be used in a sense wide enough to include a payment which the author can rightly demand, it is not satisfactory to say that the author's protection is merely a reward. And even if this were true, it still would not follow that it was not a right of property.

The Author's Work and the Public Benefit.—All rights granted should find their justification in general utility to society. The protection of the community or State should be given as a return for this and this only; so that in all ages interested persons have been anxious to show that real consideration has been required of individuals in return for rights and monopolies granted to them.

The adoption in England of this principle of general utility in the case of books was evident soon after printing was invented; but the consideration required for the privilege to print appeared in many different forms, of which some disappeared with the Revolution, and others are not recognisable at the present day.

In the case of printers, correct printing at a moderate price was one such consideration, and the issue of books which tended to encourage peaceable acceptance of the political *status quo* was another.

The author's work entitles him to the same reward as that which was formerly granted to the printer, if only from the fact that it is equally for the good of the community at large. This general utility to mankind is the basis of what has been called 'the social contract' between author and public. If any member of society offers the product of his intellect and invention for the benefit of the public, general utility demands protection for him in his works; in the case of the author this protection is represented by copyright. Having recognised this general utility, the State grants *legal* copyright by statute, in place of the *moral* right formerly acknowledged only by public opinion.

To what class of rights does Copyright belong?—The legal right thus given to the author, like other legal rights, may form the subject of assignment[1] and devolution; and, since not only the rules of law as to assignment[1] and devolution, but even the code to be applied according to Private International Law, may differ with the kind of property involved, it becomes necessary to consider in what class of rights copyright should be placed.

Copyright, as we have seen, is not an ordinary right of property, since the author's conception exists only in contemplation of the mind, and finds no place in the external world of material things. 'The author's right is a mere right unaccompanied with the possession of anything corporeal.[2] In the formal language of Jurisprudence the rights which are

---

[1] The Copyright Act 1842, sec. 2, defines 'assigns' as including 'every person in whom the interest of an author in copyright shall be vested, whether derived from such author before or after the publication of any book, and whether acquired by sale, gift, bequest, or by operation of law, or otherwise.'

[2] Williams, *Personal Property*, 15th ed., p. 40.

opposed to rights of property are designated 'obligations.'[1] These are not rights in or over things, availing against anyone who seeks to interfere with the free use and disposition of the owner, but are rights to the performance of, or the abstinence from, certain acts, on the part of specific individuals. It will thus be seen that copyright is not a mere obligation, since, being enforceable against anyone who infringes it, it is valid against the general public, not simply against ' a person or persons certain or determinate.'

Again it has been suggested that copyright partakes of the nature of a monopoly,—that it is a privilege, secured to a given individual, enabling him to prohibit a certain class of acts on the part of the public, for his own benefit. This view, however, while doubtless accurately representing the author's actual position in relation to the public, involves the notion that, in its very origin, the author's right is a mere artificial creation of the State, i.e. a 'reward,' and not, as we have attempted to show, an antecedent right of property deriving only its legal protection from the State.

The most reasonable theory seems to be the one which was indicated in *Millar v. Taylor*, viz. that the right in question is indeed a right of property, but one of an anomalous kind, exercised over no definite object.

Some foreign jurists have thought to evade the difficulty by adding a fourth class of 'intellectual rights' (including patents, designs, trademarks, etc., as well as copyright)[2] to the division of rights into real rights, personal rights, and obligations, which is accepted on the Continent. But this does not help us much. If by an ' intellectual right' is

---

[1] This term, derived from the Roman Law, is in current use on the Continent, where the accepted division of rights is into real rights, personal rights, and obligations. Its vogue in England is mainly academic.

[2] See Lyon-Caen, *Lois françaises et étrangères*, p. 169.

meant a right over an intellectual subject, then copyright undoubtedly belongs to this class.   In such case, however, the division turns on the physical nature of the subject over which the right is exercised, rather than on the jural nature of the right itself : so that, for the sake of logical consistency, it is necessary to add many other classes, such as rights over land, over furniture, over houses, and so on.   This reduces the principle to an absurdity.[1]   On the other hand, if ' intellectual rights' does not mean this, it is not apparent what it does mean,—all rights are ' intellectual' in the sense that they themselves, as distinguished from their subjects, exist only in contemplation of the intellect.

In England, copyright has been declared by statute to be ' personal property,'[2] so that it descends upon death according to the rules which regulate the devolution of personal estate.

Much learning has been spent in discussing the question into which of the two accepted classes of personal property— *choses in possession,* *e.g.* books, horses, clothes, and *choses in action,* *e.g.* debts and rights of action,[3]—it should go.   At

---

[1] A French author, evidently well instructed in logic, in commenting on the French Copyright Bill of 1841, wondered that no one was found to say : ' If we make a law on literary property, there is no reason why we should not make a special law for every form of property, so I propose to you a law on each of the following forms : property in hats, property in peaches, property in peaches in brandy, property in the green coat belonging to M. Anguis '—and so forth.— Darras, *Du Droit des Auteurs et des Artistes,* p. 27.

[2] ' Be it enacted that all copyright shall be deemed personal property, and shall be transmissible by bequest, or, in case of intestacy, shall be subject to the same law of distribution as other personal property, and in Scotland shall be deemed to be personal and moveable estate.'—The Copyright Act, 1842, sec. 25.

[3] ' *Choses in possession* are moveable goods, of which their owner has actual possession or enjoyment, and which he can deliver over to another upon a gift or sale ; tangible things, as cattle, clothes, furniture, and the like. . . . The term *choses in action* appears to have been applied to things, to recover or realise which, if wrongfully withheld, an action must have been brought ; things, in respect of which a man had no actual possession or enjoyment, but a mere right enforceable by action, . . . *e.g.* money due from another, the benefit of a contract, and compensation for a wrong.'—Williams, *Personal Property,* 15th ed., p. 27.

first sight it would seem that it cannot be a *chose in posses-sion*, since there is no definite thing to be possessed ; still, looking to the essence of the right, it is clear that it is a right against the general public to prohibit the doing of certain acts in respect of a given intellectual work.   In any case it cannot be a *chose in action*, since it holds good, not against a particular person, but against the world at large ; and has moreover always been assignable, while *choses in action* were originally not transferable, and even now can only be assigned under certain very definite restrictions.[1]

It is true that the right is not actively exercised till an infringement has been committed ; still, to say that the only right which exists is the right of action created by the infringement is to deny the possibility of infringement alto-gether.   If this is the ground upon which the theory that copyright is a *chose in action* is based, it would be equally reasonable to call a right of property over a piece of land a *chose in action* ; for here too a right of action lies against a definite individual upon infringement.   We must conclude that copyright is a personal thing ' in possession.'   In any case the question is of little practical importance, since, for many purposes, copyright is *sui generis*, its incidents being regulated by statute.

[1] For a discussion of the whole question see an article by Mr. Spencer Brod-hurst in the *Law Quarterly Review* for January, 1895.

SECTION IV.

EVOLUTION OF THE LEGAL RIGHT.

WITH SPECIAL REFERENCE TO ENGLAND.

Printing and copyright—Protection by royal privileges—Early privileges granted to authors—The Stationers' Company—The Licensing Act, 1662 —The Act of Anne, 1709—Progress since 1709.

The moral right of the author to property in his work has already been considered. The history of the recognition of the legal right by the State, *i.e.* of the conversion of the moral right into a legal right, will now be briefly traced.[1]

Printing and Copyright.—The sole and exclusive right to multiply copies was of little value until the introduction of printing. Yet copyright was a subject of property in ancient times, when the only means of multiplication was copying by hand, for we learn from the Classics that Terence sold his plays—presumably these were purchased for the performing rights, as in one case the assignment was to an actor. Juvenal also tells of the sale of a tragedy, the Agave, from Statius to the player Paris.[2]

Again in the Middle Ages, long before the invention of printing,[3] 'multiplying and increasing books by writing was a privilege of the University of Oxford, and all men and trades employed thereon were privileged persons of the University, as it is accorded 18 Edward I. "Coram ipso domino rege et ejus concilio ad Parlamentum."'[4]

---

[1] The development of International copyright in various countries is treated in Chap. iii. of this part.

[2] 'Esurit, intactam Paridi nisi vendit Agaven.'—Juvenal, *Sat. VIII.* 87.

[3] Introduced into England in 1474 by Caxton. Some say Corsellis came to Oxford, and issued a book as early as 1468; but the weight of authority is against this view.

[4] Letter from Dr. Fell, the Bishop of Oxford, to the Archbishop of Canterbury, 6th January 1679, quoted in Gutch's *Collectanea Curiosa*, vol. i., p. 273.

Nevertheless the early history of copyright, in so far as it is of real importance, is bound up with the history of printing.

Protection by Royal Privileges.—Progress towards the modern conception of copyright was tardy, and it was not until the eighteenth century that statutory copyright was granted in any country. England led the way in 1709, the example being followed at some distance of time by several States of America and then by France. But before this statutory copyright protection was given to authors at a very early date by means of royal privileges or patents, this being the recognised mode of safeguarding the interests of the owner until the time when public opinion became so strong as to force statutory recognition of copyright. The royal prerogative died hard; in France up to the year 1789 no one was allowed to print a book without first securing a privilege, while in Würtemberg protection was accorded in this way as recently as 1836.

The consideration for these privileges was supposed to be correct printing at a reasonable price for the public benefit, and the advantage to the authorities was the restraint put upon seditious and other objectionable works. The means used to obtain the royal protection were often corrupt. Thus many cases have been handed down where money payments were made to Court favourites in return for their good offices in securing these privileges.

Early Privileges Granted to Authors.—In the beginning, however, the printer, not the author, was the direct recipient of the privilege; though, of course, indirectly the author was benefited, since he was at liberty to make his own terms with the printer before letting him have the manuscript. It was some time before the conception of copyright as a printer's monopoly developed into the idea of it as an author's property. The first recorded privilege granted direct to the

author was given in 1491 by the State of Venice to Peter of
Ravenna; by it the exclusive right to print and sell his
Phœnix was assured to him.   In Germany the first privilege
was issued at Nuremberg in 1501.   In England the earliest
privilege given to an author of which any account is preserved is a patent of 1530, granted in favour of 'Maistre
Jehan Palsgraue Angloys natyf de Londres, et gradue
de Paris,' for a book to teach the French language, which
he is said to have 'made with a great and long continued dyligence,' and which, 'besydes his great labours,
payns, and tyme there about employed, he hath also at his
proper cost and charge put in prynt.'[1]   As a rule however the printer was the primary object of protection; and
he often received privileges in respect of works which were
rightly in the public domain.

It has been contended that these privileges, rarely given to
authors, revocable at the King's pleasure, and frequently granted
only for a few years or for one edition, were not strictly in
the nature of copyrights.   But the powerful protection of the
King's prerogative, as shown by the patent, was of special
value in days when the legal remedy was slow and difficult to
obtain; and the right of the patentee falls well within the
accepted definition of copyright as 'the sole and exclusive
liberty of printing or otherwise multiplying copies.'

The Stationers' Company.—Everywhere the power of the press
for good and evil was soon recognised, and in England the
Stationers' Company was chartered by Philip and Mary in
1556 for the declared purpose of preventing the publication
of heretical and seditious books.

For nearly two hundred years after the introduction of
printing, the action of the authorities in granting privileges,
and in making ordinances in connection with the multiplica-

---

[1] Herbert's *Typographical Antiquities*, vol. i., p. 470.

tion of books, was governed mainly with a view to censorship. In France the Edict of Moulins in 1566 prohibited any person from printing or causing to be printed any book or treatise without the leave and permission of the King and Letters of Privilege, and in other countries privileges were refused to any book which, in the opinion of the authorities, was either heretical or seditious or obnoxious to the Government for any other reason.   Even with all these restraints on printing, however, the number of books multiplied at this time was considerable.   In England, between 1576 and 1595, no fewer than two thousand different books were entered on the register of the Stationers' Company as the property of particular persons ; and this in spite of the fact that the prohibition of Elizabeth, issued in 1559, against printing books without a licence was renewed from time to time by the Star Chamber.

'Till the year 1640, the Crown exercised an unlimited authority over the press ; which was enforced by the summary powers of search and confiscation and imprisonment given to the Stationers' Company all over the realm and the dominions thereunto belonging, and by the then supreme jurisdiction of the Star Chamber, without the least obstruction from Westminster Hall or the Parliament in any instance.'[1]   And, when in 1640 the Star Chamber was abolished, and 'all regulations of the press, and restraints of unlicensed printing, by proclamations, decrees of the Star Chamber, and charter powers given to the Stationers' Company, were deemed to be and certainly were illegal,'[1] 'the licentiousness of the press was carried to the greatest height.'[2]

In 1643 it was found that, in addition to the mass of libellous and licentious matter which had appeared since the restraint was removed, divers persons, ' contrary to former orders and the constant custom used among the Stationers'

---

[1] Willes, J., in *Millar v. Taylor*.   [2] Carte's *Letters*, published 1739.

Company, had taken liberty to print, vend, and publish the most profitable vendible copies of books belonging to the Company and other Stationers,'[1] and an ordinance dealing with the abuse was passed in that year by the two Houses.

But though right-minded people believed in 'the just retaining of each man his several copy, which God forbid should be gainsaid,'[2] much indignation was felt against the appropriation of 'copies,' *i.e.* copyrights, and the monopolisation of the printing trade, by the members of the Stationers' Company. In 1644 Milton published his *Speech for the Liberty of Unlicensed Printing.* It should be carefully noted that in this he does not advocate that it should be open for others than the author or his assignees to print copyright works, but that the latter shall have complete control over the printing of their own works.

The Licensing Act, 1662.—The Ordinance of 1643 was followed by others to the same effect in 1647 and 1649. The Ordinance of 1647 was characteristic of the time ; it decreed that all books concerning sports should be burnt, and that the kingly office and House of Lords should be abolished.

The next piece of legislation in England was the Licensing Act of 1662. Although introducing little that is novel, this must be regarded as a prominent landmark in the history of copyright, for its language plainly recognises literary property ; the 'owner' is referred to again and again, and the words 'any book or books the right of printing whereof doth solely and properly belong to any particular person or persons,' expressly acknowledge the common-law right. The author's claim is strengthened, too, by a clause in the Act which prohibits the unauthorised use on copies of a book of the mark of the person solely privileged to print that

---

[1] Scobell's *Acts and Ordinances*, 1658 edition, p. 44.
[2] Milton's *Areopagitica,—a Speech for the Liberty of Unlicensed Printing.*

particular work, thus clearly contemplating a right of property in the work. This Licensing Act was continued to 1679, when, owing to the disturbed state of the country, it was allowed to lapse. It was revived in 1685 for seven years, and afterwards extended to 1694.

The Act of Anne, 1709.—After the expiration of the Licensing Act in 1694, repeated attempts were made to renew it. Although the owners of copies had a legal right to them at common law the lapse of the statute left them without adequate protection, and numerous petitions were presented by the proprietors praying that fresh enactments should be made for securing their property. They had so long been protected by penalties that they considered an action at law an inadequate remedy. Thus an application for a Bill, made in 1709, closed as follows : ' The liberty now set on foot of breaking through this ancient and reasonable usage is in no way to be effectually restrained but by an Act of Parliament. For by the common law a bookseller can recover no more costs than he can prove damage ; but it is impossible for him to prove a tenth, nay perhaps a hundredth, part of the damage he suffers, because a thousand counterfeit copies may be dispersed into as many different hands all over the kingdom, and he may not be able to prove the sale of ten. Besides, the defendant is always a pauper ; and so the plaintiff must lose his costs of suit. No man of substance has been known to offend in this particular, nor will any ever appear in it.'

In 1709 the Act of 8 Anne, c. 19 was passed, this being the first Act passed in any country to grant protection to authors. The first section of the Act is as follows :—

8 Anne, c. 19.—' An Act for the encouragement of learning, by vesting of the copies of printed books in the authors or purchasers of such copies, during the times therein mentioned.

' Whereas printers, booksellers, and other persons have of late frequently taken the liberty of printing, reprinting, and publishing books without the consent of the authors or proprietors of such books, to their very great detriment, and too often to the ruin of them and their families : for preventing therefore such practices for the future, and for the encouragement of learned men to compose and write useful books, be it enacted that from and after the tenth day of April, 1710, the author of any book or books already printed, who hath not transferred to any other the copy or copies of such book or books, shall have sole right and liberty of printing such book and books for the term of one-and-twenty years, to commence from the said tenth day of April, and no longer.

'And that the author of any book or books already composed, and not printed or published, or that shall hereafter be composed, and his assigns, shall have the sole liberty of printing and reprinting such book and books for the term of fourteen years, to commence from the day of the first publishing the same, and no longer.

'And that if any other bookseller, printer, or other person whatsoever, shall print, reprint, or import any such book or books, without the consent of the proprietor first had and obtained in writing, signed in the presence of two or more credible witnesses ; or shall sell, publish, or expose to sale any such book or books, without such consent ; then such offender shall forfeit such book or books to the proprietor of the copy thereof, who shall forthwith damask and make waste-paper of them ; and farther, that every such offender shall forfeit one penny for every sheet which shall be found in his custody.'

This Act was of an altogether different character from the old Licensing Act and Star Chamber Decrees. The importance of the printing press had before been recognised, but now for the first time a plain acknowledgment was made of the rights of authorship. The distinction between the abstract conception of the author's work and the tangible product, the book, which was the sole subject recognised in early times as capable of ownership, was definitely made.

Progress since 1709.—Since this, the only great advance in legislation for literary copyright in England was the badly-drafted Act of 1842, but statutory protection has been granted to other classes of intellectual property, and of recent years great progress has been made in the recognition of international copyright. The passing of the Act of Anne however settled the nature of copyright in England and hall-marked the author's moral right as a legal right.

CHAPTER II.

INTERNATIONAL INFRINGEMENT.

SECTION I.

COPYRIGHT AS A NATIONAL RIGHT.

THE fitness of an intellectual production as a subject of property and the moral right of the author to property in his work having been established, copyright laws were made by the civilised countries of the world granting to authors a sole exclusive right to multiply copies. But domestic laws cannot be enforced outside the territory[1] by the State which makes them, and any compulsory protection of foreign works is purely a matter of international arrangement—generally under condition of reciprocity.

'As soon as a copy of a book is landed in any foreign country all complaint of its republication is in the absence of a treaty fruitless, because no means of redress exist. . . . It becomes public property, not because the justice of the case is changed by the passage across a sea or boundary, but because there are no means of enforcing the private

---

[1] The old maxim of feudal times was : *Leges non valent extra territoriam.*

right.'[1] So wrote Curtis in 1847, and even at the present
day territoriality generally regulates the protection.

In former times merchandise cast upon a foreign shore was
held to be the lawful[2] prey of the finder, and now, though in
the case of goods the law of nations enforces the owner's
claim, yet for literary piracy committed abroad the author
has no remedy apart from international agreements, except
in a few countries which treat foreign authors with unusual
liberality.

The English Act of 1842, though designed ' to afford greater
encouragement to the production of literary works of lasting
benefit to the world,' was, like the statutes of other countries,
intended primarily not for the protection of authors throughout the world but for the benefit of British subjects ; in
time, however, both at home and abroad, commercial considerations and other national interests caused the extension
of the principle of protection to all persons within the
jurisdiction of the State, even in cases where there was no
direct allegiance or citizenship.

[1] Curtis, *Law of Copyright*, p. 22.
[2] 'The law of nations being a body of customary rules depends upon the
practice of nations ; and what has not been practised cannot be affirmed to be
a part of that law.'—Curtis, *Law of Copyright*, p. 22.

SECTION II.

THE ETHICS OF UNAUTHORISED REPRINTING OF FOREIGN WORKS.

Though piracy at sea was at one time considered an honourable profession, general morality has so far advanced that at the present time this barbaric practice is regarded as criminal. But intellectual property has not yet been acknowledged as worthy to rank with material goods in respect of international protection, progress towards a general recognition of international copyright being much more slow than the advancement of domestic recognition of copyright, confined to the subjects of the protecting State.

In the light of modern opinion the unauthorised reprinting of foreign copyright works is entirely opposed to the principles of justice ; [1] but it is scarcely fair to charge our predecessors with dishonesty of purpose in an age when a royal privilege was necessary to protect books against infringement in the author's own country, and when the reprinting of foreign works was not only generally regarded as just but even received royal support. In the sixteenth century the right to reprint foreign books in France belonged to the King's printer ; and early in the nineteenth King William of Holland encouraged the reprinting of foreign works by subsidising this form of literary piracy.

---

[1] The anomalous attitude of the United States of America will be discussed later.

Views like that expressed by Putter, a jurist of Augsburg, who in his treatise on Literary Property (1774) declared that, from the ethical point of view, as little difference existed between the piratical treatment of foreign authors and that of natives as between breach of faith committed against a citizen and one of which a foreigner was the victim,[1] were therefore far in advance of the time. The reprinting of foreign works was for centuries regarded as an honourable business[2] and engaged in by honest citizens[3] without any thought of the wrong they were committing.

After the doctrine of the royal monopoly had been broken down in France, trade in foreign reprints was governed almost entirely by ordinary commercial rules of outlay and return. The old privileges extended to aliens as well as to subjects, but the copyright law which superseded them gave to the native author as such the sole right to make copies of his work. Thus the foreign author was quite at the mercy of native booksellers, who reprinted any foreign work which they thought would repay them.

No better proof of the ethics of the time could be given than that furnished by a Commission of the French Chamber of Peers appointed to examine a proposed new Copyright Bill. It was proposed to establish a system of reciprocal protection between France and England, but the opinion of

[1] Darras, *Du Droit des Auteurs et des Artistes*, p. 181.

[2] In Belgium Haumann and Company—a firm engaged in reprinting foreign copyright works on a large scale—had a President of the Court of Cassation, who had been Minister of the Interior, as its Chairman, and a member of the Senate, an Inspector of Public Instruction, and several magistrates amongst its directors. The boards of other companies were similarly composed.—Darras, *Du Droit des Auteurs et des Artistes*, p. 151.

[3] It is narrated that when Liège was a centre of the printing industry an honest printer of that town met the author Marmontel, who protested against the theft of his works. 'Liège is a free country,' was the reply; 'its inhabitants have the right to print anything they think good; that is our trade.'—Darras, *Du Droit des Auteurs et des Artistes*, p. 148.

the Commission proved unfavourable. The following is an
extract from its report issued in 1839 :—' The only English
books reprinted at Paris, and sold at a very moderate price
compared with English editions, give buyers and French
booksellers a real advantage. In England, where the cost
of manufacture is greater than in France, no French work
is reprinted. Reciprocity between the two countries will
so be most favourable to Great Britain ; and will deprive
us, without any compensation, of the means of procuring at a
reasonable price English books of which the price is excessive
when it is necessary to import them from beyond the seas.'[1]
It was on these grounds that the Commission decided against
reciprocity. This from a country which since 1793 was
supposed to have discountenanced the unauthorised reprinting
of all works, both domestic and foreign, leaves no doubt as to
what was the current opinion.

[1] Darras, *Du Droit des Auteurs et des Artistes*, p. 214.

SECTION III.

FORMER IMPORTANCE OF THE TRADE IN FOREIGN
REPRINTS.

International piracy formerly general—Enterprise shown in reprinting
of foreign works—Magnitude of the trade in foreign reprints—Reprisals
suggested where reciprocal protection refused.

International Piracy formerly general.—It is only in very
recent times that any attempt has been made to secure international protection for authors. Reprints made for sale in
the country of production were formerly regarded as no
infringement of a foreign author's rights; and even when
these spurious reproductions were exported to other countries
the author had no means of redress. Holland and Germany,
the nurseries of the printing trade, led the way in this
piratical industry; and other countries were not slow to
follow. Belgium in the eighteenth century has been described
as 'a veritable hotbed of Infringement.'

Certain conditions offer special temptations to piracy—thus
when two or more nations speak the same language[1] trade in
literary reprints can be most profitably carried on. In former
times Germany suffered from the depredations of Austria;
the Prussian States continually laid one another under contribution; Belgium 'showed itself extremely solicitous that
French ideas should be propagated in all branches of learning'; and before the *Act of Union* one of the ways in which
Ireland asserted its independence of England was by printing English books, not only for her own use, but also for
exportation.

---

[1] Musical, artistic, and dramatic works need little adaptation to suit a foreign
market and thus provide ready material for the foreign pirate.

Even to-day England's literature is to American publishers a store of wealth upon which many still draw freely, in spite of the so-called reciprocity[1] brought about by the Chace Act of 1891, while the existence of a large immigrant population of various nationalities in the United States of America makes it possible to reproduce at a considerable profit unauthorised copies of the works of several other countries.

Fifty years ago the reprinting of any foreign work depended almost entirely on its attractiveness, the cost of its reproduction, and the extent of the market to which it would be likely to appeal: these matters being found satisfactory, little hesitation was felt on account of the injury which the alien author might suffer. This applied especially to countries where printing was an important national industry.

Enterprise shown in Reprinting Foreign Works.—The enterprise and business ability shown by pirates was worthy of a better cause. Agents were appointed in foreign countries to obtain new works at the earliest opportunity; in 1841 English books were reprinted at Paris, France being in a convenient position for securing its neighbour's new publications without delay. In 1884 an American firm sent special correspondents to England for the purpose of securing a new book about to be published by the Queen immediately upon its appearance; it was cabled across the Atlantic ocean in twenty-four hours, and was printed and put on sale within twelve hours of the receipt of the last words.[2] Printers belonging to the United States have frequently set up the type of English works on the steamers from Liverpool to New York, so that the new books have been

---

[1] The chief clause of the Chace Act—that in order to gain American copyright every work must be set up in type within the States—involves a double expense, if the work is also to be printed off in its native country.

[2] Darras, *Du Droit des Auteurs et des Artistes*, p. 143.

issued to the American public within a week after their appearance in England.

In addition to the piracy itself, the methods adopted to further quick reproduction have not always been above reproach. Employees have been bribed to furnish proof-sheets,[1] and stenography and telegraphy have been illicitly pressed into service. Thus Ponsard's *Agnès de Méranie* was printed in Belgium before it appeared in France, its native country,[2] and later on Zola's *l'Assommoir* was represented in Antwerp before the drama had been printed, stenography having been employed to commit the piece to writing during its performance.[3]

Great ingenuity was often displayed by the literary pirate in the prosecution of his business. 'Printing beyond the seas' of infringements intended for exportation into the country of origin used to be a special source of anxiety,[4] and to nullify its injurious effects measures were often taken to cut off the foreign reprints at ports and frontier towns. The vigilance of the customs officers was however frequently evaded by importations at unlikely places. Thus in 1837 some Belgian publishers, by the adoption of a circuitous route and by the pretence of re-importation,[5] for a time defeated the efforts of

---

[1] The printer Richardson in 1753 told how, notwithstanding the extraordinary precautions he had taken, some Irish printers contrived to get proof-sheets from some of his servants as a certain work was in the press, and announced it for publication in Dublin almost contemporaneously with his own London edition. —Lowndes, *Law of Copyright*, p. 39.

[2] See the *Journal des Economistes* for March, 1847.

[3] Darras, *Du Droit des Auteurs et des Artistes*, p. 164. Cf. the English case of *Macklin v. Richardson*, Amb., 695.

[4] That printing beyond the seas was a matter of grave concern to English authors is shown in Sec. 4 of this Chapter.

[5] There is a present danger to English authors that cheap reprints authorised in any particular colony by special arrangement may be imported thence to others in which the book sells at full price. In spite of customs officers thousands of Tauchnitz and other English books published abroad at a low price find their way into England.

the French authorities to prevent the importation of reprints ; and quite recently song folios and other books 'lawfully printed' in America, but not allowed to be imported into England, have been brought here by a circuitous route *via* Antwerp and other European ports with a view of eluding detection at the ordinary ports of importation from America.

Magnitude of the Trade in foreign Reprints.—The extent to which the trade in foreign reprints was at one time carried on was enormous.   The Belgian pirate companies formed between 1834 and 1838 employed fourteen million francs in type-founding, printing, and paper-making.[1]   In 1840 the catalogue of Méline, a Belgian bookseller, embraced 1290 works, seven-eighths of which were piracies of French works ; and two other lists—issued respectively by Haumann and Wahlen—which together made mention of over 1800 books, exhibited quite the same proportion of infringements.[2]

Reprisals suggested where Reciprocal Protection refused.— In view of these facts, it is scarcely surprising to find that international differences have been frequent. These have most often been provoked by the United States.   In 1836 a Committee of writers was formed in England to check American piracy ; it proposed to establish between the United States and Great Britain a reciprocal guarantee for intellectual rights.   It is almost needless to say that the project came to naught.   Deliberate reprisals have been suggested where, as in the case of the United States, the attacks have been one-sided.   But the principle which forms the foundation of copyright law ought not to be abandoned by one country because it has been violated by another ; this was perceived by the English Copyright Commission of 1876, which in response to complaints on the part of English authors against American

---

[1] Darras, *Du Droit des Auteurs et des Artistes*, p. 150.   [2] *Ibid.*, p. 155.

piracy gave it as its opinion that reprisals in the matter of literary plunder were illegitimate.

The feeling of resentment against the conduct of the United States of America is not confined to England. In 1878 'l'Association pour la Réforme et la Codification du Droit des Gens,' in a congress held at Frankfort, passed a resolution to the effect that the Commission upon the International Code of New York should report to its Government the progress made by other countries in the direction of international equality in matters of literary copyright, and should use its influence to bring about the insertion in treaties with foreign powers of a clause by the terms of which each contracting State should be bound to grant to authors belonging to the other the rights assured by it to its own subjects. Four years later the International Literary Congress of Rome, 1882, lodged a protest against the absence of international protection in the United States, 'which is not compatible with the sentiments of honour and of dignity of a great free country.'[1]

---

[1] Darras, *Du Droit des Auteurs et des Artistes*, pp. 164, 165.

SECTION IV.

EARLY PIRACY OF ENGLISH WORKS.

Irish and Dutch piracies—French and Belgian piracies—German piracies—American piracies—Piracies in other countries.

Every nation with a literature of any value has at some time or other suffered from literary piracy on the part of foreign publishers ; and, although such piracies were till recently internationally lawful, a feeling of resentment has invariably been the result.

Down to the middle of the eighteenth century England suffered greatly from the importation of unauthorised copies of its best works printed beyond the seas, and later on, when this had been restrained, the export of authorised editions to foreign countries suffered from the competition of cheap foreign reprints.   In 1537 Grafton, one of the King's printers, petitioned Lord Cromwell to obtain protection for him against the reprinting by Dutchmen of copies of *Matthew's Bible*, which work he had published.   This, he pleaded, had been brought out with great study and labour, and at an expense amounting to over £500 ; while others had printed it again at less than half the charges in 'a lesser letter to the entent that they maye sell their lytle books better chepe' (*i.e.* cheaper) than the original copies.

That this was not a solitary case the frequent decrees and ordinances against unlawful reprinting, which were issued successively in 1556, 1585, 1623, 1637, 1641, 1643, 1647, and

1649 proved. Then came the Licensing Act of 1662 which contained clauses forbidding the introduction of books printed abroad, but neither this nor the Act of Anne[1] in 1709, which imposed a penalty of 'one penny per sheet and the forfeiture of the book,' succeeded in suppressing the objectionable traffic.

Indeed in 1735 foreign reproduction of English popular works was so systematic, and so damaging to the sale of the originals, that application was made to Parliament for more efficacious legislation. 'A committee being appointed, pirated editions, printed abroad, of no fewer than twenty-nine different English authors were placed before them.'[3] On the recommendation of this committee a Bill was introduced into Parliament which after much alteration and curtailment finally became the Act of 1739.[2] The Act consisted of only two clauses, one of which forbade the importation from abroad of any book first printed in England within twenty years on penalty of forfeiture of books, £5, and double the value of each copy so imported or knowingly sold.[3]

Irish and Dutch Piracies.—Though importations into England from Ireland and Holland, which had been the principal offenders, were checked by this Act, booksellers of these countries still continued to print and sell outside England. We are told that in 1753 the 'scramble of the Irish booksellers' as to 'who should first entitle himself[4] to the reprinting of a new English book' was still keen; and 'happy was he

---

[1] Nothing in this Act was to extend to prohibit the importing or selling any books in Greek, Latin, or any other foreign language, printed beyond the seas.—Sec. 7.

[2] 12 George ii. c. 36, re-enacted by 27 George ii. c. 18, 33 George ii. c. 16, and 29 George iii. c. 55. Later Acts checking importation are 41 George iii. c. 107, 5 and 6 Vict. c. 45, 39 and 40 Vict. c. 36 (Customs Consolidation Act, 1876), 52 and 53 Vict. c. 42 (Revenue Act, 1889).

[3] Lowndes, *Law of Copyright*, pp. 37, 39.

[4] That is by the 'courtesy of the trade' in Ireland. Cp. Part ii., Chap. i., sec. 6.

who could get his agent in England to send him a copy of a supposed saleable piece as soon as it was printed and ready to be published.'[1]

French and Belgian Piracies.—It is significant of the extent of the advance in the international protection of copyright made in recent years that such a country as France should, little more than half a century ago, have considered that the interests of its trade and of its general public furnished sufficient reason for permitting international pillage. 'English books reprinted at Paris and sold at a very moderate price compared with English editions give buyers and French booksellers a real advantage,' is the statement of the French Commission of 1839. Books manufactured in England, it adds, are very dear on account of the price of labour; the author's right to remuneration being altogether ignored. Since 1852, however, except for a few books imported before the Decree of that year was held to prohibit the importation as well as the manufacture of unauthorised reprints of foreign works, English authors have had no ground of complaint against France.

German Piracies.—In respect of the piracy of foreign works Germany was no better than its neighbours. Indeed in the first half of the nineteenth century Leipzig, like Brussels, was to the front in the work of international infringement : and until recently an active trade in editions of the most attractive English works has been carried on by German publishers without any payment to authors, though some houses such as Tauchnitz have made a practice of securing the consent of the latter.[2]

American Piracies.—Much has already been said with regard to the conduct of the publishers of the United States. A bare

---

[1] Statement made by Richardson, the printer of Sir Charles Grandison, in 1753, cited by Lowndes, *Law of Copyright*, p. 39.

[2] See Part ii., Chap. i., sec. 6, *Courtesy Copyright*.

list of the titles of the English books which have been appropriated by them would occupy many pages, for, with many who do a cheap trade, piracy is the rule rather than the exception. Whatever will sell is taken without any thought of the English author, who is thus deprived of the profits which he might reasonably expect from the sale of his work among the millions in the States. In order that an English work may appeal to the American public it is not of course necessary that it should be translated ; and cheap reprints of English books are turned out daily with no expense on account of authorship. The competition amongst the booksellers is keen, and ' cut prices ' are so low as to render the sale of authorised imported copies at a fair price impossible.[1]

The state of affairs in the publishing trade on the one hand, and the steady advance towards the recognition of international copyright which is becoming apparent amongst the educated classes on the other, alike tend to bring about the improvement of the present inequitable state of affairs ; and many economic considerations of a reactionary nature strengthen this tendency. Any substantial amelioration must proceed from internal progress in thought : little can be expected from the pressure of external interest, for America's capacity for self-support, due mainly to its geographical position, gives it the power in many matters to dictate its own terms, a circumstance of which, when entering into diplomatic arrangements, it has frequently taken full advantage.

Piracies in other Countries.—England also suffers from the depredations of several minor States with which it has hitherto made no copyright treaties. A striking example of this is the extensive infringement of Sir Arthur Sullivan's music which is carried on at the present time by the Argentine

---

[1] The price of imported works is enhanced by the 25 per cent. *ad valorem* duty which the United States of America levies on English books.

Republic.   In this case however England has the remedy at hand.   It has only to become a party to the Montevideo Convention, which has been signed by the Argentine Republic, in order to obtain copyright protection in that country for English subjects.   Amongst the countries of Europe, France, Italy, and Spain have already signified their adhesion to the Montevideo Convention.

SECTION V.

EARLY PIRACY OF FRENCH WORKS.

Dutch and Belgian piracies—German piracies—Spanish and American piracies.

France, like England, has suffered greatly from international pillage : in close proximity to the centres of the printing industry, it has struggled with even less success to keep out foreign reprints from its confines. Gifted as France is with a brilliant and versatile literature, it is small wonder that, before the modern development of international copyright, its most famous authors were freely laid under contribution by bordering States.

French booksellers, in a Memoir of 1764 to M. de Sartines, stated that they regarded the issue of cheap foreign reprints with apprehension. As Darras says, the sight of Swiss copies of Corneille's works sold at six sous (threepence), in competition with the authorised edition at ten times the price, created quite an 'economic disturbance.' Occasional attempts were made by the victims to export their goods to foreign markets and there undersell the piratical editions, but it was difficult to carry out this operation successfully. The situation was such that French publishers had often to supply copies of French works at a low price to foreign houses in order to prevent the latter carrying out a threat to reprint them on their own account. Authors had to complain not only of money losses, but also of the mutilation of their works at the hands of foreign printers.[1]

---

[1] The following passage from the preface of *Atrée et Thyeste*, by Crébillon, dated March 1707, aptly illustrates this : 'For nearly three years I steadfastly

E

Dutch and Belgian Piracies.—In Corneille's time Switzerland, Avignon, and Holland were the countries[1] which pirated French works most freely.[2]   The injury inflicted by these countries however was small compared with the subsequent appropriations of Belgium.   'Full of solicitude for the propagation of French ideas,' says Darras, 'she speculated on every French name renowned in Europe, on the authority of our jurists, our physicians, and our *savants*, on the happy *verve* of our historical school, on the versatility of our literary taste, and above all on the charms of a language exact and graceful.' The Belgians not only carried on their trade unblushingly,[3] but, holding that they had a right to print all that was good, even boasted of their share in the promotion and dissemination of literature.

The temporary annexation of Holland and Belgium which took place during the French Revolutionary Wars produced but little good effect.   When the independence of the Low Countries had been restored, King William of Holland directly countenanced the trade in foreign reprints, and

withheld my *Atrée*, and I would never have yielded had I not seen it printed in Holland with so many faults that my paternal feelings were moved.   I could not in pity see it thus mutilated; printers' faults added to those of the author; too much by half!   At the same time I decided to publish my *Electre*, to save it from a similar fate.'—Darras, *Du Droit des Auteurs et des Artistes*, p. 146.

[1] See Darras, *Du Droit des Auteurs et des Artistes*, p. 140.

[2] From a letter of Voltaire addressed to the King of Prussia in 1750 we learn that the Dutch printers had become so independent that one of them refused to return a MS. of *l'Anti-Machiavel*, a work composed by the King of Prussia. The King, having changed his opinions, wished to withdraw the work, and delegated Voltaire to approach the printer with a view of preventing its publication; but the attempt was unsuccessful.—Darras, *Du Droit des Auteurs et des Artistes*, p. 147.

[3] Reference has already been made to the bookseller of Liège who introduced himself to Marmontel as a publisher of his works, telling him with pride that his *Bélisaire* had reached a third edition, and his *Contes Moraux* a fourth. After Belgium had been merged in the Low Countries by the Congress of Vienna, Chateaubriand, when passing through Brussels, was presented by a publisher with the first copies of a reprinted edition of his own *Atala* and *René!*

even went so far as to assist it financially. Nor were Belgian[1] booksellers slow to take advantage of their newly found freedom from the French dictation. Copyright works were multiplied by thousands. All sorts of works were reproduced; indeed, it is said that at this time, when the censorship in France was strict, the Paris police index of prohibited books greatly resembled the current catalogues of the Brussels bookshops.

After Belgium had been declared independent of Holland, the friendly intervention of France in bringing this about was, according to French writers, repaid by continued attacks on the literature of her subjects. Between 1834 and 1838,[2] millions of francs were sunk in the Belgian piratical trade, and the resultant output was enormous.

The Cessation of Belgian Infringements.—The state of affairs was so serious that in 1836 a Commission was appointed by the French Government to consider the best means of checking the reproduction of French works abroad; in its report, presented in the following year, the formation of treaties was strongly advocated, and certain other measures proposed which were eventually embodied in the laws of 1841 and 1842. In 1840 preliminary negotiations for copyright treaties were entered into with both Belgium and Holland, but, although a commercial treaty of that year with the latter country definitely contemplated the establishment of international relations, it was not until 1855 that Holland signed a treaty granting protection to French works.

After 1842 the Belgian trade in infringing reprints sensibly decreased, owing in some measure to the stringency of the new French laws, which made importation into France much

---

[1] 'Sans doute, à cette époque, il était vrai de dire de ce pays qu'il était moitié singe, moitié bédouin.'—Darras, *Du Droit des Auteurs et des Artistes*, p. 150.

[2] 'The Dutch were protectors, the Belgians assassins,' says Balzac in 1836.

more difficult. Still this did not go to the root of the trouble. Legislation on the part of Belgium itself was necessary ; and this was secured under a commercial treaty of 1852 between France and Belgium, whereby considerable commercial benefits were assured to the Belgians in return for a sacrifice of the profits they had so long derived from international pillage.

German Piracies.—Although the German booksellers could not find so ready a market for reprints of French works as their fellow tradesmen of Holland and Belgium, they yet showed great enterprise. At the beginning of the nineteenth century the fairs of Leipzig[1] were noted for the sale of reprints of foreign works, and traffic in them was also extensively carried on in many other towns of Germany, Austria, Würtemberg, and Baden.

In more recent times, if we are to believe M. Tissot in his *Journey to the Annexed Countries*,[2] the business of infringement was carried on in the most unscrupulous manner. Just as in the United States many a 'Select Library of English Literature' now exists, so in Germany *Bibliothèques Choisies*[3] of French literature were formerly to be found. At Biefeld, under the title of the *Théâtre Français*, all the popular pieces of France were reprinted.

Spanish and American Piracies.—Though the international copyright policy of Spain is liberal enough, that country does

[1] To appreciate the value of the treaty of 1856 between France and Saxony it is necessary to remember that, in the palmy days of infringement, Leipzig was, next to Brussels, the centre of the trade. The Saxon publishers distinguished their victims only by the merit of their works.—*Journal des Economistes*, vol. xlviii., p. 116.

[2] See Darras, *Du Droit des Auteurs et des Artistes*, p. 160.

[3] One contained reprints of the best French copyright works brazenly ornamented on the last page with a crest surrounded by the words *Contrefaçon interdite* ('Infringement forbidden'), while on the title page Paris was given as the place of publication. Another piratical collection, entitled *France Littéraire*, carried the fidelity of the reprint to the extent of copying a vignette of the *Maison Didot*, the institute from which the original copies were issued.

not exercise sufficient supervision to assure an efficient protection to foreign authors.   Alphonse Daudet's *Sapho*[1] and
l'Evangéliste are quoted by Darras as notable works that have
suffered from this laxity.

France, like England and Germany, has reason to complain of the attitude of the United States of America towards
the international protection of copyright, but not nearly to
the same extent, since in the United States the number of
French-speaking inhabitants is small.

---

[1] The pirate of *Sapho* actually fabricated a letter in praise of his translation,
purporting to come from Daudet himself.

SECTION VI.

EARLY PIRACY OF GERMAN WORKS.

Value of German intellectual works—Inter-State and Austrian piracies —American piracies.

Value of German Intellectual Works.—The magnitude of Germany's depredations on English and French works must not exclude attention to the fact that other nations still continue to pillage German literature to an enormous extent.

These latter appropriations may not be always flagrant, and the decision whether they are plagiarisms or piracies may often hang in the balance, but their net value is none the less substantial. The laborious research that German scholars bring to bear in every branch of learning, and the skilled investigations that their academic system promotes, produce a wealth of information which offers a peculiar temptation to journalists and bookwriters of other countries. In many countries publishers of text-books could tell of author's copy sent to them with German double commas for quotation marks and with other undoubted signs of Teutonic extraction, while the work of journalists, statisticians, and historians often shows on its face that it is derived from German sources. Baedeker is of German origin, though many of the Tauchnitz novels so familiar to the English are not.

Inter-State and Austrian Piracies.—Up to 1837 the piratical trade in works first issued in the Germanic States was mainly internecine : each State carried on its industry unrestrained by any respect for the literary property of the others.

At the beginning of the nineteenth century, Austria was

to Germany in respect of piracy what Belgium was to France before 1852 and what America is to England at the present day ; in each case the identity of language enhancing the temptation to steal.   Not only were the reprints used in Austria itself, but a regular trade in them was carried on with other countries.[1]   The takings of Austria were so substantial that in 1815 the German publishers presented an urgent memoir on the matter to the Congress at Vienna. The Austrians replied to this in a manner which left no doubt as to their view of the situation.   ' A publisher,' they said, ' buys of the author, for the price agreed on, merely the copy of the manuscript and not the right of publication.   This right is granted to him by his government for his own territory : that government has no power to grant the said right for foreign States.   The subject of a foreign State buys a copy of the printed edition with a view of reprinting it if his government permits.'

American Piracies.—Among present-day infringements of German works those carried on by the United States of America are particularly notorious.   Germany, like every other country whose literature is valuable, is freely preyed upon by the Republic.   In view of the large Teutonic immigrant population there is obviously a wide-spread demand for German books in the United States.   If any evidence of this were required the facts brought out in the celebrated American case of *Stowe v. Thomas* (1853) would provide it ; in addition to the authorised German translation of Mrs. Beecher Stowe's famous *Uncle Tom's Cabin*, an unauthorised one had been made in the same language.

According to an article[2] in the *Deutsche Rundschau* of

---

[1] Lieber's *Political Ethics*, p. 125.

[2] *Der Deutsche-Amerikanische Buchhandel*, by M. Fried. Kapp.—See Darras, *Du Droit des Auteurs et des Artistes*, p. 162.

January, 1878, though the American papers were full of German tales and articles of every kind, the reprinting in book form of German works in the States was at that time on the decline. It is doubtful how far this holds good at present, but in any case the contemporary author is not much benefited, since as a rule it is copies of the old classics that are now imported from Germany instead of being reprinted in America, the American output of modern German works probably remaining the same.[1]

In 1892 Germany concluded a treaty with the United States of America, but since this, like England's arrangement with the same country, is dependent on the American Act of 1891 with its protective manufacturing clause, it is questionable whether German authors derive much advantage from it.[2]

[1] Darras, *Du Droit des Auteurs et des Artistes*, p. 162.
[2] See Part V., Additional Section.

CHAPTER III.

NATIONAL PROGRESS TOWARDS PROTECTION OF FOREIGN WORKS.

FROM the foregoing outline of the history of literary piracy it will be gathered that the tolerance formerly conceded to international infringement has been gradually withdrawn. This process has been carried out in greater or less degree throughout every civilised State of the world. It has been greatly facilitated of recent years by improved methods of communication, which have led to a comparative uniformity of opinion throughout all countries interested in literature.

In each State where the principle of protection for foreign works has been established the history of its recognition has been much the same. At first the liberty to reproduce all work was made dependent on privileges, granted sometimes to authors but more frequently to booksellers. These privileges were given for old as well as for new books, and were occasionally bestowed on foreigners for the purpose of attracting valuable works to the country. Next the State gave protection to copyright by positive legislation. This was at first confined to the subjects of the protecting State or to works published within the territory.   Afterwards it was extended, under various conditions, largely through the influence of treaties, to aliens and foreign works.   And in 1852 France set an example to the world by completely assimilating the rights of foreigners to those of its own subjects.   Belgium and Luxemburg have more recently followed its lead.   Apart from these domestic statutes, the Berne Convention has now established a substantial uniformity amongst the principal nations of the world in their treatment of foreign works. How much further the assimilation and unification of the domestic laws of the different countries can be carried with advantage will be the subject of discussion in a later chapter.

The development of the recognition of foreign copyright in each of the important countries of the world will now be treated.

SECTION I.

PROGRESS OF PROTECTION IN GREAT BRITAIN.

Talfourd's Bill—The International Copyright Acts—Treaties.

Great Britain was, in virtue of her Copyright Act of 1709, 8 Anne, c. 19, the first great nation to legislate for the rights of authors, but for more than a century the domestic protection established by this Act was not extended to foreign works, though the protection of the works of foreign authors, if first published in the United Kingdom, was by many believed to be part of our common law from the beginning.[1]

Talfourd's Bill.—Thus Sergeant Talfourd, in introducing his Copyright Bill of 1837, said : 'There is only one other consideration to which I will advert as connected with this subject—the expedience and justice of acknowledging the rights of foreigners to copyright in this country and of claiming it from them for ourselves in return. If at this time it were clear that our law afforded no protection to foreigners first publishing in other countries, there would be great difficulty in dealing with this question for ourselves, and we might feel bound to leave it to negotiation to give and to obtain reciprocal benefits. But if a recent decision on the subject of musical copyright[2] is to be regarded as correct, the

---

[1] It will be remembered that, although the Act of Anne was passed in 1709, an independent copyright in perpetuity under the Common Law was successfully claimed for British subjects up to the case of *Donaldson v. Beckett* in 1774.

[2] *I.e.* the decision in *D'Almaine v. Boosey*, 1835.

principle of international copyright is already acknowledged here, and there is little for us to do in order that we may be enabled to claim its recognition from foreign States. It has been decided . . . that the assignee of foreign copyright, deriving title from the author abroad to publish in this country, and creating that right within a reasonable time, may claim the protection of our courts against any infringement of his copy. If this is law . . . we shall make no sacrifice in so declaring it, and in setting an example which France, Prussia, America, and Germany are prepared to follow. Let us do justice to our law and to ourselves.'[1] The protection referred to rested upon the judgment of Lord Abinger in *D'Almaine v. Boosey* (1835). In that case it was ruled that an assignee of the work of an alien could gain copyright if the work were first published in the United Kingdom. But this does not go very far, as the assignment to an English publisher is a requirement which detracts greatly from the value of international recognition.

The International Copyright Acts.—The International Copyright Acts of 1838 and 1844, however, put matters on a more satisfactory footing. The Act of 1844 (7 and 8 Vict. c. 12) enabled Her Majesty by Order in Council to direct that authors of works first published in foreign countries should have copyright therein within Her Majesty's dominions ; such Orders in Council to have no effect unless they stated that reciprocity was granted for British publications. Authors of works published in foreign countries were not to be entitled to copyright except under this Act. It cited the International Copyright Act,

---

[1] *Talfourd's Speeches*, pp. 26, 27. In order to guard against any misapprehension of Sergeant Talfourd's meaning it may be necessary to emphasise the fact that the copyright in question in *D'Almaine v. Boosey* was assigned *before* publication, and that the work was first published in this country—protection in such a case is obviously very different from international protection as we now understand it.

1838, which it repealed, the Copyright Amendment Act, 1842 —which was to apply to books to which the Order related, except so far as excluded by the Order—and the Acts relating to performing right, engravings, and sculptures; delivery of copies at the British Museum and other libraries was not exacted, the one copy required to be delivered at Stationers' Hall under the Act being transmitted to the British Museum by the officer of the Stationers' Company. Nothing in the Act was to be construed to prevent the publication of any translation of a foreign work, or of any foreign article of political discussion.

Pursuant to this Statute of 1844, Orders in Council were promulgated, with the object of carrying out no fewer than sixteen treaties. These were with France, Belgium, Spain, Italy, and a number of separate Germanic States, including Prussia.

In 1852 an Act was passed to 'extend and explain the International Copyright Act and to carry into effect a Convention with France on the subject of copyright.' Under this statute, translations were expressly protected but adaptations of plays for the English stage were not to be prevented, and it was provided that all articles in newspapers relating to politics and other contributions might be republished or translated freely, unless the author conspicuously notified his intention to reserve his rights in them. A clause was made to reduce in favour of France the duty payable on books and engravings imported into England, with the further proviso that if any reduction were made to other countries, it should be extended to France.

In 1875 came 'an Act to amend the law relating to international copyright' by which authors of foreign countries named in Orders in Council issued under the Act could, if the Order so directed, prevent the representation in British dominions of any unauthorised translation of a dramatic piece for the period named in the Order in Council, which period was not to exceed five years.

The International Copyright Act, 1886.—The most important step in English copyright legislation made since the passing of the great Literary Copyright Act of 1842 was undoubtedly the International Copyright Act, 1886. This Act was passed to enable Her Majesty to accede to the Berne Convention, which had been finally settled by a great international conference in that year, and to issue Orders in Council granting protection to foreign works. The Convention established an International Union 'for the protection of the rights of authors over their literary and artistic works' between nine States, including nearly all the great countries of Europe. It is provided that authors of any of the countries of the Union shall enjoy in the other countries the same rights as natives. The Berne Convention and the International Act of 1886, which still remains in force, are fully considered in Parts III. and IV. of this work.

Treaties.—Great Britain has now a treaty with Austria-Hungary (1893), and an arrangement with the United States of America (1891), taking effect under the Act of Congress, 1891. It is also a party to the Berne Convention, though not to that of Montevideo.

SECTION II.

PROGRESS OF PROTECTION IN FRANCE.

It was not until 1793 that France replaced the old system of privileges by an express statutory enactment, which protected the works of foreigners, if published in France, in addition to those of subjects. In 1836 a Commission was appointed 'to consider the best means of checking foreign infringements'; the Belgian piracies at that time being particularly injurious to French authors. This Commission was in favour of the principle of reciprocity; but the subsequent Commission, appointed in 1839 by the French Chamber of Peers, regarded such a principle as disadvantageous when applied to some countries, such as England, and so no immediate progress was made. In 1841 unconditional recognition was suggested in the Chamber of Deputies, but was dismissed as impracticable. Learned societies and men of letters however continued their efforts to bring about a reform in the law, and in 1852 a most liberal decree was issued which gave more than reciprocity : it fully recognised the rights of foreign authors by placing them on the same footing as those of subjects, giving protection to aliens even for works published in foreign countries.

Treaties.—Reciprocity, however, though not made a condition of protection, was not despised in practice. From 1852 to 1857 France entered into twenty treaties with foreign countries, and even since 1886 others have been effected.

Among the countries with which treaties relating to Copy-right now obtain are : Holland (1855 and 1860); Portugal (1866); Austria-Hungary (1866, 1881, and 1884); Spain (1880); Germany (1883); Sweden (1884)[1]; Italy (1884). France is a party to both the Berne and Montevideo Conventions.

[1] A Commercial treaty of 1881 with Norway and Sweden also contains pro-visions relating to copyright.

SECTION III.

PROGRESS OF PROTECTION IN GERMANY, AUSTRIA, AND HUNGARY.

Copyright progress in Germany—Establishment of Inter-State protection —The modern Copyright Code—Treaties—Copyright progress in Austria— The Act of 1895—Treaties—Copyright progress in Hungary—The Hungarian Act of 1884.

COPYRIGHT PROGRESS IN GERMANY.

Establishment of Inter-State Protection.—In Germany the history of the recognition of copyright is particularly interesting, the method by which the various constituent States have arrived at a common Copyright Code being typical of the general development of international copyright.

At the beginning of the nineteenth century inter-State relations existed amongst the various Germanic countries in many different forms. Upon the formation of the Confederation in 1815, by Art. 18 of the Constituent Code the German Diet recognised[1] the necessity for copyright legislation; but, owing to the diversities between the various copyright laws in force and the difficulty found in reconciling the views of so large a number of States, a federal code of copyright was then out of the question.

Hence no substantial advance was marked until 1827, when the King of Prussia issued an Order setting forth that, as no satisfactory result had been accomplished by the resolution of the Diet, negotiations should be opened up by Prussia with those States in which the infringement of copyright was

---

[1] Again in 1820 by Art. 65 of the Act of that year.

F

prohibited, so as to bring about provisionally the abolition of all distinctions between natives and foreigners in the contracting States. As a consequence of this, in 1827, 1828, and 1829 some thirty States signed treaties with Prussia, thus clearing the way for the important Federal Act of 1832, which adopted the terms of the Prussian Order of 1827. Henceforth each of the States which then composed the Germanic Confederation[1] was bound to respect the rights of authors belonging to the other States in the same manner as it did those of its own.

The reciprocity thus established was a great step forward, but even then, owing to the difference in the laws of the various States, inter-State protection was far from complete. Where copyright was not accorded to natives, obviously alien authors received no protection ; again it might happen that protection was altogether dependent on privileges. The latter condition of things obtained in Würtemburg; but even there by 1835 opinion had so far advanced that the booksellers addressed a circular to the German newspapers requesting them to refuse the announcement of any piratical work. In 1835 these anomalies were removed by a federal law which gave six years' provisional protection to authors, and in the following year this term was increased to ten years, with a promise that it should be extended before 1842.

The Modern Copyright Code.—In 1870 a comprehensive code was promulgated for the new German Empire. Its protection extended to the works of German authors, wherever published, but not to the works of aliens, unless first published in Germany by German publishing houses. This, however, has now in great part been superseded by a recent Act of 1901 which does protect the literary, musical, and dramatic works of aliens, imposing only the condition of first publication in the Empire.

---

[1] Of these, twenty-five were constituent members of the famous Zollverein or Customs Union.

Treaties.—Germany has treaties with Belgium (1883), France (1883), Italy (1884), the United States of America (1892), and Austria-Hungary (1899). It is also a member of the Berne Convention.

COPYRIGHT PROGRESS IN AUSTRIA.

The Act of 1895.—In 1836 Austria extended to all countries under its rule the Ordinances made by the German Diet in 1832 and 1835, which protected all works printed in States of the Confederation; and again in 1846 it adopted the extensions made by the Diet in 1841 and 1846. Indeed up to the passing of the German law of 1870 the copyright legislation of Austria was bound up with that of Germany.

Some new legislation was however long desired, and when Hungary led the way in 1884 it was expected that the sister State would soon follow its example. No comprehensive law, however, was passed till 1895,[1] when the period of protection was enlarged to a term consisting of the life of the author *plus* thirty years; this applies to the works of Austrians published abroad, and, under condition of reciprocity, to the works of foreign authors published in the German Empire, though in this case the period of protection is limited by the term of the country of origin.

Treaties.—For all other works protection is regulated by treaties. Austria's treaty of 1887 with Hungary is still in force, and Austria-Hungary as one State has treaties with France (1866,[2] 1881, and 1884), Italy (1890), Great Britain (1893), and Germany (1899).

---

[1] The 1846 law gave only ten years' protection in performing rights after the author's death. An extension of the duration of rights had already been contemplated, and the approaching expiration of the copyright period in Wagner's works brought about the provisional Act of 1893, giving a twelve years' period in performing rights.

[2] This treaty was at this date concluded with Austria alone, but was declared applicable to Hungary in 1879.

Progress in Hungary.

The Hungarian Act of 1884 by Sec. 79 applies to the works of Hungarian citizens even when they have been first published in a foreign country, but does not apply to the works of foreign authors generally. The works of foreigners who have lived continuously in Hungary for at least two years and paid taxes there without interruption and also all works which have first appeared with native publishers nevertheless enjoy the protection provided by the law.

SECTION IV.

PROGRESS OF PROTECTION IN ITALY.

After the political unification of Italy (1861) the first general law of copyright was promulgated at Florence, then the seat of Government, in 1865. This law was extended successively to Venice and the Papal States. Before this the various States of which the Kingdom of Italy now forms the embodiment had each a separate law.[1] After 1865, with the exception of a law in 1875 relating exclusively to dramatic works, no legislation took place until 1882, when an Act was passed authorising the codification of the two laws of 1865 and 1875 with some modification of their substance.

International copyright is now regulated by Sec. 44 of this Act, which runs (§ 1) : 'The present law is applicable to the authors of works published in any foreign country with which no special treaty now exists, provided that in the country in question laws exist which recognise for the benefit of authors rights more or less extended, and these laws are applicable by reciprocity to works published in Italy.' If reciprocity is held out by a foreign State to other States on condition that the latter assure to the authors of works published in its territory the same privileges and guarantees as those recognised by its own laws, the Government of the King is authorised to grant both by a royal decree under condition of reciprocity, provided that these

---

[1] Lombardy and Venice however came under the Austrian Copyright Law of 1846.

privileges and guarantees are temporary (*i.e.* limited to a term) and do not differ essentially from those recognised by the Italian law.

If the law of the foreign country in question prescribes deposit of copies of the work or declaration of particulars at the time of publication, it is sufficient, in order to render the right of the author effective in Italy, that proof should be given that the one or the other has been carried out conformably to that law.   In the alternative case ' the deposit or the declaration prescribed by the present law may be made either in Italy or before Italian consuls abroad.'

Treaties.—Italy has treaties with Spain (1880), Germany (1884), France (1884), Austria-Hungary (1890), and Norway and Sweden (1894).   An 'Exchange of Notes' with the United States of America took place in 1892.   Italy is a party to the Berne Convention.

SECTION V.

PROGRESS OF PROTECTION IN SPAIN.

Copyright in Spain now rests upon a law of 1879, supplemented by various articles of the Penal and Civil Codes. Sec. 50 of the law of 1879 reads thus : ' The citizens of the States whose legislation recognises for Spaniards the right of intellectual property, as provided for in the present law, shall enjoy in Spain the rights accorded by the said law, without the necessity of a treaty and without having recourse to diplomatic intervention, by means of an ordinary action brought before a competent judge.' Art. 51, after providing for the denunciation of several treaties already existing, announces that as many new treaties as possible shall be entered into upon the following bases : (1) complete reciprocity between the contracting parties ; (2) mutual treatment on the footing of ' the most favoured nation ' ; (3) every author establishing his right in one of the two contracting countries to be protected in the other without fresh formalities ; (4) printing, sale, importation, and exportation of works in the languages or dialects of the one country to be forbidden in the other, unless made with the authorisation of the proprietor of the original work.

Treaties.—Spain has treaties with Belgium (1880), France (1880), Italy (1880), and Portugal (1880). With the United States of America it has carried out an ' Exchange of Notes ' (1895) ; the copyright relations of the two countries are also regulated by Art. 10 of the Treaty of Peace of 1898. Spain is also a member of the Berne Convention.

SECTION VI.

PROGRESS OF PROTECTION IN BELGIUM.

Belgium, which in the first half of the nineteenth century had been the greatest of literary pirates against the French, was the first country to follow the French law of 1852 in freely extending copyright protection to aliens. This was done in 1886, previous to which year Belgium had no statutory legislation on international copyright. Since 1852, however, when a commercial treaty was made with France containing provisions for the international protection of the works of authors of the two countries, numerous treaties had been entered into which recognised the rights of foreign authors : indeed the spirit displayed was so very liberal that by these treaties authors were placed in a better position than subjects.

The law of 1886 gives to foreigners the same rights as natives[1] without any condition of reciprocity ; and enlarges the term of translating right to a period equal to that obtaining for the original work.

---

[1] The Government Bill employed the expression *propriété littéraire et artistique*, but the law as passed uses the term *droit d'auteur* ('the author's right'). M. de Borchgrave in his report to the Chamber of Representatives dilates upon the nature of the 'author's right.' He refutes the theory that this right is a privilege created by positive law ; but while admitting that, like property, it is a natural right, he seeks to demonstrate that it is not a right of property. He is of opinion that it belongs to a new class of rights called 'intellectual rights' (including the rights of patentees, authors, artists, and inventors of designs or industrial models).—(Lyon-Caen, *Lois françaises et étrangères*, p. 169.) This theory was first developed by a Belgian lawyer, Edmond Picard, in an article appearing under the title 'Des droits intellectuels à ajouter comme quatrième terme à la division classique en droits personnels, réels, et d'obligation.'— (*Pandectes Belges*, Vol. ii., Introduction, p. 26.)

Treaties.—Belgium has now treaties with Holland (1858), one with Portugal (1866), one with Spain (1880), and one with Germany (1883). The benefits of the United States Act of 1891 have also been extended to it by Proclamation. A former treaty of 1881 with France was denounced in 1891 on account of objections to French tariffs; and the only treaty now subsisting between the two countries is the Berne Convention, to which both are parties.

SECTION VII.

PROGRESS OF PROTECTION IN SWITZERLAND.

Up to 1856 there was no mutual recognition of copyright among the Swiss cantons, and even when federal legislation was attempted the various governments were not unanimous. The federal law of 1883, which came into force in 1884 for the whole of Switzerland, superseded the separate laws of the cantons and the partial attempts at federal legislation. Under this law, authors domiciled in Switzerland, as well as subjects, are protected, whatever the country of origin of their works; while foreign authors, domiciled abroad, gain copyright only for works first published in Switzerland. Apart from these provisions, foreign works are protected if the country of origin accords copyright to Swiss works.

Treaties.—Switzerland entered into a Convention with France in 1882 which was to hold good until February 1st, 1892; it was, however, denounced in 1891. A commercial treaty of 1896 with Japan deals with the subject of copyright. In 1891 Switzerland gave to the United States of America the assurance necessary to secure the advantages of the Chace Act. Switzerland is a party to the Berne Convention.

SECTION VIII.

PROGRESS OF PROTECTION IN VARIOUS OTHER COUNTRIES.

Copyright progress in Denmark—Treaties—Copyright Protection in Greece—Copyright progress in Norway and Sweden—Treaties—Unsatisfactory position of Russia—Copyright progress in the United States—The Chace Act, 1891—International arrangements.

Copyright Progress in Denmark.

Amongst the minor States, Denmark, in virtue of its claim that of all nations it was the first to protect the rights of foreigners, demands the first consideration. Since the passing of its domestic law of 1741 foreign copyright has in practice enjoyed recognition, but no express legislation on the subject was carried out until 1828, when an Order of Frederick II. of Denmark was issued, which recited that 'infringement of foreign literary works has never been tolerated in this country,' and stated that its provisions were generally applicable to all infringing literary works of which the publication was forbidden in Denmark, particularly those which belonged to the subjects of other States in which Danish works enjoyed reciprocal protection. It went on to forbid infringements of writings, the copyright in which belonged to aliens, under a penalty therein provided, on condition that in the countries to which the aliens in question belonged infringements of those of Danish subjects were reciprocally forbidden.[1] Denmark has recently enacted a new Copyright Code (19th December, 1902) with the object of clearing the way for adhesion to the

---

[1] Darras, *Du Droit des Auteurs et des Artistes*, p. 191.

Berne Convention. The law of Denmark provides for the establishment of diplomatic reciprocity by royal Ordinance.

Treaties.—Royal Ordinances have been issued in favour of France (1858 and 1866) and Norway and Sweden (1879), while the assurance required by the Chace Act has been given to the United States of America (1893); and in 1903 Denmark accepted the Berne Convention.

COPYRIGHT PROTECTION IN GREECE.

Greece has no copyright law except that contained in the Penal Code of 1833. Art. 432 of this provides for a period of fifteen years' protection of the works of art and intellect, such period being capable of extension by the grant of a special privilege. And Art. 433 adds : 'The provisions of the preceding article are further applicable : (1) in favour of foreigners, even when they have not obtained a privilege in Greece, but only when the State to which the stranger belongs accords the same protection to Greek subjects ; (2) to all other inventions, works, or products of science and art, in so far as they are protected by special privileges granted in Greece against all injurious imitation.'

COPYRIGHT PROGRESS IN NORWAY AND SWEDEN.

The present law of Norway, which was promulgated in 1893, is mainly a codification of two Acts of 1876 and 1877. Most of the changes effected in the latter were carried out in order to remove the obstacles which had previously stood in the way of adhesion to the Berne Convention. The law of Norway adopts the principle of diplomatic reciprocity and protects its subjects whatever the country of origin of their work.

Treaties.—Norway has copyright relations with Sweden under Royal Ordinances of 1877 and 1881. Norway and Sweden, acting jointly as one State, have entered into arrangements with Denmark and Italy in 1879 and 1884 respectively. A commercial treaty concluded with France in 1881 also contained an article dealing with copyright. This treaty was to expire in 1892 ; but in January of that year was extended by a further agreement. Norway adhered to the Berne Convention in April 1896, but refused to accept the alterations effected by the Additional Act of Paris in May, 1896, on the ground that in certain respects these were inconsistent with its domestic law ; the chief divergency being in the matter of translating right. Norway by its Act of 1893, which gave an absolute translating term of ten years,[1] had brought its domestic law into line with the Convention of 1886, but was not prepared for the further extension of the international term which was carried out by the Act of Paris.

Sweden.—The domestic law of Sweden, which country has recently joined the International Union, is substantially the same as that of Norway.

UNSATISFACTORY POSITION OF RUSSIA.

Of Russia Darras says : 'If its law is consulted it seems to protect foreigners to a certain extent, but if the reality of the facts alone is taken into consideration its place is marked side by side with the United States and Turkey.' Italy in 1865 and Prussia in 1869 made overtures to Russia for copyright treaties, but both without effect. Russia absolutely refuses to enter into copyright treaties. Two formerly existed, one with Belgium and the

---

[1] Or a period equal to that of the copyright in the original work on condition of translating within one year.

other with France, but the 'Bulletin of the Laws of the Empire' announced their abrogation two years before the time arranged for their expiration.

COPYRIGHT PROGRESS IN THE UNITED STATES.

The United States was the first of the great countries of the world to follow in the wake of Great Britain with a Copyright Act, and for nearly a century it has had under consideration the question of international copyright recognition. Nevertheless the present attitude of this country is extremely unfair towards foreign authors, though an educated section of the people have long advocated a change. In 1837 a Committee[1] of the Senate took up the matter; their Report stated 'That authors and inventors have according to the practice among civilised nations a property in the respective productions of their genius is incontestable; and that this property should be protected as effectually as any other property is by law, follows as a legitimate consequence.' . . . 'It being established that literary property is entitled to legal protection, it results that this protection ought to be afforded wherever the property is situated.'[2]

Much was said and written in the few years before the passing in 1891 of an Act providing for a measure of

---

[1] This Committee was composed of Clay, Webster, Buchanan, Preston, and Ewing.

[2] 'A British merchant brings or transmits to the United States a bale of merchandise and the moment it comes within the jurisdiction of our laws they throw around it effectual security. But if the work of a British author is brought to the United States, it may be appropriated by any resident there and republished without any compensation whatever being made to the author. We should be all shocked if the law tolerated the least invasion of the rights of property in the case of the merchandise, whilst those which justly belong to the works of authors are exposed to daily violation without the possibility of their invoking the aid of the laws.'—Report of the Senate Committee, 1837, quoted in Putnam, *The Question of Copyright*, p. 105.

international protection. Ex-President Cleveland strongly expressed his personal disapprobation of the lethargy of his country in regard to legislation for international copyright, and his feeling was shared by President Harrison, who, in his message to Congress in 1889, wrote: 'The subject of an international copyright has been frequently commended to the attention of Congress by my predecessors. The enactment of such a law would be eminently wise and just.'

Native authors and composers, too, were loud in their clamours for the substantial advantages which an international copyright law would give. Universities petitioned Congress for such a measure, the leading educationalists and divines freely expressed opinions in favour of international protection, and a large section of the American publishers and printers acknowledged that they held the same views. The last-named, however, added to their suggestions for new legislation the significant proviso that any modification by which American copyright 'should be secured for foreign books should impress as an essential condition that the books should be printed in the States.'[1]

The Chace Act, 1891.—The Act of Congress which resulted from the Chace Bill of 1891, though unsatisfactory in many respects,—particularly in its stipulation that all books must be set up in type in the States in order to gain copyright,—nevertheless to some extent recognises the rights of aliens by its abolition of the former requirement of citizenship as a condition precedent to copyright. Even in order for aliens to take advantage of its greatly qualified protection, the Act demands general reciprocity on the part of the States to which they belong. Great Britain through its law officers has given

---

[1] 'The intelligent voice of the whole country asks for the passage of a measure substantially the same as this,' is Putnam's verdict in recapitulating the arguments adduced for the International Copyright Bill.

an assurance that it satisfies in this respect the conditions of the Statute, and many other countries have done the same.

In a recent Statute of March 3rd, 1905, the United States has made some advance upon the Chace Act by allowing authors of works first published abroad in any language other than English to gain an interim protection for twelve months, upon complying with certain conditions. At any time during this period they may fulfil the type-setting requirement and the formalities of the American law and so gain full copyright in the United States. But, for obvious reasons, the relaxation is not extended to English works.

International arrangements.—Under this Act arrangements for international protection have been completed by the United States with Great Britain, France, Belgium, and Switzerland, in 1891; with Germany and Italy in 1892; with Denmark and Portugal in 1893; with Spain in 1895 (with a renewal in 1898); and with Holland, in 1899.

The relations set up by these treaties are generally in favour of America. Since 1891, however, the agitation for the establishment of complete international protection has not diminished; and, in view of the fact that many publishers have shown a sense of moral obligation to foreign authors by compensating them for the appropriation of their works, it may well be hoped that before long a more liberal policy will be adopted.

PART II.

THE THEORY OF INTERNATIONAL COPYRIGHT.

CHAPTER I.

THE POLITICAL ECONOMY OF COPYRIGHT.

§ 1. Balance of Interests to be considered by the State.
§ 2. Enrichment of the Stock of Literature.   Cheap Books.
§ 3. Home Industries.   § 4. Protection of Native Authors.
§ 5. The Economic Aspect of Universal Protection.
§ 6. Competition.   Courtesy of the Trade.   Courtesy Copyright.

CHAPTER II.

INTERNATIONAL PROTECTION BY MEANS OF TREATIES.

§ 1. The Contractual Nature of Treaties.
§ 2. Universal Protection compared with Reciprocity.
§ 3. Methods of Establishing International Recognition.
§ 4. Modes of Reciprocity.   Protection without Reciprocity.
§ 5. Protection by Treaty.   § 6. Possible Conflict of Treaties.
§ 7. Registration, Deposit of Copies, and other Formalities.

CHAPTER III.

THE POSSIBILITY OF A UNIVERSAL LAW OF COPYRIGHT.

§ 1. The Present Prospect of a Universal Law of Copyright.
§ 2. The Development of International Copyright.
§ 3. The Ideal Universal Law.
§ 4. Practical Advance towards a Universal Law.
§ 5. Central Authority and Administration.

CHAPTER IV.

ALIEN AUTHORS AND ALIEN LAWS.

§ 1. The Author and the Work.
§ 2. The Conditions of Protection in various countries.
§ 3. Formalities specially imposed upon Aliens.
§ 4. Conflict of Jurisdiction and of Laws.

G

CHAPTER I.

THE POLITICAL ECONOMY OF COPYRIGHT.

SECTION I.

BALANCE OF INTERESTS TO BE CONSIDERED BY THE STATE.

THE previous chapters furnish many facts with regard to international infringement and international protection that will go far to provide the necessary data from which the general principles regulating the policy of a State with respect to foreign works may be deduced. The early conception of copyright as a royal privilege, the breach of which would be punished only in the country of origin, put on intellectual works a narrow and inadequate economic value. Immediate self-interest excluded the adoption of any far-seeing policy on the part of the State, but cosmopolitan utility with its international action and reaction demands a more liberal view. With greater intellectual activity and increased facilities for intercourse between different countries the recognition of international copyright gradually advanced. Its acceleration and retardation may be traced to definite economic causes which will be examined in this chapter.

Immediate utility not the only consideration.—Self-protection is a primary law of nature : the adoption of the principle is intuitive, and its application calls for little abstract reasoning. It is only when the need for this self-protection becomes less pressing, and abstract ideas have free play, that a liberal view of economic questions is possible. Though generosity is excluded from the sphere of political economy,[1] yet a reputation for honourable dealing, broad-mindedness, and stability is a valuable asset to nations as well as to individuals in dealing with one another.

Exclusive protection by a State of the immediate interests of its subjects,—of its authors, publishers, and printers,—and legislation and administration immediately directed to the welfare of its industry and commerce, proceed from a comparatively simple policy ; but the establishment of sound principles of protection, which shall secure the greatest ultimate benefit to all classes of the community, is a matter which requires deep consideration and intelligent foresight.

Supply of Literature an important consideration.—From the economic point of view, the great advantage of international protection to foreigners is the acquirement of a wider and better controlled market for their works. The non-recognition by a country of copyright in foreign works largely deprives its inhabitants of the best foreign books, except in the few cases where native publishers find it profitable to reprint them on their own account. It is impossible for a foreigner to decide what books will sell in a country as well as a publisher who is constantly doing business there, or to know how to introduce his publications with the same advantage.

Non-protection may also tend to check the output of the works of native authors, because of the competition of the cheap reprints of foreign works which it allows ; for although

---

[1] Many intangible elements such as pleasure, glory, and other forms of self-gratification, which were formerly excluded from consideration in the study of economics, are now recognised as factors within its scope.

the self-gratification, glory, or reputation which the author's work brings may sometimes be his reward, yet even in this intellectual sphere of labour the supply is largely governed by the price paid.

Ultimate effects cannot be neglected.—The injurious effects on public taste and morals, arising from the wholesale reprinting of the more popular and sensational literature, which unfortunately sells most readily, to the exclusion of the best works, the demand for which is generally slow, cannot be neglected by a nation. It is a truism that the influence of utility upon value preponderates, but the acquisition of a work cannot be said to be a gain, if its ultimate effects are to prove harmful to the best interests of the people. Indirect consequences may either discount or enhance present utility. Future interests and derivative results must both be considered in estimating value. The protection of subjects, the enrichment of the stock of literature, the provision of cheap and good books for the people, and the protection and encouragement of native industry, are the chief national considerations which retard the progress of the recognition of foreign copyright; but unreasoning protection of home industries at the expense of other nations, and unwillingness to grant international reciprocity, have often been found suicidal.

SECTION II.

ENRICHMENT OF THE STOCK OF LITERATURE.
CHEAP BOOKS.

Desirability of securing the works of foreigners—Fair expropriation from foreign works—Injurious consequences of withholding International Protection—Dangers connected with cheap books.

Two important motives which influence the attitude of a nation towards international copyright are the desire to enrich its stock of literature and the wish to provide its public with cheap books. But in acting upon these it is well for the State to keep in mind the necessity of preserving its domestic supply of literature from impoverishment. In the adoption of any particular line of policy, its indirect as well as its direct effects should be carefully considered.

The history of international infringement supplies abundant examples of one method by which a plentiful supply of new foreign books can be obtained, namely, by allowing the unauthorised reprinting of foreign works; but, with a few notable exceptions, all civilised nations have now abandoned this method of self-enrichment, as belonging to an age when rights in intellectual works were little understood.

Desirability of securing the works of foreigners.—A second and fairer method is for the State to hold out a general inducement[1] to foreign authors to publish their works first in its territory and to secure these against the competition of unauthorised reprints so that a profitable sale may reasonably be anticipated.

---

[1] The law should be such as to induce men of learning everywhere to send their productions for first publication.—Drone on the American law prior to 1891, *Treatise on Copyright*, p. 95.

The Berne Convention recognises the advantages of attracting the works of non-Union subjects to the territory of the International Union. Art. 3 of that Agreement, as revised by the Act of Paris 1896, stipulates that 'Authors not belonging to any country of the Union, if they shall have published their literary or artistic works, or caused them to be published, for the first time in one of these countries, shall enjoy for such works the protection granted by the Berne Convention and by the present Additional Act.' This is an advance on the old Art. 3 of 1886, which protected directly only the publishers, not the foreign authors, of such works.

Fair expropriation from foreign works.—Even when a State fully protects all foreign works, it is but reasonable that it should reserve to its own subjects a certain liberty of expropriation, —that is, that it should allow the latter to make use of foreign copyright works in certain well-defined cases, but so as not to interfere with the normal sale of the latter. Cosmopolitan utility demands that, for the sake of the advancement of knowledge and the diffusion of science, greater latitude should be allowed in the making of extracts from foreign works than can be tolerated in respect of those which are of domestic origin. The Berne Convention allows a liberty of expropriation to be conceded in favour of works destined for educational and scientific purposes and for chrestomathies.

In international arrangements it is necessary to define somewhat strictly the limits within which the principle of expropriation is to be allowed to operate. It is obvious that if it is left for each State to determine these for itself there will be very great danger that the interpretation would in some countries be so wide as practically to turn the permitted expropriation into ordinary piracy. Until recently, international expropriation by translation was the common rule, and as such found its way into treaties,[1] and the making of adaptations[2] from foreign works was also regarded as legitimate. Even now Norway and Sweden, which are party to the Berne Convention of 1886, regard the amendment carried out by the Additional Act of Paris, providing for the almost complete international recognition of translating right, as an insuperable obstacle to the adoption of that Act ; and England permits a domestic as well as an international freedom of abridgement, novelisation, and dramatisation. The principle of expropriation has received some curious applications in the history of domestic law : thus, in the early part of the seventeenth century, Holland, while generally protecting the intellectual works of its subjects from infringement, expressly excepted school and church books with the view of their better diffusion.

Injurious consequences of withholding International Protection. The injury done to the foreign author by denying him all opportunity of controlling the circulation of his works, so that there is little inducement for him to correct initial mistakes, and to make alterations and improvements, may not appear to be very great. But more serious consequences ensue from the tolerance of free reproduction of foreign works. In view of the possibility of other editions being put on the market at a lower price, a publisher will often refuse to risk his capital in reprinting foreign works of more than ephemeral interest : a premium is thus put upon the publication of sensational and trashy literature. Bad works often pay better

[1] The English Act of 1852, which enabled Her Majesty Queen Victoria to carry into effect the treaty made with France in 1851, contained provisions so onerous that the liberty of translation which was allowed under the Act of 1844 practically remained in force.

[2] Sec. 6 of the 1852 Act reads 'nothing herein contained shall be so construed as to prevent fair imitations or adaptations to the English stage of any dramatic piece or musical composition published in any foreign country.' The Section was construed, as might be expected, with considerable liberality.

than good ones, and where a publisher can acquire no property in his productions he is likely to let a prospect of immediate profit influence him, to the prejudice of the best interests of literature.

Of the effect of the selfish policy of the United States on the American people, Sir Henry Maine says, in his *Popular Government*, that 'their neglect to exercise their power for the advantage of foreign writers has condemned the whole American community to a literary servitude unparalleled in the history of thought.'[1]   The reactionary effect of freely permitting foreign reprints is strikingly exemplified in the United States.   It is impossible to determine exactly the results of such a policy, but three distinct effects can be traced : (1) the issue of inferior and unrevised—and in some cases mutilated—reprints ; (2) the impoverishment of native literature ; and (3) the demoralisation of ideas and literary taste, which is caused by the reproduction of popular sensational works, to the exclusion of healthy literature and works of real intellectual value.

In the ordinary course, a book is published under the auspices of a publisher who uses his best endeavours to produce the work in a form that will reflect credit on his firm and enhance his reputation, while the author takes advantage of new editions to revise and bring it up to date.   In the hands of a piratical foreign publisher these fostering influences largely disappear.   Further, there is a net loss to the community where the same book is set up in type by a number of rival printers.   Competition leads to underselling, and this in turn to deterioration in the production itself.

Dangers connected with cheap books.—Whatever the force of the motive which the desire for the enrichment of its literature may present to a country, it is inferior to that

[1] See Putnam, *The Question of Copyright*, p. 97.

which the prospect of obtaining cheap books holds out to its people and the chance of realising large profits to its booksellers and publishers. Specious arguments pointing to such superficial advantages as immediate economy in production, and quick return for capital, have done more to retard the international recognition of copyright than everything else put together. A desire for monetary gain, the predominant counter in the science of economics, has been previously shown to exist in certain countries—notably Holland, Germany, and Belgium—in which printing is or has been an important national industry. It will be seen that in the past free competition amongst pirates has always brought about deterioration in the works produced. A similar result will probably sooner or later compel even that great section of the American public which looks only to present material advantages to accept an equitable international copyright Act. 'The cheapest books to be bought to-day in the United States are mostly inferior stories by contemporary English novelists ; while the cheapest books to be bought to-day in England, France, and Germany are the best books by the best authors of all times.'[1]

In addition to the demoralisation of literary taste which directly ensues from the free reproduction of foreign works, a real impoverishment of native literature also results. For years America has possessed 'libraries,'[2] each of which issues

[1] See the paper by Brander Matthews—'Cheap books and good books'—in Putnam, *The Question of Copyright*, p. 430.

[2] 'Among the chief of these collections are the " Franklin Square Library " and the " Harper's Handy Series." In 1886 there were issued fifty-four numbers for the " Franklin Square Library," only one of which was by an American. In the same year there were sixty-two numbers in " Harper's Handy Series." Deducting four by American authors, we have fifty-eight cheap reprints issued in the latter as a consequence of the absence of international protection. Of these fifty-eight fifty-two were works of fiction, and only six belonged to other branches of literature.'—Matthews, in Putnam, *The Question of Copyright*, p. 425.

new works, mainly of foreign origin, at short and regular intervals. The number of English works reprinted in America is alone enormous. Under a continuance of these circumstances it is not difficult to foresee a speedy exhaustion of the native supply of best books, ousted by inferior substitutes. The unequal competition of reprints of English books, for which the American publisher pays the author nothing, must have its effect on the creative energies of native writers. To this further reference will be made.

SECTION III.

THE PRINTING TRADE. ENCOURAGEMENT OF HOME INDUSTRIES.

The American type-setting clause—The condition of simultaneous publication—Printing for exportation—Publishing interests—Mechanical musical instruments.

The solicitude of the State for the public benefit generally finds its legitimate outlet in provision for the needs of the public at large; but as the prosperity of every country is dependent upon its commerce the importance of special attention to the interests of its industries must not be overlooked.   The chief trade connected with copyright is of course printing; indeed, copyright would have had little commercial importance if printing had not been invented.

At first the printer alone, not the author, reaped the benefit derived from the multiplication of books.[1]   For many years printers were the recipients of royal privileges which, in return for the capital and labour involved in the production, secured them the sole right to print a particular book.   In England, up to 1644 the proprietors of the presses contrived to keep 'copies,' *i.e.* copyrights, almost entirely in their own hands, as Milton's *Speech for the Liberty of Unlicensed Printing* in that year plainly proves; and England, it may be said, was only typical of most countries in this respect.

---

[1] In early days printers generally combined their trade with that of publishing and bookselling.

That copyright protection depended in other countries than England upon control of the printing presses is clear from the anxiety formerly displayed by printers to obtain privileges from the King of Saxony. The great book fairs of Leipzig, though largely supplied from the home presses, dealt in the works of many nations; and in view of the enormous sales which were effected at the fairs, the King's privilege, protecting authors from the unauthorised multiplication of their works throughout his territory, including Leipzig, was of great value.

The printing trade is undoubtedly an important industry, advancing with civilisation and education, but foreigners should not be called upon to support that trade in order to gain the advantage of a so-called reciprocity of copyright protection. It is not difficult for the intelligent to realise that immaterial property is entitled to the same reverence as that which is material. The tolerance of such inequitable treatment by the educated classes of the country which gets the worst of the bargain is due merely to a feeling that two wrongs do not make a right.

The American Type-setting Clause.—The reasons adduced for the introduction of the type-setting clause in the American law of 1891 are not based on justice, but on the immediate advantage derived from levying a tax on foreigners. The technical line of argument is indicated by the testimony given by Mr. J. L. Kennedy, on behalf of the International Typographical Union, before the Judiciary Committee of the House of Representatives, when the present Act of Congress was in contemplation. In reply to the question, 'Why do the printers favour this Bill?' Mr. Kennedy replied, 'For several reasons. The first and principal reason is the selfish one. How rare is the human action that has not selfishness for its motive force! Its effect as a law will be given to greatly stimulate book printing in the United States. . . . Indeed, it has been conspicuously stated in the London *Times* that, if this Bill becomes a law, the literary and book-publishing centre of the English world will move westward from London and take up its abode in the city of New York. That would be a spectacle which every patriotic American might contemplate with complacency and pride.

'The Englishman who writes books for the money he can get out of them as well as the fame—and I think it fair to presume that the great majority of authors are actuated by both of those motives—will recognise that here is the richest market, and he will not think it a hardship to comply with the provisions of this proposed law in view of the substantial benefit it is to him, and the printers do not consider it a hardship to require of him that he shall leave upon our shores so much of his profits at least as will pay for his printing. . . . In short, it is not difficult for printers to see that such a law will confer inestimable benefits upon their own and allied trades.'[1]

A strange but characteristic opinion to present for the consideration of the legislature of a great Republic! A recommendation of a truck system with its objectionable features openly presented! Nevertheless, in spite of the obviously interested character of the arguments adduced, the printers, forming only a small class of the public, were allowed to dominate the whole, though the chief motive of their persistence was simply private gain; and the type-setting clause was inserted in the Chace Bill of 1891.

The condition of Simultaneous Publication.—In addition to the onerous clause of the Chace Act (1891) that all works

---

[1] Putnam, *The Question of Copyright*, pp. 78, 79.

which are to gain American copyright must be set up[1] in
the United States, the securing of American copyright by
the English publisher is fraught with the anxiety of assuring
himself that the condition of simultaneous publication imposed by the American law is fulfilled, and of supervising
the printer to make him carry out spelling and other typographical details according to the English mode.[2]

Should the English publisher be unwilling to have his
type set up in the States, his only chance of appealing to
its market is to export copies of his works to that country.
On payment of an *ad valorem* duty of 25 per cent. upon
importation of the books into America he will be allowed
to enter the market, in competition with American publishers
who can produce the same works free from duty and without
remuneration to the author.

Printing for Exportation.—In such a case the injury to
the copyright owner is sufficiently keenly felt when in one
country the works of another are copied for home consumption ; but it is accentuated when reprints are exported to
other countries and smuggled on a large scale into the country
of origin, or into its colonies and dependencies. Such a
piratical traffic with the country of origin used to be extensively carried on in French works by the Belgians,[3] and

---

[1] The truck system is generally accompanied by exorbitant prices, but under
the American type-setting clause exorbitant prices are not exacted from English
publishers and authors ; indeed in some branches of the book-producing trade,
e.g. electro-typing, American prices are not greater than those which obtain
in other countries, and the same holds good for certain kinds of paper.

[2] The latter task may be avoided if the whole of the type is set up separately
in each of the two countries. This however involves a double outlay, and the
risk of failure in simultaneity of publication still remains.

[3] After the treaty with France in 1852, by which the Belgian piracies were
checked, the Belgian export trade declined from an annual value of 2,238,000
francs to one of 1,306,000 francs in 1856. It is pleasing, however, to note that
under the healthier influences subsequently instituted the legitimate trade gradually increased and brought up the total value of exports to its old volume.

now a great number of unauthorised copies of English works
find their way into Canada from the United States. No
complete remedy for such an evil can be found : experience
shows that the most vigilant supervision on the part of
customs officers may be eluded. The only effectual preventive
lies in the prohibition of unauthorised reproduction by the
country in which it is carried on.

Publishing interests.—The State has to consider the
publishing as well as the printing trade ; but in the long
run the interests of the publisher are so intimately bound
up with those of the native author that it is not necessary
to take them into separate account. The best interests of
both are opposed to those of the cheap printer.

It is true that a publisher may at first find it most
profitable to make his output as large as possible, even
by preying on foreign works ; but such a course is not
likely to pay in the long run. As Von Bar says, with reference to this policy, ' Experience has in fact shown . . .
that in the end booksellers are forced into a ruinous system
of underbidding each other, or to the payment of *honoraria*
to foreign authors and agents . . . without securing themselves against further reprints by rivals in the trade.' [1]
Hence even the argument of trade-interest is not altogether
incompatible with the protection of foreign authors by the
State.

Mechanical Musical Instruments.—The Berne Convention
furnishes an example of the extent to which commercial
interests can affect the international protection of copyright.
§ 3 of its Closing Protocol runs :—' It is understood that
the manufacture and the sale of instruments serving to reproduce mechanically musical airs in which copyright subsists

---

[1] Von Bar, *Theory and Practice of Private International Law*, trans. Gillespie,
p. 748.

shall not be considered as constituting musical infringement.'
This is doubtless a concession to Switzerland, in which the
manufacture of these instruments is a national industry.   It
is the counterpart of a provision to the same effect contained in a commercial treaty of 1866 between Switzerland
and France.

SECTION IV.

PROTECTION OF NATIVE AUTHORS.

American authors suffer from the national policy—Retorsion and reprisals
—Reciprocity the safest principle.

It is quite reasonable that the immediate interests of its
members should be the first care of a community.   Indeed
it is possible that the very existence of society is due to the
necessity for self-preservation.   But with the advance of civilisation, States become less exclusive; and intercourse with
foreign nations teaches that there are many advantages to be
derived from a wider interpretation of the need for mutual
tolerance and protection.   In fact for matters of common
interest, such as literature, society may be considered universal,
and, with the increasing realisation of this fact, the maxim
that 'where there is society there is law' is being justified
in the development of a uniform international law of copyright.   In the meantime States are recognising their moral
duties towards foreign authors through the medium of their
domestic law.

Between the extremes of alienage and citizenship there are
one or two intermediate grades of relationship to the State
which have under various qualifications been held to entitle
authors to copyright protection.   These will be dealt with at
length in Chapter IV., entitled, 'Alien authors and alien
laws.'   The economic aspect of the crude policy of confining
protection to subjects, or of admitting foreigners only upon
condition of their fulfilling onerous conditions within the
territory, will be considered in this Section.

H

American Authors suffer from the National Policy.—The United States is at the present day prominent amongst the countries which refuse equitable protection to foreign authors, and its refusal to protect them, which on the surface would seem to establish a valuable monopoly in favour of American authors, has in reality done them more harm than good. Thus Mr. W. E. Simonds, in a Report on the International Copyright Bill of 1890-1891, presented on behalf of the House Committee on Patents, says : ' It is shown that . . . our present procedure represses authorship by putting the products of the labour of American authors into untrammeled competition with the products of English labour, for which nothing is paid ; that our present procedure deprives American authors of the advantage of the British market ; that our present procedure vitiates the education and tastes of American youth ; that our present procedure bars our people from the benefits of the good literature of England ; and that our present procedure prevents the cheapening of good and desirable books in the United States.'[1]

To buy in the cheapest market is a rule of economics which even a child is quick to recognise. The existence of a market where goods can be obtained for nothing involves ruin for other markets. Hence it is impossible for American authors to contend with the constant supply of reprints of foreign works, since these are free of the cost of authorship. ' The main difficulty undoubtedly arises from the fact that, although the language of the two countries is identical, the original works published in America are as yet less numerous than those published in Great Britain. This naturally affords a temptation to the Americans to take advantage of the works of the older country, and at the same time tends to diminish the inducement to publish original works. It is the opinion,

[1] Quoted in Putnam, *The Question of Copyright*, p. 130.

of some of those who gave evidence on this subject, and it appears to be plain, that the effect of the existing state of things is to check the growth of American literature.'[1]

In a petition to Congress the American authors themselves complained of the impoverishment of native literature which had resulted from the refusal of the United States to protect foreign works, and in self-defence urged Congress to pass an International Copyright Bill 'which will protect the rights of authors.'[2] This petition, presented in favour of the Chace Act, came from one hundred and forty-four of the leading American authors 'who earn their living in whole or in part by their pen, and who are put at a disadvantage in their own country by the publication of foreign books without payment to the author, so that American books are undersold in the American market to the detriment of American literature.'[3] Such a statement, originating with an influential body of native authors, affords remarkable testimony to the evil of withholding international recognition.[4]

Retorsion and Reprisals.—While American authors besought the American Government to protect them from the results of

---

[1] Report of the British Commission of 1876, § 236.

[2] A somewhat similar state of affairs existed in Belgium in 1839. A petition of this date addressed to the National Chamber asks for a grant of 30,000 francs to be divided between Belgian authors. At this time the poverty of the native literature was attributed to the fact that the printing presses were so fully occupied in issuing reproductions of French books that the Belgians could find no one who would print their own works. Ten years later a similar complaint was made in a number of petitions addressed to the Chamber.—Darras, *Du Droit des Auteurs et des Artistes*, p. 79.

[3] Putnam, *The Question of Copyright*, p. 107. As Von Bar says, 'Experience has in fact shown that the reprinting of foreign works on a large scale . . . damages native authors, since their work has difficulty in competing with the printed works which are not burdened with any honorarium to the author.'— *Theory and Practice of International Law*, p. 748.

[4] 'An impulse to defend ourselves is linked to many forms of danger by a sequence of cause and effect.'—Westlake, *Chapters on the Principles of International Law*, p. 5.

its generosity, the subjects of other nations were urging their governments to adopt means which would compel the United States to establish a more equitable state of affairs. Before the days of the general protection of foreign authors these means had been ready to hand ; some nations having even made express enactments against offending countries. Thus the Prussian Code of 1791, after a clause providing for general reciprocity, makes the following restriction by Sec. 47 of the Introduction : 'Should a foreign State make laws onerous to foreigners in general and to the subjects of Prussian States in particular, or if it suffers knowingly a similar abuse, the law of reprisals shall take effect' ; while Sec. 1033 of the Code enacts that 'Infringements are permitted with respect to publishers of works in foreign countries, in so far as, in those States, they are permitted to the prejudice of Prussian booksellers.'

But such means are hardly available at the present day. A State cannot without changing its law make specific retorsion against another in copyright matters, and the best opinion is against the justice of such action. The difficulty of the matter is well expressed in the Report of the English Copyright Commission of 1876, which says, in connection with the American piracies : 'When deciding upon the terms in which we should report upon this subject we have felt the extreme delicacy of our position in expressing an opinion upon the policy and laws of a friendly nation, with regard to which a keen sense of injury is entertained by British authors. Nevertheless we have deemed it our duty to state the facts brought to our knowledge, and frankly to draw the conclusions to which they lead.'[1] The Commission gave its full consideration to the just complaints of British authors, and dispassionately states its conclusions as to the

---

[1] *Report of the Royal Commissioners on Copyright*, 1876, § 234.

best line of policy to be pursued. ' It has been suggested to us that this country would be justified in taking steps of a retaliatory character, with a view of enforcing, incidentally, that protection from the United States which we accord to them. This might be done by withdrawing from the Americans the privilege of copyright on first publication in this country. We have, however, come to the conclusion that, on the highest public grounds of policy and expediency, it is advisable that our law should be based on correct principles, irrespective of the opinions or the policy of other nations. We admit the propriety of protecting copyright, and it appears to us that the principle of copyright, if admitted, is one of universal application. We therefore recommend that this country should pursue the policy of recognising the author's rights, irrespective of nationality.' [1]

Reciprocity the Safest Principle.—If a nation wishes its authors to enjoy protection in foreign countries as well as at home it is highly advisable for it so to shape its law as to be able to offer recognition to foreign copyright in return for a reciprocal recognition of its own. Under any other circumstances it is only in a few foreign countries, *i.e.* in those which freely accord protection to all authors without condition of reciprocity,[2] that its authors will get any protection at all ; and in those countries which adopt the ' principle of universal protection,' protection is given as a mere matter of grace, not in fulfilment of an international obligation. It is not compatible with the dignity of a State to allow the international protection of its authors to depend on the unrequited generosity of foreign States ; its own law should enable it to claim copyright recognition from other countries for its subjects as a matter of international reciprocity. Hence the domestic law

---

[1] *Report of the Royal Commissioners on Copyright*, 1876, § 251.
[2] France, Belgium, and Luxemburg.

of every country[1] should at least duly provide for the establishment of reciprocal protection by international agreement with other countries ('diplomatic reciprocity'), if not for the protection of foreign authors as a matter of course where the law of their own country satisfies the condition of reciprocity ('legal reciprocity').

[1] *I.e.* every country in which the making of a treaty does not *ipso facto* involve the alteration of the domestic law so far as is necessary to enable the treaty to take effect.

SECTION V.

THE ECONOMIC ASPECT OF UNIVERSAL PROTECTION.

The Principle of Universal Protection—No direct disadvantage results from the principle—It opens the way for treaties—And attracts intellectual works to the country adopting it—Limited application of Universal Protection in France and Belgium—Universal Protection regarded as a matter of common justice—Reciprocity under the Berne Convention.

The Principle of Universal Protection.—There are three nations—France, Belgium, and Luxemburg—which grant statutory protection to the works of foreigners without imposing any direct condition of reciprocity. They adopt what has been termed by some Continental authors 'the generous policy of recognition of copyright.' But, as 'generous' connotes elements which are generally considered incompatible with 'policy,' and as, besides, the term is eulogistic rather than descriptive, it seems preferable to adopt another phrase, 'the principle of universal protection.' This almost explains itself : when applied to copyright it denotes the principle by which protection is extended to all works irrespective of the nationality of the author.

It would be idle to deny that the conferment of such a universal protection proceeds in part from purely altruistic motives ; but, while recognising this, it will be found that motives which are strictly economic may also be discovered in the liberality dispensed in this way.

A reputation for broad-mindedness is as valuable in diplomacy as in ordinary commercial transactions. Although the conduct of an individual may be prompted entirely by philanthropy or by a desire for distinction, these motives are outside the sphere of international action. The first care of a government should be the interests of its subjects, and it is a matter of duty for it to see that a proper return is secured for any benefit it accords to foreign States. Therefore any course of conduct which appears to be disinterested will, upon close examination, probably disclose some elements which do not enter into the idea of generosity.

Conduct which is apparently generous sometimes springs from an appreciation of the advantages to be derived from it. At first sight, the open recognition of the rights of authors of all countries without any condition of reciprocity plainly appears to be quite altruistic, but on examination it will be found that the risk of loss is not great, and may be more than compensated for by advantages attendant on the policy. In any case, of course, if the policy is unsuccessful the grant of protection can be readily withdrawn or restricted.

A State may be expected to seek for its subjects as much as it gives to aliens ; but if the gift costs nothing, then the absence of the return which we call reciprocity is the renunciation of a possible benefit, rather than an actual loss. A country adopting the principle of open recognition of the right of authors without reference to this return, may realise also that the reproduction in, and importation into, its territory of protected foreign works may stimulate its own authors and artists to competition, and thus ultimately advance the education and culture of its people. Again, the subjecting of foreigners to high court fees[1] on coming into court and the depriving them of the ordinary penalties offer a means of discounting the general protection to an almost unlimited extent ; and the imposition of vexatious formalities, such as

---

[1] Von Bar suggests these as legitimate means of placing subjects in a comparatively favourable position.—Von Bar, *Theory and Practice of Private International Law*, pp. 749, 750.

the deposit of security for costs, may still further detract from the completeness of the assimilation of aliens to subjects. These qualifications are not mere products of the imagination, but are actually adopted in the procedure of many countries.

By the suggestion that the grant of universal protection may depend on interested motives, or may in practice fail of completeness, it is not intended to detract from its actual value. In order, however, to show that it does not depend on any particular superiority of character on the part of the States which carry it out it is necessary to enter into an analysis of the conditions which produce it. From this it will be seen that, though it always calls for commendation, its commercial advantages do not necessarily lie solely on the side of the recipients of protection.

No direct Disadvantage results from the Principle.—On examining the consequences of the adoption by a State of the principle of universal protection, it at first sight appears that such a policy must result in substantial loss ; but here as in other transactions there are underlying factors, which, upon closer consideration, will be seen greatly to modify the first estimate. The case in which the injury appears greatest is where a country which benefits by the protection refuses reciprocity, by denying rights to authors belonging to the liberal country ; but here the same unsatisfactory state of affairs will exist whatever copyright policy be adopted by the latter. Therefore, since the detriment in question would necessarily have been sustained, it cannot be regarded as a consequence of the grant of universal protection. Even if one State makes an offer of reciprocal protection to another, the offer may be rejected or ignored. And if the contract is eventually completed it will often be impossible to obtain adequate consideration. The protection mutually given by the two parties to an international agreement for reciprocity may be regarded as an indeterminate equation, satisfied by various values dependent on the resources and goodwill of either State.

Upon a calculation of the advantages and disadvantages of the principle of universal protection, and a comparison of them with those which attach from following other lines of policy, it appears that that principle, although not so satisfactory as that of reciprocity in its best aspect, is by no means without benefit to the country granting it.

It opens the way for Treaties.—In one respect, indeed, the principle of universal protection provides, though indirectly, a great increment of advantage. The adoption of such a principle by any country at once proclaims an awakened interest in international copyright. And, although the principle is in strictness all-sufficient in itself, it is in practice often an introduction to treaty-making on a large scale. It is, in fact, almost equivalent to a general invitation to enter into diplomatic arrangements, coming from a country with open credentials for broad-mindedness.

Thus of the generous policy of the French Decree of 1852 Von Bar says : ' French diplomacy has not, by reason of this liberality, found any difficulty in arranging advantageous conventions, as the result has shown, although formerly her literary and artistic productions fell victims in a marked degree to reprints and to piracy. The task of arranging these treaties has on the contrary been made easier. Completely unselfish testimony was thus given to the objectionable character of this piracy, and to the mischief it did to the country whose trades availed themselves of it, and most States have not been able to resist the force of this argument.'[1]

The principle of universal protection possesses the great

[1] Von Bar, *Theory and Practice of Private International Law*, pp. 748, 749.

advantage of simplicity, in that it is an offer of free and
unconditional protection to all. No doubt is left as to what
State may avail itself of its provisions ; but an open offer of
reciprocity may lead to difficulties with countries accepting it,
unless the agreement is sanctioned in a definite treaty.

An offer of unconditional protection is not necessarily
followed by reciprocal offers from the benefited States, but in
general the latter show no desire to abuse the liberality of the
other nation, as is indicated by the large number of treaties
now in force with France.

And attracts intellectual works to the country adopting it.—
The protection of the rights of foreigners by a State is
necessarily valid only within its own territory, and much of
the resultant benefit of the protection is reflected upon its own
people. The fact that it is *only* in the countries which grant
protection to foreign works, and not outside them, that the
right is enjoyed seems sufficiently easy of comprehension, but
does not appear always to have been firmly grasped by
writers on copyright. In no foreign country will the general
public benefit by the extension of protection, which will affect
the authors alone, and only a minority of those. The gain to
foreign authors as a class may thus be small.

Most of the arguments that have been used in the early
part of this chapter against the narrow policy which refuses
to give protection to foreign works may be turned in favour of
the principle of universal protection. As might be expected,
the countries which grant a wise protection to foreigners are
also the most liberal in their domestic treatment of works of
literature and art. The tendency is for such countries to
attract the best foreign works. As a result a healthy spirit of
competition is likely to be engendered amongst their own
authors and artists ; and in this way their literature may
be benefited and their trade increased.

The loss on account of foreign infringement resulting to a
country which adopts the principle of universal protection is
more apparent than real. In a country like France, which is
sufficiently advanced to follow a policy of unconditional recognition of foreign copyright, art and literature are usually
highly developed, while on the other hand a country which is
likely to lend itself to piracy has as a rule little good literature of its own and no demand for good foreign literature.[1]
Hence the works of the liberal country are likely to find
a comparatively small sale in the other State. Thus the
detriment suffered from the non-establishment of reciprocity
by the country granting universal protection is usually not
very serious.

**Limited application of universal Protection in France and
Belgium.**—The principle adopted by France and Belgium in
1852 and 1886 respectively is not that of the complete
assimilation of the rights[2] of foreigners to those of natives.
Foreign works are not admitted to copyright in France unless
their authors have performed in respect of them the conditions
and formalities imposed by the country of origin, and both in
France and in Belgium the term[3] of copyright accorded is

---

[1] This of course can hardly be said of the United States, which, in spite of its
extensive borrowing from the countries of Europe, has nevertheless a fair claim
to rank as a literary nation.

[2] It does not follow that a country which adopts the principle of universal protection will as a matter of course refuse to protect foreign works which have no
copyright in their own country. France, according to Lyon-Caen, Pataille,
Renault, and Darras, does not protect such works; but Pouillet is of a contrary
opinion.

[3] It is noteworthy that France, Belgium, and Luxemburg, which are generally
in favour of a unification of laws, should treat the duration of the foreigner's
rights each in a different manner. The French decree of 1852 is silent on the
point, but the general, though not the universal, opinion interprets the period of
protection for the foreigner as limited in two ways: (1) that it must not be
greater than France gives to its own natives, viz. life *plus* fifty years, and (2) not
greater than that of the country of origin. Belgium expresses the same rule

limited by that given in the country of origin.   Substantially,
however, in these countries aliens enjoy the same rights as
natives.   In Luxemburg the performance of the conditions
and formalities of the country of origin is not expressly
required, while the domestic term of protection is not limited
by that of the country of origin.

Universal Protection regarded as a matter of common Justice.
—Both Darras and Von Bar think a mode of protection even
more generous than that adopted by France, Belgium, and
Luxemburg to be practicable ; but this view rests upon a
chimerical assumption that all men would act justly in the
absence of any constraining self-interest.   Darras believes
it to be a retrogression for a State to make copyright
laws when it already protects copyright as 'a matter of
course,' particularly when the new laws subject international
protection to the condition of reciprocity.   It is extremely
doubtful however whether there ever has been a State
which gave a prompt and adequate remedy as 'a matter of
course.'

Darras characterises the conduct of Frederick VI. of Denmark, who, while claiming that infringements of foreign works
had never been permitted in his country, legislated in 1828
against them, as a backward step.   And even of the French
Decree of 1852, which was the first French legislation for the
protection of works printed abroad, he writes : 'Far be from
us any intention to under-estimate its merit, but we must
nevertheless say that the aliens' question had been threshed
out long ago, and that long ago their rights had been affirmed.'[1]
Like Von Bar, he thinks that 'the immorality of the piracy
of a foreign work is brought much more sharply forward if it

---

specifically in the Act of 1886, while Luxemburg has no limitation whatever to
the period of the country of origin.

[1] Darras, *Du Droit des Auteurs et des Artistes*, p. 212.

is as a matter of course reprobated by the State, than if the
repression of it seems to be merely the result of an international treaty.' [1]

Reciprocity under the Berne Convention.—The basis of
the Berne Convention is practically a universal reciprocity,
embodying in every country the assimilation of the
rights of aliens to those of subjects. Until every country
freely adopts the principle of universal protection, reciprocity
appears to be the only equitable principle upon which an
international agreement can be framed.

[1] Von Bar, *Theory and Practice of Private International Law*, p. 750.

SECTION VI.

COMPETITION. COURTESY OF THE TRADE.
COURTESY COPYRIGHT.

Courtesy of the trade—Courtesy Copyright—Percentage systems—Integrity of leading American publishers.

Referring to the publisher's position with regard to books not of a popular character, Putnam says : ' Almost every such work, separately considered, appeals to a limited class only. The republication of one of them involves, as a rule, a very considerable outlay. No publisher dare undertake the necessary outlay—the publication of a book always being an experiment, financially—unless he is sure he can have the whole limited field to himself.'[1] Many years ago the risk of competition was reduced in Ireland, Holland, and Belgium by agreement[2] among the publishers themselves ; and more recently it has been dealt with in similar fashion by the publishers of the United States of America. In Holland a ' Mutual Protection Society' was founded, to which publishers, when they discovered a foreign book which seemed a good subject for translation, gave notice of their intention to reproduce it ; the Society thereupon guaranteeing that no other publisher should compete with them.[3]

---

[1] Putnam, *The Question of Copyright*, p. 100.

[2] In 1753 Richardson complained that the Irish booksellers were agreed among themselves that he who should first obtain an English work should be considered to have a sufficient title to it.

[3] M. Van Zuylen, in the *Bulletin de l'Association Littéraire*, 1880, p. 60.

Courtesy of the Trade.—In the printing countries just re-ferred to, the importance of the courtesy of the trade, *i.e.* the mutual arrangement among the publishers that the 'title' of the first producer of a foreign reprint shall be respected, was small compared with its latter-day importance in the United States of America. The English Royal Copyright Commission of 1876, after a preamble on the ruinous effects of mutual underselling, reports that 'American publishers were thus obliged to take steps for their own protection. This was effected by an arrangement among themselves. The terms of this understanding are that the trade generally will recognise the priority of right to republication of a British work as existing in the American publisher who can secure priority of issue in the United States. The priority may be secured either by arrangement with the author, or in any other way. The understanding, however, is not legally bind-ing, and is rather a result of convenience and of a growing disposition to recognise the claims of British authors, than of actual agreement.'[1]

Fortunately and unfortunately, this American courtesy of the trade has now become of less importance. In Ireland more than a century ago, 'now and then a shark was found who preyed upon his own kind,' as the newspapers of Dublin have testified; and in America, particularly in the Western States, disregard for the courtesy title became more general, the 'courtesy of the trade' having now been largely replaced by what is euphemistically styled 'courtesy copyright.'

Courtesy Copyright.—'Courtesy copyright' is not a legal right, but a claim to monopoly on the part of the publisher, derived from the author's authorisation to reprint his work in return for an agreed sum. No doubt payments have often

---

[1] *Report of the Commission of 1876,* § 241.

been made as a mere matter of justice to the author,[1] but in the case of 'courtesy copyright' there is a commercial reason for them.

Reference has already been made, in the historical account of international infringement contained in a previous chapter, to the competition amongst publishers to obtain the first copies of new foreign works so as to forestall each other in the market of their own country ; to their employment of agents to facilitate the achievement of this object ; and to their expenditure of large sums of money in telegraphing 'copy' and securing advance proofs. The advantages obtained even by such means as these were important, but in recent times publishers have adroitly gone still further and have enlisted the services of the authors themselves in consideration of a money payment. The latter, finding that nothing is gained by withholding their consent, are generally willing to permit the reproduction of their works, to furnish advance proof-sheets, and to undertake to give early intimation of the corrections and alterations made in subsequent editions which may appear in the country of origin. The publisher derives obvious benefits from such an arrangement. In addition to the advantage of being the first in the field, and of securing greater accuracy for his reproductions, he is able to announce works issued by him as 'author's edition' or 'authorised edition.' This serves as a guarantee for the accuracy of the reproduction, and is an excellent advertisement.

Hence, even before the general recognition of 'courtesy copyright,' many American publishers found it profitable to offer English authors a fraction of the value of their work in return for the American 'rights.' Darras attributes the origin of the practice to the authors themselves, but it will be seen

---

[1] Courtesy copyright was paid for by Tauchnitz of Leipzig long before England had any treaty relations with Germany.

that in all probability negotiations for securing the sanction and co-operation of authors in return for a small consideration were generally begun by the publishers.[1]

Under the Chace Act of 1891, English authors and publishers are now able to render themselves independent of all such arrangements by securing legal copyright in the United States. The privilege, involving as it does the necessity of setting up the type of the work in the United States, is however taken advantage of only in particular cases, as for most books a person resident in England is hardly in a position to judge in advance whether the circulation is likely to repay the cost of composition.

Percentage Systems.—In connection with this subject certain devices, which have been adopted by countries with a view of rendering the copyright works of their own authors open to reproduction upon certain conditions, are worthy of note. According to a system now in vogue in Italy, an exclusive right of publication belongs to the author of a work during his life ; and, in the event of his death before the end of forty years from the date of first publication, his successors derive a title for the remainder of that period. When the term of forty years, or (if the author outlives this) the author's life, has expired, a second period of forty years commences, during which anyone can republish the work upon paying to the author a fixed percentage (*tantième*). On the Continent this is generally known as the system of the

---

[1] 'In view of this state of the relations among the American houses,' says Darras, ' English authors conceived an ingenious system by which they obtained from the United States of America some pecuniary advantages. They procured for an American house the means of first publishing a reprint of their works, for which service they exacted payment. In this manner the first leaves of Livingstone's last work cost £1000. But this payment was made, not as Klostermann has thought, for the satisfaction of an unquiet conscience: its object was merely to assure considerable benefits to the publisher.'

domaine public payant.[1] In Switzerland it obtains with regard to the performing right in published plays. Anyone is at liberty to perform such plays on assuring to the author a royalty of 2 per cent. on the gross receipts.[2]

In Canada, as far back as 1872, a Bill was passed to permit Canadian publishers to reprint English copyright works, on payment of a royalty to the owner of the copyright. This, however, failed to obtain the consent of the Crown. Again in 1889, another Act, also as yet devoid of legal force, provided for the issue of licenses authorising persons, on payment of a royalty, to print and publish works in which, though eligible for protection, Canadian copyright should not have been completely acquired.

A similar ∠system has been advocated for the United States of America in respect of the reproduction of foreign copyright works. It has been suggested by Mr. R. Pearsall-Smith (in the *Nineteenth Century*) 'that any American publisher shall be at liberty to print editions of the works of a foreign author under the condition of paying to such author a royalty of 10 per cent. of the retail price. That this royalty shall be paid by the purchase from the author, in advance of the publication of the American edition, of stamps representing the above rate, as many stamps being bought as there are copies printed in the edition, and each copy of the book that is placed in the market by the publisher bearing one of these stamps conspicuously affixed.'[3]

Integrity of leading American Publishers.—In the course of this chapter it has been shown that the present inequitable law of America not only countenances, but directly encourages, native publishers to make use of foreign works without authorisation or payment. Still, it must be remembered that liberty conceded by law is not always used—that, even if the

[1] Lyon-Caen, *Lois françaises et étrangères.*—Introduction, p. xxxv.
[2] Swiss Copyright Code of 1883, sec. 7.
[3] Quoted in Putnam, *The Question of Copyright*, p. 65.

law of a country is illiberal, the conduct of its people may differ. The actual practice of American publishers is considerably in advance of their legal possibilities. It is true that, in many cases where payment has been made, English authors, knowing the absence of legal claims, have accepted insignificant sums for the American ' rights ' in their works, although the literary value to the American publisher in some of these has been almost or quite equal to that of the English copyright.

But it is directly within the author's personal knowledge that at the present day leading publishing firms in the large cities of America pay substantial sums to English authors for their American 'rights,' well knowing that in America these rights are moral only, not legal.

In some cases within the last few years, payments made to authors by the American publisher have nearly equalled the price which has been obtained for the English copyright ; the fact that some of these works have a larger circulation in America than in England does not detract from the integrity of the American publishers' action. As this applies also to works in the higher branches of education, literature, and philosophy, there is reason to hope that the time is not far distant when the American people will call for a more enlightened and equitable egislation than that which at present exists.

CHAPTER II.

INTERNATIONAL PROTECTION BY MEANS OF TREATIES.

SECTION I.

THE CONTRACTUAL NATURE OF TREATIES.

The two views of Copyright—Copyright primarily a municipal right—
A Copyright Treaty is a contract.

The Two Views of Copyright.—Before considering copyright as the subject-matter of treaties it is advisable to discuss the views which may be taken as to the character of the right. The two conceptions of copyright may be set out thus :—

A Prohibitory Right.—	**A Right of Property.—**
(i) Municipal, when the right is established by domestic law.	(i) Enforced by the law of a particular State, as a matter of justice to the native author.
(ii) International, when the right is established by agreement with foreign States, generally based on reciprocity.	(ii) Enforced by the customary law of nations, as a matter of justice to all authors.

In the previous chapters, where the history of international infringement and international recognition has been discussed from the national point of view, copyright has tacitly been regarded as a right of prohibition against the public, and not as a private right of property which should be valid all the world over, even in the absence of treaty. As to its true character, however, there is amongst nations a considerable difference of opinion, which has had its effect upon international practice. If copyright is a right of prohibition, it is a right of prohibition only against the public of a particular country, and is therefore solely municipal. If on the other hand it is a right of property, the general principle that all States should respect property wherever it is situated gives it a moral claim to be protected everywhere.

Copyright primarily a Municipal Right.—The right of prohibition, though it is primarily municipal, may of course be extended to foreign works. Sometimes this is done without any conditions, but much more frequently it is made to depend upon reciprocity. Where this is so the reciprocal interchange of protection is, it should be remarked, a contract based on the ordinary rule of consideration.

On the other hand, if the private right of property is acknowledged, the situation is radically different. Here the matter is no longer one of value given and received on either side, as in the purchase of a bookcase or a volume of a book. The concession of international copyright is now merely the independent recognition of an existing right of property, which becomes valid in each country as its law provides it with the means of protection. Where this view of the nature of copyright is taken its infringement must be regarded as analogous to the unauthorised seizure of a tangible article.

The former theory, however, seems the better. There is no such universal recognition of its proprietary character as would entitle copyright to call upon every State to protect it as a mere matter of justice—though several States have in fact done so—in the absence of international relations with the country of origin of the work. If copyright is property, it is property of an anomalous kind, and, as the story of its evolution shows, its claim to protection cannot be placed on the same ground as that of most other kinds. The opposing theory does not correspond with the facts, and tends to confuse law and morality. Therefore the only safe and permanent basis on which international copyright can exist is to be found in a formal agreement,[1] *i.e.* a convention or treaty.[2]

A Copyright Treaty is a Contract.—A treaty is 'a bargain in which something is bought by one party at the price of an equivalent given to the other,' though the exact consideration is not always expressed. In a copyright treaty reciprocity provides the consideration necessary to bind the bargain, since it imports a value given and received on each side. One of the parties may, it is true, derive more advantage from the bargain than the other; but *adequacy* of consideration is not usually considered necessary to a contract.

It is often through fear that the protection received may not be an adequate consideration, as well as through ignorance and apathy on copyright matters, that nations are slow to enter into international copyright treaties. It is difficult to

---

[1] The offer and acceptance of reciprocity may be made in a number of ways; amongst others by proclamation, exchange of notes, or official assurance following an offer. The *form* of the treaty is however unimportant.

[2] There seems to be no well-marked distinction between the terms 'treaty' and 'convention.' According to Hall (*International Law*, p. 344) the former is used for the larger political or commercial contracts, and the latter for those concerning more specific objects, *e.g.* copyright, or of smaller importance. In English statutes reference is made to copyright 'conventions' with foreign countries, and in the French language *convention* and *traité* are both used, the latter less frequently. On account of its paramount importance, the Berne Convention is regarded as *the* Convention in matters of copyright. It would be convenient if the term 'convention' could be reserved for a treaty to which more than two nations are parties.

assess the value of such an abstract subject of property as copyright even in the country of origin of the work. It must vary with the passing taste of the public and the current appreciation of particular authors. This is true even where the protection accorded to copyright is regulated according to a uniform standard, but in the case of two different nations the value of the protection itself will vary owing to differences in their laws, in their legal procedure, and in the efficiency of their administration. But though in particular cases these difficulties may seem almost insuperable, yet the consideration given and received by each party can usually be gauged with sufficient accuracy, each State negotiating for the totality of its subjects, and estimating their various interests and expectations as a whole.

In the absence of a sense of moral obligation to protect the works of foreigners on the part of a State, the value of the reciprocity to be received is generally the chief factor which enters into the question of the establishment of such protection. Sometimes, however, the gain regarded may even be independent of reciprocity, *e.g.* where it consists in the suppression of trashy literature in favour of the best and most desirable foreign works, or the protection of native authors against the unfair competition of foreign reprints. But in such cases there is no question of contract, these motives being sufficient to induce the country to grant protection spontaneously by its domestic law. These considerations have been treated in the preceding chapter on 'The Political Economy of Copyright.'

SECTION II.

THE PRINCIPLE OF UNIVERSAL PROTECTION COMPARED WITH THAT OF RECIPROCITY.

Dangers connected with the Principle of Universal Protection—Reciprocity compared with the Principle of Universal Protection—Reciprocity regarded as unsound.

As has been pointed out above, if copyright is regarded as a personal right of property, every country ought unconditionally to protect foreign authors. This is the theory upon which the principle of universal protection, *i.e.* the protection of the copyright of aliens without condition of reciprocity, is based.

If the claim to copyright is to be upheld, say the advocates of this principle, it must be enforced by each State without awaiting any promise of reciprocal recognition on the part of others. In the words of a French authority, 'Literary piracy is a theft. In order for us to punish theft from foreign authors, is it necessary that foreign governments should do the same for our authors ? Morality would thus be no longer a duty, but a market.'[1] This view had been previously expressed by Lamartine in 1841.

Dangers connected with the Principle of Universal Protection.—But while it must be acknowledged that each new adoption of the principle of universal protection marks real progress, at the same time it cannot be overlooked that the absence of reciprocity as a condition of protection affords a temptation to other nations. A country granting unconditional recognition deprives itself of the power of withholding that

---

[1] Lherbette, quoted in Darras, *Du Droit des Auteurs et des Artistes*, pp. 81, 82.

protection which it might otherwise have offered as a consideration for a similar protection of the rights of its own authors.

In practice, however, these dangers may be reduced by well-calculated plans and wise diplomacy. Despite the absence of consideration, in some ways the adoption of the principle which universal protection involves is found to stimulate the development of treaties[1]; and with each fresh treaty that is made the inconvenience resulting from the principle is proportionally diminished. Still the derogation from its liberality which is thereby caused materially reduces the moral value of the advance towards a universal law which the adoption of the principle marks.

Reciprocity compared with the Principle of Universal Protection.—Experience has amply proved that the condition of reciprocity provides in general a good working basis for international agreements. The Berne Convention has adopted it as its fundamental principle. Besides the fact that when there is no such condition attached to the protection of aliens no means of defence against foreign piracy exist, it is patent that 'in applying it unjust nations are punished, while those which apply fair principles in their dealings are recompensed.'

While no doubt the principle of universal protection serves as an excellent example, yet it accentuates the difference between the copyright law of a country which adopts it and that of another which does not, and so acts as a deterrent to advance on the part of the more backward countries.[2]

---

[1] When France adopted the principle of universal protection in 1852 she was, says Darras, 'able to treat, not as an industrial nation bargaining for a tariff from mercantile peoples, but as sovereign of a moral empire, summoning, one might almost say forcing, Europe to sign a second declaration of intellectual rights.'—Darras, *Du Droit des Auteurs et des Artistes*, p. 83.

[2] Though on the other hand it is clear that the French Decree of 1852 has not stood in the way of the conclusion of treaties between France and other States. See last chapter, sec. 5.

Reciprocity regarded as Unsound.—Reciprocity is considered an unsound principle by many jurists, including Von Bar and Darras ; but the line of argument they adopt is one of such lofty morality as to be inapplicable to practical conditions. According to them, if piracy is held by the State to be wrong, all authors, including aliens, should be protected against it without the intervention of reciprocity.

Von Bar holds, as we have seen, that the immorality of the piracy of a foreign work is brought much more sharply home where, being punished according to fundamental principles, it is reprobated by the State as a matter of course, than in a country where its protection depends on a treaty. The practical disadvantages of the principle of universal protection are not ignored by Von Bar ; but he propounds certain means whereby the disadvantage to native authors which is a consequence of the non-existence of reciprocity may be minimised. Thus, amongst other devices by which foreigners might be placed under disabilities, Von Bar suggests that upon seeking redress they might be required to pay ' exceptionally high court fees,' and that when successful they might be deprived of any penalties awarded, which should go to the public treasury instead.[1]

---

[1] With regard to the imposition of a similar disability, i.e. *cautio judicatum solvi*, or deposit of security for costs, which is frequently exacted from aliens, much adverse criticism has of late been expressed in copyright conferences.

SECTION III.

METHODS OF ESTABLISHING INTERNATIONAL RECOGNITION.

The development of International Protection—Protection by Statute and by Agreement—Unions for International Protection—Factors in the establishment of Protection—An indefinite declaration of intention is unsatisfactory—Domestic conditions affect value of agreement—Differences in the domestic interpretation of terms.

The development of International Protection.—In a perfect community ethics would doubtless take the place of law, and moral wrongs would be punished as a matter of course without need of special legislation. Under existing conditions, however, where a moral right exists and general opinion has been brought to recognise that it is of such a nature as to be a proper subject for positive law, it becomes a national and international duty to convert this into a legal right by providing a remedy for its infringement. Copyright is no exception to this rule. The most flagrant outbreaks of literary piracy in the last century, by compelling attention to the serious detriment suffered by authors under the existing state of affairs, prepared the way for great progress in the development of international recognition. So, too, the important Conventions made by the German Confederation in 1832 and 1835 and the series of treaties formed by Belgium, including one with France in 1852, were the outcome of a natural reaction against the extensive piracy of foreign works which had previously been carried on in these States.

In France the primary investigation into the 'best means of checking injury done by reproduction of French works abroad,' undertaken by the Commission of 1836, was followed by the adoption of severe measures against the importation of French reprints and resulted indirectly in the formation of commercial treaties with Belgium in 1852 and Holland in 1855,[1] stipulating for the protection of French authors. The measures in question, though dictated by pure self-interest, resulted in the development of broader views upon international copyright. This ultimately led to the grant of universal protection to aliens, for in 1852 Parliament took the matter seriously in hand and enacted a decree which gave the same protection to foreigners as to natives, without any condition of reciprocity. This advance on the part of France was only the beginning of a more general forward movement.

In 1858 the International Literary Congress, attended by many delegates from governments and learned societies, men of letters, jurists, and others, met at Brussels, the old 'workshop of infringements.' The congress passed five resolutions, all of them of an optimistic character : the one with which we are immediately concerned demanded the universal and absolute assimilation of the rights of foreign authors to those of subjects. The principle thus expressed is unobjectionable as an ideal, but in practice international recognition must for well-founded reasons fall far short of it.

Protection by Statute and by Agreement.—Legal protection of aliens may be established directly in any of three ways :

> (1) By Statute;
>
> (2) By Treaty ; including
>
> (3) By Convention, forming an International Union.

A STATUTE may declare :

> (*a*) Its willingness or intention to protect the rights of
> foreigners upon condition of reciprocity ; or

---

[1] The negotiations for these treaties were begun in 1840.

(*b*) Its willingness or intention to protect the rights of foreigners without any condition of reciprocity.

A TREATY establishing recognition may contain either :

(*a*) Provisions for specific reciprocity, or

(*b*) Provisions for general reciprocity.

Continental writers, such as Darras and Nicolau, classify the methods in which protection may be granted to foreigners as follows :

(1) Diplomatic reciprocity, *i.e.* treaty ;

(2) Legal reciprocity, *i.e.* unilateral declaration of intention to recognise the rights of foreigners without treaty but subject to reciprocity ;

(3) Unilateral declaration of intention to protect the rights of foreigners without any condition.

Unions for International Protection.—Ambiguity is much less likely to exist in a convention which is drawn up by an International Union comprised of a number of States than in a treaty between two States alone. An agreement between a number of States is only settled after much discussion in international conferences : and at such conferences the presence of a large number of negotiators leads to an exhaustive examination of the draft of the agreement, so that nearly every important point is raised by some one or other before a definite result is achieved. The fact that an International Union binds a number of countries at once by identical obligations is all in favour of simplicity and saving of time and labour. On the other hand, the difficulty of arriving at a treaty which shall be accepted by all, increases in direct proportion to the number of the parties ; and the bringing together of conferences and the preservation of good feeling amongst their members are matters of great difficulty.

In considering the processes which lead to the formation of such a Union, it is necessary first to look to the individual

States, which usually possess different systems of legislation and administration, and different legal ideas, but which exhibit certain points of identity.   With the diffusion of thought and the scientific examination of a subject like copyright, the differences begin to disappear and the points of identity to increase in number.   Eventually it becomes possible for some States to enter into treaties with one another.   Other countries follow their lead, and a network of treaties is established. Thus the ideas of the various countries concerning the right of aliens to protection and the proper mode of granting them protection become assimilated to one another.[1]   At this stage some one country must take the lead and convene the other States, or enter into a large number of treaties, with the object of bringing about the conclusion of a multiple convention.[2]

Factors in the Establishment of Protection.—There are two important factors which usually enter into the recognition by a country of the rights of foreign authors.   In the first place there is the declaration of intention to grant such recognition, whether with or without condition of reciprocity.   As such a declaration has an international significance, it is necessary that great care should be taken to state its exact force and scope, otherwise there will be a risk of serious misunderstanding with other States.   Next there is reciprocity itself, which,

[1] But, while the existence of a number of treaties between various States inevitably tends to a unification of their views, it nevertheless in another direction tends to impede the formation of an international union, since no such union can stand on a sound basis, while many independent treaties between its members are in force.

[2] Attention may again be called to the important step taken by Prussia in 1827, with a view to bringing about the establishment of a federal code of copyright for Germany.   The Diet having proved unable of itself to cope with the difficulties in the way of this, between 1827 and 1829 Prussia induced thirty-one States to enter into treaties with it, thus clearing the way for the important Federal Act of 1832, which abolished all differences between foreigners and natives throughout the Germanic Confederation : see Part I., Chap. III., sec. 3.

though not required when international protection results from unilateral action on the part of one country, is always present when it depends upon arrangement between two or more States. This reciprocity varies in mode—for each of the contracting States may agree to grant the other or others the rights of its domestic law, or it may agree to grant a set of rights, independently defined and fixed in the agreement itself. The subject of reciprocity is sufficiently important to be treated in a separate section.

An Indefinite Declaration of Intention is Unsatisfactory.—Considering now the first of these two factors, it appears that a declaration of willingness or intention may or may not require a corresponding declaration of acceptance, by treaty or otherwise, as a condition precedent to its taking effect, and in this fact there lies a danger. An expression of mere willingness, being an invitation to others to offer rather than a definite offer, can rarely occasion serious misunderstanding, but a declaration of intention to protect the rights of foreigners upon condition of reciprocity is liable to be taken as an offer, and a country actually granting general reciprocity to foreigners may consider tacit acquiescence, without more, to be a sufficient acceptance thereof.

The official list of countries which protect foreign works upon condition of reciprocity, even without treaty, contains the names of some sixteen,[1] including Great Britain, Italy, Norway, Spain, Sweden, Switzerland, and the United States, and in the early history of copyright where protection was accorded to foreign works at all it was generally in this vague way. In practice, however, many of these sixteen States, e.g. Great Britain, the United States of America, and the Scandinavian

---

[1] The office of the International Union also gives a list of countries protecting foreign works only under treaties : these are twenty in number, and amongst them are to be found Austria, Germany, Holland, Hungary, and Japan.

countries, require an answer in some form or other before they will regard the international agreement as complete.

If the agreement be complete and expressed in definite terms the establishment of international protection is assured ; but this may not be so if the second nation simply acts on the intention expressed in the offer without officially signifying its acceptance.

Domestic conditions affect value of Agreement.—Again, even when a system of reciprocal protection has been satisfactorily established, variations in the formalities of the two countries may lead to the destruction of the protection in a particular case. Thus one country may require deposit as a condition of copyright and the other have no such condition ; or they may even entertain different views as to a broad principle, *e.g.* one may hold that judicial decisions establish a general law, while the other may consider them more or less weighty statements of opinion, which cannot have any such effect. A declaration by two countries that they mean to extend to each other the benefits of their domestic law implies that their domestic protection is substantially the same in quality and amount, and if this is not so the declaration cannot well have its proper effect.

An example of this is a case which arose under the Belgian law of 1855, giving protection to French limited companies under condition of reciprocity. Belgian limited liability companies were in France allowed a *locus standi* only in virtue of judicial decisions, which in that country are not binding as law ; in consequence, Belgium, considering the protection thus accorded to rest on too insecure a basis, held that the condition of reciprocity had not been satisfied, and refused to recognise the rights of French companies.

Differences in the Domestic Interpretation of Terms.—The stability of the international contract may be threatened not only

K

by differences regarding the nature of the protection for which it provides, but also by differences regarding the capacity of the persons whom it is intended to benefit. Where this is so, the rule of international law, that terms having a different legal meaning in different States are to be understood in the sense given to them in the State to which they apply, may sometimes meet the case. 'Domicile' in connection with copyright is an important subject, and the meaning of the term varies widely in different countries : even 'inhabitant' receives diverse interpretations, *e.g.* under Austrian law a person must be domiciled to rank as such, while in Italy the word is applied to everyone living in a commune and registered as a resident.[1] And so with international copyright, the interpretation of terms included in the agreement for reciprocity may, in cases where there is conflict, be settled by this rule ; the law of the country with respect to which the meaning is to be applied defining the circumstances under which a person is entitled to protection.

[1] ' By the treaty of 1866 it was stipulated between Austria and Italy that inhabitants of the provinces ceded by the former power should enjoy the right of withdrawing with their property into Austrian territory during a year from the date of the exchange of ratifications. . . . The language of the treaty . . . had not an identical meaning in the two countries. As the provision referred to territory which was Austrian at the moment of the signature of the treaty the term " inhabitant " was construed in conformity with Austrian law.'—Hall, *Treatise on International Law*, p. 353.

SECTION IV.

RECIPROCITY AND ITS MODES.   PROTECTION WITHOUT RECIPROCITY.

Reciprocity, specific and general—Reciprocity is in theory unsatisfactory because indefinite—But in practice satisfactory—Unconditional protection by statute—The French Decree of 1852—Assimilation of *rights* and assimilation of *protection.*

The difficulty of estimating what is the exact value of the willingness or intention of any given country to grant reciprocal protection, and the uncertainty as to whether a proper acceptance has been made, or as to the construction of an established treaty, are small compared with that of discrepancies which of necessity exist between the values of protection in different countries.   Such discrepancies necessarily impair the completeness of the reciprocity which forms the consideration binding the agreement.

Reciprocity, Specific and General.—Reciprocity may be either (1) specific or (2) general, and may range in value from the complete assimilation on each side of the rights of foreigners to those of natives to the mutual concession of a few definite rights to authors.   General reciprocity is often accompanied in practice by specific provisions on certain matters, as in the early days of the German Confederation, when the Decree of 1837 added a specific protection for ten years throughout the Germanic States to the general reciprocity which was agreed upon in the Decree of 1832.

In the case of specific reciprocity the danger of inequality is minimised, but general reciprocity is open to the objection indicated above ; though there may be a perfect agreement, the contents of the respective protections afforded by the two States may vary greatly. It may even be found, as was the case with Würtemberg in 1832, that one of the countries grants no statutory protection to its own natives and that therefore on its side the reciprocity, which consists in granting to authors belonging to the other country the same protection as it gives its own, is absolutely barren. Apart from such flagrant cases of inequality as this, it is obvious that in the absence of specific provisions reciprocity may often be incomplete. Where this is so delicate problems are likely to arise from which international complications will sometimes result.[1]

Reciprocity is in theory unsatisfactory because indefinite.— One of the objections raised against reciprocity is based on its necessary incompleteness. Where it obtains, one of the two contracting States is generally obliged to give to the foreign author rights greater in both duration and content than its own authors get in return—this is because of the impossibility of estimating accurately the value of any given domestic protection, which puts the establishment of a perfectly fair agreement out of the question. The value of protection in a given State depends on the number and average intellect of its people, on the extent of the domestic recognition accorded to various literary and artistic works, and on its ideas as to the admission to copyright of certain classes of subjects, such as photographs, works of architecture, etc.

But is in practice satisfactory.— The opponents of the doctrine of reciprocity close their eyes to the existence of any reciprocity short of the absolute ; they reject reciprocity

---

[1] It must be mentioned that, instead of involving the grant of the same *right* to foreign authors as to natives, general reciprocity may take the form of a concession of the same *protection* to the established rights of foreigners as that which is accorded to those of natives. In the former case foreigners may get rights unrecognised by their own domestic law, while in the latter they can obtain no further rights beyond those already gained by them in the country of origin.

as it exists, but fail altogether to provide a suitable substitute. Moreover they tax the principle with the disadvantages of conditions which do not properly attach to it.

According to Von Bar, who decries reciprocity, desirable results cannot be obtained from it unless the municipal laws of the different States are to a considerable extent identical in content. We may well admit that reciprocity cannot exist in the absence of some common elements, since it is on these that it is based ; but we cannot on that account agree with Von Bar that the principle is therefore practically fruitless. It is fairly obvious that all civilised codes present many common features ; and especially is this so in the case of copyright. In spite of all the arguments against the principle, it is clear therefore that, except in the few cases where universal protection is freely granted, the choice inevitably lies between recognition on such a basis and no protection at all. Hence a country has nothing to lose and something to gain by the adoption[1] of reciprocity ; for, however inadequate the protection it gets in this way may be, so far as it goes it acts as a deterrent to piracy.

Few publishers and authors are aware of the exact extent of the protection to which the works of a particular foreign country are entitled under its domestic law, even when they know that some protection exists. ' All rights reserved ' is generally a sufficient warning, and does not call for an exact knowledge of the rights of the work in its country of origin. Therefore, although reciprocity has been characterised as unsound and incompatible with the true principles of the recognition of the right to copyright, it is the most satisfactory basis of international protection. It might be dispensed with

---

[1] The effect of a merely impending treaty embracing the condition of reciprocity was seen in the desertion of the printers and publishers of piratical reprints from Brussels, the centre of the trade in international infringements, prior to the Belgian treaty with France in 1852.

if every nation would on its own account consent to assimilate
the rights of foreigners to those of its own subjects, or even
to assimilate the protection given in two cases, without treaty
or other contract conditional on reciprocity.   This speculation,
however, does not belong either to the science of law or that of
practical economics.

Unconditional Protection by Statute.—The method of establishing international recognition by unilateral declaration of
intention to protect the rights of foreigners without condition
of reciprocity has, however, actually been adopted by the
three countries mentioned above, *i.e.* France, Belgium, and
Luxemburg.

But even here, as we have shown, its full effect has in
practice been derogated from by means of treaties in the
case of certain important countries.   The absence of the other
countries from the list is, it may safely be surmised, due either
to apathy or to unwillingness on their part to pay for what
they could get for nothing : it can scarcely have been doubt
as to the permanency of the statutory protection.   Nor is it
just to suppose, as has been suggested, that those countries
which entered into treaties did not know the real state of
affairs.   Doubtless many of them were perfectly willing to
make a return for the protection which was given to them, even
in the absence of means of compulsion.

Pouillet and other leading French writers on the subject of
International Copyright forcibly express their views upon the
practical and well calculated application of the wise generosity
of their country which, from whatever motives, has adopted
the highest standard of recognition of the rights of authors
both in its domestic law and in its international relations.
But to give protection without condition of reciprocity, and
then to qualify it, as France has done, by particular arrangements in the case of those countries which are willing to act

justly, leaves the advantage with those which refuse to enter into any agreement, and detracts from the consistency of the principle.

The French Decree of 1852.—The French law embodying the principle of universal protection, which was also adopted by Belgium in 1886 and by Luxemburg in 1898, has frequently been interpreted as bringing about complete assimilation of the rights of foreigners to those of natives, whatever the rights which the former enjoy in the country of origin. A glance at the articles of the Decree of 1852 would at first sight appear to confirm this view. These articles run as follows :—

> *Art. 1.* 'The infringement on French territory of works published abroad and mentioned in the penal code constitutes an offence.'
>
> (*Art. 2* deals only with sales, exportation, and forwarding.)
>
> *Art. 3.* 'The offences dealt with in the preceding article shall be punished conformably with the penal code.'
>
> *Art. 4.* 'Nevertheless no action shall be admitted unless with the accomplishment of the conditions required with reference to works published in France, especially by Sec. 6 of the law of the 19th July 1793.'

Assimilation of 'Rights' and Assimilation of 'Protection.'— But Darras maintains that the 'liberal principle' of the Decree is merely to permit the alien to enjoy in France the rights given him by his own country, and this view is supported by Lyon-Caen and other authorities.[1] Darras' contention is that the Decree 'accords simply the same penal protection' to both foreigner and native ; if, he says, the preceding articles of the Decree had brought about complete assimilation, the legislator would not have introduced Art. 4 by the adversative

---

[1] See Lyon-Caen, *Lois françaises et étrangères sur la propriété littéraire et artistique*, p. 37, n. 3.

'nevertheless,' but would have employed such a term as 'consequently.' The argument scarcely appears irresistible; but, supported as it is by the opinion of the best authorities and by diplomatic practice, the view of 'assimilation of protection' as against total 'assimilation of rights' may safely be adopted as correct.

It is extremely important to distinguish between these two things; for, while assimilation of the *rights* of aliens to those of natives may result in the former gaining rights which they do not enjoy under their own domestic law, assimilation of *protection* can confer no right whatever beyond those already gained in the country of origin. Both modes of recognition however furnish an absolute protection which is measured by a definite standard indicated by the terms (*a*) the rights, and (*b*) the protection, accorded to native authors.

SECTION V.

PROTECTION BY TREATY.

Position of Treaties in English law—Advantages and disadvantages of Treaties—The effect of settled arrangements—Treaties draw attention to disputed points—Treaty-making a slow process—Copyright should not be dealt with in commercial Treaties—Injustice of such inclusion adversely criticised—The ' most favoured nation clause'—Effect of war on commercial Treaties.

According to the rules of international law a treaty may be validly made by agreement between State negotiators accredited, either for the specific purpose, or in virtue of general power belonging to their office, followed by express or tacit ratification[1] on the part of the supreme treaty-making power of the State.[2]

Usage has not prescribed any necessary form of international contract : definite offer and acceptance[3] by competent authorities are its only essentials. ' Between the binding force of contracts, which barely fulfil these requirements, and those which are couched in solemn form, there is no difference. From the moment that consent on both sides is clearly established, by whatever means it may be shown,

---

[1] This is interpreted very liberally on occasions, *e.g.* a truce may be made by acknowledgment of the white flag, when it takes effect as a treaty merely in virtue of a general recognition by the supreme power of the validity of this method.

[2] See Hall, *Treatise on International Law*, p. 345.

[3] ' A valid agreement is therefore concluded as soon as one party has signified his intention to do or to refrain from a given act, conditionally upon the acceptance of his declaration of intention by the other party as constituting an engagement, and as soon as such acceptance is clearly indicated.'—Hall, *Treatise on International Law*, pp. 343, 344.

a treaty exists of which the obligatory force is complete.'[1]
Hence a valid international agreement may be made by
declaration and answer or by exchange of notes : thus the
assurance of reciprocal protection which was given by Lord
Salisbury to the United States in order to satisfy Section 13
of the Act of Congress of 1891, was accepted as creating
a binding arrangement with Great Britain, which country was
therefore admitted by proclamation of the President to the
benefit of the Act.

Position of Treaties in English Law.—In this chapter the
modes of establishing international recognition have been
divided into protection by statute and protection by treaty ;
but in the English law of international copyright there
is not that distinction between diplomatic, legal, and de-
clarative measures which is made by French writers. Our
International Copyright Acts have always been made with
treaties in view, some to adopt[2] those already made, *e.g.*
the Act of 1852, which gave a legal sanction to the
treaty made with France in 1851, and others to give power
to the Crown to carry out contemplated arrangements by
means of Orders in Councils, as was done by the Acts of
1844, 1852, and 1886. Treaties usually become law in
virtue of Orders in Council made under general powers
given by Acts of the latter class.

Advantages and Disadvantages of Treaties.—There can be
no doubt that in copyright as well as in other matters
treaties possess great advantages. They can be arranged for
a period long enough to give the publisher sufficient time
to reap the advantage of his venture on the foreign
market, while provision may be made for their renewal at

---

[1] Hall, *Treatise on International Law*, p. 344.
[2] The Monkswell Bill of 1901 provides for the complete adoption of the Berne
Convention as revised at the Paris Conference in 1896.

intervals sufficiently short to provide opportunities for that
frequent revision which continuous advance in international
conceptions of copyright makes necessary. A copyright
treaty presents an opportunity for a direct and honest
solution of the various questions which are at issue with
regard to the rights of authors of the contracting countries;
and the international arrangement, being of full contractual
force, puts matters on the most substantial basis.

The effect of settled arrangements.—It has been objected
that treaties retard progress, revision being impossible until
the expiration of the stipulated term. The obvious reply to
this is that at the outset the contracting parties may fix whatever number of years they think convenient, or may even
follow the rule of the Berne Convention and make the treaty
terminable at a year's notice. Moreover, when the parties
are ready for progress they can always by mutual consent
cut short the interval fixed. Apart from this, the objection
in question applies to all copyright Acts, whether international
or municipal : experience has shown that the institution and
revision of copyright statutes is difficult and slow compared
with legislation on matters which command the popular
attention.

The inability on the part of a State to denounce a treaty at
will is not without a corresponding advantage, for the other
contracting party is equally bound for the same time. It is
significant of the development of modern commerce that
calculations and arrangements are often now made in anticipa-
tion of transactions in the far future, in many cases even
beyond the life expectation of the parties. A fair degree of
permanency in diplomatic arrangements which affect trade is
therefore essential : and this is particularly true in reference
to copyright, which, in the absence of international agreement, entirely loses its commercial value in a foreign country.

Treaties draw attention to disputed points.—The fact, claimed by some as an advantage, that copyright treaties finally settle delicate matters of dispute between the parties, is regarded in the contrary way by others. According to the latter, to call public attention to details of controversy may wound national susceptibilities and is therefore unwise. But, on the other hand, not to do so is merely to postpone the evil and to give repeated occasion for friction. In any case a treaty is a contract ; and it presents the ordinary opportunities for including or excluding any particular matter.

Treaty-making a slow process.—It is sometimes urged that the making of treaties is slow and cumbrous, and many instances of this fact may be given. Thus the task of securing treaties with the German States in connection with the establishment of copyright recognition throughout the Confederation occupied Prussia for three years. But it must be remembered that this particular case was the first of its kind, and it may fairly be asked what substitute for the tedious process can be suggested.

The labour may be reduced, as France's negotiations after 1852 show, by excellence of the domestic legislation of one or both of the parties ; and while the success of the first treaty may operate to induce other States to enter into negotiations, the extra trouble involved decreases in proportion to the number of treaties. In fact, as in the case of the Berne Convention, it is possible for a multiple treaty to be contracted between a large number of States at a time.

Copyright should not be dealt with in Commercial Treaties.—Though there is a stage when, owing to the growth in human needs, even intellectual productions become ordinary objects of commerce, yet the question of the rights which exist in intellectual works and that of their international treatment need separate consideration : the protection of copyright should not be made dependent upon the changes in the world's market. It is only by regarding copyright apart from other matters that it is possible to give it that delicate consideration which such an abstract commodity requires.

In international relations particularly this holds good. The custom of nations makes a marked distinction between its treatment of the private rights of foreigners where bales of cotton[1] and foreign intellectual publications are concerned: property in the latter is recognised grudgingly.

Even when a State rises superior to the general custom in this respect, it often, clumsily enough, treats commercial matters and author's rights together in such a way as to work injury to the latter. On the motion of M. Renault, the International Congress held at Paris in 1878 recommended the abolition of the practice of incorporating copyright provisions with commercial treaties, but, in spite of its evils, this still continues. Stipulations for the recognition of intellectual rights are frequently mixed up with questions of tariffs on various classes of goods and those affecting many other trade interests.

To this there would be less objection if the nature of the problems involved in the protection of author's rights was fully known, and if these, together with the relative values of the intellectual and material products, could be settled by the draftsman at the outset. But, in addition to the risk of the proper data not being within his knowledge, it is to be feared that, if in the process of negotiation any of the proposed

---

[1] 'The law of nations, being in great part a body of customary rules, depends upon the practice of nations; and what has not been practised cannot be affirmed to be part of that law. But the real equity of the case, founded in the principles which govern other rights, requires that the author's interest in his book should be respected throughout the globe, as much as the interest of a merchant in a bale of goods.'—Curtis, *Law of Copyright*, p. 22.

contents of the treaty have to be sacrificed, the provisions dealing with intellectual rights will be eliminated in favour of the
others.   However, this is not always the case ; the action of
France in reference to its commercial treaty of 1852 with
Belgium provides an illustration of the making of commercial
concessions in order to secure international recognition, though
here the commercial value of the intellectual productions in
question was undoubtedly great.

Injustice of such Inclusion Adversely Criticised.—The injustice of embodying provisions relating to intellectual rights in
commercial arrangements has often been emphasised by literary
and artistic Conferences.   Attention has been drawn to the
lack of a right conception of the nature of intellectual rights
which is indicated by their incorporation in commercial treaties,
and to the difficulties which, when the exigencies of trade and
the pecuniary interests of the parties have to be taken into
account, beset the commencement and termination of the
treaty at appropriate times.

In a commercial treaty 'discussion may be limited to the
difficulties arising out of commercial relations and the principles of intellectual rights ignored almost entirely ; in such a
case the interests of copyright would have no assured to-
morrow.'[1]   Why should the fate of literary and artistic
agreements follow the fluctuations of markets, and be bound
up artificially with that of matters with which the subject has
no connection ?   Romberg's report presented to the Copyright Congress at Brussels in 1884 shows the inconvenience
of such treaties as that between France and Holland[2] in

---

[1] Darras, *Du Droit des Auteurs et des Artistes*, p. 657, n. 1.

[2] 'In Art. 14 of the treaty of commerce and navigation between France and
Holland (July 25, 1840), the regulation of the question of intellectual rights was
promised at a later date.   Owing to various circumstances, into the details of
which we need not now enter, the literary convention did not come into force
until 1855.'—Darras, *Du Droit des Auteurs et des Artistes*, p. 202.

which copyright matters were mingled with questions relating to shipping and commerce. ' On the day when the merchants of Havre and the shipowners of Rotterdam are no longer able to agree, literary infringement will once more be at liberty to set up its workshops at the Hague.' [1]

The ' Most Favoured Nation Clause.'—According to Von Bar, the most favoured nation clause is entirely unsuited for conventions relating to copyright. But, though the insertion of this clause in a treaty with one State ' may, perhaps, impair the full operation of the treaty concluded with another State, there need be little fear of this being the case with regard to intellectual property.' [2] The most favoured nation clause presents a perfectly fair consideration on either side in an international agreement, but if this is inserted difficulties may arise when revision of arrangements with the same party is desirable, and obstacles may present themselves to the making of treaties with other States unless it is convenient to introduce the clause there also. Of the fairness of the clause, Darras says : ' If the Spaniards are more completely protected in France than are the English, there results certainly an inequality, but this fact does not by itself cause any prejudice to the English.'

The policy of introducing the most favoured nation clause into treaties has been fully adopted by France. In 1891 it had no fewer than five Conventions embodying the principle, those with Spain 1880, Germany 1883, Italy 1884, being still in existence : the Belgian treaty of 1881, however, was denounced in 1891, and in the same year the Swiss agreement of 1882 was also repudiated, Belgium and Switzerland taking this action as a measure of retorsion, on account of commercial disputes.

---

[1] Darras, *Du Droit des Auteurs et des Artistes*, p. 657, n. 1.
[2] Paquy, *Thèse de doctorat*, p. 187.

The copyright treaty of 1851 between France and Great Britain, now no longer in force, contained preferential clauses ; it provided for a reduction in the duties payable on books, prints, drawings, and musical works published in France and imported into Great Britain. It further enacted that 'the rates of duty . . . shall not be raised during the continuance of the present Convention ; and that if hereafter, during the continuance of this Convention, any reduction of those rates should be made in favour of books, prints, drawings, or musical works published in any other country, such reduction shall be at the same time extended to similar articles published in France.'[1]

Effect of War on Commercial Treaties.—Treaties of commerce are generally annulled by a declaration of war ; and this fact becomes of great importance to the author where copyright provisions are contained in a commercial treaty.

The idea that on the declaration of war all the subjects of one State were supposed to be enemies of the other has been replaced in modern times by a more tolerant view. The example set by the English Government in 1756, when it allowed French persons then in the country to remain during the war, has frequently been copied ; and now it is practically certain that, if separate copyright arrangements were in force at the commencement of hostilities, the intellectual work of a foreigner would be free from molestation.

Commercial treaties are, however, as has been stated, usually annulled by the outbreak of war, and this fact has great bearing upon our subject, for when copyright provisions are embodied in them these naturally lapse with the treaties. For example, during the Franco-Prussian war of 1870 and 1871 the commercial treaties in which the copyright relations between France

---

[1] Burke, *The Law of International Copyright between England and France*, p. 92.

and the Germanic States were determined became inoperative. When they were renewed in 1871, nine States were not included, and it was not until after a lapse of twelve years that the omission was remedied in a fresh treaty.

The injury caused to the best interests of copyright by dealing with it in commercial treaties is therefore not solely the direct result of war. The effect of war is not always repaired at its close, for with the restoration of peace pressing matters of trade have to be adjusted, and copyright protection is then not usually regarded as of the most urgent importance. Copyright is of such cosmopolitan nature that it should be rendered independent of such influences, and form the subject of a separate agreement.

SECTION VI.

THE POSSIBLE CONFLICT OF TREATIES.

Possible conflict with domestic law—Possible conflict with other Treaties —The Rules of the Berne Convention as to conflicting Treaties.

Possible conflict with Domestic Law.—It is out of the question for two countries to think of entering into any sort of copyright treaty with one another, unless their domestic systems of law have many elements in common. The general idea of the nature of copyright, and the general principles upon which the author's protection is based, must at least be the same in both systems—and, in matters of detail, the more closely the provisions of the two codes approach one another the better will be the chance of success for the treaty. If there is any great divergence between the two systems of law, the establishment of the treaty will be difficult, and even when it has been completed there will be great danger of misunderstandings and of disputes as to the way in which it is to be carried out. Under arrangements for reciprocity, a country cannot well know what it is going to receive unless it can take its own law as at least a rough guide. That Russia has at the present time no copyright treaties with other countries is doubtless due to the fact that her copyright legislation is altogether out of harmony with that of the more highly civilised countries of the world.

In order to make the negotiation of treaties easy and to secure success for them when made, it is necessary for every country to keep well abreast of the times, to take note of the development of international opinion on the subject of copyright, and, when opportunity offers for the reform of its own law, to give its full consideration to the existing laws of other States, with a view to imitating what is best in them and rejecting what is worst. In this way the process of assimilation and advance is carried on.

When the domestic laws of two States are sufficiently alike to admit of the conclusion of a satisfactory treaty between them, it is still necessary for each to take care that, in entering into such a treaty, it does not pledge itself to provisions conflicting with that part of its domestic law which is dissimilar from that of the other State. At the present time countries are not given to examining their laws exhaustively as a preliminary to treaty negotiations. Hence it sometimes happens that in accepting what appears to be a perfectly harmless proposal a State involves itself in future difficulties, simply because the proposal in question embodies the other party's view of the law and not its own. This is a danger against which it is necessary to take adequate precautions.

Possible conflict with other Treaties.—When a country which is thinking of entering into a treaty has one or more treaties with other States already in force, it is necessary for it to use all due care in order to prevent the insertion in the new treaty of any provisions which shall conflict with its existing obligations under the old agreements. As an example of the anomalies which may result from carelessness in this respect, Darras points out that a German author who publishes his work in Belgium has, under the rules of the treaties made by France with Belgium and Germany respectively, the choice of one of two periods of protection in France. As the author of a Belgian *work*, he may claim the domestic period of the Belgian Law, *i.e.* life *plus* fifty years : while as a German *author*, he can claim only the domestic period of the German Law, *i.e.* life *plus* thirty years. As a matter of fact he would probably get the longer period of protection, but the example shows that it is advisable for a country which is contemplating the conclusion of a number of treaties to adopt at the outset certain definite lines of policy and to follow them out in every case ; so that each treaty becomes part of a consistent whole and not an isolated transaction which may come into conflict with others.[1]

The rules of the Berne Convention as to conflicting Treaties.— Where an International Union is established, it is usually part of the object of its members to secure uniformity of treatment for their authors throughout the territory of the Union. The success of any such purpose is likely to be impaired by the existence of separate treaties between the countries of the Union. In the case of the International Union formed at Berne in 1886, the Berne Convention permits such separate treaties to subsist so long as they confer upon authors, or their representatives, rights more extended that those granted by the Convention, or include other stipulations not contrary to that agreement. This is a sacrifice of the principle of uniformity to the paramount object of advancing the international rights of authors. As a matter of fact, however, the Convention is superseding all separate treaties between Union countries. No fresh ones are being concluded, and year by year those which already exist are being denounced.

---

[1] According to the general rules of International Law, when one country has made separate treaties with two different States and a conflict arises between these agreements the earlier in date takes precedence over the later.

SECTION VII.

REGISTRATION, DEPOSIT OF COPIES, AND OTHER FORMALITIES.

Vexatious conditions should not be imposed on foreigners—Difficulties connected with deposit of copies—Formalities under the English International Acts.

Vexatious conditions should not be imposed on foreigners.— An international agreement for reciprocal protection should be made as simple as is compatible with definiteness : each State should extend to subjects of the other exactly the same rights as it grants to its own [1] and should not seek to introduce any complications in the shape of conditions and formalities into the treaty. It is unreasonable that a State, under an open or veiled threat to refuse to enter into a projected treaty, should make stipulations for the acceptance of provisions drawn up in the interests of its manufacturing trade or tariffs, whether it wishes these to be inserted in the treaty itself or to take effect separately. Copyright arrangements should not be hampered by such provisions as the one insisted upon by the United States in 1891 to the effect that aliens must set up the type of their books in the country in order to gain protection.

In addition to such unreasonable stipulations as these, there are others which are commonly adopted, in spite of the fact that many persons, even in the countries which insist upon them, regard them as troublesome and vexatious. The principal of

---

[1] It is only reasonable that an author who wishes to have his work protected in a foreign country should make himself acquainted with the conditions on which the protection of native works depends ; though it is desirable that in all countries these conditions should be made as uniform as possible.

these relate to deposit of copies of the work, registration of title, and other formalities, which have almost as many variations in mode as there are contracting States. The confusion created by these restrictions is such that the total abolition of them has been strongly advocated; but it is submitted that this would mean a present simplification at the expense of an increase of doubt and confusion in the future: some formality by which the commencement of the term of copyright for each work may be dated seems absolutely necessary.

Difficulties connected with Deposit of Copies.—In practice authors who wish to have their works protected in a foreign country must have regard to the following possible contingencies :

(1) Deposit may be required in the country of origin ; and

    (*a*) may also be required in the foreign State; or

    (*b*) may not be required in the foreign State.

(2) Deposit may not be required in the country of origin ; but

    (*a*) may be required in the foreign State; or

    (*b*) may not be required in the foreign State.

(3) In countries where deposit is required it may be either

    (*a*) A condition for the vesting or protection of the copyright; or

    (*b*) A separate obligation incurred by the fact of publication, with separate penalties attached—as is the case in England.

An author who belongs to a country which does not exact deposit of copies as a condition of the vesting of copyright must be particularly careful, lest, ignorant of any such requirement, he should lose the protection of his rights in foreign countries; and even an author who belongs to a country which itself requires deposit, may wrongly consider the performance of this formality in the country of origin sufficient to fulfil the demands of a foreign State which also requires deposit of copies within its own borders.

The need for a careful examination by each of the contracting parties of the requirements of the other's domestic law is illustrated by a misunderstanding which arose under the Prussian Law of 1837. This Act adopted the principle of general legal reciprocity; and it was thought in France that the Decree of 1852, which granted universal protection to aliens, fulfilled its requirements and entitled French authors to protection in Prussia.[1] This view was, however, found to be erroneous.[2] The Decree exacts deposit from aliens as a condition of protection, while the Prussian law imposed no such condition; therefore, as an absolute reciprocity did not exist, it was held by the Prussian Courts that France could not claim protection under the Prussian statute, although that country, pursuing its policy of universal protection, made no difficulty about extending the protection of its own law to Prussian authors.

Formalities under the English International Acts.—In Great Britain, deposit of copies and registration are no longer exacted from the authors of foreign books entitled to the protection of the law. This is clear from the terms of the International Act of 1886 (sec. 4), which provides that 'Where an order respecting any foreign country is made under the International Copyright Acts, the provisions of those Acts with respect to the registry and delivery of copies of works shall not apply to works produced in such country except so far as provided by the order.' The exemption is recognised in practice at Stationers' Hall and the British Museum.

[1] Pataille and Huguet, *Code International de la Propriété Industrielle Artistique et Littéraire*, p. 297.
[2] Klostermann, *Das geistige Eigenthum* (Berlin, 1871), vol. i., p. 59.

It is important to note this, as the section of the International Act of 1844 which refers to registration and deposit[1] is not expressly repealed by the 1886 Act—a fact which may account for the existence in foreign countries of a widespread opinion that deposit is still necessary to enable foreign works to gain protection in Great Britain.

It has, however, been suggested that, as under the 1886 Act a foreign work is to have the same rights as if produced in the United Kingdom, and as these rights only exist in virtue of various domestic Acts, the provisions of those Acts as to registration and delivery of copies must apply, apart altogether from such *extra* formalities as were formerly

---

[1] **Registration and Delivery of Copies under the English Acts.**—As there seems to be some doubt, even in England, as to the effect of the provisions of those prior Acts, we insert them here :—

1844 Act (secs. 6-9) unconditionally provides for the registry and delivery of copies at Stationers' Hall. The effect of sec. 4 (i) of the 1886 Act, combined with the present Orders in Council, is to make this inapplicable to works of the present treaty countries.

1852 Act (sec. 8) enacts that no author shall be entitled to the benefit of the Act in respect of the translation of any book unless registration and deposit of the original work be made within three calendar months of its first publication in the foreign country, and also registration and deposit of a copy of the authorised translation in the United Kingdom within a time to be mentioned in the Order in Council. This section is repealed by sec. 12 of the International Act of 1886.

Art. 8 of the treaty of 1852 with France was quite clear. It ran :—' Neither authors, nor translators, nor their lawful representatives or assigns, shall be entitled in either country to the protection stipulated by the preceding articles, nor shall copyright be claimable in either country, unless the work shall have been registered in the manner following, that is to say :—(1) If the work be one that has first appeared in France, it must be registered at the Hall of the Company of Stationers in London. (2) If the work be one that has first appeared in the Dominions of her Britannic Majesty, it must be registered at the *Bureau de la Librairie* of the Ministry of the Interior at Paris . . .'—Burke, *Law of International Copyright between England and France*, p. 88.

But, however plain were the directions to the foreign author for registration and deposit under the old Acts, it is equally clear from the 1886 Act that, in the absence of any special provision in the particular Order in Council relating to the foreign country, the International Acts do not now require registration and deposit.

required by the International Statutes. After receiving some support from judicial authority,[1] this view of the law has now been overruled by the Court of Appeal, which has decided that no registration or deposit whatever of foreign works is necessary in Great Britain, unless it is expressly required by the Order in Council granting protection.[2]

[1] *Fishburn v. Hollingshead* (1891), 2 Ch. 371.
[2] *Hanfstaengl v. American Tobacco Company* (1895), 1 Q.B. 347.

CHAPTER III.

THE POSSIBILITY OF A UNIVERSAL LAW OF COPYRIGHT.

SECTION I.

THE PRESENT PROSPECT OF A UNIVERSAL LAW OF COPYRIGHT.

The comparison of national systems of Copyright—A universal law is an all-embracing International Code—The two factors in International Copyright—The true conception of Copyright—Copyright Conventions and voluntary Universal Protection—National obstacles to international progress —Danger of too rapid progress.

The comparison of National Systems of Copyright.—A rapid survey of the present position of copyright protection in the civilised countries of the world yields the conclusion that in essence the rights conceded to authors are everywhere identical. All countries forbid unauthorised copying, all limit the duration of the author's right to a certain term, and all grant some recognition to subsidiary rights like performing right or translating right.

But when we come to the details of protection, we find that the laws of the various States differ very considerably from one another. The term of protection varies from the author's life *plus* 80 years of Spain to the 28 years (with a conditional extension for a further 14 years) of the United States and the life (or 40 years) period of Italy. Some countries impose formalities, some do not ; and those which do are by no means at one as to the nature of the formalities to be exacted, and the part which they are to play. Thus in England registration is a 'condition precedent to suing,' in the United States it is a condition of the vesting of copyright, and in Austria it is not required for any purpose. Again, the law of the United States contains a 'manufacturing clause,' according to which no work can gain protection unless its type has been set in America.

There are differences between the laws of various countries as to the liberty of extract for educational and scientific works, as to the need for express reservation for musical performing right, as to the treatment of newspaper and magazine articles, as to the relation of translating right to copyright, as to the author's right to prevent the conversion of his novel into a play or of his play into a novel: everywhere there are differences. And, in default of the imposition upon all countries of a common code by some extraneous power possessed of a world-wide authority, a universal law can only be brought about by harmonising all such differences and by assimilating all details according to some certain pre-arranged standard—some 'model law'—through the ordinary means of international negotiation.

A Universal Law is an all-embracing International Code.—As to the treatment of the rights of foreign authors, this process of assimilation has already made considerable headway in a number of countries. Every State on entering into a treaty agrees to fashion that part of its law which regulates the protection of foreign authors, in such a way that it may conform to the standard set up by the treaty itself. As to the protection of *native* authors, however, there has so far been no attempt to unify the rules relating to this in any two or more countries.

Hence in the present state of affairs all that can be considered is the unification of the protection of foreign authors in every civilised country. When this has been achieved, then will be the time to look to the question whether a common code can be established for the regulation of all copyright matters, national and international, throughout the world. Once such a code were established, there would of course be no longer any distinction between national and international affairs : for purposes of copyright the whole civilised world would then be one nation. Meanwhile attention must be confined to a project for the elaboration of one common law of international copyright of such a character as to secure to foreign authors everywhere a fixed and liberal protection.

The two factors in International Copyright.—International copyright involves two distinct factors :

> (i) The subject-matter with which the law is concerned ; and
>
> (ii) The parties to the international agreement by which the law is established.

A universal law is reached only when the first is made to embrace a complete copyright code, and the second to include every State throughout the civilised world. The essential process in the establishment of a universal law is international assimilation, which, in its simplest form, may be accomplished by the unification of a single element in the domestic copyright codes of two countries.

The true conception of Copyright.—At the present time, it is often said that the international protection of copyright is a mere matter of common justice, but such a conception of the author's rights has only been laboriously reached, and even now the protection of the works of foreign authors is by no means universally regarded as a mere recognition of a personal right of property attaching to the author simply in virtue of his creative work. Whatever the true ethical view as to the nature of copyright, as a matter of fact it is only upon an existing international agreement that a foreign author can safely base his claim to protection.

Copyright Conventions and Voluntary Universal Protection. —Though, as we have seen, such an agreement is most simply completed by means of a treaty, some danger of perplexity and conflict arises, if the process of treaty-making is separately repeated with other countries. If, however, instead of a number of separate treaties, a copyright Convention—one agreement for a number of countries—is established, then this danger is considerably reduced. Still, even the making of multiple Conventions is a slow road to a universal law of copyright.

The unilateral assimilation of the rights of foreign authors to those of natives, independently of international negotiations, which was initiated by France in 1852, has since been followed by only two countries—Belgium (1886) and Luxemburg (1898). It is doubtful whether any great progress will ever be achieved by this means alone. The sudden and artificial advance in the recognition of international copyright increases the difference which has to be removed by other countries before assimilation of domestic laws becomes possible, and may serve to create a reluctance towards progress on the part of such other countries.

National obstacles to International progress.—Whether advance towards a universal law is made by domestic legislation or by treaty, there are many practical obstacles which have first to be removed. Economic considerations—some sound, some fallacious—play an important part in inducing nations to adopt an attitude of determined inaction. And any peculiarities in the various systems of law which are deeply rooted in the national life will often be found very difficult to eradicate.

Danger of too rapid progress.—Though, of course, progress is to be desired, any advance in international legislation proceeding much more rapidly than the development of national laws is likely to re-act with undesirable results. Hence, even in a great International Convention, absolute specific rules can only be made on subjects as to which there is a real international consensus of opinion, other matters being left to the general rule of reciprocity. National development of thought, stimulated by international communication of ideas, will then enable this minimum of binding rules to be enlarged gradually under the safe guidance of experience.

SECTION II.

THE DEVELOPMENT OF INTERNATIONAL COPYRIGHT.

Unification of laws—Formation of a Copyright Union—The Berne Convention.

Unification of Laws.—A universal law is reached by the development of the subject-matter of the law, and the successive conclusion of treaties between the various States of the civilised world. In the development of the subject-matter, an important process is the unification of the laws of different States : the matters upon which the several national laws are agreed are most easily embodied in an international convention. Before it is possible to measure the extent to which this unification can be carried, it is necessary to examine the attitude of the various States with regard to copyright. This is largely determined by the manner in which copyright is regarded—whether as a right of prohibition against a given public or as a personal right of property—since the countries which hold the former view will generally treat the right as purely municipal, while those which adopt the latter will consider it to be valid all the world over. It has been shown that the view usually taken is that copyright is a right of prohibition ; hence most countries by their domestic law limit protection to native authors or native works.

As a consequence, in order to secure protection for the works of its subjects in foreign countries other than these, a

State must enter into agreements with other States, whereby an assimilation of international rights ranging in extent from a single specific provision to the whole content of the several domestic laws may be effected.

There are even cases in which States have allowed this international assimilation to outstrip their domestic law. Thus, Germany until 1901 conferred upon the subjects of other countries of the International Union translating rights under the Berne Convention, considerably more extended than those which under its domestic law it granted to its own.

Formation of a Copyright Union.—The development in the international recognition of copyright which leads to the making of Conventions proceeds by well-marked stages. At first the single independent State is to be considered. This may possess a system of law generally incompatible with those of its neighbours, although some points of similarity must necessarily exist. A distinct advance is achieved when, by the introduction of commonly accepted provisions, its domestic law is harmonised with those of other countries so as to render international negotiation feasible. When in a number of States this process of international negotiation has gone some way, it will be found that throughout them all the protection of foreign authors presents the same general features. Then the time is ripe for the assimilation of all the various systems of international copyright in one great Convention.

The Berne Convention.—Development of ideas and increased facility of intercourse have already to a large extent broken down the barriers between the different nations. Thus, the International Union for the Protection of Literary and Artistic works, created in 1886 by the Berne Convention, now comprises not only all the principal countries of Europe, except Russia and Austria, but also Japan, Haiti, and Tunis. And the Berne Convention was followed in 1889 by the Convention of Montevideo, which embraces the Argentine Republic, Paraguay, Peru, and Uruguay, and also France, Spain, and Italy.

SECTION III.

THE IDEAL UNIVERSAL LAW.

One law for all countries—Cosmopolitan nature of copyright—Obstacles in the way of advance—The effect of national environment—Methods of advance—Danger of too rapid extension—Importance of a precise law.

One Law for all Countries.—The ideal universal law of copyright is a single code, binding throughout the world, and giving the fullest protection to the authors of every country, without distinction of nationality. Such a universal law would present the great advantage of simplicity as well as that of international equity. Under it, the rights of authors in every country would be known without reference to foreign systems of law. But the project has been characterised by Bluntschli as 'a beautiful dream of the idealists,' and it has been urged that, as it begins to be realised, the need for any international agreement whatever vanishes. This, however, raises no valid objection to progress in that direction ; if, with the advance towards a universal law, States grant international protection of their own free will, rather than as a matter of obligation, the effect can only be for good.

Cosmopolitan nature of Copyright.—Although copyright is municipal in its origin, and therefore available only against a given public and limited to a particular territory, it is so cosmopolitan in its nature that the territory of protection for it might well be extended so as to include the whole world ; and a general acknowledgment be bestowed upon every portion of the content of the right which reasonably admits of it.

Obstacles in the way of advance.—Reluctance on the part of a nation to enter into treaties for the protection of foreign authors may be due to mere apathy ; but, as we have seen, it usually arises from considerations of domestic advantage. These are largely dependent upon the economic conditions of the country in question, which will frequently shape its policy solely with a view to present material interests.

The most prominent motives considered in Chapter I. as tending to retard the recognition of foreign copyright by a State are the protection of subjects, the enrichment of the stock of literature, the provision of cheap and good books for the people, and the protection and encouragement of native industries. But history has shown that a refusal to admit the works of foreigners to copyright may well be followed by a serious reaction which will injure the native author and the native public ; as in the case of the United States, which, after long restricting protection to American subjects, was, in 1891, ultimately forced to grant some measure of international recognition, for the sake of its own public, its authors and publishers.

The effect of National Environment.—Economic considerations, however, are not the only ones which serve to produce reluctance to enter into international conventions on the subject of copyright. Such a reluctance is also largely the outcome of national environment, which embraces customs, institutions, traditions, religion and culture, often inseparable from the land to which they are attached. Copyright can claim no direct connection with the physical features of a country or the temperament of its people, yet a nation's views of art and literature are greatly influenced by such elementary and ultimate facts as these.

An artificial process of levelling, which would offend the susceptibilities of a people and necessitate the sudden eradication of deep-rooted convictions, is likely to be neither acceptable nor profitable. Legal systems and principles, amongst other things, are deeply rooted in the national regard ; and it is not only substantive rules that bear the imprint of the national character, but this is also in some degree the case with rules of procedure and other matters of adjective law. The view that international treaties have no intrinsic legal force, the recognition of common law and case law, and the use of Injunctions, all of which obtain in England and the United States of America, must often appear strange to the continental lawyer.

Methods of Advance.—When all such obstacles have been removed a nation is in a position to make a definite advance in the direction of a universal law of copyright. The effacing of conflicting elements in the various systems of domestic law must necessarily be a slow and gradual process, for generally progress can only be effected through the growth of a coherent international opinion which is fostered by the increasing facility of international inter-communication.

The various private International Associations for the protection of the interests of authors, publishers, and others, which are growing in number and importance, contribute greatly to this development of thought. And before everything else in this connection must be placed the periodical conferences of the International Literary and Artistic Association. Apart from these private societies, the work done by the office of the International Union at Berne in collecting and circulating all manner of information upon all subjects connected with international copyright is of the greatest service.

Danger of too rapid extension.—It is a well established principle that legislation should not outstrip public opinion, unless under extraordinary and temporary conditions. So in a convention like that of Berne it is necessary to keep prominently in view that too rapid extension of the copyright protection internationally demanded may involve a falling off in the number of adherents. If due regard is paid to the speed of development of the various domestic laws, a steady progress may safely be made by the gradual addition of further elements of protection to the international code.[1] On the other hand, if this advance is not kept within due limits, the numerical strength of the union will diminish.

The necessity for cautious advance is illustrated by the dissatisfaction expressed in the National Council of Switzerland when discussing the ratification of the Additional Act of Paris, which effected certain important amendments in the Berne Convention. Feeling also ran high in Germany ; and in Denmark, on account of the advanced provisions which had been introduced, a powerful section of the press opposed the projected adherence of that country to the Berne Convention, which nevertheless has since taken place.[2] In France, Belgium, and Spain[3] dissent was also freely expressed in influential quarters. Again, Great Britain refused to sign the Interpretative Declaration of 1896, while Norway refused to accept the Additional Act ; and, very recently, the example of Norway in this respect has been followed by Sweden.

Importance of a precise Law.—It should be remembered also that the provisions of a convention should be as

---

[1] The interest evinced by those countries which are not already members of the Union was demonstrated in 1896 by the presence at the Conference of Paris in that year of representatives of the Argentine Republic, Bolivia, Brazil, Bulgaria, Columbia, Greece, Guatemala, Mexico, Peru, Portugal, Roumania, Sweden, and the United States, none of which are members of the International Union.

[2] Denmark joined the Union in 1903.

[3] Report of Congress of Monaco, p. 205.

definite as possible.   In the words of the Secretary of the
International Office, 'A precise law, though less advanced,
is preferable to an undigested mass of so-called liberal provisions.   The first can be reformed, and when the right
moment comes will surely be revised ; the second will evoke
general uneasiness, and is likely some day to produce a retro-
grade movement.' [1]

[1] M. Ernst Röthlisberger in a paper presented to the Congress of the International Literary and Artistic Association at Monaco, 1897.—Report of the
Congress, p. 211.

SECTION IV.

PRACTICAL ADVANCE TOWARDS A UNIVERSAL LAW.

Reciprocity a sure means of advance—Reciprocity may be either general or specific—Matters for Assimilation—(i) Persons to be protected—(ii) Works to be protected—(iii) Period to be given—(iv) The Content of the copyright to be granted—The various kinds of provisions in Treaties—National advance—Copyright Conferences—The Berne Convention.

Reciprocity a sure means of advance.—Protection of the rights of foreign authors must of necessity be either contractual or voluntary. Contractual protection is the safer, for, while gratuitous voluntary protection marks an appreciable advance in the direction of a universal law, progress by this means must necessarily be somewhat precarious.

As we have seen, reciprocity has proved a sound principle of international action and a great number of treaties have been made with it as a basis. These have not only extended a recognition of the rights of foreign authors, but have also done much to stimulate advance in the direction of a general international copyright. Voluntary universal protection is doubtless a very good thing for authors, but it will be a long time before it will become general. In the present state of affairs, where every nation is primarily, if not solely, concerned with its own interests, protection by treaty seems to be the surest and safest means of advance, while the adoption of universal protection by a State here and there only

serves to increase the existing differences in the various
international systems of law.   If every nation would consent
without agreement to assimilate the rights of foreign authors to
those of its own subjects then treaties would be of little use,
but on such a hypothesis the prospect of bringing about a
universal law for international copyright would vanish with
the need for it.   By means of reciprocity considerable progress
has been made towards realising the conception of universal
international copyright, and it is to this principle that we must
look for further advance.

Reciprocity may be either general or specific : therefore when a
treaty based on reciprocity has been made between two States
it becomes necessary to enquire into the extent of the protection
thereby provided.   The engagement may range in value from
a mere promise to grant to foreign authors the rights of the
domestic law to an agreement to administer the whole of a
specially elaborated code, itself making provision for international protection and carefully delineating the features of
such protection.   In practice, however, complete assimilation
is found impossible on account of national peculiarities, which
prevent a country from departing very far from the provisions
of its own domestic law.   Hence general reciprocity is the rule.
If this is defined as the granting by each country of the same
protection to the rights of foreigners as that which is accorded
to those of natives, the protection granted under it on each
side must be relative.

Matters for Assimilation.—The chief questions which arise
when assimilation is proposed are :—

    (I) What persons should be protected.

    (II) What works should be protected.

    (III) What should be the duration of the protection.

    (IV) What is the nature of the protection which should
        be allowed.

A full discussion of these matters would lead us too far afield : but the chief considerations are as follows :—

I. Persons to be protected.—The persons to be protected are easily determined under international agreements; the admission of all subjects of the contracting States is a simple solution of the question. The international protection may also be extended to the works of authors who do not belong to the contracting countries, when the works are first published in one of the States.

II. Works to be protected.—A broad statement as to what works are to be protected can be made with ease ; but it is considerably more difficult to arrive at an exact definition of the fit subjects for copyright. Even among the members of the International Union, there are some countries which deny complete protection to photographs, unless they are of works of art, and others which admit works of architecture themselves (as distinct from their plans) and choregraphic works to copyright protection. The rule however that a State must grant the same rights to foreign authors as to its own subjects brings about a relative assimilation which is sufficiently definite.

III. Period to be given.—As to the period of protection to be given to a copyright work, the greatest divergency prevails. Thus, for ordinary works, Austria, Germany, Japan, and Switzerland grant a period of the author's life *plus* thirty years ; Belgium, Denmark, France, Hungary, Norway, Russia, and Sweden, author's life *plus* fifty years ; Spain, author's life *plus* eighty years ; Great Britain, forty-two years, or life *plus* seven years, whichever is the longer ; the United States, twenty-eight years from registration, with a possible extension of fourteen years ; and Italy, forty years or the author's life, whichever is the longer, with a modified protection for a further forty years. The principle of relative assimilation, however, will furnish a uniform rule under which either the period of the country of origin of the work or that of the country of importation may be adopted.

In this respect the Berne Convention modifies its general rule of reference to the law of the country where protection is sought, and provides that if the period given by that country be greater than that of the country of origin, it shall be cut down to equal the latter. But it is difficult to see why the law of the place where protection is claimed by a foreigner should not entirely regulate duration as well as other matters. Though absolute assimilation in this matter is at present impossible, it is worthy of note that the States which have recently legislated on copyright, including Germany in 1901, have given one of two periods—either life *plus* thirty years or life *plus* fifty years ; and the former is the term of protection prescribed in the recent English Bills brought forward in the House of Lords.

IV. **The Content of the copyright to be granted.**—In the matter of extent of protection, *i.e.* the content of copyright, countries differ greatly ; but even here the differences are largely arbitrary, the existence of anomalies being for the most part due to dilatoriness in domestic legislation. The copyright of an author in his books should include the rights of translation, of dramatisation, of novelisation, and of abridgement ; whilst an artist should be protected against reproductions of his picture by lithography, drawing, photography, *tableaux vivants*, and every other process of copying. The principal right should in every case carry with it all its derivative rights.

The various kinds of Provisions in Treaties. Jus cogens minimum.—It is quite conceivable that a copyright Convention should consist merely of one Article, providing for the reciprocal extension of the ordinary domestic rights as between the contracting parties.   In order to make the agreement acceptable to as many countries as possible it is, however, usually necessary to incorporate other provisions invested with lesser degrees of binding force.   And, on the other hand, when there are a number of parties with domestic laws in all stages of advance, it is generally found advisable to insert certain provisions securing an absolute minimum of protection in certain repects.   This is known as a *jus cogens minimum*. The danger of too rapid advance being kept in sight, it is desirable, with a view to a universal law, to extend this mandatory portion of the Convention as far as is compatible with safety.

Hence the articles of a Convention may range from provisions laying down an absolute international rule to provisions expressly relegating authority to the various domestic laws, and between these two extremes there may be several grades.   In this connection, the possible contents of a Convention may be classified in descending scale as follows :—

I. Absolute provisions which make no reference to any external standard.

II. Specific provisions which depend for their actual content upon some appointed external standard like the domestic law of the country granting protection.

III. Provisions making an absolute rule relating to matters which are expressly left to each country to define.

IV. Provisions allowing the regulation of certain matters by domestic authority, subject to conditions imposed by the Convention.

V. Provisions relegating certain matters entirely to domestic legislation.

The gradations in this list present an easy means for the adaptation of international protection to national progress.

This method has been applied with considerable success in the Berne Convention.

Discretionary Provisions.—Beginning with the provisions that have the least degree of binding force, and working upwards, we find that the fifth class, which embraces subjects left entirely to domestic legislation, includes certain matters of administration which do not admit of advance. However much a universal law is to be desired, there are many things which are patently not capable of international treatment. Seizure of offending copies is one of these. The idea of a general police and customs administration under some central authority can only be regarded as visionary.

Apart from these executive affairs, each nation has certain principles which are inherent in the national life ; and in some cases legal rules, though not really inherent, may be the subject of such an attachment on the part of a people that they cannot be dissociated from the national life. In time, under the influence of a wider and sounder knowledge of economics and a general intellectual development, rules like these latter may mature into proper subjects for international codification.

To apply international binding force to peculiarly national elements is in some cases impossible and in others unwise. Where assimilation is obviously desirable, and the differences between the various national laws are only arbitrary, mere suggestion will frequently effect what is wanted in the way of stimulus. Resolutions passed at Conferences, especially when the latter are of such importance as those of the International Union, indicate the lines of progress which appear most practicable. At the Berne Conferences it was originally intended to insert in the official text of the Convention a number of recommendations (*vœux*) indicating the lines on which future progress in national legislation should take place, but it was afterwards decided that, although the changes thus advocated were highly desirable, it would be inadvisable to make them the subject of formal resolutions.

Various Classes of Mandatory Provisions.—The fourth class of provisions, which comprises matters left to domestic authority subject to certain conditions imposed by the treaty, marks the first step in the direction of complete assimilation.

The third class constitutes a further advance, though this may be small, for here the Convention takes the initiative instead of allowing the particular country to do so. The binding force of the provisions yet falls far short of the absolute, domestic interpretation being still allowed. Thus the Berne Convention forbids the adaptation of copyright works, but allows the courts of the various countries to enforce the reservations of their respective domestic laws; therefore, although Great Britain, for instance, is bound to prohibit adaptation under this rule, yet, since the dramatisation of a novel does not constitute an infringement under its domestic law, it is not bound to protect Union authors against that form of adaptation.

The second class includes specific provisions which depend on some appointed external standard for the determination of their actual content. Thus Art. 2 of the Berne Convention provides that a subject belonging to any one of the Union countries shall enjoy in the others the rights which the respective laws give to natives, and goes on to say that the conditions and formalities to be fulfilled are those required by law in the country of origin of the work.

The first class has the highest possible degree of binding force. Its provisions are absolute and are not dependent on any external standard, national or otherwise. In totality these constitute the minimum of protection which all the countries, whatever the state of their respective domestic laws, are bound to give ; hence they are called the *jus cogens minimum* of the treaty.   On account of the total absence of the domestic element, this group in particular cannot safely include any provision which does not meet with the ready acquiescence of all the parties.

National Advance.—It must not be thought from what has gone before that, apart from treaties, the recognition of international copyright has already made no substantial progress. The chief European countries all accord a considerable measure of protection to aliens by their own domestic laws. France, Belgium, and Luxemburg, as we have seen, grant an unconditional recognition to foreigners, and there are many other States which, even in the absence of treaties, protect the works of foreign authors generally with the stipulation that such works shall be first published in their territory.

Thus Germany, Italy, Spain, Switzerland, and other States grant copyright to foreign authors simply on the latter condition; according to an official declaration made by Great Britain to the United States the English rule is the same, but this statement is somewhat too sweeping.   Italy, Spain, and Switzerland protect alien authors even when their works are published abroad, but in this case only on condition that the countries to which they belong accord a reciprocal protection.   Switzerland grants an unconditional recognition to alien authors of such works if they are domiciled in the country.

Copyright Conferences.—Important conferences have from time to time been held for the discussion of international copyright, amongst which those of Brussels 1858, Paris 1878, Rome 1882, Berne 1884-1886, and Paris 1896 are, perhaps, of the greatest importance.   The first of these, which is interesting in view of its very early recognition of advanced principles of international copyright, was attended by influential representatives from most of the principal countries, and passed the following resolutions :—

' The principle of international recognition of property in literary and artistic works in favour of their authors ought to find a place in the legislation of all civilised nations.

' This principle ought to be admitted from country to country even in the absence of reciprocity.

' The assimilation of foreign authors to native authors should be absolute and complete.

' In addition to the completeness of the subject-matter the universality of the subscribing States is a necessary factor of a universal law.'

In this connection it is interesting to note that the International Literary and Artistic Association—the chief amongst authors' international societies—has for some time had the question of a universal law under its consideration. M. Georges Maillard, one of the members, has drawn up a ' model law ' embodying the ideas of the Association as to the contents of such a law ; and this model law is from time to time re-considered at the Conferences of the Association.[1]

The Berne Convention.—The Berne Conferences were far less ambitious : still, if only by the adoption of the principle of reciprocity, they succeeded in establishing a sound basis for international copyright protection. The Berne Convention of 1886, which created the International Copyright Union, is the nearest approach to a Universal Law which has yet been made.

The original signatories to this Convention were Great Britain (with its dominions), Belgium, France (with its colonies and Algeria), Germany, Haïti, Italy, Spain, Switzerland, and Tunis. Luxemburg adhered in 1888, Monaco in 1889, Norway in 1896, and Japan in 1899. The latest accessions are

---

[1] See also Part III., Chap. VI., sec. 3, and the Appendix.

Denmark (with the Faröe Islands) and Sweden, which became members of the Union in 1903 and 1904 respectively. It is significant of the low state of ethics with respect to copyright in the United States, Russia, and Austria, that these countries have not yet entered the Union.

In 1896, ten years after the last Conference at Berne, the International Copyright Union held a further Conference at Paris, as a result of which several important alterations were made in the Convention. For an account of the Berne Convention as a whole, and of the changes effected by the Paris Conference, the reader is referred to Part III. of this work, where the subject is treated in full detail.

SECTION V.

CENTRAL AUTHORITY AND ADMINISTRATION.

National bias—The establishment of an International Court—Other international matters—International Registration—International Records—An International Library and Bibliography—An International Vocabulary.

Even if a Universal Law were achieved, in the absence of some central authority with power to interpret and enforce its provisions, copyright protection throughout the countries of the world would still be far from uniform ; for no two nations would take exactly the same view of the meaning and construction of the common code, and no two nations would carry it out with exactly the same degree of efficiency.   An international court would thus be an almost necessary appendage of a Universal Law, to say nothing of an international system of registration, an international vocabulary, and other matters. These things, however, have a present and practical interest, apart from the shadowy importance which attaches to them as part of the scheme for a Universal Law; for they may be of considerable service in the carrying out of the great Copyright Conventions which already exist.

National Bias.—Differences of opinion between the parties to international agreements are inevitable, just as between parties to private contracts.   Indeed, among the former, on account of the extent of the field left open to interpretation and the absence of decisions possessing international binding force, differences are even more likely to occur.   Treaties are essentially based on reciprocity ; but it would be impracticable or presumptuous for the parties to attempt to prescribe the exact way in which the equality of treatment thereby provided

N

for should be carried out. Without impugning international impartiality, it must be pointed out that domestic ideas and legal systems are likely to influence the result of litigation, and it is obvious that in the interpretation of the provisions of a Convention the national interests at stake will, to some extent, influence the issue.

At the Annual Conference of the International Literary and Artistic Association held at Vevey in 1901, M. Dieffenbach gave several recent examples of misinterpretation and mis-application of foreign laws. He cited a case where the Court of Appeal at Brescia, in Italy, feeling an uncertainty with regard to the interpretation of the German law, applied to Germany for the opinion of a competent authority. But when the case eventually came before the Appeal Court of Milan the judges there refused to accept this opinion, and even declared that it was manifestly erroneous. Differences of opinion of this nature have often arisen on account of the prejudices of local courts and the difficulty of interpreting foreign laws ; and their number is liable to increase.

The establishment of an International Court.—The establishment of an International Court has been suggested as a solution of the difficulty. At the Conference of the Institute of International Law held at Cambridge in 1895, this question was raised by a Report on the amendment of the Berne Convention presented by MM. Renault and Roguin. The Conference appointed MM. Darras and Roguin to receive opinions, and to report to the next session. Since 1895, until quite recently, the matter has unfortunately been crowded out at the meetings of the Institute ; in 1904, however, at the meeting at Edinburgh, it came again under discussion. The possibility and limits of an international jurisdiction, have also been frequently discussed at ordinary copyright conferences.

Authority of the Court.—It is difficult to conceive of a Supreme International Court, the decisions of which would be accepted as binding by all States. Still, although a Supreme International Court may at present be considered as impracticable as a universal law, an international tribunal with a more or less restricted authority is certainly possible. Any such tribunal, even if its powers were little more than to settle differences submitted to it by both parties, or to express opinions at their request, would serve a useful purpose.

Assuming that an International Court is to be established, many questions arise as to the authority with which it should be invested :

> (i) Should it give binding decisions or merely opinions ?
>
> (ii) What force should its decisions have as precedents ?
>
> (iii) Should it be set in motion at the request of individuals as well as of States ?
>
> (iv) Should the request of both parties be necessary ?

The nearest approach to an International Court which is at present practicable is a court that shall have power to give binding decisions, but only on the application of both parties. Still, if this were to perform the ordinary work of a court, its cost would be altogether disproportionate to its utility. Such a state of affairs would be entirely opposed to the English notion that civil courts should pay their own way. Still, the advantages to be derived from the settlement of international differences by a body of jurists of mixed nationalities would compensate for the deficit between the cost and the receipts of the court. It is not impossible, however, that an International Court should be instituted with power to decide on all matters of private international law, under which arrangement copyright would contribute only a share of the cost. This project has often been mooted, but the time does not yet seem ripe for its fulfilment.

Board of Arbitration.—But although international solidarity is not yet sufficiently advanced for the establishment of an International Court, there is no reason why some central authority should not be constituted for the settlement of differences in connection with copyright arising between parties of different nationalities. Such central authorities have already been established by the International Postal Union and by the International Union for the Railway Carriage of Goods.

If such a tribunal were established for the Copyright Union it might take any one of the following forms :—

    (i) A Board of Arbitration ;

    (ii) An Advisory Court consisting of experts ; or

    (iii) The International Office at Berne, acting in either of the preceding capacities.

At its formation in 1865, the International Postal Union empowered its Bureau to give opinions upon questions of difference between its members. And again in 1891 arbitration with binding authority was established by the Postal Union for certain matters. This was especially meant to apply to cases of disagreement relative to the interpretation of the Convention and to the settlement of disputes respecting responsibility for the loss of registered letters and packets.

Similarly the Union for the Railway Carriage of Goods, on the application of both parties, gives decisions through its Central Office in cases arising between the railways of the Union, such as those relating to the use of their waggons.

Other International Matters.—From time to time suggestions have been made with a view to placing many other matters connected with international copyright under a central authority. Some of these are practicable, and their adoption would doubtless further the work of unification; but others are evidently prompted by an infatuation for centralisation, even at the expense of economy and utility.

The matters propounded fall under four heads :—

    I.   International registration,

    II.   International records,

    III.   International library and bibliography,

    IV.   International vocabulary.

I. **International Registration.**—International registration of works published within the International Union might well be placed in the hands of the Central Office at Berne. Such a centralisation, in conjunction with a periodical publication of a list of the works registered, would provide a most useful means of information; particularly with respect to (i) the date of publication of works in other countries, from which (ii) the date when they would fall into the public domain could be calculated, and, (iii), the question whether an authorised translation of a particular work had been made before the expiration of the author's restrictive period (*délai d'usage*).

If law and morality are to work hand in hand it should not be considered dishonourable to copy or translate a book after the copyright or translating right has expired; and therefore any system by which the dates of such expiration are exactly noted would be an excellent thing, whether the author's term of protection has expired or is still in force.

In connection with its work of registration, the International Office might also issue international certificates, stating the performance of the requisite conditions and formalities. This, however, would be hard to carry out unless formalities were very much simplified throughout the Union; at present it is felt that this would entail too much extra work for the Office. It has also been suggested that the Office should investigate the title to any particular work submitted

to it. But this, while also being a great tax upon the time of
the staff, would necessarily be dependent upon the co-operation
of local officers in the various countries.

II. **International Records.**—Some centralisation of documents
and authoritative collection of statistics would prove of great
value and would assist in the development of information concerning international copyright. Official translations of the
domestic copyright laws of each country should also be made.

This work has already been commenced by the International Office for all recent laws, French translations of these
having been published in *Le Droit d'Auteur*, the useful organ
of the International Union.[1] It should also be mentioned
that the Office has recently published a collection of all the
Copyright Treaties now in force, each being set out in the
original language and in French.[2] Indeed, in the collection
and circulation of all sorts of information bearing on international copyright, the Office has done much, and is still
doing, good work ; but its present resources do not admit of
a satisfactory discharge of any further important functions.

III. **An International Library and Bibliography.**—The request
of certain literary societies for an international library, containing copies of all books published in the Union countries,
is not worthy of much consideration : the territory being so
large, no city would be convenient as a centre. For general
purposes the International Library at Brussels satisfies all
reasonable requirements.

It is desirable, however, that the authorities at Berne should
have ready access to all such documents and books of reference
as may be required for purposes of information ; this would

---

[1] Lyon-Caen, *Lois Françaises et Etrangères* contains an exhaustive collection
of the copyright laws of all the countries of the world, done into French.

[2] *Recueil des Conventions concernant la propriété littéraire et artistique*, Berne,
1904.

necessitate only a small fraction of the cost that a fairly complete international library would involve.

The value of an international bibliography, published by the Central Bureau, of all works relating to copyright is unquestionable, and this work is now proceeding under the supervision of M. Morel, the Director of the Office.

IV. **An International Vocabulary.**—The obstacles presented to the unification of copyright laws by difference of national institutions, customs, and legal systems have already been discussed. But the effect of this difference does not end here. The same idea, when regarded from different points of view, needs different modes of expression; and when it becomes necessary to represent the same idea in several languages further ambiguity is likely to arise. It is not every word that can be translated with exactness by a single word; literal translations often convey meanings which vary with the language in which they are rendered.

An international vocabulary of juridical terms would help to remove the danger of ambiguity, to advance the work of unification, and to secure a clear expression of its results. A literal translation of single words in each of the principal languages would be of little use, but an International Law Lexicon with short explanations of the terms translated would be of service. Such a juridical vocabulary should be done in English, French, and German, at least; while Italian and Spanish have also a good claim to be included. The production of a vocabulary of legal terms relating to copyright would demand an immense amount of labour on the part of expert linguists possessing a thorough acquaintance with comparative law. The task, however, is not insuperable, and the result would prove of great international advantage.

CHAPTER IV.

ALIEN AUTHORS AND ALIEN LAWS.

SECTION I.

THE AUTHOR AND THE WORK.

Should the State regard the author or the work ?—Territoriality the better principle—Nationality and Domicil—The Principle of Territoriality —Convention Territoriality.

Introduction.—The causes and conditions which affect international copyright, together with the various modes of establishing protection, have now been sketched. It remains to consider the practical results of their operation and to examine the actual position of alien authors in the various countries of the world. Akin to this subject is that of the 'Application of Alien Laws,' *i.e.* the adoption by the municipal law of any country of the provisions of the municipal law of another to regulate certain matters which, while they fall under its own jurisdiction, nevertheless seem to bear such a close relation to the foreign country as to call for a special application of the law of the latter. That part of the subject-matter of this chapter which falls under the head 'The Position of Alien Authors' relates to the extension of domestic protection to aliens, while that entitled 'The Application of Alien Laws' relates to the extension of the domestic code to embrace the provisions of a foreign body of law.

Conventions would seem to call for treatment in this chapter, since they affect the position of the alien author, being in fact ready-made codes which it is necessary for the parties to adopt as a whole into their domestic law ; but as the Berne Convention is the only existing Convention of widespread international importance, the subject will only be treated here incidentally with regard to the general principles which regulate the relation of international agreements to national law. The Berne Convention, which forms almost a complete international code, is left over to Part III., where it will be treated as a separate whole.

The history of international copyright shows that the general attitude of a country towards the protection of alien authors depends to a great extent upon its views as to the conduct which will best serve its own interests. Such views, moreover, often affect specific provisions of the municipal law, which may owe their shape to the opinion held by the country as to the best way of attaining the particular economic ends it has in view. Economic considerations more obviously govern the question of adherence to an international convention, for here the matter is one of deliberation and reasoned decision.

So long as States[1] remain independent of one another, progress towards a universal law, though perhaps directly connected with the establishment and expansion of large conventions, must ultimately rest on a corresponding enlargement and expansion of domestic law in each separate State, made with the object of taking in the provisions of such

---

[1] The term 'state' is more exact than 'country' or 'nation,' and it has a definite significance in international law. The three words all denote the same idea ; but while 'country' emphasises the element of territory, and 'nation' that of the people which inhabit the territory, 'state' gives prominence to that aspect in which the people are regarded as an organisation, existing under a settled system of government, and forming an international unit.

conventions and investing them with the authority of the legislature. Such an expansion however does not necessarily require an express enactment : there may be a general principle of law that treaties shall *ipso facto* be adopted into the domestic code.[1] In each country, as it advances in civilisation, convention law is in this way gradually superseding the old domestic law with respect to the protection of aliens : the result is that the international parts of all national codes are becoming uniform in shape and content. When this process has reached its consummation there will no longer be any peculiar 'position of alien authors.' Meanwhile it is necessary to determine what protection is accorded to aliens under the domestic law of the more important States.

Should the State regard the Author or the Work?—It will be found that there are two main principles by which, in the absence of reciprocity, a State determines the individuals who are to enjoy copyright protection, the one that all persons standing in a personal relation—subject or domiciled —to the State should be protected in virtue of their personal capacity, the other that copyright should be granted to all works published within the State territory irrespective of the personal capacity of their authors. In several countries both these principles are adopted and co-exist in the law. Thus according to the Austrian law an author gains protection if either (*a*) he is an Austrian citizen, or (*b*) his work has first appeared on Austrian territory; while in Switzerland the condition of domicil supersedes that of citizenship as the alternative to first publication in the country.

The whole question seems to be whether the State in

---

[1] In England treaties which cannot be carried out without a change in the domestic law require an Act of Parliament to give them effect.—Anson, *Law and Custom of the Constitution*, vol. ii., pp. 297 *seq.*

granting protection should look primarily to the author or to the work or to both : and a somewhat similar question arises with reference to the application of alien laws. Here the chief thing to be decided is whether the country to which the parties owe allegiance or in which they are domiciled, or that in which the infringement of the work has taken place, is to be regarded.

Territoriality [1] **the better Principle.**—It seems that on the whole the view which recognises copyright as attaching directly to the work is the better one : for, while it is undoubtedly of advantage to a State to secure the publication of as many works as possible within its dominions, the publication of works abroad by its subjects or persons domiciled in it results in no gain whatever to its literature. As long as the country obtains the work, the nationality of the author matters little : and whether copyright is regarded as property gained by original creation or as a reward given to the author for his services to the public, there seems no reason of principle why the mere fact of publication should not be sufficient to secure protection throughout the country in which that publication has taken place. If copyright is to be regarded as attaching to the work in this sense, it follows that the jurisdiction and the law to be applied when these are at conflict in two countries should be those of the country where the infringement in question has taken place.

Nationality and Domicil.—Where, however, protection is made to depend on the personal capacity of the author, the

---

[1] The sense in which the term 'territoriality' is here used must be very carefully distinguished from that which is more given to it as denoting the principle that the jurisdiction of a state begins and ends with the boundaries of its territory. Though there is some connection between the two meanings, the former has reference to the conditions under which the State accords certain rights, the latter to the conditions under which it may enforce certain duties.

exclusive adoption of the principle of nationality would put out of the question any 'protection of alien authors,' since an alien author is of course an author belonging to another country than the one in which protection is claimed. Nevertheless it is important to consider that principle, both because in the application of alien laws it is often used to determine personal capacity, and because, when an author belonging to one country is domiciled in another, or publishes his work in foreign territory, he may for certain purposes be regarded by his own State as an 'alien author': at any rate he has not that complete title to protection which would render his relations with his own country normal and the discussion of them superfluous.

Nationality is the relation subsisting between an individual and the State with which he is politically identified.[1] Domicil is the relation subsisting between an individual and the country which he has made his home. Of course in the majority of cases domicil coincides with nationality, in which case it is merged in the latter relation. Hence the subject only comes into separate importance when the individual under consideration has left his country of origin. In this state of affairs 'residence taken up with an intention that it shall be permanent'[2] is required to constitute a domicil; and this may be analysed into the following two factors: (1) The intention to choose a place for a permanent abode and thus to make it the centre of relations. An abode which is regarded as merely temporary is thus insufficient, even if it is of prolonged duration. (2) The realisation of this intention by acts which correspond with it, e.g. taking a house. Length of

---

[1] This use of the term 'nationality' must be carefully distinguished from its use to denote a community possessing common feelings, aspirations, and origin; e.g. the Irish people.

[2] Von Bar, *Private International Law*, p. 111.

residence has no intrinsic importance, but may serve as an
evidence of intention ; the same may be said of interruptions
by absence.[1]   In some countries, however, the notion of domicil
is arbitrarily defined by law.   Thus in Hungary two years
residence is required by the Act of 1884 (sec. 79), together
with payment of taxes during that period.

It will be found that some countries rest their protection
of copyright upon the principles of nationality and domicil
at the same time : so that under their law any author who is
either subject or domiciled obtains copyright.   On the other
hand the majority of States adopt one of the two principles
and reject the other : thus Austria limits its ordinary domestic
protection to Austrian citizens, and Switzerland to persons
domiciled in the country.[2]

There seems little reason why a State should not, if it
wishes, extend the advantages of its laws to authors connected with it by a personal tie, even when their works
have not been published in its territory—and in the case
of unpublished works it is obviously necessary to rely solely
upon the personal criterion.[3]   If any choice has to be made
between the principle of nationality and that of domicil,
the latter should be adopted : for by becoming domiciled
in a country a person, as regards his commercial and domestic
affairs, casts in his lot with his adopted home, and should
therefore be accorded all rights which are not purely political
in character.

The Principle of Territoriality.—Whatever view a State may
take of its obligations to its subjects and persons domiciled
within it, in awarding copyright protection it should have

---

[1] Von Bar, *Private International Law*, p. 113.

[2] Though in both these countries all *works* first appearing on the territory gain
protection whatever the status of their author.

[3] Unless a suggestion of Von Bar's be adopted, and every country protect the
work on the ground that it *may* be published in its territory.

first regard to the principle of territoriality—the principle
that all works published within the country are to be granted
copyright,—both on account of its theoretical soundness and
because of its practical utility.   Most States now enforce it
by their domestic law, either alone or in combination with
nationality or domicil ; and, except in the case of unpublished works, it has been adopted by the Berne Convention
as the only criterion of title to protection.   Art. 3 of that
agreement, as amended by the Act of Paris, gives full
protection to all works first published within Convention
territory ; while even an author belonging to a Union country
cannot gain Convention copyright if his work is first published outside the Union.   A State of the Union which does
not by its municipal law enforce the principle of territoriality
is thus obliged by the convention to employ it in the regulation of international affairs.

Convention Territoriality.—The solidarity of the Union is
much increased by the adoption of the territorial principle
of protection.   The exclusion from Convention copyright of
works of Unionist authors published without the Union and
the inclusion of works of non-Unionist authors published
within it combine together to make the territory of the
Union a sort of precinct, publication in any part of which
secures protection throughout its whole extent.   So far as
concerns the essential conditions of protection the Union may
thus be regarded as one homogeneous whole.   Publication in
any country of the Union means publication for the united
area, and will ensure protection throughout that area ; and in
this respect there is no more profit in considering the constituent countries as separate entities than there would be in
distinguishing between publication in Yorkshire and publication in Middlesex as regards the title which they confer to
the protection of the English Law.

SECTION II.

THE CONDITIONS OF PROTECTION IN VARIOUS COUNTRIES.

The conditions of protection in England—The conditions of protection in France, Belgium, and Luxemburg—The conditions of protection in Italy, Spain, and Switzerland—The conditions of protection in Germany, Austria, Hungary, Norway, Denmark, Japan, and Tunis—The conditions of protection in Sweden and Greece—The conditions of protection in the United States and Holland.

Most of the States of Europe whose literature and art are of importance are members of the International Union established by the Berne Convention. This agreement determines the position throughout the Union of authors and works belonging to any one of the signatory States.

For these States, therefore, in their relations to each other, the rules of domestic law relating to the treatment of alien authors are of little importance, though those which define the rights granted to native authors are of interest as determining the rights given to authors of the Union under the Convention. In so far, however, as rules of the former class lay down the conditions upon which the attainment of municipal copyright depends, they affect the title of works to copyright under the Convention. A short consideration, then, of the fundamental grounds of protection in each of those States is not without its importance, even in the settlement of their mutual relations.

Outside the sphere of the Convention such a consideration is undoubtedly necessary—for, except within the limited domain of particular treaties, the position of aliens in non-Union countries and of non-Unionist authors (publishing their works outside the Union territory) in Union countries depends entirely upon the attitude taken up by the various domestic laws towards such principles as reciprocity, nationality and domicil, and territoriality. This attitude also serves to indicate the general degree of advancement to which countries have attained in their copyright legislation.

A brief summary of the essential conditions which obtain in each of the principal States of the world in reference to the granting of copyright protection will therefore now be made. The domestic laws of the various countries alone will be examined : no attempt will be made to include the provisions of ordinary treaties, while the Berne Convention will be dealt with subsequently.

THE CONDITIONS OF PROTECTION IN ENGLAND.

It seems well in the first place to consider how our own English law treats the alien author. The English copyright law differs from that of most other countries in that it is contained in many separate statutes, so that there is one rule for literary, musical, and dramatic works, another for prints, another for paintings, drawings, and photographs, and yet another for works of sculpture. There are few of the important States of Europe which have not now codified their law of copyright, and, though of course the various classes of works are dealt with separately in these codes, some general disposition, applicable indiscriminately to all classes, concerning the conditions under which the alien shall enjoy protection is usually to be found as well.

Summary of the English Law.—The English law provides for the establishment of diplomatic arrangements with foreign countries, based on reciprocity. Under such arrangements, it is possible for works first published abroad to obtain protection in Great Britain ; otherwise it is necessary for the foreign author to satisfy the ordinary conditions of the domestic law.

For literary, musical, and dramatic works, first publication in the British dominions is required. Prints must be 'engraved, etched, drawn, or designed' in Great Britain. In the case of paintings, drawings, and photographs, it is necessary both that the author shall be a British subject or resident within the dominions of the Crown, and also, probably, that the work shall be published in the British dominions. For works of sculpture the rule seems to be that they must be ' put forth and published' within the British dominions.

Diplomatic Reciprocity.—To begin with, the English law recognises the principle of 'diplomatic reciprocity.' An Act of 1838 empowered Her Majesty by Order in Council to extend copyright to the authors of books published in any foreign country which should be named therein for a term not exceeding that granted to British subjects. It will be noted that this provision applied only to *books*. It was repealed by the International Copyright Act of 1844 (7 Vict. c. 12), which enabled Her Majesty by Order in Council to grant copyright to the authors, etc., of ' Books, Prints, Articles of Sculpture, and other Works of Art ' for a term not exceeding that secured to British subjects for the respective classes of works. Her Majesty was also empowered to extend to aliens the benefit of the Dramatic Literary Property Act of 1833 and of the provision of the Copyright Amendment Act of 1842, granting performing right to dramatic works. Orders in Council made under this Act were to be laid before Parliament within six weeks of issue.[1]

---

[1] Or if Parliament should not then be sitting, within six weeks after the commencement of the next Session.—7 Vict. c. 12, s. 16.

The next statute on this subject is one of 1852 (15 Vict.
c. 12), 'to enable Her Majesty to carry into effect a Convention with France on the Subject of Copyright ; to extend
and explain the International Copyright Acts ; and to explain
the Acts relating to Copyright in Engravings.' Its title
sufficiently explains its aims; its chief effect was to empower
Her Majesty to alter certain of the stipulations of the Copyright Act of 1842 which stood in the way of the enforcement
of the recently concluded Convention with France.

The last and most important of all the International
Copyright Acts is still wholly in force. It is an Act of
1886 (49 and 50 Vict. c. 33) giving power to the Crown
to accede to the Berne Convention. Before making any
Order in Council under this Act, the Crown is to be satisfied
that the foreign country in question 'has made such provisions (if any) as it appears . . . expedient to require for
the protection of authors of works first produced within the
United Kingdom.' The intention which runs through all the
International Copyright Acts is to prepare the way for the
Crown to enter into diplomatic arrangements for reciprocity
with foreign countries.

First publication essential.—In the absence of such arrangements, the English law makes first publication within the
British Dominions (or simultaneous publication in a foreign
country and the British Dominions) a condition of copyright
for literary works. The Act of 1842 required publication
within the United Kingdom, but the International Act of
1886 (s. 8) provides that 'The Copyright Acts shall . . .
apply to a literary or artistic work first produced in a British
possession in like manner as they apply to a work first
produced in the United Kingdom.'

A British subject, wherever resident, secures copyright
by the mere fact of publication within the British Dominions ;

but it has never been established at law that residence within the British Dominions at the time of publication may be dispensed with in the case of aliens. According to the opinion of Lords Cairns and Westbury expressed in *Routledge v. Low*, 1868,[1] the mere fact of publication within the British Dominions suffices in every case ; and their *obiter dictum* was followed by the English law officers in an opinion which was communicated to the United States in 1891.[2] As a matter of fact, works of Americans first published in England are invariably treated by English publishers as copyright works, without reference to the place of residence of their authors.

In the previous case of *Jefferys v. Boosey*, 1854,[3] which was decided on the statute of 1709 (8 Anne c. 19), however, it had been held that the foreign author must be resident at the time of publication. The opinion of Lords Cairns and Westbury seems mainly to rest upon the preamble of the Act of 1842, passed to encourage 'the production of literary works of lasting benefit to the world,' but these words hardly seem to warrant the conclusion that that Act meant upon this point to alter the rule deduced in *Jefferys v. Boosey* from the Act of Anne, which was itself passed ' for the encouragement of learning.'

Whichever opinion as to the effect of the Act of 1842 be right, there is no doubt that the Naturalisation Act of 1870 enables an alien friend to acquire and hold personal property in the same way in all respects as a British subject. According to one view,[4] this makes it possible for a foreign author to secure British copyright by mere publication within the

---

[1] *Routledge v. Low*, L. R. 3 H. L. 100.

[2] With the object of satisfying the conditions required to secure the benefits of the Chace Act of that year. This assurance was perfectly general in its terms, and, even if it correctly represents the law as to the conditions of protection for literary works, it will be seen that it clearly fails to do so for works of fine art.

[3] *Jefferys v. Boosey*, 4 H. L. C. 815.

[4] See Scrutton, *The Law of Copyright*, 4th ed., p. 129.

British Dominions, for copyright is personal property and no residence is needed in order to enable a British subject to obtain it. Still, in this case the question is not so much the acquisition of personal property already in existence, as the *creation* of such property *ab initio*. Copyright is not personal property till it is obtained, and, if being a British subject is a condition of the *obtaining*, the Naturalisation Act does not affect the matter.

As regards performing right in musical and dramatic works, the law is probably the same as for literary copyright.

The Rules as to Works of Art.—With reference to artistic works, the rule differs according to the nature of the work. In order to gain copyright, Prints must, by the Act of 1776 (17 Geo. III. c. 57, s. 1), be 'engraved, etched, drawn, or designed in Great Britain,' though the words of the Act contain no restriction to British subjects or persons resident in Great Britain at the time of publication.

Paintings, drawings, and photographs, besides being, in all probability, subject to the condition of first publication in the British Dominions,[1] do not gain copyright unless their maker is 'a British subject or resident within the Dominions of the Crown' (Fine Arts Copyright Act, 1862).[2] Accordingly, in *Geissendörfer v. Mendelssohn*[3] an entry of copyright in a floral border, painted for certain cards by a German subject resident in Germany, was expunged from the register. Hence works of

---

[1] See the International Copyright Act of 1844 (s. 19).

[2] 25 and 26 Vict., c. 68, s. 1. Assuming—what is very unlikely—that the Naturalisation Act of 1870 would by itself have the effect of enabling aliens to gain copyright in literary works without residence, it would seem, by parity of reasoning, that it also has the effect of abrogating this express disposition of an earlier statute. As regards works of the fine arts, the view of the law conveyed to the United States can only be supported on this dubious hypothesis.

[3] *Geissendörfer v. Mendelssohn*, 13 T. L. R. 91.

art by American authors cannot gain copyright in Great Britain even by first publication there. So far, then, the opinion expressed by our law officers in 1891 was plainly wrong, and the reciprocal arrangement with the United States fails on our side. Under the Fine Arts Act no action is maintainable in respect of any infringement committed before registration at Stationers' Hall.

With reference to works of sculpture, the Act of 1813 (54 Geo. III. c. 56, s. 1) enacts that 'every person or persons who shall make or cause to be made any new and original sculpture . . . shall have the sole right of property . . . for the term of fourteen years from first putting forth and publishing the same,' provided the name of the proprietor and the date are put on the work produced. A court of law would probably interpret the Act as requiring that the 'putting forth and publishing' should take place within the British Dominions; but it may be conjectured that no condition of British nationality would be imposed.

Rule as to Unpublished Works.—As regards common law right in unpublished works, no definite rule has been laid down concerning the capacity of aliens; but many of the dicta in *Jefferys v. Boosey* draw a distinction between the author's right in his manuscript before publication and his copyright after publication, and seem to suggest that, while the latter cannot vest in an alien without residence,[1] no such condition attaches to the former.

The English Copyright Bill, which has now been before Parliament for several years, provides anew for the enforcement of the Berne Convention throughout His Majesty's dominions, and once more enables the Crown to make regulations for the protection of works first published in another country, upon being satisfied that the latter makes due

[1] *I.e.* according to the view of the law taken in this case.

provision for the protection of works first published in His Majesty's dominions. This is a fresh recognition of 'diplomatic reciprocity.'

Treaties.—Great Britain is a member of the International Union, and its international relations with the other members are wholly regulated by the Berne Convention. It has also a Treaty of 1893 with Austria-Hungary and an arrangement for reciprocity, dating from 1891, with the United States. Protection secured under a treaty must be carefully distinguished from protection secured under the domestic law of the country granting it. The two may be equivalent in content, but the conditions of the one are regulated by treaty, those of the other by domestic law. It is with the latter kind of protection alone that we are here concerned.

THE CONDITIONS OF PROTECTION IN FRANCE, BELGIUM, AND LUXEMBURG.

As has already been stated, the countries which by their domestic law are most liberal to the alien author are France, Belgium, and Luxemburg. These States attach to their copyright protection no condition either of reciprocity on the part of foreign States, or of residence or publication within their territory on the part of foreign authors.

France.—Where the work of an alien is first published in France, it is protected by the ordinary French law ; no residence on the part of the alien is required, and the mere fact of publication in France confers on the foreign author exactly the same right as would be gained by a Frenchman.

But even where the work is not first published in France, it may, in virtue of a Decree of 1852, secure the same *protection* as that accorded to native works. The author however is in this case placed under certain disabilities. By Sec. 4 of the Decree the French domestic formalities must be carried out ; and in addition to these, as the Decree presupposes a title to copyright, it is necessary that the formalities which are imposed by the country of origin of the work as conditions of copyright shall have been fulfilled. Moreover the rights of the work in France cannot be greater than those which it enjoys in its own country.[1]

French Treaties.—France is a party to the Conventions of Berne and Montevideo.[2] Apart from these, it has established international relations with Austria-Hungary, Bolivia, the Congo, Costa Rica, Denmark, Ecuador, Germany, Guatemala, Holland, Italy, Mexico, Monaco, Montenegro, Norway and Sweden, Portugal, Roumania, Salvador, Spain, and the United States.

Belgium.—Sec. 38 of the Belgian Law of 1886 runs : ' Aliens enjoy in Belgium the rights secured by the present law, although the duration of the latter cannot exceed the duration fixed by the Belgian law. Nevertheless if their rights expire sooner in their own country they shall lapse at the same time in Belgium.' It will be seen that this contains no express requirement as to the fulfilment of the formalities of the country of origin.

Belgian Treaties.—Belgium is a member of the International Union and has copyright relations with the Congo, Germany, Holland, Mexico, Portugal, Spain, and the United States.

Luxemburg, by Sec. 39 of its Law of 1898, puts foreigners on absolutely the same footing as subjects in respect of

---

[1] That is, according to the view taken by Darras and others. But whether the Decree gives aliens the same *rights* as subjects, or, as Darras represents, only the same *protection*, is a matter of some controversy.

[2] Its accession to the latter Convention has, however, been accepted only by the Argentine Republic and Paraguay.

copyright protection, without any condition as to the formalities of the country of origin.[1]

Luxemburg is a party to the Berne Convention, but has no other treaties.

The Conditions of Protection in Italy, Spain, and Switzerland.

Italy, Spain, and Switzerland protect works of foreign authors published within their respective territories ; and apply the principle of 'legal reciprocity' with regard to works published abroad.

Italy.—Sec. 1 of the Italian Decree of 1882 grants copyright to 'the authors of intellectual works' without any requirement as to nationality. As, however, Art. 44 enacts that the law is applicable to the authors of works first published in a foreign country, *provided that a reciprocal protection is granted by the laws of that country to works first published in Italy*, it is clear that the ordinary protection is meant to apply to works first published in Italy and to these alone. Art. 44 requires that the laws of the foreign country in question should recognise as belonging to authors 'rights more or less extended,' and that they should be applicable by reciprocity to works published in Italy. In order that works first published in a foreign country may gain the protection of the Italian law, it is therefore necessary that the country of first publication should be one which protects the copyright in its own works and is willing to extend its protection reciprocally to Italian works. Where the foreign law itself requires as a condition of reciprocity that the rights and remedies of its own law shall be granted to its authors by the other country, the Italian

---

[1] See Part II., Chap. i., sec. 5.

Government may effect this by Decree, so long as the rights and remedies accorded are temporary (*i.e.* limited as to term), and do not differ essentially from those of the Italian law.

Italian Treaties.—Italy is a member of the International Union, a party to the Montevideo Convention,[1] and has international relations with Austria-Hungary, Columbia, France, Germany, Mexico, Norway and Sweden, San Marino, Spain, and the United States.

Spain.—The Spanish Law is in a similar position to that of Italy in that it grants protection to the 'authors' of original works without express qualification. The qualification to be deduced by implication is however different in the two cases. In Spain the principle primarily applied is that of nationality. The law makes special provisions with regard to *subjects of foreign States,* from which it may be concluded that under ordinary circumstances Spanish subjects alone enjoy the benefit of its protection, and that they obtain copyright whether they publish their works in Spain or abroad.

The Act of 1879, Sec. 50, grants protection to subjects of States which recognise by their legislation in favour of Spaniards such a right of intellectual property as is established by that Act. If this condition is to be construed strictly it would appear to be almost incapable of realisation ; but probably a substantial correspondence in the protection given would in practice be allowed to suffice. Sec. 51 of the Act contains a very distinct recognition of the principle of 'diplomatic reciprocity.' This article lays down the following bases for the diplomatic arrangements it holds in contemplation : (1) Complete reciprocity, (2) Mutual treatment upon the footing of 'most favoured nation,' (3) Formalities of country of origin alone to be imposed, and (4) Printing, sale,

---

[1] Its accession to the latter has been accepted only by the Argentine Republic and Paraguay.

importation, and exportation, in each country, of copyright works in the languages or dialects of the other to be forbidden.

Spanish Treaties.—Under this Act Spain has adhered to the Conventions of Berne and Montevideo,[1] and has established copyright relations with Belgium, Columbia, Costa Rica, France, Guatemala, Italy, Portugal, Salvador, and the United States. Many of these agreements were made soon after the enactment of the law of 1879,—a high tribute to the reasonableness of the principles laid down by that Act.

Switzerland.—The Swiss law of 1883 by Sec. 10 grants its protection to all works of which the authors are domiciled in Switzerland and to all works first published there. Other authors enjoy protection for works published abroad only if their country treats authors of works published in Switzerland on the same footing as authors of works published in its own territory.

Swiss Treaties.—Switzerland is a member of the Berne Convention, and has copyright relations with Japan and the United States.

THE CONDITIONS OF PROTECTION IN GERMANY, AUSTRIA, HUNGARY, NORWAY, DENMARK, JAPAN, AND TUNIS.

The laws of Germany, Austria, Hungary, Norway, Denmark, Japan, and Tunis also protect, under varying conditions, works which are first published in their respective territories ; but they contain no provision for 'legal reciprocity.' Hungary and Norway will not protect works of aliens first published in the country unless they have appeared with

---

[1] Its accession to the latter Convention has been accepted only by the Argentine Republic and Paraguay.

native publishers; and the German law contains a similar condition with regard to works of art. Germany, Austria, Hungary, Norway, and Denmark recognise the principle of nationality concurrently with that of territoriality.

Germany.—The German law of 1870 relating to literary, musical, and dramatic works and designs, protected (Sec. 61) only such works of foreign authors as should have first appeared with publishers having their houses of trade situated in Germany.[1] Nearly the whole of this law has recently been repealed by an Act of 19th June, 1901,—which also only applies to literary, musical, and dramatic works and designs, —s. 55 of which provides that 'An alien enjoys protection for any work published within the Empire provided that he has not already caused the work itself or a translation thereof to be published in another country,'[2] while s. 54 protects all subjects of the Empire for all their works.

With regard to works of art and photographs, the German law, contained in statutes of less recent establishment, is by no means so reasonable. The Act of 9th January, 1876, which regulates copyright in works of art, protects only such works of foreign authors as appear for the first time with native publishers; while the Act of the 10th January of the same year, relating to photographs, restricts protection for these to native authors. As Germany is a member of the Berne Convention these limitations do not lessen the protection due under that agreement to authors belonging to Union countries.

German Treaties.—Germany is a member of the International Union, and has separate copyright relations with Austria-Hungary, Belgium, France, Italy, and the United States.

---

[1] Special provision, however, being made by Art. 62 for legal reciprocity with other States which should have formed part of the old German Confederation, *e.g.* Austria.

[2] Translation published by Longmans, Green, and Co., 1902.

Austria has also recently codified its law of copyright, though, unlike Germany, it has embraced in its new law works of art and photographic works as well as works of literature and of music.

The Austrian law of 1895, Sec. 1, makes the provisions of that law applicable to all works of literature, art, and photography first appearing on the territory. By the same Article an Austrian citizen is given protection for all his works wherever published. Sec. 2 of the Act provides for a limited legal reciprocity, applicable only to the German Empire ; also for a general diplomatic reciprocity.

Austria has a treaty with Hungary, and the two countries, in their international capacity as a single State, have entered into several agreements mentioned below.

Hungary.—The Hungarian law still makes the personal relation of the author to the State the chief determinant of protection. By the Act of 1884 (Sec. 79), the works of Hungarian citizens and of aliens domiciled in Hungary are protected even if published abroad ; though a foreign author who is not domiciled only gains protection for works which first appear with a native publisher. Sec. 80 of the same law is also worthy of note. It reads ' The present law applies even when a Hungarian subject violates its provisions in a foreign country to the prejudice of a Hungarian subject.' This shows the attitude of Hungary towards the questions treated in Sec. 4 of this chapter.

Austro-Hungarian Treaties.—Although Austria and Hungary have distinct codes of domestic copyright law, as already stated Austria-Hungary constitutes one State for international purposes. This dual State is not a member of the International Union, but has entered into particular treaties with France, Germany, Great Britain, and Italy.

Norway.—Copyright in Norway is granted by Sec. 37 of

the law of 1893 to all works of Norwegian subjects and also to all works of aliens which first appear with Norwegian publishers.[1] The Article also provides for the establishment of 'diplomatic reciprocity' by Royal Ordinance.

Norwegian Treaties.—Norway is a party to the Berne Convention of 1886, though it has refused to accede to the Additional Act of 1896. Internal reciprocity is established between Norway and Sweden. These countries form a dual State,[2] and have joint treaties relating to copyright with Denmark, France, and Italy.

Denmark.—The law of Denmark is similar to that of Norway. The recent Act of 19th December, 1902, Sec. 36, provides for the application of that Act to all works of Danish subjects and to works of foreign subjects published by a Danish publisher.[3] Provision is made for 'diplomatic reciprocity' by Royal Ordinance.[4]

Danish Treaties.—Under this Act Denmark has entered the International Union. It has also copyright relations with France, Norway and Sweden, and the United States.

Japan.—As to the persons protected, the law of Japan is identical with that of Denmark. By Sec. 28 of its Act of 1899 the former country protects all works first published upon its territory, without any condition as to the nationality of their publisher. The same section contemplates the establishment of diplomatic reciprocity. Following this out, Japan in 1899 adhered to the Berne Convention. A commercial treaty of 1896 with Switzerland, which is still in force, also deals incidentally with copyright.

---

[1] Where the publishing house is a firm all the partners, or in the case of a limited company all the directors, must be domiciled in Norway.

[2] Until quite lately, however, Sweden was not a party to the Berne Convention.

[3] The rule for determining the nationality of a firm is the same as in the Norwegian law.

[4] The consent of the Diet however is necessary where the contemplated arrangement involves the undertaking of pecuniary obligations.

Tunis, by its law of 1899 (Sec. 1), protects works first published on its territory and recognises the principle of diplomatic reciprocity. It is a member of the International Union.

The Conditions of Protection in Sweden and Greece.

In Sweden and Greece the ordinary copyright protection seems to be limited to subjects, but the laws of both countries provide for the extension of protection to foreign authors upon condition of reciprocity.

Sweden.—The Swedish Literary Copyright Code of 1877 (Sec. 19) states that it applies to the works of Swedish citizens (presumably wherever published); and that its provisions may under condition of reciprocity be extended by the King to the works of aliens. Protection therefore is not given as a matter of course to the literary works of aliens published in Sweden.

On this point the rule is somewhat different for works of art. The Artistic Copyright Act of 1867 by Sec. 8 provides that 'The provisions of the present law may, under condition of reciprocity, be extended by the King in whole or in part to the reproduction of the artistic works of aliens resident abroad.' From this it may be gathered that works of aliens domiciled in Sweden, as well as works of Swedish subjects, are protected in the ordinary course of the law.

Sweden is now a party to the Berne Convention. Apart from this, it has issued a royal edict admitting Norwegian works to copyright, and jointly with Norway has entered into several copyright arrangements with other countries, the names of which have already been given, under Norway.

Greece.—Act 433 of the Greek Penal Code of 1833 recognises the principle of 'legal reciprocity.' It applies the protection given by the preceding article of the code against the 'infringement and imitation of works of art and intellect' to aliens whose government affords the same protection to Greek subjects.

The Conditions of Protection in the United States and Holland.

The laws of the United States and Holland attach to the acquisition of copyright by aliens certain peculiar conditions made in the interests of domestic industries.

The United States.—The American Act of Congress of 1870[1] applied only to citizens of and residents in the United States. The protection then given was extended in 1891 by the Chace Act, and now alien authors can gain copyright protection in America if their country grants reciprocal protection to citizens of the United States.[2] If the work is in the English language, it is necessary that it should be published in America either first, or simultaneously with its publication in another country, and, besides this, that on or before the day of publication a copy of the title (*i.e.* title-page) of the work, and also two copies of the work itself, *which latter must be printed from type set within the limit of the United States, or from plates made therefrom, or from negatives or drawings on stone made within the limits of the United States, or from transfers made therefrom*, shall be deposited with the

---

[1] Incorporated into the Revised Statutes in 1874.

[2] *I.e.* the foreign country must either (i) grant copyright to American citizens on substantially the same basis as to its own, or (ii) be a party to an international agreement for reciprocity, which the United States may join at will. When a country satisfies either of these conditions the American President will issue a proclamation in its favour, and thereafter its subjects will be admitted to the benefit of the American Law.—Sec. 13 of the Chace Act.

Librarian of Congress.[1] Since March, 1905, works in t. foreign language first published abroad may, under certain conditions, gain full protection, provided that the ordinary requirements of the law are fulfilled within twelve months.

The Act of 1891, in providing an amended reading for that section of the previous statute[2] which embodies a general grant of protection to authors, omits those words in the former Act which conferred that protection expressly upon citizens or residents of the United States who should be authors; Sec. 13 of the amending Act provides that the latter shall only apply to 'a citizen or subject of a foreign State or nation' when such foreign State or nation shall grant reciprocal protection. Thus it would seem that subjects of those States which do not acknowledge reciprocity get no protection, even when resident[3] in the United States.[4]

The matter is, however, by no means free from doubt. Sec. 4 of the amending Act provides that a registration fee of one dollar shall be charged upon every person 'not a citizen *or resident* of the United States,' and this can only be regarded as imposing a special disability upon persons enjoying an international copyright protection, persons whose copyright arises under the ordinary domestic rule being exempt. It is, no doubt, rather in order to make room for the inclusion of aliens satisfying the conditions of Sec. 13 than in order to effect the exclusion of residents not satisfying these conditions that Sec. 1 of the Chace Act leaves out the phrase granting protection to citizens or residents of the United States.

---

[1] Sec. 3 of the Chace Act, 1891.—Sec. 4956 of the Revised Statutes.

[2] S. 4952 of the Revised Statutes.

[3] The American Courts will not consider a person as 'resident' unless he has an intention of permanently remaining in the country. This interpretation makes residence practically equivalent to domicil.

[4] In any case it seems clear, as Mr. MacGillivray points out, that a foreigner resident in, but not a subject of, a country with which reciprocity is established cannot obtain copyright.—MacGillivray, *Treatise on Copyright*, p. 249.

International Arrangements.—Under Sec. 13, Proclamations have been issued admitting subjects of Belgium, Chili, Costa Rica, Denmark, France, Germany, Great Britain, Holland, Italy, Mexico, Portugal, Spain, and Switzerland to the benefit of the amended Act.

Holland.—The Dutch law (1881 Act—sec. 27) makes 'publication by means of printing'[1] in Holland or the Dutch Indies the condition of copyright in published works;[2] hence it would seem that a work first published in Holland by a Dutchman does not gain protection unless printed on Dutch territory, while, on the other hand, a work first published in Holland by a foreign author will gain protection if it has been printed on Dutch territory.

Holland, while rejecting the invidious principle that the law should look only to the nationality of the author, clings to a rule which is infinitely worse, since it makes protection depend on the condition of printing in the country—a matter which in strictness is independent of literary considerations.

In respect of unpublished works and lectures, the 1886 Act does, however, regard the personal status of the author; for Sec. 27 grants protection for these to authors domiciled in Holland or the Dutch Indies.

Dutch Treaties.—Holland has copyright relations with Belgium, France, and the United States.

[1] According to the interpretation of the International Office, the Act requires the first publication, *i.e.*, issuing to the public, as well as the printing, to take place in Holland or the Dutch Indies.

[2] The Canadian Copyright Act, 1875, which cannot, of course, impair the validity in Canada of British Imperial Copyright, requires printing and publication in the country as a condition of Canadian copyright. It has been decided in *Frowde v. Parrish* (1896), 27 Ont. Rep. 526, that printing and publishing from stereotype plates imported into Canada is a sufficient 'printing' within the meaning of the Act.

SECTION III.

FORMALITIES SPECIALLY IMPOSED UPON ALIENS.

Formalities relating to the inception of copyright—Competing formalities—Formalities of protecting country not usually required—The English rule as to formalities—Formalities in France, Belgium, and Luxemburg—Extraneous formalities rarely required—Formalities relating to Procedure in Court—In matters of procedure special formalities may be useful—Deposit of Security for Costs.

FORMALITIES RELATING TO THE INCEPTION OF THE RIGHT.

Whatever general principles a country adopts in deciding if protection shall be granted to foreign authors, when it gives them any protection at all, it has to determine whether they shall be required to fulfil merely the same formalities as subjects, or whether, in virtue of their exceptional position, special formalities shall be imposed upon them or special exemptions granted them.

Competing Formalities.—A State which protects all works published within its territory, and only these, since it does not regard the personal capacity of the author and has nothing to do with foreign works, would naturally apply to all protected works alike its domestic formalities without modification. In such a case there is no reason for imposing any disability or for granting any exemption to a protected work on the ground that its author is an alien.

The position is somewhat different where a country grants protection to works of aliens published abroad. Here there are obviously two sets of formalities, either or both of which might possibly be required—that of the country of origin and that of the country granting protection. The fact of distance and difference of language generally renders the fulfilment of the formalities of the latter a somewhat difficult operation : there is also the general ignorance, prevalent everywhere, of foreign formalities to be taken into account. On the other hand, since the object of formalities is usually either to make known certain facts connected with the coming into existence of the right, as in the case of registration, or to benefit the State at the expense of the author, either by exacting fees or by requiring deposit of one or more copies of the work, there is considerable reason for subjecting even works published abroad to the formalities of the municipal law.

It is difficult to see why a country granting protection should not require foreign authors as well as natives to conform to its own ideas of what is necessary for such purposes as registration. Nor is it obvious that the author of a work published abroad has, in virtue of his choice of a foreign country, any claim to exemption from a tax levied on native authors in return for copyright protection. It may therefore be concluded that where a State consents to forego the fulfilment of its own formalities in respect of works published abroad to which it grants protection, it does this merely as a matter of grace, and not as a necessary part of its original concession of copyright.

Formalities of protecting country not usually required.— Still, as a matter of grace, there is much to be said for such a proceeding in view of its obvious simplicity and convenience : a fact which has generally been recognised in copyright treaties. Thus the Berne Convention provides that the fulfilment of the formalities of the country of origin shall be sufficient to establish protection throughout the Union,

and the majority of copyright treaties make a similar stipulation.[1]   Moreover the general tendency of domestic law is
towards the protection of copyright gained abroad without
any fresh formality.   Thus Spain (Act of 1879, sec. 51) lays
this down as one of the bases on which copyright arrangements are to be made.   And Italy, by its Act of 1882, sec.
44,[2] will, when reciprocity is established, accept deposit of
copies of the work or declaration of copyright, when performed
according to the law of the country of origin, in lieu of the
similar formalities imposed by Sec. 21 of the Act, which are
required to be carried out in Italy.[3]

The English Rule as to Formalities.—In Great Britain the
law empowers the King to issue Orders in Council giving
protection to works first published in any foreign country,
and makes no reference to the fulfilment of formalities there;[4]
but the only two Orders in Council at present in force are
concerned with treaties—the Berne Convention of 1886 and
the Treaty of 1893 with Austria-Hungary—which protect
only works that have complied with the formalities of the
country of origin.[5]

As to the fulfilment of the English domestic formalities, the
present law, as settled in *Hanfstaengl v. American Tobacco*

---

[1] The general adoption of this rule would, *cæteris paribus*, lead all authors to
publish in one country, viz. that which imposed the least burdensome
formalities.

[2] Sec. 44, § 3, reads: 'If, in the foreign country, the law prescribes deposit
or declaration at the time of the publication of a work, it is sufficient, in order to
gain a copyright in the work, enforceable in Italy, that proof should be given that
the one or the other has been carried out conformably to the laws of the foreign
country.'

[3] The declaration contemplated by Art. 21 is a statement of intention to retain
the copyright in a work, accompanied by an exact description of the latter and
a mention of the year of publication.

[4] Act of 1844, 7 Vict. c. 12, sec. 2.

[5] The arrangement with the United States is not a treaty.   On the part of
Great Britain it consists simply of an assurance given to the United States,
having reference to the state of the English domestic law.

Co.,[1] is that where no special mention of them is made in the Order in Council on which the protection of the work depends they are not required.

The International Copyright Act of 1844 (sec. 6) imposed upon authors of foreign works to whom English copyright should be extended the formalities of registration and of deposit of one copy of the book; thus requiring from such authors practically the ordinary domestic formalities. The International Copyright Act of 1886 (49 and 50 Vict. c. 33, sec. 4) enacted that the provisions of the International Copyright Acts as to formalities (which are contained in the Act of 1844) should not apply to protected foreign works, except in so far as provided in the Order in Council granting protection. This apparently gives to the Crown power to relieve foreign works altogether from the performance of British formalities; and the Order in Council adopting the Berne Convention must be taken as having done this, at the same time requiring foreign works to fulfil the formalities of their country of origin.

On the other hand, it has been argued that, as an Order of Council made under the International Copyright Acts simply has the effect of extending to the foreign works to which it applies 'all and singular the enactments' of the Copyright Amendment Act[2] of 1842, and as that Act itself requires registration (s. 24) and deposit (s. 8), these formalities are still obligatory under the general rule, although the special and additional formalities imposed by the Act of 1844 (s. 6) are no longer thus necessary. It is probable, however, that Sec. 6 of the 1844 Act was meant to supersede the provisions of the Act of 1842 with reference to formalities: and in *Hanfstaengl v. American Tobacco Co.*[3] affirming *Hanfstaengl*

---

[1] *Hanfstaengl v. American Tobacco Co.* (1895), 1 Q.B. 347.
[2] International Act of 1844 (7 Vict. c. 12, s. 3).
[3] *Hanfstaengl v. American Tobacco Co.* (1895), 1 Q.B. 347.

v. Holloway [1] it has been decided that for the countries comprised in the Order in Council of 1887 the ordinary English formalities are no longer necessary. It is doubtful whether this principle can be held to apply to sculptures and engravings, for which the formality prescribed by the statutes is not registration, but the imposition of the author's name on the work.

Under the law of Great Britain, then, the formalities requisite for foreign works are determined for the works of each country by the particular Order in Council which deals with them. There is a possibility of total exemption from all formalities whatever; but the Orders in Council will doubtless generally require the fulfilment of the formalities of the country of origin, not those of the national law of Great Britain. [2] This represents the policy of all the Orders now in force; under them the formalities of the country of origin, and no others, are imposed.

Although Spain, Italy, and Great Britain do not by their ordinary domestic law protect the works of aliens published abroad, they yet recognise the principle of reciprocity and determine the formalities to which such works shall be subjected where that principle applies. The majority of countries make no provision on the subject by their domestic laws, the formalities to be imposed on foreign authors being left to be decided at the making of each particular treaty.

Formalities in France, Belgium, and Luxemburg.—France, Belgium, and Luxemburg, which extend their domestic copyright to all foreign works wherever published, have, however, naturally had to make some rule on the subject. France grants

---

[1] *Hanfstaengl v. Holloway* (1893), 2 Q.B. 1.

[2] The Treaty of 1893 with Austria-Hungary provided that, while, for obtaining protection in England and Austria, the fulfilment of the formalities of the country of origin were to be sufficient, English works claiming protection in Hungary should be required to fulfil the formalities of both these latter countries.—See Art. 5 of the Treaty.

to such works only the same *protection* as that accorded to works published in her territory ; it assumes that the works it protects have already gained copyright in their own country, and proceeds by way of extending to them its domestic remedies rather than by granting to them a separate copyright. In order to profit by the liberality of this country, it is therefore necessary for foreign writers to have established their copyright in their country of origin, and hence to have fulfilled all the formalities imposed by that country as conditions of the attainment of copyright.[1]

Besides imposing upon the author of a foreign work the formalities of the country of origin, the French law expressly obliges him, as a condition precedent to suing, to perform the ordinary French domestic formalities (1852 Decree, sec. 4).[2]

The foreign author of a work published in France gains the ordinary domestic protection, and is subjected only to the ordinary domestic formalities.

The Belgian Law of 1886 (sec. 38) grants to aliens the *rights* secured by that law, without making any express stipulation as to formalities. Hence it is possible that Belgium does not exact from authors of works published abroad the fulfilment of the formalities of the country of origin, but only requires that its own domestic formalities should be complied with. The latter have been abolished altogether by the law of 1886 as regards works published in the lifetime of the author, but for posthumous works and works published by the

---

[1] It will be seen that it is doubtful whether, in order to gain protection in France, it is necessary for the author of an English book either to register it or to make deposit of copies in Great Britain. Neither registration nor the delivery of the stipulated number of copies of the work is, by English law, a condition of copyright. The former is only a ' condition precedent to suing ' : the latter a separate duty with separate penalties, imposed upon the author by a Copyright Act it is true, but not carrying with it loss of copyright in the event of default.

[2] Deposit of two copies as a rule—of three for certain kinds of works.

State or public bodies a Royal Decree of the 27th March, 1886, issued in accordance with Secs. 4 and 11 of the law, requires registration within six months of publication, under penalty of loss of copyright.

The new copyright code of Luxemburg, issued in 1898, very closely follows the Belgian Law of 1886. Section 39 in the former code, relating to the protection of foreign authors, is almost word for word the same as the corresponding section in the Belgian Law;[1] and, like Belgium, Luxemburg dispenses with all formalities whatever, except for posthumous works and works published by the State or by public bodies, which must be registered within six months under penalty of loss of copyright.

Extraneous Formalities rarely required.—Very few countries impose upon the alien author any special extraneous formalities beyond those of the country of origin and of their own domestic law. The granting of copyright to works published abroad may be regarded, either as an extension of the protection which they already enjoy in their own country, or as a distinct and separate concession of domestic copyright. If the protecting State takes the former view, it is generally content with the performance of the formalities of the country of origin of the work,[2] while if it adopts the latter, it will usually impose merely its own domestic formalities.

As to the works of aliens published in the country itself and not abroad, the States which grant copyright to such works usually treat them in every respect as native works, subjecting them to the ordinary formalities imposed upon such works. It is not clear what justification a State, which protects by its domestic law all works first appearing in its territory, can

---

[1] Except that the latter contains a clause restricting the duration of the foreign author's rights to the period accorded by the country of origin, a limitation which the other omits.

[2] Though sometimes it imposes its own as well, *e.g.* France.

have for imposing special conditions upon their authors when the latter are aliens. The theory upon which the grant of copyright is based is that the fact of publication within the State places the work of the alien on a level with that of a subject, in respect of title to protection ; and it would seem that it should equally do this in respect of formalities to be performed. This view is generally accepted ; very few States which protect all works first appearing in the territory at the same time make special regulations for the case of alien authors. As we have seen, however, the United States, by Sec. 4 of the Chace Act 1891, exacts from alien authors of works 'copyrighted' according to that Act one dollar as a registration fee, while for citizens and residents the charge is only fifty cents.

Formalities relating to Procedure in Court.

In respect of procedure there is not the same objection to the imposition of special formalities upon the authors of protected foreign works as in respect of the substantive right.

The author of a work admitted to copyright by a country other than that in which it first appeared may reasonably expect the recognition of his abstract claim to protection to carry with it the recognition of its practical validity, upon the fulfilment of those formalities which the protecting country imposes upon its own works—it being of course required of him that he should furnish those dues, in the way of deposit of copies, which, in the public interest, that country has felt itself entitled to levy upon authors of native work. At all events, he may at least expect to be freed from all further formalities except such as are imposed by the country of origin in respect of its domestic protection and which therefore

may be exacted without reproach by any foreign State granting an extension of that protection.

In matters of Procedure special Formalities may be useful.—As
regards the substantive right, then, there is nothing in the
peculiar position of the author of a foreign work that can
warrant the imposition of any special formality by a State
which grants the work protection. But when the author
presents himself in Court, asking for remedy in respect of an
infringement of that substantive right, his case assumes a
different aspect. In the first place, the fact that his work
first saw the light abroad—joined perhaps to the fact that,
under the law of the protecting State, the formalities of the
country of origin alone were requisite and these alone have
been fulfilled—may render the ordinary methods of proof and
disproof, *e.g.* calling of witnesses and production of extracts
from the Register, either inapplicable or else very difficult
to put into operation. In such circumstances, partly in order
that the defendant may not be embarrassed by having to go
to foreign countries to investigate the title set up by the
plaintiff, and partly for the advantage of the plaintiff himself,
it is not unusual for countries to lay down a special mode of
proof for the establishment of the plaintiff's right.

Thus it is provided by the English International Copyright
Act of 1886 (sec. 7) that an extract from a register or certificate or other document stating the evidence or proprietorship
of the copyright, if authenticated by the official seal of a
minister of state of the foreign country or by the official seal
or signature of a British diplomatic or consular officer acting
in such country, shall be admissible as evidence of the facts
contained therein, and all courts shall admit it as evidence
without proof. The Berne Convention (Art. 11) contains a
provision that the appearance of the name of any person on the
work as author shall give him a *prima facie* title to copyright

therein, and that in cases where the Courts are in doubt as to the fulfilment of the formalities of the country of origin they shall have power to call for the production of a certificate from a competent authority showing that those formalities have been fulfilled.

Strictly speaking, such provisions as these can hardly be said to impose special formalities; it is more accurate to look upon them as permitting than as requiring a certain mode of proof. Apart from them, it has been suggested that a country would be justified in subjecting foreign authors to special court fees on a higher scale. The greater work which is thrown on the Court when the proofs involve two languages, and when in other respects the proceedings are of a more elaborate character, may perhaps provide a good reason for demanding an increase of fees.

Deposit of Security for Costs.—Besides such regulations as these, there are others which impose particular formalities upon the alien author, on the ground that his belonging to another nation renders it more difficult to fix him with whatever responsibilities in the way of costs, etc., he may incur in the prosecution of his suit. He can withdraw himself from the jurisdiction of the Court more easily than a native; hence it is often deemed advisable to require him before the suit commences to make special provision for the satisfaction of its incidents. Formalities imposed with this object are, however, something more than mere matters of form, for they generally involve the deposit on the part of the foreign plaintiff of some substantial sum as security: but, like the former class, they do not affect the substantial existence of the right and only regulate the procedure by which it may be made good in practice.

Deposit of security for costs is less often exacted from aliens in England than on the Continent, where it passes

under the Roman law term *cautio judicatum solvi.* Thus, in
France, Sec. 16 of the Civil Code makes it obligatory, with
certain exceptions, wherever an alien is the plaintiff and a
Frenchman the defendant.[1]   The Decree of 1852 seems only
to enable the alien to claim the benefit of a remedy which till
then had been limited to the authors of works published in
France, without freeing him upon appearance in Court from
conditions attaching to all alien plaintiffs merely in virtue of
their alien status.   It will be noted that the French rule as to
cautio only applies where the defendant is a Frenchman and
hence does not affect the case where one alien sues another in
the French Courts.[2]

In this respect the Belgian law is the same as that of France ;
Germany however exacts the *cautio* from the foreign plaintiff
even where the defendant is an alien.   In the English Courts
a plaintiff may be required to find security if he is beyond
the jurisdiction of the Court or if his presence within it is
merely temporary, and it would seem that at the discretion
of the Court security may be exacted from the plaintiff where
the defendant is likewise resident abroad.

Though, however, *cautio judicatum solvi* finds a place in
the law of nearly every European country, there are signs in
the Union countries of a tendency to do away with it.   In
Italy it has already been abolished.   Germany will dispense
with it in respect of subjects of countries granting a like dis-
pensation in respect of German subjects.   The matter has long
engaged the attention of Societies formed to promote the
interests of literature and science ; thus as early as 1877 the
Institute of International Law passed a resolution to the effect
that it should be abolished.[3]   Since then many treaties have

---

[1] Darras, *Du Droit des Auteurs et des Artistes*, p. 299.
[2] Von Bar : *Principles and Practice of Private International Law*, p. 876.
[3] *Ibid.*, pp. 878, 879.

provided for its remission as between contracting States. The most important of these is the Convention which was signed at the Hague on the 14th Nov. 1891, and which has been ratified by Austria-Hungary, Belgium, Denmark, France, Germany, Holland, Italy, Luxemburg, Norway and Sweden, Portugal, Roumania, Russia, Spain, and Switzerland, many of them members of the International Copyright Union. This treaty provides (Art. 11) that no security or deposit shall be imposed on the subjects of any of the contracting States, having their domicil in one of these States, who may be plaintiffs or defendants before the Courts of any other of these States ; while (Art. 12) the parties agree to execute within their respective territories the judgments of each other's Courts against persons thus exempt from security or deposit.

SECTION IV.

CONFLICT OF JURISDICTIONS AND OF LAWS.

The bases of Private International Law—A Court cannot always justly apply its own ordinary rules—The Appropriate Court and the Appropriate Law—Copyright from the standpoint of Private International Law—A country can only place duties upon its own public—The country where the infringement is committed should have jurisdiction—The Appropriate Law that of country where infringement committed—The Appropriate Law for Contracts—Inheritance—Law of the Country of Origin.

The Bases of Private International Law.

It now becomes necessary to consider the subject of 'The Application of Alien Laws,' which is often designated 'Private International Law' or the 'Conflict of Laws.' A subject of one State may commit on the territory of another an act to the injury of a fellow subject ; or the matter may be more involved,—for example, a subject of one State may make with a subject of another in the territory of a third a contract which is to be performed in that of any of the three, or even in that of a fourth. In such cases there is an obvious conflict as to which State should exercise jurisdiction over the matter. In the former example, the native State may, in virtue of the nationality of the parties to the suit, claim to assume jurisdiction, and the same claim may be made by the other State on the ground that offences committed within its territory are properly cognisable by itself ; while, in the latter example, there are no less than four countries which each have some reasonable claim to the exercise of jurisdiction. There is nothing in International Law proper to prevent the case being decided by each country for itself; but obvious inconvenience and injustice would result from the enforcement of its own claims by any State, without regard to the probable action of the other or others.

Private International Law.—With a view of reconciling the various claims to jurisdiction which arise where the parties to a suit are connected by different ties with more States than one, a system of 'Private International Law'[1] has been elaborated, which affects to determine precisely the appropriate Court for each case of conflict. Upon the main principle of this system the majority of modern civilised States are agreed: so that where, for example, the rule of private international law points out the country where an offence has been committed as having the primary right to jurisdiction, other States, basing their claims on different grounds, will remain passive, at any rate until the courts of that country have definitely refused to undertake the decision of the matter.

A Court cannot always justly apply its own ordinary Rules. —It will not however necessarily be just for the Court which undertakes jurisdiction to apply the rules of its own domestic code to the decision of the case. If, for example, the State to which the defendant owes allegiance assumes the right of determining the question at issue, and if its ordinary law regards as an infringement of copyright an act of his, which was not an infringement according to the law in force at the place where it was committed, then it may fairly be argued that the defendant ought to be acquitted, on the ground that in copyright the law of a country effects an adjustment of

---

[1] 'Private International Law' comprises a system of rules for the selection from among several competing codes of the one appropriate to govern any given matter. It differs from 'International Law' proper (*public international law*) in that it deals with the relations of States and private individuals, not with that of States *inter se*.

claims, holding good only for the conditions obtaining among its own people, and ceasing to be equitable when applied to the conditions obtaining in another State; and that, therefore, as the act complained of does not constitute an offence at the place of commission, it ought not to be regarded as an offence by any tribunal. This is an extreme case, the conflict here being as to the whole infringing character of the act complained of; but, since the laws of two countries exactly coincide in very few matters, there will nearly always be some difference in result, more or less substantial, between the application by a country of its own law and the application by it of the law of another State.

It is clear, then, that the mere fact that a State is properly entitled to exercise jurisdiction over a case does not justify the conclusion that in so doing it will be acting most fairly to all parties by applying the rules it has laid down for the regulation of the normal conduct of its subjects, or of persons territorially connected with it. It is found advisable on many matters to apply the rules embodied in a particular foreign code of laws. In such case, these become in an auxiliary fashion part of the law of the State which applies them.

There are certain general principles which determine with regard to each case of conflict what country is to have jurisdiction, and what law is to be applied. The majority of civilised States adopt these principles in regulating the authority of their courts and the law they put in force, and thereby avoid a considerable amount of confusion and contradiction which would otherwise be inevitable.

The Appropriate Court and the Appropriate Law.

The Appropriate Court.—By the 'Appropriate Court' is meant that country which Private International Law selects from among all countries which might claim jurisdiction as the one entitled to take cognisance of a particular case.

The Appropriate Law.—By the 'Appropriate Law' is meant that code which Private International Law selects from among the whole number of domestic codes as the one suitable to govern a given legal relation.

Copyright from the standpoint of Private International Law.—Private International Law is a highly academic science, its principles being usually first formulated by theorists and then adopted into the practice of States. In copyright there is little actual practice to crystallise the principles in force, and these latter are therefore at present mainly of a theoretical character.

Before any specific rules can be laid down to determine the choice of jurisdictions and laws in matters of copyright, it is necessary to enter into some general investigation of the nature of the right, viewed from the standpoint of Private International Law. When a country grants to an author copyright in his work it grants him not so much the liberty to multiply copies—which in the normal course of things he would enjoy irrespective of special legislation—but the right to exclude others from so doing. In other words the essence of copyright is the legal power to prevent copying on the part of the general public. Hence the recognition of copyright by law in reality consists of a prohibition against copying, addressed to the general public.[1]

[1] In the language of jurisprudence this is expressed by designating copyright a 'right *in rem*'—'a right availing against the world at large.'

Q

A Country can only place Duties upon its own Public.—Now the prohibition addressed to the general public by any country can only be directed to its own public, because it has not the power of interfering in the relation between its own authors and the inhabitants of foreign countries. The sum total of the prohibition addressed by a State to its public in reference to copyright rightly constitutes the sum of their duties in respect of it. One qualification must be added to these statements. When an inhabitant of one country commits an act taking effect upon the territory of another, he falls so far as that act is concerned under the law of that other : the law of a State extends to the whole of its territory and embraces in its purview all the acts done within that territory. Hence 'the public,' as used above, must be taken to exclude residents of the country in respect of acts committed abroad, and to include residents of a foreign country in respect of acts committed on the territory of the State in question. The fact is that the State aims its prohibition at acts rather than at persons, and that its prohibition extends to all such acts as it has power to prevent, viz. to all which are committed upon its territory.[1]

The Country where an Infringement is committed should have Jurisdiction.—Each State fixes for its own territory the nature and extent of the duties to be imposed on the public. The conditions of life and society vary with different States, and it is reasonable to accept from each country within its own territory its own estimate of the rights and duties which its public is to have. Hence, in matters of copyright, it is the country where the offence complained of is committed that has

---

[1] Of course no State can actually exercise jurisdiction over a person resident abroad until that person enters its own territory ; thus, in the English case of *Morocco Bound v. Harris* (1895), 1 Ch. 534, an English court refused to grant an injunction against the performance of a copyright play in Germany, on the ground that an English injunction could not operate in that country. This however does not affect the question as to what acts are abstractedly to be considered unlawful.

the primary right to jurisdiction.[1] Of course it can exercise no effective jurisdiction if the offender with all his property is abroad and remains there ; but so soon as he enters the territory action can be taken against him, or, if action has already been taken, judgment can be executed.

Besides the *forum delicti comissi* (the country in which the offence was committed), the *forum ligiantiae* (the country of allegiance of the defendant) or *forum domicilii* (the country of domicil of the defendant) may also take jurisdiction, *i.e.* a State may reasonably assume authority over acts of its subjects or persons domiciled within it committed abroad ; but, as will be seen later, it will generally put into force the *lex loci delicti comissi*, refusing to punish acts which are innocent according to the law of the country where they are committed. It would seem to accord better with principle to leave the case altogether to the courts of the country where the offence is committed.

The Appropriate Law that of country where infringement committed.—The appropriate law to be put in force is, for the ordinary case of acts committed in the territory of one State by subjects of another, determined in the same way as the appropriate *forum*, *i.e.* that of the country where the offence has taken place is applied. Under the Berne

---

[1] If copyright be regarded from the standpoint of Private International Law as in essence a right of property, its position at first sight appears somewhat different. In respect of real property, the country where the land, etc., is situated determines the principles to be applied ; and, in respect of personal property, some States look to the country of situation and others to the country where the owner is domiciled. In neither case does the country where the offence is committed have authority as such. Copyright is however an exceptional species of property. The copyright in a given work has no definite location or country of situation (*locus rei sitae*). If indeed it can be said to have any situation at all, it must be regarded as situated in every State to the extent, and only to the extent, to which it is recognised by the domestic law. Hence there are a multitude of different *loci rei sitae*, and for each case it becomes necessary to determine the one which has priority of claim. This would naturally be the country where the infringement had taken place. Thus, even regarding copyright as a right of property, the conclusion is the same, though reached by a roundabout route.

Convention the appropriate law is the *lex fori*[1]—the law of the country from which protection is sought—but as the appropriate *forum* must be determined according to the rules just laid down, the administered *lex fori* is practically equivalent to the law of the country in which the infringement has been committed.

The Appropriate Law for Contracts.—It is obvious, however, that in respect of contracts and succession[2] there is no such law. There is no reason why the ordinary rules of Private International Law upon these matters should not be applied. A contract is a contract whatever its subject-matter, and the principles upon which the law regulating it is determined, based as they are upon the probable expectation of the parties, do not in general vary with its subject-matter. The same can hardly be said of succession, in respect of which legal theory in many countries recognises a sharp distinction between movable (or personal) property and land : but even here copyright ranks constructively as a movable, and follows the general rules laid down for movable property.

For contracts, the decisive law is ' the law of the citizenship or the domicil, as the case may be, or the law of the place where the bargain which regulates the matter was concluded or is to be fulfilled.'[3] This, however, is not the place to enter into a detailed exposition of the rules of Private International Law upon the subject of contracts, which is not directly connected with copyright. It is sufficient to say that different countries adopt different criteria for this subject : thus the system of France and Italy takes as its foundation the law of the place in which the contract is concluded, and

---

[1] See *Études sur la revision de la Convention de Berne*, published at Berne (1896) by the International Office, p. 51.

[2] Copyright, like nearly every right, may, of course, be the subject of assignment and may pass by inheritance or bequest.

[3] Von Bar, *Principles and Practice of Private International Law*, p. 742.

that of Germany adopts the law of the place of performance ; while many authorities urge that, as a general principle, the personal law of the parties (the law of the country of allegiance, or, preferably, that of the country of domicil) ought to hold, and Great Britain decides the matter according to the circumstance of each particular case.[1] It is of course open to the parties to enter into a special agreement that the legal effect of the contract shall be regulated according to the law of a particular country ; the general rules only hold in the absence of such agreement. The principle *locus regit actum*—'the place governs the act'—applies to the form of contract, so that the satisfaction of the formal requirements of the country where it is made is sufficient to give an agreement validity.[2]

Inheritance.—Succession to real property generally follows the law of the country of location (*lex rei sitae*), but the difficulty of fixing the situation of such an intangible subject as copyright has already been indicated. Copyright, however, is regarded as personal property by the law of Great Britain, and a similar view is taken in most other countries. Hence for it the ordinary principles enable us to neglect the *lex rei sitae* altogether and to apply directly the personal law of the deceased.

Law of the Country of Origin.—The enforcement by many States of the law of the country of origin with reference to formalities and duration has already been dealt with. It is obviously a case of the 'application of alien laws.'

---

[1] Von Bar, *Principles and Practice of Private International Law*, pp. 539, 552.

[2] But the agreement, though valid, will be unenforceable unless *evidenced* in the manner required by the English Law.—*Leroux v. Brown* (1852), 12 C.B. 801.

PART III.

THE BERNE CONVENTION:
Acceded to by Great Britain under the International Copyright Act, 1886.
(With a Chapter on the Montevideo Convention.)

CHAPTER I.

THE INTERNATIONAL COPYRIGHT UNION.

CHAPTER II.

GENERAL PRINCIPLES OF THE BERNE CONVENTION.

CHAPTER III.

THE PROTECTION GIVEN BY THE BERNE CONVENTION.

CHAPTER IV.

WORKS PROTECTED BY THE BERNE CONVENTION.

CHAPTER V.

INFRINGEMENTS, REMEDIES, AND PROCEDURE UNDER THE BERNE CONVENTION.

CHAPTER VI.

THE REVISION OF THE BERNE CONVENTION.

CHAPTER VII.

THE MONTEVIDEO CONVENTION, 1889, AND OTHER AMERICAN CONVENTIONS.

CHAPTER I.

THE INTERNATIONAL COPYRIGHT UNION.

SECTION I.

HISTORY OF THE BERNE CONVENTION.

The character of the Berne Convention—History of the formation of the International Union—The International Literary and Artistic Association—International Copyright Union mooted—First International Conference at Berne, 1884—Conferences of 1885 and 1886—The Progress of the Convention—New adherents and revisions—Effect of the Convention on domestic legislation—The Montevideo Convention, 1889—Revisions : The Conference of Paris, 1896—The Additional Act and the Interpretative Declaration—Signature and Ratification of these agreements—Subsequent adherents to the Convention—The coming Conference at Berlin.

The character of the Berne Convention.—The international copyright relations of most of the principal States of the world are at the present day governed almost entirely by the multilateral treaty which has already been alluded to as the Berne Convention. It is true that in various points the domestic laws of certain States among its signatories surpass it in the liberality of the protection accorded to authors and works : but its own provisions are so broad that the general scope of its protection is, as between its parties, capable of little further extension. It establishes only a minimum of international protection as between its parties, but the minimum is large and on several points approaches a maximum.

Moreover, while purely domestic extensions of the minimum are immediately revocable at the will of the country which is their author, the minimum itself, established as it is by international agreement, cannot be withheld without a grave breach of international obligation.[1] The provisions of a treaty to which there are only two parties are internationally binding as between the parties: and it is obvious that, other things being equal, neglect to fulfil the requirements of a multilateral agreement like the Berne Convention is a much more serious matter than the breach of the provisions of a bilateral treaty.

Again, domestic law has full scope—except as affected by treaties external to the Convention—in regulating the relations of Union countries with non-Union countries, as well as those between non-Unionist countries *inter se*: but, as nearly every country which possesses intellectual works worth protecting is a member of the Union, this free exercise of domestic law can hardly be held to constitute a serious derogation from the international importance of the Convention.[2] If in every respect the Convention provided a maximum of international protection, exceeded in no point by domestic law or by treaty stipulations, and if every State of the civilised world had subscribed it, it would constitute for international copyright such a universal code as has been contemplated in a preceding part of this work. As it is, the Convention, though it does not reach complete universality, approaches sufficiently near thereto to justify its being treated as a substantive and independent code of international copyright.

While, then, in one aspect the Berne Convention is nothing more than a multilateral treaty, in another it is a code of

---

[1] Unless, of course, the State desiring to withhold protection withdraws from the Union. For this however, under Article 20, a year's previous notice is necessary.

[2] The United States, Austria, and Russia are the only great powers which are not members of the Union.

international copyright constituting the common law for the territory of the 'International Union for the protection of the rights of authors over their literary and artistic works,' which covers the major part of the civilised world. The advantages of belonging to such a Union may, to some extent, be gathered from what has already been said on the subject of reciprocity. But, in so far as the Berne Convention is more than a mere treaty, the subject is not exhausted there. It is clear that enlightened motives and honest intentions combined with motives of policy to bring about the formation of the Union : and that they still combine to induce the accession of countries now outside it.

As was pointed out by the late M. Numa Droz, in a Presidential address delivered to the second Conference of Berne, 1885, after the text of the Convention had been agreed on : 'The creation of the Union, which establishes a tie between all its members and will serve to stimulate them, is . . . the most important step in the progress achieved : it is a striking affirmation of the universal conscience in favour of copyright.'[1] Hence the matter cannot be treated simply as a matter of policy. It must be recognised that the Union has in view not only the present carrying out of a mere bargain between its members, but also the advancement of the best interests of copyright throughout the world.

HISTORY OF THE FORMATION OF THE INTERNATIONAL UNION.

The influences which have induced the principal nations of the world to widen their sphere of action beyond the immediate protection of domestic copyright are many and

---

[1] *Actes de la Conférence réunie à Berne*, 1885, p. 65.

varied.   The treaties and the domestic law of the more
advanced countries have set an example of progress to
other States, and have played an important part in the
creation of that body of general opinion which made the
Convention possible.   Regarding the Convention as a definite
and specific expression of such general opinion, however,
it must be admitted that most of the credit attaching to
its construction belongs to an international society of authors
and artists, having its headquarters at Paris.

The International Literary and Artistic Association.[1]—This
Society, already referred to under the name of the International Literary and Artistic Association,[2] was founded in
1878 under the presidency of Victor Hugo.   Though so long
ago as 1858 a Literary Congress held at Brussels declared that
uniform legislation on the subject of copyright throughout the
countries of the world was a thing to be desired, and though
that opinion has been echoed by Congresses held at Antwerp
in 1861 and 1877,[3] yet to the International Literary and
Artistic Association was immediately due that persistent
advocacy of the claims of literary property to universal recognition which brought international opinion to the point of
action.

The Association was the outcome of the first International
Congress organised by the French Société des Gens de
Lettres ; and, from that date till this, it has held year

[1] The present Secretary of this society is M. Jules Lermina, and the offices of
the society are at 22, Rue de Châteaudun, Paris.

[2] The Association is composed of a permanent honorary committee, an
executive committee, ordinary members, and affiliated societies; the administration of affairs being in the hands of the executive committee. The members of
the Association are of various nationalities. At the time of its formation, this
society directed its efforts solely to the protection of literary property, and then
bore the name 'International Literary Association,' but at the Congress of
Brussels in 1884, having extended its sphere of action to artistic property, it
altered its name to that set out in the text.

[3] See *Le Droit d'Auteur*, 1888, p. 3.

by year a Congress in some one of the great cities or convenient centres of Europe.[1]   Its rules declare that 'it exists for the defence and propagation of the principles of international literary and artistic property, and is especially concerned with the execution of the resolutions of the international literary congresses.   It protects the interests of authors and artists in every country, and establishes between them ties of confraternity.'[2]

International Copyright Union mooted.—In 1882, at the Congress at Rome, the Association definitely took up the project of an International Copyright Union.   At that Congress a resolution was passed, instructing the Bureau of the Association to invite the co-operation of the press, and to take steps for the institution of an international conference, composed of representatives of interested bodies, for the purpose of concerting a scheme for the creation of an International Union.

Berne having been chosen as the seat of this Conference, the Swiss Government was approached, and gave its countenance to the project, with the speedy result that in 1883 the Conference took place.   The outcome of its labours was a draft convention for the contemplated Union,[3] which was placed in the hands of the Swiss Government, and through this medium was brought before the notice of the civilised States of the world.   The Swiss Government then invited the

---

[1] London, Lisbon, Vienna, Rome, Amsterdam, Brussels, Antwerp, Geneva, Madrid, Venice, Paris, London, Neuchatel, Milan, Barcelona, Antwerp, Dresden, Berne, Monaco, Turin, Heidelberg, Paris, Vevey, Naples, Weimar, and Marseilles (1904) have, in the order named, been the seats of the Congresses of the Society.

[2] See *Association Littéraire et Artistique Internationale.   Son Histoire—Ses Travaux*, 1878—1889, p. vii.

[3] 'Pour constituer une Union générale pour la protection des droits des auteurs sur les œuvres littéraires et manuscrites.' See *Association Littéraire et Artistique Internationale.   Son Histoire—Ses Travaux*, p. 182, where the whole text of this draft is set forth.

various Governments to take part in a diplomatic conference upon the matter.

First International Conference at Berne, 1884.—As a result of this action an International Conference was held at Berne in 1884, the following twelve States being represented : Austria-Hungary, Belgium, Costa Rica,[1] France, Germany, Great Britain, Haïti, Holland, Norway and Sweden, Paraguay, Salvador, and Switzerland. Italy, Spain, Portugal, Brazil, and the Argentine Republic had intended to send delegates, but were prevented by circumstances from taking part. The Swiss Government submitted to the Conference a draft convention essentially similar to the one drawn up in 1883, though somewhat more elaborate in detail.

The Conference met on September 8th, 1884, and at its second sitting proceeded to discuss a comprehensive paper of fourteen questions, submitted by the representatives of Germany.[2] It at once became evident that considerable difference existed between the views of the various States, especially with respect to the treatment to be accorded to translating right. France on the one hand took an extremely liberal view of the author's claims to an exclusive right of translating his own work : Norway and Sweden on the other were prevented by the state of their domestic law from granting a greater protection than was imperatively demanded by justice.[3]

---

[1] This State was represented only at the last sitting of the Conference.

[2] It is noteworthy that one of the German delegates—M. Reichardt—submitted a resolution to the effect that instead of drawing up a Convention the Conference should elaborate a universal law. It was soon seen however that this was impracticable.

[3] Sec. 5 of the Norwegian law of 1876 ran as follows : 'A person who translates a literary work from one language into another enjoys the rights of an author over his translation provided that he has not infringed the provisions of the present law.' The provisions in question were contained in Sec. 15, which ran : 'The translation of a literary work, without the consent of the author, from the original language into a dialect of this language, and *vice versa*, is considered as a reproduction to which the prohibition against

Germany took up an intermediate position and strove to arrive at a compromise.

The majority of the disputed points were eventually referred to a Committee which had been appointed for the purpose of making a detailed examination of the convention scheme. That Committee suggested many modifications in the draft issued by the Swiss Government. These were then submitted to the Conference, where, despite the serious difference of opinion on the question of translating-right and on many points of detail, a general spirit of compromise led to the completion of a document which, with a few alterations, ultimately became the International Agreement known to us as the Berne Convention of 1886.

Conferences of 1885 and 1886.—The form of the Berne Convention was settled at a second Conference, which commenced its session on the 7th September 1885, and it only remained for a third Conference, meeting on the 6th September 1886,

---

infringement applies. For this purpose, Norwegian, Swedish, and Danish are considered as dialects of one and the same language. Translation is also treated as infringement: (*a*) when the work translated was unpublished, (*b*) when a work first published in a dead language is translated and published in a living language, (*c*) when a work published simultaneously in several languages is translated and published in one of those languages.'

The Norwegian law of 1893, after making a somewhat similar prohibition, adds: 'In every other case no translation may be published without the consent of the owner of the copyright during ten years from the end of the year of the first publication of the original work.' This brought the Norwegian law into line with the Berne Convention, but did not satisfy the demands made later on by the amending Act of Paris. In the law of Sweden the successive stages in the growth of the period of translating right are exceedingly instructive. As the law stood in 1877, no translating right whatever was recognised. In 1883, however, a five years' right was given, subject to a *délai d'usage* of two years. Later this was extended to eight years, with the same *délai d'usage*, by the important Act of 1897. And now by a Law of the 29th April, 1904, it is provided that 'Within ten years from the first publication of the work, it is forbidden to publish, through the medium of printing, translations thereof in other languages, without the consent of the author.' This enactment has enabled Sweden to accept the Berne Convention, though it is not yet able to adopt the amendments of the Additional Act of Paris.

to proceed with the formal business of signature.[1] The following States signed the agreement : Belgium, France, Germany, Great Britain, Haïti, Italy, Liberia, Spain, Switzerland, and Tunis. Before the Convention could come into force it was still necessary for it to be ratified. Art. 21 provided that ratification should take place within a year, and it was duly carried out by all the above countries with the exception of Liberia.

The Progress of the Convention.

The Berne Convention, established in 1886, represented a compromise between the conflicting views of its various signatories. It was put forward as embodying a 'minimum' of international protection, individual members of the Union being of course left free to grant to foreign authors by their domestic legislation rights more extended than those secured by the Convention. In the words of Numa Droz, in his closing speech to the International Conference of 1885, 'Doubtless, as is the case with every agreement between sovereign States, our work presents the character of a compromise. It was not in our power, neither could it form part of our intention, to eliminate the various peculiarities which exist in the law of the contracting countries, peculiarities which are connected with diversities of doctrine, of usage, and of procedure, in relation with the institutions of

---

[1] At the second Conference neither Austria-Hungary nor Salvador was represented : but the Argentine Republic, Spain, the United States, Honduras, Italy, and Tunis sent delegates for the first time. Holland, Honduras, and Norway and Sweden took no part in the third Conference ; but Liberia was represented, and Japan sent a delegate to watch and report upon the proceedings. The third Conference was necessary in order to leave time for the delegates to obtain from their respective States the powers necessary to enable them to sign the Convention.

each country and with its juridical culture. On no point, then, have we prejudiced the essential principles upon which the juristic conception of copyright rests ; hence no country is called upon to choose in this respect between a sacrifice painful from the point of view of principle and complete abstention. On the contrary, all can enter the Union and still preserve in their laws and in their legal theories that which is dear to them, provided that, on the other hand, they consent to guarantee an efficient protection to authors in the matters regulated by the Convention. We did not wish to become divided upon words, when it was possible for us to have the substantial thing.'[1]

New adherents and revisions.—The future extension of the sphere of the Convention, both as to territory and as to protection accorded, was regarded as desirable : for Art. 18 provides for the admission to the Union of countries which did not take part in its foundation, if their domestic law protects the rights secured by the Convention, while, under Art. 17, this Act may be submitted to revisions 'made with the view of introducing into it amendments calculated to perfect the system of the Union.'[2]

The Closing Protocol to the Convention (§ 6) provided that the next conference of the Union should take place at Paris, within a period of from four to six years from the coming into force of the Convention. As a matter of fact, the actual interval exceeded the extreme limit thus fixed, and it was not until 1896 that the Conference of Paris was held.[3]

---

[1] See *Actes de la Conférence de Berne*, 1885, p. 65.

[2] See Chapter vi. on ' The Revision of the Berne Convention.'

[3] There are strong practical reasons in favour of allowing long intervals to elapse between successive conferences of the Union. The Conference of Paris has profited by an experience that the Conference of Berne lacked, providing for an interval of from six to ten years before the next conference to be held at Berlin.

That Conference, which made several important revisions in the text of the Convention, forms a landmark in the history of the Union. During the interval from 1886 to 1896, the personal strength of the Union—and consequently the territory throughout which the Convention obtained— was increased by the accession of Luxemburg (1888), Monaco (1889), Montenegro (1893), and Norway (1896).[1] On the other hand, it is noteworthy that no withdrawals were made between 1886 and the Conference of Paris in 1896.

Effect of the Convention on domestic legislation.—For some little time after the Convention came into force, it seems that its importance was considerably underrated. Outside the Union it was regarded as little more than an ordinary copyright treaty, and even within the Union authors often remained in ignorance of their new rights under it. Soon, however, the efforts of the International Literary and Artistic Association brought it into prominence, and, long before the Conference of Paris, it came to be regarded throughout the world as a sound practical code of international copyright law.[2]

It had its effect upon domestic legislation, as the various copyright enactments issued between the years 1886 and 1896 show. The Law issued by Tunis in 1889 bears on its face the evidence of having been inspired by the Convention ; and it may be conjectured that the contemplated adhesion of Belgium to the Union in course of formation in 1886 was largely responsible for the liberality of its Act of that date. The English Act of 1886 is primarily designed to enable Great Britain to discharge its international duties under the Convention ; but it also confirms previous international Acts

---

[1] Montenegro however has since retired from the International Union (on the 1st April, 1900) 'for motives of economy.'—See *Le Droit d'Auteur*, 1899, p. 61.

[2] See *Le Droit d'Auteur*, 1898, p. 3.

R

which adopt reciprocity as a general principle. A reformation of the Norwegian law of copyright was undertaken in 1893 with the express object of bringing that law into harmony with the Convention. In the interval before the Act of Paris Denmark and Sweden also contemplated the reform of their domestic law as a preliminary to joining the Union; but in neither case was this carried out till quite recently. On the 28th May, 1897, Sweden issued a whole series of copyright enactments; but even then it was unable to join the Union, owing to the shortness of its term of translating right. On 29th April, 1904, however, a new Law was passed, which extended the period of translating right to equal that prescribed in the 1886 Convention. Shortly after this (on the 8th July, 1904), Sweden accepted the Berne Convention of 1886, together with the Interpretative Declaration. The accession, which did not include the Additional Act of Paris, took effect as from the 1st August, 1904. Denmark, having first reformed its law of copyright by an Act of the 19th September, 1902, entered the Union on the 13th June, 1903, accepting all three instruments; its adhesion took effect as from the 1st July, 1903.

The Montevideo Convention, 1889.—The Berne Convention of 1886 was followed by the Montevideo Convention in 1889. This latter convention on international copyright was formed in the first instance between four South American States, and afterwards subscribed to by France, Spain, and Italy. In the main it is modelled on the Convention of Berne, although it exhibits several important points of difference. A full account of it and its relation to its prototype is given in Chapter VII.

Revisions.—The Conference of Paris, 1896.—From the time of the coming into force of the Berne Convention, literary and artistic societies and congresses, led by the International

Literary and Artistic Association, have given careful and searching consideration to the whole of its provisions and have suggested many subjects for reform. Their resolutions served to indicate to the Conference of Paris the points on which the Berne Convention fell short of satisfying the claims of authors and artists. In this way the work of revision was greatly facilitated. The International Office of the Union also proved of invaluable service, and, through the medium of its monthly magazine, *Le Droit d'Auteur*, which be it said looks at most questions from the author's point of view, stimulated the development of thought and lent publicity to copyright matters.

The Paris Conference of the Union was organised by the French Government with the able assistance of the International Bureau. It has already been explained that circumstances prevented the holding of this Conference within the limit of six years, originally fixed for it by the Berne Convention ; indeed it was not until August, 1895, that the French Government issued two preliminary circulars, one addressed to the governments of the various countries of the Union and the other to those of certain non-Union countries, each stating that the 15th April, 1896, had been fixed as the date of the Conference of Paris, and inviting the Governments to whom they were addressed to send representatives.

The International Bureau also sent various circulars to the countries of the Union, enclosing the French scheme of amendment. This stated at the outset that in the opinion of the French Government the time had not yet come for an exhaustive revision of the Convention, and that in the provisional work of amendment it would be well to keep in mind the desirability both of preserving the coherence of the Union and of facilitating new accessions. Any radical measures of reform would defeat both these ends. Into the specific propositions of the French scheme it is hardly necessary to enter, since, in face of the actual results of the Paris Conference, the stages by which these results were reached become insignificant.[1]

In response to the invitation of France, all the thirteen countries of the Union, except Haïti,[2] together with fourteen non-Union countries, including Denmark, Portugal, Sweden, and the United States, each sent one or more delegates to the Conference. The French scheme, together with the resolutions of the various congresses, formed the material upon which the Conference had to work.

The Committee of Draftsmanship appointed by the Conference prepared four documents :

> (1) A general report drawn up by M. Renault and presented in the name of the Committee ;
> (2) The draft of an 'Additional Act' introducing substantial amendments into the text of the Convention ;
> (3) The draft of an 'Interpretative Declaration' purporting to make clear the meaning of the original articles of the Convention on certain points that were more or less obscure ; and
> (4) A series of suggested Recommendations (*Vœux*).

The Additional Act and the Interpretative Declaration.—The drafts of the Additional Act and the Interpretative Declaration have now both been adopted by all the countries of the Union, except Great Britain, Norway, and Sweden. Norway and Sweden have accepted the Interpretative Declaration and rejected the Additional Act, while Great Britain has accepted

---

[1] The results achieved by the Conference are set out at length in Chapter VI., on 'The Revision of the Berne Convention.'

[2] Haïti had intended to be represented, but her delegate was prevented from attending the Conference.

the Additional Act and rejected the Interpretative Declaration. These countries are prevented by the state of their domestic law from completely falling into line with the rest of the Union.

The Recommendations were unanimously adopted by all the countries of the Union which were represented at the Conference of Paris.

Signature and Ratification of these Agreements.—A detailed statement of the contents of the various instruments is contained in a subsequent chapter. Here it only remains to note that the Additional Act and the Interpretative Declaration were duly signed on the 4th May, 1896. The *Vœux* were not signed, since, being merely expressions of deliberate opinion, they were not in the nature of a formal agreement.

On the 9th September, 1897, the Additional Act and the Interpretative Declaration were ratified by all the States which had signed them the year before.

Subsequent adherents to the Convention.—Haïti, which had not signed the Additional Act and the Interpretative Declaration with the other countries of the Union, accepted both these instruments on the 17th January, 1898. Japan, which had for some time past shown an interest in International Copyright,[1] upon joining the International Union on the 15th July, 1899, adopted the Convention as amended by the Conference of Paris. On the 1st July, 1903, Denmark became a party to the Convention in its amended form. More recently still, on the 1st August, 1904, Sweden joined the Union; but it has accepted only the Convention of 1886, not incorporating the Additional Act.

---

[1] It will be remembered that this country sent a delegate to the Berne Conference of 1886. Several commercial treaties concluded by it with countries of the Union in 1896 contained an article pledging Japan to enter the Union as soon as possible.

The amendments effected by the Conference of Paris are the only modifications in the Convention itself which have been carried out since its establishment.

The coming Conference at Berlin.—The existing state of affairs, however, is not intended to be final ; another Conference of the Union for purposes of revision is to be held at Berlin within from six to ten years from the coming into force of the Additional Act of Paris.[1]   The matters which have been suggested as subjects for the consideration of this Conference are discussed in Chapter VI.

[1] Probably this will take place in 1906.

SECTION II.

CONSTITUTION AND BASIS OF THE INTERNATIONAL UNION.

Membership and Administration—List of Union Countries—Future Accessions—The United States and Art. 18—Recent Accessions to the Union—The Admission of Colonies—The Coming into Force of the Convention : Denunciations—The Revision of the Convention—The requirement of unanimity—Effect of Art. 17.

MEMBERSHIP AND ADMINISTRATION.

List of Union Countries.—At present the International Union comprises the following fifteen countries :—Belgium, France, Germany, Great Britain, Haïti, Italy, Spain, Switzerland, Tunis, Luxemburg, Monaco, Norway, Japan, Denmark, and Sweden.　Of these, the first nine have been members from the foundation.　At the formation of the Union, the Republic of Liberia signed the Convention, but it has not yet ratified it.[1] Luxemburg, Monaco, Montenegro, Norway, Japan, Denmark, and Sweden were admitted later under Art. 18 of the Convention ; but of these Montenegro has since withdrawn.

Future accessions.—This Article allows countries not members of the Union, but which 'assure in their own territory legal protection to the rights which form the object of this Convention,' to become parties to the Convention, upon making a request in writing to the Swiss Government, which undertakes to communicate the notice to the other members of the

---

[1] It is stated that the representative of Liberia declared that his powers only authorised him to sign the Convention, and did not extend to permit him to pledge his country to bear any share in the expense of administration.— *Actes de la Conférence de Berne*, 1886, p. 44.

Union.   Accession implies complete acceptance of the obligations of the Convention, and, of course, carries the right to participate in all its advantages.[1]   The clause which stipulates that the domestic law must confer the rights which the Convention protects apparently means nothing more than that States which do not protect copyright by their domestic law are not to be allowed to join the Union.   It can hardly mean that the domestic protection is to be of the same character in every respect as the international protection conferred by the Convention; although every State which accepts the Convention must of course make due provision by its domestic law for carrying out its engagements under that agreement.

The United States and Art. 18.—The latter obligation arises from the very fact of acceptance,—not, it would seem, from Art. 18, which apparently relates to *domestic*, not *international*, protection.   The United States, however, when considering whether Sec. 13 of the Chace Act of 1891[2] authorised it to admit the countries of the Union *en bloc* to the benefit of that Act, seems to have been under the impression that, in view of the existence of the type-setting clause in the Act, Art. 18 of

---

[1] Art. 18 runs as follows: ' Countries which have not become parties to the present Convention, if they assure in their own territory legal protection to the rights which form the object of this Convention shall be permitted to accede thereto upon their request.   This accession shall be notified in writing to the Government of the Swiss Confederation, and by the latter to all the others.   It shall imply, as a necessary consequence, adhesion to all the clauses and admission to all the advantages stipulated for in the present Convention.'

[2] The words of this Section are as follows: ' That this Act shall only apply to a citizen or subject of a foreign State or nation, when such foreign State or nation permits to citizens of the United States of America the benefit of copyright on substantially the same basis as its own citizens, or when such foreign State or nation is a party to an international agreement which provides for reciprocity in the granting of copyright, *by the terms of which agreement the United States of America may at its pleasure become a party to such agreement.*   The existence of either of the conditions aforesaid shall be determined by the President of the United States, by proclamation made from time to time, as the purposes of this Act may require.'

the Convention debarred it from adhering thereto 'at its pleasure.' The United States may have been quite right in holding that it could not thus accept the Convention: but if so, this was not because Art. 18 did not give it permission to accede to the Union at will. It was a consequence of the fact that for the United States to take advantage of that permission would be for it to pledge itself to an extension of its domestic protection which it was unable to carry out.[1]

Recent accessions to the Union.—Luxemburg gave in its acceptance under Art. 18 in 1888, while its domestic law was still unsatisfactory. No change in that law followed until 1898; still, in Luxemburg, as treaties take effect without express legislation, no alteration would be necessary to make the Convention part of the domestic law. Monaco signified its adhesion in 1889, immediately after it had issued a new copyright code making provision for reciprocity. Similarly Japan acceded to the Union on the 15th July, 1899, four months after issuing a new domestic copyright code. On the 13th April, 1896, immediately before the Conference of Paris began its sittings, Norway accepted the Berne Convention proper, i.e. the original agreement of 1886. Denmark, having been for several years contemplating entry into the Union, enacted a new copyright code on the 19th Sept., 1902, which paved the way for acceptance of the Convention, the

---

[1] The situation was made clearer by a telegram sent on the 23rd June 1891 by the Swiss Federal Department for Foreign Affairs to its Minister at Washington, in reply to an inquiry whether the United States could adhere to the Convention without modifying its domestic law. That telegram contained the following passage: 'The adhesion of the United States, which is heartily desired, is always possible under the conditions of Art. 18 of the Berne Convention, but it appears to be incompatible with the application of Sec. 4956 [of the American revised statutes] to Unionist works, since Art. 2 of the Convention considers the Union as one single territory for purposes of publication and exacts no other formalities than those of the country of origin of the work. . . .' See *Le Droit d'Auteur*, 1891, p. 94, on this and the whole subject.

Additional Act and the Interpretative Declaration on the 1st July, 1903. Sweden, having extended its period of translating right by a Law of 29th April, 1904, accepted the Convention in its original unrevised form, together with the Interpretative Declaration, on the 1st August, 1904. Montenegro is now no longer a member of the Union, having retired in 1900 'from motives of economy.'

The admission of Colonies.—Art. 19 of the Convention contemplates the probability that countries having colonies and foreign possessions will desire to secure the benefits of the Convention to these as well as to themselves. With this in view, it provides that 'countries acceding to the present Convention shall also have the right to accede thereto at any time for their colonies or foreign possessions. To this end they may either make a general declaration, by which all their colonies or possessions are comprised in the accession, or expressly name those which are included therein, or limit themselves to indicating those which are excluded therefrom.' The Convention thus offers every facility for the incorporation of colonies and foreign possessions into the International Union. Of this full advantage has been taken, for Spain, France, and Great Britain, all of which possess extensive foreign dominions, each acceded at the formation of the Union for all their dependencies[1]; and, more recently, Denmark has brought the Faroë Islands into the Union with her.[2] In view of the convenience attaching to the establishment of uniform international relations throughout the whole of the territory of each State, the rule that a country which has colonies and foreign possessions

[1] Together with its colonies, France brought in Algiers. The acquisition of the Transvaal and of the Orange River Colony by Great Britain *ipso facto* brought them into the Union. This was recognised by the English Government in a letter of 6th May, 1903, addressed to the International Office.

[2] See *Le Droit d'Auteur*, 1903, p. 73. The accession has no effect with regard to Iceland, Greenland, and the Antilles.

may carry them along with itself into the International Union is of considerable value.

The Coming into Force of the Convention. Denunciations.— Art. 20 provided that 'The present Convention shall be put into effect three months after the exchange of the ratifications,[1] and shall remain in force for an indeterminate time, until the expiration of one year from the day on which it may have been denounced. This denunciation shall be addressed to the Government charged to receive accessions.[2] It shall only take effect in respect of the country which shall have made it, the Convention remaining operative for the other countries of the Union.' Thus, as might have been expected, the withdrawal of one of the members is not to involve the dissolution of the whole Union. The Convention has been found to work satisfactorily in practice; up to the present there has been only one denunciation.

Ratifications were exchanged on the 5th September, 1887, and the Convention accordingly came into force on the 5th December of that year.[3] During this interval of three months, Great Britain issued the Orders in Council necessary to make the Convention enforceable in the British Dominions. The result of Art. 14,[4] combined with the Closing Protocol,

---

[1] Art. 21 runs: 'The present Convention shall be ratified, and the ratifications thereof shall be exchanged at Berne, within one year at the latest.'

[2] By the Act of Paris the words 'the Government of the Swiss Confederation' have been substituted for 'the Government charged to receive accessions.'

[3] The Additional Act of Paris, which was ratified on the 9th Sept., 1897, came into force on the 9th December, 1897. In England, however, by the terms of the respective Orders in Council the Berne Convention did not come into force until the 6th September, 1887, and the Additional Act not until the 10th December, 1897.

[4] Art. 14 runs as follows: 'The present Convention, under the reservations and conditions to be determined by a common agreement, applies to all works which, at the time of its coming into force, have not yet fallen into the public domain in their country of origin.' The 'reservations and conditions' in question are set out in § 4 of the Protocol, for which see Sec. 5 of this chapter, on Retroactivity.

§ 4, is to make the Convention applicable to all works which at the time of its coming into force have not yet fallen into the public domain in their country of origin, subject however to any reservations contained in independent treaties between any of the countries of the Union, or in the various systems of domestic law. The question of retroactivity is discussed at length later in this chapter.

THE REVISION OF THE CONVENTION.

Besides making due provision for possible changes in the *personnel* of the International Union the Berne Convention also contains dispositions fixing the mode in which changes in its own text are to be effected.

Article 17 contemplates future revisions made in order to introduce 'amendments calculated to perfect the system of the Union.' It provides that questions of this kind, together with others relating to the development of the Union, shall be considered in conferences to be held successively in the various countries of the Union. As we have already seen, the first of these conferences was held at Paris in 1896, and the next is to be held at Berlin before 1907.

The requirement of unanimity.—Article 17 of the Convention also provides that no amendment shall be valid for the Union in the absence of the unanimous consent of its members.[1] In this connection, it is interesting to consider the position of the Additional Act, which was rejected by Norway and Sweden,

---

[1] The full text of Art. 17 is as follows: 'The present Convention may be submitted to revisions with the object of introducing therein amendments calculated to perfect the system of the Union. Questions of this kind, as well as those which concern the development of the Union from other points of view, shall be considered in Conferences to be held successively in the countries of the Union by delegates of the said countries. It is understood that no alteration in the present Convention shall be binding for the Union in the absence of the unanimous consent of the countries composing it.'

and of the Interpretative Declaration, which was rejected by Great Britain. Under Art. 17, these are not binding on the Union as a whole, each of the additions merely constituting a separate and distinct agreement between the countries which have subscribed to it; yet the Additional Act is now generally incorporated in the Convention text, and the Interpretative Declaration is set out together with the matter in the original Convention to which it relates. These agreements are looked upon as acts of the whole Union, the machinery of the Union is employed on their behalf, and Great Britain, Norway and Sweden, rather than the other members of the Union, are regarded as outside the Union for certain particular purposes.

Effect of the requirement of Article 17.—Hence the practical result of Art. 17 is not, as it would appear, that no amendments have any force in the absence of unanimity amongst the members of the Union, but simply that revisions which are not unanimous are not binding upon those members of the Union which have not consented to them—a thing obvious apart from any special provision—and that the majority in such a case must not force upon the minority the choice of observing their amendments or being excluded from the Union. It does not mean that no alteration in the Convention can have any force unless and until it receives the assent of every country in the Union; though doubtless if a revision is to form part—even an optional part—of the Convention text, and to enjoy the advantages of the machinery of the Union, the States supporting it must be in such a majority that the dissentients can be looked upon as isolated exceptions to a general rule.

Even where this is so, it is conceivable that, if the dissentient States chose to object to the name and organisation of the International Union being identified with the provisions to which they had refused to subscribe, the majority would, under Art. 17, be obliged to give heed to the objection. In order to carry out their project, the majority would then have to form themselves into a separate Union for the points in dispute.[1]

---

[1] Such a case is not likely to arise. Great Britain and Norway were prevented by their domestic law from assenting to provisions which in the main they approved, and did not wish to prevent their adoption by the Union at large. In the case of Great Britain a Bill which, appearing in various forms, has now for some time been before the House of Lords, will, when it becomes law, largely remove the difficulties in the way of the acceptance of the Interpretative Declaration. For many sessions the Bill has been crowded out in the press of business, but as yet it has met with no serious opposition.

SECTION III.

THE BERNE CONVENTION AND CONFLICTING TREATIES.

The rules of the Convention as to treaties between Union countries —Existing and future treaties—Treaties now subsisting between Union countries—The Convention merely a minimum of international protection —No fresh treaties between Union countries since 1886—Treaties between Union and non-Union countries—The Convention is silent as to these— American International arrangements—The effect of treaties upon the Convention.

The Rules of the Convention as to Treaties between Union Countries.

Existing and future Treaties.—It is obvious that, if the Berne Convention is to retain its character as a minimum, it cannot forbid treaties between members of the Union as long as these do not derogate from the protection it establishes. Accordingly, an 'Additional Article' provides that 'The Convention concluded this day does not in any way affect the maintenance of the treaties actually existing between the contracting countries, so far as those treaties confer upon authors or their representatives rights more extended than those accorded by the Union, or embrace other stipulations which are not contrary to this Convention,' and Art. 15 states that 'It is understood that the Governments of the countries of the Union reserve to themselves respectively the right to make separately particular arrangements, between themselves, so far as such arrangements confer upon authors or their representatives more extended rights than those accorded by the Union or embrace other stipulations not contrary to the present Convention.'

The Additional Article states expressly what would otherwise have been a matter of fair inference—that the Union, in framing a Convention which was to be one law for its members, did not mean to supersede all the treaties which had been concluded by and between individuals amongst the latter, but merely to abrogate those which fell short of the Convention in respect of the international protection assured. Agreements of this class would probably have been superseded by the Convention in any case, by the application of the ordinary rule of international law that of two conflicting treaties the latter alone is to rule the points upon which there is contradiction.[1]

The Convention merely a minimum of International Protection. —In addition to expressing a rule with regard to treaties, Art. 15 is also intended to guard against the misconception that the Berne Convention is intended to be the sole law for its parties. We have already seen that the real character of the Convention is that of a code embodying a *minimum* of international protection, and it is this character that the Additional Article and Art. 15 seek to make clear. From the words of the latter Article, ' so long as they contain other stipulations not contrary to the present Convention,' it would appear that members of the Union are prohibited from

---

[1] **Treaties now subsisting between Union countries.** — The following separate treaties relating to copyright are still subsisting between Union countries: Treaties of 1883 between Belgium and Germany, 1880 between Belgium and Spain, 1879 between Denmark and Norway and Sweden, 1883 between France and Germany, 1884 between France and Italy, 1880 between France and Spain, 1884 between Germany and Italy, 1880 between Italy and Spain, and 1884 between Italy and Norway and Sweden; together with Art. 8 of the Customs Convention of 1865 between France and Monaco, an Additional Article to the Commercial Treaty of 1881 between France and Norway and Sweden, and Art. 11 of the Treaty of Amity of 1896 between Japan and Switzerland.

entering into separate arrangements derogating from the minimum protection secured by the Convention. If this had been an ordinary treaty, it would scarcely have contained such a rule : for there seems to be no reason why two or more parties to a treaty signed by a number of States should be forbidden to make what further provision they choose for the regulation of their own affairs. In such a case, provided that the effect of any subsequent agreement was limited to the States making it, it is hard to see what ground the other parties to the original treaty could have for objecting to it. So long as the Convention is regarded simply as a multilateral treaty, it is hard to see why, say, France and Great Britain should not if they choose make a separate arrangement between themselves, to the effect that the authors of each country should not enjoy protection in the other. Germany and the other parties to the Convention could hardly make it a ground of complaint against France that English authors did not receive convention rights from it ; or against England that French authors were in the same way denied protection.

But the Berne Convention is something more than a multilateral treaty. It is an Act by which a number of States have bound themselves together into a ' Union for the protection of the rights of authors over their literary and artistic works.' The members of the Union have not merely made a bargain among themselves ; they have joined together to further the recognition throughout the world of certain principles applicable to the protection of intellectual property. Any particular arrangement derogating from the rights secured by the Convention, though it would not affect the material interests of those States of the Union which are not parties to the arrangement, would serve to retard the work of the Union as a whole. Hence the principle embodied in Art. 15 is not without its force.

No fresh Treaties between Union countries since 1886.—There is every indication that as time goes on increasing protection will be given to foreign authors, and it is unlikely that any two States will in the future desire to make any arrangement derogating from the Convention. Indeed up to the present the members of the Union have been so satisfied with the Convention system that they have not attempted to make any treaties whatever, even of the kind which Article 15 permits. Since 1886 no particular arrangements have been concluded between individual States of the Union.[1]

Treaties between Union and non-Union Countries.

The Convention is silent as to these.—The Convention makes no provision as to treaties by a State belonging to the Union with one which is outside. It cannot well forbid such treaties, though the result of allowing them is to lessen or remove the inducement for the non-Union country to adhere to the Convention. It is obvious that, if by means of separate arrangements a State can secure the international protection which it desires without entering the Union, it is not likely to do this unless the system of the Union is specially adapted to its peculiar requirements.

American International arrangements.—The United States has established international relations with Belgium, Denmark, France, Germany, Great Britain, Italy, Spain, and Switzerland, as well as with several countries which are not members of the Union. In this way, while it secures for its works an international protection which extends over as large an area as that covered by the Convention, it has also been able to

---

[1] Japan concluded several treaties with Union countries before it adhered to the Convention in 1899, but has entered into none since.

mould its treaties to its own views in a way that would be impossible with a rigid international Act like the Convention.

But it is impossible for the Union to compel all nations to submit to its ruling in the matter of international protection. It cannot apply a system of boycotting, with the object of compelling backward countries to come in. All that it can do is to make its system as perfect as possible, so that the advantages of membership may be patent even to those States which are inclined to view with disfavour the general object of the Convention.

The Effect of Treaties upon the Convention.

Treaties not to be encouraged at the expense of the Convention. —As regards their effect upon the Convention, treaties made by Union countries amongst themselves differ from treaties made by Union countries with countries outside the Union. It is obvious that, while agreements of the latter class tend to prevent any extension of the Union, those of the former imperil its very existence. So soon as, to any large extent, Union countries begin to regulate their copyright relations by arrangements separate from the Convention, so soon the Convention is liable to become discredited and to lose value as a universal code of international copyright law. It fails to be the sole criterion of international duty ; and a process thereupon sets in which threatens to disintegrate the Union.

So long, however, as the number of particular arrangements between Union countries is kept within due bounds, it is probable that, if such arrangements are not in disagreement with the Convention, they will do more good than harm. An agreement made by two Union countries, which is more advanced than the Convention, is valuable as an example to others and may lead the way to improvements in the Convention itself.

But Supplementary Treaties may be useful.—The Convention is but a minimum, and may well serve as a nucleus round which States may gather arrangements satisfying their own individual needs, but it ought to be borne in mind that there is always a danger that such arrangements will supersede or encumber the Convention.   Their only proper function is to supplement it.   It has already been pointed out that since the date of the Convention there have been no separate agreements made by the countries of the Union amongst themselves. Several which had been made before the coming into force of the Convention, however, still subsist, and it is desirable that these should be examined and brought into harmony with the Convention.

SECTION IV.

ADMINISTRATION OF THE AFFAIRS OF THE UNION.

Organisation of the International Office—Some Central Office necessary for the Union—Particulars relating to the Office at Berne—Apportionment of expenditure.

ORGANISATION OF THE INTERNATIONAL OFFICE.

The fundamental principle of the Berne Convention that each of the signatory States shall extend to the works of all the others its own domestic protection renders it unnecessary to construct new executive machinery specially for the Union, since in each country that which already exists for the enforcement of its own law serves equally well for the enforcement of the Convention. Still, though it is no part of the business of the Union to see to the carrying out of the Convention, it will be seen that some organisation is necessary to enable it to fulfil its purpose of promoting the development of International Copyright.

Some Central Office necessary for the Union.—Though international agreements in general work without the aid of any central office to see to their observance, it must be remembered that the International Copyright Union, which was formed by the Berne Convention, is more than a mere aggregation of States united only inasmuch as they are pledged to grant each other one and the same measure of protection. It may almost be regarded as a Society—having a *quasi-corporate* existence—with a common interest in all that relates to copyright, and a common desire to contribute to the advancement of international protection by the best means in its power.

Hence it has need to be informed of all movements in regard to copyright that may take place throughout the world, since these both indicate the position of domestic copyright in the various States and, in some cases, suggest the lines of a possible improvement in the Convention itself.

This is a sufficient reason for the institution of a central office. An even stronger one lies in the fact that under the Convention system every country of the Union is directly interested in obtaining information concerning the copyright law of every other : for the international protection of the Convention is measured by the domestic protection of the various signatories, and it behoves authors of each State to investigate the domestic laws of the others in order to find out what is the extent of the international rights. Hence Art. 16 [1] of the Convention provides for the establishment of an international office under the name 'Office of the International Union for the protection of literary and artistic works.'

Particulars relating to the Office at Berne.—The office is located at Berne and placed under the authority and direction of the Government of the Swiss Confederation. Its official language is French. Its functions are to collect, arrange, and publish all kinds of information relative to copyright, to study questions of general utility to the Union, and to issue a periodical in French treating of questions likely to be of interest to the Union. [2] It is to give information on special

---

[1] Art. 16 runs, ' An international office is established under the name of *Office of the International Union for the protection of literary and artistic works.* This office, the expenses of which will be borne by the Governments of all the countries of the Union, is placed under the high authority of the Superior Administration of the Swiss Confederation, and works under its supervision. Its functions shall be determined by common agreement between the countries of the Union.'

[2] This periodical, published at the International Bureau, 7 Helvetiastrasse, Berne, is entitled *Le Droit d'Auteur*, and appears on the 15th of each month, price 50 centimes.

points to any of the members of the Union upon request to that effect.[1] It is also to assist the Government of the country where a Conference of the Union is to be held in preparing the programme for that Conference. The Director attends the sittings of the Conferences and takes part in the discussions, though without a deliberative voice ; he compiles an annual report of his administration which is communicated to the various members of the Union.[2] The expenses of the office are shared by the countries of the Union according to a system by which six different rates of contribution are established, and each country is allowed to declare which of them it will accept for itself. The position thus adjusts itself, for the more important States, for the sake of their own dignity, naturally subject themselves to the heavier rates.

Apportionment of Expenditure.—The expenses are not to exceed 60,000 fr. a year. The proportion paid by each of the six classes of States is as follows : First class 25 units, second 20, third 15, fourth 10, fifth 5, sixth 3. The number of units for each class is multiplied by the number of countries in it, and the whole of these results, when added together, gives the denominator of a fraction which determines the proportion to be paid by each State, the numerator consisting in the number of units for the class to which it belongs. The accounts of the Office are in the hands of the Swiss Government, which communicates a yearly statement to the governments of the other countries of the Union. The following shows in what classes the various States have ranged themselves : First class—France, Germany, Great Britain, and Italy. Second class—Japan and Spain. Third class—Belgium, Sweden, and Switzerland. Fourth class—Denmark and Norway. Fifth class—Haïti. Sixth class—Luxemburg, Monaco, and Tunis.

[1] It may be mentioned that the courteous officials of the Bureau take a liberal view of their duties in this respect, and are willing to furnish any information in their power, even to private individuals belonging to Union countries.

[2] The present Director is M. Henri Morel, and the Secretary M. Ernst Röthlisberger.

SECTION V.

RETROACTIVITY.

The rule of the Convention—The need for Retroactivity—Retroactivity under Article 14—The Additional Act of Paris and Retroactivity—The application of Retroactivity in England—Retroactivity under the International Copyright Act, 1886—*Hanfstaengl v. Holloway*—English rule compared with that of Convention—Can an expired right be revived? —Valuable subsisting interests are protected—A small expenditure may create a valid interest—The interest may be derivative or indirect.

The Rule of the Convention.

The need for Retroactivity.—One of the objects which the framers of the Convention had to keep in mind was the protection of works which had been published before it came into force and were at that time in enjoyment of domestic copyright in their country of origin. The foreigner's right to protection apart from domestic law and convention has already been discussed—undoubtedly a moral right exists, but it is destitute of legal force. Works previously published have therefore a claim to participate in the advantages of any international arrangement entered into ' for the protection of the rights of authors over their literary and artistic works'; but in admitting them it is necessary to take precautions not to do an injustice to those who have previously copied them lawfully in the past.

Retroactivity under Article 14.—The Berne Convention recognises this claim under Art. 14, which provides that ' The present Convention, under the reservations and conditions to be determined by a common agreement, applies to all works which, at the time of its coming into force, have not yet fallen into the public domain of their country of origin.' The 'reservations and conditions to be determined by a common agreement' may be gathered from § 4 of the Closing Protocol,[1] which enacts that the application of the Convention to the works indicated by Art. 14 'shall take effect according to the stipulations relative thereto contained in special treaties existing or to be concluded for the purpose,' and that in default of such stipulations each country shall determine for itself by means of its domestic legislation the manner in which the principle contained in Art. 14 is to be applied.

These qualifications of the principle of retroactivity proceeded from a desire to safeguard vested interests. In the absence of international protection foreign works had at one time been universally looked upon as lawful subjects for native reproduction, either in their original form, or by adaptation or translation. Capital had been sunk, labour had been employed in making these valuable reproductions; lawful interests had been thereby created, and a quasi-property had thus been acquired. A State which had tolerated the indiscriminate reproduction of foreign works would hardly be justified in giving an unqualified consent to the principle of retroactivity, without making due provision for the securing of this quasi-property. Hence the rule of Art. 14 was not made absolute, and it was left to each country to regulate by particular agreement or by domestic law the mode in which it should be applied.

[1] The full wording of this article as it appeared in the 1886 Convention is as follows : ' The common agreement provided for in Art. 14 of the Convention is determined as follows :—" The application of the Convention to works not fallen into the public domain at the time of its coming into force shall take effect according to the stipulations relative thereto contained in special treaties existing or to be concluded for this purpose. In default of such stipulations between countries of the Union, the respective countries shall regulate, each for itself, by domestic law, the manner in which the principle contained in Art. 14 is to be applied." '

The Additional Act of Paris and Retroactivity.—At the
Conference of Paris in 1896 it was proposed by France and
Belgium to abolish the qualifications and reservations of
Art. 14 and to give full effect to the principle of retroactivity.
By this time the hardship of the application of unconditional
retroactivity would have been much reduced, the number of
extant works in which lawful vested interests existed having
become much less, since none could have been created within
the previous ten years at the expense of authors belonging
to Union countries. Germany and Great Britain objected
that, in spite of the lapse of time, absolute retroactivity
might do injury to some vested interests which, even after a
decade, still subsisted. In face of this objection it was decided
to leave Art. 14 in its original form.

In § 4 of the Closing Protocol, however, several modifications were introduced.[1] A few words were imported into the
first line serving to make clearer its reference to the works
indicated in Art. 14. Two new clauses were added. One
was necessitated by the extension of the author's exclusive
right of translation in his original work which was effected by
the Additional Act of Paris. It provided that the stipulations
of the Convention as to retroactivity applied equally to translating right, as assured by the Additional Act. The other,

---

[1] The amended reading is as follows : ' The common agreement provided for
in Art. 14 is determined as follows : The application of the Convention of Berne
and of the present Additional Act to works not fallen into the public domain
in their country of origin at the time of the coming into force of those Acts shall
take effect according to the stipulations relative thereto contained in special
Conventions existing or to be concluded for the purpose. In default of such
stipulations between countries of the Union, the respective countries shall
regulate, each for itself, by domestic law, the manner in which the principle
contained in Art. 14 is to be applied. The stipulations of Art. 14 of the Convention of Berne and of this paragraph of the Closing Protocol apply equally
to the exclusive right of translation, as granted by the present Additional Act.
The above-mentioned temporary provisions are applicable in case of new accessions to the Union.'

which was the final clause, made the previous clause of § 4 of
the Closing Protocol applicable in the case of new accessions
to the Union.[1] None of these alterations represent modifications of the original principle of the Convention. Their
object is merely to throw light on those principles, to carry
them out in detail, and to secure their application to the
condition of things set up by the amending Act.

THE APPLICATION OF RETROACTIVITY IN ENGLAND.

Great Britain was one of the countries which availed
themselves of the permission of § 4 of the Closing Protocol
to regulate by their domestic law the mode in which the
principle of retroactivity should be applied. The English law
is particularly instructive, both on account of its intrinsic
importance, and because the qualifications which it attaches
to retroactivity form an excellent illustration of the object of
the provision contained in the Closing Protocol.

Retroactivity under the International Copyright Act, 1886.—
The intention of § 4 of the Closing Protocol as to retroactivity was carried out in Great Britain by the International
Copyright Act of 1886, which enabled the Crown to accede
to the Convention, and the Order in Council of November
28th, 1887, which adopted the Berne Convention. The Act
of 1886 (sec. 6) provides that ' Where an Order in Council is
made under the International Copyright Acts with respect

---

[1] It was proposed in the Committee of Draftsmanship to add to this Article
a proviso that ' countries which should not have taken measures (to apply
the principle of retroactivity) within a period of two years should be deemed
to have accepted the principle of absolute retroactivity.' This proposition
received the assent of the great majority of the Committee; but the scruples of
one of its members, who thought that its adoption might deter some of the States
from joining the Union, led to its being abandoned.—See *Actes de la Conférence de
Paris*, pp. 174, 175.

to any foreign country, the author and publisher of any literary or artistic work first produced before the date at which such Order comes into operation shall be entitled to the same rights and remedies as if the said Acts and this Act and the said order had applied to the said foreign country at the date of the said production : Provided that where any person has before the date of the publication of an Order in Council lawfully [1] produced any work in the United Kingdom, nothing in this section shall diminish or prejudice any rights or interests arising from or in connection with such production which are subsisting and valuable at the said date.' Sec. 3 of the Order in Council adopting the Berne Convention gives effect to the provision.[2] The retrospective force to be given to the Convention in England is therefore regulated by it.

Hanfstaengl v. Holloway.—In the case of *Hanfstaengl v. Holloway*[3] the rule of the English Act as to retroactivity was applied. The defendant had, before the coming into force of the Order in Council, photographed a picture entitled *The Guardian Angel* belonging to the Hanfstaengl Co., first produced in Germany before 1887, and had copied this on cards used for advertising purposes. After 1887 he made fresh copies, but the plaintiff was protected against the issue of these, it being held that the latter had not in 1887 a 'direct subsisting, pecuniary interest' in the continuation of the production. It was suggested, however, that if the defendant had not recouped himself for his outlay

---

[1] 'Lawfully' here means 'without contravening any existing copyright.' *Moul and Mayeur v. Groenings* (1891), 2 Q.B. 443.

[2] Sec. 3, § 3 of the Order is as follows : 'The author of any literary or artistic work first produced before the commencement of this Order shall have the rights and remedies to which he is entitled under sec. 6 of the International Copyright Act, 1886.'

[3] *Hanfstaengl v. Holloway* (1893), 2 Q.B. 1.

he might have been entitled to do so, even by printing from fresh stones.

English rule compared with that of Convention.—Since under the Convention (Art. 2) the term of international protection cannot in any country exceed that granted by the country of origin, the general rule of the English International Act, protecting foreign works as if the Order had been in force at the date of their production, would seem to have the same effect as the general rule of Art. 14 of the Convention, providing that that agreement applies without exception to all works which at the moment of its coming into force have not yet fallen into the public domain in the country of origin. This conclusion is strengthened by the facts that the Order specifically adopts the Berne Convention of 1886, and that the Act of 1886 was passed, as appears from its preamble, for the purpose of carrying into effect the Convention.

Can an expired right be revived?—But though the English rule as to retroactivity is the same in substance as that of the Convention, the two do not quite coincide, as the case of *Lauri v. Renad*[1] shows. In this case protection was claimed for the translating right in a French work, entitled *Le Voyage en Suisse*, which had not yet fallen into the public domain in France. The work had already enjoyed a translating right of five years from its registration in England under the International Act of 1852, and this term had lapsed in 1884. The Court of Appeal, upholding a decision of Kekewich, J., expressly refused to 'revive or recreate' the translating right, on the ground that a copyright which had already existed in England and had expired could not be renewed without express words in a Statute requiring its renewal. The general rule of retroactivity laid down in Sec. 6 of the Act of 1886 and Sec. 3 of the Order in Council did not suffice, Kay,

---

[1] *Lauri v. Renad* (1892), 3 Ch. 402.

L. J., even going so far as to suggest that the effect of these sections was limited to works published in the interval between the passing of the Act and the coming into force of the Order in Council.

But this would seem to be a mistaken view. The suggestion of Kay, L. J., refuses to give to the sections in question their natural connection with Art. 14 of the Berne Convention with § 4 of the Closing Protocol, and assumes that no provision was made to carry those articles into effect in the sense intended by them.[1] The contention that a right which has already been enjoyed cannot be renewed—or rather that another right of the same character cannot be conferred—under the general rule of retroactivity places works belonging to countries with which we have already concluded conventions in a worse position than those of countries with which the Berne Convention forms our first copyright arrangement. It is hardly to be supposed that this was the intention of the Act of 1886. It may perhaps fairly be concluded that the rule laid down in *Lauri v. Renad* will probably be reversed, if occasion arises, by the House of Lords. In the meantime, however, that case forms the only authoritative indication of the law upon the point it decides. As matters stand at present, then, a work belonging to any country to which an Order in Council made under the International Acts applies will, *pace* Kay, L. J., gain the same protection as if the Order in Council and those Acts had been in force at the time of its publication : unless it has already enjoyed protection in England and the protection has expired, in which case it cannot gain a renewed protection in virtue of the words in the Act of 1886.

Valuable Subsisting Interests are protected.—The proviso

[1] Cf. Charles, J., in *Hanfstaengl v. Holloway* (1893), 2 Q.B. 1, at p. 7.

in the English statute that no application of the principle
of retroactivity shall diminish or prejudice subsisting and
valuable rights or interests is of special importance in that
it forms an express and direct modification of that principle
and shows the qualifications which it was thought necessary
to impose in order to make its application just. The result
of decided cases is to limit the application of the term
'rights' in the statute to *legal* rights obtained by some
such process as the translation or adaptation of the original,[1]
and of the term 'interests' to cases where the producer,
though he may have no legal right, can set up some special
claim distinct from that of the rest of the public, acquired,
for example, by the expenditure of capital or skill upon
the production.[2]

A small expenditure may create a valid interest.—*Moul v.
Groenings*[3] and *Hanfstaengl v. Holloway*[4] decide that the
interest contemplated by the proviso must have a pecuniary
value.

A very small expenditure may, however, suffice to create
a valid subsisting interest. Thus, in *Moul v. Groenings*,[3] it
was held that a bandmaster who before the coming into force
of the Order in Council had bought a piece of music for
five shillings, made band parts from it, and practised his band
in performing it, had a 'direct, subsisting, pecuniary interest'
therein which would enable him to take advantage of the exemption contained in Sec. 6 of the International Act of 1886.

The Interest may be derivative or indirect.—Thus, in
Schauer v. Field,[5] registration before December 6, 1887, of a

---

[1] Per A. L. Smith, J., in *Moul and Mayeur v. Groenings* (1891), 2 Q.B. 443, at
p. 449.
[2] Per Chitty, J., in *Schauer v. Field* (1893), 1 Ch. 35, at p. 41.
[3] *Moul and Mayeur v. Groenings* (1891), 2 Q.B. 443.
[4] *Hanfstaengl v. Holloway* (1893), 2 Q.B. 1.
[5] *Schauer v. Field* (1893), 1 Ch. 35.

picture as a trade-mark, coupled with its employment on show cards, etc., for purposes of advertisement, was held sufficient to create a 'subsisting and valuable interest.'

It would appear from *Moul v. Groenings*[1] that the defendant will gain judgment even where the subsisting and valuable rights or interests belong to persons other than himself, provided only that a verdict against him would tend to impair them.[1]

---

[1] *Moul and Mayeur v. Groenings* (1891), 2 Q.B. 443.

CHAPTER II.

GENERAL PRINCIPLES OF THE BERNE CONVENTION.

SECTION I.

SCOPE OF THE CONVENTION.

Inter-relation of the Convention and the Union—Administrative provisions—The Convention deals only with copyright—Performing right.

Inter-relation of the Convention and the Union.—It is interesting to consider, as a matter of theory, whether the International Union was the creation of the Berne Convention or the Berne Convention the creation of the International Union. A declaration to the effect that 'The contracting States are formed into a Union for the protection of the rights of authors over their literary and artistic works' stands at the head of the Convention (as Art. 1); and from this it would appear that the point of precedence must be settled in favour of that agreement. On the other hand some sort of union—if only a very loose one—must have existed between the parties to the Convention before they set themselves to the task of elaborating a common code for the protection of the rights of authors.

The Convention may perhaps be regarded in two lights : as

a legal agreement turning a union *de facto* into a union *de jure*, and fixing the lines upon which it is to be conducted, and as an expression of the policy which the members of such a union have mutually contracted to carry out.

Administrative Provisions. — As a matter of fact, the Convention contains two distinct sets of provisions: Art. 1 creating the Union, Art. 15 relating to particular arrangements between Union countries, Art. 16 constituting the International Office, and the rest of the Articles treated in the preceding chapter, serve to determine the conditions precedent to the carrying out of that scheme for the international protection of copyright works which is unfolded in the other articles, to settle the constitution of the Union as distinguished from the principles it intends to enforce. Whatever the respective priority of the Convention and the Union, it is clear that, as between the two classes of dispositions of the Convention itself, those that merely deal with the constitution and working of the Union, and make provision for the due carrying out of the Convention, ought to be treated first.

Accordingly, Chapter I. has been devoted to an account of the International Union and its relations to the Berne Convention. Before treating in detail the various rules which go to provide the substantive protection of that agreement, it is now proposed to investigate the general principles which run through the whole.

The Convention deals only with Copyright.—The Berne Convention is strictly a *copyright* agreement. The functions of the Union, as defined by Art. 1, are limited to the protection of 'the rights of authors over their literary and artistic works.' As all States may not be agreed as to what works fall under this category and are proper subjects for copyright, care has been taken to explain the phrase 'literary and artistic works.' Art. 4 of the Convention contains a more or less exhaustive enumeration of the works which are regarded as enjoying this character, together with a comprehensive definition which is meant to cover any *lacunae* which may exist in the other part of the Article.[1] The essential idea of the definition is that of *reproduction* in printed or cognate form, and probably capacity for reproduction is the best criterion of fitness for copyright.

Performing right.—Performing right in dramatic and musical works has nothing to do with the issue of copies to the public, except in so far as it is necessary to guard against such issue of copies being construed into a surrender of the performing right. The right in question is, however, so closely allied to copyright that the Convention, like most domestic codes, has found it necessary to deal with the subject, and by Art. 9 extends its protection to the public representation of dramatic, dramatico-musical, and musical works.

[1] Article 4 is dealt with at considerable length in Chapter IV., to which the reader is referred for a discussion as to its actual effect. The text of the Article is as follows : ' The expression "literary and artistic works" comprises books, pamphlets and all other writings ; dramatic or dramatico-musical works and musical compositions with or without words ; works of design, painting, sculpture, and engraving ; lithographs, illustrations, geographical charts ; plans, sketches, and plastic works relating to geography, topography, architecture, or the sciences in general ; finally, every production whatsoever in the literary, scientific, or artistic domain which can be published by any mode of impression or reproduction whatever.'

SECTION II.

FUNDAMENTAL PRINCIPLES OF THE CONVENTION.

The standard of international protection—Law of protecting country adopted—The rule as to duration—Registration and deposit of copies—The various classes of provisions—The *jus cogens minimum* of the Convention—Absolute provisions expressly admitting domestic intervention—Provision reserving full scope to domestic law—Anomalous provisions.

The Berne Convention is essentially of a contractual nature, being founded on a basis of reciprocity. On certain matters it establishes an absolute minimum of protection throughout the composite territory which falls under its control, but its general rule is that each country shall accord to foreign Unionist authors the rights which by its domestic law it accords to natives.

The Standard of International Protection.—When the choice between setting up one arbitrary and independent standard of protection for every country, and making the standard in each case the domestic law of one of the countries involved, was considered at the Berne Conferences of 1884 and 1885 the former alternative first found the greater favour on account of its apparent simplicity. But a closer consideration of the four elements of protection, viz.

(1) the persons protected,

(2) the works protected,

(3) the period of protection, and

(4) the rights granted,

disclosed many matters which, on account of the differences between the various national systems of law, did not readily lend themselves to this mode of treatment. Hence ultimately the

principle of relative assimilation, *i.e.* of regulating protection
in each case by the law of one of the countries concerned, was
adopted. It then became necessary to decide what law should
be chosen for the standard of assimilation. The choice lay
between

> (1) the law of the country of origin of the work, and
> (2) the law of the protecting country.

Law of Protecting Country adopted.—The law of the country
of origin of the work would at first sight appear to be the most
suitable standard of protection. The Montevideo Convention [1]
adopts the rule that the law of the country of origin of the
work shall follow it wherever it seeks protection. But this
rule involves the application by the protecting country of a
foreign law, which is a difficult process and is in practice
attended with great risk of misinterpretation. It would be
unwise to call upon each country of an International Union
comprising fifteen countries to administer international protection in a way that would involve the separate investigation
of the law of every other country. Hence for the Berne
Convention the alternative course was chosen, and the appropriate law for the determination of international protection
became that of the country from which protection is sought ;
although in two specific matters, *i.e.* the period of protection
and the conditions and formalities to be fulfilled, this rule is
modified, effect being given to the law of the country of
origin.

The rule as to duration.—As to the conditions and formalities to be fulfilled, the law of the country of origin is to be
the sole criterion ; but the term of copyright is to be adjusted

---

[1] This was concluded on the 11th January, 1889. It has been ratified by the
Argentine Republic, Paraguay, Peru, and Uruguay. Bolivia, Brazil, and Chili,
though they signed the Convention, have not yet ratified it. France, Spain, and
Italy have also adhered to it, but up to the present their adhesion has only been
accepted by the Argentine Republic and Paraguay.

by the law of the protecting country, except where the
domestic period of that country is greater than that of the
country of origin, when it is to be cut down to equal the
latter.[1]

Registration and Deposit of Copies[2] are certainly most con-
veniently performed in the place of first publication, but the
limitation of the period of protection accorded in any country
by that of the country of origin of the work seems, at first
sight, to be contrary to the true spirit of the Convention. In
all other matters, the rights of foreign authors throughout
the Union are assimilated to those of subjects ; even in the
case where rights not admitted in the country of origin are
claimed as part of the copyright, they must be conceded by
those countries of the Union which recognise them by their
domestic law. Still, one of the underlying principles of the
Convention is that only works which are actually in enjoyment
of copyright in their country of origin shall be entitled to
claim protection from other countries. It is through the
country of origin that an author derives his claim to international protection—and when that country itself has refused
or has ceased to give protection, it is hardly in a position to
claim protection for its authors from others. In this principle
lies the explanation of the rule of the Convention relating to
conditions and formalities, as well as of the rule relating to
duration.

---

[1] The rule is often represented thus : the question of duration is to be
regulated by the domestic laws of the countries concerned, but when the country
of origin and the protecting country have different periods of protection, there is
a conflict and the shorter period is chosen.—See *Études sur la revision de la
Convention de Berne*, p. 49.

[2] Recent laws show a tendency to dispense with registration and deposit.
Their abolition has been strongly advocated in international Conventions as the
simplest means of bringing about uniformity in respect of formalities, but it is
submitted that to adopt this course would be to sacrifice convenience to academic
simplicity.

The Various Classes of Provisions of the Convention.

The provisions of the Convention display various well-marked degrees of binding force. Art. 2, which contains the fundamental rule of the Convention, provides that 'Authors belonging to any country of the Union, or their lawful representatives, shall enjoy in the other countries for their works, whether unpublished or published for the first time in one of those countries, the rights which the respective laws do now or may hereafter grant to natives.'

As a general principle, then, each country is required simply to extend its own domestic protection to Unionist authors, but this is somewhat qualified by the series of articles which follow Art. 2 in the Convention. Some of these articles, indeed, simply repeat the rule of Art. 2 for certain special subjects, the fitness of which for copyright is or has been matter of controversy. Thus the Closing Protocol provides that photographs, works of architecture, and choregraphic works shall be protected in those countries which grant them copyright by their domestic law. But, besides merely declaratory provisions like these, on certain subjects the Convention makes absolute rules having no relation to any domestic system, and on others it expressly provides for the intervention of the domestic law of the protecting country in cases where perhaps this would not be warranted by the general principle. Public law and administration are necessarily left to domestic authority.

The 'jus cogens minimum' of the Convention.—The absolutely binding provisions of the Convention form what is called its *jus cogens minimum*, i.e. that portion of its system which, being entirely independent of any external standard, every country, whatever the state of its domestic law, is obliged to adopt as a whole. This *jus cogens minimum* embraces certain dispositions concerning the establishment, organisation and functions of the International Union, which may for the present be dismissed as outside our particular purpose, and others that affect the actual substance of the protection accorded by the Convention. These are set out by the authorities of the International Office in the *Études*[1] prepared by them for the Conference of Paris as follows :—

(1) The protection of non-Unionist authors for works published anywhere in the Union. This is established by Art. 3.

(2) The definition of 'literary and artistic works,' which is to include 'every production whatsoever in the literary, scientific, or artistic domain that can be published by any mode of reproduction whatever.'—Art. 4.

(3) The rule that the exclusive right of translation belongs to the author during the whole duration of his copyright in the original work, subject to the proviso that if it is to be retained it must be exercised within ten clear years of the publication of the original.—Art. 5.

(4) The protection—the same as that in the original work —which is accorded in the literary form of translations lawfully made.—Art. 6.

(5) The protection of serial novels appearing in newspapers or magazines, and the conditional protection of other newspaper and magazine articles (except articles of political discussion, news of the day, and miscellaneous items), which is established by Art. 7.

(6) The protection of the performing right in plays,

---

[1] *Études sur la revision de la Convention de Berne*, p. 50.

published or unpublished dramas ; and also in music when the right has been expressly reserved.—Art. 9.[1]

(7) The rule that copyright belongs *primâ facie* to the author whose name is on the work, and that in respect of anonymous or pseudonymous works the publisher may sue ; though a foreign court may require a certificate showing that the formalities of the country of origin have been fulfilled.— Art. 11.

(8) The protection of authorised photographs of protected works of art for the whole duration of the copyright in the principal work.—Closing Protocol, § 1 B.

(9) The rule that the manufacture and sale of mechanical musical instruments reproducing copyright airs shall not be considered as constituting an infringement.—Closing Protocol, § 3.

Absolute Provisions expressly admitting Domestic Intervention. —In addition to these provisions, which do not in any way allow of individual variation, there are others in which, while an absolute rule has been laid down, its definition, interpretation, or administration has been expressly left to the domestic law of the protecting country. These are as follows :

(1) The prohibition of unauthorised indirect appropriations, *e.g.* adaptations and arrangements of music, when the alterations do not confer the character of a new original work. These are definitely forbidden, but the Convention provides that the countries of the Union may enforce any reservations which may be contained in their respective domestic laws.— Art. 10.

(2) The seizure of piratical copies on importation, which,

---

[1] The authorities at the office include Art. 9 in their list of absolute dispositions but, since that Article simply applies the rule of Art. 2—itself a relative disposition—to performing right, it is submitted that it should not be placed in this list.

though made obligatory, is left to be carried out in the manner prescribed by the domestic law of each country.— Art. 12.

(3) The application of the principle of Art. 14, that the Convention shall apply to all works not in the public domain in the country of origin at the time of its coming into force. Each country is allowed to regulate by separate treaties or by its own domestic law the manner in which this principle of retroactivity shall be enforced.—Closing Protocol, § 4.

Provision reserving full scope to Domestic Law.—The countries of the Union have reserved to themselves full power to control, on grounds of public policy, the circulation of all works within their territory. This reservation is embodied in Art. 11.

Anomalous Provisions.—There are two matters with regard to which the Convention seems unreasonably to diminish the author's international rights. In the first place, although unauthorised indirect appropriations are forbidden generally by Art. 10, they are regarded by Art. 8 as permissible—if not even to be encouraged—when made for certain specific purposes, *i.e.* for insertion in educational or scientific works or in chrestomathies.[1] Each country of the Union is expressly allowed to decide for itself how far extracts shall be permitted for such purposes. Again, as we have seen, § 3 of the Closing Protocol provides for the free toleration of the manufacture and sale of mechanical musical instruments, even when these serve to reproduce copyright airs. These provisions, which allow the free use of the authors' property in certain ways without his consent or control, are contrary to the true spirit of the Convention.

---

[1] A chrestomathy is defined in Murray's *Oxford Dictionary* as 'a collection of choice passages from an author or authors, especially one compiled to assist in the acquirement of a language.' The French definition given by Littré is 'Un recueil de morceaux, choisis dans des auteurs réputés classiques.'

SECTION III.

PERSONS ENTITLED.

Different classes of persons protected—General rules as to persons entitled
—Persons included in Art. 2—The evolution of Art. 2—Nationality the
criterion of capacity—Unionist authors to enjoy same rights as natives—
Persons included in Art. 3—The evolution of Art. 3—Art. 3 and the
country of origin.

Different classes of persons protected.—It is a great advance
for a country which has hitherto limited its copyright to the
works of native authors to extend its protection to the works
of foreigners, even when this protection is limited by the condition that such works must be first published in the territory.

The International Union, unconsciously following the usual
order of domestic development, after duly providing for the
protection of the native author, turned its attention towards
the commercial interests of the native publisher, granting him
copyright in the works of non-Unionist authors first published
by him within the Union.

But after the lapse of ten years this rule was altered and
protection was extended to non-Unionist authors in their
own right for all their works which should be first published
in any Union country.

General rules as to persons entitled.—The progress of this
development will be sketched in the following Sections. Meanwhile the total effect of the rules of the Berne Convention
with respect to the persons entitled to protection may be stated
as follows : For works published within the territory of any of
the countries of the Union, an author, even if he himself does
not belong to any Union country, gains the protection of the
Convention ; in order to gain protection for his *unpublished*

works, however, he must belong to a Union country. From
this it may be seen that, in order to gain international protection under the Convention for his work, an author about
to publish must publish it in Belgium, Denmark (or the Faroë
Islands), France (or its colonies or Algeria), Germany, Great
Britain (or its dominions), Haïti, Italy, Japan, Luxemburg,
Monaco, Spain (or its colonies), Switzerland, or Tunis[1];
that is, in one of the countries which have accepted the
Berne Convention as amended by the Additional Act of
Paris. If he belongs to a Union country, he will also gain
protection by first publishing his work in Norway or Sweden ;
if not, first publication in either will secure him protection,
but only indirectly, in virtue of a special arrangement with
the publisher.[2]

The author of an unpublished work will not gain protection
unless he is connected with one of these countries, or with
Norway, by the tie of nationality.

Persons Included in Art. 2.

The Evolution of Art. 2.—The persons for whom the countries
of the Union primarily desired to secure international protection were of course their own authors. By Art. 2 of the

---

[1] The protection given by the Convention must be carefully distinguished from
the domestic protection conferred by individual countries. In order to gain this
in any country, it is necessary to comply with the requirements of the municipal
law, which usually exacts either that the author of the work shall be a subject or
that the work itself shall be published in the country. France, Belgium, and
Luxemburg, however, protect all works, wherever published and whatever the
nationality of their author.

[2] Norway and Sweden are members of the International Union, but, as they
have not accepted the Additional Act, their relations with the other members are
regulated by the Convention of 1886 in its original form. The author of a work
published in Norway or Sweden will therefore not necessarily gain from any
country protection under the Convention on his own account, though the publisher
of the work will, under the old Art. 3, be protected throughout the Union.

original draft of the Convention, as presented by the Swiss Government to the Berne Conference of 1884, international protection was in the first place secured to 'the subjects or citizens of each of the contracting States.'[1]

In the Committee appointed by the Conference of 1884 for the purpose of considering the draft of the Convention in detail, the delegates of Germany pointed out that ' subjects or citizens ' would not in every country be exactly equivalent to natives, whom it was the intention of the Convention to protect, and also that no country could reasonably expect to secure Union copyright for such works of its authors as were published in countries not belonging to the Union.   They therefore submitted to the Committee an amended version of Art. 2 protecting authors 'belonging (*ressortissant*) to any of the contracting countries,' and limiting the protection to such of their works as should be unpublished, or should have been first published in one of the countries of the Union. The amended version was accepted by the Committee and ultimately reproduced in the final text of the Convention, with a few slight verbal alterations which do not concern us here.[2]   The import of the condition as to publication within the Union will be dealt with in Chapter III.

[1] See *Actes de la Conférence de Berne*, 1884, p. 11.

[2] Amongst other things, the phrase 'contracting countries' was altered into 'countries of the Union.' It is perhaps worth while to suggest that this was dictated by a desire to emphasise the solidarity of the Union. The Convention was more than a mere contract: the *personnel* of the Union might change, but still the Convention would hold good and the Union itself would stand. The full text of Art. 2 as it stood in the 1886 Convention is: 'Authors belonging to any country of the Union, or their lawful representatives, shall enjoy in the other countries for their works, whether published in one of those countries or unpublished, the rights which the respective laws do now or may hereafter accord to natives. The enjoyment of these rights is subjected to the accomplishment of the conditions and formalities prescribed by the law of the country of origin of the work ; it cannot exceed in the other countries the duration of the protection accorded in the said country of origin. The country

Nationality the criterion of capacity.—The substitution of the words 'Authors belonging to any of the contracting countries' for the words 'The subjects or citizens of each of the contracting States' was dictated by a desire to make clear that it was such persons as enjoyed *nationality* in any Union country, and only such persons, that the Convention meant to include in its protection.   Art. 3 as it stood in the Swiss draft[1] might in some countries have had the effect of assimilating to such persons, authors whose only connection with the Union was the fact that they were domiciled in one of the countries belonging to it; but Germany objected to this, and in the Committee of draftsmanship the clause granting protection to authors domiciled in the Union was struck out.   The result is that only authors who are connected with a country of the Union by the tie of nationality (*l'indigénat*) enjoy for all their works (whether unpublished or published within the Union) the protection of Art. 2.

Unionist Authors to enjoy same rights as natives.—It is to be noted that, although in determining what works shall be protected the Convention adopts the principle of territoriality, it nevertheless regards protection as due from each country to the Unionist author in virtue of his own nationality, rather than in virtue of the nationality of his work; so that, when an author belonging to one country of the Union publishes his work in another, the latter, whatever the state of its domestic

of first publication, or, if that publication takes place simultaneously in several countries of the Union, that one of them in which the shortest period of protection is granted by law, is considered to be the country of origin of the work. For unpublished works, the country to which the author belongs is considered to be the country of origin of the work.' For the amendments effected by the Conference of Paris, see Chap. iii., sec. 2.

[1] 'The subjects or citizens of States not forming part of the Union, who are domiciled in, or cause their work to be published on the territory of, any State of the Union are assimilated to the subjects or citizens of the contracting States.'—*Actes de la Conférence de Berne*, 1884, p. 11.

law, is bound to grant him the protection prescribed by the Convention.[1]

This was of considerable practical importance before Germany enacted its new law upon literary, musical, and dramatic copyright in 1901.   Before that date foreign authors who first published their works in Germany—unless this publication was made through a publisher having his house of trade situated in Germany—failed to obtain protection under the domestic law.   Hence a Swiss author publishing in Germany through the agency of a Swiss publishing house had no claim to protection in Germany except under Art. 2 of the Convention. The German law of literary, musical, and dramatic copyright has now been amended, and first publication in Germany, however made, secures domestic protection ; but this is not so with either works of art, which, if they are to gain copyright, must appear with native German publishers, or photographs, which will only be protected if produced by native German authors. Moreover, in Norway domestic copyright, even in literary works, is conceded to aliens only on condition that their works first appear with Norwegian publishers ; and the law of Sweden is somewhat similar.[2]   The Convention requires that all countries shall give foreign authors—however and wherever they publish, so long as it is in the Union—the same protection as that which they give to natives.

PERSONS INCLUDED IN ART. 3.

In respect of such of their works as are published for the first time in one of the countries of the Union, non-Unionist authors enjoy protection under Art. 3 of the Convention, as amended by the Act of Paris.

---

[1] 'Authors belonging to any country of the Union . . . shall enjoy *in the other countries* . . . the rights that the respective laws accord to *natives.*'

[2] See Part III., Chap. iv., sec. 2.

The Evolution of Art. 3.—The original text of this Article, as it appeared in the draft of the Swiss Government, placed not only all non-Unionist authors domiciled within the Union, but also all non-Unionist authors publishing their works on Union territory, on the same footing as the persons protected under Art. 2. The opposition of Germany to the inclusion in the protection of the Convention of authors merely domiciled in the Union has already been mentioned. It proceeded, ostensibly at least, from a feeling that to grant protection to authors not belonging to countries of the Union would be to lessen materially the inducement for non-Union countries to become parties to the Convention.

On the same ground, Germany objected to the inclusion of non-Unionist authors publishing their works within Union countries. The German delegates intimated, however, that that country saw no reason why publishers belonging to the Union should not be accorded protection in respect of works of non-Unionist authors published by them and appearing for the first time on the territory of the Union.

Art. 3 was amended by the Committee of 1884 and brought into harmony with the ideas of Germany.[1] In its amended form it provided that 'The stipulations of Art. 2 apply equally to the publishers of literary or artistic works published in any country of the Union, though the author

---

[1] Sec. 61 of the German law of 1870 runs: 'The present law applies to all works of native authors, whether such works have appeared within the country or abroad, or have not been published at all. The works of foreign authors which appear at the house of a publisher having his business establishment in the territory of the North German Confederation shall also enjoy the protection of the present law.' In extending the benefits of its law to the other countries of the Union, Germany, while willing to widen its sphere of protection to include all Unionist authors, was not willing to sacrifice the principle laid down in the law of 1870 that the works of outsiders could only claim protection through an inside publisher. In later years its policy has changed. In 1896, as will be seen, it found itself able to agree to the amendment of Paris, and its new law of 1901 embodies the principle of territoriality pure and simple.

belongs to a country which is not a party to the Union.'
It is almost in this shape that Art. 3 appears in the final text
of the 1886 Convention.[1]

The wording of the Article seems to go beyond the original
intention of Germany and to secure protection for the publishers of works of non-Unionist authors first published within
the Union, even when they themselves are not natives of
any Union country. This, however, was the definite object
of the Conference, for the Committee of 1885 expressly
considered the question, and unanimously agreed that the
nationality of the publisher was a matter of indifference,
so long as he had a 'permanent and durable' establishment
in a Union country.[2]

At the Paris Conference of 1896, however, it was suggested by Belgium and Switzerland that the author of the
work, even though a subject of a country not belonging
to the Union, should receive protection directly instead of
through his publisher; and Germany had so far changed
its views that it was now able to admit the soundness of this
principle. Hence the Article was amended, and now reads,
'Authors not belonging to any country of the Union,
if they shall have published their literary or artistic
works or caused them to be published[3] for the first time

---

[1] The only difference is 'The stipulations of the present Convention' for 'The
stipulations of Art. 2.'

[2] See *Actes de la Conférence de Berne*, 1885, p. 42. At the Conference of 1884,
M. Lavollée, a French delegate, expressed the opinion that the word 'publisher'
in Art. 3 was to be taken in the widest sense so as to apply it to the producer
(*entrepreneur*) of plays.—*Actes de la Conférence de Berne*, 1884, p. 44.

[3] The proposition of Belgium and Switzerland extended to protect works
represented or executed, as well as works published, for the first time on Union
territory. If this proposition had been adopted, a non-Unionist playwright
producing his work in a Union country would have been safeguarded from
what, under the present Article, are lawful infringements. It was, however,
objected that the fact of representation or execution was not sufficiently
notorious to make it a practicable basis of protection; and the words 'repre-

in one of those countries, shall enjoy for such works the protection granted by the Berne Convention and by the present Additional Act.' All the countries of the Union, except Norway and Sweden, are bound by the amendment.

Art. 3 and the Country of Origin.—Where a country of the Union does not by its domestic law protect all works first published within the territory, a question arises whether Art. 3 binds it to grant protection to the works of non-Unionist authors published there for the first time. Before 1901, the work of a Russian author first published in Germany (unless by a publisher having his house of business in that country) failed to obtain domestic protection under the German law —was Germany obliged under Art. 3 to grant such a work the same protection as that given to native authors? In the report of the proceedings of the Committee of Draftsmanship appointed by the Conference of Paris, it is laid down that in such a case the work gains protection throughout the whole extent of the Union, and the country of origin, as well as the other Union countries, is bound to grant it the ordinary rights of the domestic law.[1]

This interpretation of the amended Art. 3 derives great weight from the fact that it takes origin with the very body which was responsible for the wording of that Article : but still it is rather remarkable that the Convention, which regards the claim to international protection of a work written by a non-Unionist author as based on the fact that it is protected in the country of origin, should itself attempt to compel the country of origin to grant protection.

sented or executed' were accordingly left out of the article. Sir H. Bergne, a British delegate, was of opinion that the change did not alter the effect of the article in securing protection for all works represented or executed, provided that in the country of production they are regarded as published.—See *Actes de la Conférence de Paris*, pp. 112, 113, 165.

[1] See *Actes de la Conférence de Paris*, p. 165.

In any case, the question is no longer of much practical importance, since Germany, which, with the exception of Norway, has, till lately, been the only country of the Union to make its domestic protection depend upon a condition of nationality, has by its Act of 1901, sec. 55, extended protection to all literary, musical, and dramatic works of aliens published within its territory.[1]

---

[1] But even now works of art by foreign authors gain protection only if they appear with native publishers, and photographs only if they are produced by native authors. See Part II., Chap. iv., sec. 2.

CHAPTER III.

THE PROTECTION GIVEN BY THE BERNE CONVENTION.

SECTION I.

NATURE OF THE PROTECTION.

Protection given by Article 2—Assimilation of rights—The necessary examination of foreign laws—The foreign author to benefit by future extensions of domestic protection—The author's exclusive translating right—Primary and derivative rights—Translating right under Article 5—The author's restrictive translating term—International importance of translating right—Performing right in dramatic and musical works—Its international importance—Article 9—The benefit of Article 2 extended to performing right—Notice of reservation of musical performing right in England—The policy of requiring notice—Lecturing right—The treatment of infringements affects the content of copyright.

PROTECTION GIVEN BY ARTICLE 2.

THE general object of the Berne Convention is to secure protection throughout the Union for all works published within the Union territory. In considering the provisions by which that object is achieved, it seems well, first, to deal with the protection given, its nature, conditions, and extent; and then to treat of the specific subjects to which it is accorded, together with the variations of the general rule established in respect of some of these subjects.

This is the substantive part of the law of the Convention.

The adjective part consists of the rules relating to infringements, remedies, and procedure.

The protection given by the Convention, the works protected, the acts which the Convention characterises as infringements, and the remedies and procedure available, will each form the subject of a separate Chapter. The Convention is not a final statement, incapable of variation, of the law relating to international copyright ; but, on the contrary, it expressly provides for its own revision. The conditions of revision will be dealt with in a separate Chapter, which will also contain a short account of the revisions that have already taken place, and of matters which may be expected to form subjects of future revisions.

The fundamental principle of Art. 2 : Assimilation of rights.— In this Chapter, the protection given by the Berne Convention will be treated. The cardinal principle relating to this is to be found in the first paragraph of Art. 2, which declares that 'Authors belonging to any country of the Union, or their lawful representatives, shall enjoy in the other countries for their works, whether unpublished or published for the first time in one of those countries, the rights which the respective laws do now or may hereafter grant to natives.'

Each State has formed its own estimate of the kind and amount of protection due to authors. In the Convention it was not thought advisable to force upon any country views which were not in accordance with its own domestic theory, and so, as a general rule, no State is required to give a greater protection to aliens than it is accustomed to grant to its own subjects. A country cannot be expected to make invidious exceptions to its ordinary rules of law in favour of foreign works. On the other hand, it is but reasonable that a country which admits a duty to protect foreign works should interpret that duty in the light of its conduct in its own affairs, and freely place foreign works on the same level as its own. This is the principle on which Art. 2 is based.

The necessary examination of foreign law.—In practice, there is one obvious objection to the rules laid down in that Article. If authors are to get to know their rights under the Convention, it will be necessary for them to undertake investigations, which may be involved and difficult, into the domestic laws of foreign countries ; and so the international protection held out to them may be rendered useless.

The difficulty however seems more formidable than it really is. It is not necessary for the proper protection of an author that he should have a detailed knowledge of his rights. In the case of his foreign rights under Art. 2, the fact that the copyright laws of all the countries of the Union are based on the same principles, and are more or less similar in detail, gives him a fair notion of their extent ; and even in the case of his domestic rights in his own country it is rarely indeed that he has much more than this. Except in cases of dispute, a knowledge of general principles usually suffices for all practical purposes. And when it becomes necessary for the author to enforce his rights in his own country, he usually goes to an expert and commissions him to make the necessary investigation. A precisely similar course is open to him when he has to enforce his foreign rights, though in this case it may be attended with greater difficulty and expense. Moreover the International Office provides a ready means of information upon the copyright laws of the various countries of the Union, and is always ready to give advice in matters which come reasonably within its functions.

The foreign author to benefit by future extensions of domestic protection.—It will be noted that the protection of the alien author is to be *kept* on a level with that of the native, the last few words of the clause of Art. 2 quoted above making it obligatory on States to grant to foreigners the benefit of any further advance in their domestic law.

The Author's Exclusive Translating Right.

The rule of Art. 2 is the general rule of the Convention. As such it determines what works are to gain protection, what rights are to be embraced in the general grant of copyright, what acts constitute infringements, what procedure is to be adopted in suing, what remedies are to be applied, and other cognate questions. It is, however, only a general rule, and on some points of particular international importance the Convention has made special dispositions which modify it.

Thus Art. 7 (as amended by the Additional Act of Paris) prohibits the reproduction of serial stories in newspapers and magazines, and therefore even countries which do not grant copyright to such stories by their domestic laws are bound to protect them—at any rate when they have first appeared on foreign territory—under the Convention. There are several other provisions of this kind, most of which find a place in subsequent Chapters. But there are two, relating respectively to translating right and performing right, which, since they affect the actual content of the protection given by the Convention, will be treated here.

Primary and Derivative Rights.—The primary rights in an ordinary work are determined by the general rule of Art. 2. But Translating right and Performing right are derivative and not primary, and receive special treatment under Arts. 5 and 9 of the Convention. It will be seen that translating right is strictly a part of the copyright in the original work. It is an exclusive right of translating the latter, vested in the author, and enabling him to prevent all others from making translations.

For this, it is not necessary for the author to translate the work personally; but if he does so, or authorises another to produce a translation, his exclusive translating right, so long as it lasts, serves to protect the translation he has thus made or authorised. When this exclusive right has expired, any person may go back to the original work and translate it at will. All translations lawfully made[1] will be protected in their text as original works: that is to say, their producer can prevent other persons from copying them though he cannot prevent anybody from going back to the original work and making a fresh translation on his own account. The distinction between the translating right and the right in a translation lawfully made should be carefully noted.

Translating Right under Art. 5.—Article 5 in its present form as amended by the Act of Paris runs as follows :—

'Authors belonging to any country of the Union,[2] or their lawful representatives, shall enjoy in the other countries the exclusive right of making or authorising translations of their works, during the whole duration of the right in the original work. Nevertheless, the exclusive right of translation shall cease to exist when the author shall not have made use of it within a period of ten years from the time of the first publication of the original work, by publishing or causing to be published, in one of the countries of the Union, a translation in the language for which protection is claimed.

'For works published by instalments, the period of ten

---

[1] There are three cases in which a translation may be lawfully made, (i) where the author of a work, in which both copyright and translating right still subsist, has given his consent or authorisation ; (ii) where the translating right, though not the copyright, in the work has lapsed ; (iii) where the work has fallen into the public domain.

[2] See Sec. 2 of this Chapter for a discussion of whether this extends to prevent non-Unionist authors from getting translating right for works published within the Union.

years does not begin to run until the publication of the last instalment of the original work.

'For works composed of several volumes published at intervals, as well as for reports or papers published by literary or learned societies or by individuals, each volume, report, or paper, is, with regard to the period of ten years, considered as a separate work.

'In the cases provided for by the present Article, the 31st December of the year in which the work was published is considered to be the date of publication for the purpose of calculating the period of protection.'

The Convention thus expressly binds members of the Union to recognise an exclusive right of translation as part of the copyright in every work which claims their protection under Art. 2, whether or not they do the same in respect of works protected only by their domestic law.

The Author's Restrictive Translating Term.—The effect of Art. 5 is to secure to authors a period of ten clear years from the publication of their original work, during which they are protected against all unauthorised translations appearing any-where in the Union, in whatever language. If during this ten years' period—commonly called *délai d'usage*—the author does not himself publish a translation of his work, his exclusive translating right lapses altogether, and anyone is at liberty to translate his work into any language ; if, however, he does exercise his translating right, he will get protection, during the whole of the remaining period of copyright in the original work, against all other translations *in the same language* as that which he himself has published. He will get no protec-tion against translations in *other* languages after the expiration of the ten years *délai d'usage*.

Thus, if the author of a work published in England translates it into French or German, at the end of five years from publication his rights are as follows :—(1) A right for a further five years (the balance of the *délai d'usage*) to prevent the publication of any translation of his work *in any language* ; (2) a right extending beyond this and running with the copyright in the original work, to prevent the publication of any translation of his work *in French or German* ; and (3), besides this, a further right for five years more in the text of his translations,[1] which, however, does not concern us here. Before the Act of Paris, right No. 2 did not exist—the author had only an exclusive period of ten years, during which he was protected against all translations, and a right in the text of such translations as he himself chose to make. The inability of Norway and Sweden to give more than this prevented them from accepting the Act of Paris.[2]

It will be seen that the *délai d'usage* introduced by the Act of Paris can be regarded in either of two ways, *i.e.* as an absolute period of protection given to the author so as to enable him to make his own translations, thereby entitling himself to a further term, or as a period of protection to which the full term of translating right may become contracted, if certain conditions are not fulfilled.

International importance of translating right.—To ensure a general international protection of translating right and to fix a minimum term for its duration was a matter of especial importance. The domestic translating right accorded by any country to its own works is not of very great value, for it can only avail against other translations appearing in the territory of the protecting State, and translations in a foreign language are in no country likely to gain a large sale. It is usually not worth while for an author to issue translations of a work first published in the native tongue in

---

[1] See Chap. iv., sec. 3.   [2] See Chap. i., sec. 1.

the same country as that in which he published the original. On the other hand, the protection by a country of translating right in works appearing in another is of the greatest value, since such works need translation in order to appeal to the foreign public. An international copyright which did not include the right to prohibit translation for a greater or less term would be illusory.

PERFORMING RIGHT IN DRAMATIC AND MUSICAL WORKS.

International importance of performing right.—The protection of plays and music from unauthorised performance is even more valuable than the protection of books from unauthorised translations. Works belonging to the former class appeal to a very wide public, and in the case of music, which is printed in an international notation, there is no need of any adaptation whatever in order that it may suit the requirements of a foreign public.

Article 9. The rules of the Convention as to performing right are contained in Article 9. That Article runs as follows : 'The stipulations of Art. 2 apply to the public performance of dramatic or dramatico-musical works, whether such works be published or not. Authors of dramatic or dramatico-musical works, or their lawful representatives, are, during the existence of their exclusive right of translation, in like manner protected against the unauthorised public representation of translations of their works. The stipulations of Art. 2 apply equally to the public performance of unpublished musical works, and of published works as to which the author has expressly declared upon the title-page or at the commencement of the work that he forbids their public performance.'

The benefit of Art. 2 extended to Performing Right.—Art. 9 is not designed to include plays and music among the works protected by Art. 2,—they are specially mentioned in the list of subjects given by Art. 4,—but to extend the copyright already given by Art. 2 to include *performing right* in plays and music. If a country does not grant any performing right to its own dramatic and musical works,[1] Art. 9 does not bind it to concede such a right to the musical and dramatic works of other countries; if it does, it must put musical and dramatic works belonging to subjects of other States of the Union on the same level as native works.[2] For performing right the Convention prescribes no minimum period of protection.

Notice of Reservation of Musical Performing Right in England.—Like the Convention, English law demands notice of reservation as a condition precedent to the retention of performing right in published pieces of music. This rule is designed to serve as a safeguard against the extortionate demands of such owners of musical copyright as the late Mr. F. J. Wall.

In England, before the rule requiring express reservation came into force, it was by no means unusual for private persons to purchase music and to perform it publicly in connection with amateur theatricals, concerts, etc., little thinking that by so doing they were bringing themselves within reach of the law. Mr. Wall bought up a large number of the performing rights that were available and obtained large sums by way of compensation from the persons who had thus unknowingly invaded his acquired rights. The result was a scandal which led to the passing of the Musical Copyright Act, 1882, commonly known as the 'Wall Act,' as a result of which notice of

---

[1] As is the case with Japan, Luxemburg, Norway, and Tunis.

[2] Except that it may require the fulfilment of the conditions and formalities of the country of origin (alone), and may limit its period of performing right by that given by the country of origin.

reservation is now required. The practical advantages of the rule in question would seem to be considerable.

The Policy of Requiring Notice.—Nevertheless opinion on the Continent has of late come to regard the requirement of express notice for the reservation of performing right in works of music as unfair to the composer. It is argued that performing right is a normal part of the copyright in a piece of music, and that it is unreasonable to require the owner of a right to proclaim his ownership in order to secure himself protection. It is for the person who wishes to reproduce the music to ascertain whether he can legitimately do so, not for the author to make a declaration on the subject for the assistance of would-be infringers.

On the other hand, it is true that the purchaser of a piece of music generally has in view not its mere perusal, as in the case of a book, but its actual performance. He intends to buy the right to play it, at any rate in private, and it is not to be expected that, in the absence of express prohibition, he shall draw a clear line of distinction between the right to play in private, which is normally his as a result of his purchase, and the right to play in public, which his purchase does not extend to secure him.

Already much of the best music is in the public domain, and day by day more falls in. As time goes on, the difficulty of distinguishing between pieces which anybody may perform and pieces in which the composer still retains his exclusive performing right becomes greater and greater. The law does not require any statement to be placed upon pieces in which the performing right has lapsed or has been abandoned by the author; and so the requirement of express notice of reservation for pieces in which that right still subsists confers an inestimable benefit upon the general public, in that it enables any purchaser to see at a glance exactly what are his rights in a musical work he has bought or is about to buy.

In this view, performing right is not a primary incident of the copyright in a piece of music, but a special right, which the author may keep if he chooses, but which, in the absence of express notification, the public will assume not to be withheld on the sale of sheet music. A notice of reservation, which involves little trouble or expense to the author, and which may save the purchasing public from unknowingly committing an infringement, may therefore fairly be required to be placed in a conspicuous place on every sheet of music sold in which it is desired that performing right shall be retained.[1]

These arguments for and against the abolition of the Convention rule will probably be discussed at length at the next conference of the Union, to be held at Berlin in 1906 at latest.[2] The matter is almost certain to be mooted by Germany, which in 1901 issued a new copyright law, requiring no mention of reservation and making other rules for the regulation of performing right.[3]

Lecturing Right.—Another question which will doubtless be dealt with by the Conference of Berlin is that of lecturing right. A lecture is not essentially a dramatic work, though sometimes the line of distinction may be hard to draw; it is clearly neither a dramatico-musical nor musical work. Hence it does not come within the scope of Art. 9,

---

[1] It will be noted that the argument does not apply equally to dramatic and musico-dramatic works, which are often bought for mere perusal. For these, moreover, the public performance which usually precedes issue in printed form is a warning to the public that the acting right belongs to the author.

[2] The whole subject of performing right will probably then be discussed; this may include the extent to which private performances, performances to limited audiences, performances for charities, etc., are to be allowed.

[3] See Secs. 11, 27, and 28 of the Act in question.

though, if it has been reduced to literary form, it gains *copyright* under Art. 2 either as a published or unpublished literary work, according as it has or has not been issued to the public in printed form.[1]

Whether the general rule of Art. 2 extends without further provision to give such a work lecturing right in countries which accord that right to the lectures of their own subjects is not at first sight clear, but in view of the fact that it has been found necessary to introduce a special article in order to secure performing right for musical and dramatic works, it would seem that the 'rights' referred to in Art. 2 cannot logically be held to include lecturing right.

The Treatment of Infringements affects the Content of Copyright.

Since the copyright in a work is, from one point of view at least, merely the right to prevent all forms of reproduction that are forbidden, its content necessarily varies with the provisions of the law as to what constitutes infringement. The Convention, while leaving the rule of Art. 2 in general operation, lays down special rules as to how far certain classes of works, which are on the border line between the infringing and the lawful, *e.g.* educational treatises containing extracts from copyright works, are to be allowed. These rules however look directly to the derivative work—deciding whether it is or is not lawful—and only by way of consequence to the original—deciding whether its copyright does or does

---

[1] Great Britain, though it regards the lecture as published from the time of first delivery in public, dates its protection under the Literary Copyright Act from the time of first publication in printed form.

not extend to prevent the particular form of reproduction.[1]
They are therefore appropriately treated in Chapter V. on
'Infringements, Remedies, and Procedure.' It only needs
to be pointed out here that that Chapter, so far as it deals
with infringements, is a necessary complement to this.

[1] A mere difference in *mode* of treatment leads to a difference in legal theory,
and may lead to a difference in the substance of the law. Thus a prohibition of
works of a given class would be construed strictly, while a statement that
copyright included the right to prevent works of a given class would be
construed liberally.

SECTION II.

INVESTITIVE FACTS[1] *OF PROTECTION.*

The general conditions of protection—The country of origin—Simultaneous publication—Posthumous works—The investitive facts of protection—Work enjoying domestic copyright in several countries—Simultaneous publication within and outside the Union—Constructive simultaneity—The conditions and formalities of the country of origin—Ambiguity of 1886 text—Can other conditions and formalities be required?—What amounts to publication—The International definition—The English rule as to publication—Need for unanimous agreement—The Convention rule for unpublished works—Territoriality as applied to unpublished works—Von Bar's theory of potential publication—Practical reasons against this.

THE GENERAL CONDITIONS OF PROTECTION.

In a description of the protection given by the Convention, its conditions and duration are as important as its actual nature. The rules which determine the coming into existence and the expiration of protection affect its character as much as those which determine its content. The Articles of the Convention which treat of the investitive facts of protection are Arts. 2 and 3, and the principles they lay down are very simple. An unpublished work has a right to protection if its author belongs to a Union country (Art. 2, § 1); a published work if the first publication took place in a Union country, whether the author belong to a Union

---

[1] The expression ' investitive facts ' is borrowed from Bentham, who uses it to denote ' those facts on which, by the dispositions of the law, rights arise or come into being,' while he employs the counterpart, ' divestitive facts,' to denote ' the facts upon which rights terminate or are extinguished.'—Austin, *Jurisprudence*, vol. ii., p. 882.

country or not (Art. 2, § 1, and Art. 3).[1]   Probably all
works published in Union countries can claim translating
right under Art. 5, though that Article appears to apply
only to 'authors belonging to any country of the Union':
for Art. 3 gives non-Unionist authors of such works the
(whole) protection of the Convention and not merely that
of Art. 2.   In no case can the right to protection become
effective—in no case does copyright under the Berne Convention vest—until the conditions and formalities of the country
of origin have been fulfilled (Art. 2, § 2) ; and, from the
Interpretative Declaration, it is clear that these are the only
conditions and formalities which can be required.

The Country of Origin.—Published works are, according to
the general system of the Convention, identified with the
country in which they make their first appearance.   For them
the country of origin is determined by Art. 2, § 3, to be the
country of first publication.   In the case of unpublished works,
the territorial principle will not hold, and for these, therefore,
it is necessary to fall back upon the test of nationality.   By
Art. 2, § 4, the country of origin of an unpublished work is
the country to which its author belongs.

Simultaneous Publication.—When a work is published simultaneously in two or more countries of the Union, the Convention
adopts an artificial criterion for determining the country of
origin, which is defined as the country that grants by its
domestic law the shortest term of copyright (Art. 2, § 3).[2]

---

[1] Art. 2 protects only such of the published works of Unionist authors as have
first appeared in Union countries.   Art. 3 protects such works of *non-Unionist*
authors as have first appeared in Union countries.

[2] The reason of this is doubtless connected with the rule which limits the
duration of Convention copyright in each country to the term of protection
accorded in the country of origin.   Any one of the countries in which the simultaneous publication takes place may be considered the country of origin, and the
one which a State wishing to perform no more than its bare duty under the
Convention would naturally choose, in the absence of express provision, would be

Posthumous works are protected by Art. 2, § 5.[1] This clause was added by the amending Act of Paris; it only serves to make clear what was under the old Convention a matter of fair inference.

The investitive facts of protection.—The following table gives a clear idea of the 'investitive facts of protection' :—

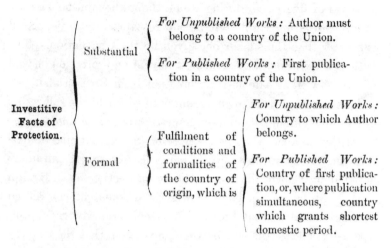

Investitive
Facts of
Protection.

Substantial

For Unpublished Works: Author must belong to a country of the Union.

For Published Works: First publication in a country of the Union.

Formal

Fulfilment of conditions and formalities of the country of origin, which is

For Unpublished Works: Country to which Author belongs.

For Published Works: Country of first publication, or, where publication simultaneous, country which grants shortest domestic period.

Work enjoying domestic Copyright in several countries.—From the point of view of the rule laid down for the determination of the country of origin, it is interesting to consider the position of a work receiving domestic protection from two or more countries at the same time. The case may be taken of a work published in Spain—which country protects all works first appearing in its territory—by an author domiciled in Switzerland, which protects all works of persons domiciled

the one granting the shortest term of protection. The Convention makes a specific disposition on the matter, in order to prevent misunderstanding. According to the theory upon which the rules of Art. 2 are based, it would be an anomaly for any country to be obliged to continue its protection of a foreign work, after the moment at which it is able to point to any country of origin and say that there the copyright has expired.

[1] 'Posthumous works are included among the works protected.'

within it.[1] Both countries accord to the work the protection of
their domestic law ; the question is whether either is bound to
grant it the protection provided for by the Convention, which
in some respects exceeds that of the domestic law.   The Swiss
domestic term of translating right, though equal to that given
in the original work, is subject to a restrictive period (*délai
d'usage*) of five years, during which the author must make use
of his translating right if it is not to lapse, and this period
is shorter than the similar one given by the Convention.   The
author will thus gain by securing Convention protection instead
of—or as well as—domestic protection from Switzerland.

It is of course open to any country to withhold the full rights
of the Convention from purely domestic works ; but no country
is entitled to abate the due measure of its international obligations merely by calling a work domestic, when under an international agreement it is entitled to protection as a foreign
work.   In the case in point, Switzerland would be confronted
by the contention that the work was not properly Swiss, but
Spanish ; and as the rule of the Convention, that the country
of first publication shall be considered the country of origin,
seems to attach the work to Spain, it is probable that
Switzerland would be bound to accept this view.

The principle may therefore be laid down that when a work
is entitled to international protection under the Convention, no
grant of domestic protection to it by any country can derogate
from its international rights.

SIMULTANEOUS PUBLICATION WITHIN AND OUTSIDE THE UNION.

A nice point arises with regard to works which are simultaneously published in a Union and a non-Union country.   It

---

[1] See Part II., Chap. iv., sec. 2.

is not immediately clear whether such works can be brought within the words of Art. 2, 'published *for the first time* within one of those countries' [of the Union], for, while the author can always point to the Union country and say that first publication took place there, the country from which he claims protection can with equal force point to the non-Union country and say that the work first appeared outside the Union.

The Convention itself does not directly assist to settle the question. It certainly says that, when publication takes place simultaneously in several countries *of the Union,* the one granting the shortest term of domestic protection shall be considered as country of origin, but this rule applies only in cases where the countries of simultaneous publication all belong to the Union. Its object is merely to define the position of works simultaneously published, in respect of the requirement of the conditions and formalities of the country of origin and the limitation to the term conceded by that country; it does not affect to determine the circumstances under which such works will gain the protection of the Convention.

On general principles, it would seem that the wish of the Union to secure literary works fresh from the hand of their authors is satisfied by simultaneous publication within its territory and outside it. It cannot well complain if non-Union countries enjoy a like advantage in respect of the same works. It is not for the International Copyright Union to adopt a 'dog-in-the-manger' policy. A work which has a Union country to stand sponsor for it to the Union should not be denied protection, on the ground that another and ineligible sponsor can also be put forward.

Though this seems the true solution, the words of the Convention leave the question open; and so each country must decide the matter for itself. It is, however, very improbable

that any country will feel itself entitled to withhold protection
from a work protected by the ordinary domestic law of the
Union country of origin.[1]

Constructive Simultaneity.—The question becomes more
complicated when, as under the English Copyright Bill, a
Union country declares that it will regard works first
published elsewhere as simultaneously published, if they are
published on its own territory within a certain term from
the date of first publication.[2] It would seem, however,
that even if a country of the Union in which a work is
actually published simultaneously with its publication in a
non-Union country can claim Convention protection for it,
no country can force other countries to recognise a mere
'constructive simultaneity' which is the artificial creation
of its own domestic law.   A recognition on the part of other
countries of any such constructive simultaneity must be a pure
matter of grace.   The question is one of some importance for
Great Britain, since there is good ground for expecting that,
when its new Copyright Bill becomes law, many authors will
take advantage of its disposition on simultaneous publication,
in order to secure domestic protection in both England and the
United States of America, with greater economy and convenience than is possible under the existing system.

[1] In the case of *Osgood McIlvaine and Co. v. Fehsenfeld* (1897) the Imperial
Court of Germany recognised the claim to Convention protection of a work
simultaneously published in England and the United States of America.—See
Le Droit d'Auteur, 1898, p. 45.

[2] Sec. 49 of the House of Lords Copyright Bill, 1900, reads: 'For the purposes of this Act, publication or performance out of the United Kingdom within
fourteen days after publication or performance within the United Kingdom shall
be deemed to be simultaneous, and *vice versa*.'

The Conditions and Formalities of the Country of Origin.

Ambiguity of 1886 text.—In the original text of the Berne Convention (1886), the first paragraph of Art. 2 suggested that the publication within the Union territory of a work of a Unionist author, previously published outside the Union, would be enough to secure it the protection of that Article.[1] It cannot be supposed that this was the intention of the Convention.[2] The Additional Act of Paris has made the position clear by altering the wording of Art. 2[3] so as to make *first* publication within the Union an express condition of protection for published works.

Can other conditions and formalities be required?—The original wording of the Convention left open another matter of considerable importance. Art. 2, § 2, in exacting the accomplishment of the domestic conditions and formalities of the country of origin, did not say that no other conditions and formalities were to be imposed. Without breach of the *letter* of the law, therefore, a country granting protection was at liberty to require foreign works to perform registration,

[1] The 1886 text reads: 'Authors belonging to any country of the Union, or their lawful representatives, shall enjoy in the other countries for their works, whether published in one of those countries or unpublished, the rights which the respective laws do now or may hereafter grant to natives,' in which, it will be observed, the phrase '*first* published' does not appear.

[2] It is of course open to Union countries to grant any protection in excess of that of the Convention, which is only a *minimum*. When a work published in Roumania was reproduced in Germany, and thence exported to Belgium, where all foreign works are protected by the domestic law, that country protected the Roumanian author against the Belgian publisher.

[3] This now reads: 'Authors belonging to any country of the Union, or their lawful representatives, shall enjoy in the other countries for their works, whether unpublished or published for the first time in one of those countries, the rights which the respective laws do now or may hereafter grant to natives.'

deposit of copies, etc., according to its own domestic rules.[1] The intention almost certainly was that, once the demands of the country of origin were satisfied, every work should at once gain copyright throughout the Union. This, however, was not made clear.

Great Britain, at any rate, considered the question an open one; and, though *Hanfstaengl v. American Tobacco Co.*,[2] affirming *Hanfstaengl v. Holloway*,[3] has for the time decided it in accordance with the almost certain intention of the Convention, these cases, turning mainly on the interpretation of the English domestic law, give little insight into the English view of the effect of the Convention. By its treaty of 1893 with Austria-Hungary, however, Great Britain is pledged to exact no further conditions and formalities for the protection of Austrian and Hungarian works than those of the country of origin.[4]

The Interpretative Declaration of Paris has at length settled the matter by declaring that 'with reference to the terms of Art. 2, § 2, of the Convention, the protection assured by the aforesaid Acts [*i.e.* the Convention and the Additional Act] depends solely upon the accomplishment, in the country of origin of the work, of the conditions and formalities which

[1] Art. 2, § 2 runs: 'The enjoyment of these rights is subjected to the accomplishment of the conditions and formalities prescribed by the law of the country of origin of the work; it cannot exceed, in the other countries, the duration of the protection granted in the said country of origin.'

[2] *Hanfstaengl v. American Tobacco Co.* (1895), 1 Q.B. 347.

[3] *Hanfstaengl v. Holloway* (1893), 2 Q.B. 1.

[4] Art. 5 of this treaty runs: 'In the British Empire and in the Kingdoms and States represented in the Austrian Reichsrath, the enjoyment of the rights secured by the present Convention is subject only to the accomplishment of the conditions and formalities prescribed by the law of that State in which the work is first published; and no further formalities or conditions shall be required in the other country. . . . In the dominions of the Hungarian Crown, the enjoyment of these rights is subject, however, to the accomplishment of the conditions and formalities prescribed by the Laws and Regulations both of Great Britain and of Hungary.'

are prescribed by the law of that country.' This rule now obtains throughout the Union, for, though Great Britain has not accepted the Declaration, it does not object to the provision in question—with which its domestic law, as settled in *Hanfstaengl v. American Tobacco Company*,[1] is quite in accord.[2]

WHAT AMOUNTS TO PUBLICATION.

The International Definition.—Clause 2 of the Interpretative Declaration defines the requirements of the Convention with respect to publication. According to it 'by *works published* is to be understood works issued to the public (*éditées*) in one of the countries of the Union. Consequently the representation of a dramatic or dramatico-musical work, the execution of a musical work, and the exhibition of a work of art do not constitute publication in the sense of the aforesaid Acts.'[3]

---

[1] *Hanfstaengl v. American Tobacco Co.* (1895), 1 Q.B. 347.

[2] The reason why Great Britain refused to accept this particular interpretation is stated on p. 111 of the *Actes de la Conférence de Paris* to be connected with colonial affairs. Canada has long been endeavouring, though so far without success, to subject all protected non-Canadian works—British, Colonial, or foreign—to certain very stringent conditions, involving, amongst other things, printing and publishing in Canada within a given period after publication elsewhere.—See Part IV., Chap. ii., sec. 3. Great Britain holds that the rule of the Interpretative Declaration is just, as is shown by the fact that it was embodied in the treaty of 1893 with Austria-Hungary.

[3] The question whether a rule imposing the formalities of the country of origin as a condition precedent to copyright can be held to necessitate the performance of such formalities as the registration and deposit of copies required by the English law has already been discussed (in Part II., Chap. iv., sec. 3). It only remains to point out here that the particular wording of the Berne Convention : 'The *enjoyment* of these rights is subjected to the accomplishment of the conditions and formalities prescribed by the law of the country of origin of the work'—might be considered to require performance, not only of those conditions and formalities which are necessary to the vesting of the right, but also of those which are necessary to its effective exercise. This would necessitate registration, though not deposit, for works first published in England. Deposit in England has nothing to do with the vesting or the exercise of the copyright in a work, and is in reality an independent obligation with separate penalties, connected with copyright only in that it attaches to the author of every original work and is imposed by the Copyright Act.

The English Rule as to Publication.—Under the English law, however, as laid down in *Boucicault v. Delafield* (1863),[1] affirmed by the Court of Appeal in *Boucicault v. Chatterton* (1876),[2] representation in public constitutes publication for dramatic works : by analogy, it would doubtless be held that the public performance of musical works constitutes publication for them, while *Blanchet v. Ingram*,[3] and *Blank v. Footman* (1888),[4] go to set up the rule that unconditional exhibition to the public has a like effect in the case of artistic works. The English interpretation of 'publication' is thus altogether at variance with that embodied in the Interpretative Declaration of Paris.[5]

The acceptance of that Declaration by England would therefore have brought its domestic law into serious conflict with its international duties ;[6] for, though, in form, to subscribe the Declaration would only have been to agree to certain rules of interpretation, in effect it would have been to promise to enforce certain rules of substantive law. The acceptance of the Interpretative Declaration would not only have compelled Great Britian to *regard* as unpublished works it has hitherto regarded as published ; it would have compelled it to *treat* as unpublished works which its own law only allows it to treat as published. All the countries of the Union except Great Britain have adopted the Interpretative Declaration.

[1] *Boucicault v. Delafield*, 1 Hem. and Miller, 597.

[2] *Boucicault v. Chatterton*, 5 Ch.D. 267.

[3] *Blanchet v. Ingram*, 3 T.L.R. 686.

[4] *Blank v. Footman*, 39 Ch.D. 678.

[5] As was pointed out in the French memorial, presented to the Conference of Paris, upon the interpretation of the word 'publication,' the language of Art. 9 of the original Convention gave rise to a strong inference in favour of the view of the majority. The French memorial also remarks that there were grave practical difficulties in the way of the application of the English interpretation. —See *Actes de la Conférence de Paris*, pp. 191 seq.

[6] See *Actes de la Conférence de Paris*, pp. 161 seq., for a statement of the divergent views entertained by England and the other members of the Union.

Anomalies caused by different interpretations.—The state of affairs set up by the lack of unanimity presents some curious anomalies.[1] Not only does the international protection granted by England to musical, dramatic, and artistic works, performed or exhibited and not yet printed, differ largely in substance from that given by the other countries, but the conditions on which the protection itself depends are different in England and other countries.

Some particular cases of this divergence will now be considered. If a Unionist author writes a play and performs it for the first time in a Union country, without issuing it in printed form, Great Britain will regard and treat it as published, while the other States of the Union, taking a different view of its character, will protect it as an unpublished work. Thus it will be secured against infringement throughout the Union, including England, though the ground of its protection will not everywhere be the same.[2]

If, however, the play, written by a Unionist author, is first produced in a non-Union country—say in the United States of America—it will not gain international protection in Great Britain, since, according to the English view, the rule of Art. 2 protecting the unpublished works of Unionist authors does not apply, for the work is published—while the rule relating to published works, which requires first publication within the Union, excludes the work, first published outside it. But the

---

[1] Some of these were brought before the notice of the Conference of Paris by Germany.—See *Actes de la Conférence de Paris*, pp. 189, 190.

[2] This difference, however, itself complicates the rule as to the application of the conditions and formalities and the term of the country of origin. Since every Union country other than Great Britain regards a work first represented in England as unpublished, while Great Britain holds it to be published, it is not clear whether or not such a country, in giving protection, is entitled to exact the accomplishment of the conditions and formalities imposed by England, the country of origin, upon *published* plays and to limit its grant of acting right by the term obtaining in England for the acting right in *published* plays. It is very possible that these questions must both be answered in the affirmative.

other countries of the Union will protect the play under
Art. 2, as the unpublished work of an author belonging to
the Union.

The position is exactly reversed when an author belonging
to a country outside the Union produces a play for the first
time within a Union country.   In this case, England will grant
protection to it, under Art. 3, as a work published within the
Union, and the other members will withhold protection, because
in their view Art. 3 does not apply, and Art. 2, which protects
the unpublished works of Unionist authors only, excludes the
work.   But if the author afterwards issues his play for the
first time in printed form within a Union country, Art. 3 will
come into general operation, and the play will thenceforward
gain protection throughout the whole of the Union,[1] including
England, where it had previously enjoyed protection.

Need for Unanimous Agreement.—The numerous anomalies
springing from such a slight divergence of opinion on a matter
of principle well illustrate the need for unanimity concerning
the interpretation of doubtful terms.[2]

The definition of publication contained in the recent
English House of Lords Copyright Bill[3] raises a hope that

---

[1] It will be seen that the rules just enunciated exclude from international protection American plays and music produced for the first time in England and
not issued in printed form.   Sir Henry G. Bergne, one of the British representatives at the Conference of Paris, holds that the other countries of the Union
would be bound under Art. 3 of the Convention to protect such plays, in view of
the fact that in England they would be regarded as published works.—See
Actes de la Conférence de Paris, p. 165, n.   But it is difficult to see how Great
Britain can force its own ideas of publication upon other members of the Union,
especially in face of the express statement of opinion embodied in the Interpretative Declaration.

[2] One of the Recommendations of the Convention of Paris was to the effect that
at the next Conference the various texts of the Convention now in force should be
made one.

[3] 'Publication means the first offering, with the privity of the owner of the
copyright, a book for sale or distributing copies of it or otherwise making it
accessible to the public.'

before long Great Britain will see its way to come into line with the general opinion of the Continent.

The Convention Rule for Unpublished Works.

Territoriality as applied to Unpublished Works.—Much of the diversity obtaining in the Union with regard to the protection of musical, dramatic, and artistic works would have been obviated if the Convention had freely extended its benefits to unpublished works, without any condition that their author should belong to a Union country. But it could hardly have been expected to take such a course. It must be borne in mind that, although the Berne Convention is a great advance on previous international treaties in the protection given to foreign works, nevertheless it is essentially a contract, and as such any advantages which it brings to third parties are merely incidental to its main objects. From this point of view, the unpublished works of non-Unionist authors can hardly be regarded as having a good claim to protection under such an agreement.

Von Bar's Theory of Potential Publication.—As we have seen, the only sound principle of protection is that which looks to the work rather than to the author, requiring that the former, not the latter, shall be connected with the country granting protection or some other State with which reciprocity obtains. At first sight, however, it seems that this principle cannot apply to unpublished works—since they have not yet established a connection with any country whatever.

But Von Bar[1] points out that the international treatment of the work should be based upon the fact that it is capable of publication everywhere—that foreign countries should look to its potential connection with their own territory rather than to its actual connection with an author belonging to another

---

[1] Von Bar, *Principles and Practice of Private International Law*, p. 754.

country,—and that therefore every State should protect un-published manuscripts, without regard to the nationality of their author. Whether the author's right in an unpublished work is regarded as a mere incident of his property in his manuscript, or whether it is looked upon as a copyright in a work hereafter to be published, it seems clear that, in theory, Von Bar's conclusion is just. It is somewhat anomalous that a country should at first withhold protection from a manuscript work on the ground that its author is an alien, and afterwards grant copyright to it because the fact of publication within the territory has supervened.

Practical reasons against this.—But, however sound this argument may be from a theoretical point of view, the Convention must pay some regard to the commercial aspect of affairs ; it cannot well adopt a course of conduct which, by giving its members no advantage over non-members, would destroy the inducement for the latter to join the Union.

In practice the intrinsic international value of the protection of an unpublished work is small. It is only of importance with regard to the fact that the work may be expected subsequently to be published. If the unpublished work of a non-Unionist author is first published in a Union country, it is reasonable to say, looking at the question retrospectively as from the date of publication, that the Convention ought to have protected the work, even in its unpublished state. In the converse case, where the work of a Unionist author is published in a non-Union country, its protection by the Con-vention before publication is proved by the result to have been undeserved. But, of course, while a work is unpublished, it is impossible to forecast with certainty where publication will take place. Any rule must be based on probability, and the probability is that an author will publish in the country to which he belongs.

SECTION III.

THE TERM OF PROTECTION.

The general rule as to duration of protection—Difficulties of application in certain cases—The rule of the Convention : Article 2—A disadvantage attaching to simultaneous publication—Illustrations of this—Difficulty created by introduction of life term—General advantage of simultaneous publication—Case where both countries give same domestic period—Case where one country subsequently extends its period—Simultaneous publication within and outside the Union—Term of translating right—Author's restrictive translating period—Copyright in translations—Translating right under Art. 5—Case where domestic translating term less than that of the Convention—Effect of the Convention of 1886—Term of translating right under the English Act of 1886—Exceeded that given by 1886 Convention —Convention term extended by Additional Act of Paris, 1896—Difference between the existing International rule and the English rule.

THE GENERAL RULE AS TO DURATION OF PROTECTION.

Difficulties of application in certain cases.—The general rule of the Convention as to the duration of international protection is clear enough. In the application of this rule to specific cases, however, a number of difficulties crop up, chiefly with reference to the determination of the country of origin where works are published in two or more countries of the Union, or in Union countries and non-Union countries, at the same time. It will be seen from what follows that the law of the country of origin is an important factor in the calculation of the period of protection to be accorded to each work. It is proposed, therefore, after giving a short account of the general rule of Art. 2, to deal with several cases in which the determination of the country of origin is complicated by simultaneous publication.

The Rule of the Convention : Article 2.—It is provided by Art. 2, § 2, that the international protection given shall not in any country of the Union exceed the term of protection accorded in the country of origin. Hence each country is merely required to grant to foreign works either the domestic period which it grants by its own law to native authors, or that granted by the law of the country of origin of the work, whichever is the shorter.[1] It is only reasonable that, if a country protecting foreign works under an international treaty, it should withhold nothing of what under the domestic law it conceives to be due to works of its own; but it is hardly to be expected that any country will continue to accord rights to a foreign work after the country of origin has shown, by terminating its own protection, that it considers the claims of the work to have been satisfied.

Under the rules of the Convention the determination of the country of origin is perhaps of even greater importance in respect of duration than in respect of the conditions and formalities to be fulfilled—but of course the country of origin for the one matter is the country of origin for the other, and what has been previously said on the point in reference to conditions and formalities holds good in reference to duration.

[1] In attempting to carry out the provisions of the Convention the English International Act of 1886 has gone beyond them. Sec. 2 (iii.) of that Act enacts that 'The International Copyright Acts and an order made thereunder shall not confer on any person *any greater right* or longer term of copyright in any work than that enjoyed in the foreign country in which such work was first produced.' The ordinary construction of these words would limit the *content*, as well as the duration, of the copyright granted to foreign works by the law of the country of origin, and would thus, *e.g.* result in the withholding of performing right from plays published in a country like Japan, which does not recognise performing right. See Sec. 1 of this Chapter.

A Disadvantage attaching to Simultaneous Publication.—This seems the appropriate place to point out that the Convention rule as to the country of origin in cases of simultaneous publication renders it of questionable advantage for an author to make simultaneous publication in two or more countries which differ in the period of protection accorded. Where this course is adopted, so soon as the domestic copyright in the work expires in the country which gives the shortest period, the international protection of the work throughout the Union will also cease and determine ; for that country of simultaneous publication which grants the shortest term of protection by its domestic law is to be considered the country of origin, and in no country can the term of international protection exceed the term of domestic protection given in the country of origin. If, on the other hand, an author publishes in the country which gives the longest period and afterwards in the others, the decisive term will be the longest period instead of the shortest.

Illustrations of this.—Thus if an author publishes simultaneously in Germany (domestic period, author's life[1] *plus* thirty years) and in France (domestic period, author's

---

[1] **Difficulty created by introduction of life term.**—As between countries which grant protection for a certain fixed number of years, and countries which introduce the element of the author's life, some arbitrary principle, based on a calculation of each author's expectation of life, would have to be adopted for the determination of the country of origin. As a matter of fact, however, the life element enters into the laws of all the countries which are at present members of the International Union ; and though for works of sculpture Great Britain grants an absolute term of fourteen years from creation or publication (capable of prolongation if the author continues to live), and for engravings an absolute term of twenty-eight years from publication, these periods are so short that they cannot possibly enter into competition with those given by the other countries. In the case of literary works, difficulty may spring from the fact that Great Britain concedes an absolute term of forty-two years as an alternative to the ordinary one of

life *plus* fifty years), then in Belgium and Norway, the domestic period of author's life *plus* fifty years is, under the Convention, shortened by twenty years, in accordance with the rule that it shall not exceed the domestic period of the country of origin, viz. Germany.[1] On the other hand, if the author first publishes in France, and any time afterwards in Germany, however short the interval may be, he will get the full domestic term of life *plus* fifty years in both Belgium and Norway, without any reduction.

General advantage of Simultaneous Publication.—The advantage of absolutely simultaneous publication is, of course, that simultaneity secures domestic protection from each of the countries of first publication, while, when a work is published successively in two or more countries, it generally gains domestic protection in the country of first publication alone, obtaining only Convention rights from the others. Thus, the publication of a work in Spain simultaneously with its publication elsewhere will secure for the author, under the domestic law of that country, an exclusive right of translation, for a term equal to the full term in the original work, unqualified by any condition requiring the exercise of the right within a certain number of years : while if the publication is made first in the other country, and only subsequently in Spain, the author will gain no right under the domestic law of the latter, and, under the Convention, his

author's life *plus* seven years ; while, in a similar way, the law of Italy grants (for all classes of works) a period of forty years as an alternative to the ordinary one of author's life. It cannot be known at the time when a work is published whether the absolute or the life term will be the longer ; or whether the former, if it turns out the better, will be worth more than a period like that given by the law of Germany, *i.e.* life *plus* thirty years.

[1] As a matter of fact, Belgium would protect the work throughout the whole of the period which it grants to domestic works, but the protection for the increment of twenty years would depend merely on domestic law and could not be claimed under the Convention.

enjoyment of a full term of translating right in his work
is subject to the condition that that right shall be exercised
within ten clear years.[1]

Case where both countries give same Domestic Period.—The
Convention contains no rule for determining the country of
origin where simultaneous publication takes place in two
or more countries, all of which give the same domestic
period : in all probability the choice in such a case would
lie with the author, who would be entitled to claim protection throughout the Union, on fulfilling the conditions
and formalities of any one of such countries.

Case where one country subsequently extends its Period.—
Another nice point arises when a work is published simultaneously in two countries of the Union having different
domestic periods, and the one with the shorter term afterwards
legislates so as to extend it beyond that given by the other.[2]
The former country is undoubtedly the country of origin to
begin with.   Does it remain so after the positions are reversed ?
If so, is the limiting term for the duration of international
copyright in the work to consist in the domestic term as
altered or in that term as it originally stood ?   In the

---

[1] It has been suggested that in cases of simultaneous publication the author,
in order to gain protection under the Convention, is bound to perform the
domestic formalities of *each* of the countries of simultaneous publication : but the
rule that the country with the shortest term is for the purposes of the Convention
the country of origin, when combined with the rule (made plain by the Interpretative Declaration) that the conditions and formalities of the country of origin
alone need be fulfilled, seems conclusive against this.   Since the author is not
allowed to derive any benefit from the connection of his work with countries
other than that which grants the shortest term, it would be unreasonable
to make his international protection conditional on the performance of the
formalities of such other countries.

[2] This question may arise between Great Britain and Haïti when the House
of Lords Copyright Bill, granting a term of author's life *plus* thirty years,
becomes law.   Haïti's domestic period is the author's life and that of his widow,
together with twenty years from the author's death in favour of his children,
and ten years from death in favour of other heirs.

absence of any specific disposition in the Convention itself, it is impossible to attain to any final solution of these questions.

It seems clear that where the conditions and formalities imposed by the country originally granting the shorter term have been fulfilled before the alteration in the law of the other is made, an effective copyright throughout the Union has already vested, and the author cannot afterwards be required to fulfil any further formalities. Beyond this one cannot venture to be certain. From the fact that no effective right vests until the conditions and formalities of the country of origin have been fulfilled, it would appear that in any case the country which grants the shorter period at the time when the performance of these is completed is the one to be looked to in this respect; and, with regard to duration, since the aim of the Convention (Art. 2, § 3) is to allow any country protecting the work under the Convention to withdraw its protection as soon as it is able to point to *any one* country of origin and say that there protection has ceased, it is likely that the limiting period under Art. 2, § 2, is that of the country which ultimately, *i.e.* after the legislative change, concedes the shorter term. But if, before the other extends its period, the term given by it to the work has expired, it could hardly be argued that the subsequent extension revives the right.[1]

Simultaneous Publication within and outside the Union.—When a work is published simultaneously in a country within the Union and in a country outside it, the work derives any claim it may have to the protection of the Convention from the Union country alone; hence for Union purposes this is the

---

[1] It is possible that several lawful editions might have been produced in the interim, and it would be obviously unjust for subsequent events to be allowed to convert these into infringements.

country of origin.[1]   The rule of Art. 2, that the country which grants the shortest period is to be considered the country of origin is worded so as to apply only to simultaneous publication within two or more Union countries ; and, for the rest, in matters of this kind countries within the Union cannot well take any cognisance whatever of the state of affairs which may exist in countries outside it.[2]

TERM OF TRANSLATING RIGHT.   AUTHOR'S RESTRICTIVE TRANSLATING PERIOD.   COPYRIGHT IN TRANSLATIONS.

Translating Right under Art. 5.—In a later chapter the subject of translations will be considered with regard to the copyright in their text, that is, in their phraseology and form. Such works, when lawfully made, receive in each country of the Union the same protection as that given to original works. The rights thus given endure for the ordinary term of copyright, and call for no special treatment under the heading of duration ; but, apart from these rights in translations already made, the author of every protected work enjoys for a certain period an exclusive right to prevent other people from publishing translations of his work, if made without his consent.

---

[1] But if the non-Union country afterwards enters the Union, the application of the principle of retroactivity might make it necessary to determine the country of origin according to the rules which obtain in the case where the relative position of the countries of simultaneous publication is changed after the publication has taken place which has been considered above.

[2] Hence if a work is published simultaneously in the United States (primary term, twenty-eight years) and in Great Britain (term, author's life *plus* seven years or forty-two years, whichever is the longer), Spain (term, author's life *plus* eighty years) will protect it for the period given by Great Britain, though that of the United States is the shorter.

The rule as to translating right is contained in Art. 5, which, in its original form,[1] granted to authors of the Union an exclusive right of making or authorising the translation of their works until the expiration of ten clear years from the publication of the original work, and in its present shape[2] confers a conditional right of translation during the whole duration of the right in the original work.

Translating Right and Copyright in Translations.—For a period of ten years, then, the author of an original work is protected against would-be translators ; during this ten years it is left to him to decide whether he will allow his right to lapse, or whether he will make or authorise a translation, which, if published, will secure him protection against all other translations in the same language during the whole duration of the copyright in the original work, and in addition will, as we have just seen, itself gain protection *in its literary form* as an original work. This restrictive translating period of ten years, during which the author must make a translation in order to secure the full right of preventing translating into the same language, is frequently referred to in discussing the Berne Convention as the *délai d'usage*, *i.e.* the period allowed to the author in which to

[1] The original text of Art. 5, § 1, ran : ' Authors belonging to any country of the Union, or their lawful representatives, shall enjoy in the other countries the exclusive right of making or authorising translations of their works until the expiration of ten years from the publication of the original work in one of the countries of the Union.' The other paragraphs of Art. 5 have not been altered by the Additional Act of Paris.

[2] In its present amended form, Art. 5, § 1, reads thus : ' Authors belonging to any country of the Union, or their lawful representatives, shall enjoy in the other countries the exclusive right of making or authorising translations of their works during the whole duration of the right in the original work. Nevertheless, the exclusive right of translation shall cease to exist when the author shall not have made use of it within a period of ten years from the time of the first publication of the original work, by publishing or causing to be published, in one of the countries of the Union, a translation in the language for which protection is claimed.'

avail himself of his rights. As will be pointed out later, this *délai d'usage*, together with the possible extension of it to cover the whole period in the original work, is strictly not so much a derivative right as an integral part of the copyright in the original work.

If the author has produced a translation within the ten years' period, he is further protected against all other translations in the same language until the copyright in the original work is terminated by the efflux of its term. Such termination, it must be noted, rarely corresponds with the end of the term of copyright in the literary form of the authorised translation, as this dates from the publication of the translation itself, an event which may not occur till some time after the publication of the original work.

Case where Domestic Translating Term less than that of Convention.—Countries which grant to domestic works a translating period less than that of the Convention are bound to extend that period to the required length in favour of foreign works, while countries which grant more are *at liberty* to give foreign works the benefit of their generosity in the matter.[1] Countries which take the former course are in an anomalous position. They are obliged to grant to works of other countries a greater protection than they grant to their own.

This was the case with Germany until 1901, for its law as it stood before that year gave only a translating right of five years from the publication of the translation, at the same time imposing upon the author a restrictive translating period, or

---

[1] It seems to be the opinion of the International Office that the extension by any country to alien authors of its domestic rights when these exceed the rights provided for by absolute articles of the Convention like Art. 5, is more than a matter of liberty, and is in fact obligatory under Art. 2. It is difficult to hold, however, that specific rules, such as that of Art. 5, are not meant to supersede *pro tanto* the general rule of Art. 2.—See *Études sur la revision de la Convention de Berne*, p. 49.

DIAGRAMS OF TERMS OF PROTECTION UNDER THE BERNE CONVENTION.

A. ORIGINAL LITERARY WORK.

Ex. 1. First published in Germany . . . . $x(=$ A.'s life$)+$ 30 years.

2. First published in England . . . . $\Big\{$ $x(=$ A.'s life$)+7$ yrs.

         or, if longer,   42 years.

In the following examples the German period of protection is taken as a type.

B. AUTHORIZED TRANSLATIONS

(Published within 10 years of publication of original work).

(a) *Protection in the particular text only.*

Ex. 1. If translated by T. in German only, then protected in its text from any other German translation for . . . . . . $y(=$ T.'s life$)+$ 30 years.

(b) *Protection against any other translation in same language.*

Ex. 2. Protection against any other German work, however different its text . . . $z(=$ rem. of A.'s life$)+$ 30 years.

Ex. 3. If published simultaneously with original work, protection against other translations exactly that of original work . . . . . $x(=$ A.'s life$)+$ 30 years.

Ex. 4. If published 5 years afterwards . . . $x-5+$ 30 years.

Ex. 5. If published nearly 10 years afterwards . $x-10+$ 30 years.

Ex. 6. Authorized translation published within 10 years, but after A.'s death . . . . $x(=0)+$ 30 years.

(c) *Protection of the original work against translations in languages other than German.*

Ex. 7. If translated in German only, protection against other translations in other languages is . . . .   *Nil.*

C. LAWFUL TRANSLATIONS

(Other than authorized translations published within 10 years of the original work).

Ex. 1. Protection against succeeding translations in the same language, if text be different, is . . . .   *Nil.*

Ex. 2. If translated by T. in German, then

(a) Protection in its text . . . . . . $y(=$ T.'s life$)+$ 30 years.

(b) Protection against translations in other languages is . . . . . .   *Nil.*

D. PROTECTION IN *TEXT* OF TRANSLATION
COMPARED WITH THAT IN THE ORIGINAL WORK.

Original work pub^d 1900, author dying 1925 . $x(=25$ years$)+$ 30 years.

Translation pub^d 1910, translator dying 1945 . $y(=35$ years$)+$ 30 years.

E. PROTECTION UNDER THE ENGLISH ACT OF 1886.

Ex. 1. If translated in English and published within 10 years, then protected in its text from other translations in any language . $\Big)$ $y(=$ T.'s life$)+7$ yrs.

     or, if longer,   42 years.

Ex. 2. And against any other translation, however different in its text . . . . . . $\Big\{$ $z(=$ rem. of A.'s life$)+7$ yrs.

    or, if longer, 42 years, less delay in issuing translation of the original work.

Ex. 3. If English translation not published within 10 years, English protection against unauthorized translations is . .   *Nil.*

délai d'usage, of three years (or, for dramatic works, six months) within which he had to exercise his right if this was not to lapse. Norway and Sweden at the present time grant to the author of the original work, a sole translating right for ten years only;[1] but these countries have refused to add to the difficulties of their position by accepting the Additional Act of Paris. Denmark, however, in entering the International Union in 1903, accepted the Additional Act, though its translating term was then the same as that of Norway; with the result that early in 1904 a new law was passed to extend this term to the length required by the Additional Act.

Effect of the Convention of 1886.—The net result of the Convention of 1886 in its original form was to give to the author of a work the right to exclude others from translating it during a period of ten (clear) years[2] from its publication, irrespectively of whether he did or did not exercise that right. If he did exercise it, the author was still able to prevent the making of other translations for the rest of the period of ten years, and, in addition to this, he got (Art. 6) a distinct right in the literary form of his translation for just as long a term as if the translation had been an original work. That is to say, until the end of the ten years he had a right to prohibit all translations whatever : while, after this, he had a

---

[1] In Norway, however, the author gets a term of translating right equal to the full term of copyright, in respect of translations published simultaneously with the original work, or within a year from the publication of the latter.

[2] The main disposition of Art. 5 is contained in its first paragraph, set out above. The rest of the Article, which was left untouched by the Additional Act of Paris, runs : ' For works published by instalments, the period of ten years does not begin to run until the publication of the last instalment of the original work. For works composed of several volumes published at intervals, as well as for reports or papers published by literary or learned societies or by individuals, each volume, report, or paper, is, with regard to the period of ten years, considered as a separate work. In the cases provided for by the present Article, the 31st December of the year in which the work was published is considered as the date of publication for the purpose of calculating the period of protection.'

right, for as much of the ordinary term of copyright as was
left unexpired since the publication of the translation, to prohibit all such translations as were copied directly from his
own rendering, and did not go back to the ultimate source,
i.e. the original work.[1]

TERMS OF TRANSLATING RIGHT UNDER THE ENGLISH ACT OF 1886.

English term exceeded that given by 1886 Convention.—The
English International Act of 1886 (Sec. 5, sub-sec. 1), however, went beyond the provisions of the Convention in respect
of translating right, and gave to the author the *same* right of
preventing the production in and importation into the United
Kingdom of unauthorised translations of his work, as of preventing the production and importation of the original, but
with the proviso that, if no authorised translation in English
appeared within ten clear years from the publication of the
original work,[2] the right to prohibit unauthorised translations
should cease.   It also enacted, by Sec. 5 (iii), that lawfully
produced translations should have the same protection as that
granted to original works (*i.e.* should be protected against
copying, though not against other translations directly made
from the original work).[3]

---

[1] Take as an example the case where the author published a translation three
years after the publication of the original work.   For seven years (*i.e.* until ten
years had elapsed since the first appearance of the original) no other person could
make any translation whatever.   After that time, anyone might translate from
the original: but no person might publish a copy of the author's translation in
any country, until three years had elapsed from the expiration of the copyright
in the original in that country.   See Diagrams on p. 28.

[2] Or within any other term provided by the Order in Council.

[3] The text of Sec. 5 of the International Copyright Act, 1886, is as
follows : ' (1) Where a work being a book or dramatic piece is first produced in

Hence, the effect of the Act was : (1) to give to the author a clear term of ten years, during which he would be protected against all unauthorised translations of his work ; (2) upon the production during that term of an authorised translation in English, to make that exclusive period of protection capable of extension, so as to be co-terminous with the period in the original work ; and (3) by the side of this, to grant a right for the ordinary term of an original work[1] in the text of every translation, whether made by the author himself or by any others acting lawfully.

Convention term extended by Additional Act of Paris, 1896.— In its draft of amendments presented to the Conference of Paris in 1896, the French Government proposed that the term of translating right under the Convention should be extended to cover the whole duration of the copyright in the original work ; or, if the Conference could not agree to such a great advance, that the assimilation of the two rights

a foreign country to which an Order in Council under the International Copyright Acts applies, the author or publisher, as the case may be, shall, unless otherwise directed by the order, have the same right of preventing the production in and importation into the United Kingdom of any translation not authorised by him of the said work as he has of preventing the production and importation of the original work. (2) Provided that if after the expiration of ten years, or any other term prescribed by the order, next after the end of the year in which the work, or in the case of a book published in numbers each number of the book, was first produced, an authorised translation in the English language of such work or number has not been produced, the said right to prevent the production in and importation into the United Kingdom of an unauthorised translation of such work shall cease. (3) The law relating to copyright, including this Act, shall apply to a lawfully produced translation of a work in like manner as if it were an original work. (4) Such of the provisions of the International Copyright Act, 1852, relating to translations as are unrepealed by this Act shall apply in like manner as if they were re-enacted in this section.'

[1] Not of *the* original work, for, after the copyright in this had determined, there would still be a period, varying in length with the time when the translation was issued, during which the translation would be protected in its text ; the two would coincide in the solitary case where the author published a translation at the same time as his original work. See Diagrams on p. 328.

should be made conditional upon the exercise of his right
by the author during a restrictive translating period (*délai
d'usage*) of twenty years from the first publication of the
original work. Germany, which, having then a very small
domestic term of translating right, was contemplating the
extension of this to equal the duration of the copyright in
the original work,[1] lent its support to the proposal for complete
assimilation. Great Britain, however, in view of the state of
its law, as set out above, stood in the way of this, urging
that its adoption would have the effect of preventing new
States from joining the Union. In the result, the Conference
accepted an Article framed on the lines of the English International Act (Sec. 5). This, as has been pointed out before,
provides for the assimilation of translating right to the copyright in the original work, subject to a restrictive translating
period of ten years.

**Difference between the existing International Rule and the
English rule.**—The only substantial difference in effect between
the provision of the Convention and that of the English Act is
that, while the latter will apparently, for the remainder of the
term of copyright, protect a work of which an authorised
translation in English has appeared during the restrictive
period of ten years against other translations in any language
whatever, the Convention as revised protects works of which
authorised translations have appeared during the restrictive
period, against other translations *in the same language* only.[2]
In the case of a translation appearing in English within the

---

[1] This extension has since been carried out by the Act of the 19th June, 1901
(Sec. 12).

[2] See Diagrams on p. 328. A minor point of difference is that for a book
published in numbers the English Act dates the restrictive period separately for
each number from the time of its publication, while the Convention, both in its
original and in its revised form, dates the restrictive period for the work as a
whole from the publication of the last number.

restrictive translating period, the Convention would therefore only extend to prevent other translations in that language, whilst, on the other hand, in the case of a translation appearing in any other language than English, it would nevertheless require England to forbid other translations in the same tongue.

CHAPTER IV.

WORKS PROTECTED BY THE BERNE CONVENTION.

SECTION I.

VARIOUS DEGREES OF PROTECTION ACCORDED.

The need for a general definition—Protection of 'literary and artistic works'—National views differ as to the character of various works—Special treatment accorded to certain works—The various modes of treatment adopted—The Convention divides works into three classes.

THE NEED FOR A GENERAL DEFINITION.

Protection of 'Literary and Artistic Works.'—The International Union, as the Convention sets out in Art. 1, has for its object the protection of 'the rights of authors over their *literary and artistic works.*' It is essentially a *Copyright* Union, and so, while all works susceptible of copyright fall within its range, it does not concern itself with any others. If then the phrase 'artistic works' be taken, in the broad sense, to include musical and dramatic productions, the statement in the opening Article adequately expresses the aim and functions of the Union.

National views differ as to the character of various works.—
The varying tastes and modes of thought of different countries
naturally lead them to place the same species of work in
different categories : so that while one State, such as Germany,
makes incorporation into an industrial work the criterion of
the industrial character of an ambiguous work, such as a
chromo-lithograph, another, like France, makes the question
depend upon whether the work itself is employed for industrial
purposes.[1]

Such inevitable divergences of view presented some difficulty
to the framers of the Convention.   It seemed hardly just to
allow a member of the Union to refuse protection to a work
generally adjudged literary or artistic, on the plea that its own
law took, if not an unenlightened, at any rate an anomalous,
view of the matter.   The difficulty was met by the insertion
of a comprehensive definition of 'literary and artistic works'
in Art. 4 of the Convention.[2]   The question of the precise
relation of this definition to the rule of Art. 2, that the rights
to be accorded by each country to authors of works protected
by the Convention shall be those which by its domestic law it
grants to natives, will be discussed in a subsequent section.
It is sufficient here to say that the express inclusion of Art. 4
in the Convention shows that the definition therein contained
was meant to take effect as a rule, binding either legally or
morally.

[1] This latter view, however, is a subject of controversy even in France.—
See *Le Droit d'Auteur*, 1899, pp. 132, 133, also the French case *May's Sons v.
Landsberg*, reported in the same volume, p. 134.

[2] 'The expression " literary and artistic works " comprises books, pamphlets,
and all other writings; dramatic or dramatico-musical works, and musical compositions, with or without words; works of design, painting, sculpture, and
engraving ; lithographs, illustrations, geographical charts ; plans, sketches, and
plastic works relating to geography, topography, architecture, or to the sciences
in general ; finally, every production whatsoever in the literary, scientific, or
artistic domain which can be published by any mode of impression or reproduction whatever.'—Art. 4, Berne Convention.

The Special Treatment Accorded to Certain Works.

The various modes of treatment adopted.—In respect of certain matters, however, such as photographs, the views and opinions of the members of the Union were found to be so much at variance that it became necessary definitely to concede to each country the right to deal with them in the manner adopted by its domestic law. The Convention expressly recognises the doubtful claim to copyright of these debated works, and, refusing to set up a common standard, requires each country to regulate its international protection by the rules of its ordinary domestic law.

Certain other classes of works are, with or without conditions, specifically deprived of protection, as is the case with the several kinds of newspaper matter mentioned in Art. 7. Rightly or wrongly, these are regarded as cosmopolitan property, and their diffusion throughout the world is considered to stand precedent in importance to the creative interest of the individual author in the particular form in which he has clothed them.

In the last place, there are certain derivative works, *i.e.* works which, while original in form, derive their substance directly from other works previously published. Of this nature are translations and photographs of works of art. The anomalous character of such works—from one point of view original, and from another unoriginal—coupled with their paramount international importance, entitled them to special treatment ; and so the Convention has specifically assured to them an absolute protection.

These derivative works are merely particular cases of the works embraced in Art. 4. If that Article is legally binding, their peculiar mode of creation, which might give rise to doubt, accounts for their special treatment ; while, if, on the other hand, the general definition of 'literary and artistic works' has only a moral force, they doubtless owe their special legal protection to the fact that they are objects which have pre-eminent claims to international recognition.

The Convention divides Works into three Classes.—Putting aside such works as these for the moment, the Convention deals with the works which fall within its scope in three distinct ways :

(1) The majority it includes in the general definition of Art. 4, and (according to the view taken of the force of that Article) either protects directly or holds out as objects worthy of general protection ;

(2) As to several, it expressly permits each country to decide for itself whether they shall be protected or not, according to the rule applied in the case of domestic works ; and

(3) A few it specifically deprives of protection.

In order to estimate accurately the material results of these differences in mode of treatment, it is necessary first to examine Art. 4, which has also an independent importance, in that it affects to determine the range of the whole Convention.

SECTION II.

THE GENERAL DEFINITION OF ARTICLE 4.

The form of the Article—Five classes of works enumerated—Concluding definition—History of Article 4—Meaning of *enfin*—Defects of the definition—Ambiguity of the Article—Its force—D'Orelli's view that it is part of the *jus cogens minimum*—The opposite view—Intermediate theories of Darras and Kohler—Criticism of Kohler's view—Criticism of Darras' view—Criticism of D'Orelli's view—The special treatment of photographs and choregraphic works—The true object of Article 4—Effect of Article 4 on domestic legislation.

THE FORM OF THE ARTICLE.

Five Classes of Works enumerated.—A reference to Art. 4 will show that in form it clumsily combines enumeration with definition proper. It begins with a statement that the expression 'literary and artistic works' comprehends the following five classes of works : (i) books, pamphlets, and all other writings ; (ii) dramatic or dramatico-musical works and musical compositions with or without words ; (iii) works of design, painting, sculpture, and engraving ; (iv) lithographs, illustrations, geographical charts ; and (v) plans, sketches, and plastic works, relating to geography, topography, architecture, and the sciences in general.

Concluding Definition.—Then, any *lacunae* which might be found in this enumeration are provided for by a generalisation of the whole class, the species of which have just been set forth : 'Finally, every production whatsoever in the literary, scientific, or artistic domain which can be published by any mode of impression or reproduction whatever.'[1]

History of Article 4.—Little discussion was expended on the wording of the Article at the Conferences of Berne. It is substantially a reproduction of Art. 1 of the Franco-German Treaty of 1883, and of the Franco-Italian Treaty of 1884.[2] The Conferences allowed themselves to be guided by the experience of former negotiators, and did not undertake the task of framing a new definition for themselves. The Article in the Swiss Federal draft was accepted almost as it stood, the only amendments being the insertion of 'illustrations' and 'plastic works relating to geography, topography, architecture, or to the sciences in general.' These additions were suggested by a question in the list submitted by the German delegates. Article 4 of the Convention has since been substantially reproduced in several treaties,[3] and domestic codes.[4]

Meaning of 'Enfin.'—The official English translation of the Convention renders the word *enfin* by the phrase 'in fact.' This, however, seems to misrepresent the intention of the Conferences of Berne. If the general definition is introduced

---

[1] The original French of the Article is as follows: 'L'expression "œuvres littéraires et artistiques," comprend les livres, brochures, ou tous autres écrits; les œuvres dramatiques ou dramatico-musicales, les compositions musicales avec ou sans paroles; les œuvres de dessin, de peinture, de sculpture, de gravure; les lithographies, les illustrations, les cartes géographiques; les plans, croquis et ouvrages plastiques, relatifs à la géographie, à la topographie, à l'architecture ou aux sciences en général; enfin toute production quelconque du domaine littéraire, scientifique ou artistique, qui pourrait être publiée par n'importe quel mode d'impression ou de reproduction.'

[2] The alterations are the insertion of 'with or without words' after 'musical compositions'; the substitution of 'sciences in general' for 'natural sciences,' and the insertion in the last clause of the Article of the words 'which can be published by any mode of impression or reproduction.'

[3] *E.g.* the Montevideo Convention, 1889 (Art. 5), and the Treaty between England and Austria of 1893 (Art. 4).

[4] *E.g.* those of Monaco and Tunis.

by the phrase 'in fact,' it loses a great deal of its force.   It
was intended to do more than merely sum up the preceding
enumeration—the object was to widen the scope of this.
Otherwise there would be little reason in making the objects
comprised in the enumeration anything more than mere
examples of the definition.   The *enfin* can only be properly
rendered by some connective word like ' finally.'[1]

Art. 4 includes five specific classes of works, and then, to
provide for possible omissions, a comprehensive descriptive
clause is inserted, embracing other modes of perpetuating the
results of intellectual labour, perhaps not yet devised.

Defects of the Definition.—In itself, the enumeration of Art. 4
is unobjectionable.   It is clear, precise, and comprehensive.
The same cannot be said of the definition, which errs in
that, attempting to interpret the expression ' literary and
artistic works,' it contains the terms to be defined ('literary' and ' artistic')—adding the limitation to ' every production which can be published by any mode of impression or
reproduction whatever' instead of an explanation—and offers
no sufficient test by which the objects comprised by those
terms can be ascertained.

Ambiguity of the Article.—A more serious objection to the
Article lies in the ambiguity which results from this very
coupling of enumeration with definition.   There is considerable
difficulty in determining the relative importance of the two
modes of expression.   It may at once be admitted that no
such recital of species as that aimed at by the authors of the
Convention can be altogether exhaustive, and that, consequently, if the method of enumeration is to be employed, some
general clause is necessary, to cover those cases that have been

---

[1] This was the opinion of such authorities as MM. Droz, Pouillet, and Lermina,
as appears from remarks made by them at the Conference of the International
Literary and Artistic Association at Berne in 1889.

omitted through oversight, or through inability to forecast the future development of thought and ideas.   But to throw such a general clause into the form of a definition is directly to impair the validity of the enumeration, while, at the same time, the employment of a definition in such a connection deprives it of the intrinsic force that it would otherwise have.   A country may regard a class of works specifically mentioned in the enumeration as out of the literary, scientific, or artistic domain, and in such a case may well refuse it protection, on the ground that the definition is paramount, and that the enumeration is meant only to illustrate its effect.

Thus the French Court of Cassation in *May's Sons v. Landsberg*, 15th June, 1899,[1] gave as one of its grounds for rejecting an appeal against a judgment of the Court of Douai, which refused international protection to German chromo-lithographs, ' That even if this Article (4) of which the object is to define the expression "literary and artistic works," contains an enumeration of works of this kind, amongst which works of design and of painting are included, this enumeration is not restrictive and is not of an imperative and absolute character ; indeed, the last paragraph of Art. 4 indicates that the Convention is to be applicable to every production whatsoever in the literary, scientific, or artistic domain which can be published by any mode of impression or reproduction whatever, and the application of the Convention is always subject to one condition, viz. that the work is a literary or artistic work ; it is only to protect works of this character that the treaty of Berne has been concluded ; and hence it is not enough that a publisher should present any design whatever in order to be in a position to claim the benefit of the treaty, which can only be accorded to him if the design produced is an artistic work.'

[1] See *Le Droit d'Auteur*, 1899, p. 134.

It has been urged that this reading of Art. 4 is wrong ; [1] but in any case it is clear that the peculiar form in which that Article is couched is itself, in part at least, responsible for the ambiguity which rendered such a construction possible.

On the other hand, a country might justifiably take the view that the definition was meant simply to provide for *lacunae* in the enumeration, and therefore that objects comprised in the wording of the former are not entitled to protection, unless they are either specially mentioned in the latter or are akin to some object that is so mentioned. The definition would thus be construed narrowly as a sort of amplification of the enumeration; and the fact that a work was considered to be in the literary, scientific, or artistic domain would not of itself be enough to secure it protection. There is little to be said in favour of either of these two readings of Art. 4. It is sufficient here to point out that both are possible.

The Force of Article 4.

The objections to the form of Art. 4 hold good whatever its actual force. If it imposes on every Union country an obligation to protect all the works it comprises, its faults provide an excuse, if not a justification, for the withholding of protection from some of these ; while if its object is merely to indicate the sense attached by the International Union as a whole to the phrase 'literary and artistic works,' its ambiguity prevents it from adequately fulfilling its purpose. Assuming, however, that the meaning of the Article may be definitely ascertained, there yet remains the difficulty of determining the extent to which it is binding.

The clear object of the Union (Art. 1 of the Convention)

---

[1] See *Le Droit d'Auteur*, 1899, pp. 130 seq.

is to protect 'the rights of authors over their literary and artistic works.' Art. 4 affects to determine the meaning of literary and artistic works. Is it then part of the *jus cogens minimum* of the Convention—does it compel the countries of the Union to grant protection to the works it comprises,—or does its force in any way fall short of this?

D'Orelli's view that the Article is part of the 'jus cogens minimum.'—Upon this question several theories have been put forward. On one side the extreme view was taken by the late M. D'Orelli, formerly Professor of law in the University of Zürich, who was one of the Swiss delegates to the Berne Conferences of 1884 and 1885. According to his interpretation, Art. 4 is part of the *jus cogens minimum* of the Convention, both its parts are equally obligatory, and all members of the Union are obliged, not merely to recognise its validity as a definition of literary and artistic works, but to give protection to all the works it comprises, independently of the state of their domestic law, and, presumably, also of that of the country of origin.[1] This in spite of the rule of Art. 2 which exacts from each country merely the same protection for the works of Unionist authors as that granted to natives by the domestic law, and limits the duration of protection by the period given by the country of origin. As regards that Article, it is to be presumed that D'Orelli held that its function was merely to determine the *kind* and *amount* of protection to be given, while the question whether protection should be given at all was to be decided by Art. 4 alone.

In this view every State is supposed to give some domestic protection to the 'literary and artistic works' of Art. 4, and the fact that it does not do so is not to entitle it to neglect the

---

[1] As to the law of the country of origin the position taken up by D'Orelli is not clear from his articles (cited below) in *Le Droit d'Auteur*; but M. Darras, whose theory is a modification of that put forward by D'Orelli, holds that, so far as Art. 4 is obligatory, it is independent of all domestic law.

international duties which it has implicitly pledged itself to perform by subscribing to an Article purporting to determine the scope of the Convention.

This theory was suggested in an undeveloped form by M. D'Orelli at the second sitting of the Berne Conference of 1885, when the draft of Art. 4 was under discussion. France had proposed that photographs should be included in the enumeration of the Article, and Italy had made a similar suggestion with regard to choregraphic works. Upon a statement by M. Reichardt, the German delegate, to the effect that, since its law did not regard photographs as artistic works, Germany could not consent to this, MM. Renault and Lavollée, the French delegates, remarked that they did not see how any inconvenience would result to that country from the inclusion of the works in question, since Art. 4 was entirely subordinate to Art. 2, and therefore no country was obliged to grant international protection to works of Art. 4 unprotected by its domestic law. In reply, M. D'Orelli, with M. Reichardt, stated that he considered Art. 4 to be absolutely imperative. Sir Henry Bergne, who represented England, thereupon suggested that a general definition would be preferable to the enumeration contained in that Article.[1] Ultimately photographs were dealt with separately, though it is doubtful whether this fact can be taken to imply adhesion on the part of the Conference to M. D'Orelli's views. The whole discussion is valuable, as illustrating the position taken up by the various countries, and the division of opinions which has prevailed from the first.[2]

The opposite view.—The theory which stands at the opposite extreme from that of D'Orelli seems to have been held by

---

[1] See *Actes de la Conférence de Berne*, 1885, p. 22.

[2] See *Le Droit d'Auteur*, 1889, p. 2, and 1891, p. 15, for a subsequent statement of D'Orelli's view.

the French delegates.   According to this, Art. 4 merely states
the scope which it was intended that the Convention should
have: all members of the Union are required to recognise
that the works comprised in the Article are objects to which
the Convention applies, but from the very fact that the Convention, and with it the rule of Art. 2, applies to them, no
country is bound to grant international protection to any of
these objects, unless by its national law it protects domestic
works of the same character.

The force of the authoritative interpretation of ' literary
and artistic works' is thus rather to prevent any State of
the Union, which by its domestic law grants protection
to works of a given character as literary or artistic, from
refusing them international recognition on the ground that
such works are outside the protection of the Convention,
than to compel any State which excludes such works by its
domestic law to concede such recognition on the ground that
the Convention expressly requires it.

Darras considers that the enumeration alone is binding.—
Reason will be adduced later for the belief that this view is
the right one.   Meanwhile two intermediate theories must be
noticed and dismissed.   MM. Darras,[1] Nicolau,[2] and others,[3]
hold that the *enumeration* of Art. 4 is part of the *jus cogens
minimum* of the Convention, and is binding on all countries
irrespective of the state of their domestic law, and of that of
the country of origin of the work, while the *definition*—the
enfin clause—is so general that it is practically subject to

---

[1] *Du Droit des Auteurs et des Artistes*, pp. 535, 536.

[2] Nicolau, *La Propriété littéraire et artistique*, p. 79.

[3] The view taken by the International Office seems to be that, without regard
to the state of their domestic law, countries are obliged to protect all works
specifically mentioned in Art. 4 which are protected in the country of origin—
while, for other works, protection need be granted only if the domestic laws of
the foreign country and the country of origin agree in recognising their copyright character.—See *Le Droit d'Auteur*, 1899, pp. 132, 133 ; and 1900, p. 35.

the rules of Art. 2, assimilating international protection in each country to that given to native authors, and limiting it by that of the country of origin in respect of duration and conditions and formalities.

Kohler adopts interpretation of Country of Origin.—M. Kohler[1] would make the rule as to the country of origin absolute in every case, so that no work comprised in Art. 4 should gain protection in any country, unless it was protected (as a literary or artistic work) in its country of origin. On the other hand, all works comprised in Art. 4 which satisfied the condition of protection in the country of origin would be entitled to protection throughout the Union, even in countries which refuse to recognise the literary or artistic character of similar domestic works.

Criticism of Kohler's view.—The cardinal objection to these two theories is that they attach varying degrees of importance to different parts of the same Article. M. Darras treats the enumeration of Art. 4 in one way and the definition in another, while M. Kohler does the same in respect of the two rules of Art. 2, that international protection in each country is to follow domestic protection and that it is to be limited as regards conditions and formalities, and duration, by the rules in force in the country of origin.

The latter assumption is without any support whatever from the wording of Art. 2. No doubt it is a fundamental principle of the Convention that no work which is unprotected, or which has ceased to be protected, in its country of production shall enjoy protection internationally ; but, with equal certainty, it is a fundamental principle of the Convention that a work protected by it shall only enjoy in each country the ordinary domestic rights. If then Art. 4 is regarded as imperatively

---

[1] *Die Immaterialgüter im internationalen Recht (Zeitschrift für internat. Privat-und Strafrecht)*, 1896, p. 350, cited in *Le Droit d'Auteur*, 1899, p. 132.

demanding international protection for the works it comprises, why should its inconsistency with both rules of Art. 2 be explained at the expense of one and not at that of the other ? Why should it be incumbent on a country to protect one of the works of Art. 4 when the sum of the rights which are granted to natives in such a work stands at zero, and not when the period of protection conceded in the country of origin stands at zero ?

Criticism of Darras' view.—For M. Darras there is more to be said. The anomalous form of Art. 4 does afford some justification for supposing that its two parts were meant to have different degrees of binding force, and if M. Darras went only so far as to assert that, both parts being imperative, the vagueness of the latter allows of considerably more latitude of interpretation on the part of the various domestic tribunals than is possible with the former, he would doubtless receive the cordial support of those who believe that the result of Art. 4 is to do more than merely interpret ' literary and artistic works ' ; although in that case his theory would consist simply in a statement of the obvious. He seems, however, to go further ; for he says definitely[1] that, in his opinion, while the works mentioned in the enumeration are to receive an absolute protection, those embraced in the definition ' need be protected only if the laws of the countries of origin and of importation are agreed in safeguarding the rights in them.'

In order to confute this theory, it seems sufficient to say that, whatever the difference in form between the two parts of Art. 4, they are both employed in the elucidation of the phrase ' literary and artistic works,' that there is nothing in the Convention to justify the attaching to them of any difference in binding force, and that, on the contrary, the introduction

---

[1] Darras, *Du Droit des Auteurs et des Artistes*, p. 536.

of the definition by the word *enfin* goes to show that it
was intended as a summation of and complement to the series
of works mentioned in the enumeration. M. Darras indeed
practically admits as much when he treats[1] a similar Article in
the Franco-German agreement of 1883 as forming one homogeneous whole.

Criticism of D'Orelli's view.—We may then conclude that
Art. 4 must be regarded as 'all of a piece,' and, the way
being thus cleared, may proceed to consider whether, in
conjunction with Art. 1 or Art. 2, or both of them, it has, as
D'Orelli thought, the effect of compelling protection for the
works it comprises. Its mode of expression—'the phrase
"literary and artistic works" *comprises*, etc.'—is certainly
that of a definition ; and, as a definition, it may be part of the
Convention *jus cogens minimum* without having the substantive
force that D'Orelli attributed to it. That is to say, it may
impose on all Union countries an absolute obligation to *regard*
all the works it comprises as 'literary and artistic works' for
the purpose of the Convention without imposing on those
countries any further obligation to *protect* such works.

By itself, this is all it affects to do ; and any attempt to
give it a greater force must be based upon a combination of it
with other articles of the Convention. The only Articles that
can be used to form such a combination are Arts. 1 and 2.
Now Art. 1 determines the function of the Union as 'the
protection of the rights of authors over their literary and
artistic works'; but this is only a general statement of the
aim of the Union, and does not of itself impose any obligation
upon its members. The binding provisions of the agreement
are contained in the subsequent Articles. Art. 2, § 1 runs :
'Authors belonging to any country of the Union, or their
lawful representatives, shall enjoy in the other countries for

---

[1] Darras, *Du Droit des Auteurs et des Artistes*, pp. 535, 579.

their works, whether unpublished or published for the first time in one of those countries, *the rights that the respective laws do now or may hereafter grant to natives.'* Art. 4 defines what is meant by ' their works,' but it is clear that works as thus defined only gain in each country the same rights as are conceded to natives. In order to support D'Orelli's theory it is necessary to assume that this rule of Art. 2 applies only to the mode in which protection is to be enforced, and has nothing to do with the giving or withholding of protection itself. But if Art. 2 does not confer protection, no other Article does ; and it is almost incredible that such a crucial matter as the general rule of protection should be left to be deduced by implication, to say nothing of the fact that no rational ground for implication of the sort can be found in any part of the Convention.

On the other hand, if Art. 2 is simply *regulatory,* it is strange that it should proceed directly by way of *conferring* rights, instead of by way of stating how far rights conferred else-where are to extend. This being so, a country surely cannot be blamed if it takes Art. 2 to mean what it says, and if, in the absence of any other provision exacting protection, it con-siders that it has fulfilled its international duties (except in certain matters of detail, *e.g.* translations, specifically regulated by other articles) when it has freely extended the benefit of its domestic law to all the ' literary and artistic works' of the Union. Where any domestic protection whatever is already given, D'Orelli himself would not have required a country to extend its domestic rights in favour of foreign works ; so that, to take an extreme case, a State in which the domestic law gave to lithographs only a week's protection would not be bound to give more than a week under the Convention. If, then, D'Orelli recognised that the rule as to the extent of protection might contract the actual protection until it became infinitely small, why should he not have recognised that it might contract it out of existence altogether ?[1] And if it cannot do this, how is the extent of international protection to be determined in respect of works to which a State denies protection by its domestic law ? If by the general rules prevailing for copyright in the country, the anomaly results that a State may be bound to give a greater protection to works in which it recognises no domestic copyright whatever than to works which it invests with some domestic copyright, though of small extent ; and if by the unfettered wishes of the protecting State, the protection becomes simply illusory.

The special treatment of Photographic and Choregraphic Works. —The whole tenor of the three Articles of the Convention which bear on the question at all is thus opposed to the theory that the result of the interpretation of 'literary and artistic works' in Art. 4 is to bind countries to grant international protection to all the works it comprises ; and it may fairly be held that a State would be justified in following the rule which issues from a natural construction of these Articles, singly and in combination. But, in order to establish the academic truth of the theory which has been implicitly adopted here, that the effect of Art. 4 is simply to provide an authoritative *definition*, nothing more, it is necessary to deal with a further argument put forward by D'Orelli, based upon the fact that photographs and choregraphic works, as to the protection of which the domestic laws of the various countries differed, were removed from the sphere of Art. 4 and made the subject of special provisions contained in the Closing Protocol to the Convention. These provisions expressly allow

---

[1] The same argument applies in respect of the rule limiting the duration of protection under the Convention to the period accorded by the law of the country of origin, which is, so far as one can gather, equally held by D'Orelli to have no effect in impairing the mandatory force of Art. 4, *i.e.* in cases where the period of the country of origin is *nil*.

countries to regulate their protection of such works by their domestic law ; and it is urged that if, where such permission was to be given, it was found necessary to provide for it expressly, it cannot exist in respect of the works comprised in the general rule.

To this contention there are two answers. The first is that the Union as a whole not being agreed in recognising the literary or artistic character of the works in question, it would hardly have acted with theoretical consistency if it had placed them in a definition or enumeration of such works on the character of which it professed to be agreed. The second and practical objection is that, if such a course had been adopted, although no country would have been obliged to grant to these works any protection which it did not give to native works of similar character, yet all countries which did give them domestic recognition would have been bound to protect them internationally, even when the national treatment of them was based on the conception that they were *industrial*, not *artistic*, works. A State which had subscribed an international recognition of photographs as artistic works could not withdraw from its international obligations under Art. 2, on the plea that, though it protected such works, it regarded them as industrial rather than artistic in character.

The same holds good with regard to the limitation of international protection in respect of conditions and formalities by the law of the country of origin of the work : no State which protected photographs and choregraphic works by its domestic law could have refused them the benefit of the Convention on the ground that, though they were in enjoyment of protection in the country of origin, that country denied to them all artistic character and treated them simply as industrial works. Those members of the Union which regarded the works in question as industrial, or as of dubious character, naturally objected to giving them protection under a *copyright* agreement ; while those which regarded them as artistic in like manner objected to binding themselves to protect works which enjoyed no *copyright*—but only a *patent-right*—in the country of origin.

The difficulty was met in the original Convention (1886) by the insertion of §§ 1 and 2 of the Closing Protocol, which bound those countries that regarded the works in question as proper subjects for copyright mutually to give them international protection.   The effect of this was to create for each class of works a sub-Union, or *union restreinte*—*i.e.* a Union within the Union proper, existing in touch with the latter, and enjoying all the advantages of its organisation and administration ; this was composed of the countries regarding the works in question as 'artistic' or 'dramatico-musical' respectively, which agreed amongst themselves to grant them reciprocal protection.   It is admitted even by M. Fliniaux, who holds that the enumeration in Art. 4 is obligatory,[1] that the effect of those two paragraphs of the final Protocol is as stated ; and this being granted, it is unnecessary to say more, in order to show that their object is distinguishable from that which in our opinion is to be attributed to Art. 4.

The true object of Art. 4.—It may in the last place be contended that, unless the object of that Article is to confer an absolute protection on the works it comprises, it can have no useful object, and becomes merely superfluous.   If, it may be asked, the obligations of each country under the Convention are regulated by Art. 2, what is the use of such an Article as Art. 4 ?   No authoritative definition of 'literary and artistic works' is necessary, since in every case the fitness of a work for protection is to be determined by the domestic law.

But, while it is simpler and easier to adopt the domestic

---

[1] Fliniaux, *La Propriété littéraire et artistique internationale*, pp. 277, 284, 285.

law of each country as the criterion of the fitness of a work for protection therein, it is clear that the force of the Convention would have been much diminished by the omission of all statement of its scope. In the first place, countries might have withheld international protection under Art. 2 from works recognised and protected by the domestic law as copyright subjects, on the ground that their literary and artistic character was not generally recognised throughout the Union, and that therefore the Convention did not apply to them. At present, Art. 4 is binding as a *definition*—though only as a definition—of the subjects which are to enjoy the benefit of the Convention, and no such plea can be urged in respect of any of the works it comprises. Then, in the manner indicated above, it also seems to result from the insertion of the Article that countries which protect any of its subjects as industrial works are not at liberty to deny them international protection, on the ground that the Convention deals only with 'literary and artistic works.' Having been designated as within its scope by the Convention itself, such works cannot be excluded from its benefits. Thus States granting any domestic recognition to a given work are prevented from alleging individual difference from the general conception of its character as excuses for the withholding of international recognition, and as much uniformity is secured as is consistent with the standard of domestic law set up by Art. 2.

Effect of Art. 4 on Domestic Legislation.—Finally, though Art. 4 does not directly enforce protection of its subjects, yet, as a definite expression of opinion as to the content of the phrase 'literary and artistic works,' to which each country has by international agreement committed itself, there is little doubt that it will react on domestic legislation and ultimately bring it into harmony with the Convention.

A A

A country in revising its law cannot well ignore the fact that it has embraced the definition of the Article, and is pledged to regard the works comprised therein as 'literary and artistic.' It is not, of course, compelled to bring its domestic definition into line with that of the Convention: but it is likely to remember that that Act is something more than a mere contract, professing as it does to form a Union for the impartial advancement of the interests of copyright throughout the world. Art. 4 has a moral force as well as a legal one.

SECTION III.

DERIVATIVE SUBJECTS OF COPYRIGHT.

Works accorded special treatment—Copyright in translations—Translations protected as original works—'Lawful translations' and 'authorised translations'—The question of translating right in translations—Copy of translation may infringe rights in original work—Copyright in translation usually outlives copyright in original work—Article 6 is part of the *jus cogens minimum*—Authorised photographs of protected works of art—Authorised photographs protected throughout the Union—History of the Convention rule—These photographs are derivative works—The Convention rule part of the *jus cogens minimum.*

Works accorded Special Treatment.—There are certain works which call for separate treatment, since, while they enter into the general terms of Art. 4, in that they belong to the 'literary, scientific, or artistic domain' and are capable of reproduction, they derive their claim to separate protection from their particular form, being substantially reproductions of other original works. Of this nature are translations, adaptations, arrangements of musical works, and photographs of works of art.[1] Such works consist in the re-presentation of borrowed copyright matter in an original form : and by reason of their derivative character their title to copyright is not quite clear. The intrinsic international importance of the three chief species

---

[1] All photographs have some claim to be protected as artistic works. Authorised photographs of protected works of art have a double claim, since they present an independent artistic character as photographs, and a derived artistic character as reproductions in a special form of other artistic works. Their derived character secures them an absolute protection, — merely as photographs they would only get a protection dependent on the view taken of them by the domestic law of each country.

just referred to rendered it highly advisable for the Union definitely to determine their position in the scheme of the Convention : hence this was not left to be regulated in accordance with the individual views of the various members of the Union, under Arts. 2 and 4, but was made the subject of separate Articles forming part of the *jus cogens minimum* of the Convention.

In the case of adaptations, arrangements of music, etc., however, where the derivative works themselves often embody a good deal of original work on the part of the adapter, the Convention proceeded by way of prohibiting unauthorised reproductions of this kind, not by way of granting protection to authorised ones. It is important to notice this, for, while an unauthorised adaptation competes to some extent with an authorised one, it does far more damage to the original work, especially when it is sold at a much lower price than the latter.

The legal position of derivative works naturally differs according to the amount of original work they contain, which may vary in quantity ; another important consideration turns on whether the borrowed matter is taken from the public domain or with the author's consent, or from some copyright work without authorisation. Looking at these factors, there are thus four classes of works to be taken into account : (1) Works containing a preponderance of original matter, together with borrowed matter, legitimately taken ; (2) Works containing a preponderance of original matter, together with borrowed matter, taken without authorisation from a copyright work ; (3) Works containing a preponderance of borrowed matter, legitimately taken ; (4) Works containing a preponderance of borrowed matter, taken without authorisation from a copyright work. Where the borrowed matter is legitimately taken, as in classes (1) and (3), there is no question of infringement. The only question left is what amount (if any) of originality is sufficient to confer on the derivative works a copyright of their own ; and with this the Convention does not directly deal. On the other hand, where the borrowed matter is taken without authorisation from a Copyright work, it is a question to be considered whether any proportion of original work to borrowed matter, however great, shall be allowed to exempt the derivative work from the charge of infringement ; and again, whether the derivative work may, under any circumstances, be a fit subject of Copyright. The Convention treats the subject from the point of view of infringement, ruling that there is an infringement where the new material is not sufficient to confer on the whole work the character of originality, but allowing each country to give effect to the reservations of its own domestic law.

This mode of treatment renders it necessary to postpone the consideration of adaptations to the next Chapter.

COPYRIGHT IN TRANSLATIONS.

The rule of Art. 6 of the Convention in respect of translations has already been touched upon, and the translating right of Art. 5 has been distinguished from the copyright in authorised translations conferred by Art. 6. The distinction is that the former avails to protect the original work against translations, while the latter protects authorised translations themselves against copying : the former is a right *against* unlawful translations, the latter a right *in* those that are lawful. The former is thus part of the content of the copyright in the original work, and as such has already been dealt with : the latter, which is a right in a derivative work, belongs to this Chapter.

Translations protected as Original Works.—Article 6 of the Convention runs :

'Lawful translations are protected as original works. Hence they enjoy the protection stipulated for in Arts. 2

and 3 as regards their unauthorised reproduction in the countries of the Union.

'It is understood that, in the case of a work for which the translating right has fallen into the public domain, the translator cannot oppose the translation of the same work by other writers.'

' Lawful Translations ' and ' Authorised Translations.'—In the First Schedule to the English House of Lords Copyright Bill dated the 18th April, 1899, where a translation of the Berne Convention is printed, the original French of Art. 6, 'Les traductions *licites* . . .' is rendered '*Authorised* translations . . .' This construction is both inaccurate and misleading. A *licit*, or lawful, translation is one that is made without any infringement of the rights of the author : an *authorised* translation one that has been prepared by the author or has received his consent. Since under the Convention (Art. 5) an author's exclusive right of translation expires if not exercised within ten clear years from the publication of the original work, when this term has expired without any exercise of his right on the part of the author, all translations are lawful whether authorised or not.[1] As Art. 6 stood in (Art. 8 of) the first draft of the Convention,[2] presented by the Swiss Federal Council to the Berne Conference[3] of 1884, it gave protection to *les traductions autorisées*, and we cannot suppose that the subsequent alteration of its wording in the Conference of 1885 was purposeless. *Authorised translations* in the English Bill is therefore a misrepresentation of *les traductions licites* : the rendering *lawful translations* is obviously correct.

---

[1] In order to be able to advertise 'author's authorised edition,' a publisher may ask an author's permission to issue a translation of his work, and may pay for it, even after the author's translating right has fallen into the public domain.

[2] Discussion led to many changes in this draft, so that the numbering of the Articles in the settled Convention differs considerably from the original numbering.

[3] See *Actes de la Conférence de Berne*, 1884, p. 49.

The Question of Translating Right in Translations.—According to one construction, the words of Art. 6—'such works enjoy the protection stipulated for in Arts. 2 and 3'— limit the substantive protection conferred on translations to that included in those Articles—though doubtless remedies and procedure are affected by such Articles as Nos. 11 and 12.[1] Hence it may be contended that lawful translations do not themselves enjoy the benefit of Art. 5 of the Convention : that is to say, that they do not gain any exclusive right of translation (apart from that which may exist in the original work). Of course no such right could avail to prevent would-be translators into another language from making this use of the original work itself, when the exclusive translating right in this had expired : but it would serve to protect the first translation from employment as the basis of any fresh translation into a language different both from its own and from that of the original. The question is not without practical importance.[2] For example, a Swiss who knew only French and German would be unable to translate an English work from the original into German : but if his task had been facilitated by a prior translation into French, he might without difficulty produce a German rendering from this. The true view seems to be that, while the first clause of Art. 6 assimilates the protection of lawful translations to that of original works, the fact that in

---

[1] Art. 11 gives the person whose name appears on a book as author a *prima facie* title to copyright—with the qualification that the Court may exact the production of an official certificate showing that the conditions and formalities of the country of origin have been fulfilled ; Art. 12 provides for the seizure of infringing works.

[2] It has been suggested that, as 'lawful' translations have copyright only in their form, not in the matter, translations of them can hardly be regarded as infringements, except with respect to the original work. It would seem, however, that to take the example given above, a Swiss who makes a translation into German from a French version of an English work avails himself of the *form* of the French version and of the *substance* of the original work, committing thereby a double infringement, unless the original has fallen into the public domain.

the following clause, which proceeds to set out the consequence, of this, they are accorded only the protection stipulated for in Arts. 2 and 3, is probably due to neglect on the part of the International Conference to perceive that Art. 5 might have some bearing on the position as well. In view of the general words, ' Lawful translations are protected as original works,' it is probable that Art. 6 covers Art. 5, from which the extension to lawful translations of a translating right of their own necessarily follows. Of course, as is explained later on by Art. 6, when the translating right of the principal work has fallen into the public domain, a translator cannot prevent others from going back to the original source and translating the work for themselves, either into the same language as that of his translation, or into a different one : but he can prevent others from *copying* his translation, and also, it is suggested, since lawful translations are to be protected as original works, from *translating* it.[1]

Copy of Translation may infringe Rights in Original Work. —So long as the exclusive translating right of Art. 5 subsists in an original work, the only lawful translations are those which have been authorised or allowed by the author of the original work ; and so long a mere copy of a lawful translation not only constitutes an infringement of the translator's rights in the latter, but forms an infringement of the author's rights in the original work as well.[2] On the other hand, a fresh translation into the same language as that of the authorised translation, though it infringes the right of the author of the

---

[1] Of course, while the copyright in the translation endures for the ordinary term, the translating right therein is, under Art. 5, limited to ten years from the publication of the translation itself, with an extension to equal the duration of the copyright in the translation itself, as regards all languages in which translations of the latter have been published within that ten years' period.

[2] Because by Art. 5 the author is given, during his translating term, the exclusive right of making or *authorising* the translation of his works ; and consequently all reproductions of the latter in a translated form to which his authorisation did not extend would be held to invade his exclusive right, even when they were derived indirectly through the medium of an authorised translation.

original work, does not infringe that of the authorised translator.

When the exclusive translating term of the author has expired, his exclusive rights with respect to translations have gone : after that, while copying a lawful translation still constitutes an infringement of the translator's rights, a fresh translation from the original work injures no one, and is itself *licit*.

Copyright in Translation usually outlives Copyright in Original Work.—It follows from the fact that a lawful translation is protected as an original work that its rights begin to run from the time of its publication, not of that of the original : so that, as already pointed out, an author's right in a translation made or authorised by him will endure for some time after his copyright in the original has expired, except in the rare case where the translation is published at the same time as the original work, when of course the two rights will expire together.

Art. 6 is part of the 'Jus Cogens Minimum.'—Art. 6 absolutely assimilates the protection of lawful translations to that of original works, leaving no latitude for domestic interpretation ; hence it forms part of the *jus cogens minimum* of the Convention.

AUTHORISED PHOTOGRAPHS OF PROTECTED WORKS OF ART.

Authorised Photographs protected throughout the Union.— The international rule as to authorised photographs of protected works of art[1] is contained in the Closing Protocol (§ 1, B) of the Convention, where it figures rather as a declaratory clause subsidiary to the general rule for photographs than as a separate provision. After granting a general protection to photographs,

---

[1] A photograph as an original work is, under the Berne Convention, as amended by the Additional Act of Paris, to be accorded protection in each country so far as the domestic law permits (see Sec. 5 of this Chapter), but in this Section we are concerned with a special class of photographs of which the claim to protection is derived from works which are themselves original.

regulated by the domestic protection in each country, § 1, B of the Protocol goes on to state that ' It is understood that an authorised photograph of a protected work of art enjoys legal protection in all the countries of the Union, within the meaning of the Berne Convention and the present Additional Act, so long as the principal right of reproduction of this work itself lasts, and within the limits of private agreements between the parties entitled.'

History of the Convention Rule.—The position of these authorised photographs, which is somewhat akin to that of authorised translations, formed a subject of discussion when the definition of ' literary and artistic works ' in Art. 4 was first considered by the 1884 Conference. In the course of the debate, M. Ulbach, one of the French delegates, remarked : ' It is well understood that even if you do not yet wish to protect commonplace (*banale*) or commercial photography, you consider the artistic photograph which reproduces a masterpiece as a reflection of that masterpiece, worthy of respect, if not in virtue of the same title, at least by a kind of distant relationship.'[1] The Conference recognised that authorised photographs of protected works of art ought to enjoy protection : but it was not until the second Conference of 1885[2] that they were made the subject of a special provision in the Protocol, expressly conferring protection upon them.

These Photographs are Derivative Works.—Photographs of protected works of art have always been placed on a footing different from that of ordinary photographs : and this is undoubtedly due to their derivative character. They are protected, not because of any special claim of their own to treatment as artistic, but because the content of the right in the original work of art embraces the right to prohibit and hence to authorise the making of copies of

[1] See *Actes de la Conférence de Berne*, 1884, p. 45.
[2] See *Actes de la Conférence de Berne*, 1885, pp. 43, 55.

it by means of photography, in a somewhat similar way to that in which the content of the right in an original literary work embraces the right to prohibit and to authorise the making of translations of it.

The position of an authorised photograph is very similar to that of an authorised translation.   So long as the principal right in the picture itself exists, it derives its protection from that right, just as an authorised translation, made within the restrictive translating period, derives protection from the right in the original ; when the principal right is lost, the photograph continues to enjoy protection as an ordinary photograph, for the remainder of the period granted in each country to ordinary photographs, in the same way as an authorised translation continues to enjoy protection under Art. 6 after the right in the original has expired.   During this final term other photographs of the same work can be made, and will themselves enjoy protection as ordinary photographs just as during the remainder of the period of Art. 6 other translations can be made which will themselves be protected in their text as lawful.

The only difference in the two cases is that, while Art. 6 definitely and in a binding manner assimilates the protection of translations properly made to that of original works, the Closing Protocol leaves the amount of protection of ordinary photographs not made from artistic works to be regulated for each country by its own domestic law.

The Convention Rule part of the 'Jus Cogens Minimum.'—While, however, the clause of § 1, B of the Protocol which deals with ordinary photographs is thus not absolute, the clause which deals with the photographs of works of art forms part of the binding minimum (*jus cogens minimum*) of the Convention.

SECTION IV.

NEWSPAPER AND MAGAZINE ARTICLES.

The original rule of the Convention (1886)—The consideration of cosmopolitan benefit—History of Article 7—The two classes of newspaper and magazine articles—Position of serial novels—Discussion of the Article amongst international societies—The Paris Amendment—Its effects— Reproduction in other newspapers or magazines alone contemplated— Systematic appropriation.

THE ORIGINAL RULE OF THE CONVENTION (1886).

The consideration of Cosmopolitan benefit.—Ordinary newspaper and magazine articles present themselves in a peculiar light to the framers of an international Convention.[1] They embody current thought and current information in a form more or less ephemeral ; and the public to which their appeal is addressed is usually the public of the country and of the hour. Hence, while the author may fairly set up a claim to protection for such articles in his own country, in the absence

---

[1] In this Section it is intended to deal with the rule laid down in the Convention of 1886, which has since been altered by the Additional Act of Paris. The present rule is treated in the next Section, but for convenience of reference and comparison its text is given here. It runs : 'Serial novels (*romans-feuilletons*), including short stories, published in newspapers or periodical magazines of any country of the Union, cannot be reproduced, in original or in translation, in the other countries, without the authorization of the authors or their lawful representatives. This applies equally to other articles in newspapers or magazines whenever the authors or publishers shall have expressly declared in the newspaper or magazine in which they have published them that they forbid their reproduction. For magazines, it is sufficient if the prohibition is made in a general way at the beginning of each number. In the absence of prohibition, reproduction will be permitted on condition of indicating the source. No prohibition can in any case apply to articles of political discussion, news of the day, or miscellaneous items (notes and jottings).'

of any express reservation on his part there is much to be urged against granting him internationally a set of rights which the form of publication suggests that he does not contemplate ; rights which might be of small advantage to himself, yet a serious deprivation to others.[1]

Any general prohibition directed against the copying by periodicals of one country of the contents of newspapers and magazines belonging to another would tend to retard the diffusion of much thought and knowledge for which only a speedy diffusion can be useful.[2] A literary work of permanent interest to the world may safely be granted a liberal period of international copyright ; but this scarcely applies to articles appearing in periodicals upon current events or current phases of thought. Such articles, though important in their own way, are frequently only of passing interest, and are rarely collected into book form, and so made accessible to the foreigner.

On account of the insight into the position and contemporaneous ideas of their country given by articles containing news and opinions of local interest, it may be highly desirable that other nations should be made familiar with them, and that they should be made accessible to the general public before their interest is lost through any delay arising from a necessity of securing consent to reproduce them from the author or the publisher. As to news of general international interest, the advantage of permitting free circulation between nations is even more obvious. As will be seen later, these considerations of cosmopolitan benefit have led

---

[1] Of course, by express reservation the author indicates that he intends to appeal to a larger public than that of his own country : and, as he is the creator of the article, he should be able to do what he likes with it. The point is, not that he has no claim to property in newspaper and magazine matter, but that, unless he expressly reserves it, there is a presumption that he does not wish to avail himself internationally of his right.

[2] The information as to the situation of affairs in a given country which is contained in articles of its own newspapers and magazines is of course much more reliable than that obtained by foreigners in other ways.

to the total exclusion of political articles, news of the day, and miscellaneous items (notes and jottings) from the protection of the Convention, while it forms the reason, just as the temporary expectations of the author form the justification, for the qualified exclusion of other newspaper and magazine articles from the benefits of international recognition.

History of Art. 7.—In the original project of the Convention, drawn up by the Swiss Federal Council and presented for the consideration of the Conference of 1884, no special treatment was meted out to the contents of newspapers and magazines. The peculiarity of their position was first indicated by Germany in the list of questions already referred to,[1] in which it was suggested that, with the exception of serial novels and works of science and art, all such contents should be left open to free reproduction.[2]   Upon discussion, the matter was sent to the Committee of Draftsmanship for examination ; and as a result an Article (then appearing as Art. 9) was drawn up, containing :

(i) A free permission to reproduce, in original or in translation, articles extracted from newspapers or periodical magazines :

(ii) A statement that this permission was not to extend to the reproduction of serial novels or articles relating to science or art ;

(iii) A similar statement with regard to other articles included in (i) to which the authors or publishers should have attached an express reservation ; and

(iv) A proviso that no such reservations could apply to articles of political discussion.

---

[1] See No. 6 of the List.—*Actes de la Conférence de Berne*, 1884, p. 25.

[2] Germany had for a long time taken a special interest in the question : thus a treaty concluded by this country with Switzerland in 1869 contained a provision upon the subject, which is again dealt with in the German law of 1870, in German treaties of 1883 with France and Belgium, and in one of 1884 with Italy.— See *Études sur la revision de la Convention de Berne*, pp. 57, 58.

The Conference accepted the Article without amendment, rejecting an earnest plea, on grounds of cosmopolitan benefit, by the delegate of Haïti for the exclusion of scientific articles from the prohibition against reproduction. As a result of the reconsideration of the Article which took place during the Conference of 1885, it was embodied as Art. 7 of the Convention, in the following final form :—

'Articles in newspapers or magazines, published in any country of the Union, may be reproduced, in original or in translation, in the other countries of the Union, unless the authors or publishers have expressly forbidden it. For magazines, it is sufficient if the prohibition is made in a general manner at the beginning of each number of the magazine.

'No prohibition can in any case apply to articles of political discussion or to the reproduction of news of the day or miscellaneous items (notes and jottings).'

The two classes of Newspaper and Magazine Articles.—So far as it goes, the result of this provision of the Convention of 1886 is clear. It divides newspaper and magazine articles into two classes : (i) those dealing with political discussion, news of the day, and miscellaneous facts, and (ii) all others. Articles included in the first class it leaves absolutely open to reproduction, while those in the second may be copied freely only when their author or publisher has not expressly forbidden it. It is necessary to explain, however, that, though the *prohibition* to copy articles comprised in (ii) which have been provided with notice of reservation is part of the *jus cogens minimum* of the Convention, and must therefore be enforced by every member of the Union in respect of foreign takings by its own periodicals, the clause relating to the general *permission* to copy other articles is optional, and each country may take advantage of it or reject it by its domestic law at will ; though, if it forbids its journals to copy these other articles, it cannot demand reciprocity from States which do not.

It is not the object of the Convention to prevent any country from forbidding its own periodicals to copy foreign articles. This is a mere matter of domestic policy ; and the Convention is concerned, not with binding countries to look after their own interests, but with binding them to respect the interests of others.[1] This point was considered in the debate upon Art. 7 which took place at the Conference of 1885, when it was also recognised that the term 'articles of political discussion' applied only to writings concerning the politics of the day, not to essays or articles treating of questions of political science or social economy, and that it was not intended to permit the reproduction, e.g. in the form of a miscellany, of a *series* of articles which had appeared in the same paper.[2]

Position of Serial Novels. Finally the question of the position of serial novels has to be considered. Although such novels appear in the form of newspaper and magazine articles, they differ from ordinary articles in that they are works of the imagination, possessing a separate and permanent value independent of passing events. They have not seldom previously appeared in volume form, and in all cases they have exactly the same claim to protection as other works of fiction.

As we shall see later, the Additional Act of Paris, at least as regards all countries of the Union except Norway and Sweden, has now made clear the position of these articles, but at the earlier Conferences much time was spent in discussing whether the liberty of reproduction in the absence of reservation given by Art. 7 applied to them, or whether they fell under the general rule of Art. 2. In order to make this matter clear, the

---

[1] At the Conference of 1885 the English delegates asked for the suppression of Art. 7, on the ground that the law of England required articles borrowed from newspapers to be provided with an indication of the source whence they were taken. It was then explained, doubtless on the principle indicated above, that it was not intended to prevent countries from requiring their own papers to indicate the source of borrowed matter.—See *Actes de la Conférence de Berne*, 1885, p. 46.

[2] See *Actes de la Conférence de Berne*, 1885, p. 46.

French delegate, at the third Conference of 1886, proposed to introduce an express declaration that they were 'regulated, not by Art. 7, but by Arts. 2, 5, 10, and 11 of the Convention.' A difference of opinion, however, manifested itself among the delegates and, since the project of 1885 was regarded as definitive, the proposal was withdrawn. As, however, the only objections urged against it were that it was superfluous, and that its discussion would hinder the adoption of the 1885 draft, it may perhaps be assumed that the general opinion of the Union was on the side of France.[1]

The Modifications Effected by the Additional Act of Paris, 1896.

Discussion of the Article amongst International Societies.— In the interval of ten years which elapsed before the next Conference of the International Union, the position of serial novels under the Convention was much discussed by the various societies interested in the matter.[2] The general trend of their opinion may perhaps be expressed in the words of a resolution passed by the assembly of German authors which met at Vienna in 1893: 'Serial novels should be recognised

---

[1] See *Actes de la Conférence de Berne*, 1886, pp. 16, 17. But Germany at least took another view. It was its delegates who urged the objection that the French proposal would provoke discussion and so hinder the adoption of the text, which had already been settled. Later, Bismarck, in the explanatory memorial, dated 6th May, 1887, by which he submitted the Convention to the German Diet for approval, stated that the protection of serial novels under the Convention depended on express reservation. The same opinion was held by the German authorities, MM. Dambach and Scheele. In this connection it is interesting to note that the International Office suggests the following definition of a newspaper article: 'A short and cursory article, bearing upon a subject of the day, more especially upon a political, administrative, or critical subject.' See on the whole matter, *Études sur la revision de la Convention de Berne*, pp. 58-60.

[2] See their resolutions, collated in *Actes de la Conférence de Paris*, pp. 57, 58.

by a special declaration as being literary works, not newspaper
articles.' At the same time, it may be gathered from resolutions of an International Literary Congress which met at
Paris in 1889, and of the Institute of International Law,
meeting at Cambridge in 1895, that there was a movement in
favour of making it obligatory upon periodicals to indicate the
source whence matter, lawfully copied, was derived.

The Paris Amendment.—The French Government in its draft
of amendments to the Convention went far beyond these
suggestions. It proposed that no articles except articles of
political discussion, news of the day, and miscellaneous items
(notes and jottings), should be open to reproduction without
the express authorisation of the author.[1] This proposition was
too sweeping for the Conference. The delegates of Germany,
Belgium, Holland, and Monaco all made alternative suggestions
embodying a less radical reform,[2] and the ultimate result was
the framing of a new Article, couched in the following terms :
' Serial novels (*romans-feuilletons*), including short stories, published in newspapers or magazines of any of the countries
of the Union cannot be reproduced, in original or translation,
in the other countries without the authorisation of the authors
or their lawful representatives. This applies equally to other
articles in newspapers or magazines whenever the authors or
publishers shall have expressly declared in the newspaper or
magazine in which they have published them, that they forbid
their reproduction. For magazines it is sufficient if the prohibition is made in a general way at the beginning of each
number. In the absence of prohibition, reproduction will be
permitted on condition of indicating the source. The prohibition cannot in any case apply to articles of political
discussion, news of the day, or miscellaneous items (notes and
jottings).'

---

[1] See *Actes de la Conférence de Paris*, pp. 41, 42.
[2] See *Actes de la Conférence de Paris*, pp. 115, 116.

Effects of the Amendment.—This Article differs from the original Art. 7 of 1886, in that it definitely and absolutely forbids the reproduction of serial novels and short stories[1] without the authorisation of the author, and in that for other articles which, when unprovided with reserve, it leaves open to reproduction in the terms of the 1886 Convention, it requires that the source whence they are taken shall be indicated.[2]　In form it is also changed—to prohibitory from permissive.

The wording of the new Article leaves some doubt as to whether it was meant to exact indication of source in respect of reproductions of articles of political discussion, etc.　Upon the point being raised by M. de Borchgrave, one of the delegates of Belgium, it was definitely stated that such articles were to remain under the old *régime* and that it was not intended to require indication of source for such reproductions.[3]

Reproduction in other Newspapers or Magazines alone contemplated.—Another point worthy of note—also elucidated by M. de Borchgrave—is that it had been assumed all through, not only in the proceedings at Paris, but previously in 1884, 1885, and 1886 at the Conferences of Berne, that the

---

[1] These latter, designated in the Act of Paris by the word *Nouvelles*, are thus defined by M. Renault in his report drawn up for the Paris Conference in the name of the Commission of draftsmanship : ' Short romances and tales and works of fiction, often compressed into a single article in a newspaper or review.'—See *Actes de la Conférence de Paris*, p. 171.

[2] The reason for the absolute protection of serial novels is practical as well as theoretical in character. Arrangements in many cases exist between newspaper proprietors and authors by which the former are allowed to reproduce, as serial stories, novels which have already appeared in volume form. If, then, serials are only to be protected when provided with notice of reservation, the authors, in cases where such arrangements are made, are likely to undergo the hardship of seeing their works copied by other magazines, through the negligence of the newspaper proprietors, over whose actions they have no immediate control.

[3] The point, as raised, only affected articles of political discussion ; but it follows *a fortiori* that the rule laid down applies also to news of the day and miscellaneous facts. It seems desirable that indication of source should be exacted for articles of political discussion at least.—See *Actes de la Conférence de Paris*, p. 138.

permission given by the Article applied only to reproductions in other newspapers and magazines; and that, therefore, the omission of any express limitation to this effect was to be attributed rather to a feeling on the part of the Conference that it was unnecessary, than to any idea that it was not consonant with the intention of the Article.   In the Report of the Committee, drawn up by M. Renault, it is, indeed, mentioned that the Committee 'thinks that, although it is not expressly stated, the reproduction which is permitted is reproduction in other newspapers or magazines.   The publication of a volume composed of a series of articles without the authorisation of the author is not allowed.'[1]

Systematic Appropriation. —It would seem that the permission of Art. 7 would warrant a systematised and regular borrowing of articles by the same periodical from the same source.   The difference between such a reproduction as this and an occasional borrowing of an occasional article or two is not one of kind, but one of degree.   On the other hand, it is clearly not desirable that one journal should make a substantial and frequent use of another as a source of newspaper matter, without paying for what it takes.   If articles are worth taking they are worth paying for ; and, in cases where the taking is wholesale, the consideration that no one should be allowed to derive profit from the labour of another without making some recompense may well outweigh the consideration of cosmopolitan benefit.[2] In any case, it is to be hoped that this question of organised 'tapping' for material will be dealt with at the next Conference of the International Union.

[1] Report of the Committee, *Actes de la Conférence de Paris*, p. 171.

[2] Under the Swiss law the abuse may be met under Art. 50 of the *Code des Obligations* by prosecution for illicit profit-making : ' Quiconque cause sans droit un dommage à autrui, soit à dessein, soit par négligence ou par imprudence, est tenu de le réparer.'

SECTION V.

PHOTOGRAPHS, ETC.

The Convention rule a compromise—Photographic works—Combination of artistic and industrial elements—Various views taken by different countries —History of the 1886 rule—Effect of this is to create a sub-Union—Change in the German view—The rule of the Additional Act, 1896—Recommendation that all countries should protect photographs—Semi-official view as to effect of Paris amendment—Criticism of this view—Choregraphic works —Indeterminate position of these works—Definition—The German view— Choregraphic works to be protected where recognised by domestic law —Effect of Convention to create a sub-Union for these works—The protection of choregraphic works throughout the Union—Works of architecture—Buildings as subjects of copyright—Works of architecture protected by Additional Act of Paris—A sub-Union created.

The Convention Rule a Compromise.—In regard to photographs, choregraphic works,[1] and works of architecture proper (as distinguished from their plans) the rule laid down by the Convention represents a compromise between the countries which recognise the claim of these works to domestic copyright protection, and those which deny to them all copyright character. The former naturally advocated their inclusion in Art. 4, while the latter, holding that they were not 'literary or artistic,' refused on principle to consent to any mention of them in the definition of 'literary and artistic works.' The ultimate result was that in each case the subjects in question were not included in Art. 4, but were dealt with by separate provisions, providing for their protection by the countries which gave them domestic recognition. Other

---

[1] Descriptive representations on the stage, in which the story is expressed by the postures and movements of the ballet.

States are relieved from any obligation to protect them, but
the Articles regulating their position, being all inserted in
the Closing Protocol, are to be regarded as merely provisional,
suggesting future reform of domestic law for the backward
countries.

PHOTOGRAPHIC WORKS.

Combination of Artistic and Industrial elements.—In photographs, an artistic element is combined with an element
purely mechanical, in varying degrees of proportion. In
photographs of landscapes, etc., the selection of a suitable
subject exacts from the photographer an appreciation of
artistic effect; while, in photographs from life, the pose
and grouping of the subjects, the arrangement of the
background and setting, and the distribution of the light
are artistic processes of no small importance. In retouching
the negative the skill of the photographer is again called
into exercise : but in the actual process by which the impression is obtained he plays a very small part, his functions
being confined to setting the camera in motion. Where the
operator neither selects or arranges his subject with an
eye to artistic effect, nor retouches the negative, the artistic
element disappears altogether : but the mechanical element
can never disappear, and therefore, though some photographs
may be partially artistic in character, others may be entirely
devoid of the artistic element.

On the other hand, all photographs owe their origin to
the industry of the operator : hence even those which are
in no sense works of art have some claim to protection as
industrial works. Moreover in practice some intellectual
element must always be present. Thus, the question
usually being one merely of degree, it is often difficult to
determine in the abstract whether a given photograph should

be granted an extended measure of protection as a work of art, or regarded as industrial and invested with a period of protection which is comparatively short.

Various views taken by different countries.—The difficulty is usually solved once for all by a statutory decision as to the category in which photographs shall be placed : and, as this is almost entirely an arbitrary matter, it is not to be wondered at that we find divergences in the views taken by various countries.[1] Thus Germany and Switzerland regard all photographs as industrial works, and protect them as such, giving them a period of only five years ; while Spain, Great Britain, and Monaco treat all photographs indiscriminately as artistic works and accord them the full term of artistic copyright.

History of the 1886 Rule.—The question of the international protection of original photographs was raised by France, upon the discussion of Art. 4 by the 1884 Committee of draftsmanship. It was then suggested that they should be included among the works enumerated in that Article : but the German delegates objected, on the ground that the present state of the domestic law of Germany would not allow that country to consent to their being placed in the class of artistic works. The result was that the Committee decided to leave the question open for the time, but to draw up a resolution indicating the desirability of including original photographs in the protection of the Convention. This resolution was adopted by the Conference and embodied in the draft Convention of 1884.[2]

---

[1] In Belgium, France, and Italy, however, it is left to the Courts to decide in each case whether the photograph is an artistic work or not. This method, though the only one that is theoretically correct, presents numerous practical difficulties, and, as M. Pouillet says, 'exalts the Courts into academies by making them judges of the beautiful, when they should only be judges of the right.'

[2] See *Actes de la Conférence de Berne*, 1884, p. 63.

In 1885 France again proposed that photographs should
be included in Art. 4, and again upon objection by Germany
the question was shelved. This time, however, the Committee
inserted a definite provision in the Closing Protocol, requiring
the countries which did not deny the character of artistic works
to the works in question, to admit them to the benefit of the
Convention.

The 1886 Rule.—The provision in question was adopted by
the Conference, and stands as No. 1 in the Closing Protocol
to the Convention of 1886, in the following terms :—

' With reference to Art. 4, it is agreed that those countries
of the Union in which the character of artistic works is
not refused to photographic works, bind themselves to admit
them, from the coming into force of the Convention concluded
this day, to the benefit of its provisions. They are, however,
only bound to protect the author of the said works in so far
as their law permits, saving the international arrangements
at present existing or hereafter to be entered into.' (The
second paragraph treats of authorised photographs of protected works of art, and is dealt with in Sec. 3 of this
chapter.)

Effect of the Rule to create a sub-Union.—As M. Numa
Droz has pointed out,[1] the effect of the Article is to create
a limited Union (*Union restreinte*) between the countries
which do not reject the claim of photographs to be treated
as artistic works.[2] From the wording of the Closing Protocol, and from the consideration that the general principle
of the Convention is to require each country to extend its

---

[1] *Journal de Droit International Privé*, 1885, p. 489.

[2] The negative wording of the article—' in which the character . . . is not
refused,' etc.,—is worthy of note, both on account of the practical effect it has
in binding countries in which the position of the works in question is not clearly
defined by law, and because it indicates the view of the Convention that photographs have a *primâ facie* claim to protection, so that the relegation of the matter
to domestic legislation is a *concession* made to those countries which refuse to
recognise their artistic character.

own domestic protection to Unionist works, it would appear that the members of this sub-Union are not, as suggested by M. Darras,[1] merely obliged to protect photographs, *inter se*, but that they are also bound to admit the photographs of the other Union countries to the benefits of the Convention.[2]

The result of this is not, however, to secure any protection for photographs of countries which grant them no protection whatever by their domestic law—for, though due in principle, such a protection would in fact be excluded by the rule of Art. 2, providing that the duration of the rights to be accorded cannot exceed that of the country of origin,—but only for those belonging to countries which grant them some domestic protection, though this may be based on the idea that they are, *e.g.*, industrial works. Thus a German photograph, having fulfilled the conditions and formalities of the German law, would probably be protected by France for a period of five years, this being the term granted by the domestic law of Germany, although that law only protects photographs as industrial works. The reverse would not hold good ; a French photograph would gain no Convention protection whatever in Germany.

Change in the German view.—In a treaty with the United States of the 15th January, 1892, Germany agreed to accord to the photographs of American citizens the benefits of its domestic law. This indicated a change of attitude on the part of Germany, and it is therefore not surprising to find that, at the Paris Conference of 1896, that country consented to a change in the wording of § 1 of the Closing Protocol, though it still refused to agree to the proposal of France to include photographs in the enumeration of Art. 4.[3]

---

[1] Darras, *Du Droit des Auteurs et des Artistes*, pp. 586, 587.

[2] See *Études sur la revision de la Convention de Berne*, p. 40.

[3] See resolutions of the International Literary and Artistic Association and the International Photographic Union in *Actes de la Conférence de Paris*, p. 55, for various suggestions.

The Rule of the Additional Act, 1896.—This refusal placed
the adoption of that measure out of the question : and the
Article ultimately accepted by the Conference of Paris, which
now stands as No. 1, B, of the Closing Protocol, runs :

('With reference to Art. 4 it is agreed as follows') :—
'Photographic works, and works obtained by analogous processes, are admitted to the benefit of the provisions of those
Acts,[1] in so far as domestic law allows this to be done, and
in the measure of the protection that it accords to similar
national works. . . .' (The proviso dealing with authorised
photographs of protected works of art remains, in the same
terms as before.)

Recommendation that all countries should protect Photographs.
—In view of the diversity of domestic law in respect
of the protection of photographs, the Conference of Paris
also issued the following Recommendation (*Vœu*) : 'It is
desirable that, in all the countries of the Union, the law
should protect photographic works, or works obtained by
analogous processes, and that the duration of the protection
should be at least fifteen years.' Clause 1 of the Interpretative
Declaration of Paris, which provides that the protection of
Art. 2 depends *solely* upon the fulfilment of the conditions
and formalities of the country of origin, is also made applicable
to the protection of photographic works.[2]

Semi-official view as to effect of Paris Amendment.—The
effect of the Act of Paris is thus described by M. Renault,

---

[1] *I.e.* the Berne Convention and the Act of Paris.

[2] It may be well, in this connection, once more to point out that Norway
and Sweden have refused to accept the Additional Act of Paris, and England the
Interpretative Declaration, so that the relations of Norway and Sweden with
the other countries of the Union are regulated solely by the original Berne Convention and the Interpretative Declaration, and those of England by the Berne
Convention and the Act of Paris (but see, *contra*, *Le Droit d'Auteur*, 1899,
p. 64). As to conditions and formalities, however, England interprets the Convention in the sense of the Interpretative Declaration (see a statement by Mr.
Howard, one of the English delegates at the Paris Conference, in *Actes de la
Conférence de Paris*, p. 111).

in the Report of the Committee : 'Thus, in the relations between the countries of the Union, the protection accorded to photographs or to works obtained by analogous processes can be demanded, whatever it is. No country sacrifices its principles, though every country accords its domestic treatment to Union countries. The essential thing is that protection should be assured ; the nature of the protection is of secondary importance.

'From the fact that protection must be claimed in virtue of the Convention, it follows, on the one hand, that protection cannot be claimed for a longer period than in the country of origin, and, on the other hand, that it is sufficient to fulfil the conditions and formalities prescribed in that country, conformably to the interpretation . . . of Art. 2, § 2, of the Convention. . . . It is useful to note that, according to the clause submitted to the Conference, the countries of the Union in which as a matter of fact no protection is granted to photographs by law, are not obliged to protect the photographs of the other countries of the Union, and nevertheless will profit by the protection accorded in these latter countries. Here again there is a concession made without reciprocity.'[1]

Criticism of this view.—The first part of this extract contains a lucid statement of the actual position : but the latter portion seems somewhat inconsistent, since, where the term of protection granted by the country of origin is *nil*, any positive term, however short, must exceed it, and therefore, under the rule of Art. 2, § 2, countries in which the law gives no protection whatever to photographs, though in theory they may be entitled to profit, will in fact profit nothing by the Convention protection accorded by other countries, in compliance with the Protocol. The general principle that, in order for a work to have a *locus standi* to claim international protection, it must be in the enjoyment of *some* protection in its

---

[1] See *Actes de la Conférence de Paris*, p. 167.

own country, supports the unambiguous wording of Art. 2, § 2, in this respect.

The final statement of the passage in M. Renault's Report set out above must therefore be explained by supposing that it treats only of the primary obligation of the Article,—by which countries protecting photographs are obliged to admit all Unionist photographs *to the benefit of the provisions of the Convention,*—not of the way in which that obligation works out. If there is any contradiction, it would seem that the revised Convention, which alone constitutes a binding act, must override the official report, which only aims at explanation. It is, therefore, difficult to agree with the view expressed in *Le Droit d'Auteur*,[1] that the effect of the Articles in question, in view of the Report, is to make it obligatory upon countries which themselves protect photographs to grant any protection to photographs emanating from countries which themselves grant none by their domestic law.

CHOREGRAPHIC WORKS.

Indeterminate position of these works.—As regards choregraphic works (descriptive ballets),[2] it was the fact that their position as a class was in most countries still undetermined, rather than any positive difference of opinion as to their nature, that stood in the way of their inclusion in Art. 4 of the Convention. The extent to which the development of the choregraphic art had attained in Italy led this country to propose at the 1885 Conference that these works should be enumerated among the 'literary and artistic works' of that

---

[1] *Le Droit d'Auteur*, 1899, pp. 64, 65.

[2] **Definition.**—A choregraphic work is defined by the International Office in *Le Droit d'Auteur*, 1899, p. 14, as a work which 'represents . . . a processional dance, sometimes also a dancing group, the object being to reproduce on the stage a determinate subject, often an allegory or a symbolic grouping.'

Article[1] ; the objection then made, which, as in the case of photographs, originated with the German delegacy, was that 'the task of defining these works, which in certain countries have only quite recently been admitted to protection, still presents serious difficulties.' [2]

The German view.—The following remarks of M. Reichardt[3] clearly express the position taken up by Germany : 'A thorough examination of the question has shown us that, instead of providing for the protection of these works expressly and generally by the Convention, it would be preferable, in the interests of the development of the matter, to leave this question to the judgment of the Courts. The Convention already protects the *libretto* and the music of ballets upon another ground. What else is there then to protect? It would be the *ensemble* of dances, poses, and living pictures, etc. In proclaiming the protection of choregraphic works unreservedly and indiscriminately, would not the Conference run the danger of including implicitly in this protection such and such a *pseudo*-choregraphic work which would not merit inclusion amongst works of art ? Do you wish to protect upon this ground every pantomime, every choregraphic scene, represented in the circus, at fairs, in booths, even in the open street ? There does not exist in science, in the various systems of law, or . . . in jurisprudence, any clear definition of choregraphic works.

'In view of the imperative need to exercise discrimination in granting the protection claimed by the Italian delegacy, it will be necessary, at least until the problem of a definition is solved, to reserve to the Courts the power of deciding, when the question arises, if, and under what conditions, the protection accorded to dramatic or dramatico-musical

---

[1] In Art. 5 of the Montevideo Convention, choregraphic works are mentioned amongst the works to be protected.

[2] *Actes de la Conférence de Berne*, 1885, p. 43.   [3] *Ibid.*, pp. 21, 22.

works against illicit reproduction applies to choregraphic works.'

Choregraphic Works to be protected where recognised by domestic law.—Hence this subject too was dealt with in a provision of the Closing Protocol (§ 2), which runs thus :

' With reference to Art. 9, it is agreed that those of the countries of the Union the law of which implicitly includes choregraphic works amongst dramatico-musical works, expressly admit the said works to the benefit of the provisions of the Convention concluded this day.

' It is, however, understood that disputes which may arise upon the application of this clause shall be reserved for the decision of the respective Courts.' [1]

Effect of the Convention is to create a sub-Union for these Works.—In spite of a further effort on the part of Italy, made at the Paris Conference, to secure the inclusion of choregraphic works in Art. 4, this provision remains unaltered, and at present stands part of the Convention, as § 3 of the Closing Protocol. Its effect is to create a sub-Union, similar in character to that created for photographs, between the various States of the Union in which the domestic law recognises the dramatico-musical character of choregraphic works. It is to be noted that the domestic protection which the Convention has in view need not flow from an express statutory provision, but may be the result of general principles of law including choregraphs in the interpretation of dramatico-musical works, whether declared in decisions of the Courts or not. In any case, it will be for the Courts to decide whether a given choregraphic work falls within the protection of the law.[2]

The Protection of Choregraphic Works throughout the Union.—Among the countries of the Union, Belgium, Haïti, Luxemburg, Monaco, Switzerland, and Tunis have not yet found it

---

[1] A German Treaty of 1884 with Italy contains an analogous disposition.
[2] See Le Droit d'Auteur, 1899, pp. 13 seq., on the whole question.

necessary to lay down any rule as to the status of chore-graphic works. Italy grants an express protection to such works ; Denmark and Norway protect 'ballets, pantomimes, and other analogous works for which special music has been composed'; and the definition of 'dramatic piece'[1] in the English Act of 1842 is wide enough to include all ordinary choregraphic works. In Spain and France such works are protected under general principles of the law.[2] In Germany it is for the Courts to decide, for each case as it arises, whether the choregraphic work can be regarded as dramatic or dramatico-musical or not, and to grant or withhold the pro-tection of the law accordingly.

WORKS OF ARCHITECTURE.

Buildings as subjects of Copyright.—While the claim of the architect to copyright in his plans and designs has for some time been widely recognised, it is only recently that the ques-tion whether he should be accorded any protection in his buildings as such has received notice. It was not brought for-ward in the Conferences of Berne ; but between the last of those conferences and the Conference of Paris a plea was raised by M. Jules de Borchgrave, in *Le Droit d'Auteur*,[3] on behalf of such works in question, and in the *Études* compiled by the Inter-national Office in view of the latter Conference a full discussion of the matter was undertaken, in which the same conclusions as those of M. de Borchgrave were reached. At the time of the Conference of 1886 'the right of re-edification'—as the

---

[1] 'The words "dramatic piece" shall be construed to mean and include every tragedy, comedy, play, opera, farce, or other scenic, musical, or dramatic entertain-ment.'—Stat. 5 and 6 Vict. c. 45, sec. 2.

[2] As to France, there are decisions to support this view. Moreover, in the treaty of 1884 with Italy choregraphic works are expressly included amongst protected works, and their unauthorised representation in public is forbidden.

[3] *Le Droit d'Auteur*, 1890, pp. 13 seq.

architect's exclusive right to reproduce imitations of buildings which he has erected has been called—was not expressly recognised by the domestic law of any country of the Union, though it was protected implicitly by the law of France, Belgium, and and Spain, and, probably, by that of Italy and Switzerland ; and up to the present the new law of Luxemburg, enacted in 1898, is the only one which contains a specific mention of ' works of architecture ' among the works to be protected.

There is no need here to enter into a lengthy consideration of the reasons upon which the claim of such works to protection is based. It is sufficient to say that an edifice may embody an original conception on the part of the architect, just as a book may embody an original conception on the part of the author, or a plastic work such a conception on the part of the sculptor ; and that, whatever the form of a work, it is unfair to deny to its creator an exclusive right in it, unless from its nature and purposes it is reasonable to presume an intention to throw open the work to free reproduction. The architect is provided with a remedy against the unauthorised reproduction of his plans, which are protected as works of art (in England as drawings), but the protection of the plan of a building is not the protection of the building itself.[1] The making of plans, again, though a usual preliminary, is not absolutely essential to the construction of architectural works.[2]

Works of Architecture protected by Additional Act of Paris.— The International Office having called attention to these principles, and having demonstrated at length that the works in question should be protected internationally, the French Government took the matter up, and, in its draft of amendments pre-

---

[1] In England the fact that the plans have to be passed by the local authority before any building is begun renders it possible for the first architect to prove copying on the part of the second from the outset.

[2] Thus, for a wager, M. O. Mothes, an architect of Saxony, erected a turret with a spiral staircase in 1848, without any preliminary plan or model.—See *Le Droit d'Auteur*, 1899, pp. 2, 3.

sented to the Paris Conference, proposed that works of architecture should be included in Art. 4[1] ; Germany again refused to accept the French proposal, and again a compromise was arrived at. Its results are embodied in § 1, A, of the amended Closing Protocol, which runs :

' With reference to Art. 4 it is agreed as follows : .

' " In the countries of the Union in which protection is accorded, not only to architectural plans, but also to works of architecture themselves, those works are admitted to the benefit of the provisions of the Berne Convention and of the present Additional Act." '

A sub-Union created.—The effect of this is again to create a sub-Union, similar in character to those established for photographs and choregraphic works.[2]

[1] This proposal was foreshadowed in resolutions of the International Literary and Artistic Association, at Neuchatel 1891, Milan 1892, and Antwerp 1894, collated in *Actes de la Conférence de Paris*, p. 55.

[2] It is worth while to consider the position of works of architecture under the original Convention of 1886. The International Office takes the view that the general rule of Art. 4 bound countries whose domestic law regarded works of architecture as artistic to protect them if they were in enjoyment of protection in their country of origin (*Études sur la revision de la Convention de Berne*, p. 30). This may be so ; but it is pertinent to ask why then it was found necessary to insert a special Article in the 1886 Convention, in order to set up a similar rule for choregraphic works. Another view of the definition of Art. 4 is that it is to be interpreted in the light of international opinion, so that a country which itself holds that a certain work is in the literary, scientific, or artistic domain, is nevertheless not bound to protect it if it can show that this view is not generally accepted by the countries of the Union.

CHAPTER V.

INFRINGEMENTS, REMEDIES, AND PROCEDURE UNDER THE BERNE CONVENTION.

SECTION I.

THE GENERAL RULE OF THE CONVENTION.

Relation between right and infringement—Remedies and procedure should be left to domestic law—Infringements may be internationally defined—The rules of the Convention as to infringements.

Relation between Right and Infringement.—Since it is a necessary consequence of the existence of a right that all acts interfering with its free exercise are illegal, every grant of a right necessarily implies a corresponding prohibition of infringements. Hence the general rule of Art. 2, which provides that in each country Unionist authors are to enjoy the same rights as those granted to natives, serves also to determine the acts which constitute infringements. At the same time, it has the effect of assuring to Unionist authors the same treatment on the part of each country in respect of remedies and procedure as that accorded to natives, for the term 'rights' is not limited to primary rights, but includes as well rights to remedies and rights connected with procedure.[1]

Remedies and Procedure should be left to Domestic Law.— These last two matters, indeed, the Convention leaves almost entirely to domestic law; for though, besides Art. 2, Arts. 11, 12, and 13 all relate to remedies and procedure, Arts. 12 and 13 are purely permissive, and Art. 11 alone purports to lay down an absolute rule forming part of the Convention *jus cogens minimum*.   It is, of course, hardly within the province of an ordinary international agreement to dictate to its parties the means to be employed for securing the rights it confers : it is assumed that they each possess an efficient system of judicature, and that their own remedies are well adapted to enforce obedience to law.

Infringements may be internationally defined.—With regard to infringements the case is different, for a Convention naturally aims at widening the area of the author's protection, so that acts against aliens which were formerly tolerated may henceforth be forbidden in all the contracting countries.   To say this is only to say that the usual object of a Convention is to secure to authors rights previously denied to them in countries other than their own.   The correlation of right and obligation makes every extension in the domain of rights involve an extension in the domain of infringement ; and thus all Articles which, forming part of the *jus cogens minimum* of the Convention, serve to secure certain international rights over and above those of Art. 2, have some claim to be dealt with in this Chapter, since they embody absolute rules widening the domain of international infringement.   As the substantial effect of such Articles has already been set out in the two previous Chapters,

---

[1] It is therefore doubtful whether a member of the Union would, under the Convention, be entitled to exact from authors belonging to another Union country any such special formalities as the *cautio judicatum solvi* referred to above ; see, however, Nicolau, *La Propriété littéraire et artistique*, pp. 318 seq., and Part II., Chap. iv., sec. 3, of this work.

it is, however, only necessary to point out that those Chapters are complementary to this.

The Rules of the Convention as to Infringements.—The only absolute rules couched in prohibitory form that the Convention contains are embraced in the revised Art. 7, relating to newspaper and magazine articles ; and it has been pointed out in the last Chapter that in their original shape these too were permissive. It is true that Art. 10 begins with a special prohibition levelled against adaptations, arrangements of music, etc., but the rule is qualified by a clause declaring that, in its application, the reservations of the various domestic laws may be taken into account. Art. 8, on educational and scientific works and chrestomathies, which is also matter for this Chapter, allows countries, in derogation of the general rule as to infringements, to make provisions by their domestic law, or by treaties, for an international liberty of extract in favour of such works. It is in no sense part of the *jus cogens minimum* of the Convention. Lastly, § 3 of the Closing Protocol, which provides that the manufacture and sale of mechanical musical instruments are not to be considered as constituting infringements of the musical copyright, though it creates an absolute rule, aims, not at forbidding certain acts, but at securing that certain acts, which might otherwise be forbidden by the various domestic laws, shall be tolerated internationally. It subtracts from— and does not add to—the list of international infringements.

SECTION II.

REPRODUCTIONS WHICH ARE SPECIFICALLY PROHIBITED.

Adaptations, arrangements of music, dramatisations, etc.—Nature and treatment of these works—Distinction between these and chrestomathies— History of the rule relating to adaptations—Indirect appropriations generally unlawful—National reservations to be applied—Dramatisations and noveli- sations in England—Dramatisation, etc., discussed at the Paris Conference— Compromise by means of the Interpretative Declaration—Educational and scientific works : Chrestomathies—The nature of expropriation—The necessity of a special international rule—The history of the Convention rule —Each country to determine the extent of lawful expropriation—Art. 8 not a codifying article—Union countries which allow expropriation—The right of quotation not affected—In strictness international expropriation is unjust—The plea of public benefit.

ADAPTATIONS, ARRANGEMENTS OF MUSIC, DRAMATISATIONS, ETC.

Nature and Treatment of these Works.—Works which are in substance reproductions of others under a different form stand in a somewhat ambiguous position, by virtue of the conflict between their original and their unoriginal elements. It is therefore necessary for any Copyright Act or Agreement which affects to be comprehensive to fix their mode of treatment, by a definite and express rule.

The most enlightened view seems to be that no amount of novelty of form can extend to justify a substantial appropria- tion of the results of the labour of another.[1] The fact, however,

---

[1] See an article by M. Henri Rosmini in *Le Droit d'Auteur*, 1895, p. 21, with the comments of the International Office.

that at first sight the works in question present the appearance of new and original works gives them at least a *primâ facie* independence, and because of this *primâ facie* independence they are more effectually prohibited by an express designation of them as infringements than by an express extension of the rights in the original work, involving merely by implication that they are to be treated as illegal.

Distinction between these and Chrestomathies.—Hence the Convention, in dealing with adaptations, arrangements of music,[1] etc., does not proceed by way of conferring on the author of the original work an exclusive right to carry out the processes which their manufacture entails, but by way of prohibiting such works themselves, when produced without the consent of the author of the original work.

On the other hand, works made up of extracts from others taken *en bloc*, which rest their claim to independence on the plea that they are meant to achieve a different purpose, or to appeal to a different public, are primarily of an infringing character. Hence, where these are to be disallowed, there is no need to make any express provision on the matter ; they fall under the general rule of law giving the author of an original work the exclusive right to multiply copies of it. It is only where they are to be permitted—as is the case in the Convention, with certain qualifications, for works composed of extracts for educational and scientific purposes and chrestomathies—that it becomes necessary to accord to them a specific treatment. If ever the plea of 'different purpose' can avail to warrant unauthorised takings, it is only when the consideration of 'public benefit' is to over-ride the author's claim to copyright in his conception ; and where this is so, and only where this is so, it becomes necessary for a copyright code to make an express statement on the matter.

---

[1] It is hardly necessary to point out that, in view of the catholicity of musical taste and universality of notation, these are of special international importance.

History of the Rule relating to Adaptations.—The importance of dealing with the process of adaptation in the manner indicated above has been recognised from the beginning. Art. 10 of the original Swiss draft read : 'Adaptation shall be considered as constituting infringement, and proceeded against as such.' The German delegacy, in its list of questions (No. 10), suggested that, in view of the difficulty of adequate definition,[1] it would perhaps be better to leave the matter to the cognizance of the various domestic tribunals.

The matter was relegated to the Committee of draftsmanship, with the result that an Article (§ 3) was inserted in the Closing Protocol,[2] leaving it to the Courts to estimate in each case the amount of injury to the author resulting from the 'adaptation.' Meanwhile the position of arrangements of music had also been mooted by Germany,[3] and settled in a similar way by an Art. 10 inserted in the body of the Convention.

Indirect Appropriations generally Unlawful.—At the 1885 Congress, the Article in the Protocol dealing with adaptation was fused with Art. 10, and in this form was ultimately embodied as Article 10 in the 1886 Convention. The following is the Article as it now stands :

'Unauthorised indirect appropriations of a literary or

---

[1] At the third sitting of the 1884 Conference, M. Ulbach, a French delegate, suggested the following definition : 'Adaptation is the arrangement or disarrangement of the primary work, with the aim of adapting it to the taste or the capacity of another public ; it is a particular and personal arrangement, which takes the substance of the work without taking its form.' This definition is obviously far from satisfactory, and one is almost forced to agree with the Committee of German experts referred to by M. Dambach, which, having lately discussed the question, had come to the conclusion that no satisfactory definition could be constructed. The general opinion of the Conference seemed in favour of the German view, the French delegates themselves ultimately recognising that no definition could be complete.—*Actes de la Conférence de Berne*, 1884, pp. 34, 58.

[2] See *Actes de la Conférence de Berne*, 1884, pp. 57, 58, 63.

[3] See No. 2 in the German list of questions and the Article proposed by Germany as No. 11 A.—*Actes de la Conférence de Berne*, 1884, pp. 25, 55.

artistic work designated by various names, such as *adaptations, arrangements of music*, etc., are specially included among the unlawful reproductions to which the present Convention applies, when they are merely the reproduction of such a work, in the same form or in another form, with non-essential alterations, additions, or abridgements, without in other respects presenting the character of a new original work.

'It is understood that, in the application of the present Article, the Courts of the various countries of the Union will, if occasion arises, take into account the reservations of their respective laws.'

Art. 10, though since 1886 it has been made a subject of interpretation by Clause 3 of the Interpretative Declaration of 1896, remains unaltered at the present day. It establishes the comprehensive principle that derivative works such as adaptations, are illegal, unless, of course, they can be regarded as new original works.

National Reservations to be applied.—In the application of the principle, however, each country is left free, through the medium of its Courts, to give effect to any particular deviations from the principle which may find a place in its domestic law.

As regards the works which are specifically mentioned in Art. 10—adaptations and arrangements of music—it seems to be obligatory upon every country to enforce a general prohibition against them, though in the application of such a prohibition it may introduce the qualifications of its own law ; but as regards the general definition of that Article, the proviso as to the mode in which the Article is to be applied would, presumably, warrant a country in refusing to prohibit, even in principle, an indirect and unauthorised reproduction allowed by its domestic law.

Dramatisations and Novelisations in England.—A situation of this kind exists in England with regard to 'dramatisations' of novels, and possibly also, although there is no express decision on the point, with regard to 'novelisations' of dramas. Dramatisations, by established decision,[1] and novelisations, by analogous reasoning, both seem to be regarded in England as not constituting infringements of the works upon which they are based.

The state of the English law explains the motives of the English delegacy in asking, upon the discussion of Art. 10 by the Committee of 1885, whether dramatisation should be considered as constituting an illicit indirect reproduction. It was then recognised that, subject to circumstances, this might be so, and in Art. 4 of the explanatory declaration put forward by France in 1886 an express statement to that effect, which also extended to the case of novelisation, was made. It has already been pointed out that the French declaration was not accepted.

The matter was allowed to rest, but, in the interval between the last Conference at Berne and the Paris Conference of 1896, the English decision in *Warne v. Seebohm*,[2] to the effect that, though in practice there might be some difficulty in carrying it out without an infringement of copyright, dramatisation was permissible in principle, reopened the agitation for the embodiment in the Convention of a definite statement upon it.[3]

Dramatisation, etc., discussed at the Paris Conference.—Accordingly, in the French draft of alterations prepared for the consideration of the Paris Conference, it was proposed specifically to include novelisations and dramatisations in the first paragraph of Art. 10, and to suppress the second

---

[1] *Tinsley v. Lacey* (1863), 1 Hem. & M. 747, and *Warne v. Seebohm* (1888), 39 Ch.D. 73.

[2] *Warne v. Seebohm* (1888), 39 Ch.D. 73.

[3] See an article (cited above) by M. Henri Rosmini in *Le Droit d'Auteur*, 1895, p. 21, with the comments of the International Office, and the resolutions of various societies, collated in *Actes de la Conférence de Paris*, pp. 62, 63.

paragraph which provided for the application by the various domestic tribunals of the reserves of their respective laws. England, however, objected to both these amendments, its delegates stating that, though it agreed in principle with the suggested prohibition of the derivative works in question, the actual state of its law prevented it from promising to enforce any rule such as would issue from Art. 10, as modified by the French proposals.

Compromise by means of the Interpretative Declaration.— Hence no change in the Article was made by the Additional Act of Paris itself, but the desires of the majority were met by the inclusion in the Interpretative Declaration of 1896 of a Clause 3, to the following effect :—

' The transformation of a novel into a play, or of a play into a novel, comes within the stipulations of Art. 10.'

The statement of Clause 3 constitutes an authoritative interpretation of Art. 10, binding on all the members of the Union except Great Britain, which is the only country that has rejected the Interpretative Declaration.

From the mode of treatment adopted, it follows that none of the signatories to the latter Act would be warranted in availing itself of the proviso at the end of Art. 10, sanctioning the reservations of the various domestic systems of law, in order to refuse to the author of an original work all protection against the processes in question. It is only in the *application* of Art. 10 that the various reservations are to be operative ; and though, so long as dramatisation and novelisation were dealt with only by the general rule, it was open to any State to interpret that rule so as to permit them, the express inclusion of them in Art. 10 entails a specific prohibition, which cannot be disregarded.

Educational and Scientific Works. Chrestomathies.

The Nature of Expropriation.—The liberty of abstracting fragments of literary and artistic works, without the consent of the author, which is conceded by some systems of law[1] in respect of works destined for education, or having a scientific character, and chrestomathies, is in the nature of an exceptional privilege, derogating from the ordinary rights included in copyright. Every country of the Union recognises in principle the author's exclusive control over the product of his brain, and, as a general rule, forbids all appropriation and expropriation in respect thereof which is made without his consent. Where expropriation is allowed for educational and scientific works, etc., the author's right still remains, but is nullified *pro tanto* by a special permission accorded to the compilers of such works, on grounds of public interest. It is not that the State wishes to deprive the author of part of his copyright, but that it wishes to free the hands of educationists and others whose work it is desirable to facilitate for the sake of the public good.

The necessity of a special International Rule.—From this point of view, it was necessary for the Convention, in order to authorise the application by each country of special rules upon international expropriation, to state its intention by a special article. It would not have been enough to leave the matter under the *régime* of Art. 2, since that Article would have obliged each country to grant to the author its full domestic rights, while (probably) it would not have allowed it to derogate from those rights by conceding special exemptions to certain works, freeing them from the general prohibition of unauthorised

---

[1] *E.g.* those of Austria, Germany, Hungary, Norway, Sweden, and Switzerland.

takings.[1]   This,   together   with   the   desire   to   preserve
particular arrangements providing for expropriation, accounts
for Art. 8, which at first sight seems merely to enunciate a
special case of the general principle of Art. 2, and therefore to
be superfluous.

The History of the Convention Rule.—The question whether
any liberty of making extracts for scientific or educational
purposes and for chrestomathies should be conceded to the
public, like the analogous question with regard to newspaper
and magazine articles, was first raised by the German delegates
in their list of questions submitted at the first sitting of the
1884 Conference.[2] The consideration of the matter having
been referred to the Committee of draftsmanship, the German
representatives drew up and presented to this body an Article
which provided for freedom of expropriation, upon condition
that the name of the author, or the source of the extract, should
be indicated. This Article contained no reference to domestic
law or treaties.

As it then stood, Art. 8, by its last paragraph, expressly
exempted musical compositions from liability to expropriation in selections destined for schools of music.[3]   The

---

[1] It is interesting to note that so early as 1844 a proposed reform of the law
of Sweden, having for its object the establishment of the principle of legal
reciprocity, was admitted only with the exclusion of Church books and works
of education from its scope.—Darras, *Du Droit des Auteurs et des Artistes*, p. 203.

[2] See Question 6, *Actes de la Conférence de Berne*, 1884, p. 25. The German
law of literary, dramatic, and musical copyright was then contained in the Act
of 1870, which conceded (Secs. 7, 44, 47) a large liberty of expropriation. Expropriation was also sanctioned in the Franco-German Treaty of 1883 (Art. 4).
The new German Act of 1901, which has superseded the 1870 Act, is even more
liberal than its predecessor (Secs. 19-26).

[3] The official report states that 'The introduction of the above provision has
been proposed by the German Delegacy, because it seemed to be for the universal
interest that certain borrowings should be left free to be made from authors,
within reasonable limits, for the needs of education. The Committee has
recognised the existence of such an interest. It has considered, moreover, that
it was preferable to regulate this liberty of reproduction by the general Convention, rather than to leave the provisions relative thereto to special agreements

Committee adopted the Article with a few modifications, including the introduction of a word which would have placed *artistic* works amongst those liable to fragmentary reproduction. Upon discussion by the Conference of the Committee's draft, the French delegates showed themselves strongly averse to the insertion of any such stipulation as Art. 8 contained.[1] Ultimately, however, the proposition of the Committee was adopted by the 1884 Conference.

In the Conference of 1885 Great Britain and Italy joined France in objecting to Art. 8. In default of its total suppression, M. Henri Rosmini, on behalf of Italy, strongly urged in the Committee of draftsmanship that the last paragraph, relating to selections for schools of music, should be eliminated. He represented the provision therein contained as establishing 'an unjustifiable anomaly, to the detriment of musical education.' The inconsistency was so obvious that, by a considerable majority, the Committee accepted M. Rosmini's motion,[2] and then rejected the Article altogether, Germany voting against it in its amended form.[3]

Each country to determine the extent of Lawful Expropriation. —As a consequence the Committee decided to substitute a new Art. 8, leaving each country to determine the whole question of

---

and to the domestic law of each country.—See *Actes de la Conférence de Berne*, 1884, p. 50.

[1] It was pointed out at the time that this action on the part of France was somewhat invidious, in view of the fact that that country had already consented to the inclusion of a similar provision in its Treaty of 1883 with Germany. To this the French delegates replied that, while such a treaty is merely a matter of convenience between its parties, a Convention like that aimed at by the Union ought to look to the establishment of sound and liberal principles.—See *Actes de la Conférence de Berne*, 1884, p. 51.

[2] The majority was 9—Belgium, France, Great Britain, Honduras, Italy, Norway, Sweden, Switzerland, and Tunis—against 3—Germany, Haïti, and Spain.—See *Actes de la Conférence de Berne*, 1885, p. 47.

[3] The majority here was 7—Belgium, France, Germany, Great Britain, Italy, Switzerland, and Tunis—against 5—Haïti, Honduras, Norway, Spain, and Sweden.

international expropriation by its domestic law and by treaties. The substituted Article stands as Art. 8 of the present Berne Convention, and reads :

'As regards the liberty of lawfully making extracts from literary and artistic works for publications destined for education, or having a scientific character, or for chrestomathies, this matter is reserved to the law of the countries of the Union, and to particular arrangements existing or to be concluded between them.'

Art. 8 not a codifying Article.—It is plain from the Report of the Committee [1] that even this qualified admission of expropriation was dictated, not so much by abstract respect for the principle, as by the fear lest silence should endanger the security of treaties permitting some measure of mutual expropriation between the parties,[2] which, in order to be valid under Art. 15, or the Additional Article, as the case might be, were required to confer more extended rights than those of the Convention, or to contain other stipulations not contrary to the latter Act.[3] It is difficult, therefore, to agree with *Le Droit d'Auteur* [4] that Art. 8 is an Article in which codification is admitted in principle, though circumscribed by the direct applicability of domestic law. Having regard to its history it would be more correct to say that it is an Article which bears witness to the abandonment of the principle of codification in regard to its subject, and which owes its very existence to the need for allowing free scope to domestic law and particular treaties.

Union Countries which allow Expropriation.—Among the members of the Union, Germany, Norway, Sweden, and

---

[1] *Actes de la Conférence de Berne*, 1885, p. 47.

[2] Such as the French treaties of 1883 with Germany and Spain respectively.

[3] In *Actes de la Conférence de Berne*, 1884, p. 52, however, M. Lavollée, one of the French delegates, says that a stipulation in a treaty for liberty of extract ought to be regarded not as *contrary* to the Convention, but as bearing on matters *other* than those regulated thereby.

[4] *Le Droit d'Auteur*, 1895, p. 64.

Switzerland recognise, under varying conditions, the liberty of expropriation by their domestic law,[1] and it is sanctioned in many international treaties.

The Right of Quotation not affected.—It must be mentioned, by way of explanation, that Art. 8 does not affect the right of quotation for purposes of criticism and comment, and that its phrase 'destined for education' is to be construed in a wide sense to cover the case of works destined for elementary education and for self-instruction as well as that of works with a higher object. Statements to this effect were made in the Conference of 1885, when the form of the Article was settled.[2]

In strictness International Expropriation is unjust.—At the Conference of Paris no suggestion was made with a view to the modification of Art. 8. The principle upon which liberty of expropriation rests was therefore not discussed. It may, however, be pointed out that, in strict justice to the author, no plea of 'different purpose' or 'public benefit' should extend to legalise the unauthorised appropriation of any part of his work.

If the work of one man is to be exploited by another for any purpose, it should only be when the consent of the former has been obtained, if necessary by means of a money payment. It is true that newspaper and magazine articles of a certain kind constitute an exception to this rule, but that is only because their objects and the mode of their publication usually preclude their being regarded as of permanent literary value.

---

[1] Sec. 25 of the German law of the 19th June, 1901, and Sec. 11 of the Swiss law of 1883 require a clear indication of source. The Norwegian law of 4th July, 1893, allows expropriation from a work, only after the expiration of 10 years from its publication (*Le Droit d'Auteur*, p. 136). A common condition in treaties permitting extracts for chrestomathies is that every extract shall be accompanied with explanatory notes in another language than that in which it was originally published (Nicolau, *La Propriété littéraire et artistique*, p. 303).

[2] See *Actes de la Conférence de Berne*, 1885, p. 47.

A writer of articles of political discussion for a newspaper cannot complain if another journal reproduces them, for, from the manner in which they are set forth, it is reasonably clear that he meant unreservedly to contribute his ideas to the hotch-potch of general opinion. Even here, however, the 'different purpose' does not altogether hold ; for, directly such articles are considered from the point of view of general literature, instead of from that of current politics, their reproduction—in the form of a miscellany, for example—seems obviously to be an infringement. Generally speaking, then, the fact that an author may have left undeveloped the possibilities of his work is no reason for taking the control of their development out of his hands.

The plea of 'public benefit.'—As to the 'public benefit,' the public ought not to be benefited at the expense of the author and to the profit of pirates. The 'public benefit' may serve as a secondary consideration when, as in the case of news, there is some independent justification for denying to the author the ordinary literary rights ; but it can never serve to over-ride a just claim to protection, for the simple reason that, whatever its immediate advantages, interference with individual rights really results to the detriment of the public in the long run.

The plea in question is one that has been urged throughout the history of copyright in respect of every case in which literary misappropriation has been left unpunished by law ; and in every case up to the present it has been found impotent of itself to prevent the amendment of the law. It is possible that at some future date the International Union will reject it, and that all extracts, for whatever purpose, made without the consent of the author of the work which supplies them, will be pronounced internationally illegal.[1]

---

[1] An able article by M. Rosmini, exposing the fallacies of most of the arguments put forward in favour of the principle of Art. 8, appears in *Le Droit d'Auteur*, 1894, p. 134.

SECTION III.

MECHANICAL MUSICAL INSTRUMENTS.

The nature of mechanical musical instruments—Manufacture of these instruments allowed—Distinction between manufacture and performance—The former strictly an unlawful adaptation—Development of the industry since 1886—The Convention provision a concession to Switzerland—The rule of the Convention—The two points of view—The history of the Convention rule—The Article does not permit *performance* of copyright airs—The device of interchangeable parts—Popularity of the improved instruments—The interpretation of the rule by the Courts—Musical copyright, not performing right, involved—German decisions—The predominant German view—The recent German domestic Act permits interchangeable parts — International importance of German decisions — French decisions permit interchangeable parts—American and English cases—Suggested alteration of the rule—Proposal to except interchangeable parts—Attempted distinction between the instrument and the discs, etc.—No mechanical musical instrument whatever is an infringement—But the Convention rule should be abolished—All unauthorised reproductions of copyright music violate a moral right—No essential difference between modern and old instruments—Suggested system of royalties.

The Nature of Mechanical Musical Instruments.

Manufacture of these Instruments allowed.—One of the most remarkable provisions of the Convention is contained in § 3 of the Closing Protocol, which indicates a notable survival of old ideas, in that it legalises a form of piracy. The Article reads : ' It is understood that the manufacture and sale of instruments serving to reproduce mechanically musical airs in which copyright subsists shall not be considered as constituting musical infringement.'

D D

Distinction between Manufacture and Performance.—The supporters of the rule are careful to explain that it is only the *manufacture and sale* of these mechanical musical instruments which is freed from liability to be treated as an offence against musical copyright, while the *performance* of copyright airs by this means falls under the general rule of Art. 9, protecting the performing right in musical and dramatic works. In considering the Article, this distinction must be accepted and carefully borne in mind, though the framers of the Convention can hardly have overlooked the fact that the manufacture and sale of a mechanical musical instrument is only an ordinary preliminary to the performance of the pieces which it is capable of reproducing.

The former strictly an Unlawful Adaptation.—It would seem that whether the manufacture and sale of musical instruments mechanically reproducing copyright airs should be permitted, is a question which, like the kindred one with reference to adaptations, arrangements of music, etc., might well be left to the various domestic legislations to decide. From one point of view at least, that part of a musical box or of a barrel organ of which the mechanical adjustment determines and produces the tune is only a particular form of adaptation suited to the requirements of a peculiar instrument, just as the Tonic Sol-fa notation of the melody of a piece of music is an adaptation of it to the needs of vocalists who prefer to adopt that system.

Development of the Industry since 1886.—The importance of the legal position of mechanical musical instruments is immeasurably greater to-day than it was when the Convention was framed. In 1886 complete consideration had not been given to the matter by any of the Union countries, nor were they then fully alive to the consequence of the step they were taking. Of late, since the appropriation of pieces of copyright music for mechanical instruments has, through the development of the arts of manufacture, become of more than

trifling importance for the composer, a great divergence of
view has manifested itself between several countries as
regards their domestic treatment of the more modern and
elaborate of such instruments; and this has led to a corresponding divergence in the interpretation of the Convention
itself. These differences have almost nullified the practical
importance of the original provision dealing with mechanical
musical instruments, and have stood in the way of its further
elucidation.

The Convention Provision a Concession to Switzerland.—The
immaturity of international thought on the subject at the time
of the Convention, however, instead of contributing to the
rejection of the article in the rigid form proposed, was probably
the occasion of its acceptance. The article was a concession
to Switzerland,[1] which had large interests at stake in the
musical box industry.[2] If the disinterested States had foreseen the logical results of the principle involved, they would
hardly have accepted it with such an easy complacency.

THE RULE OF THE CONVENTION.

The Two Points of View.—The interference with the right of
the owner of the musical copyright may be regarded in either
of two distinct ways.

In the first place, there is, on general principles of law, an
infringement of the copyright in the sheet music. Where the
tune parts are interchangeable, the perforations, spikes, and
grooves in the rolls, discs, and other interchangeable parts,
though more solid than the ink which represents the notes
between the staves in the sheet music, correspond exactly to

---

[1] M. Chenet puts its acceptance down as 'a slight act of courtesy' to Switzerland. See Nicolau, *La Propriété littéraire et artistique*, p. 285.

[2] The cantons of Vaud and Geneva were at that time the centres of the manufacture.

them in the function which they perform, and it is therefore
urged that the rolls, discs, etc., are substantially reproductions
of the sheet music.   And, if not adapted to interchangeable
parts, there is some ground for holding that the instrument
itself, considered as a whole, constitutes an infringement of the
musical copyright.

Besides this, if the mechanical musical instrument is set in
motion in public there is an infringement of the performing
right—the sounds produced are the same as those in the
original composition ; this is sufficient to constitute an infringement, whatever the medium through which the sounds are rendered.   Even if the performance be to a limited public it is
illegal.   Thus in the French domestic case, *Society of Authors,
Composers, and Publishers of Music v. Decharanne*,[1] where copyright music had been executed by an automaton in a *café*
at St. Étienne, the proprietress set up the defence that the
sounds were so feeble as to be incapable of penetrating any
distance ; but the Court held that it was sufficient that the
sounds should, under normal circumstances, be capable of
being heard by persons seated near the instrument.

Here, as has been pointed out, we are only concerned with
the *manufacture and sale* of mechanical musical instruments,
not with their employment when they reach the hands of the
purchaser ; hence we have only to consider them from the
former point of view, *i.e.* as interfering with the copyright in
the sheet music.

The History of the Convention Rule.—The proposal to exempt
mechanical musical instruments from the ordinary rules of
the Convention as to infringement originated with the Swiss
Federal Government, which in § 2 of the Closing Protocol
of its draft stated that ' (The undersigned Plenipotentiaries are
agreed) : " To define that the words ' arrangements of music '

---

[1] See *Le Droit d'Auteur*, 1901, p. 52.

. . . do not apply to pieces reproduced by automatic instruments, such as electric pianos, musical boxes, barrel organs, etc." '

The Conference of 1884 re-worded this, and brought it, except for a few slight verbal differences, to the following form, in which it stands at present : ' It is understood that the manufacture and sale of instruments serving to reproduce mechanically copyright musical airs are not considered as constituting musical infringement.' [1] The Conference of 1885 took into consideration the question whether it should be made clear that the Article extended to permit the *performance* of copyright airs by means of these instruments, as well as the manufacture and sale of instruments appropriating such airs ; but here such a difference of opinion manifested itself that no agreement could be reached. The original wording was therefore allowed to remain without addition.

The Article does not permit Performance of Copyright Airs. —The very fact that there was such a difference of opinion shows that the Article, which forms part of the *jus cogens minimum* of the Convention, cannot be read to require members of the Union to exempt performances on these instruments from the ordinary rules as to infringement of performing right, as well as to discharge their manufacture and sale from liability as infringements of musical copyright. The wording of the Article does not go thus far, and, altogether apart from the question of intention, it must be interpreted strictly, since it confers an exceptional licence.

The Device of Interchangeable Parts.—Not long after the completion of the Convention, the device of making the tune-determining parts in mechanical musical instruments detachable and interchangeable, which had hitherto been almost

---

[1] The small alterations which brought the 1884 reading into this form were effected by the Conference of 1885.

unknown, quickly sprang into prominence.[1] Where this device was adopted, the body of the instrument was constructed in such a way that when the detachable and interchangeable parts —in the form of discs, rolls, sheets, bands, or cylinders, perforated, engraved, or studded with points—were revolved in the instrument, certain notes were produced, each with a certain degree of relative duration, the whole making up a musical composition. Any number of discs, rolls, sheets, bands, or cylinders of the same size could be fitted to each instrument, so that the musical capacity of the machine was only limited by the willingness of manufacturers to produce the necessary tune-parts.

Popularity of the Improved Instruments.—The popularisation of instruments constructed in this manner, which, being, in virtue of their infinite versatility and their great delicacy of organisation,[2] far nearer perfection than the old-fashioned musical boxes, for the first time offered a serious menace to musical copyright, awakened composers and publishers into action for the defence of their interests. Proceedings were taken against the manufacturers of the offending cylinders, bands, discs, etc., on the ground that these were in reality nothing but adaptations, in a peculiar notation, of the pieces

---

[1] The extent to which the industry has been carried is attested by the great variety of forms and names under which these improved instruments appear. The following are names of some of the better known kinds : — Herophone, ariston, aristonette, orchestrion, orchestrionette, phœnix, manopan, pianophone, melodiophone, aerophone, symphonion, polyphone, organette, aeolian, clariophone, automatic piano, pianista, pianola, orpheus, sicilian, angelus, stella. To these may be added the phonograph, gramophone, graphophone, etc., which, though of slightly different nature, in that they will reproduce words as well as music, present all the essential features of the other class.

[2] In a paper presented to the Publishers' Conference at Leipzig in 1901, Mr. Boosey, the well-known English music publisher, stated that interchangeable rolls representing the music of songs could be obtained in different keys to suit various voices, and vocalists are thus enabled to dispense with accompaniments on the piano. He also pointed out that the aeolian was now used to play the music for dances.

they served to reproduce.[1]   A crop of cases sprang up in Germany, the chief centre of manufacture for the improved instruments, and in France, the United States, and Great Britain the Courts were also called upon to deal with the question.

THE INTERPRETATION OF THE RULE BY THE COURTS.

Musical Copyright, not Performing Right, involved.—In all the cases with regard to mechanical musical instruments which are cited here, the question has been simply whether the manufacture and sale of interchangeable parts—discs, rolls, bands, or cylinders—constitutes an infringement of the copyright in the pieces of music which they serve to reproduce ; the question whether the use of the instrument in public constitutes an infringement of the performing right has not been raised.

German Decisions.—German cases are by far the most numerous, and the decisions which have been given in them present some inconsistencies.

As early as 1885, the Superior Court of Leipzig (Penal Chamber) had pronounced perforated cards for use with mechanical musical instruments to be infringements.[2]   The other German cases took place subsequently to the Berne Convention, and in them, though in all except one the infringement alleged was committed in Germany, the Courts interpreted the rule of § 3 of the Closing Protocol, deciding for each case whether or not this rule should be construed to cover the

---

[1] If an unauthorised disc, roll, band, or cylinder can be regarded as an infringement of copyright in sheet music, it is fair to conclude that such an article, when lawfully made, is a subject of musical copyright.   On this assumption it is interesting to consider whether—in England and under the Convention rule—discs, etc., made with the consent of the composer of the original piece of music, must bear notice of reservation if the performing right is to be preserved intact.

[2] See *Études sur la revision de la Convention*, p. 24.

objects brought into question. For the one international case, that Article had, of course, a direct application as part of the Convention: for the domestic cases, its applicability resulted from the view taken of it by the German Courts as being an authoritative interpretation of the law of 1870, which itself contained no express statement on the question.[1]

In 1888[2] the Imperial Court (1st Civil Chamber) decided against perforated discs for use with the 'herophone.'

In 1890 (10th March) the case of *Waldmann v. Schmidt and Co.* resulted in a judgment by the Superior Court of Leipzig (4th Civil Chamber) in favour of interchangeable discs for the ' orchestrionette ' or ' phœnix,' the conclusions of the Imperial Court being rejected, on the ground that, since instruments with interchangeable parts were known in Switzerland before the coming into force of the Convention,[3] there was no reason for withholding full force from § 3 of the Closing Protocol.

On the 23rd May of the same year, in *Waldmann v. Späthe*, the Superior Court of Géra (1st Civil Chamber) ruled that toothed bands of metal for the ' clariophone ' were not infringements, holding that, whether the instruments in question were known in Switzerland in 1887 or not, the words of the Closing

---

[1] The reasoning by which the German Courts brought themselves to regard the provision of the Protocol in this light is indicated by the following passage from the judgment of the Superior Court of Leipzig (4th Civil Chamber) in *Waldmann v. The Leipzig Musical Instrument Manufactory (Paul Ehrlich and Co.)*, 1891 : 'If Germans are not to manufacture such instruments, and, on the other hand, their sale in Germany by the subjects of other countries is to be permitted under the Convention, outstripping the German law, the industry of this country will be vitally affected.'—See *Le Droit d'Auteur*, 1895, p. 59. In a note to this case, the International Office expresses a doubt whether the ground alleged will support the conclusion, and suggests that the silence of the 1870 law on the matter was of itself sufficient to authorise the Courts to adopt the rule of the Convention.

[2] In the appeal case *Pietschmann v. Waldmann*, reported in *Le Droit d'Auteur*, 1889, pp. 111 *seq.*

[3] This was stated by M. Seifert, an expert.—See *Le Droit d'Auteur*, 1890, p. 119, for the whole judgment.

Protocol laid down a clear and comprehensive rule which could not be subjected to restrictive interpretation.[1] This judgment was upheld on appeal to the immediately superior Court.

M. Waldmann then carried the case to the Imperial Court (1st Civil Chamber), which, on the 31st January, 1891, reversed the decisions of the lower Courts, and decided that the bands in question were infringements. As regards the Convention, this Court stated that 'even supposing that the authors of this declaration in the Protocol had already known of the musical instruments with interchangeable discs containing the notes, they did not intend to include the latter in their declaration, but rather musical boxes, barrel organs, and other mechanical musical instruments, playing a limited number of airs, and at that time generally known'; the Court went on to distinguish the discs in question from these.[2]

On the 28th May, 1890, in *Waldmann v. The Leipzig Musical Instrument Co.*, the Superior Court of Leipzig (4th Civil Chamber) gave a decision in regard to perforated cards for the 'ariston' contrary to its decision of the 10th March in the same year as to interchangeable discs for the 'phœnix.' In this case it followed the Imperial Court in the 'herophone' case, and decided that the cards in question were infringements.[3] Despite the ruling on the point of infringements, judgment was found for the defendant company, on the ground that the advantages accruing to the plaintiff from its illegal proceedings outweighed the damage suffered.

On appeal the 7th Civil Chamber of the Supreme Court of Saxony (22th Oct., 1894) upheld this judgment, both on the point of infringement and on that of damage, and again gave judgment for the defendant Company.[4]

---

[1] See *Le Droit d'Auteur*, 1890, p. 120.
[2] See *Le Droit d'Auteur*, 1891, pp. 81 *seq.*
[3] See *Le Droit d'Auteur*, 1890, pp. 120 *seq.*
[4] See *Le Droit d'Auteur*, 1892, pp. 62 *seq.*

A further appeal, however, led to a verdict completely in favour of M. Waldmann, the Imperial Court (1st Civil Chamber) ruling that he was entitled to recover the amount by which the defendant company was enriched as a consequence of its piratical acts, and on this point reversing the decisions of the lower Courts.[1]

In another Waldmann case—*Waldmann v. Pietschmann*,— which arose out of the declaratory judgment given in 1888 as between the same parties, their relative positions then being reversed, the Imperial Court (1st Civil Chamber) on appeal decided that 'herophone' and 'manopan' discs were infringements, overruling the decision of the lower Courts to the effect that the defendants had not been negligent, and therefore only liable in damages to the extent of their enrichment.[2]

On the 31st December, 1891, the case *Waldmann v. The Leipzig Musical Instrument Manufactory* (Paul Ehrlich and Co.) came before the 4th Civil Chamber of the Superior Court of Leipzig, and this time it was decided that discs with minute raised points arranged in concentric circles for the 'symphonion' were not infringements.[3] Though the decision in this case draws a close analogy between the 'symphonion' and the Swiss musical box, and adverts to points of difference which distinguish its discs from those of the 'herophone' and the 'clariophone' (and therefore *a fortiori* from the perforated cards of the 'ariston'), the grounds on which it is based

---

[1] See *Le Droit d'Auteur*, 1897, pp. 104 *seq.*

[2] See *Le Droit d'Auteur*, 1892, pp. 78, 79.

[3] 'It matters little that the legislator may not have thought of aristons, herophones, symphonions, etc., and it is useless to say that, in all probability, if he had thought of them, he would have treated them differently from the instruments that were present to his mind in the elaboration of the law. Perhaps it would have been more prudent to have chosen a less general expression. But this general expression has now become law ; it alone can operate as a rule,— not the intentions of the legislator, which do not in any way manifest themselves in the law and cannot be controlled.' This is a noteworthy passage from the judgment, setting forth clearly what, in our opinion, are the proper limitations to be imposed upon the suggested interpretation of the Convention rule.

are sufficient to cover all interchangeable parts.[1]   It therefore tends to conflict with the last decision of the same Court, and with decisions of the Supreme Court of Saxony and the Imperial Court.

The German case of *Litolff v. Reissner*, heard before the Superior Court of Leipzig (4th Penal Chamber) on the 8th October, 1898, was of direct international importance, inasmuch as the composition which had been appropriated for reproduction upon discs studded with minute points,—this time for the 'polyphone'— was of French origin, although the rights in it had been assigned to a German publisher.   The Court agreed with the Imperial Court and the Supreme Court of Saxony that § 3 of the Closing Protocol did not apply to instruments, like polyphones, with interchangeable discs, and so gave judgment for the plaintiff, ordering the confiscation of the offending discs.[2]

The Predominant German View.—This decision stands in direct contradiction to that of the same Court in the last cited case, and it can only be concluded that the latter represents a crude state of thought, and that, upon mature consideration, the Superior Court of Leipzig has come over to the views of the Imperial Court and the Supreme Court of Saxony.   The Imperial Court in particular has consistently ruled that Art. 3 of the Closing Protocol does not apply to mechanical musical instruments with interchangeable parts : and now that the Superior Court of Leipzig has followed its lead, this may perhaps be put down as the accepted German view.

The Recent German domestic Act permits interchangeable parts.— As far as the domestic law of Germany goes the matter has now been finally settled by the new Act of 19th June, 1901, which reads (Sec. 22) : 'Reproduction is permitted when a musical composition is, after publication, transferred to such

---

[1] See *Le Droit d'Auteur*, 1895, pp. 65 *seq.*, for the whole case.
[2] See *Le Droit d'Auteur*, 1899, pp. 10 *seq.*

discs, plates, cylinders, bands, and similar parts of instruments for the mechanical rendering of pieces of music. This provision is applicable also to interchangeable parts, provided that they are not applied to instruments by which the work can, as regards strength and duration of tone and *tempo*, be rendered in a manner resembling a personal performance.'[1]

International importance of German Decisions.—From the point of view of international copyright, the German cases, nearly all of which have involved a construction of the Berne Convention rule, are the most important as well as the most numerous. Germany, of all countries, has the largest interests involved in the manufactures of the improved instruments, and therefore any decisions of its Courts against them are most likely to contain an impartial statement of the law. The few cases which have arisen in other countries are not, however, without importance, since they at once illustrate the view taken and tend to throw more light upon the actual truth of the matter.

French Decisions permit interchangeable parts.—On the 2nd August, 1893, the French Court of the Seine decided in favour of perforated cards for 'pianistas,' 'orchestrions,' etc. The judgment, though based upon the French Law of 16th May, 1866, bears on the Convention, in virtue of the similarity between the wording of the rule laid down in that law, and that of § 3 of the Closing Protocol.[2]

On the 2nd August, 1893, the same Court gave a similar

---

[1] In view of the state of opinion indicated by this Section, it is not surprising that, at the Conference of Paris in 1896, Germany objected to amend § 3 of the Protocol so as to exclude from its scope instruments with interchangeable parts.

[2] See *Le Droit d'Auteur*, 1893, pp. 154, 155, where the International Office takes exception to the conclusion of the Court. It is interesting to note that, even in 1866, the principle of perforated cards was known, since in France it was the object of two patents, one taken out by Seetu or Seytre in 1842, the other by Thomasson in 1864.

judgment in another case ; and this was upheld on the 9th January, 1895, by the Paris Court of Appeal.[1]

In France, then, it may be gathered by analogical reasoning, that the widest interpretation is given to the Convention Article.

American and English Cases. In the United States, the Circuit Court of Massachusetts (27th January, 1888) has decided that perforated cardboard bands for the 'organette' are not infringements,[2] and in the recent English case of *Boosey v. Whight*,[3] the High Court of Justice, confirmed by the Court of Appeal, has arrived at the same conclusion in respect of similar bands for the 'aeolian.'

The judgment in this case was based mainly on the wording of the Literary Copyright Act, 1842, and does not directly involve the Berne Convention. But, if the bands in question are not infringements in England according to the domestic law, it would seem *a fortiori* that the English Courts can hardly treat them as such under the Berne Convention. From the decision in *Boosey v. Whight* we can conclude nothing as to the interpretation the English Courts would give to this article : but we can conclude that foreign manufacturers will be accorded full liberty in England to make and sell interchangeable discs. The English view as to the nature of such objects, regarding them merely as accessories of the instruments to which they relate, is at one with that of France and at variance with that of Germany. The English view as to the meaning of § 3 of the Closing Protocol has received no authoritative statement, but on this point again France differs from Germany.

---

[1] The case was *Maquet and others v. Thibouville*, reported in *Le Droit d'Auteur*, 1895, pp. 63 *seq.*

[2] *Études sur la revision de la Convention de Berne*, p. 24.

[3] *Boosey v. Whight*, 16 T.L.R. 82.

Suggested Alteration of the Rule.

Proposal to except interchangeable parts.—At the Conference of Paris, France proposed to add to the Article in the Protocol a second paragraph exempting from its benefits 'instruments which can reproduce airs only by means of the additions of perforated bands or cards, or other devices independent of the instrument, sold separately and constituting musical renderings in a particular notation.'[1] The German delegates objected to this proposition on various grounds, practical as well as theoretical.[2] In the result the French proposition fell to the ground, and the Article was left in its original form.[3] The old difficulties of interpretation, therefore, still present themselves.

Question whether included in existing Rule.—The arguments in favour of limiting § 3 of the Protocol to the older kind of mechanical musical instruments seem to resolve themselves into :

(1) A statement that in 1887 (the date of coming into force of the Convention) instruments with interchangeable parts were practically unknown.

---

[1] See *Actes de la Conférence de Paris*, p. 47. It is objectionable in that it is aimed against the instrument itself, instead of against the bands, etc., which are really the subject of the composer's complaint; so that, at first sight, it would extend to prohibit mechanical instruments with interchangeable parts reproducing only airs from the public domain. This point was raised in Committee by the delegate of Belgium.—See *Actes de la Conférence de Paris*, p. 175.

[2] See *Actes de la Conférence de Paris*, p. 199, for a memorial setting them forth. France seems to have seen, from the point of view of the composer, the defects of the Article, as interpreted by its own Courts; while, on the other hand, Germany, partly no doubt moved by its material interests, shrunk from definitively embodying in the Convention the result of the decisions of its own Imperial Court, and aimed at enlarging the statement of the Protocol, so as expressly to include the new kind of instrument.

[3] See *Actes de la Conférence de Paris*, p. 175. Belgium, Italy, and Monaco ranged themselves with France; while Spain, Great Britain, Norway, and Switzerland supported Germany. A heated discussion took place 'in which certain of the incriminated instruments even took part,' but no agreement could be reached.

(2) A contention that, even if this were not so, the actual wording of the Article, interpreted in the light of the original reading in the Federal draft, does not cover such instruments; and

(3) A distinction drawn between the instruments themselves —to which alone, in the failure of arguments (1) and (2), it is acknowledged that the Article applies—and the appurtenant discs, etc., which are looked upon as having a separate existence, and considered to be themselves infringements—of the sheet music.

Urged that interchangeable parts were unknown in 1886.— As to (1), there is evidence to show that the instruments in question had made their appearance before the Berne Conference in France, Germany, and Switzerland.[1] And it may be presumed that the delegates of these three States at least, who should have been conversant with the actual position of affairs in their own country, were aware of this. Even if this were not so, it is submitted that the words of that Article are clear, and that, in the absence of ambiguity, there is no place for restrictive interpretation. Where a general rule has been laid down by the legislature in definite and precise terms, it must be presumed that the principle on which it is based has received full consideration, and it is not for the functionaries charged with the carrying out of the law to except particular cases from the *régime* of that principle on the ground that possibly they may not have been foreseen. For the rest, even when the logical application of the principle is unsatisfactory, the Courts still should not depart from it, though it is time for the legislator to amend it.

It is admitted, even by M. Rosmini, one of the most strenuous advocates of the narrower view, that the letter of the

---

[1] In *Waldmann v. The Leipzig Musical Instrument Manufactory* an expert gave evidence that interchangeable cylinders were known in Switzerland long before the Convention.

Convention favours the manufacturers.[1] It may well be contended that it is the international duty of members of the Union to administer the letter of the law, unless they have definite means of knowledge that in the circumstances of the case the rule intended by the framers of the Convention would have been otherwise.[2]

The contention that the words do not include these.—As regards the second contention, that, apart from all question of intention, the wording of the Article, when interpreted in the light of the original Federal draft, does not cover instruments with interchangeable parts, a glance at the Article as it now stands is sufficient to show that it contains no suggestion of any such limitation ; and though the 'etc.' in the phrase of the Federal draft 'electric pianos, musical boxes, barrel organs, etc.' might demand a restricted interpretation, the fact that in the Convention reading the enumeration is dispensed with, and a general rule laid down, puts this out of the question for the Article in its present form.

Attempt to distinguish between the Instrument and the Discs, etc.—The third argument put forward by the advocates of the narrower view, which regards the interchangeable parts as distinct, and to be distinguished, from their appropriate instruments, goes too far. It assumes that the Convention wished to leave the rights of authors in their integrity, and only to exempt from the charge of infringement such instruments as would not prejudice them ; for, in other respects, both instrument and interchangeable part are on the same footing, being mechanical devices adapted to an identical end, viz., the

---

[1] See *Lettre d'Italie*, in *Le Droit d'Auteur*, 1890, p. 94.

[2] M. Numa Droz, at the 1889 Conference of the International Literary and Artistic Association held at Berne, expressed himself in favour of the narrower view, but it is noteworthy that the Society passes a resolution that ' It is to be *desired* that Art. 3 of the Closing Protocol should be limited to musical boxes and barrel organs, and should not be extended indiscriminately to all instruments serving to reproduce mechanically musical airs,' thus seeming to admit that in its actual force the Article in question had this indiscriminate application. —See *Le Droit d'Auteur*, 1895, pp. 60, 61.

reproduction of the copyright music. The fact that it was found necessary to interpolate a special provision to carry out the intention of the Convention shows of itself that it was intended to derogate in some measure from the author's rights, and such an intention would naturally include the tune-determining part in an instrument which, without that part, would be harmless.

For the rest, the discs, rolls, bands, etc., in question can hardly be conceived as performing any function apart from the instruments to which they belong. It is for those instruments that they are sold, it is only as parts of those instruments that they have any meaning, and it is simply because they so largely increase the versatility of those instruments that they seriously threaten the interests of composers. In the English case of *Boosey v. Whight*,[1] cited above, it was, indeed, contended that, since a specially skilled person could read the original music from the perforations in the rolls of paper used with the 'Aeolian,' these rolls should be regarded as copies of the original sheet-music ; but the Court of Appeal refused to regard the rolls in any other light than as particular parts of their appropriate instruments, having no individuality of their own. In the words of the Master of the Rolls : 'Conceding, for the sake of argument, that a person might be trained to play, or even to sing, from the perforated sheets, it is clear that they are not made to be so used, nor are they ever so used in fact ; and we ought, in my opinion, to deal with the case on broad business lines, and not on unpractical, though theoretically possible, assumptions.' The Court therefore held that the rolls could not be regarded as copies of the plaintiffs' sheets of music.

No Mechanical Musical Instrument whatever is an Infringement under the Convention.—The plain conclusion to which the

---

[1] *Boosey v. Whight*, 16 T.L.R. 82.

previous discussion leads is that States which desire completely to carry out their international engagements under the Convention of Berne should exempt all kinds of mechanical musical instruments from treatment as infringements.

But the Convention Rule should be abolished.—No doubt the serious damage to musical composers and publishers caused by the modern instruments is mainly responsible for the various attempts made to differentiate the improved devices from those of more ancient origin.   This fact, though it affords no justification for a fallacious interpretation of the law, offers very good reason for its amendment.   Were it not for the fact that industrial interests stand in the way,[1] it is submitted that the members of the Union would before this have perceived that the whole immunity accorded to the instruments in question is based upon an injustice to the composer.   The logical working out of the principle of the Convention should have served to demonstrate its fallaciousness.   The proposal of France to withdraw the sanction of the Convention from the more advanced class of instruments was a half-hearted attempt to get rid of the more serious consequences of the rule ; and the German delegates were undoubtedly logical in urging as they did[2] that the Article of the Protocol should either be left in its original form or abolished altogether.

All Unauthorised Reproductions of Copyright Music violate a Moral Right.—In effect, any arrangement of music for a mechanical instrument, whether the part of the instrument in

---

[1] The business of manufacturing the more modern instruments has become of remarkable magnitude.   M. Litolff, a German manufacturer, in a petition of 29th May, 1899, addressed to the Imperial Office of Justice, stated that the Polyphone Musical Instrument Company at Wahren, mainly devoted to the manufacture in question, realised a profit of 33·15 per cent. in 1897, and of 39·71 per cent. in 1898.   In eighteen months M. Litolff's own house had sold 13,564 copies of perforated cards of one popular air, and 18,657 of another, while the sale of the original editions had fallen from 7,647 to 890 copies, and from 25,698 to 13,729 copies respectively.—See *Le Droit d'Auteur*, 1899, p. 128.

[2] See *Actes de la Conférence de Paris*, pp. 199, 200.

which it is embodied is fixed or separable, interchangeable or non-interchangeable, is carried out only by an interference with the moral rights of the composer.[1] It is substantially an adaptation of the piece to suit an instrument of another kind than that for which it was written, and differs from ordinary cases of such adaptation only in that the instrument for which it is made exacts no special knowledge or skill from the performer. The sale of such instruments enables the purchaser to reproduce at will airs of which the right to permit reproduction should be solely under the control of their creator.[2] The question of damage done to the latter does not enter into the argument— at least he is deprived of a legitimate percentage on sale, and the profanation of his composition may seriously depreciate its value.[3] It is sufficient that the air is appropriated without his consent.

[1] The interests of the makers of mechanical musical instruments are not paramount, and should not be allowed to over-ride the ordinary rights of composers. Mr. Boosey pointed out at the recent Publishers' Conference of 1901 that, in matters of literary copyright, the interests of the printer, typefounder, etc., are rightly made subservient to those of the author, and that the case of mechanical musical instruments was exactly parallel.

[2] The perforated cards, known as 'the automatic piano,' etc., through the medium of which an unskilled performer is enabled to reproduce pieces of music *upon an ordinary pianoforte*, serve in almost every respect as substitutes for the pieces themselves.

[3] In *Waldmann v. The Leipzig Musical Instrument Company* (*Le Droit d'Auteur*, 1890, p. 121) the following four grounds of injury were alleged by an expert :— (*a*) Diminution of sale of the original pieces of music ; (*b*) Restriction of the copyright of the plaintiff, who would have wished to stamp the perforated cards for his compositions himself ; (*c*) Vulgarisation of the latter ; (*d*) Impossibility of translating them profitably into a foreign notation, since they would have been already too much diffused by the sale abroad of the perforated cards. Mr. Boosey in his paper stated that his firm had refused to supply sheet music to the manufacturers of barrels for barrel-organs, on account of the resultant vulgarisation. Besides all this, as he acutely remarked, there is apparently nothing to prevent a manufacturer from appropriating a melody and distorting it by adding a harmony of his own, thus threatening serious damage to the composer's reputation—unless possibly an action for libel would lie. It is at present a fairly common thing for manufacturers to cut short, to alter, and otherwise to maltreat the pieces which they appropriate, with the object of suiting them to the capabilities of the various instruments.

No essential difference between Modern and Old Instruments.—
As for the attempted distinction between the two kinds of
instruments in respect of their invasion of musical copyright,
the distinction is one only between offending adaptations sold
separately from their appropriate instruments, and offending
adaptations which are so embodied in their appropriate instruments that they cannot easily be detached.[1] Both kinds of
adaptation are morally unfair, but the facilities for the manufacture of the former are infinitely greater than those for the
manufacture of the latter, and so the former has had to bear
the brunt of the blame. The only fair way to deal with them
is to prohibit both, leaving the manufacturer to make a bargain
for the right of reproduction with the owner of the musical
copyright.

It is, therefore, to be hoped that, at some future Conference
of the Union, § 3 of the Closing Protocol will be suppressed.
This would leave the whole question to the domestic rules of
each country, under Art. 2 of the Convention ; but, in view
of the international importance of music, it might be found
well to make an absolute and express provision on the subject
aimed indiscriminately *against* all mechanical musical instruments, instead of in their favour.

Suggested system of Royalties.—It will probably be some
time before such a sweeping reform as this is carried out, even
though its justice speedily becomes patent. Meanwhile it may
be found that the adoption of some such system of obligatory
percentages as that sketched by M. Litolff in his petition to the
German Imperial Office of Justice, already referred to, will
serve to reconcile conflicting interests. M. Litolff suggests that
the manufacture and sale of instruments reproducing copyright

---

[1] As the German delegates pointed out at the Conference of Paris, in view
of the fact that some countries mainly devote themselves to the manufacture of
instruments with interchangeable parts and others to those with fixed parts, it is
internationally unfair, as well as logically unsound, to establish different treatment for the two classes.—*Actes de la Conférence de Paris*, p. 200.

airs, and performances by them, shall be allowed, but only on payment to the owner of the copyright of a maximum percentage of $7\frac{1}{2}$ per cent. on the gross, or $12\frac{1}{2}$ per cent. on the net, value of each copy of the reproducing part.[1] This proposal refers only to instruments with interchangeable parts, but it might well be extended to cover all kinds.

---

[1] *Le Droit d'Auteur*, 1899, p. 128. The chief objection to any percentage system is that, owing to the difficulty involved in the collection of the sums due to the author, he is often defrauded of his rights. Under the Colonial Copyright Act of 1847, arrangements were entered into between Great Britain and many of her colonies by which the importation of foreign reprints of English works into the colonies was allowed on payment to the author of a certain percentage of their value (in Canada, $12\frac{1}{2}$ per cent.). The duty of collecting these percentages was entrusted to the Customs officers, and was carried out so negligently that it ceased to be worth while for authors and publishers to concern themselves about their colonial rights. In Canada, for instance, 11d. was the whole amount that had been collected for Archbishop Trench during a number of years, though his works had a large sale in Canada.

SECTION IV.

REMEDIES AND PROCEDURE.

Remedies under the Convention—The general rule as to remedies—Seizure of infringements under Article 12—Control of circulation under Article 13 —Presumption of authorship under Article 11—The 1886 rule as to seizure of reprints—The Paris Amendment to this—Each country is bound to seize piratical works—Control of circulation of works is reserved for domestic administration—Rules as to procedure—Each country to protect aliens on same conditions as its own subjects—Each Court to follow its own procedure—May special Security for Costs be exacted from aliens?—Name on work raises presumption of authorship—Utility of the presumption—History of Article 11—Article 11 not in conflict with Article 2—An illustrative Italian case—Certificate of accomplishment of formalities may be required—Proposed that the International Office should grant certificates.

Remedies under the Convention.

The General Rule as to Remedies.—It has already been pointed out that the general rule of the Convention with regard to the remedies to be accorded to foreign authors, and the rules of procedure to which the latter are to be subjected, is furnished by Art. 2, which in these as in other matters secures to aliens the same treatment from each country as that accorded by its domestic law to natives. It is not usually within the province of an international agreement to dictate to its parties the means they are to adopt for the safeguarding of the rights it confers ; and, therefore, in respect of remedies and procedure, the Convention contains few Articles tending to modify Art. 2. There are, however, some points of particular international importance connected with the enforcement of Convention protection upon which it has been deemed advisable to lay down special rules.

Seizure of Infringements under Article 12.—In view of the fact that Convention protection may expire in one country sooner than in another, and so lay the author open to injury from the wholesale exportation of copies of his work,—lawful in the place where they have been produced,—into a place where they still have a claim to protection, an Article (12) has been inserted providing for the seizure of the offending works in countries where they constitute infringements.[1] This Article at once concedes an international right and imposes an international duty.

Control of Circulation under Article 13.—Art. 13, which states that each country is free to control the circulation, representation, and exhibition of works, is merely declaratory in its purport. It lends its sanction to domestic rules punishing the publication and dissemination of seditious, blasphemous, obscene, or libellous works, requiring printers and publishers to conform to administrative regulations, such as provisions for the maintenance of a censorship, the enforcement of which in respect of foreign works might otherwise have been regarded as a breach of international duty.

Presumption of Authorship under Article 11.—Finally, the difficulty which attaches to proof of authorship by an alien has given rise to Art. 11, providing that the author whose name appears upon the work shall be entitled *prima facie* to be treated as the true author. This Article also contains a provision indicating a means of proof of the fulfilment of the formalities imposed by Art. 2 of the Convention.

The 1886 Rule as to Seizure of Reprints.—In the 1886 Convention, Art. 12 reads :

' Every infringing work shall be subject to seizure upon

---

[1] See *Actes de la Conférence de Berne*, 1884, p. 57. The original aim of the Union, as expressed in the Act of 1886, was to enable copies to be seized upon *importation* into countries where the author's copyright still subsisted ; but at the Conference of Paris a wider view led to the suppression of all indication as to point of time.

importation into those countries of the Union in which the original work has a right to legal protection.

'The seizure will take place in accordance with the domestic law of each country.'

The words in the original French are 'Toute œuvre contrefaite *peut* être saisie, etc.,' which would appear to place the acceptance of the principle of seizure upon importation at the discretion of each country. This, however, as was explained at the Conference of Paris,[1] was not the intention of the Convention. Art. 12 was drawn up in the interests of the owner of the copyright, being meant to provide the latter with a means of defence against the transport of infringements from one country to another. It forms part of the *jus cogens minimum* of the Convention, and the permissive form in which it is couched, while it fixes infringements with liability to a very stringent form of remedy, does not leave countries free to hold their hands, when to do this would be contrary to the wishes of the author of the original work.[2]

For the rest, the second paragraph of the Article allows each country to regulate the carrying out of the seizure,—to determine the necessary form and the competent authority,—according to its domestic law.

The Paris Amendment to this.—The Additional Act of Paris suppressed the words 'upon importation,' with the object of

---

[1] See *Actes de la Conférence de Paris*, p. 173.

[2] In the first draft of Art. 12 the latter paragraph read—'The seizure shall take place upon the request either of the public minister or of the interested party, in conformity with the domestic legislation of each country.' This appeared to limit the liability to seizure of offending works to cases where an express request was made by a person belonging to one of the two specified classes, and therefore the English delegates objected to it, in view of the fact that in England after general notice seizure takes place without the direct intervention of the copyright-owner or of a Minister of State for each case. The result of their objection was that the paragraph in question was brought into its present form.—See *Actes de la Conférence de Berne*, 1885, p. 51.

making it clear that countries were to have a free hand as to the time of seizure of infringements ; it also effected one or two slight verbal alterations in § 1 of the Article. In its present form that paragraph reads thus:

'Every infringing work shall be subject to seizure by the competent authorities of the countries of the Union in which the original work has a right to legal protection.'

The latter paragraph of the Article remains unaltered.

Each country is bound to seize piratical works.—The effect of the amendment seems to be to oblige countries of the Union to seize infringing works anywhere within their territories at any point of time, subject to the proviso that they are to be allowed to perform the seizure in their own way. The English delegates, however, in accepting the amended Article, stated that Great Britain could not hold itself bound to carry out its requirements in colonies where the laws did not permit seizure in the interior of the country.[1]

Control of circulation of works is reserved for domestic administration.—Art. 13 arose out of a proposition made by the German delegacy in the 1884 Committee of Draughtsmanship. It has undergone no change since its acceptance by the Conference of 1884 in the following form :

'It is understood that the provisions of the present Convention cannot in any way derogate from the right which belongs to the Government of each country of the Union to permit, to supervise, and to prohibit, by legislative measures or police regulations, the circulation, representation, and exhibition of every work or production in respect of which the competent authority may find it necessary to exercise that right.'

[1] See *Actes de la Conférence de Paris*, p. 173, where is also reported an ingenious amendment by the Swiss delegacy, prohibiting the seizure of works, lawful in their country of origin, when merely in process of transit through a country in which they are unlawful. This amendment was withdrawn, upon a representation that the question it raised was one of considerable nicety, which would rarely present itself in practice.

It constitutes simply an express declaration of the right of Union countries to enforce, in respect of foreign works claiming Convention copyright, any regulations for the administrative control of the press and the stage which domestic policy may dictate,[1] and to subject all publications to the criminal liability

RULES AS TO PROCEDURE.

In order that an author may effectively avail himself of the machinery created by the State for the enforcement of his rights, he must consider not only his 'remedy,' which may be likened to the arm of the engine by which its operations are immediately carried out, but also the appropriate 'procedure,' or the means to be adopted for setting the engine in motion and making it work in the right way. In this connection the first question that arises, when the wrong is an international matter, relates to the determination of the country to which the demand for redress should be referred—or, to continue the simile, to the selection, from a number of kindred machines, of that one which is best suited to the operation in hand.

Each Country to protect aliens on same conditions as its own subjects.—On this the Convention contains no special provision. The matter is therefore regulated by Art. 2. Each State is bound to throw open its Courts to alien authors of the Union under the same circumstances as to its own subjects. The principles upon which such intervention depends have already been considered in Part II., Chapter iv., from which it will have been gathered that the right rule is for States to take jurisdiction over all wrongs committed within their boundaries,

---

[1] Such a control is almost unknown in England, though traces of it are to be found in the censorship of plays by the Lord Chamberlain, and the statutory requirement that printers shall attach their name and address to the works printed by them—a requirement which, as is well known, is not rigorously enforced.

—in other words, that the appropriate forum is the *forum delicti*.[1] This was the view taken by the English Court of Chancery in *Morocco Bound Syndicate v. Harris*,[2] when the Court refused to intervene to protect the plaintiffs from threatened infringements of their performing rights in Germany.

Each Court to follow its own procedure.—When the right Court has been decided, it follows almost as a matter of course that the procedure to be adopted is the procedure of that Court ;[3] for it is quite natural that, in asking redress of a foreign Court, an author should be required to prefer his request in the form established by the rules of the Court. As regards the International Union, this view is supported by the general rule of Art. 2. In this connection, it is worthy of note that § 1 of the Closing Protocol reads thus in the Swiss draft of the Convention : ' It is understood that the final provision of Art. 2 of the Convention (relating to the accomplishment of the conditions and formalities of the country of origin) does not affect the law of each of the contracting States, so far as concerns the procedure followed before the tribunals and the competence of those tribunals.' This declaration was however omitted by the 1884 Conference as superfluous.[4] Its purport was simply to make it clear that, while the performance of the *substantive* conditions and formalities of the country of origin was, under Art. 2, sufficient to establish the author's right to protection throughout the Union, as regards the conditions and formalities *of procedure*, he was bound to conform to the rules of the country from which he claimed the enforcement of his right.

May special Security for Costs be exacted from Aliens?—It is hardly necessary to dwell upon the distinction between the

---

[1] *Forum delicti* = country where the offence has been committed.

[2] *Morocco Bound Syndicate v. Harris* (1895), 1 Ch. 535.

[3] This is expressed by the maxim of Private International Law, *Ubi forum, ibi lex*.

[4] See *Actes de la Conférence de Berne*, 1884, p. 63.

conditions and formalities upon which the birth of the copyright depends, and those which merely relate to its enforcement
against infringements.[1]   To the latter class belongs the *cautio
judicatum solvi*, or deposit of security for costs, required in
many countries from foreign plaintiffs.   The policy pursued by
the Union of equalising aliens and subjects before the law seems
inconsistent with the continued exaction of a special security
in matters of copyright coming under the Convention.   Still, it
would seem that some safeguard against vexatious proceedings is necessary in the case of alien plaintiffs, who may
easily depart from the country without leaving any effects
to answer for the costs of the suit.   But the general rule
of Art. 2 is against the imposition of special formalities on
alien authors of the International Union : and the superfluous
§ 1 of the Protocol in the Swiss draft was directed rather
towards forestalling any claim on the part of foreign authors
to exemption from the ordinary rules of procedure applicable to
subjects, than towards retaining any special disability imposed
on them and not imposed on subjects.   Hence, in spite of one
or two adverse decisions of the French and Belgian courts,[2] it
seems tolerably clear that it is a breach of contractual duty for
a State of the Union to exact any exceptional security from a
Unionist author, on the ground that he is an alien.[3]   Where
the deposit is exacted from subjects resident abroad as well as
from aliens, as is the case in England, the spirit of the Convention is scarcely departed from.

[1] The English registration, which is merely a condition precedent to suing,
presumably belongs to the latter class, but the English Courts do not require it
of alien members of the Union suing under the International Copyright Act of
1886.

[2] See *Le Droit d'Auteur*, 1889, p. 46, and 1892, pp. 48, 78.

[3] See in support of this view M. Louis Cattreux, then Secretary of the International Literary and Artistic Association, in *Le Droit d'Auteur*, 1889, pp. 73,
87, 95, and *contra* M. Darras, in *Le Droit d'Auteur*, 1892, p. 48, and M. Nicolau,
La Propriété littéraire et artistique, p. 319.—See also *Actes de la Conférence de
Paris*, p. 70.

Name on Work raises presumption of Authorship.—The general rule of the Convention in respect of procedure is thus that of the equalization of aliens with subjects, which is adopted by Art. 2 as the basis of the Convention. The only special provision on the matter contained in the Convention is to be found in Art. 11 :

'In order that the authors of works protected by the present Convention may, in the absence of proof to the contrary, be considered as such, and consequently admitted to institute proceedings against infringements before the Courts of the various countries of the Union, it is sufficient for their name to be indicated on the work in the accustomed manner.

'For anonymous or pseudonymous works, the publisher whose name is indicated on the work is entitled to safeguard the rights belonging to the author. He is, without other proof, reputed the lawful representative of the anonymous or pseudonymous author.

'It is understood, nevertheless, that the Courts may, if necessary, require the production of a certificate from the competent authority, stating that the formalities prescribed, according to Art. 2, by the law of the country of origin have been fulfilled.'

Utility of the presumption.—The need for some such Article was first suggested by Germany in its list of questions for the Conference of 1884.[1] Even in his own country it is so difficult for an author to prove his title to copyright, *i.e.* to demonstrate the originality of his work, the fact of authorship, etc., that, where their own subjects are concerned, most States set up presumptions in favour of authorship.[2] Where an

---

[1] See No. 14 of this list. *Actes de la Conférence de Berne*, 1884, pp. 26, 36.

[2] In England registration establishes a *primâ facie* ownership of copyright under Sec. 11 of the Literary Copyright Act, 1842. The German law sets up an elaborate system of presumptions. Thus Sec. 7 of the Copyright Act of 1901 reads : 'If a published work contains on the title-page, in the dedication or preface, or at the conclusion, the name of an author, the presumption is that he

author is proceeding, in virtue of international rights, before a foreign Court, his difficulty is considerably increased. Under the general rule of the Convention, countries would, no doubt, have extended the benefit of their own domestic presumptions to foreign authors: but in view of the diversity of their various systems of law, this relief would have been somewhat illusory. Hence the demand for a uniform international rule on the subject.

History of Article 11.—The German delegates framed an Article in pursuance of the suggestion conveyed in their question, and this was accepted by the Conference of 1884.[1] It was almost identical with that actually included in the Convention, except that it contained no reference to the exaction by the Courts of certificates that the formalities of the country of origin have been fulfilled.[2]

Article 11 not in conflict with Article 2.—In the Conference of 1885, M. Rosmini observed that Art. 12 (as Art. 11 was then numbered) was not in harmony with Art. 2.   In this, as M. Reichardt pointed out, M. Rosmini confused substantive conditions and formalities with rules of procedure.[3]   In reality

is the originator of the work. If the work consists of articles by several contributors, it suffices if the name is given at the beginning or end of the article.   In the case of works published under any other than the author's real name, or without an author's name, the editor, or, should no such editor be mentioned, the publisher is entitled to defend the rights of the originator.   In the case of works which, before or after publication, are performed or recited in public, the presumption is that the originator is the person who was described as author on the occasion of the announcement of the performance or recitation.'

[1] In this its first shape, Art. 11 was identical with Art. 7 of the Franco-German Treaty of 1883, and with the two first paragraphs of Art. 7 of the Italo-German Treaty of 1884.—*Le Droit d'Auteur*, 1899, p. 50.

[2] It specified the places in which the appearance of the author's name would secure him the benefit of the presumption, thus: 'Upon the title-page of the work, below the dedication or the preface, or at the end of the work' (*Actes de la Conférence de Berne*, 1884, p. 56).   From these words it was deduced by Sir H. G. Bergne (*Actes de la Conférence de Berne*, 1885, p. 35) that the Article did not apply to works of art.   The clause in question has now, however, been left out, and the name is to be indicated 'in the accustomed manner,' which would appear to mean in *any* manner that is usual.

[3] See *Actes de la Conférence de Berne*, 1885, p. 35.

the intention of Art. 11 is not to set up any new formality
or to interfere with any old one.   In order to gain copyright
an author must perform the conditions and formalities prescribed by Art. 2.   When he has done this, his right is
established and he is not required to do anything else.   But
when he comes into Court to enforce his copyright, he has,
in the absence of any presumption in his favour, to enter
into a formal and elaborate proof of his ownership—of his
identity as the author of the work which has been infringed.
All that Art. 11 does is to provide that, when his name
appears on the work, he shall be dispensed from this proof
of identity, and the burden of showing that his title is bad
shall fall upon the defendant.   He is not exempted from
the performance of the substantive formalities of the country
of origin, and is still bound to prove that these, which do
not affect his actual right but only its practical validity, have
satisfactorily been fulfilled.   The indication of name is thus
entirely within the discretion of the author, and the only result
of its omission is that he is deprived of the useful presumption
of authorship which it carries with it.

An illustrative Italian case.—On this point attention may
be drawn to the Italian case *May's Sons v. The Italian
Institute of Graphic Art*, which came before the Milan Court
of Appeal on the 10th January, 1899.[1]   The Court ruled that, in
order for a work to gain protection under the Convention, it
was necessary for the author, or, where the work was anonymous or pseudonymous, for the publisher, to indicate his name
upon it.   On this and another ground, it gave judgment against
the plaintiffs, who had only put the letter ' M,' the initial of
their name, upon the chromo-lithographs for which they
claimed protection.[2]

[1] See *Le Droit d'Auteur*, 1899, p. 54.

[2] It thought that ' Art. 11 of the Convention of Berne . . . indicates simply
that *one* of the principal formalities which are essential and fundamental for
assuring to the work the protection provided by Art. 2 of the Convention . . .

Upon appeal to the Court of Cassation at Rome (7th June, 1900), this interpretation of the Berne Convention rule was declared to be erroneous, and the judgment of the lower Court was reversed.[1]   The following passage from the decision of the Court clearly sets forth the true principle of Art. 11 :

'Whoever brings an action against another person, imputing to him the infringement of a literary or artistic work, would, according to the general rules of law, be bound to prove that he himself (the plaintiff) is author of the work ; but, by a favour granted to authors by Art. 11 of the Convention, it is enough simply to have indicated on the work the name "In the accustomed manner," to be dispensed from furnishing the proof exacted by the common law ; and then the duty of establishing that the plaintiff is not the author of the work falls on the defendant.'

Certificate of accomplishment of Formalities may be required. —In order to make it quite clear that Art. 11 provided no relief from the substantive conditions and formalities of Art. 2, and afforded no presumption of their accomplishment, the Conference of 1885 thought it advisable to add a third paragraph to that Article, providing for the exaction by Courts, in case of necessity, of a certificate setting forth that those conditions and formalities had been fulfilled ; and with this the Article was brought into its present form.

The words 'in case of necessity' in the final provision probably have the effect of preventing any demand on the part of the Court for a certificate, when the plaintiff has proved

consists in the imposition upon this work of the name of the author, or in its place that of a third party (publisher). In this way the authorship of the work, the desire to have it considered as an intellectual work, to remove it for a certain time from the public domain, and to warn others against imitating it are affirmed in a formal manner against the world at large . . . This indication does not set up a presumption of the existence of the right, in the sense of a facility to be accorded for the institution of the action : on the contrary, it is the condition necessary to *establish the proof* of the right and to make it effective.'

[1] See *Le Droit d'Auteur*, 1900, p. 145.

that, in the country of origin, no conditions or formalities whatever are required.[1] This is the case in Monaco and Tunis for all classes of works, while in Norway photographs, in Germany anonymous and pseudonymous works and photographs, in Belgium posthumous works and State publications, and in Switzerland posthumous works, State publications, and photographs, alone are subjected to formalities.[2] The case is the same when the defendant does not deny that the plaintiff has fulfilled the formal requirements of the law.

Proposed that the International Office should grant Certificates.—In the Conference of 1885 M. Rosmini proposed that the International Office should be entrusted with the duty of providing certificates required under Art. 11. 'In delivering certificates which should serve as substitutes for those of the country of origin, the International Office would facilitate the exercise of their rights for authors.' After some discussion, however, it was agreed that the proposed task would be too heavy for the Office, though it was stated that the latter would always be ready to assist authors in obtaining the necessary certificates.[3]

At the Conference of Paris the question was raised again, in connection with the whole subject of entrusting the Office with the duty of registering copyright works.[4] M. Morel, the Director of the International Office, then declared that, in his opinion, without undue trouble, the Office could usefully act as

---

[1] This may be done *arguendo* or by expert legal evidence, or by the production of an official statement from the authorities of the country of origin.

[2] See *Le Droit d'Auteur*, 1897, pp. 38, 39.

[3] See *Actes de la Conférence de Berne*, 1885, p. 37.

[4] An international register would be of considerable advantage in the case of anonymous and pseudonymous works, with regard to which it is usually desired to prevent the disclosure of the author's name. This was suggested by the Congress of German Authors at Vienna in 1893.—*Actes de la Conférence de Paris*, p. 49. It is noteworthy that, according to the German Law (Act of 1901, Sec. 31), if the real name of the author is not indicated within thirty years, the copyright expires.

an intermediary between plaintiffs requiring a certificate and the law of the country of origin.[1]   After various suggestions for *Vœux*, or ' Recommendations,' the whole matter was dropped, it being understood that the Office was always ready to serve the interests of authors in any way within its power.

[1] He estimated the number of cases in which a certificate is required at about twelve or fifteen per annum.—See *Actes de la Conférence de Paris*, p. 130.

CHAPTER VI.

THE REVISION OF THE BERNE CONVENTION.

SECTION I.

THE CONDITIONS OF REVISION.

The progress of international thought—The imperfection of the Convention—The nature of the advance of the Convention—Recommendations of the Conferences—Relation between national and international progress—Preliminary Recommendations of the Conference of 1884—The Recommendations of the Conference of Paris—Sub-Unions—The function of sub-Unions—Sub-Unions for the Additional Act and the Interpretative Declaration—Recommendations and sub-Unions only provisional measures—Various domestic influences affecting international progress—Effect of domestic law—Treaties and the Convention—Resolutions of literary and artistic societies.

THE PROGRESS OF INTERNATIONAL THOUGHT.

The Imperfection of the Convention.—The substance of the Convention as it stands at present has now been set forth. Though that agreement establishes throughout a wide area a very full measure of protection for literary and artistic works it cannot be claimed for it that it is a perfect and definitive code of international copyright rules. A careful examination of it shows that, in many respects, the moral rights of authors have suffered derogation owing to extraneous considerations,

the chief of which has been the desire to secure unanimity
among the contracting parties.   Still, it must be remembered
that public international benefit and the wishes of the contracting States are not among the least of the things to be
taken into account in the formation of an International Copyright Union.

The following are put forward by authors as instances in
which their just claims have been abated by the Convention :
the restrictive translating period (*délai d'usage*) of Art. 5,
the rule of Art. 7 that articles of political discussion in
periodicals may be reproduced without indication of source,
the liberty of extract sanctioned by Art. 8, and the exemption
of mechanical musical instruments from the ordinary rules as to
infringement which is carried out by the Closing Protocol, § 3.
The qualified character of the protection accorded to works
of architecture, photographs, and choregraphic works by §§ 1
and 2 of the Protocol is admittedly due to the difficulty of
securing agreement throughout the Union in the treatment
of these subjects.

The nature of the advance of the Convention.—As has already
been pointed out in Part II., it is impossible to arrive at a
complete and definitive international agreement between the
civilised countries of the world while the domestic law of
those countries remains diverse and improves at varying rates
of progress.   In this connection, it may once again be remarked that it is only when national systems approach a
common perfection that it is possible for an international
system to approach completion.   In the meantime a common
civilisation subjects all the States to which literature is an
object of care to nearly the same set of influences : and, as
a result, their copyright legislation is based on identical
principles.   It is this which makes possible such an agreement as the Convention of Berne.   Concurrently with the

advance of the domestic codes of countries within the Union, the intension of that agreement will increase—the protection it accords will become more complete : concurrently with the advance of the domestic codes of countries outside the Union its extension will increase—the area it covers will widen.

Provision for advance in both directions has been made by the Convention itself, in Art. 17, which deals with revisions of the Convention, and Arts. 18 and 19, which deal with new accessions to the Union. In the work of revision, the necessity of preserving the cohesion of the existing Union and the desirability of facilitating new accessions should both be kept in mind : the intension of the Convention is not recklessly to be increased, without due regard to its extension.

RECOMMENDATIONS OF THE CONFERENCES.

Relation between National and International Progress.—In practice, the progress of an international Convention like that of Berne generally keeps a little in advance of the domestic progress of the most backward of its signatories : for a country is often ready to accept a principle and to embody it in an agreement, before it is able to establish it in its own law. Where, however, the principle is one of great moment, this state of things cannot well exist unless a change in the conflicting domestic system has already been definitely projected. Hence in regard to certain matters of importance, in the domestic treatment of which there is little approach to uniformity among the countries of the Union, it has been found well, however plain the need of uniform international rules, to refrain from embodying such rules in the Convention.

The Recommendations of International Conferences.—In such cases the desire for perfection in the international system has been reconciled with the exigencies of convenience by putting forward Recommendations (*Vœux*). These indicate what the Union conceives to be the ideal rules on certain matters, with the object of paving the way for their ultimate adoption into the Convention, when the various domestic hindrances shall have been removed. They are not legally binding, but are merely expressions of opinion, to which the parties concerned have pledged themselves and which there-fore they can reasonably be expected to support when occasion arises.

Preliminary Recommendations of the Conference of 1884.— The Berne Conference of 1884 passed two such resolutions, under the name 'Principles recommended for an Ulterior Unification.' They run as follows :—

' 1.   The protection accorded to the authors of literary or artistic works should endure for the whole of their life, and after their death for a number of years, which should not be less than thirty.

' 2.   It would be well to favour as much as possible the tendency towards the complete assimilation of translating right to the ordinary right of reproduction.'[1]

The Conference of 1885, however, while stating that it still accepted these principles, thought it futile to reproduce their text in the completed instrument, and they were accord-ingly abandoned.[2]

These Recommendations have had their effect on domestic law,[3] and the second of them has now, under qualification of a

---

[1] See *Actes de la Conférence de Berne*, 1884, p. 88.

[2] See *Actes de la Conférence de Berne*, 1885, p. 57, where another Recommenda-tion, suggested by the Italian delegacy and informally accepted by the Conference, is also reported.   This was to the effect that it was desirable to introduce into the Union the system of preliminary licence, according to which no person can per-form the work of another, without first producing to the local authorities the written consent of the author, and obtaining their sanction for the proposed representation.

[3] In the Japanese Act of 1899 the copyright period has been fixed at the author's life and thirty years, and, subject to a ten years' restrictive translating period, the period of translating right has been assimilated to this.   In the

ten years' restrictive translating period, been embodied in the international system.

The Recommendations of the Conference of Paris.—At the Conference of Paris the system of Recommendations was again adopted, and three Recommendations were put forward. These are set out in the next Section, where the results of the Paris revision are treated as a whole.

Subsidiary Unions.

The Function of sub-Unions.—While Recommendations, such as those passed at the Conferences of the Union, are undoubtedly an excellent incentive to progress where a general agreement exists throughout the Union upon a matter of principle, combined with some reluctance on the part of a number of the members to embody it in a binding rule, it is not so where either of these two conditions is lacking. If there is much disagreement as to a principle, it is of course impossible for the Union to lay down a rule embodying it in any shape or form. On the other hand, if there is complete agreement as to the desirability of enforcing a principle, there is nothing to hinder its immediate incorporation into the Convention. Where, however, the great majority of members of the Union are at one as to the desirability and practicability of laying down a certain rule, and only one or two take up a different attitude, the rule cannot be made part of the Convention without imperilling the stability of the Union; still, at the same time it seems a pity to sacrifice possible progress by omitting it altogether. In such cases, the International

English Copyright Bill lately before Parliament, the same period has been adopted, and an absolute assimilation of translating right to the ordinary copyright has been decreed for domestic works (international relations being regulated under the Bill by the Convention rule). In the German Act of 1901 the translating period has been absolutely assimilated to the ordinary period for copyright (which is retained at author's life and thirty years).

Copyright Union, following the example of the Universal Postal Union and the International Industrial Union,[1] has adopted the system of subsidiary Unions or 'sub-Unions.'

The principle of these sub-Unions has already been explained. Each consists of a number of States, members of the principal Union, banded together by a common agreement to carry out certain provisions in advance of, or subsidiary to, those of the original Convention. Its existence is recognised by the principal Union, and it is allowed to avail itself of the machinery constructed by the latter for the preservation of its system.

Sub-Unions for the Additional Act and the Interpretative Declaration.—According to Art. 17 of the Berne Convention, alterations in that Act are not binding unless they receive the unanimous consent of its parties. Hence the refusal of Norway and Great Britain at the Conference of Paris in 1896 to accept the Additional Act of Paris and the Interpretative Declaration respectively has in strictness prevented either of those agreements from becoming part of the system of the original Union. Hence, too, Sweden, in joining the Union in 1904, was able to accept the Convention and refuse the Additional Act. Under these circumstances two separate sub-Unions are formed, the one consisting of the signatories to the Additional Act and the other of the signatories to the Interpretative Declaration. The fact that there is only one dissentient to the Declaration and only two to the Additional Act tends to throw into the background the fact that neither of these revisions really affects the Union as a whole.[2]

[1] See *Le Droit d'Auteur*, 1898, p. 33.

[2] Reason has already been given for the belief that the Articles in the Closing Protocol, dealing with the protection of works of architecture, photographs, and choregraphic works, have also the effect of setting up sub-Unions between the countries that grant protection to these works. The fact that these Articles are placed in the Protocol, not in the body of the Convention, brings into prominence their provisional character.

At the Conference of Paris a Recommendation was carried expressing the need felt by the Union for one single text, accepted by all its members: and it is possible that, before the next Conference of the Union, the present dissentients by carrying out the necessary alterations in their domestic law, will have made it feasible to incorporate the two subsidiary agreements into the original Convention.

Recommendations and sub-Unions only Provisional Measures.— It is obvious that Articles binding only certain countries, Recommendations, and sub-Unions, can only be regarded as provisional measures, marking in a definite manner the lines of progress for the Union as a whole : and that great care must be exercised in adopting such measures, lest they seriously threaten the cohesion of the principal body. With this in view, they must never be applied to principles of which there is not a distinct prospect of acceptance on the part of the dissentient States in the future.[1]

Various Domestic Influences affecting International Progress.

Effect of Domestic Law.—For the countries which are tardy in the recognition of international copyright, the Convention, the subsidiary Acts, and the Recommendations of Conferences urge on domestic progress ; while the domestic law of the more progressive States leads the way to the development of the Convention itself.[2]

---

[1] Unless however they embody arrangements between certain States which, deriving their value from purely local or otherwise special considerations, would fail to apply to the others. Such a situation is obviously not likely to arise in matters of copyright.

[2] **Treaties and the Convention.**—In the initiation of the Convention particular treaties played an important part—preparing States for some general international regulation of copyright, and indicating the most suitable lines for this to follow. The Franco-German Treaty of 1883, the form of which was almost

Resolutions of Literary and Artistic Societies.—The resolutions of the various literary and artistic associations, which represent the views of authors, publishers, and artists themselves upon the treatment that is due to them, exert a great influence upon general opinion. Some of these societies are indefatigable in suggesting improvements in the existing state of affairs, and are often primarily instrumental in setting to work the forces of national and international legislation.

Reference has already been made to the part played by the 'International Literary and Artistic Association' in the movement which led to the formation of the International Union, and to the work since done by that and kindred institutions in suggesting amendments of the Convention. It only remains to add that the purely national societies, through their effect on domestic systems of law and modes of thought, also contribute, though in an indirect way, to the development of international opinion.[1]

identically followed in subsequent treaties between Germany and Belgium and Germany and Italy, was the basis upon which the Convention was drawn up. The assimilation of the period of translating right to that of copyright, which has been carried out subject to certain conditions by the Additional Act of Paris, was foreshadowed in treaties between Spain and Belgium, and Spain and France, so long ago as 1880. The whole period between 1880 and 1886 was marked by a revival of interest in copyright throughout the civilised world, which was productive of a large crop of treaties.

Since 1886 the Convention has, throughout the Union, practically superseded all particular agreements : and the denunciation of old, rather that the creation of fresh treaties, is the order of the day.

Treaties may, however, facilitate the entry into the Union of countries outside ; thus Japan in two treaties of 1896 with Germany and Switzerland respectively and one of 1894 with Great Britain definitely promised to make that accession to the Convention which it carried out on the 15th July, 1899.—*Le Droit d'Auteur*, 1896, p. 152.

Within the Union, the energy of the various States is now concentrated directly on the development of the Convention.

[1] Attention may here be called to a movement on the part of the Co-operative Society of Austrian Authors in the German Language, and the Austro-Hungarian Association of Publishers, in favour of the adhesion of Austria-Hungary to the Berne Convention.—See *Le Droit d'Auteur*, 1892, p. 73 ; 1900, pp. 9, 54.

It must be remembered that the views of all literary and artistic societies represent mainly one set of interests, and are usually far in advance of those which it is possible for the Union to take. Nevertheless it is the expressed object of the Union to protect the rights of authors and artists, and therefore the statement of their grievances by authors and artists themselves is of value in promoting the development of the Convention system along practical lines.

SECTION II.

THE REVISION OF PARIS.

The Conference of Paris—Revisions under Art. 17 of the Convention—Delay in holding Paris Conference—The legislative results of the Paris Conference—The Additional Act—The four Articles of the Act—Amendments effected—All Unionist works protected—Author's exclusive translating right extended—Indication of source required for borrowed newspaper articles—Works of architecture conditionally protected—The Interpretative Declaration—Effect of the Declaration—Conditions and formalities of country of origin alone are required—Definition of 'works published'—Dramatisation and novelisation prohibited—The Recommendations of the Conference of Paris—Recent progress on these lines—Treaties which have been superseded—Present tendency is against making of separate treaties.

THE CONFERENCE OF PARIS.

Revisions under Art. 17 of the Convention.—The Convention not only foresaw the necessity for its own revision and laid down the conditions on which that revision is to proceed,[1] but also indicates the machinery for the operation by providing (Art. 17, § 2) that :

'Questions of this kind [relating to revisions], as well as those which concern the development of the Union from other points of view, shall be considered in Conferences to be held successively in the countries of the Union by delegates of the said countries.'

[1] This is done by Art. 17, which runs : 'The present Convention may be submitted to revisions with the object of introducing therein amendments calculated to perfect the system of the Union. . . . It is understood that no alterations in the present Convention shall be binding for the Union in the absence of the unanimous consent of the countries composing it.'

Delay in holding Paris Conference.—At each Conference the place of the next, together with the limits of time within which it is intended to hold it, is to be fixed, and it is then left to the Government of the country selected, acting in conjunction with the International Office, to make the necessary preliminary arrangements.

In the original Convention, § 6 of the Closing Protocol provided that the next meeting of the Union should be held at Paris, within from four to six years after the coming into force of the Convention. That the limits of time fixed in this way are not absolute, but are dependent on circumstances, is clear from the fact that the Paris Conference was not actually held until 1896,[1] some nine years after the Convention came into force.[2] So far the revision effected at that Conference is the only one that has taken place : but at Paris it was arranged that the Union should meet again at Berlin within from six to ten years.[3] The next Conference may accordingly be expected to meet at some time in the near future—this is not likely to be before 1906.

On the whole, it was probably a good thing that the Conference of Paris did not take place so soon as was originally contemplated. If Conferences are held at too frequent intervals, general opinion has not time to formulate, with the result that revisions may be carried out without due consideration, so leading to unsatisfactory consequences. The Convention

[1] The following passage appears in the first Circular, dated August 1895, issued by the French Government in convening this Conference : 'The Government of the Republic has not failed to take up the task entrusted to it by the States of the Union, but circumstances not having appeared to it to be favourable, it has not thought it well to convene these States within the period fixed by the Protocol. None the less it has carried out at its convenience, in concert with the Office of the Union, a thorough consideration of the questions to be submitted to the coming Conference.' The circular goes on to fix the 15th April, 1896, for the date of the Conference.

[2] 5th December, 1887.

[3] See *Actes de la Conférence de Paris*, p. 146.

is a product of such careful deliberation that subjects for revision are few in number and of comparatively little importance. Moreover the individual countries of the Union must be given time to enable them to bring their domestic law into harmony with the Convention.

The legislative results of the Paris Conference.—As a result of the revision of Paris, three separate instruments were put forward. Of these the most important is the Additional Act[1] proper, which effects several important changes in the substance of the Convention. The Interpretative Declaration,[2] as its name suggests, affects merely to make clear ambiguities in the existing rules of the Convention. Great Britain, however, interprets two of these rules in a different way by its domestic law. Hence for that country the Declaration represents a change in the substance of the Convention which it is at present unable to accept. The purport of the *Vœux* has just been explained. They are merely formal expressions of opinion, which have not been signed, and therefore are not to be found in the official instruments.

THE ADDITIONAL ACT.

The four Articles of the Act.—The Additional Act modifies Arts. 2, 3, 5, 7, 12, and 20 of the Convention of 1886 together with §§ 1 and 4 of the Closing Protocol annexed thereto. It is adopted by all the States of the Union, with the exception of Norway and Sweden. It embraces four Articles, of which the first provides for the modification of the Convention proper and

---

[1] Or, to give it its full title, the 'Additional Act of the 4th May 1896, modifying Arts. 2, 3, 5, 7, 12, and 20 of the Convention of the 9th September 1896, and Nos. 1 and 4 of the Closing Protocol annexed thereto.'

[2] Or the 'Declaration interpreting certain provisions of the Convention of Berne of the 9th September 1886, and of the Additional Act signed at Paris on the 4th May 1896.'

the second for that of the Closing Protocol, while the third permits countries of the Union which are not parties to the Additional Act to accede thereto, and the fourth deals with ratification, etc.

Amendments effected.—The results of the first two articles have been treated specifically in their appropriate places. Here they may be summarised as a whole. The following are the amendments in the Articles of the Berne Convention effected by Art. 1 of the Additional Act :—

I. **Ambiguities in Art. 2 removed.**—The wording of the first paragraph of Art. 2 is re-cast, so as to make it clear that the intention is to protect only works *published for the first time* in a Union country, and unpublished works. It is specifically stated in an additional fifth paragraph that posthumous works are included amongst the works protected.[1]

II. **All Unionist Works protected.**—Non-Unionist authors are given protection, under Art. 3, for their works first published in the territory of the Union in their own proper person, and not, as formerly, only through the medium of the publishers.[2]

III. **Author's exclusive Translating Right extended.**—The ten years' restrictive translating-term conferred by Art. 5[3] is now

[1] Art. 2 now runs : [§ 1] 'Authors belonging to any country of the Union, or their lawful representatives, shall enjoy in the other countries for their works, whether unpublished or published for the first time in one of those countries, the rights which the respective laws do now or may hereafter grant to natives.'

[Sec. 5] 'Posthumous works are included among the works protected.'

[2] Art. 3 now runs : 'Authors not belonging to any country of the Union, if they shall have published their literary or artistic works, or caused them to be published, for the first time in one of those countries, shall enjoy for such works the protection granted by the Berne Convention and by the present Additional Act.'

[3] Art. 5 now runs : 'Authors belonging to any country of the Union, or their lawful representatives, shall enjoy in the other countries the exclusive right of making or authorising translations of their works during the whole duration of the right in the original work. Nevertheless, the exclusive right of

extended so as to endure for the whole duration of the right in the original work, subject however to the proviso that the exclusive right shall lapse if not exercised within ten clear years from the publication of the latter.

IV. Indication of source required for borrowed Newspaper Articles.—Novels appearing in periodicals are now specifically mentioned in Art. 7,[1] and receive an unconditional protection. For other newspaper or magazine articles, the copying of which is not expressly prohibited, reproduction is subjected to the condition that the source whence they are taken shall be acknowledged. The paragraph in Art. 7 stating that no prohibition can apply to articles of political discussion, news of the day, and miscellaneous items, is left unchanged ; no clear rule is laid down about indication of source where such articles are reproduced.

V. Reprints may be seized at any time.—The words 'upon importation' which formerly appeared in Art. 12[2] are

translation shall cease to exist when the author shall not have made use of it within a period of ten years from the time of the first publication of the original work, by publishing or causing to be published, in one of the countries of the Union, a translation in the language for which protection is claimed.'

[1] Art. 7 now runs : 'Serial stories (*romans-feuilletons*), including short stories, published in the newspapers or magazines of any country of the Union may not be reproduced, in original or in translation, in the other countries, without the authorisation of the authors or their lawful representatives.

'This applies equally to other articles in newspapers or magazines, whenever the authors or publishers shall have expressly declared in the newspaper or magazine in which they have published such articles that they forbid the reproduction of these. For magazines, it is sufficient if the prohibition is made in a general way at the beginning of each number.

'In the absence of prohibition, reproduction will be permitted on condition of indicating the source.

'No prohibition can in any case apply to articles of political discussion, news of the day, or miscellaneous items (notes and jottings).'

[2] Art. 12 now runs : 'Every infringing work shall be subject to seizure by the competent authorities of the countries of the Union in which the original work has a right to legal protection.

'The seizure will take place conformably to the domestic law of each country.'

suppressed, so that now infringing works are subject to seizure throughout the Union at any time.

VI. Swiss Government to receive denunciations.—In Art. 20[1] the Swiss Federal Government is now specifically named as the Government authorised to receive notice of denunciations.

Art. 2 of the Additional Act effects the following changes in the Closing Protocol :—

I. Works of Architecture conditionally protected.—In § 1 of the Protocol[2] a new paragraph, ' A,' is added, securing Convention protection to works of architecture in countries which grant them protection by their domestic law. The rule for photographs becomes § B, and is altered so as to secure those works protection according to the provisions of the domestic law, in countries which grant them domestic protection upon any ground instead of, as formerly, only in countries which do not refuse to them the character of artistic works.

II. Retroactivity in connection with Translating Right and New Accessions.—§ 4 of the Protocol.[3] The rule of this

---

[1] Art. 20 (§ 2) now runs : ' This denunciation shall be addressed to the Government of the Swiss Confederation. It shall only take effect in respect of the country which shall have made it, the Convention remaining operative for the other countries of the Union.'

[2] § 1 of the Protocol now runs : ' With reference to Art. 4 it is agreed as follows :

' (A) In the countries of the Union in which protection is accorded not only to architectural plans, but also to works of architecture themselves, those works are admitted to the benefit of the provision of the Berne Convention and of the present Additional Act.

' (B) Photographic works, and works obtained by analogous processes, are admitted to the benefits of the provisions of those Acts, in so far as domestic law allows this to be done, and in the measure of the protection that it accords to similar national works.

' It is understood that an authorised photograph of a protected work of art enjoys legal protection, in all the countries of the Union, within the meaning of the Berne Convention and of the present Additional Act, so long as the principal right of reproduction of this work itself lasts, and within the limits of private agreements between the parties entitled.'

[3] § 4 of the Protocol now runs :

' The common agreement provided for in Art. 14 of the Convention is concluded as follows :

paragraph upon retroactivity is made applicable to translating right as assured by the Additional Act, and it is stated that the rule is to hold in case of new accessions to the Union.

New accessions to the Additional Act.—Art. 3 of the Additional Act reads as follows :—

'The countries of the Union which are not parties to the present Additional Act shall at any time be allowed to accede thereto, on request by them to that effect. This provision shall apply equally to countries which may hereafter accede to the Convention of the 9th September 1886. It will suffice for this purpose that such accession be notified in writing to the Swiss Federal Council, which shall in turn communicate it to the other Governments.'

Ratification, etc.—Art. 4 reads as follows : 'The present Additional Act shall have the same force and duration as the Convention of the 9th September 1886.

'It shall be ratified, and the ratifications thereof shall be exchanged at Paris, in the manner adopted in the case of that Convention, as soon as possible, and within the space of one year at the latest.

'It shall come into force, as regards those countries which shall have ratified it, three months after such exchange of ratifications.'

'The application of the Berne Convention and of the present Additional Act to works not fallen into the public domain in their country of origin at the time of the coming into force of those Acts, shall take effect according to the stipulations relative thereto contained in special Conventions existing or to be concluded for the purpose.

'In default of such stipulations between countries of the Union, the respective countries shall regulate, each for itself, by domestic law, the manner in which the principle contained in Art. 14 is to be applied.

'The stipulations of Art. 14 of the Berne Convention and of this paragraph of the Closing Protocol apply equally to the exclusive right of translation, as granted by the present Additional Act.

'The above-mentioned temporary provisions are applicable in case of new accessions to the Union.'

The Interpretative Declaration.

The **Interpretative Declaration** contains but three Articles ; these throw light on the intention of Arts. 2, 10 and § 1 B of the Final Protocol in the Convention. The Declaration has been accepted by all the States of the Union except Great Britain.

The effect of its provisions is as follows :—

I. **Conditions and Formalities of Country of Origin alone are required.**—Art. 2, § 2, is to be read as making Convention protection *solely* dependent upon the accomplishment of the conditions and formalities of the country of origin. The same rule is to hold for the protection of photographs under § 1 B of the Protocol.[1]

II. **Definitions of ' works published.'**—The Declaration defines ' works *published*' as works *issued to the public* in one of the countries of the Union ; so that the representation of a dramatic or dramatico-musical work, the performance of a musical work, and the exhibition of a work of art do not constitute ' publication ' under the Convention.[2]

III. **Dramatisation and Novelisation prohibited.**—Dramatisation and novelisation are expressly included in the prohibition against indirect appropriations contained in Art. 10.[3]

---

[1] Clause 1 of the Declaration runs :

' With reference to the terms of Art. 2, § 2, of the Convention, the protection accorded by the aforesaid Acts depends solely upon the accomplishment, in the country of origin of the work, of the conditions and formalities which are prescribed by the law of that country. The same shall hold good for the protection of the photographic works mentioned in § 1, B of the revised Closing Protocol.'

[2] Clause 2 of the Declaration runs :

' By works *published*, is to be understood works *issued to the public* in one of the countries of the Union. Consequently, the representation of a dramatic or dramatico-musical work, the performance of a musical work, and the exhibition of a work of art do not constitute *publication* in the sense of the aforesaid Acts.'

[3] Clause 3 of the Declaration runs : ' The transformation of a novel into a play, or of a play into a novel, comes within the stipulations of Art. 10.'

The Recommendations of the Conference of Paris.

The Recommendations passed by the Conference of Paris, which, it must be remembered, have no legal force, are five in number, viz. :

I. **Minimum Protection for Photographs.**—'That in all the countries of the Union the law should protect photographic works, and works produced by analogous processes, and that the duration of the protection should be 15 years at least.'

II. **Notice of Reservation for Music should be abolished.**— 'That the laws of the countries of the Union should fix the limits within which the next Conference may adopt the principle that published musical works should be protected against unauthorised performance without the author being obliged to make mention of reservation.'

III. **Treaties should be harmonised.**—'That the special treaties concluded between countries forming part of the Union should be examined by the respective contracting parties, with the object of determining which of their provisions may be considered to remain in force in conformity with the Additional Article of the Convention; and that the result of this examination should be embodied in an authentic instrument, and communicated to the countries of the Union, through the agency of the International Office, before the meeting of the next Conference.'

IV. **Forgery of Authors' Names and Marks should be Punished.** —'That penal provisions should be inserted in domestic systems of law, with the object of suppressing the misappropriation of names, signatures, or marks of authors in respect of literary and artistic works.'

V. **One Text for whole Convention.**—'That the deliberations of the next Conference should result in the issue of one single text of the Convention.'

Recent progress on these lines.—Since 1896 four members of the Union—Denmark, Germany, Japan, and Luxemburg —have re-cast their domestic law, while Great Britain has for some years been engaged upon a similar task.

The new copyright code issued by Luxemburg in 1898 mentions photographic works in the definition of 'literary and artistic works' contained in Art. 1;[1] these works thus obtain protection for the ordinary period of author's life *plus* 50 years. Notice of reservation is still required by Art. 16 of the Act, for the retention of performing right in published pieces of music. The misappropriation of authors' names and marks is forbidden (Art. 25) under pain of from three months to two years' imprisonment, and a fine of from 100 to 2,000 francs (these penalties being either cumulative or alternative at the discretion of the Court), together with the confiscation of the infringing works.[2]

The Japanese Copyright Act of 1899, by Art. 23, grants a ten years' term of protection to photographs, and, by Art. 1, protects performing right in musical and dramatic works without requiring any mention of reservation; while, by Art. 40, it subjects persons issuing a work under the real or assumed name of another author to a heavy fine.[3]

The German law of the 19th June, 1901, tacitly abolishes the condition of express notice of reservation for the retention of performing right in musical works.

Denmark, preparatory to joining the Union on the 1st July, 1903, issued a new copyright Law dated the 19th December,

[1] This definition is noteworthy, in that it is a reproduction of Art. 4 of the Berne Convention, *with the addition of works of architecture and photographic works.*

[2] See *Le Droit d'Auteur*, 1898, p. 65, sec. 99.

[3] From 30 to 500 yen (about £3 to £50). See *Le Droit d'Auteur*, 1899, p. 141, for the text of the Japanese Act.

1902. In this Act nothing is said about the protection of photographs, which, under a Law of 1865, get protection for only five years, or about the misappropriation of names, signatures, and marks, while notice of reservation is still exacted for the retention of performing right in pieces of music. Denmark has found it enough to bring its law into line with the existing Convention, and has not been able to go beyond it.

The English Literary Copyright Bill, in spite of the Recommendation of the Paris Conference, still insists on notice of reservation for dramatic and musical works. The English Artistic Copyright Bill extends the term of protection for photographs to the author's life *plus* thirty years.

Treaties which have been Superseded.—As regards Recommendation No. 3, though the various States have not yet undertaken the systematic examination of their treaties which is there recommended, it is noteworthy that the particular treaties between Great Britain and Germany,[1] France and Luxemburg (1856 and 1865), Switzerland and Germany (1869), and Switzerland and Italy (1868), were denounced on the 22nd January 1898, the 9th September 1899, the 17th November 1899, and the 17th November 1899, respectively.[2] The ground of denunciation has usually been that the Convention has rendered the particular treaty useless, and it is obvious that, if the process goes much further, the examination

---

[1] These comprised ten agreements with individual Germanic States of dates 1846 (2), 1847 (4), 1853 (2), 1855, and 1861, and one of 1886 with the German Empire.

[2] See *Le Droit d'Auteur*, 1898, p. 29, and 1899, pp. 113, 144. Upon the 28th November, 1887, Great Britain, by the Order in Council which provided for the putting into force of the Berne Convention, revoked nineteen previous Orders putting in force particular treaties. As regards the German agreements, however, no diplomatic exchange of notes had taken place, and the denunciation of these was therefore merely a unilateral act on the part of England, of the validity of which there was under the circumstances some doubt. Germany, however, on its side issued a Declaration denouncing them, on the 22nd January, 1898, and this has been given in the text as the date of their suppression.

contemplated by Recommendation No. 3 will fail for lack of material.[1]

Present tendency is against making of separate Treaties.—The ideal state of things is that in which the Convention forms the one and only law for the regulation of international affairs throughout the Union. At present Great Britain, Haïti, Luxemburg, and Tunis—four out of the fifteen States of the Union—have each no treaties with any other Union country; and of the arrangements subsisting between the other States, practically none have been concluded since the date of the Berne Convention. The tendency is to get rid of existing treaties, not to make fresh ones; so that in all probability the Berne Convention will soon be the only international copyright agreement in the Union.

---

[1] As regards the collection of the treaties still in force, attention has already been called to the *Recueil des Conventions et Traités concernant la Propriété littéraire et artistique*, issued by the International Office in 1904.

SECTION III.

FUTURE REVISIONS.

Suggested alterations in the form of the Convention—No immediate call for further revision—One text and no particular treaties—Unambiguous language—Suggested alterations in the substance of the Convention— Extension of restrictive translating period—Abolition of liberty of extract —Prohibition of mechanical musical instruments—Abolition of notice of reservation—Article 4 should be made absolutely binding—Lecturing right should be protected—Security for costs—Suggestion that all formalities should be abolished—Should the Bureau supply certificates ?—Forgery of names and marks—The future extension of the International Union —The Berne Convention and a Universal Law—A model law drafted.

The present Section, on the whole, represents the Continental, rather than the English, point of view. It embodies the opinions of the authorities of the International Office, and the other chief workers in the field of International Copyright, together with the desires of authors themselves ; and, though these opinions and desires are by no means ' beautiful dreams of the idealists,' still it must be remembered that they emanate from enthusiastic advocates of a Universal Law, who, in many cases, are also interested parties. Hence the plans of these reformers are not always restrained by a judicious weighing of consequences. Nevertheless, coming as they do from those concerned in the actual work of the International Office, and from the Society to the activity of which the initiation of the Convention was mainly due, they have considerable weight, and will probably determine the direction, if not the extent, of future revisions.

The reader who has weighed the account given of the genesis, principles, and application of the Berne Convention may safely be left to form his own conclusions as to the urgency and necessity of the various matters propounded. That there are many anomalies cannot be denied, but there are hardly more than exist in the bewildering mass of English domestic Copyright Law.

Suggested Alterations in the Form of the Convention.

No immediate call for further Revision.—The thoroughness with which the Conference of Paris has performed its work may be gauged from the fact that the revised Convention has been received with general satisfaction by authors and artists, who have failed to point out any very important defects calling for immediate remedy. It is true that the protection granted by the Additional Act in respect of certain classes of authors and artists falls far short of the ideal; but for the rights of the majority it provides a measure of recognition that is fully abreast of public opinion, one that has not called forth any very sincere complaint of its inadequacy on the part of the various literary and artistic associations. Most of the matters of detail upon which the provisions of the Additional Act are defective are matters upon which general international opinion is not yet settled.

There is not at present, therefore, any urgent call for a further revision of the Convention. The Conference of Berlin, however, is approaching, and, with a view of indicating the work which will lie before that Conference and of exposing certain obvious imperfections in the present Convention, it seems well, in concluding this chapter, to advert to some of the chief suggestions made for the improvement of the existing system. In so doing, we would again caution the reader that many of the most thoroughgoing advocates of reform have at heart the interests of the author, rather than the establishment of a secure international system of law.

One Text and no particular Treaties.—In order that the Union may preserve its cohesion and its unity, it is, in the first place, highly desirable that the last of the five Recommendations passed at the Conference of Paris may be realised, to the effect that the supplementary Acts, the acceptance of which is at present optional, may ere long be incorporated into the principal agreement and be made binding on the Union as a whole.

The cohesion and the unity of the Union may also be endangered by the existence of particular arrangements between the various countries of the Union. In respect of their signatories, these treaties have the same effect as the Additional Act and the Interpretative Declaration, *i.e.* they set up particular relations, which tend to undermine the stability of the Union. It is therefore to be hoped that, in accordance with a resolution of the International Literary and Artistic Association passed at Paris in 1900, all separate agreements between members of the Union may be suppressed, and that, before a Union country enters into a treaty with a non-Union country, an effort may in each case be made to induce the latter to accept the Convention.[1]

Unambiguous language.—When the perfect unity of the

---

[1] See *Le Droit d' Auteur*, 1900, p. 106. It will be seen that the resolution of the Literary and Artistic Association, which involves (*a*) the immediate suppression of all particular treaties, except as regards those provisions which are more favourable to authors than the Convention, and (*b*) the future incorporation of such liberal provisions into the Convention itself—which would make their separate maintenance unnecessary,—goes beyond the Recommendation of the Conference of Paris, which only involves the first of these.

regulating Act has been secured, it is still necessary, in order that the corresponding unity of effect may be secured throughout the Union, that its language should be made clear and precise. On the whole this is so, even now; but some of the Articles of the Convention, as we have seen, are susceptible of more than one interpretation. The Additional Act of Paris and the Interpretative Declaration have thrown light on several doubtful points; but the precise effect to be attributed to one or two provisions still remains obscure. The definition of Art. 4 and the rule as to mechanical musical instruments contained in § 3 of the Closing Protocol are special cases in point.[1] The provisions contained in these articles peremptorily call for authoritative interpretation; and there are several other points upon which the next Conference might endeavour to throw some light.[2]

SUGGESTED ALTERATIONS IN THE SUBSTANCE OF THE CONVENTION.

Extension of Restrictive Translating Period.—Turning from the form of the Convention to its substance, we find that many Articles reduce the extent of the author's protection in particular cases to less than it would be under the general rule. The present restrictive translating term (*délai d'usage*)

---

[1] Not only is the general position of Art. 4 at present in doubt, but the actual meaning of the *enfin* which joins the general and specific parts of that Article is also vague. The adoption of an international vocabulary would remove some of the difficulties of interpretation which arise out of the Convention, but would by no means make everything clear, since many questions depend, not on the literal meaning of particular terms, but on the construction which is to be put upon them in their relation to the context and to the whole scheme of the Convention.

[2] It is possible that, in accordance with a suggestion about to be made, the exemption accorded to mechanical musical instruments will be abolished altogether, in which case the need for an interpretation of the Closing Protocol (§ 3) will, of course, disappear.

of Art. 5 is an anomaly ; the duration of the author's exclusive translating right should, it is contended, be absolutely assimilated to the term of copyright in the original work. The advocates of revision urge that, so long as copyright in a work subsists, it should be necessary to obtain the author's consent before reproducing it in any other form whatever.

Abolition of Liberty of Extract.—On the same grounds the rule of Art. 8 permitting the countries of the Union to recognise liberty of extract for educational and scientific works and chrestomathies, by their domestic law or by particular agreements, would be abolished, and all unauthorised appropriation forbidden.

Prohibition of Mechanical Musical Instruments.—The exemption accorded by § 3 of the Closing Protocol to the manufacture and sale of mechanical musical instruments should be withdrawn, and a provision substituted prohibiting the unauthorised manufacture and sale of all such instruments which reproduce copyright airs, in the same way as the unauthorised multiplication and sale of copyright books, pictures, and sculptures is forbidden. This is no more than justice demands, but if at the Conference of Berlin it is not found possible to make such a complete change, the unauthorised adaptation of copyright tunes to interchangeable parts, such as discs, bands, and rolls, should at least be forbidden.[1]

Abolition of Notice of Reservation.—The condition of express reservation established by the Convention for the protection of copyright in newspaper and magazine articles, and for the retention of performing right in music, is based on a presumption that the author does not wish to retain these rights,

---

[1] At its Congress of Monaco in 1897, the International Literary and Artistic Association passed a resolution in favour of the suppression of § 3 of the Protocol : or, in default, of the establishment of a system of royalties on the proceeds of sale of reproductions, to be paid to the composer.—See *Le Droit d'Auteur*, 1897, p. 55.

and by omitting to make any statement on the matter tacitly abandons them in the eye of the law. In both cases it has been suggested by those who look only to the author's claims that the condition should be abolished[1]; but, as we have seen, there are sound reasons of public policy[2] against such a course. Besides this, Art. 7, dealing with the protection of newspaper and magazine articles, is open to further modification. There is much to be said for removing articles of political discussion—considered as literary works—from the category of articles freely open to reproduction, and for placing them on the same footing as ordinary articles. The political views of a journalist and the political facts he collects are rightly regarded as public property; but the literary form in which he clothes his views and facts is a proper subject for copyright.

Art. 4 should be made absolutely Binding.—With reference to subjects of protection, it has been suggested that all countries shall expressly be required to give a minimum international protection to the works included in Art. 4, so that no State shall, under the rule of Art. 2, profit by the backwardness of its own legislation to avoid its international duties. In other words, it is proposed that the moral rule which issues from Art. 4 should be transformed into a legal rule. When this is done, the way will be clear for the inclusion of photographs and works of architecture in the category of works of art, and for the requirement that they shall everywhere be protected as such.[3]

---

[1] See resolutions of the International Literary and Artistic Association passed at Monaco 1897 and Turin 1898.—See *Le Droit d'Auteur*, 1897, p. 55; 1898, p. 121.

[2] Since there are very many musical works, of abiding interest, in the public domain, it is to the public benefit that notice of reservation should be given, to enable the works of which performance is free to be distinguished.

[3] Many resolutions of the International Literary and Artistic Association have been passed in favour of the absolute protection (*a*) of photographs and (*b*) of works of architecture.

Lecturing Right should be protected.—Lecturing right, which, although at times it so closely approaches performing right as to be scarcely distinguishable from it, is not mentioned in the existing Convention, should specifically be assimilated to performing right.[1]

Security for costs.—The International Literary and Artistic Association has proposed that in cases where both parties belong to the Union the plaintiff should be exempt from any liability to give security for the costs of the suit (*cautio judicatum solvi*), which may attach to him as an alien.[2] Some reason has already been given[3] for supposing that, if the rule of the Convention be strictly adhered to, each member of the Union is bound to free subjects of other Union countries from all obligation to give such security. Since, however, it appears that in many Union countries this has not yet been done, it will certainly be well, in the opinion of the International Literary and Artistic Association, for the next Conference definitely to provide that, throughout the Union, no security required of aliens as such shall be exacted from authors belonging to any country of the Union.

Suggestion that all formalities should be abolished.—The Association has even gone the length of suggesting that all

---

[1] It has been suggested that performances for charitable purposes and private performances should be allowed even without the consent of the author. These are permitted under the German law, Sec. 27 of the Act of 1901 providing that unauthorised public performances of a published musical work unaccompanied by words are lawful, if (1) they are not organised for pecuniary profit and the audience is admitted without payment, (2) they take place at popular festivals other than musical festivals, (3) the profits are devoted exclusively to charitable purposes and the performers receive no remuneration, or (4) they are organised by musical and other societies and only the members and their families form the audience. As regards performances for charitable purposes, however, the principle is one which it would seem dangerous to introduce: and as regards private performances, it is submitted that the liberty exists clearly enough under the existing law.

[2] See *Le Droit d'Auteur*, 1897, p. 56 ; 1898, p. 121.

[3] See Chap. v., sec. 4 of this Part ; also Part II., Chap. iv., sec. 3.

formalities whatever should be abolished by the Convention.[1] This, however, is a very drastic measure of reform, and so long as the majority of domestic systems of law continue to impose formalities it appears neither practicable nor useful.

Should the Bureau supply Certificates ?—It was at the same time resolved by the International Literary and Artistic Association that, so long as formalities are in fact required, the International Office should be entrusted with the duty of providing certificates relating to the fulfilment of the conditions and formalities of the country of origin under Art. 11, § 3. The matter is, however, one which, as already pointed out, is not properly within the province of the International Office.

Forgery of Names and Marks.—The suggestion of the Paris Recommendation No. 4, to the effect that the usurpation by an author of the name of another and the imitation of signatures and signs of an artist should be made the subject of penal legislation, has been left till last, because, though doubtless it is perfectly reasonable, it deals with a matter which is generally regarded in this country as not properly within the domain of copyright.[2]

The future extension of the International Union.—It must be remembered that the objects of the International Union include not only the perfecting of its own system, but the extension of its sphere so that it may become a universal code for the international protection of copyright. In order fully to effect this, it is, of course, necessary to secure the adhesion of every country which is at present outside the

---

[1] Resolutions expressed at Berne, 1896.—*Le Droit d'Auteur*, 1896, p. 126.

[2] Only one English copyright statute contains a disposition on the matter, viz. the Fine Arts Copyright Act of 1862 (25 and 26 Vict., c. 58), which by Sec. 27 prohibits fraudulent signature, etc., under a penalty of £10 or double the full price of the infringing works, together with the forfeiture of the latter.

Union : but the abstention of the less civilised States does not seriously impair the value of the Convention, since infringement committed in them cannot seriously prejudice the foreign author.   The International Literary and Artistic Association, at its Congress of Paris in 1900, declared in favour of the adoption of special efforts in order to bring about the accession of the following States : Austria, Denmark,[1] the United States of North America, Hungary, Holland, the Spanish-American Republics, Roumania, Russia, and Sweden.[2]   When these have been added to the Union, authors will receive a substantial measure of protection in every country in which piracy can materially affect their interests.

THE BERNE CONVENTION AND A UNIVERSAL LAW.

Since the mode in which the Convention advances involves the gradual extension of the minimum international protection which it is incumbent on every country to grant, and since no State is likely long to withhold from its own subjects the protection it accords to aliens, the domestic systems of the various countries of the Union tend to approximate more and more to that of the Convention and to each other.   The continuance of such a process would finally result in the establishment of an absolute identity in the copyright law of those countries ; so that in the end the Convention would expand into a Universal Law.

A Model Law drafted.—Of course the possibility of the achievement of such a ' unification of laws ' lies in the far distant future ; but meanwhile it is of interest to note that a ' draft model law ' (*projet de loi-type*) of copyright has been

---

[1] Denmark accepted the Convention on the 1st July, 1903.

[2] See *Le Droit d'Auteur*, 1900, p. 107.   Sweden accepted the Convention on the 1st August, 1904.

drawn up by M. Georges Maillard, under the auspices of the
International Literary and Artistic Association. This Model
Law is of practical importance, since it indicates the lines
upon which the development of the Convention, as well as that
of national law, may be expected to proceed. In the opinion
of M. Maillard expressed at the Congress of Paris in 1900
'this project is in no way visionary and theoretical. Its
aim is to settle the principal elements of a law upon which
unification could be established within a reasonable time,
namely the minimum of protection that it is advisable to ask
at the present time for authors and artists,—a compromise
upon which it is desirable that the unification of laws should
henceforth proceed.'[1]

The adoption of this Model Law by the International
Literary and Artistic Association shows that this society has
definitely undertaken to promote the unification desired ; and,
though the difficulties are immense, there seems little reason
why the object should not ultimately be realised. In the
meantime, the influence of the scheme upon national and international legislation cannot but be for good, for every step in
the direction of uniformity involves a simplification of the
author's position, and a substantial gain in protection for him.
A translation of M. Maillard's Model Law is given in full in
the Appendix.

[1] See *Le Droit d'Auteur*, 1900, p. 98.

CHAPTER VII.

THE MONTEVIDEO CONVENTION, 1889, AND OTHER AMERICAN CONVENTIONS.

SECTION I.

THE MONTEVIDEO CONVENTION, 1889.

Parties to the Montevideo Convention—Comparison with Berne Convention—The Montevideo Convention does not create an International Union—Law of country of origin to regulate protection—Montevideo Convention more liberal in certain matters—Certain subjects exclusively dealt with in each Convention—The value of the Montevideo Convention.

Parties to the Montevideo Convention.—In 1888 a Congress of South American States was held at Montevideo, under the auspices of the Argentine Republic and the Republic of Uruguay. It considered many subjects of international law and passed some notable resolutions; and, on the matter of copyright in particular, it drew up an important Convention for the protection of literary and artistic property. This Convention was signed by the delegates of the following seven States: the Argentine Republic, Paraguay, Peru, Uruguay, Brazil, and Chili. Of these, the last two have not yet ratified the agreement. France (1897), Spain (1899), Italy (1900), and Belgium (1903) have since signified their adhesion, by notice sent to the Argentine Republic, which is one of the two States appointed by Art. 13 to receive accessions ; their accession takes effect only with regard to the Argentine Republic and Paraguay, for no other State has yet accepted it.

Comparison with Berne Convention.—The Montevideo Convention probably owes its existence, as it certainly owes its form, to the example of the Convention of Berne. It is, however, by no means a slavish copy of its predecessor. On the contrary, it sets up a system which differs from that of the International Union in several essentials, as well as in many points of detail. These may be gathered from a comparison of the translation of its text which is given in the Appendix with that of the Convention of Berne. The most important are as follows :—

I. **The Montevideo Convention does not create an International Union.**—The Montevideo Convention is merely an ordinary treaty ; it does not affect to create an International Union. There is no provision made for the establishment of an International Office, or for future revisions. States which intend to accede are not obliged to grant by their domestic law the same rights as those secured by the Convention. There is no requirement that particular arrangements shall be made to harmonise with the principal treaty. Ratification need not be simultaneous, and the Convention is to go forward, no matter how many or how few States give in their ratifications (Art. 13). And if any party wishes to withdraw, it is required (Art. 15) to give two years' previous notice of its intention, during which period efforts are to be made to arrive at a fresh basis of agreement. All these facts are irreconcilable with the conception of a stable Union, to or from which States may come and go at will without disturbing the general system.

II. **Law of Country of Origin to regulate protection.**—The principle adopted as the basis of its protection by the Convention of Montevideo may be stated thus, in the words of Art. 2 :

' The author of every literary or artistic work . . . shall enjoy in the signatory States the rights accorded to him by the law of the State in which the first publication or production of this work shall have taken place.' This makes all the incidents of protection depend on the law of the country of origin,[1] while the rule of the Berne Convention is that each country shall grant to foreign authors the same rights as those accorded by its domestic law to natives.

Just as the latter instrument, however, provides that the period of protection granted by any country cannot exceed that of the country of origin, the Montevideo Convention enacts (Art. 4) that no State shall be obliged to grant to foreign works a longer period than that obtaining under its own domestic law : so that, in respect of the term of copyright, the ultimate result is the same under both agreements, *i.e.* the author enjoys in each country either its own term or that of the country of origin, whichever is the shorter.

Since, under the Montevideo Convention, international protection proceeds according to the rights enjoyed in the country of origin, there is no need for that instrument to lay down any specific rule as to formalities : for the non-fulfilment by the author of domestic formalities relating to copyright of necessity prevents him from gaining full rights in the country of origin, and, as a consequence, deprives him *pro tanto* of international protection. There is a good deal to be said for the adoption in a treaty of the law of the country of origin as a standard of international protection ; but in practice it is difficult for a foreign public to understand and observe such a law. The derangement of ideas and principles which this involves is more easily tolerated in the

---

[1] The principle is also carried out in the Article (No. 9) dealing with adaptations, etc., which, unlike the similar Article in the Berne Convention, does not prescribe the application by each country of the reserves of its domestic law.

Spanish-American States, with their unsettled legal convictions, than it would be in Europe, where law is a product of gradual growth, and the various national systems of law are firmly rooted.

III. **Montevideo Convention more Liberal in certain Matters.** —In some respects, the Montevideo Convention is distinctly more liberal than that of Berne, and has marked the way for the future development of the latter. It protects all works published in the Convention territory, without any condition as to the nationality of their author; it assimilates translating right to the ordinary right of reproduction (Art. 3); it enumerates photographs and choregraphic works in its general definition of 'literary and artistic works,' contained in Art. 5; it makes (Art. 7) indication of source a condition of the reproduction of newspaper articles[1]; and it does not exempt mechanical musical instruments from the ordinary rules as to infringements.

IV. **Certain Subjects exclusively dealt with in each Convention.** —The Montevideo Convention contains definite provisions on certain matters which the Berne Convention only deals with by implication, and omits to lay down rules on certain matters that the latter regulates expressly. Thus, with regard to lecturing right, it provides (by Art. 8) for the free reproduction of speeches delivered in public. It indicates (Art. 11) that the cognisance of an offence properly belongs to the Courts of the country in which it has been committed, and that the law of that country is the law to be applied. On the other hand, it has no article dealing with performing right or with the protection of unpublished works.

These two omissions, indeed, are in all probability due

---

[1] In other respects its rule as to these articles is less favourable to authors than that of the Berne Convention; for, subject to indication of source, it throws them all open to reproduction, with the exception of those treating of art or science, which can only be reproduced when unprovided with express reservation.

rather to a strict limitation of the agreement to the sphere of copyright proper, than to any intention to regulate the subjects in question by mere implication,[1] but the promoters of the Berne Convention have not been so particular.

No express provision on the matter of retroactivity is to be found in the Treaty of Montevideo ; but it is probable that the same rule may be deduced from Art. 2 of that agreement as is laid down in Art. 14 of the Convention of Berne.

The Value of the Montevideo Convention.—It will be seen that in many respects the Montevideo Convention constitutes an advance on its predecessor. It is, on the whole, considerably more favourable to the rights of authors than the Act of the International Union ; but it may be suggested that readiness to enter into such an agreement does not necessarily connote ability to enforce it. European States have, however, nothing to lose and much to gain by accepting it, for, though their own publishers are not likely to reproduce many Spanish-American works, it is certain that a piratical trade is carried on by many Spanish-American publishers in European works, especially in copyright music.[2]

---

[1] Though *Le Droit d'Auteur* suggests that the former at least comes under the general rule of Art. 2.—See *Le Droit d'Auteur*, 1899, p. 53.

[2] Sullivan's music is openly and habitually performed in Buenos Ayres without the consent of the owners of the copyright.

SECTION II.

OTHER AMERICAN CONVENTIONS.

The Central American Convention, 1897—The Congress of Guatemala—
The treatment of copyright in the Convention—The ratification of the
Convention—The Pan-American Convention, 1902—The first Conference
of 1890—The Convention of 1902—The Convention is founded on that
of Montevideo—Ratifications.

THE CENTRAL AMERICAN CONVENTION, 1897.

The Congress of Guatemala.—Since the day of the Montevideo Convention, America has produced two other treaties
running to some extent on the same lines.   On the 6th June,
1897, a 'Central-American Juridical Congress' met at
Guatemala, and drew up six treaties, of which one related to
industrial, artistic, and literary property. This had been
drafted by M. A. González Saravia, a jurist of Salvador,
and, according to a statement made by him, 'The rules
established are those generally accepted, and especially those
recorded in the Convention of Paris of the 26th March,
1883, the Convention of Berne in 1886, and the Convention
of Montevideo.'

The preamble of this Central American Convention, which
sufficiently indicates its object, runs as follows : 'The
Governments of Costa Rica, and Guatemala, and that of the
Greater Republic of Central America, animated by the wish
to lay down the most fitting bases for the unification of the

principles regulating literary, artistic, and industrial property in Central America, and to make the existing law on this subject uniform . . . . have agreed to conclude the following treaty.'

The Treatment of Copyright in the Convention.—As regards copyright, this Convention does little more than state such leading principles as that the author's right shall be protected, that infringement shall be forbidden, and that subjects of each State shall be protected everywhere in the Convention territory. It requires the fulfilment of the conditions and formalities of the country of origin, and limits the duration of protection by the term given in the country of origin.[1] Apart from its lack of detailed provisions, this treaty differs from the Berne and Montevideo Conventions in the important respect that it requires each State to set up a national registry of titles, marks, and patents, and to publish year by year the entries made thereon.

The Ratification of the Convention.—Political troubles in Central America hindered the acceptance of the treaty thus prepared. In January 1901, however, a second Central American Juridical Congress met—this time at San Salvador —and approved the Convention, which had not then been ratified by any of its signatories. Since that date Salvador (12th May, 1901)[2] and Nicaragua (2nd September, 1901) have ratified it.[3] If the ratifications have been duly communicated, the Convention is therefore now in force between these States.

---

[1] The full text is set out in *Le Droit d'Auteur*, 1898, p. 87, and also in the collection of treaties published by the International Office.

[2] With the exception of Art. 12, which Salvador would not accept.

[3] See *Le Droit d'Auteur*, 1903, p. 106.

THE PAN-AMERICAN CONVENTION, 1902.

The First Conference of 1890.—A 'Pan-American International Conference' was held at Washington in 1890, at which nearly all the countries of America were represented. This Conference appointed a Committee to draw up treaties for the international protection of intellectual works (literary and artistic works, trade marks and patents), and the result was a Recommendation that the States of America should become parties to the Montevideo Convention. The report of the Committee was adopted by the Conference, but as yet no American States other than the original signatories have acceded to the Montevideo Convention.[1]

The Convention of 1902.—On the 21st October, 1901, however, a second Pan-American Conference met at Mexico, and set itself to examine afresh the question of the international protection of copyright. The labours of this Conference resulted in the elaboration of a 'Convention for the protection of literary and artistic works,' dated 27th January, 1902, which was signed by delegates of the following seventeen States: the Argentine Republic, Bolivia, Chili, Columbia, Costa Rica, Ecuador, Guatemela, Haïti, Honduras, Mexico, Nicaragua, Paraguay, Peru, the Republic of Dominica, Salvador, the United States, and Uruguay—though the representatives of Nicaragua, Paraguay, and the United States signed merely provisionally.[2]

The Convention founded on that of Montevideo.—The contracting States were formed into a 'Union for the purpose of recognising and protecting the rights of literary and artistic property.' Upon reading the treaty it is not difficult to

---

[1] See *Le Droit d'Auteur*, 1890, p. 66, for an account of this first Conference.
[2] See *Le Droit d'Auteur*, 1902, pp. 68, 69, for an account of this Conference.

perceive that it is based on the Convention of Montevideo ; it differs from this, however, in the two important respects that it requires each country to extend its own domestic protection—not that of the country of origin—to the works of foreign authors (Art. 5), and that it requires a request for protection and a deposit of two copies to be made in respect of *each* of the countries in which protection is desired (Art. 4).[1]

Ratifications.—Guatemala was the first State to ratify the new Convention, which it did by a Decree of the 24th April, 1902. The example was followed by Salvador on the 16th May, 1902, and by Costa Rica on the 13th July, 1903 ; while Paraguay is taking steps in the same direction. If the requisite communication of ratifications has been duly made, the Convention is now in force as between the countries which have ratified it.

[1] See *Le Droit d'Auteur*, 1902, pp. 82, 83, for the full text of the Convention, which is also given in the Collection of Treaties published by the International Office.

PART IV.

INTERNATIONAL COPYRIGHT IN THE BRITISH DOMINIONS.
COLONIAL COPYRIGHT.

CHAPTER I.

THE PROTECTION ACCORDED TO FOREIGN AUTHORS IN GREAT BRITAIN.

CHAPTER II.

COLONIAL COPYRIGHT.

CHAPTER I.

THE PROTECTION ACCORDED TO FOREIGN AUTHORS IN GREAT BRITAIN.

INTRODUCTORY SECTION.

National Laws the Complement of the Convention—The English International Acts—Sketch of the Contents of this Chapter.

National Laws the Complement of the Convention.—Up to the present the treatment of international copyright in this work has been detached from all reference to the national laws of particular countries, except by way of particular illustration. International agreements in general have been analysed and their various elements examined, while the Berne Convention, which is by far the most important of all existing international agreements on the subject of copyright, has been considered in detail. The Convention forms a great international code of copyright law, which many countries have bound themselves to put into force, and therefore its provisions are of the greatest international importance. But it does not follow from the fact that a country is internationally bound to observe them that these provisions are necessarily law in that country. It is conceivable that a country may be internationally bound to incorporate them into its law, without in practice carrying out its international obligation by doing so. Such an omission rarely occurs, except in regard to small matters of detail. Indeed, it is not at all uncommon for a State to go beyond the provisions of the Convention. In order, then, to exhaust the subject of international copyright completely, and to give a full exposition of the present state of international protection of literary and artistic works, it would be necessary to enter into the details of the domestic law of every civilised country; the details not only of 'the English law of international copyright,' but of the German law of international copyright, of the French law of international copyright, and of that part of every copyright code which defines the protection to be given to foreign works.

The English International Acts.—This, however, is a counsel of perfection. But in an English work it seems necessary at least to give some account of the manner in which, and the conditions under which, foreign copyright works are protected by the English law; so far, that is, as there is any account left to give, beyond that already contained in the preceding Parts. Great Britain, as it has increased the area of its international relations, has from time to time found it necessary to frame a special set of statutes, in order to make it possible for the benefits of the domestic law to be extended to foreign works; and these 'International Copyright Acts' will here be our chief concern.

With the ordinary English domestic law we shall have little to do, except in so far as relates to the conditions of protection. So long as an author, of whatever nationality, fulfils the condition of first publication within the British dominions[1] he gets just the ordinary protection of the English law, no

---

[1] As to the question of residence at the time of publication, see Sec. 4 of this Chapter.

more and no less. The effect of the international Acts is,
put shortly, to dispense with this condition for works belonging to countries with which Great Britain has international
arrangements, *i.e.* the fourteen foreign countries of the Copyright Union,[1] Austria, and Hungary. The protection given
to such works is that of the ordinary domestic law, with
certain slight modifications made in view of the altered
circumstances ; thus, where the term of protection under the
ordinary English law is greater than that given in the foreign
country of origin, the ordinary English term is cut down
to that which is accorded in the latter country.[2] This is
in accordance with the Berne Convention, the fundamental
principle of which is that authors belonging to any of the
countries of the Union shall enjoy in the other countries the
same rights as natives, subject, however, to the proviso that
the conditions and formalities of the country of origin must
be fulfilled, and that the term of protection cannot in any
country exceed that given in the country of origin. Art. 1 of
the treaty of 1893 with Austria-Hungary contains a provision
which is substantially the same.

It will be seen, then, that the English domestic law plays a
very large part in the English law of international copyright.
But as to the nature of the protection accorded by the domestic
law, we shall have little to say ; for this part is not intended
to deal with the whole of the English law of copyright, but
only with that portion of it which bears *special* reference to
international affairs.

[1] At present these are : Belgium, Denmark, France, Germany, Haïti, Italy,
Japan, Luxemburg, Monaco, Norway, Spain, Sweden, Switzerland, and Tunis.
[2] Cf. Sec. 2, (iii.) of the International Copyright Act, 1886 :—' The International Copyright Acts, and an order made thereunder, shall not confer on any
person any greater right or longer term of copyright in any work than that
enjoyed in the foreign country in which such work was first produced,' with the
proviso to the same effect in the Order in Council of 28th November, 1887,
putting in force the Berne Convention.

Sketch of the Contents of this Chapter.—The following is an outline of the subject-matter of this chapter, in the order of treatment :—

I. The general conditions of protection under the ordinary domestic law are treated in Section 1. This subject has special importance for foreigners, in that it embraces a statement of the circumstances under which they can obtain protection without having recourse to the special provisions of the International Acts. As has already been indicated, all works published in the British dominions are protected by the ordinary domestic law, which looks only to the fact that they are British works, without seeking to enquire into the nationality of their authors.[1] The domestic law is based mainly on the Literary Copyright Act of 1842, but the common law stands also as one of its foundations. The international part of the code, representing as it does an artificial extension of the scope of the ordinary law, is made up entirely of statutes—the ' International Copyright Acts '—with a few judicial decisions which illustrate their meaning.[2] The most important of these statutes is the International Copyright Act, 1886, which paved the way for the adoption of the Berne Convention, but other Acts, of dates 1844, 1852 and 1875 respectively, are still partly in force.

II. The general effect of these International Copyright Acts, and their relation to each other, is dealt with in Section 2. They give permission to the Crown by Orders in

---

[1] There is one reservation which ought possibly to be made upon this statement, *i.e.* there is some shadow of authority for asserting that a foreign author, in order to get the benefit of the ordinary domestic law, must have been resident in the British dominions at the time of the publication. See later, Sec. 4.

[2] The fact that the English copyright law is made up partly of common law, illustrated and expounded by judicial decisions, and partly of a multitude of statutes, is likely to prove a source of difficulty to the foreigner, who can usually find the whole of his native law within the four corners of a code.

Council to enter into agreements upon copyright with foreign countries.

III. As a result, England has become a party to the Berne Convention of 1886,[1] to the Additional Act of Paris of 1896, which revised the Convention in several important particulars, and to a Treaty of 1893 with Austria-Hungary. These agreements are discussed in Section 3.

IV. The foreign works eligible for protection and the conditions under which such works gain copyright under the English International Acts, as supplemented by these Conventions, form the subject-matter of Section 4. The rule seems to be that no conditions and formalities whatever need be fulfilled, beyond those exacted in the country of origin of the work.

V. The rights accorded to protected foreign works are dealt with in Section 5, containing an account of the modifications in the substance of the ordinary domestic protection which are made to meet the special requirements of the foreign works receiving the protection of the International Copyright Acts. The chief of these will be seen to be that a special term of translating right is fixed by the International Acts for protected foreign works.

VI. In Section 6 the duration of the protection accorded to foreign works is considered. The International Acts provide that such works shall receive in England no greater right or longer term of copyright than they enjoy in their country of origin ; but apart from this restriction, they receive the same term of protection in England as that accorded to domestic works. Under the English law, however, different classes of works receive different periods of

[1] The relation between the International Copyright Act of 1886, the Order in Council of 28th November, 1887, and the Berne Convention stands thus : the Convention was legalised in England by the Order in Council, which itself drew its authority from the Act of 1886.

copyright,—an anomaly which, in view of the fact that most foreign codes give one and the same period to works of all kinds, it is difficult for an alien to grasp. It has therefore been deemed well to set out the periods which, under the English domestic law, the different classes of works actually get.

VII. The remedies open to the authors of foreign works, and the special rules of procedure applicable to them, form the subject of Section 7. It will be found, however, that over this department the domestic law holds almost uninterrupted sway.

VIII. The way in which the Act of 1886, the Order in Council of 1887, and the Berne Convention are made to apply to works published before the coming into force of the Convention will be discussed in Section 8 under the title of ' The retroactive application of international protection in England.'

SECTION I.

THE PROTECTION OF FOREIGNERS UNDER THE ORDINARY ENGLISH DOMESTIC LAW.

No statutory rule as to fundamental conditions of copyright—Questions as to nationality of author and place of publication—Rules as to conditions of literary copyright—Rules as to conditions of artistic copyright and performing right—Historical account of the status of the foreign author under the ordinary English domestic law—Domestic Acts protect only British works—Former importance of residence for the foreign author— Decided in 1854 that Act of Anne required residence of foreign author— Position of the foreign author under existing law—Dictum that residence not necessary under existing law—Assurance given to United States that no residence required—This contradicts Fine Arts Copyright Act, 1862— Special rules for works of art, sculptures, etc.

No Statutory Rule as to Fundamental Conditions of Copyright. —Whilst almost every English statute which relates to copyright has had something to say about those formalities, like registration, which must be fulfilled before works possessing all the essential elements of copyright can gain an effectual protection, it has apparently never been thought necessary, at least in the domain of *literary* copyright, to state in an Act of Parliament what are the fundamental conditions as to originality of the work, nationality of the author, place of publication, etc., upon which the very claim to copyright— the title to protection upon performance of the necessary formalities—depends. Accordingly, it is in judicial decisions alone that information as to the laws applying to these important matters can be found. The questions of nationality and place of publication are all that concern us here; and, in

respect of these, the points that have been raised before
the Courts have been various in character and variously
decided.

Questions as to Nationality of Author and Place of Publication.
—Always with reference to literary works, it has been asked
whether, in order that copyright in a work may be obtained
under the ordinary domestic law, the author must be a British
subject, and, after this question had been answered in the
negative, whether he must be resident in the British
dominions, either permanently or at the time of publication.
The Act of 1842 makes no allusion whatever to the place
in which the work must be first published, and the Courts
have had to determine whether the first publication was required to take place in the United Kingdom or in the British
dominions, or whether no such limitation was intended by
the statute. And after it had been settled, under the law
before 1886, that first publication in the United Kingdom
was necessary, it was suggested that, if the author was a
British subject, he should be exempted from this condition
and allowed to get copyright under the domestic Acts, even
if he had first published his work abroad.

Rules as to Conditions of Literary Copyright.—The result
of the decisions (as to domestic *literary* copyright) on these
questions of the nationality of the author and the work may
be briefly stated as follows : before 1886 first publication had
to take place in the United Kingdom ;[1] but the International
Copyright Act, 1886 (sec. 8) altered this, and now first publication anywhere in the British dominions suffices.[2] A
British author is not exempt from this requirement, and

---

[1] *Boucicault v. Delafield* (1863), 1 Hem. and Mil. 597 ; *Boucicault v. Chatterton*
(1866), L.R. 5 Ch.D. 267.

[2] 'The Copyright Acts shall, subject to the provisions of this Act, apply to
a literary or artistic work first produced in a British possession in like manner
as they apply to a work first produced in the United Kingdom.'

cannot get protection if he first publishes abroad.[1] And a foreign author can gain protection in the ordinary way by first publishing in the British dominions,[2] being on exactly the same footing as a native in this respect.

Rules as to Conditions of Artistic Copyright and Performing Right.—The conditions as to nationality which affect the copyright in other classes of works are in general laid down by statute, and may be briefly summarised thus : for paintings, drawings, and photographs the place of making or publication does not matter, but the artist is not protected unless he is a British subject.[3] Engravings and prints must be first published in the British dominions, and under the Engravings Copyright Act, 1777 (sec. 1), also 'engraved, etched, drawn, or designed' there ;[4] there is no condition as to the nationality of the author. Works of sculpture must be first published in the British dominions, and the author's nationality is not taken into account.[5] All that can be said with any certainty

---

[1] That is, apart from any international agreement which may exist with the country of publication. The reader must be very careful to note that this Section deals only with the English *domestic* law, and does not import the effect of the International statutes.

[2] Probably no residence is required ; see later in this Section.

[3] Fine Arts Copyright Act, 1862, sec. 1.

[4] The Act of 1777 (sec. 1) made it a condition that the work should be 'engraved, etched, drawn, or designed' in Great Britain. The Engravings Copyright Act, 1836 (sec. 1), extended the provisions of the earlier Act to Ireland, and (sec. 2) gave a right of action in respect of engravings and prints *published* in any part of Great Britain. This requirement of publication may be considered to supersede the condition of the earlier Act as to engraving, etc. ; or it may be held that as engraving, etc., in Great Britain was an express, so publication in Great Britain was a tacit, condition of protection under the Act of 1777, and that the real effect of the Act of 1836 was not to supersede either of these conditions but to widen the scope of both of them so as to take in Irish works.

[5] The Sculptures Act is silent on the questions of place of publication and author's nationality. Hence the rule is deduced by analogy from the judicial decisions upon literary copyright ; and probably the same doubt still lingers as in the case of literary copyright on the point whether a foreign author must be resident in the British dominions at the time of publication.

about the performing right in musical and dramatic works is that, when the play or piece is unpublished in printed form at the time of first performance, this must take place within the British dominions, if the performing right is to be retained, for, under the English law, performance constitutes publication.

HISTORICAL ACCOUNT OF THE STATUS OF THE FOREIGN AUTHOR UNDER THE ORDINARY ENGLISH DOMESTIC LAW.

The Development of Literary Copyright is of historical interest. —It will be seen that, taking everything into account, the English domestic law of copyright is very complicated. The only rules of importance which have grown up through the medium of judicial decisions instead of being arbitrarily fashioned by statute are those relating to the acquisition of copyright in literary works.

The history of the rules upon other branches of copyright, though short,—because its scope would be confined to the narration of one or two statutory provisions,—would be comparatively uninstructive.

Domestic Acts protect only British Works.—Until 1886 the ordinary domestic protection of the English law seems, naturally enough, to have been restricted to works first published in the United Kingdom.[1]

In *Clementi v. Walker* (1824)[2] it was held that a foreigner could obtain copyright in England, only when he had added to the stock of learning by first publishing his work in this

---

[1] Since the Act of 1886 publication in the British dominions suffices. It was, however, doubted in *Reid and Others v. Maxwell* (1886), 2 T.L.R. 790, whether a British subject was debarred from copyright by first publication abroad.

[2] *Clementi v. Walker*, 2 B. and C. 861.

country.   And in *Guichard v. Mori* (1831),[1] where music had
been first published in France and the copyright assigned
to the plaintiff, Lord Lyndhurst laid it down that
'The policy of our law recognises by statutes, express
in their wording, that the importation of foreign inventions
shall be encouraged in the same manner as the inventions
made in this country and by natives. This is founded as
well upon reason, sense, and justice as it is upon policy. It
appears that this piece of music was published in France by
Kalkbrenner, or someone to whom he sold it, so long ago as
in 1814, six years before the sale to the plaintiff. There can
be no question then of the right of the defendant or anyone
else to publish it in this country.'

Former importance of residence for the foreign author.—
Publication within the United Kingdom has thus from the
beginning been a condition of protection; but there has
always been some doubt as to whether this was the only
condition for foreign as well as for native authors, or whether
residence in the British dominions at the time of publication
was also required of the former. As regards the old Act of
Anne, 1709, the case of *Jefferys v. Boosey*,[2] which, though
decided so late as 1854, turned upon the construction of that
statute, definitely settled that some such residence was necessary; but, before that, a number of conflicting decisions had
been given on the same statute.

In *Bach v. Longman* (1777)[3] an alien resident at the time
of publication was protected. In the important case of
D'Almaine v. Boosey (1835)[4] it was held that where, before
publication, an alien had assigned his work to a subject and
the latter had duly made first publication in this country,

[1] *Guichard v. Mori*, 9 L.J. (Ch.) 227.
[2] *Jefferys v. Boosey*, 4 H.C.L. 815.
[3] *Bach v. Longman*, 2 Cowp. 623.
[4] *D'Almaine v. Boosey*, 1 Y. and C. 288.

he would get copyright in the work which the Courts would protect. Commenting on this, Serjeant Talfourd[1] pointed out that it went a great way towards establishing the principle of international copyright, and urged that it was highly expedient to accord protection to aliens. It is interesting to note that the Act of 1842, which was the outcome of Talfourd's determined efforts to bring about a complete revision of the whole of the English law of copyright, makes no allusion to the protection of aliens; and, in the subsequent cases which fell to be decided under this statute, the rules laid down have been deduced by a somewhat strained inference from the general words of its preamble.

The next case to *D'Almaine v. Boosey* was *Bentley v. Foster* (1839),[2] in which it was decided that an alien composing his work abroad and making no assignment to a British subject was entitled to copyright if he first published here, on the ground that 'he gave the British public the advantage of his industry and knowledge by so doing.' In *Chappell v. Purday* (1845)[3] Pollock, C.B., having investigated the previous cases, ruled that a foreigner first publishing in England was to be protected. In *Cocks v. Purday* (1848),[4] where the alien author is definitely stated to be *absent* at the time of publication, the same rule was laid down; as also in *Boosey v. Davidson* (1849)[5] and in *Buxton v. James* (1851)[6] (where the publication was simultaneous with publication in a foreign country and the copyright was assigned to

---

[1] In his speech on the Bill which ultimately became law as the Copyright Act of 1842.

[2] *Bentley v. Foster*, 10 Sim. 329.

[3] *Chappell v. Purday*, 14 M and W. 303, 320.

[4] *Cocks v. Purday*, 5 C. B. 860.

[5] *Boosey v. Davidson*, 18 L.J. (Q.B.) 174; 13 Q.B. 257.

[6] *Buxton v. James*, 5 DeG. and Sm. 80; 16 Jur. 15.

a British subject).   In *Ollendorf v. Black*[1] the foreign author was present when his work was published and he was protected.

So far it is clear that no condition of residence was imposed ; and the consideration of assignment to a British subject, upon which in some cases stress was laid, does not seem on the whole to have been material to the decisions. It may be stated at once that it is now considered as of no importance. The Courts regard the copyright as first vesting in the author, and if through some personal incapacity at the time of publication he is unable to acquire it, it cannot come into being at all.

The first case in which an alien was deprived of protection on the ground of non-residence was *Boosey v. Purday* (1849).[2] Here the Court of Exchequer went back on its previous decisions, and refused copyright to an alien who, though he had first published his work in England, was absent at the time of publication, the view taken by the judge being that the cultivation of the intellect of its own subjects was the aim of the law, rather than the first publication of foreign books here.   In this case Pollock, C.B., said : ' Our opinion is that the legislature must be considered *primâ facie* to mean to legislate for its own subjects, or those who owe obedience to its laws ; and, consequently, that the Acts apply *primâ facie* to British subjects only, in some sense of that term which would include subjects by birth or residence, being authors. . . . The object of the legislature clearly is not to encourage the importation of foreign books and their first publication in England as a benefit to this country, but to promote the cultivation of the intellect of its own subjects.'

---

[1] *Ollendorf v. Black*, 4 DeG. and Sm. 209 ; 14 Jur. 1088 ; 20 L.J. (Ch.) 165.
[2] *Boosey v. Purday*, 4 Ex. 145.

Decided in 1854 that Act of Anne required Residence of Foreign Author.—The last great case decided on the Act of Anne was *Jefferys v. Boosey* (1854),[1] which was carried to the House of Lords, and in which protection was refused to an alien resident abroad at the time of publication.   Lord Cranworth remarked that 'Where an exclusive privilege is given to a particular class at the expense of the rest of Her Majesty's subjects, that privilege must be taken to have been a national object ; and the privileged class to be confined to a portion of the community for the general advantage of which the enactment is made. When I say that the legislature must *primâ facie* be taken to legislate only for its own subjects I must be taken to include under the word "subjects" all persons who are within the Queen's dominions and who thus owe to her a temporary allegiance. . . . If publication, which is (so to say) the overt act establishing authorship, takes place here, the author is then a British subject, wherever he may in fact have composed his work.   But if, at the time when copyright commences by publication, the foreign author is not in this country, he is not in my opinion a person whose interests the statute meant to protect.'

The allusion to the place where the author composes his work bears reference to an untenable contention put forward in this and several of the earlier cases, to the effect that it was one of the conditions of protection that the work should have been composed, as well as published, in this country.   This contention is now quite obsolete.

As Lord Cranworth put it, in another passage of the same judgment : 'The law does not require or permit any investigation into a subject which would obviously for the most part baffle all inquiry, namely how far the actual composition of the work itself had in the mind of its author taken place here

---

[1] *Jefferys v. Boosey,* 4 H.L.C. 815.

or abroad.' The impossibility of determining from without what goes on in a man's mind at any particular time or place is a sufficient answer to those who would give prominence to the fact of composition, in deciding the claim of a work to protection in a given country.

Position of the Foreign Author under existing Law.

Dictum that Residence not necessary under existing Law.— The rules laid down in these cases, based as they were upon the Act of Anne, are of no independent validity at the present day, since that Act is now quite superseded by the Copyright Act of 1842 ; but so far as the two statutes are analogous—so far, that is, as it is not evident that a change in the law was contemplated by the latter Act—the interpretations of the earlier one serve to throw an auxiliary light upon the existing law.

Up to the present, the only case turning on the question of the rights of aliens which has been decided on the Copyright Act of 1842 is *Routledge v. Low* (1868) ;[1] and in this, though it was unnecessary to the decision of the case, certain judges expressed the opinion that an alien, even if resident abroad, gets copyright in this country by first publication. Miss Cummins, an American subject, wrote a book entitled *Haunted Hearts*, and while it was still in manuscript assigned it to Messrs. Low, the English publishers. The book was subsequently published by this firm, at a time when Miss Cummins was temporarily resident at Montreal, it being admitted that she had gone to reside in Canada simply with the idea of enabling her assignees to acquire English copyright in the work. The defendant firm pirated the book and, upon application by Messrs. Low, Kindersley, V.C., granted an injunction.

[1] *Routledge v. Low*, L.R. 3 H.L. 100.

The case was taken to the Court of Appeal and thence to the House of Lords, which finally decided in favour of the plaintiffs, on the ground that residence in the British dominions at the time of publication was sufficient to enable an alien to obtain copyright in works published here.

Indeed, Lords Cairns and Westbury went further than this, holding that no residence at all was necessary. According to Lord Westbury, 'The Act appears to have been dictated by a wise and liberal spirit, and in the same spirit it should be interpreted, adhering of course to the settled rules of legal construction. The preamble is in my opinion quite inconsistent with the conclusion that the protection given by the statute was intended to be confined to the works of British authors. On the contrary, it seems to contain an invitation to men of learning in every country to make the United Kingdom the place of first publication of their works, and an extended term of copyright throughout the whole of the British dominions is the reward of their so doing.

'So interpreted and applied, the Act is auxiliary to the advancement of learning in this country. The real condition of obtaining its advantage is the first publication by the author of his work in the United Kingdom. Nothing renders necessary his bodily presence here at the time, and I find it impossible to discover any reason why it should be required or what it can add to the merits of first publication.

'It was asked in *Jefferys v. Boosey*, why should the Act (meaning the statute of Anne) be supposed to have been passed for the benefit of foreign authors? But if the like question be repeated with reference to the present Act, the answer is, in the language of the preamble, that the Act is intended "to afford greater encouragement to the production of literary works of lasting benefit to the world"; a purpose which has no limitation of person or place. . . . If the intrinsic merits of the reasoning on which *Jefferys v. Boosey* was decided be considered (and which we are at liberty to do, for it does not apply to this case as a binding authority) I must frankly admit that it by no means commands my assent.'

Assurance given to United States that no Residence required.— The attempted distinction between the purposes of the Act of Anne, itself passed, be it noted, ' for the encouragement of learning,' and those of the Act of 1842, may or may not be valid ; however this may be, in 1891 the law officers of the Crown followed the *obiter dicta* of Lords Cairns and Westbury in advising Lord Salisbury, then Foreign Secretary, that residence in the British dominions was not a necessary condition for the acquisition of English copyright by a foreigner.   Supported by this authority Lord Salisbury gave to the United States an assurance to the same effect,[1] in order to satisfy the requirements of the American Chace Act of 1891 ; as a consequence the benefits of this Act were soon afterwards extended to Great Britain by a Proclamation of the President of the United States, dated 1st July, 1891. If in any subsequent case the Courts should refuse to support the opinion expressed by Lords Cairns and Westbury, it is obvious that a serious disturbance in our international relations would result ; but, of course, this consideration does not affect the point of law, which must still be regarded as unsettled.

The Assurance contradicts Fine Arts Copyright Act, 1862.— As regards works of the fine arts, the assurance, though given in good faith, is undoubtedly wrong.   Under the Fine Arts

---

[1] It is worthy of note that the first communication made by Lord Salisbury was worded as follows : ' Her Majesty's Government is informed that the English statutes (*lois anglaises*) grant copyright protection to a foreigner upon the first publication of his work in any part of Her Majesty's dominions . . . ,' and that a few days later this was replaced by a second declaration in which the words ' the copyright law (*législation sur le droit d'auteur*) in force in all the British possessions ' were substituted for ' the English statutes,' the rest of the wording remaining unchanged.—See *Le Droit d'Auteur*, 1891, p. 96.

Copyright Act, 1862, it is made a condition of copyright in paintings, drawings, and photographs that the author shall be either a British subject or resident within the dominions of the Crown. This has been expressly laid down in the case of *Geissendörfer v. Mendelssohn*,[1] where a floral border for certain cards designed by defendant had been painted by a German artist resident in Germany. The border was entered on the copyright register, and plaintiff succeeded in getting the entry expunged, on the ground that the author of the work was neither a British subject nor resident within the British dominions. Residence in the British dominions is therefore plainly essential for an American citizen who wishes to get protection in England for any such work, and in this respect the United States has good ground of complaint.

Special Rules for Works of Art, Sculptures, etc.—This is only one instance of the difficulties arising from the fact that the English law has different sets of rules for literary works, works of art, sculptures, etc. The historical sketch given above has been limited to literary works; but a general account of the existing conditions of protection for all classes of works is given in Section 4 of this chapter.

---

[1] *Geissendörfer v. Mendelssohn*, 13 T.L.R. 91.

SECTION II.

THE INTERNATIONAL COPYRIGHT ACTS.

The purpose of the International Acts—Act of 1838 provided for reciprocity—Act of 1844 widened international protection—Protection refused
to British authors for works previously published abroad—Publication of
a play may take place without printing—First publication in British dominions essential to copyright—The International Act of 1852—Translating
right protected—Stage adaptations and newspaper articles under the 1852
Act—A translation, to rank as such, must be complete—Stage adaptations
are prohibited by Act of 1875—Act of 1886 enforces Berne Convention—
Extension of translating right—'The International Copyright Acts'—
Orders in Council issued under International Acts—The House of Lords
Bill.

The purpose of the International Acts.—The ordinary protection of the English law is thus limited to works which have
been first published in the British dominions. Such works are
regarded as English, and it is part of the national policy of
Great Britain to protect them, irrespective of the nationality
of their author.[1] They come immediately within the sphere of
the English domestic law. Works published abroad, on the
other hand, do not gain any protection in England unless
special provision has been made in their behalf. A series of
International Acts, however, has enabled the Crown to enter
into diplomatic arrangements with foreign countries, providing
for the protection of foreign works in England upon condition
of reciprocity. The matter is now almost entirely regulated

---

[1] Subject however to the possible doubt, previously discussed, as to whether
residence at the time of publication is necessary in the case of such foreign
authors as belong to countries with which we have no international agreement in
force.

by an Act of 1886, but parts of the earlier Acts of 1844, 1852, and 1875 are still in force.

Act of 1838 provided for Reciprocity.—The first International Copyright Act was passed in 1838. A few years after it had been definitely laid down in *Guichard v. Mori*[1] that if a foreigner first published his work abroad it was open to anyone to reproduce it in England, even though the author had assigned the right to publish in this country to some definite person, this Act empowered the Crown to issue Orders in Council directing that authors of books first published in a foreign country which granted reciprocal protection to British books should have copyright within the British dominions. Thus, like later International Acts, this statute did not extend English copyright indiscriminately to all alien authors, but only to those belonging to countries with which special arrangements had been made.

Act of 1844 widened International Protection.—The Act of 1838 was defective in that it applied solely to books ; and, moreover, after the enactment in 1842 of the (domestic) Literary Copyright Act, which extended the term of copyright for British works, it was thought desirable to enable authors of foreign works to gain the benefit of this extended term.

Accordingly, the Act of 1838 was repealed by **an Act of 1844 (7 Vict., c. 12)**, entitled 'An Act to amend the law relating to International Copyright,' embracing within its scope books, prints, works of sculpture, and any other works of art which should be defined in Orders in Council issued under the Act.

The new Act (sec. 2) enabled the Queen by Order in Council to direct that authors of works first published in foreign countries should have copyright therein for any period

---

[1] *Guichard v. Mori* (1831), 9 L.J. (Ch.) 227.

not exceeding the English domestic term. It provided
(sec. 19) that authors of works first published out of the
British dominions were not to have any copyright otherwise
than under the Act. The Copyright Amendment Act, 1842,
was to apply to books to which the Order related, save so far
as excepted by the Order; the delivery of copies of foreign
books at the British Museum and other libraries was not
required, but a special registration and delivery of one copy at
Stationers' Hall was provided for. It was enacted (sec. 18)
that nothing in the Act was to be construed to prevent the
printing, publication, or sale of any translation of any book
entitled to protection thereunder.

In virtue of these provisions of the Act of 1844, a large
number of Orders was promulgated, and many copyright
treaties were made between England and other countries of
Europe.

**Protection refused to British Authors for works previously
Published abroad.**—Two important cases arose out of the rule
of Section 19—that no author of a work first published abroad
was to have copyright except under the Act. In the first—
Boucicault v. Delafield (1863)[1]—the plaintiff, a British subject,
first represented a printed play of which he was the author
at New York, and produced it in London afterwards. Now
the public performance of a play, though not publication
under the American law, constitutes publication in the eye
of the English law. Accordingly it was held that Section 19 of
the 1844 Act prevented the plaintiff from obtaining copyright
or performing right in England, the Court refusing to limit
the operation of the provision to the case of aliens. This in
spite of the fact that, as no arrangement for reciprocal protection then existed between Great Britain and the United
States, it was quite impossible for the plaintiff, having already

---

[1] *Boucicault v. Delafield*, 1 H. and M. 597.

first performed his play abroad, to fulfil the requirements of the statute.

According to Wood, V.C., 'The object of the legislature seems to have been in these cases to secure in this country the benefit of the first publication, and to extend to any other country the same benefit, only on certain conditions, namely, that reciprocity shall be afforded and that the representation shall take place for the first time in England, which may be published afterwards in another country.'

Publication of a Play may take place without Printing.—In this case the play had been printed in America before it was performed. But a few years later, in producing another play —*The Shaughraun*—in New York, Mr. Boucicault, thinking perhaps that the printing was an essential part of publication within the meaning of the International Act, took care not to print. The play having been reproduced in England by Chatterton, Boucicault brought an action against him, but was again unsuccessful, the Court holding that the case was not distinguishable from *Boucicault v. Delafield*.[1] Hence, according to the English view, publication may take place without either printing or issuing to the public in printed form.

First Publication in British Dominions essential to Copyright. —These two cases clearly established the rule that first publication within the United Kingdom[2] is essential for the acquisition of copyright in England, even if the author of the work is a British subject ; and this is the state of the law at the present time, except, of course, as regards authors belonging to countries with which we have copyright treaties in force.

Some doubt, however, as to whether first publication in

---

[1] *Boucicault v. Chatterton* (1886), 5 Ch. D. 267.
[2] Or, since 1886, within the British Dominions.

this country was required of authors who were British subjects, was raised by an *obiter dictum* in the case of *Reid v. Maxwell* (1886).[1] Captain Mayne Reid had written a novel entitled *The Finger of Fate* for Messrs. Ward, Lock, and Tyler, the English firm. The latter published it in monthly instalments in *The Boys' Own Magazine*, Captain Mayne Reid retaining the copyright. After the first few instalments had appeared in this magazine, the story began to run in an American weekly paper called *The Fireside Companion*, in virtue of an assignment by the author of his American rights. In the course of time, the American publication outstripped the English one, so that, while the first part of the story first appeared in England before any instalment had appeared in America, the story had been completed in America some months before its completion here. The novel as a whole was reprinted in England by Messrs. Maxwell, and published by them under the title *The Star of Empire* ; and Messrs. Ward, Lock, and Tyler, through Mrs. Reid, the author's representative, sought an injunction against the alleged infringement.

It was contended for the defence that the work had first appeared in America, and therefore that there never had been, and could not be, any English copyright in it. The Vice-Chancellor, however, granted the injunction, and he was upheld by the Court of Appeal, the Judges considering that the publication of the first part of a tale was in effect the publication of the tale itself,[2] and that, even on the contrary assumption, the injunction was undoubtedly right as to the first

---

[1] *Reid v. Maxwell*, T.L.R. 790.

[2] This view of the law is to some extent supported by Sec. 19 of the Copyright Act, 1842, which provides that the proprietor of a work published in parts shall be entitled to all the benefits of registration, on entering in the register the title of the work so published, and the time of the first publication of the first part thereof. Only the first number of the work was actually registered.

and greater part of the novel, which had in fact been first published in England.

They also inclined to think that, even if the work or any part of it had first appeared in the United States, the author would not necessarily have been deprived of his copyright in Great Britain. But in giving this opinion, they do not seem to have taken into consideration. Sec. 19 of the Act of 1844, the wording of which is in direct conflict with it. Hence the *obiter dictum* has little value, and may be neglected. Whatever the nationality of the author, it is—except in cases where the rules of International Copyright apply—incumbent on him to make first publication within the British Dominions.[1]

The International Act of 1852.—After the Act of 1844, an Act of 1852 was passed ' to extend and explain the International Copyright Acts and to carry into effect a Convention with France on the subject of copyright.' A treaty had lately been made with France, and the powers given by the earlier Act were not sufficient to enable the Crown to enforce it. This brought to light certain defects in the Act of 1844, and resulted in the making of some important modifications of the law as laid down in that statute.

Translating Right Protected.—The chief innovation effected by the Act of 1852 was in respect of translating right. It will be remembered that the Act of 1844 expressly stated that it did not prohibit the making of translations from protected foreign works ;[2] but the Act of 1852 (sec. 2) enabled the Crown to make provision for the protection of

---

[1] Before the International Copyright Act, 1886, it would have been necessary to read ' United Kingdom' instead of 'British Dominions.'

[2] ' Provided always, that nothing in this Act contained shall be construed to prevent the printing, publication, or sale of any translation of any book the author whereof and his assigns may be entitled to the benefit of this Act.'— Act of 1844, sec. 8.

authors of foreign works against unauthorised translations, for
a period which was not to exceed five years from the publication of a translation by the author himself; it being made
a condition of protection that the author should begin to
publish his translation within one year from the registration
of the original work, and should complete the publication within
three years from that time (sec. 8, sub-sec. 3). Sec. 4 of
the Act of 1852 extended the benefit of this provision to the
performing right in foreign plays, which might by Order in
Council be protected against performances in translation for
a term not exceeding five years from the publication or representation of an authorised translation; here, however, a
condition that the authorised translation should be published
within three months from the registration of the original work
made the protection of little practical use.

Stage Adaptations and Newspaper Articles under the 1852 Act.
—The Act also provided (sec. 6) that nothing in the Act
should be so construed as to prevent fair imitations or adaptations to the English stage of any dramatic piece or musical
composition published in any foreign country. Sec. 7 allowed
articles of political discussion appearing in foreign journals to
be re-published or translated on condition that the source
whence they are taken should be indicated; other articles
might be reproduced in the absence of express reservation
of the copyright and the translating right.

A Translation, to rank as such, must be complete.—It will
be seen that the plea of 'fair adaptation,' if made good,
formed a good defence to any action for infringement of
copyright in a protected foreign work. But in cases where
the foreign author had not secured an exclusive translating
right under the statute, by publishing a translation in English of his work within three months from publication, the
plaintiff would be unable to establish his own title and so on

special plea of adaptation would be necessary for the defence.
In the case of *Wood v. Chart* (1870),[1] the conditions on which
the exclusive translating right depended were discussed.   In
this case *Frou-Frou*, a French play, had been duly registered
in England.   It was translated into English with the author's
sanction under the title *Like to Like*, and the translation was
also registered.   The latter was not a verbatim rendering of
the original play, but had been altered to suit English conditions ; thus the scene was laid in England, the names were
changed to English names, and the dialogue was modified in
certain respects, a number of speeches and passages being
omitted, especially in the first act.   Substantially, however,
the play remained unchanged ; the defendants having made an
unauthorised English version of *Frou-Frou* and performed it,
the plaintiffs, the assignees of the original author, sought an
injunction ; but this was refused, on the ground that *Like to
Like* was not a translation within the meaning of Sec. 2 of the
Act.

James, V.C., held that it was a condition of protection that
a work which purported to be a translation must be in effect a
translation full and complete.   In the case of dramatic pieces
the publication of the translation was required by the statute to
take place within three calendar months of the registration of
the original work ; and on this provision, the Vice-Chancellor,
comparing it with the rule that for a book the publication of
the translation must commence within one year, and be completed within three years, from registration, said : ' I do not
think it is possible to say that this means that anything
which the author shall sanction as a translation must be published within three calendar months ; but that the translation
which has been authorised and sanctioned by the author shall
be published within that time. . . . What the Act required

---

[1] *Wood v. Chart*, 10 Eq. 193.

for some sufficient reason . . . when it required that a
translation should be made accessible to the English people,
was that the English people should have the opportunity of
knowing the French work as accurately as it was possible
to know a French work by the medium of a version in
English.'

Stage Adaptations are Prohibited by the Act of 1875.—By
the International Copyright Act of 1875 (38 Vict. c. 12),
however, the Crown was empowered, where any Order in
Council was made under the International Copyright Acts, to
direct that the Section of the Act of 1852 permitting fair
imitations and adaptations to the English stage should not
apply ; and such a direction was in fact made in the Order in
Council of November 28th, 1887,[1] which put in force the
Berne Convention throughout the British dominions. Nevertheless, the rule laid down in *Wood v. Chart* is still good, so
far as it decides that a translation, in order to gain protection
as such, must be complete and literal.

Act of 1886 enforces Berne Convention.—The greatest step
in the development of the English law of copyright which
has taken place since the passing of the Act of 1842 is
undoubtedly the International Copyright Act of 1886 (49
and 50 Vict. c. 33). This empowered the Crown by Orders
in Council to adopt the Convention, except as to some few
points, on which the language of the Statute diverges from
that of the Convention. In 1886 the Convention was signed
and the International Copyright Union was formed ; and in
November 1887 the English Order in Council adopting the
Convention was issued. This Order came into operation
before the end of the year.

Extension of Translating Right.—In respect of translating
right, the 1886 Act makes an important extension of the

---

[1] See Sec. 6 of the Order.

term of protection given by the Act of 1852. It enacts that the term of translating right shall equal the whole duration of the right in the original work, subject to the proviso that an authorised translation in English must be published within ten years from the publication of the original. This was in advance of the Berne Convention of 1886 (which gave only a ten years' term), but the Act of Paris has now brought the two sets of enactments into line.

'**The International Copyright Acts.**'—The Act of 1886,[1] in its preamble, recites that a draft International Convention had been agreed to at Berne in 1885, that the Convention could not be carried into effect in the British dominions without the authority of Parliament, and that it was expedient to enable the Queen to accede to it. Sec. 1 refers to a Schedule in which the International Copyright Acts of 1844, 1852, and 1875 are named, and enacts that these Acts shall be construed with the Act of 1886, and the whole four together cited as 'The International Copyright Acts 1844 to 1886.' Sections 14, 17, and 18 of the Act of 1844 [2] are, however, repealed, together with Sections 1 to 5, 8, and 11 of the Act of 1852.[3]

Accordingly, it is by the Act of 1886 and the earlier Acts of 1844, 1852, and 1875 (so far as these remain in force), together with the Orders in Council issued thereunder, that our international relations are regulated at the present day.

---

[1] For the text and a synopsis of this Act see Appendix.

[2] Secs. 14 and 17 dealt with matters that are merely formal; Sec. 18, providing that nothing in the Act should be construed to prevent unauthorised translations, had already been practically superseded by the Act of 1875.

[3] Secs. 1 to 5 dealt with the five years' copyright in authorised translations which was provided for by this Act; Sec. 8 stated the conditions and formalities to be fulfilled in order that protection for this term might be gained.

The 1886 Act also repeals Sec. 12 of the Fine Arts Copyright Act of 1862 so far as it 'incorporates any enactment repealed by this Act' (of 1886).

The following Acts, and parts of Acts, constitute 'the International Copyright Acts,' as at present in force :

(1) The Act of 1844, Sections 2 to 13, 15, 16, 19, and 20. Of these, Sections 2 to 5 define the protection to be given under Orders in Council, applying the Literary Copyright Act, the Engraving Copyright Acts, the Sculpture Copyright Acts, and the Dramatic Literary Copyright Act respectively, to the various classes of works protected. Sections 6, 8, 9, 11, and 12 relate to registration and delivery of copies, Section 7 to anonymous works, and Section 10 prohibits the importation of foreign reprints of protected foreign works. Section 13 provides that Orders in Council may specify different periods for different foreign countries and for different classes of works. Sections 15 and 16 define the conditions to be observed by the Crown in issuing Orders in Council ; Section 19 provides that works first published in foreign countries may gain copyright only under the International Acts, and Section 20 is the definition clause.

(2) The Act of 1852, Sections 6, 7, 9, 10, and 14. Of these, Section 6 provides that the Act shall not be construed to prevent fair adaptations to the English stage, and Section 7 allows the conditional reproduction of foreign newspaper articles ; while Section 9 prohibits the importation of pirated copies, Section 10 enacts that the Acts of 1844 and 1852 shall be read together, and Section 14 declares that the (domestic) Engravings Acts apply to lithographs.

(3) The Act of 1875, which enables the Crown, in issuing an Order in Council, to direct that Section 6 of the Act of 1852, permitting adaptations of foreign works to the English stage, shall not apply. And

(4) The Act of 1886, of which practically the whole is in force. The details of this statute are treated in this chapter.

It must be noted that important parts of the earlier Acts

are left unrepealed ; it has, indeed, been necessary to make reference back to the Act of 1844 in several important cases that have recently arisen.[1] Moreover, though the comprehensive Copyright Bill lately before the House of Lords confers very extensive powers on the Crown in connection with the enforcement of the Berne Convention and the making of international arrangements with countries outside the Copyright Union, yet it repeals no part of ' The International Copyright Acts.'[2]

Orders in Council issued under International Acts.—The English Order in Council of 1887, taking effect in virtue of the permission given by the Act of 1886, revoked (sec. 7) all existing Orders in Council, with a proviso that such revocation should not affect subsisting rights.[3] The Order (sec. 1) put the Convention into force throughout the British dominions, and (sec. 2) named the countries to which the Order was to apply. The countries named are those which then constituted the Union ; but as new countries have come in or old ones dropped out, fresh Orders have been issued.

The House of Lords Bill.—The International Copyright Act of 1886, with the subsequent Orders in Council, completes English international copyright legislation up to the present time, but Bills based on the Report of the Copyright Commission of 1876, which embody large alterations in the general law of copyright, though they make little change in the international part of that law, are brought before the House of Lords almost annually.

---

[1] E.g. *Fishburn v. Hollingshead* (1891), 2 Ch. 371 ; *Hanfstaengl v. Holloway* (1893), 2 Q.B. 1 ; and *Hanfstaengl v. American Tobacco Co.* (1895), 1 Q.B. 347 ; for which see later, Sec. 4 of this Chapter.

[2] See Sec. 52 of the Bill and the Schedule.

[3] This produced an anomalous result with regard to the treaties in force between Great Britain and various German States. The revocation of the Orders in Council enforcing these being merely a unilateral Act, Germany regarded the treaties as still subsisting, and they were not denounced by that country until 1898.

SECTION III.

COUNTRIES WHICH HAVE INTERNATIONAL ARRANGEMENTS WITH GREAT BRITAIN.

THE PRESENT BASIS OF OUR INTERNATIONAL RELATIONS.

Importance of the Berne Convention in English law—Discrepancies between English law and Convention—England has adopted the Additional Act of Paris—But has rejected the Interpretative Declaration—The revised Convention regulates our international relations—The provisions of the Berne Convention—Each country to grant its domestic rights to foreign authors—Conditional translating right during whole term of copyright—Conditional reproduction of newspaper and magazine articles—Performing right—Adaptations, arrangements of music, etc.—The Vienna Convention with Austria-Hungary—Resembles the Berne Convention—Relations with United States—American authors protected in England under conditions of ordinary domestic law—Effect of projected House of Lords Copyright Bill—Berne Convention to be adopted without modification—Extended treaty-making powers to be conferred on the Crown.

The importance of the Berne Convention in English Law.—As has been pointed out, works published in a foreign country have no immediate and direct claim to the protection of the English law. They can gain copyright in England only if the country of production happens to be one to which an Order in Council made under the International Copyright Acts applies. Austria-Hungary is the only country outside the International Union in favour of which such an Order has been made ; so the Berne Convention occupies a very large place in the account of our international relations.

The Order in Council of the 28th November, 1887, which gave effect to the Convention of 1886 creating the International Copyright Union, embraced the following eight countries :—Belgium, France, Germany, Haïti, Italy, Spain,

Switzerland, and Tunis,[1] which, together with Great Britain, formed the International Union at its birth. Luxemburg, Monaco, Norway, Japan, Denmark, and Sweden have since joined the Union, in the sequence in which they are named,[2] and in each case an Order in Council has been issued immediately after the accession, for the purpose of extending to the new-comer the benefits of the Convention.[3] Great Britain has thus not been backward in performing its treaty obligations.

It must be understood distinctly, however, that the Berne Convention is not, as such, part of the law of England. The mere fact that it is an international agreement to which Great Britain is a party gives it no claim to rank as law. It can only do this because and so far as it has been incorporated into the statute law of the land, *i.e.* in virtue of the International Copyright Act of 1886, and the Orders in Council issued thereunder.

Discrepancies between English Law and Convention.—In view of the fact that the Act of 1886 and the succeeding Order were passed to give effect to the Convention, it is a matter for regret that it was not possible simply to enact, in the words of Sec. 1 of the Order that 'The Convention . . . shall . . . have full effect throughout Her Majesty's dominions, and all persons are enjoined to observe the same,' and to make provision for the enforcement of this declaration, without making those substantive rules for international protection, which, in the result, have had the effect of modifying the full force of the Convention.

The most serious of the resulting discrepancies is that, while the Convention provides that works shall not enjoy the protection it affords in any country after the copyright in them has

---

[1] See Sec. 2 of the Order.

[2] Montenegro also joined the Union, in 1893, but withdrew in 1900.

[3] The Orders in Council relating to the first five countries are dated respectively 10th Aug. 1888, 15th Oct. 1889, 1st Aug. 1896, 8th Aug. 1899, 9th Oct. 1903; that for Sweden was issued on the 12th Dec. 1904.

expired in the country of origin, the English rule is that foreign works shall enjoy *no greater right* or longer term of copyright than is accorded to them in their country of origin. The Convention limits only the *duration* of protection by the law of the country of origin; the English law limits both the duration and the *content*.[1] Still, as a whole, the Berne Convention is substantially incorporated into the law of England.[2]

England has adopted the Additional Act of Paris, 1896.— Great Britain accepted the Additional Act of Paris, drawn up by the Conference which met in 1896 for the purpose of revising the Convention, and on 7th March, 1898, an Order in Council was issued directing that 'The Additional Act to the Berne Convention . . . shall, as from the commencement of this Order, have full effect throughout Her Majesty's dominions, and all persons are enjoined to observe the same.' The Order in Council goes on to name the countries to which it applies.

Of the members of the Union at that time, Norway and Haïti alone are absent from the list. Norway has not yet accepted the Additional Act, and our relations with that country are therefore regulated solely by the original Berne Convention. Norwegians, therefore, are entitled to claim throughout the British dominions only such rights as were conferred by the Convention of 1886.[3] The same now applies to subjects of Sweden, which country, in entering the Union in 1904, accepted the Convention without the amendments

---

[1] See Art. 2 of the Convention; Sec. 2 (iii.) of the Act of 1886; and Sec. 3 of the Order in Council.

[2] The House of Lords Copyright Bill makes this incorporation more complete, though it is noteworthy that in the Bill there are no signs of an attempt to repeal the present International Acts.

[3] The most important change effected by the Additional Act is the extension of the term of translating right from ten years to equal the whole duration of the right in the original work (on condition that it is exercised within ten years). Since, however, this term of protection was conferred—in advance of the Convention of that time—by the English Act of 1886, the benefits of which have been extended to Norway, Norwegians do not lose much in this respect.

effected by the Additional Act of Paris. Haïti, however, accepted the Additional Act soon after it had been ratified by the other countries, and on the 19th May, 1898, a special Order in Council was issued to include Haïti among the countries to which the amended Convention applies.

England has rejected the Interpretative Declaration.—On the other hand, Great Britain refused to accept the 'Interpretative Declaration' put forward by the Conference of Paris, as it conflicted with the English domestic law in two important respects. It limited the meaning of 'publication' to the issuing to the public in printed form, whereas in the view of the English law the performance of a dramatic piece constitutes a valid publication ; and it characterised the unauthorised novelisation of a play or dramatisation of a novel as an unlawful adaptation, whereas in England the dramatisation of a novel at least is a perfectly lawful process,[1] and nowhere in the law is the novelisation of a drama forbidden. It is most important for foreign dramatists to note that their unprinted plays will be regarded by Great Britain as published so soon as they have been publicly performed.

The Revised Convention regulates our International relations. —As regards all the countries of the Union except Norway, then, the Berne Convention, as amended by the Additional Act of Paris, is the basis of England's international relations.

---

[1] But dramatisation usually involves the making of copies of some part of the original work, which is a breach of the author's copyright (or 'sole right of multiplying copies'). A copy of the drama, containing of course the passages taken from the work, has to be made for the Lord Chamberlain, and it is usual to make copies for the performers as well. By proceeding against the dramatist on the ground of 'multiplication of copies,' the process of dramatisation can therefore be stopped. Thus in *Warne v. Seebohm* (1888), where the defendant in dramatising *Little Lord Fauntleroy* had found it necessary to make four copies of his dramatised version, the plaintiff obtained an injunction.

The Convention has already been discussed at length, but it may be well to recapitulate some of its most important rules, with special reference to their effect upon the protection of foreign works in England.

The Provisions of the Berne Convention.

Each Country to grant its Domestic Rights to Foreign Authors.—Under Arts. 2 and 3, Great Britain is obliged to give to authors of works published in the other countries of the Union, viz. Belgium, Denmark, France, Germany, Haïti, Italy, Japan, Luxemburg, Monaco, Norway, Spain, Sweden, Switzerland, and Tunis, the same rights as it gives to its own subjects, irrespective of the nationality of the authors themselves.[1] The enjoyment of these rights is made subject to the performance of the conditions and formalities of the country of origin of the work ; and where the term in the country of origin is less than the term in the country in which protection is claimed, copyright in the latter country is to expire when it expires in the country of origin.

Conditional Translating Right during the whole term of Copyright.—The rules as to the protection of the author against translations are contained in Art. 5 of the Convention. Under this Article, Great Britain and the other Union countries are bound to accord to foreign authors the exclusive right of making or authorising the translation of their works during the whole duration of the copyright in the original work, with a proviso that, if in any language an authorised translation has not been published within ten years from the

---

[1] Under the original Convention, a work published in a Union country by a non-Unionist author was protected in the other Union countries only through the publisher, but since the Additional Act of Paris the author can claim protection in his own name.

publication of the original work, the exclusive right of translating shall lapse as regards that language.[1]

Conditional Reproduction of Newspaper and Magazine Articles. —Newspaper and magazine articles are dealt with by Art. 7 of the Convention, which provides that such articles shall be freely open to reproduction in other periodicals ; provided, however, (except in the case of articles of political discussion, news of the day, and miscellaneous items) that the author has not inserted a notice prohibiting such reproduction. When articles are borrowed, the source whence they are taken must be indicated.

Performing-right in Dramatic and Dramatico-musical Works is secured by Art. 9 of the Convention, as also in musical works where a notice of reservation has been given.

Adaptations, arrangements of music, and other unauthorised indirect appropriations of literary or artistic works are prohibited by Art. 10.

THE VIENNA CONVENTION WITH AUSTRIA-HUNGARY.

The Treaty resembles the Berne Convention.—Austria-Hungary does not belong to the International Copyright Union, but it has a separate Convention with Great Britain, entered into at Vienna on the 24th April, 1893, which was put into force in the United Kingdom, most of the Colonies,[2] and India, by Orders in Council dated the 30th April, 1894, the 2nd February, 1895, and the 11th May, 1895, respectively. This treaty, which, under the first of these three Orders, takes effect as from the 11th May, 1894, is substantially similar to the Convention of Berne. Hence Austrian and Hungarian authors will find their

---

[1] In the original Convention, however, the author's exclusive right of translating was limited to a fixed term of ten years ; the rule was altered into the above shape by the Additional Act.

[2] *I.e.* all except Canada, the Cape of Good Hope, New South Wales, and Tasmania.

position under the English law approximately defined by the rules laid down in this chapter as to the protection of Unionist authors. The Austro-Hungarian treaty is to remain in force for at least ten years from the exchange of ratifications; and if it is not denounced before the expiration of this period of ten years, it is to continue in force until the expiration of a year from the day on which either party shall have given notice of its intention to denounce.[1] Ratifications were duly exchanged on the 14th April, 1894.

RELATIONS WITH THE UNITED STATES.

American Authors Protected in England under conditions of ordinary domestic law.—The United States is notoriously absent from the roll of the International Union. It has steadfastly refused to protect works first published outside its own territory. Until quite recently it refused to protect even works first published within the States, unless their authors were American citizens. But now, by an Act of 1891, it has made provision for a sort of international arrangement, under which foreign authors can get protection for works published in the States. Great Britain is one of the countries that have given to the American President the assurance required to set up such an arrangement, *i.e.* that it 'permits to citizens of the United States of America the benefit of copyright on substantially the same basis as its own citizens.'[2]

This assurance involves no special international protection for American authors. It is merely a declaration, with special reference to American authors, of the universally applicable rule of the English domestic law relating to literary copyright —that so long as first publication of the work is made in the

---

[1] See Art. 10 of the Convention.
[2] See *Chace Act*, 1891, sec. 13.

British dominions an alien author[1] is entitled to English copyright.

The American author of a literary work is treated by England on the same footing as a British author, and naturally falls under the ordinary rule which makes first publication in the British dominions a condition of protection. Moreover, in the case of works of the fine arts, where it is a condition of the English domestic law that the author shall be a British subject or resident within the dominions of the Crown,[2] the American author (unless resident) is altogether debarred from protection, on this very ground. On the other hand, a British author who seeks protection from the United States is required to fulfil the ordinary conditions of the law, which involves the setting of the type within the United States.

The relations between England and the United States, therefore, consist simply in an interchange of the ordinary domestic protection, and are essentially of a different nature from England's relations with the countries of the Copyright Union and with Austria-Hungary. The American author who has first (or simultaneously) published a book in the British dominions is entitled to the ordinary domestic copyright. He stands in exactly the same position as the English author with regard to the extent of the protection, the formalities to be fulfilled, and all the other incidents of copyright. In fact, he *is* a British author,—and is treated as such,—so far as regards such books. And, similarly, in order to get protection for works of other classes, it is necessary for him to satisfy the conditions of the domestic law with regard to such works.

---

[1] It is, however, not yet decided by authority that in the case of an alien author residence in the British Dominions at the time of publication is unnecessary ; but the law probably stands thus.

[2] *Geissendörfer v. Mendelssohn*, 13 T.L.R. 91.

Effect of the Projected House of Lords Copyright Bill.

Berne Convention to be adopted without modification.—
Owing to the fact that in England a treaty which involves
change in the law cannot be carried out without a special Act
of Parliament, the protection given by Great Britain to
Unionist authors falls short of, and is at variance with, the
protection required by the Convention in one or two small
points where the International Copyright Bill of 1886 has
failed to realise the full intention of the Convention. The
recent House of Lords Copyright Bill proposes to remedy this.
After naming the countries comprising the Copyright Union,[1]
it goes on to adopt the Convention as a whole in the fullest
possible manner,[2] and to enable the Crown by Order in Council
to make regulations for the better carrying into effect of the
Convention, and to modify the Convention in pursuance of any
further international arrangement that may be made.

This latter power is obviously one of considerable importance
if, as would seem to be the case, it empowers the Crown to
enforce any further international agreements effecting revisions
in the Convention, without any question as to whether or not
such agreements conflict with the English domestic law.

The Bill defines the Berne Convention, with regard to all
the countries of the Union except Norway,[3] to be the original

---

[1] Belgium, France, Germany, Haïti, Italy, Japan, Luxemburg, Monaco,
Norway, Spain, Switzerland, Tunis, and the British Dominions, with (now)
Denmark and Sweden.

[2] Sec. 42 of the 1900 Bill runs as follows: 'His Majesty may by Order in
Council direct that after a time named in such Order the Berne Convention shall
have the force of law throughout His Majesty's dominions with respect to books,
dramatic and musical works, and lectures published, performed, or delivered in
any foreign country of the Copyright Union, whether such publication, performance, or delivery has taken place before or takes place after the date of the Order
in Council, and all persons are required to obey such Convention accordingly.'

[3] It is now necessary to add Sweden.

Convention of 1886, as modified by the Additional Act of Paris, and, with regard to Norway, to be the original Convention without the modification made by the Additional Act of Paris.

Extended Treaty-Making Powers to be Conferred on the Crown. —And, as regards countries which do not belong to the International Union, it is provided that 'His Majesty, if satisfied that due provision has been made in such State for the protection of books, dramatic and musical works, and lectures, . . . published, performed, or delivered in His Majesty's dominions, may, by Order in Council, make such regulations as may be thought expedient for the protection in His Majesty's dominions of the owners of copyright in corresponding works published, performed, or delivered, in such foreign State.'

This would seem to confer on the Crown much more extended powers of entering into international relations than those which it possesses at present; for hitherto the Crown has not been able 'to make such regulations as may be thought expedient,' but only to extend to foreigners the benefit of the domestic and international statutes.

SECTION IV.

FOREIGN WORKS ELIGIBLE FOR PROTECTION.

CONDITIONS UNDER WHICH SUCH WORKS MAY GAIN COPYRIGHT.

In England a treaty is not an independent source of law—English domestic Acts the measure of international protection—Special international rules as to place of publication and formalities—English conditions of protection for works published abroad—Work must be a 'literary or artistic work'—Work must be published in Austria, Hungary, or a Union country—Difficulties connected with simultaneous publication—Country of origin defined to be that which gives shorter term—Simultaneous publication in England and a non-treaty country—An important foreign view of simultaneous publication in England and America—Constructive simultaneity under the Copyright Bill—Formalities imposed on foreign works—The decision between various sets of formalities—Early International Acts imposed special formalities—Formalities of country of origin alone now required—Dictum that ordinary domestic formalities are also necessary overruled—Doubt whether domestic formalities are not required for engravings and sculptures.

In the last Section we discussed the treaties and arrangements in virtue of which the foreign author can claim protection in England as a matter of right. The actual position of a protected foreign author under the rules of the English law must now be considered. And in the first place it will be well to treat of those conditions and formalities upon which the initial acquisition of copyright depends. It has already been indicated that foreign authors who first publish their works in the territory of the International Copyright Union are entitled to protection in England. For these the only formalities required are those exacted by the country of origin of the work.

Outside the Union, foreign authors can gain English copyright only by first publishing their (literary) works in the British dominions, in which case the ordinary domestic law applies, and protection will be given upon fulfilment of the ordinary conditions and formalities for literary works. In the course of this Section the rules relating to conditions and formalities will be explained in detail.

In England a Treaty is not an Independent Source of Law. —As England is a party to the Berne Convention, the Additional Act of Paris, and the Convention of 1893 with Austria-Hungary, it is morally bound to give effect to the provisions of these agreements. Practically, then, the protection of foreign works in England is regulated by the treaties mentioned ; but it must be pointed out that no one of them in itself would be regarded by the English Courts as a source of law. They are law in England only in so far as they have been made law by Orders in Council taking effect under the International Copyright Acts. It is to these statutes that we must look for ultimate authority.

English Domestic Acts the measure of International Protection. —The measure of the protection that works of the favoured countries are to receive is, with certain variations, the protection of the English domestic statutes. The International Acts do little else than extend the benefits of the domestic law to certain works which fail to satisfy the initial conditions of that law—in that they have not been first published in the British dominions—and which therefore do not fall immediately under its protection. The copyright granted is that of the domestic Acts ; the conditions imposed are those of the International Acts.

It may be asked how it is possible for Great Britain, fettered in this way by the restraints of its own domestic law, to enter an International Union, or to induce any other State to conclude an ordinary treaty with it. The answer is simple.

The Berne Convention and the Convention with Austria-Hungary, as in fact the majority of international agreements relating to copyright, are based on the principle that authors of works published in the territory of one of the contracting States shall receive from the others the same rights as they accord to their own subjects, not the rights given in the country of origin or any independent set of rights.

Such treaties, of course, contain other provisions as well, some of which specify the exact amount of protection to be given in respect of certain classes of works ; but the object of these is not to fix a high maximum, but only to state precisely some definite rule for matters of importance.   Hence, as a general rule, even such specific provisions do not come into conflict with the ordinary English domestic law as applied to aliens.   But, where necessary, the International Acts have made provision for the modification of the domestic rules in their application to protected foreign authors.

Special International Rules as to place of Publication and Formalities.—In this Section we have to do with the conditions which regulate the acquisition and enforcement of British copyright for foreign works.   It is a condition of domestic copyright that the work should be published in the British dominions ; and in this respect it was obviously necessary to make some special rule for international copyright.   This was done by the International Acts, which gave power to the Crown by Order in Council to admit to protection works published in foreign countries with which it might be desirable to make international arrangements.

As to the formalities which have to be fulfilled before a copyright which has been validly acquired can be enforced, this is a matter which might conceivably have been left to the domestic statutes.   As a matter of fact, however, the International Acts contain special provisions concerning the formalities to be fulfilled by the author of a foreign work, and the domestic rules do not apply even concurrently with these. The principle which obtains at present in England is that no formalities need be fulfilled in respect of foreign works beyond those imposed in their country of origin.

English Conditions of Protection for Works Published Abroad.

Work must be a 'Literary or Artistic Work.'—The fundamental condition for the acquisition of copyright in England by a foreign work is that the work shall be one to which the International Copyright Acts, with the Orders in Council made thereunder, apply. Such a work must therefore be a literary or artistic work ; and it must also be produced in a country to which an Order in Council made under the English International Act relates.

' Literary and artistic work ' is defined by the Act of 1886 (sec. 11) as including ' every book, print, lithograph, article of sculpture, dramatic piece, musical composition, painting, drawing, photograph, and other work of literature and art to which the Copyright Acts, or the International Copyright Acts, as the case requires, extend.' This differs slightly from the definition of Art. 4 of the Berne Convention,[1] but the discrepancy is scarcely likely to cause any difficulty in practice.

---

[1] ' The expression " literary and artistic works " comprises books, pamphlets, and all other writings ; dramatic or dramatico-musical works, and musical compositions, with or without words ; works of design, painting, sculpture, and engraving ; lithographs, illustrations, geographical charts ; plans, sketches, and plastic works relating to geography, topography, architecture, or to the sciences in general ; finally, every production whatsoever in the literary, scientific, or artistic domain which can be published by any mode of impression or reproduction whatever.' The effect of §§ 1 and 2 of the Closing Protocol to the Convention is to add works of architecture, photographs, and choregraphic works to this list.

If a doubt arises as to whether any work is a literary or artistic work, it would, of course, be decided by the definition of the English International Act and not by that of the Convention ; for it must be remembered that, although the Order in Council of 28th November, 1887, puts the Convention in force, the Order itself takes effect only by virtue of the Act of 1886, and is therefore subject to the limitations imposed by the provisions of that Act.

Work must be Published in Austria, Hungary, or a Union Country. —In order to gain copyright, the foreign literary or artistic work must have been produced in a treaty country, *i.e.* in one of the foreign countries of the Copyright Union,[1] in Austria, or in Hungary.[2] An author belonging to any other country, including the United States, must publish his work either first or simultaneously in the British dominions or some treaty country.

So long as the work satisfies this condition of first publication in a treaty country, the nationality of its author[3] does not matter. This falls in with Art. 3 of the Berne Convention (as revised by the Additional Act, 1896), which extends the benefits of that agreement to non-Unionist authors for their works first published on Union territory, and with Art. 2, which deprives Unionist authors of protection for works first published outside the Union.

---

[1] Sec. 3 of the Order in Council of 1887, giving effect to the Berne Convention.

[2] Sec. 1 of the Treaty of 1893 with Austria-Hungary, put into force by an Order in Council of 30th April, 1894.

[3] In this connection it may be noted that the Act of 1886 (sec. 11) states that 'The expression "author" means the author, inventor, designer, engraver, or maker of any literary or artistic work, and includes any person claiming through the author ; and in the case of a posthumous work means the proprietor of the manuscript of such work, and any person claiming through him ; and in the case of an encyclopaedia, review, magazine, periodical work, or work published in a series of books and parts, includes the proprietor, projector, publisher, or conductor. . . The expression "produced" means, as the case requires, published or made or performed or represented, and the expression "production" is to be construed accordingly.'

Even under the 1886 Convention, if the author of a work published within the Union was not himself a Unionist subject, the publisher of the work could claim protection.[1] The Additional Act amended the Convention so as to give the author a claim to protection in his own name; and, as a consequence, the Order in Council of 7th March, 1898, which put the Additional Act into effect, enacted that the Article of the earlier Order which limited the right of action to the publisher should cease to apply to all the countries of the Union except Norway.[2]

Difficulties Connected with Simultaneous Publication.

Country of Origin defined to be that which gives Shorter Term.—When a work is produced simultaneously in two or more countries of the Copyright Union, for the purpose of copyright it is regarded as having been first produced in that one of those countries in which the term of copyright in the work is shortest.[3] On this point the International Act simply repeats the rule of the Berne Convention. The English statute further adds that, where simultaneous publication takes place in the British dominions and some foreign country to which an Order in Council applies, and the latter gives the shorter domestic period, the copyright in the British dominions

[1] Accordingly, Sec. 4 of the Order in Council of 1887, operating in virtue of the Act of 1886, sec. 2 (ii), provided that, in such a case, the author should not be entitled to take legal proceedings in the British dominions for protecting the copyright, but, for the purpose of such proceedings, the publisher should be deemed to be entitled to the copyright, without prejudice, however, to the rights of the author and publisher as between themselves.

[2] 'The fourth article of the hereinbefore recited Order in Council of the 28th day of November, 1887, shall, as from the commencement of this Order, cease to apply to the foreign countries to which this Order extends.' The provisions of the Order now extend to all the Union countries, except Norway and Sweden.

[3] Sec. 3 (i) of the International Copyright Act, 1886, combined with Sec. 5 of the Order in Council of 1887.

is to be regulated by the International, not by the domestic, Acts.[1]

Simultaneous Publication in England and a Non-Treaty Country. —Where the British dominions is one of the places of simultaneous publication for a work, and a country with which Great Britain has no copyright treaty—*i.e.* any country except Austria, Hungary, and the countries of the Union,—is the other, the work has no claim whatever to protection under the International Acts, but it still gets copyright, in this case under the domestic statutes. And as domestic copyright is more valuable in some respects than international, a work simultaneously published in England and a non-treaty country may be better protected throughout the British dominions, than if the foreign country were a member of the International Union or had other treaty relations with Great Britain.

Thus a work simultaneously published in the British dominions and the United States of America will receive protection in the former country for the ordinary English period of forty-two years (or author's life *plus* seven years); whereas, if the United States belonged to the International Union, the protection would be regulated by the Berne Convention, and would continue only for the American term of twenty-eight years (with a *conditional* extension for a further fourteen).

An important Foreign View of Simultaneous Publication in England and America.—The question whether a work published simultaneously in the British dominions and in a foreign non-Union country with which England has treaty relations, will be protected as an English work through the Copyright Union, was raised in the German case of *Osgood, McIlvaine and Co. v. Fehsenfeld* (1897) and decided in the affirmative. General Lew Wallace's novel, *The Prince of India*, was published simultaneously in Great Britain and the United States. If

---

[1] Sec. 3 (ii) of the Act of 1886.

considered as a work emanating from the United States, a non-Union country, this could claim no protection under the Berne Convention ; but the German Courts, regarding Great Britain as the country of origin, accorded it international protection against an unauthorised translation.[1] If the principle on which this case was decided is to be adopted by the English Courts, works published simultaneously in a foreign treaty country, e.g. Austria, and a foreign country with which we have no treaty, e.g. Russia, will be able to claim the benefit of the International Acts and gain protection in England. The publication in the treaty country will vest the copyright, and the publication in the non-treaty country will not vitiate it.

Constructive Simultaneity under the Copyright Bill.—The chief difficulty in all matters connected with simultaneous publication arises when it is attempted to determine precisely what the law requires in order to establish the simultaneity demanded. The possibility of attaining a literally perfect simultaneity in two different countries in infinitely small[2] ; hence to require an astronomically accurate correspondence of time in the two publications would be to make the whole law as to simultaneous publication a mere ideal system inapplicable to the actual facts. It is with a view to extending the letter of the law to meet the needs of practical experience, that the House of Lords Copyright Bill artificially extends the meaning of 'simultaneously' to include any publication made within fourteen days of the actual first publication. The Bill provides that 'For the purposes of this Act publication or performance out

---

[1] See *Le Droit d'Auteur*, 1898, p. 45.

[2] The exact determination of simultaneity is practically impossible, as it depends upon personal accuracy and a scientific knowledge of local times in different longitudes. If an approximately literal simultaneity (by the clock) is to be preserved, the day of twenty-four hours is suggested as a convenient margin for reckoning, since this represents the maximum difference of time which can exist at the same moment in the different places of the world.

of the United Kingdom within fourteen days[1] after publication or performance within the United Kingdom shall be deemed to be simultaneous, and *vice versâ*.'

The main object of this enactment doubtless has to do with the ordinary domestic protection—the intention is to assure this protection to works (especially American works) published in this country within a reasonable interval of their publication elsewhere —but it would have some effect upon international protection as well.   It may make it necessary for the courts to regard works as simultaneously published if they appear in Great Britain within a short space of time before or after they have been published in a foreign treaty country.

If this view were adopted, whether the works in question should receive the ordinary domestic protection or the modified protection of the International Acts and the Orders in Council made thereunder would be decided, not according to the place where in fact first publication has been made, but under the rule that, of two countries of simultaneous publication, the one which gives the shorter period is to be considered the country of origin.

FORMALITIES IMPOSED ON FOREIGN WORKS.

The decision between various Sets of Formalities.—If, then, a literary or artistic work has been first produced in a foreign treaty country,[2] it possesses the essential characteristics necessary to entitle it to the benefit of the International Acts.   But Great Britain, like most other countries, imposes on its own

---

[1] This period would admit of a letter reaching England from the United States, and even after the work had been 'copyrighted' at Washington there would still be time to make the necessary publication in England.

[2] Either in the foreign country alone, or simultaneously in the foreign country and a foreign non-treaty country, or simultaneously in a foreign country and in Great Britain (but in this case only where the foreign country gives a period of protection shorter than the English).

works certain extrinsic formalities, *e.g.* registration and deposit of copies, which have to be fulfilled before the claim to copyright can be enforced.[1]

Hence the question arises—Should a foreign work which has a good title to copyright under the International Acts be exempted from all formalities whatever? Should it be subjected to the English formalities, should it be protected in England as soon as it has fulfilled the formalities prescribed by the law of its own country, or, finally, should it be made to fulfil both the English formalities and those of its own country? There are obvious objections to any course of procedure which exempts the foreign work from fulfilling the requirements of the law of its own country ; it would be an anomaly for a work which had failed to gain copyright in its own country to be protected by a foreign country under an international arrangement. Hence the choice lies between granting protection to a work on the simple condition that it has established its claim to copyright before its own law, and requiring of it in addition the English domestic formalities. To some extent the question is one of expediency, but according to the best theory of international copyright the exaction of any other conditions than those of the country of origin is out of place.

Early International Acts imposed special Formalities.—Great Britain, having adopted this view, requires in respect of protected foreign works the fulfilment of no other conditions and formalities than those of the country of origin. This has not always been so. The International Act of 1844 contained no requirement as to the fulfilment of the formalities of the country of origin, and it imposed certain special formalities of registration and deposit. The registration had to comprise the title, name and abode of the author, name and abode of the

[1] In England registration is not a condition of the vesting of copyright, but it is ' a condition precedent to suing.' Deposit is not a condition of copyright at all, but simply an independent obligation enforced (by the Copyright Acts) under a separate penalty.

proprietor of the copyright, and time and place of first publication; it differed from the ordinary domestic registration
required by the Copyright Amendment Act of 1842 in that the
latter comprised the name and abode of the publisher instead
of those of the author, and did not include the place as well as
the date of first publication.   The deposit required was deposit
of one copy only.[1]

Formalities of Country of Origin alone now required.—The
International Copyright Act of 1886, however, in combination
with the Orders in Council of November 28th, 1887, and
April 30th, 1894, adopting the Berne Convention and the
Convention with Austria-Hungary respectively, has had the
effect of nullifying the requirements of the Act of 1844 as to
formalities.   The Act of 1886 (sec. 4, sub-sec. 1) provides
that ' Where an Order respecting any foreign country is made
under the International Copyright Acts, the provisions of
those Acts with respect to the registry and delivery of copies
of works[2] shall not apply to works produced in such country
except so far as provided by the order.'

The Orders in Council do not make any provision at all for
the application of the earlier enactments respecting registration
and deposit, so that as far as our present international relations
are concerned these enactments may be left out of account.
The Orders in Council adopt the Berne Convention and the
Austro-Hungarian Convention respectively, and therefore the
rules as to formalities laid down in these treaties apply,
i.e. works seeking international protection must first fulfil the
conditions and formalities of their country of origin.[3]

---

[1] See the International Copyright Act, 1844, sec. 6.

[2] The chief of these provisions are contained in Sec. 6 of the Act of 1844.
Sec. 8 of the Act of 1852 makes some important provisions with respect to
translations, but this Section is repealed by the Act of 1886 (sec. 12).

[3] See the Berne Convention, Art. 2, and the Austro-Hungarian Convention,
Art. 5.   The provision (Art. 5, § 3) of this latter agreement that British works
seeking protection in Hungary must fulfil the formalities both of Great Britain
and of Hungary, does not concern us here.

Dictum that ordinary domestic formalities are also necessary overruled.—Not long ago, a question arose as to whether these conditions and formalities of the country of origin were all that were exacted in respect of foreign literary works, or whether the Act of 1886, in doing away with the formal requirements of the earlier International Acts, nevertheless left standing the formal requirements of the domestic law. It was argued that the only effect of the International Acts was to apply the domestic Acts to foreign works—that the domestic Acts demanded the fulfilment of certain formalities —and that therefore the special formalities which were formerly imposed by the International Acts merely stood as conditions precedent to the application of the domestic Acts, with their own separate set of formalities.

In *Fishburn v. Hollingshead*[1] this somewhat subtle view was adopted by Stirling, J., who was of opinion that foreign works were bound to fulfil the requirements of the national, as well as those of the international, Acts ; and that, after the special international formalities had been abolished by the International Copyright Act, 1886, the national formality of registration had still to be fulfilled. In this case, the plaintiffs had in fact registered their work—a painting—under the Fine Arts Copyright Act, 1862, and, as it was held that the registration was valid, they would have got the verdict in any case.

The view of Stirling, J., was dissented from by Charles, J., in *Hanfstaengl v. Holloway*,[2] and over-ruled by the Court of Appeal in *Hanfstaengl v. American Tobacco Co.*,[3] so that the law on the point may now be regarded as settled in the sense that no registration or deposit whatever, except that which

---

[1] *Fishburn v. Hollingshead* (1891), 2 Ch. 371. Cf. *Cassell v. Stiff* (1856), 2 K. and J. 279.

[2] *Hanfstaengl v. Holloway* (1893), 2 Q.B. 1.

[3] *Hanfstaengl v. American Tobacco Co.* (1895), 1 Q.B. 347.

may be prescribed by the law of the country of origin, is necessary for foreign literary works.[1]

Doubt whether Domestic Formalities are not required for Engravings and Sculptures.—With regard to certain classes of literary and artistic works, *i.e.* engravings and works of sculpture, the domestic law of Great Britain requires the performance of certain formalities other than the registration and deposit which are held to have been abolished for foreign works by the International Acts. As regards works of sculpture, the Sculpture Copyright Act, 1814,[2] requires that the proprietor of the copyright shall cause his name with the date (probably the date of first publication is meant) to be imposed on the sculpture before it is published. As regards engravings, a similar requirement is made by the Engravings Copyright Act of 1734.[3] And in *Avanzo v. Mudie* (1854),[4] the only case which has yet been decided on the point, it was held that a French print, *La Moisson Abondante*, was not entitled to protection under the International Act of 1844, since the name and date were not imposed as provided by the Engravings Act.

The ground of decision in *Hanfstaengl v. American Tobacco Co.* was simply that, for the case of foreign works, the special provisions made by the International Copyright Act of 1844 with regard to registration and deposit had superseded, and so by implication repealed, the provisions made by the domestic Copyright Act of 1842 with regard to registration and deposit ; and that when the formalities prescribed by the Act of 1844 were done away with under the Act of 1886, the obligation to

---

[1] It was undoubtedly the intention of the Berne Convention, by Art. 2, to oblige its signatories to accept this principle. There was some ambiguity about the original wording, but this was removed in 1896 by the Interpretative Declaration of Paris. Great Britain was precluded from accepting the Declaration by the state of its domestic law as to dramatisation, and its view of performance as constituting publication.

[2] 54 Geo. III., c. 56, sec. 1.

[3] 8 Geo. II., c. 13, sec. 1.

[4] *Avanzo v. Mudie* (1854), 10 Welsby's Exchequer Reports, 203.

perform the domestic formalities did not revive. There is no very good ground for supposing that the provisions of the Act of 1844 as to the registration and deposit of engravings and the registration of works of sculpture were meant to supersede the provisions of the domestic Acts requiring the imposition of name and date on such works, this being a formality of a somewhat different character; hence, in the absence of decisive authority, the only safe course is to assume that this is still necessary.

SECTION V.

CONTENT OF THE PROTECTION ACCORDED TO FOREIGN WORKS.

Translating right specially protected by International Acts—Present rule as to translating right in foreign works—Translating right under the Berne Convention—Discrepancy between English and Convention rule—Lawful translations to be protected as original works—Examples of distinction between translating right and copyright in translations—Calculation of translating period for works published by instalments—Adaptations for the stage—Newspaper and magazine articles—Performing right—Educational and scientific works, and chrestomathies—Mechanical musical instruments.

The protection accorded to foreign works which are entitled to the benefit of the International Copyright Acts is almost entirely that of the domestic Copyright Acts, in particular the Copyright Amendment Act of 1842.   This was secured as far back as 1844 by the International Copyright Act of that year, which provides for the extension to foreign literary and artistic works of ' all and singular the enactments of the said Copyright Amendment Act,' of the Engraving Copyright Acts, of the Sculpture Copyright Acts, and of the Dramatic Literary Property Act[1] ; and though the Act of 1844 itself, and the subsequent International Acts, have made sundry provisions with the object of modifying in various directions the incidents of the protection resulting from this general rule, the rights granted to protected foreign works are still substantially the same as those granted to native works.   Hence the Order in

---

[1] See the Act of 1844 (secs. 3, 4, and 5).

Council of November 28th, 1887 (sec. 3, sub-sec. 1), which
put in force the Berne Convention, provides that 'The author
of a literary or artistic work . . . first produced in one of
the foreign countries of the Copyright Union shall, subject as
in this Order and in the International Copyright Acts 1844
to 1886 mentioned, have . . . throughout Her Majesty's
Dominions the same right of copyright as if the work had
been first produced in the United Kingdom, and shall have
such right during the same period.'[1]

Translating Right under the International Acts. Copyright in Translations.

Translating Right specially protected by International Acts.—
In respect of one matter, however, which concerns the substance of the protection given rather than its incidents, most
international statutes and treaties find it advisable to make
specific rules. This is the subject of translating right. Speaking generally, it may be said that a literary work in its original
untranslated form makes little or no appeal to the public of a
foreign country. Practically its only chance of sale in such a
country lies in the publication of a good and sufficient translation into the foreign tongue. Hence a foreign copyright in a
book is somewhat illusory unless it carries with it a monopoly
of the right to translate ; and so it comes about that this right
to translate is always regarded as of supreme international
importance.

Accordingly the English International Acts have dealt fully
with the question of translating right in protected foreign
works. The Act of 1844 gave no translating right ; indeed,

---

[1] Then, however, follows the proviso to the effect that the author shall not have
any greater right or longer term of copyright in the work than that which he
enjoys in the country of origin.

in prohibiting the copying of such works in the ordinary way, it was careful to guard against any supposition that it intended to confer upon them any such right.[1]

The Act of 1852 created (sec. 2) a five years' exclusive translating right, and was almost entirely devoted to regulating the conditions and incidents of this right.   The Act provided (sec. 8) that, if the author wished to enjoy the full translating right, he should publish part at least of his translation within one year, and the whole within three years, of the registration and deposit of the original work.

Present Rule as to Translating Right in Foreign Works.— The Act of 1886 (sec. 5) extended this five years' translating right to cover the whole duration of the copyright in the original work, with a proviso that if an authorised translation in English had not been produced within ten clear years from the publication of the original, the right to prevent the making of other translations should cease.   This Act repealed the provisions of the Act of 1852 with regard to translating right, and also repealed Sec. 18 of the Act of 1844, freely permitting translations of foreign works, which had not been fully abrogated by the Act of 1852.[2]   It also enacted that

---

[1] Sec. 18 runs : ' Provided always, and be it enacted, That nothing in this Act contained shall be construed to prevent the printing, publication, or sale of any translation of any book, the author whereof and his assigns may be entitled to the benefit of this Act.'

[2] Sec. 5 of the Act of 1886 runs as follows: ' (1) Where a work being a book or dramatic piece is first produced in a foreign country to which an Order in Council under the International Copyright Acts applies, the author or publisher, as the case may be, shall, unless otherwise directed by the order, have the same right of preventing the production in and importation into the United Kingdom of any translation not authorised by him of the said work as he has of preventing the production and importation of the original work.

' (2) Provided that if after the expiration of ten years, or any other term prescribed by the order, next after the end of the year in which the work, or in the case of a book published in numbers each number of the book, was first produced, an authorised translation in the English language of such work or number has not been produced, the said right to prevent the production in and

lawful translations should be protected as if they were original works.

Translating Right under the Berne Convention.—These provisions of the International Copyright Act, 1886, were intended to carry out the requirements of the Berne Convention, Arts. 5 and 6. Of these, Art. 5 confers on works published in any country of the Union an exclusive translating right for ten clear years from the publication of the original work, and Art. 6 provides that 'authorised translations are to be protected as original works.'

In 1896, however, the Additional Act of Paris altered Art. 5, thus extending the period of protection against the making of unauthorised translations to cover the whole duration of the right in the original work, subject to the proviso that 'the exclusive right of translation shall cease to exist when the author shall not have made use of it within a period of ten years from the first publication of the original work, by publishing or causing to be published in one of the countries of the Union, a translation in the language for which protection shall be claimed.'

The effect of this amendment is to confer on the author an absolute right to prevent others from translating his work in any language, during a period of ten years from publication, while if during that period he causes a translation to be published in any language, he gets a further right to prevent others from making translations *into that language*, but into that language only, so long as copyright subsists in the original work.

importation into the United Kingdom of an unauthorised translation of such work shall cease.

' (3) The law relating to copyright, including this Act, shall apply to a lawfully produced translation of a work in like manner as if it were an original work.

' (4) Such of the provisions of the International Copyright Act, 1852, relating to translations as are unrepealed by this Act, shall apply in like manner as if they were re-enacted in this section.'

Thus the author of a French work published in France has the exclusive privilege of translating it into any language or languages during a period of ten years. And if during that time he has produced translations in, say, German and English, he will be protected throughout the Union, so long as his copyright in the original work endures, against all other translations in German or in English, though it will be open to anyone to come and translate it into any language other than German and English.

Discrepancy between English and Convention Rule.—Now it will be seen that, under the provisions of the English International Copyright Act, 1886, a man who publishes a book in a Union country receives in England the same monopoly of translating during the period of ten clear years; but that the condition which regulates the extension of this period to equal the whole duration of the copyright in the original work is under the English law simply that an authorised translation *in English* shall have appeared within the ten years' period. If such a translation has been published before this has expired, the author is protected in England against *all* translations, in whatever language appearing.

If no translation in English has been published, the author will not be protected at all against translations published after the expiration of the ten years' period, notwithstanding that during that time he may have published translations in, say, Italian and Spanish, and thus under the Convention have gained a right to call upon all the countries of the Union to protect him against other translations in those languages so long as copyright subsists in the original work. As Great Britain has made no attempt to bring the provisions of the Act of 1886 into line with the revision of the Convention effected by the Additional Act, there is here a conflict which, although not serious, is none the less to be regretted.

The Act, however, not the Convention (except in so far as this is adopted by the Act), is the law of England, and all that can be said is that in this respect England has failed to place itself in a position to carry out its international duties. The English rule seems to have taken shape under the influence of a desire on the part of the legislature to have foreign works made accessible to the British public; the author was given an opportunity to translate his work into English, but in default the work was thrown open to all the translators in the world. Still, the English public benefits little even by a translation in English, if this is published only in a foreign country: though such a translation would suffice to ensure translating right under the International Act.[1] Moreover, a certain section of the British public would benefit by a translation in a foreign tongue, if the translation were published in this country; though in this case the statutory requirements would not be satisfied.

Lawful Translations to be Protected as Original Works.— It may fairly be assumed that the intention of Art. 6 of the Berne Convention[2] is carried out in the English Act of 1886 (Art. 5, sub-sec. 3), which enacts that ‘the law relating to copyright, including this Act, shall apply to a lawfully-produced

---

[1] The Act of 1852, which, it will be remembered, gave a five years' translating right on condition that a translation was produced within three years of publication, said nothing about the language of the translation (though it seemed tacitly to assume that it can only be English), but enacted that it must be published in the British dominions (sec. 8, sub-sec. 3). The Act of 1886 says nothing as to the place of publication, but enacts that the language must be English (sec. 5, sub-sec. 2). In view of the provisions of the earlier Act and of the general policy of the law there is perhaps some possibility that the silence of the Act of 1886 as to the place of publication will be construed into a requirement of publication within the British dominions.

[2] This provides that ‘Lawful translations are protected as original works. Hence they enjoy the protection stipulated for in Articles 2 and 3 as regards their unauthorised reproduction in the countries of the Union. It is understood that, in the case of a work for which the translating right has fallen into the public domain, the translator cannot oppose the translation of the same work by other writers.’

translation of a work in like manner as if it were an original work.' The effect of this is to give to all translations lawfully made, whether by the author during his term of exclusive translating right, or by other persons after that term has expired,[1] a claim to protection *in their literary form*, though not in their matter, as if they were original works, for the same period as that enjoyed by original works ; that is to say, persons who wish to translate the original work are not to be allowed to go to translations which have already been made, and simply copy them, but they must go back to the original work and carry out the translation by their own unaided efforts.

Of course, so long as the author's exclusive translating right endures, no other person without his permission can make a 'lawful' translation. If the author himself, or his licensee, has made a translation during this period, he is protected against all other translations, whether these are mere copies of his own or fresh translations from the original work, so long as his exclusive translating right lasts. After that has expired, anyone is at liberty to make a translation direct from the original work, but the author's right in the literary form of his translation may still subsist, and, if so, the author will be protected against servile copies of his own translation.[2]

Examples of distinction between Translating Right and Copyright in Translations.—The interaction of these rules as to translating right and the protection of translations may best be made clear by a few examples. Take the case of an author who publishes a French work in France in 1890. If he publishes a translation in English in any year before 1900, say 1895, he will be able, under the Convention, to prevent

---

[1] Whether or not the work itself has fallen into the public domain.

[2] *I.e.* for the period which, on the assumption that the translation were an original work at the time of its publication, would still be left to run.

any other translation in that language from being published anywhere in the Union until his rights in the original work have expired, that is, in England, until 1932, when forty-two years [1] will have passed from the publication of the original work. Even after 1932, however, he will be able to prevent any *copies* (*i.e.* of the text) of his own translation from being published in England or elsewhere until forty-two years from the time when his translation itself was published, *i.e.* until 1937, though he will have no power to interfere with persons who go straight to the original work and translate it.

If the author's translation, instead of being a translation into English, had been a translation into German or any other language, the same rules would hold good under the Convention, and ought also to obtain in England. But here comes in the unfortunate divergence between the Convention and the English Act of 1886 ; under the latter statute it is part of the condition that the translation shall be a translation in English, so that in England the author loses his exclusive translating right altogether, unless he has published a translation in that language before 1900.

If he has fulfilled this condition, as in the example given, by publishing a translation in English in 1895, he will be protected in England against all other translations *in any language* until his copyright in the original work expires in 1932, whereas under the Convention he has only a right to claim protection against other translations in the same language.

If the original work had been first published in Norway,[2] a country that is not a party to the Additional Act of Paris, the author's treaty rights would have to be determined by the

---

[1] For the sake of simplicity the alternative English period of author's life *plus* seven years has been disregarded ; and so have all complications which relate to the cutting down of the English term by the term given in the country of origin.

[2] Or Sweden.

original Convention of 1886, which only gave a fixed translating right—incapable of extension—for ten years, not by
the Convention in its present amended form.   In England,
however, the translating right in the Norwegian work would
remain the same, as, like the translating right given in respect of works published in other countries of the Union,
it is defined, not by the Convention pure and simple, but
by the International Copyright Act of 1886 (sec. 5), in the
application of which no difference has been made between
Norway and other treaty countries.

To go back to the first example, if the author of the
French work published in 1890 had waited till after 1900 to
publish a translation in English he could not after that year
prevent other persons from publishing a translation in English,
since he has failed to fulfil the condition upon which the
extension of his exclusive translating right to equal the whole
duration of the right in the original work depends.   Hence,
after 1900, other persons than the author may translate.   All
translations then made, even if without the author's consent,
will be 'lawfully made,' and will be protected in all the
countries of the Union in their literary form, for so long a
period as if they were themselves original works, that is, in
England, for forty-two years (or author's life *plus* seven
years) from publication ; during that time no one will be
allowed to copy their literary form, though anyone will be at
liberty to make other translations from the original, in which
the same subject-matter will appear in a different form.

**Calculation of Translating Period for works published by
instalments.**—With regard to the period of ten years which is
exclusively reserved to the author in order to give him time
to exercise his right of making translations, the Convention
provides that for works published by instalments the ten
years' period is not to begin to count until the publication of

the last instalment.[1] The English International Act of 1886 (sec. 5, sub-sec. 2), however, makes the period begin to count separately for each number from the time of its publication. Here again is a slight divergence between the rule of the Berne Convention, and international protection as actually given in England.

ADAPTATION, PERFORMING RIGHT, AND OTHER DERIVATIVE RIGHTS.

Adaptations for the Stage.—There are several matters besides translations, which have been directly dealt with by the International Copyright Acts. The Act of 1852 by Sec. 6 expressly guarded against any interpretation of its provisions which should prohibit fair imitations or adaptations to the English stage of plays and musical works published abroad.[2] The Act of 1875, however, permitted the Crown to direct by Order in Council that this Section should not apply to any country or countries which should receive the benefit of the International Acts.[3] The Order in Council of November

---

[1] In this respect the Convention distinguishes between works published by instalments, each volume being incomplete in itself, *e.g.* a serial story, and works published in series, where each volume is complete in itself, though all together form a connected whole, *e.g.* the reports of learned societies. The full text of the provisions of the Convention on this point is as follows : ' For works published by instalments the period of ten years does not begin to run until the publication of the last instalment of the original work. For works composed of several volumes published at intervals, as well as for reports or papers published by literary or learned societies or by individuals, each volume, report, or paper is, with regard to the period of ten years, considered as a separate work.' It will be seen that, under the rule of the English law, there is no need to make such a distinction.

[2] ' Nothing herein contained shall be so construed as to prevent fair imitations or adaptations to the English stage of any dramatic piece or musical composition published in any foreign country.'

[3] ' In any case in which . . . any Order in Council has been or may hereafter be made for the purpose of extending protection to the translations of dramatic pieces first publicly represented in any foreign country, it shall be lawful for Her

28th, 1887, which put in force the Berne Convention, makes such a direction by Section 6 ; and the Convention itself specially prohibits the making of unauthorised indirect appropriations of literary and artistic works, such as adaptations, arrangements of music, etc.[1]   Hence unauthorised adaptations and arrangements of protected foreign plays and music are now illegal in England.   Here again it may be repeated that England has not accepted the Interpretative Declaration of 1896, which includes the dramatisation of novels and the novelisation of dramas within the prohibition of the Convention ; and in fact these processes are not forbidden by the English law.

Newspaper and Magazine Articles are dealt with by Section 7 of the International Act of 1852, which section is still in force, being left unrepealed by the Act of 1886.[2]   It is provided (1) that articles of political discussion which may appear in foreign newspapers or periodicals may be republished in newspapers or periodicals in this country, if the source whence they are taken is acknowledged ; (2) that other newspaper or magazine articles may be republished or translated in like manner, if (*a*) the author has not reserved his right by express notice in a conspicuous part of the paper, and (*b*) the source is acknowledged.[3]

Majesty by Order in Council to direct that the sixth section of the said Act shall not apply to the dramatic pieces to which protection is so extended ; and thereupon the said recited Act shall take effect with respect to such dramatic pieces and to the translations thereof as if the said sixth section of the Act were hereby repealed.'

[1] See Art. 10 of the Berne Convention.

[2] This Act repeals certain portions only of the earlier Acts.   The Act of 1886 and the earlier Acts of 1844 and 1852 (so far as unrepealed) are to be read together, and may be cited as the ' International Copyright Acts.'

[3] Section 7 of the International Act of 1852 runs thus : ' Notwithstanding anything in the said International Copyright Acts or in this Act contained, any article of political discussion which has been published in any newspaper or periodical in a foreign country may, if the source from which the same is taken

It may fairly be assumed that serial novels appearing in periodicals do not come within the scope of this permission, and so are not under any circumstances open to reproduction. If this is so, the English law is almost in line with the rule contained in Art. 7 of the Berne Convention.[1] It is true that the Convention mentions news of the day and miscellaneous items, in addition to articles of political discussion, as open to free reproduction,[2] but these are probably omitted from the provisions of the English Act only because they are not regarded as subjects of copyright by the English domestic law.[3]

be acknowledged, be republished or translated in any newspaper or periodical in this country; and any article relating to any other subject which has been so published as aforesaid may, if the source from which the same is taken be acknowledged, be republished or translated in like manner, unless the author has signified his intention of preserving the Copyright therein, and the right of translating the same, in some conspicuous part of the newspaper or periodical in which the same was first published, in which case the same shall, without the formalities required by the next following section, receive the same protection as is by virtue of the International Copyright Acts or this Act extended to Books.'

[1] 'Serial novels (*romans-feuilletons*), including short stories, published in the newspapers or magazines of any country of the Union, cannot be reproduced in original or in translation, in the other countries, without the authorisation of the authors or their representatives. This applies equally to other articles in newspapers or magazines, when the authors or publishers have expressly declared in the newspaper or magazine in which they have published them that they forbid their reproduction. For magazines it is sufficient if the prohibition is made in a general manner at the beginning of each number. In the absence of prohibition, reproduction will be permitted on condition of indicating the source. No prohibition can in any case apply to articles of political discussion, news of the day, or miscellaneous items (notes and jottings).'

[2] Whether the Convention requires indication of source in these cases is a doubtful point.

[3] In *Walter v. Steinkopf* (1892), 3 Ch. 489, however, it was held that the literary form in which news is conveyed is capable of copyright. Moreover, news procured at special expense has been protected in its substance, *e.g.* in the case of *Pall Mall Gazette v. Evening News and others*, 1895, where the *Evening News* and other papers were restrained by injunction from copying the scores of an Australian cricket match, news of which had been obtained by the plaintiffs at considerable cost. And the Copyright Bill recently before the House of Lords provided for eighteen hours' protection for all news specially and independently obtained.

Performing Right.—Dramatic and dramatico-musical works, whether published in the Union or unpublished, obtain performing right under the provisions of Art. 9 of the Convention. This also applies to musical works, but here it is made a condition of the retention of the performing right in pieces issued in printed form that a notice of reservation shall be placed at the beginning of the work. In this respect the English law is at one with the Convention.

The rules of the English domestic law relating to performing right, which, in virtue of the International Copyright Acts and the Orders in Council issued thereunder, are extended to all works first published (or performed)[1] in any country of the Union, and also to all unpublished works belonging to Unionist authors, are a fruitful source of controversy; but according to the general acceptation they may be stated thus:

(1) The performing right in plays which have been publicly performed, whether first published in book form or not, is protected under the Literary Copyright Act, 1842 (sec. 20), for a term of forty-two years, or author's life *plus* seven years (whichever is the longer), from the first public performance.[2]

---

[1] In the English law performance is regarded as publication. On the Continent and in the United States, however, a work is not considered to be published till it has been issued to the public in printed form. This latter view has been adopted in the Interpretative Declaration, to which England is not a party.

[2] As to plays published in book form before public performance, it is possible that this period of performing right, like the term of ordinary copyright, begins to run from the day of publication in book form; for all that the 1842 Act (sec. 20) has to say is that the first public representation or performance of any dramatic piece or musical composition shall be deemed *equivalent*, in the construction of this Act, to the first publication of any book; thus not clearly excluding the view that, for the purpose of calculating the duration of performing right, issuing in printed form is an alternative form of publication. The earlier Act of 1833, in conferring statutory performing right for the first time, dated the performing right in plays first published in book form from the time of such publication. The whole subject is enveloped in doubt.

(2) The performing right in unperformed plays[1] which have not been published in book form is probably of perpetual duration under an Act of 1833.[2]

(3) The performing right in musical compositions follows the above rules, except that, where a piece is published in printed form, the Copyright (Musical Compositions) Act, 1882, makes it necessary for the composer to place a notice of reservation on every copy in order to retain his performing right.

(4) These rules have nothing to do with the copyright in the printed play or piece of music, which begins and ends independently.[3]

Educational Works. Chrestomathies.—Under Art. 8 of the Berne Convention, it is left to each country to regulate, by its domestic law, the question how far the compilers of educational and scientific works and chrestomathies shall be granted permission to make borrowings from other copyright works. In the English law no such right is recognised ; though in many foreign countries regard on the part of the State for the interests of science, literature, and education has been allowed to override the special claims of the author, and the law permits takings of the kind indicated in Art. 8 of the Convention.

Mechanical Musical Instruments.—The manufacture and sale of mechanical musical instruments reproducing copyright airs

---

[1] At first sight it is difficult to see why an author should keep a play unperformed, if the performing right in it is of any value. It may be suggested that if no manager can be found to produce a play, even with the author's consent, no one is likely to wish to produce it without such consent. But it must be remembered that even a marketable play is always written some time, great or small, before it is actually performed ; and that in some special cases the interval may designedly be very large, as for example when a play is written early in view of an approaching coronation.

[2] The Dramatic Literary Property Act, 3 Will. IV., c. 15, sec. 1.

[3] Cf., however, *n.* 2 on previous page.

is specially permitted by § 3 of the Closing Protocol to the Convention, which provides that these processes are not to be considered as infringements. In view of the fact that this Article was drawn up long before the modern development of the manufacture of mechanical musical instruments,—long before the device of making instruments with interchangeable parts, which enables an infinite variety of tunes to be played on one instrument, became generally known—it has been doubted whether such instruments—or rather the tune-bearing and interchangeable discs, rolls, bands, and cylinders which actually contain the air—should be included within the exemption. The better opinion, however, seems to be that, as there is no express limitation of the scope of § 3 of the Protocol, they must be included in it.

In the English domestic case of *Boosey v. Whight*,[1] at any rate, it has been held that the interchangeable discs, etc., can only be regarded as part of the instrument to which they are adapted, so that it is no infringement of the copyright in the sheet music to make or sell them. There is nothing in the Convention, however, as there is certainly nothing in the English Law, to prevent the public performance upon these mechanical instruments of musical airs in which performing right subsists from being regarded as an infringement of the performing right; and there is little doubt that in England it would be so regarded.

Hence, while the foreign composer has no remedy if an English manufacturer chooses to make and sell discs, rolls, bands, or cylinders which, when inserted in their appropriate instruments, will reproduce his copyright music, he has a very good remedy if any purchaser of such discs, rolls, bands, or cylinders does actually insert them and by this means performs his music in public.

---

[1] *Boosey v. Whight* (1900), 1 Ch. 122.

SECTION VI.

DURATION OF THE PROTECTION ACCORDED TO FOREIGN WORKS.

The period of protection given in England varies with the nature of the work—Duration of international protection under the Convention—The English rule : 'No greater right or longer term of Copyright'—Result of the divergence between English Law and the Convention—Remedies in England not affected by law of country of origin—Rules for foreign author seeking protection in England—Duration under the English Law—The determination of the country of origin—Periods granted to different classes of works.

It is obvious that no account of the copyright protection given by a country to foreign works can be satisfactory if it stops short with describing the contents of the protection that is granted, without stating how long that protection lasts. Since, however, every country in the Copyright Union, except Haïti, gives more than thirty years' protection, the exact duration of the protection given by each State is not a subject of very great international interest, for there are comparatively few works in which after thirty years the copyright remains of substantial value.　Internationally, the author, who receives from each country of the Union the period of protection given to native works (subject to the limitation that it must not exceed the period given in the country of origin of the work), finds himself saddled with the task of investigating the domestic law of a number of foreign nations in order to ascertain the extent of his rights.　As regards the nature of the protection he gets,—the infringements he is

N N

secured against,—he may fairly take his own law as a guide, since it is only in details that the actual contents of copyright vary in the civilised countries of the world. With duration, however, this is not so; for the exact term of protection is almost entirely an arbitrary matter, and the periods given vary considerably in the different countries of the Union—from the author's life *plus* 80 years of Spain to the simple life period (with the alternative of 40 years) of Italy.[1]

Period of Protection given in England varies with the nature of the work.—In ascertaining the duration of his international copyright in England, the foreign author is especially likely to become involved in difficulties. Most of the countries of the Union, having codified their law, give one period of protection to all classes of copyright works, whether literary, artistic, musical, or dramatic.[2] In Great Britain, on the other hand, the law has been constructed piece by piece as the various classes of works have established their title to recognition, so that there is one Act for literary works, another for paintings, drawings, and photographs, another for prints and engravings, and yet another for works of sculpture; and these Acts have not yet been consolidated into a code.[3] As a consequence the periods of protection which these four classes of works receive differ considerably from each other, and the foreign author must be on his guard against the assumption that the term of protection for artistic works is the same as that which obtains for literary works.

---

[1] In Italy, after this period has expired, there are forty years more of what is known as the *domaine public payant*, under which anyone may reproduce the work at will, on paying to the author a royalty of five per cent. on the published price of each copy.

[2] This statement does not hold as regards performing right and translating right, the duration of which is in many countries of the Union not the same as that of the ordinary copyright.

[3] The House of Lords Copyright Bill aims at codification; but even here there is one Bill for literary copyright and another for artistic copyright.

Duration of International Protection under the Convention.— The rule of the Berne Convention is that each country shall accord to the authors of foreign works the same rights—for the same period—as it gives to natives, subject to a proviso that in no country is the term of protection thus given to exceed that which is accorded in the country of origin of the work.[1]

The English rule: 'No greater right or longer term of Copyright.'—Here however the English Act of 1886, no doubt by inadvertence, has departed from the intention of the Convention; for Sec. 2 (iii) of this Statute provides that ' The International Copyright Acts and an order made thereunder shall not confer on any person any greater right or longer term of copyright in any work than that enjoyed in the foreign country in which such work was first produced.'[2] Now the object of the Convention was simply to limit the *duration* of the international protection in a work by the term of its domestic protection in the country of origin. It was considered, with some reason, that when a work had ceased to enjoy copyright in its own country its author could hardly expect to continue to get protection in foreign countries under an international agreement. The English statute, however, by its employment of the phrase ' greater right or longer term of copyright ' limits the protection

---

[1] Art. 2: 'Authors belonging to one of the countries of the Union, or their lawful representatives, shall enjoy in the other countries, for their works, whether unpublished or published for the first time in one of those countries, the rights which the respective laws do now or may hereafter grant to natives. The enjoyment of these rights is subjected to the accomplishment of the conditions and formalities prescribed by the law of the country of origin of the work; it cannot exceed, in the other countries, the duration of the protection granted in the said country of origin. The country of first publication or, if that publication takes place simultaneously in several countries of the Union, that one of them in which the shortest period of protection is granted by law is considered to be the country of origin of the work. For unpublished works, the country to which the author belongs is considered to be the country of origin of the work. Posthumous works are included among the works protected.'

[2] This wording is repeated in Sec. 3 of the Order in Council of 28th Nov., 1887, putting in force the Convention.

which a foreign work may receive in England by the domestic
law of its country of origin, not only in respect of duration,
but also in respect of the contents of its copyright.

**Result of the Divergence between English Law and the Con-
vention.**—So that, for example, if the law is construed strictly,
musical and dramatic works first published in Japan or Luxemburg cannot claim performing right in this country, because
Japan and Luxemburg give no performing right to their own
works ; and literary works first published in Germany are
subject to the appropriation of fragments at the hands of
compilers of English scientific or educational works, because
the German domestic law recognises a large liberty of extract
in favour of independent scientific works and ' collections containing works of a considerable number of authors and specifically intended for use in churches or schools, or in education,
or for some special literary purpose.' [1]

Remedies in England not affected by law of country of origin.—
It has been decided by Kekewich, J., in the case of *Baschet v.
London Illustrated Standard Co.* (1900),[2] that the rule of the
International Act does not extend to remedies, so that, where
the foreign work enjoys in its country of origin rights of the
character claimed in the English Courts, it does not matter
whether the remedy sought is or is not one which might be
obtained in the country of origin.   In this case an injunction
was granted against the infringement by an English paper of
a number of pictures and photographs which had appeared
in a French publication entitled *La Panorama ;* and the
Court, in inflicting penalties, held that these must be assessed
on the English, not on the French, scale.   In delivering
judgment Kekewich, J., said : ' The principle is shortly this,
—A man cannot sue here in respect of a work published in

---

[1] See Sec. 19 of the German Literary Copyright Act of 19th June, 1901.
[2] *Baschet v. London Illustrated Standard Co.* (1900), 1 Ch. 73.

the country of origin,—in this case France,—unless he proves that he is entitled to protection in that country of origin; and, *vice versâ*, a man cannot sue in France in respect of a work published in England unless he proves to the satisfaction of the French Court that he is entitled to sue in England as the country of origin. But it is a very large step beyond that to say that, the right to sue once admitted, the plaintiff is to have no other remedies in the country in which he sues than he would have in the country of origin. Can it be contended that, sitting here as an English judge, I am only to apply the remedies of the French Court, and, *vice versâ*, that the French Court can only grant English remedies, however out of place and inapplicable in that jurisdiction?'

Rules for foreign author seeking protection in England.—The position of the foreign Unionist author who seeks protection in England is therefore this: He must first satisfy himself that under the law of the country in which his work was first published, he has a good right of the kind which he is about to claim, and that that right has not yet expired in the country of origin; he must further ascertain[1] that such a right is recognised by the English law, and still subsists in England. It is not quite clear whether he must also make sure that the act complained of is an infringement under the law of the country of origin, as well as under the English law. At any rate, when his right to redress is established, he can go to the English Courts and demand any suitable remedy of the English law. In other words, the foreign author cannot assert in England any rights of which he is not in present enjoyment in his country of origin, but all rights which he does so enjoy, and which exist under the English domestic law,

---

[1] *I.e.* by consulting the English domestic law as modified by the International Acts.

he can make good in the English Courts by the ordinary means of process.

Duration under the English Law.—As to duration, both under the Convention and under the English International Acts, the foreign author's copyright in England cannot last longer than in the country of origin. In effect, what the foreign author gets in England is the period given in the country of origin or the ordinary English period, whichever is the shorter.

In theory, the term of protection given to copyright works in England is shorter than that given in any other country of the Union[1] except Italy : so that in general it may be said that the limitation of the English term by that of the country of origin cannot apply. As a rule the foreign author will receive the ordinary English term. In practice, however, some difficulty is caused by the fact that the English law, unlike that of any other Union country except Italy and Haïti, offers an alternative. That is, to confine ourself for the moment to literary copyright, protection is given either for the author's life *plus* seven years, or for forty-two years from publication, whichever is the longer. The usual period of protection in foreign countries of the Union is life *plus* fifty years, which cannot under any circumstances fall short of the English period. Where this is so there is no trouble ; but in Germany, Japan, and Switzerland copyright endures for the author's life *plus* thirty years, without any alternative period. It is easy to see that whether this term is actually shorter or longer than the English term depends entirely upon how long after publication the author lives. If he dies within twelve years after publication, the English period is worth more than the German ; if not, the latter is the more valuable. In any case, the rule of the Convention and of the English Acts

---

[1] For the periods given in these other countries, see table in Appendix.

is clear enough—the author's rights are to cease in England immediately upon their expiration in the country of origin.

The Determination of the Country of Origin.—In view of the part played by the law of the country of origin in deciding the nature and extent of the protection accorded in England to foreign works, with the conditions and formalities to be fulfilled, the determination of the country of origin is obviously a matter of great importance. For all ordinary purposes, the definition of the country of origin as the country of first publication states, in almost truistic form, the principle which is to be applied, while the rule of the Convention that for unpublished works the country of origin is the country to which the author belongs is likewise simple enough. But what when a work is published simultaneously in two or more foreign countries of the Union, or in Great Britain and one or more of such foreign countries? In this case, as has already been stated, the country which gives the shortest domestic period is treated as the country of origin,[1] both by the Convention and by the English Order in Council of 28th Nov., 1887, which in this respect supplements the International Copyright Act, 1886.[2]

Where the question lies between Great Britain and a foreign treaty country, and by the application of this rule the foreign country is the country of origin, the work is, for all purposes of English copyright, to be deemed a foreign work, not a British one, and to get only the protection of the International, not that of the domestic, Acts.[3]

---

[1] For the discussion of a number of difficulties connected with the determination of the country of origin in certain cases of simultaneous publication, see Part III., Chap. iii., sec. 3.

[2] See Art. 2, § 3, of the Convention, Sec. 5 of the Order in Council, and Sec. 3 (i) of the International Act.

[3] See Sec. 3, sub-sec. 2 of the International Copyright Act, 1886. This is in accordance with the Convention.

Periods granted to different classes of works.—The foreign author must be guided by the above rules in determining how far he is entitled to the periods of protection granted by the English law[1] to the various classes of domestic works.   These periods are as follows :—

(1) Unpublished works receive perpetual protection—but it is to be remembered that in England the public performance of a play or of a piece of music counts as publication.[2]

(2) For works published in the lifetime of the author the following periods of protection apply :

  (a) *Literary works*—the author's life *plus* seven years, or forty-two years, whichever is the longer.[3]

  (b) *Paintings, drawings, and photographs*—the artist's life *plus* seven years, without any alternative period.[4]

  (c) *Engravings and prints*—twenty-eight years from publication.[5]

  (d) *Works of sculpture*—fourteen years from publication, with a prolongation for a further term of fourteen years if at the end of the first term the sculptor still lives and has kept the copyright in his own hands.[6]

  (e) *Plays and pieces of music* are protected against unauthorised reprinting for forty-two years, or the author's life *plus* seven years, whichever is the longer, dating from publication in literary form ; they are protected against unauthorised performance for the same period, but in this case the term

---

[1] These, with the Acts upon which they depend, are tabulated in the Appendix.
[2] Sec. 20 of the Literary Copyright Act, 1842.
[3] Sec. 3 of the Copyright Act, 1842.
[4] Sec. 1 of the Fine Arts Copyright Act, 1862.
[5] Sec. 6 of the Engravings Copyright Act, 1766.
[6] Secs. 2 and 6 of the Sculpture Copyright Act, 1814.

dates from the first public performance.[1] If never
printed, their *copyright* is perpetual ; if never
publicly performed, their *performing right* is
perpetual.[2]

(*f*) *Translations,* lawfully produced, are protected *in
their text* as original works.[3] Foreign original
works are protected against all unauthorised translations for ten years from publication ; and if by
the end of that time the author has caused a full
translation in English to be published, the protection continues until the expiration of the copyright in the original,[4] after which the author's
translation[5] may still enjoy protection in its text
for so long a period as remains of the term which
it would have enjoyed if it had really been an
original work.[6]

(3) Posthumous literary works are protected for forty-two
years from publication.[7] There is no express rule laid down

[1] Sec. 20 of the Copyright Act, 1842. It has been suggested that the performing
right in dramatic and musical works is lost altogether if they are published in book
form before they have been performed, but this view is almost certainly incorrect.

[2] The accepted views are adopted in the text, but they are very much subject
to doubt. According to a theory which has considerable plausibility, the
respective periods of performing right and of copyright both begin to run from
the same date, viz., that of first publication in book form or first performance,
whichever takes place the earlier.

[3] Sec. 5 (iii) of the International Copyright Act, 1886. Though the rest of
Sec. 5 relates solely to foreign works, there is nothing to show that the protection
of Sub-sec. 3 is limited to translations of such works.

[4] Sec. 5 (i), (ii) and (iv).

[5] Or translations : they may be done in various languages.

[6] This remainder may in practice be nothing, *i.e.* where the author does the
translation himself and lives more than thirty-five years after the publication of
the translation, in which case his rights in the original work (including his right
to prevent other translations from being made) and his right in his translation
(*i.e.* the right to prevent copies of that particular version from being made) will
expire together, seven years after his death.

[7] Sec. 3 of the Copyright Act, 1842—in effect this merely amounts to a statement of the fact that when the author dies before his work is published, the

as to the other classes of posthumous works, but no doubt,
mutatis mutandis, the ordinary periods of protection apply.[1]

period of forty-two years from publication is always longer than the alternative
of life *plus* seven years.

 [1] Thus, paintings, drawings, and photographs, whenever published, cease to be
protected seven years after the artist's death—and therefore if not published
within seven years from that event will, when they are published, get no protection at all.   Engravings and prints are protected for twenty-eight years from
publication, and it does not matter whether publication is made before or after
the artist's death.   Posthumous works of sculpture are protected for fourteen
years from publication, and cannot in any case satisfy the conditions upon which
the prolongation of protection for a further term of fourteen years depends.
Performing right, when it exists in published works, will follow the rules of
literary copyright as to duration ; and the same may be said of the copyright in
the text of translations.   Unpublished works of all classes, whether the author
is alive or not, get perpetual protection.

SECTION VII.

INFRINGEMENTS AND REMEDIES IN RESPECT OF FOREIGN WORKS.

English Courts will not issue injunctions to operate in foreign countries —Different kinds of infringements—Seizure by customs officers—Customs requirements for seizure—Penalties for unlawful importation ; injunctions —Remedy against unlawful reprinting by injunction, and by action for damages and delivery of copies—Rules of procedure for the foreign author.

As the author of a protected foreign work gets in England no greater rights than those which he enjoys in the country of origin, it may be supposed that no act can be regarded as an offence against his English copyright unless it would constitute an offence under the law of the country of origin if it were committed in that country. In this view, before he can make out a good title to the remedies of the English Courts, the foreign author will have to show that the act he complains of is regarded as an infringement both by the English law and by the law of the country of origin.[1]

English Courts will not issue Injunctions to operate in Foreign Countries.—And at the outset, it is necessary to point out that these Courts will not attempt to prevent the commission of offences against copyright by British subjects in foreign countries. Thus in the case of *Morocco Bound Syndicate v.*

---

[1] This has not yet been definitely decided by the English Courts ; for it is one thing to say that the works will not be protected in England unless they are protected in the country of origin, and quite another to say that works will only be protected in England against acts which are regarded as infringements in the country of origin. Cf. *Baschet v. London Illustrated Standard Co.* (1900), 1 Ch. 73.

Harris (1895)[1] the Chancery Division refused to restrain one British subject from infringing the English performing right of another in Germany, on the ground that its jurisdiction did not extend so far.   Moreover, it failed to see how an English injunction could be enforced in Germany.

In this case the defendant had announced his intention of performing the plaintiffs' play, *Morocco Bound*, in Germany, and had already left England for that purpose when the injunction was sought.   In support of their case the plaintiffs produced an affidavit from a German Professor of Göttingen, who stated that the unauthorised performance was an infringement according to German law ; and that in Germany the appropriate remedy for such a case would be an injunction. But Kekewich, J., refused to grant redress, saying, ' No doubt it is part of the duty of an English Court, in a proper case, to enforce German law—that is to say, enforce it in England ; and the German Courts will, similarly, enforce English law in Germany.   But to enforce German law in Germany is no more a part of the duty or power of an English Court than it is of a German Court to enforce English law in England.   If the defendants are not in England, they may set any such judgment at defiance, and unless they come to England, there will be no means of enforcing it against them.'

This case illustrates the principle that the appropriate law to apply in determining the question of infringement is the law of the country where the acts complained of are committed ; but it does not go far enough to decide that the English Courts will never, under any circumstances, assume jurisdiction over offences committed abroad.   The English Courts will not enforce German law in a foreign country : but it does not follow from this that they will not punish an Englishman *in England*, for offences previously committed in

[1] *Morocco Bound Syndicate v. Harris* (1895), 1 Ch. 534.

a foreign country, as, for example, where, the defendant having returned to England, the plaintiff asks for damages against him. For such offences, according to the rules of Private International Law,[1] the appropriate Court is undoubtedly that of the country where the offence was committed; but as yet we have no authority for saying that the English Courts have adopted this principle. Indeed, as regards the remedy by injunction, it is decided that our Courts may exercise jurisdiction over a defendant here, even in respect of acts committed, or about to be committed, abroad.[2] But, of course, they will not attempt to enforce this remedy in a foreign country.

A limitation of jurisdiction which applies to offences against the domestic rights in an English work must also apply to offences against rights granted to foreign works under the International Copyright Acts; so that it will rarely be advisable for a foreign author to come to England for protection against injuries threatened—even at the hands of a British subject—outside the British dominions.

Different kinds of Infringements.—The ordinary case of infringement is, of course, the reproduction of a work, or the appropriation of the whole or part thereof, without the author's consent.[3] Protection against such acts is of the very essence of copyright, and is given with varying degrees of completeness by the laws of all civilised nations. It is sufficient here to indicate the existence of the general principle in England, without attempting to show how its scope has been defined by the Courts. The English law differs from that of the other countries of the Union only in details, and for a full knowledge of the details of the protection given it is necessary to dive deep into the domestic law.

---

[1] See Part II., Chap. iv., sec. 4.

[2] It is held that Equity acts *in personam*—Cf. *Ewing v. Orr Ewing*, 9 A.C. 34.

[3] Sec. 15 of the Copyright Act of 1842 forbids the unauthorised printing or causing to be printed of copyright books in any part of the British dominions.

Besides the unauthorised multiplication of copies, the English law forbids several other acts in the nature of importation and sale.   Thus, with reference to books reprinted abroad, or unlawfully printed in the British dominions,

> (*a*) importing, or causing to be imported,[1] for sale or hire, from parts beyond the sea ;[2]
>
> (*b*) knowingly selling, publishing, or exposing to sale or hire, or causing to be sold, published, or exposed ; and
>
> (*c*) knowingly having in one's possession for sale or hire ;

are specially forbidden by the Copyright Act, 1842 (secs. 15 and 17).

These provisions apply to foreign protected works in virtue of the general principle laid down by the International Act of 1844 (sec. 3), incorporating 'all and singular the enactments of the Copyright Amendment Act' into the International code.[3]   Moreover, Sec. 10 of the 1844 Act specially prohibits the importation and sale of copies of any protected foreign work, when such copies have been reprinted in any foreign country except that in which the original was first published, without the consent of the owner of the copyright.[4]

---

[1] Knowledge is not essential to this offence.   Cf. *Cooper v. Whittingham* (1880), 15 Ch. D. 501.

[2] As a general principle, free importation from one part of the British dominions to another is allowed ; but, since 1875, copies of a lawful Canadian edition of a British work, though produced by a Canadian licensee, may not be imported into the United Kingdom.   Moreover, a Canadian Act of 1900 enables the Minister of Agriculture to prohibit the importation into Canada of copies, printed outside Canada, of any British (non-Canadian) work in which the sole Canadian rights have been assigned away.   Copies of the original English edition of the work would, of course, be included in such a prohibition.

[3] *Pitt Pitts v. George and Co.* (1896), 2 Ch. 866.

[4] The text of Sec. 10 of the 1844 Act is as follows : 'All copies of books wherein there shall be any subsisting copyright under or by virtue of this Act, or of any Order in Council made in pursuance thereof, printed or reprinted in any foreign country except that in which such books were first published, shall

In the case of *Pitt Pitts v. George* (1896)[1] it was contended that this section formed a complete code of the law relating to the importation of unauthorised copies of foreign protected works, so that the importation of copies unlawfully printed in the foreign country of origin could not be prevented; but the Court of Appeal held, by a majority, that this view was inconsistent with the section incorporating the rules of the Literary Copyright Act, 1842. Accordingly, they applied Sec. 17 of the latter Act, prohibiting the importation of all unauthorised foreign reprints, to the works complained of.

The plaintiff in this case was the assignee of the English rights in a German work, and he was protected against the importation of copies lawfully printed in Germany by the holders of the German copyright; the Court deciding that, where the copyright in a foreign work had been divided, the words 'the proprietor of the copyright' in Sec. 17 of the 1842 Act indicated the owner of the English rights.

be, and the same are hereby absolutely prohibited to be imported into any part of the British dominions, except by or with the consent of the registered proprietor of the copyright thereof, or his agent authorised in writing, and if imported contrary to this prohibition the same and the importers thereof shall be subject to the enactments in force relating to goods prohibited to be imported by any Act relating to the customs; and as respects any such copies so prohibited to be imported, and also as respects any copies unlawfully printed in any place whatsoever of any books wherein there shall be any such subsisting copyright as aforesaid, any person who shall in any part of the British dominions import such prohibited or unlawfully printed copies, or who, knowing such copies to be so unlawfully imported or unlawfully printed, shall sell, publish, or expose to sale or hire, or shall cause to be sold, published, or exposed to sale or hire, or have in his possession for sale or hire, any such copies so unlawfully imported or unlawfully printed, such offender shall be liable to a special action on the case at the suit of the proprietor of such copyright, to be brought and prosecuted in the same courts and in the same manner, and with the like restrictions upon the proceedings of the defendant, as are respectively prescribed in the said Copyright Amendment Act with relation to actions thereby authorised to be brought by proprietors of copyright against persons importing or selling books unlawfully printed in the British dominions.'

[1] *Pitt Pitts v. George and Co.* (1896), 2 Ch. 866.

Seizure by Customs Officers.—By the Literary Copyright Act, 1842 (sec. 17), every copy reprinted abroad and unlawfully imported or otherwise unlawfully dealt with is made subject to seizure at the hands of the customs or excise officer, and a special penalty is imposed on the offender ; and by the Customs Law Consolidation Act, 1876 (sec. 42), the importation of foreign reprints of English copyright works is altogether prohibited, and it is made part of the duty of the customs officers to carry out the seizure upon the entry of the infringing copies into the United Kingdom. In their origin, of course, these provisions related only to copies infringing the rights of English works, but the International Copyright Acts, together with the Revenue Act, 1889 (sec. 1), have made them fully applicable to the protection of foreign works which enjoy copyright in this country. The foreign author has thus a full right to prevent the importation of infringements into the United Kingdom.[1]

Customs Requirements for Seizure.—In order to have the offending reprints seized by the customs officers immediately on their arrival in the country, the author must, however, comply with the conditions of the Customs Consolidation Act, 1876 (sec. 42), which requires that he shall give to the Commissioner of Customs a notice in writing, duly declared, stating that copyright subsists in the work in question and naming the date when it will expire. The provisions of the English Law as to seizure are fully in accordance[2] with Art. 12 of the Berne Convention.[3]

---

[1] In view of the fact that foreign reprints, even of English works, may be freely imported (on condition that a royalty shall be collected for the author) into nearly all the colonies except Canada, it is impossible to say ' into the British dominions.'

[2] Except, perhaps, in the one respect that seizure cannot usually be made when unauthorised reprints are imported into the *Colonies*, if, upon entry, the author's royalties are duly paid.

[3] ' Every infringing work is subject to seizure by the competent authorities of the countries of the Union in which the original work has a right to legal

Penalties for Unlawful Importation; Injunctions.—Persons who unlawfully import offending foreign reprints, or who deal with reprints so imported in any of the ways set out above, are liable, upon conviction before two Justices of the Peace, to a penalty of £10 and double the value of every copy so unlawfully dealt with.[1]   The author, however, need not wait until an actual importation has given him the right to put into force these stringent remedies, but may, if he so chooses, go to the High Court and obtain an injunction on proof that an unlawful importation is threatened ; for it has been held that where a statutory penalty is imposed, the remedy by injunction may still be claimed.[2]

Remedy against unlawful reprinting by injunction, and by action for damages and delivery of copies.—For the more ordinary offences against copyright the author is provided with two remedies.   He may seek an injunction against the threatened or continued commission of an offence ; or he may bring an action for damages, and the delivery up to him of infringing copies.[3]   If he succeeds in his action for damages, he will usually get a perpetual injunction as a matter of course.   An *interim* injunction is often granted pending the trial of the action for damages, on *primâ facie* cause shown by the plaintiff; in the alternative, the Court may direct the defendant to keep an account of his profits, so that the amount of these may be taken into consideration if damages are awarded in the action.   It is noteworthy that, while an injunction can be obtained only in the High Court, an action can be brought in any Court of Record, including a County Court.   In

protection. The seizure will take place conformably with the domestic law of each country.'

[1] Sec. 17 of the Copyright Act of 1842.   £5 of the penalty goes to the customs officer who makes the seizure, and £5 to the owner of the copyright.

[2] *Cooper v. Whittingham* (1880), 15 Ch.D. 501.

[3] The Literary Copyright Act, 1842, secs. 15 and 23.

considering whether it shall grant an *interim* injunction, the
Court will take into account the injury which the granting
or refusing the injunction may do to the parties respectively.
Thus it may refuse to issue such an injunction when the
plaintiff's right is not quite clear, and the temporary restriction on sale would cause a disproportionate amount of loss to
the defendant; or when the defendant would be able to produce another similar work from original sources in a very
short time.[1]

Remedies attaching to artistic copyright, performing right, etc.
—Broadly speaking, the remedies here enumerated as applicable to infringements of copyright in literary works apply also
to infringements of copyright in works of fine art, engravings,
and sculptures, and to infringements of performing right; but
in most of these cases penalties are exacted upon simple
infringement, not only upon unlawful importation.

Rules of Procedure for the Foreign Author.—On the principle
that procedure follows the Court, the foreign author who
comes to England to seek a remedy must observe the
ordinary rules of procedure in the English Courts.[2]

Art. 11 of the Berne Convention[3] provides that the person

---

[1] *Cox v. Land and Water Co.* (1869), 9 Eq. 324.

[2] Though registration can hardly be considered as an ordinary processual
formality, it may be noted here that for foreign protected works this is not
'a condition precedent to suing,' no registration whatever being required for
such works.

[3] Art. 11 of the Convention runs thus: 'In order that the authors of works
protected by the present Convention may, in the absence of proof to the contrary, be considered as such, and consequently admitted to institute proceedings
against infringements before the courts of the various countries of the Union, it
is sufficient for their name to be indicated on the work in the accustomed
manner. For anonymous or pseudonymous works, the publisher whose name is
indicated on the work is entitled to safeguard the rights belonging to the author.
He is, without further proof, reputed the lawful representative of the anonymous
or pseudonymous author. It is understood, nevertheless, that the courts may, if
necessary, require the production of a certificate from the competent authority,
stating that the formalities prescribed, according to Article 2, by the law of the
country of origin have been fulfilled.'

whose name is indicated on a work shall, in the absence of proof
to the contrary, be deemed to be the author and permitted
to take proceedings in the Courts of the Union ; while for
anonymous and pseudonymous works the publisher whose
name is indicated on the work shall be entitled to act as
the representative of the author. These presumptions relate
only to the fact of authorship, and are not to prejudice the
right of the Courts to demand proof, by an official certificate,
that the conditions and formalities of the country of origin
have been fulfilled, as required by Art. 2.

There is nothing in the English Copyright Acts which
expressly authorises the Courts, in the absence of registration,
to presume that the person whose name is on the work is in
fact the author or publisher as the case may be, and in our
international copyright system registration finds no place.
Nevertheless, the rule of Art. 11 of the Convention is in effect
realised by the Literary Copyright Act (sec. 16), which
enacts that the defendant in any action relating to copyright
shall give notice in writing to the plaintiff of the objections
on which he proposes to rely ; and, further, if he alleges that
the plaintiff is not the true owner of his copyright, that he
shall specify the name of the person whom he alleges to be
the owner, together with the title of the book and the time and
place of publication.

As to the means of proof that the conditions and formalities
of the country of origin have been fulfilled, the International
Copyright Act, 1886 (sec. 7), provides that where it is necessary to prove the existence or proprietorship of any foreign
protected work, an extract from a register, or a certificate, or
other document, shall, if duly authenticated, be admissible in
the English Courts as evidence of the facts named therein.[1]

---

[1] ' Where it is necessary to prove the existence or proprietorship of the copyright of any work first produced in a foreign country to which an Order in

Thus the production of such an extract, certificate, or other document from his own country is for the foreign author the appropriate means for the proof of his title in the English Courts.   Where no formalities are required in the foreign country of origin, the evidence of a legal expert belonging to that country, given in person or by affidavit, will be accepted as proof of the state of the law.[1]

Council under the International Copyright Acts applies, an extract from a register, or a certificate, or other document stating the existence of the copyright, or the person who is the proprietor of such copyright, or is for the purpose of any legal proceedings in the United Kingdom deemed to be entitled to such copyright, if authenticated by the official seal of a Minister of State of the said foreign country, or by the official seal or the signature of a British diplomatic or consular officer acting in such country, shall be admissible as evidence of the facts named therein, and all courts shall take judicial notice of every such official seal and signature as is in this section mentioned, and shall admit in evidence, without proof, the documents authenticated by it.'

[1] Cf. *Morocco Bound Syndicate v. Harris* (1895), 1 Ch. 534, where an affidavit was filed by Dr. Cruesemann of Göttingen, stating that the performance complained of was an infringement according to German Law.

SECTION VIII.

THE RETROACTIVE APPLICATION OF INTER-
NATIONAL PROTECTION IN ENGLAND.

The general principle of retroactivity—Subsisting and valuable rights and interests protected—Courts will not recreate an expired right—Definition of 'subsisting and valuable rights or interests'—The conditions of retroactive protection.

The General Principle of Retroactivity.—When an Order in Council is issued in favour of a foreign country, its effect would normally be limited to such works of that country as should be first published after the date of its coming into force. It is, however, undesirable to draw an invidious distinction in favour of such works, as against all those works published before that date which are still in enjoyment of copyright in their country of origin.[1] Those works which would still get protection in England if there had always been an Order in force ought to get protection when an Order actually comes into force ; although the protection which is given to them should not be allowed to interfere with the subsisting and valuable interests which may have been lawfully created in unauthorised reproductions before the coming into force of the new Order. Provision has accordingly been made

---

[1] The number of these, and with it the practical importance of the subject of retroactivity, is, of course, decreasing year by year. And there are many works in which, though the copyright still subsists, the translating right has expired, owing to neglect on the part of the author to publish a translation in English within the allotted period of ten years. Retroactivity, however, will always find some application while new countries continue to join the International Union.

in England—with due regard for the latter consideration—
for the retroactive application of Orders in Council made
under the International Copyright Acts.

Subsisting and Valuable Rights and Interests Protected.—
The Berne Convention, while recognising the general principle
of retroactivity,[1] left each country to decide for itself under
what reservations the principle should be put into practice.[2]
And in England some qualifications to the full application of
the principle have been introduced, in order to safeguard subsisting and valuable rights and interests acquired before
protection was extended to foreign works.

The International Copyright Act, 1886 (sec. 6), after enact-
ing that, where an Order in Council is made with respect to any
foreign country, works published before the date at which it
comes into force shall be entitled to the same rights and
remedies as if the Order had been in force at the time when
such works were produced, goes on to make a reservation in the
following words : ' Provided that where any person has before
the date of the publication of an Order in Council lawfully produced any work in the United Kingdom, nothing in this section
shall diminish or prejudice any rights or interests arising from

---

[1] Art. 14.—' The present Convention, under the reservations and conditions
to be determined by a common agreement, applies to all works which, at the
time of its coming into force, have not yet fallen into the public domain in their
country of origin.'

[2] § 4 of the Closing Protocol : ' The application of the Berne Convention and
of the present Additional Act to works not fallen into the public domain in their
country of origin at the time of the coming into force of those Acts, shall
take effect according to the stipulations relative thereto contained in special
conventions existing or to be concluded for the purpose.   In default of such
stipulations between countries of the Union, the respective countries shall regulate, each for itself, by domestic legislation, the manner in which the principle
contained in Art. 14 is to be applied.   The stipulations of Art. 14 of the Berne
Convention and of this paragraph of the Closing Protocol apply equally to the
exclusive right of translation, as granted by the present Additional Act.   The
above-mentioned temporary provisions are applicable in case of new accessions
to the Union.'

or in connection with such production which are subsisting and valuable at the said date.'

Courts will not recreate an expired Right.—The English Courts have held that the rule of retroactivity thus laid down does not apply to rights which, though they have under some arrangement made before 1886 already enjoyed protection, have lapsed before the coming into force of the Order in Council; even when the Act of 1886 so extends the term of protection that, if that Act had been in force at the time when such works were first produced, they would still enjoy the rights in question in England.

This was decided in the case of *Lauri v. Renad* (1892),[1] where protection in England against a translation was claimed for a French work entitled *Le Voyage en Suisse*, which was still in enjoyment of copyright in its country of origin. The work had already enjoyed a five years' translating right in England under the International Act of 1852, and this had expired in 1884; but under the Act of 1886, retroactively applied, it would get a translating right equal to the whole duration of the copyright in the original work, which still had some years to run in England. It was urged that the rule of retroactivity must be enforced in this sense, but the Court refused to 'revive or re-create' the translating right which had expired, holding that, in order to enable them to do this, express words in the statute were necessary.[2]

Definition of 'Subsisting and valuable Rights or Interests.'—Apart from this one question as to the revival of an expired right, the Courts have been chiefly occupied with defining the effect of the reservation in favour of reproductions lawfully

---

[1] *Lauri v. Renad* (1892), 3 Ch. 402.

[2] Kay, L. J., went so far as to suggest that the effect of the rule as to retroactivity was to be limited to works published in the interval between the passing of the Act of 1886 and the coming into force of the Order in Council. But this opinion is now generally disregarded.

made [1] before the establishment of international protection in which subsisting and valuable rights or interests have been acquired.

It has been held that the term 'rights' applies to cases where a *legal* right—an 'exclusive right in a particular person'—subsists, *e.g.* by the translation or adaptation of the original,[2] and the term 'interests' to cases where some special claim, over and above that of the ordinary public, has been established in the reproduction of the original work, *e.g.* by the expenditure of capital and skill upon its reproduction.[3]

Where capital or skill has thus been expended it does not matter how small the amount may be. Thus in *Moul v. Groenings* (1891),[4] a bandmaster who, having purchased for 5s. a piece of music called 'The Caprice Polka,' which was copyright in France, and from it made band parts, had instructed his band in it, and performed it on Brighton pier —all before 6th December, 1887,—was held to have obtained such an interest as to afford him protection from the claims of the author of his original work.[5] In *Schauer v. Field* (1893),[6] a German oil-painting named 'Lisette' had been reproduced by photography on a small scale by the defendants,

---

[1] *I.e.* 'without contravening any existing copyright.' *Moul and Mayeur v. Groenings* (1891), 2 Q.B. 443, *per* A. L. Smith, J.

[2] *Per* A. L. Smith, J., *Moul and Mayeur v. Groenings.*

[3] *Per* Chitty, J., in *Schauer v. Field* (1893), 1 Ch. 35.

[4] *Moul and Mayeur v. Groenings* (1891), 2 Q.B. 443.

[5] In this case an English publisher (Lafleur) had, before the coming into force of the Berne Convention, printed and published the French polka in question and the bandmaster had bought his copy of this publisher. A. L. Smith, J., in the Divisional Court, suggested that Lafleur's interest alone, apart from that of Groenings, might serve as a defence to the latter. 'If all the bandmasters in the Kingdom,' he said, 'are to be prevented from playing the polka, it might be that Lafleur's interest in his unsold copies, if such there be, would be seriously affected, and it seems to me that this would also prevent this action from succeeding if Lafleur were in such a position at the date of the order.'

[6] *Schauer v. Field* (1893), 1 Ch. 35.

and registered as their trade mark; and it was afterwards widely employed by them on show cards and trade lists for purposes of advertisement. The plaintiffs limited the scope of their action to certain show cards which had admittedly been produced subsequently to December, 1887. But the Court held that the defendants had a valid interest in the trade mark as such, and in its use for purposes of advertisement by means of show cards; it refused to take into consideration the date at which the show cards themselves were produced.

The interest must be a 'direct, subsisting, pecuniary interest,' as was laid down in *Moul v. Groenings* (1891)[1] and *Hanfstaengl v. Holloway* (1893).[2] In this latter case the defendant had, before the coming into force of the Order in Council, reproduced a German picture, 'The Guardian Angel,' by photography, for purposes of advertisement. He printed copies from fresh stones made after 1887, and it was held that plaintiff—the owner of the copyright in the original picture—was entitled to protection against these, because in 1887 the defendant could not be said to have a direct subsisting pecuniary interest in reproducing the picture as he subsequently did.[3]

The Conditions of Retroactive Protection.—Hence the position of the foreign author with regard to works published before the coming into force of the Order in Council relating to the country of first publication[4] is this. He will get the protection of the English Law on the conditions :

> (*a*) that copyright still subsists in the work in the country of origin ;

---

[1] *Moul v. Groenings* (1891), 2 Q.B. 443.

[2] *Hanfstaengl v. Holloway* (1893), 2 Q.B. 1.

[3] It has been suggested that in deciding if a valid right or interest still subsists, the Court should take into consideration whether the edition of the work last lawfully produced before the application of retroactivity has been exhausted, and whether the producer has been recouped for his outlay.

[4] The date is 6th December, 1887, for most of the countries of the Copyright Union, *i.e.* for Belgium, France, Germany, Haïti, Italy, Spain, Switzerland, and

(*b*) that if the Order in Council and the International
Acts had been in force at the date of its production, the work would under these still be in
enjoyment of English copyright ; and

(*c*) that if the work has already obtained in England
a right of the character claimed, that right has
not yet in fact lapsed at the date at which the
Order comes into force.

The protection obtained by a work which satisfies these
conditions avails against all reproductions, except those which
are protected by (*a*) legal rights or special interests, (*b*) subsisting at the date of the coming into force of the Order, and
(*c*) of some pecuniary value at that time.

Tunis ; 10th August, 1888, for Luxemburg ; 15th October, 1889, for Monaco ;
1st August, 1896, for Norway ; 8th August, 1899, for Japan ; 9th October, 1903,
for Denmark ; and 12th December, 1904, for Sweden.   Most of these later
Orders, however, operate retroactively from the actual date of the new country's
accession.   The Copyright Convention with Austria-Hungary was put in force
as from the 11th May, 1894.   The amendments in the earlier Orders carried out
by the Order in Council enforcing the Additional Act of Paris are made to
operate retroactively by that Order, the date of which is 7th March, 1898.   This
latter Order applied to all the above-mentioned countries except Haïti, Japan,
Denmark, Norway, and Sweden.   For the first three countries, however, separate
Orders were issued on 19th May, 1898, 8th August, 1899, and 9th October, 1903,
respectively.   The benefits of the Additional Act have not been extended by
Order in Council to Norway ; but by the Order of 12th December, 1904, they
are applied to Sweden, though that country is not itself a party to the Additional
Act.   The Order in Council of 16th May, 1893, extending the benefits of the
International Copyright Acts to Montenegro, was revoked when that country
announced its intention of withdrawing from the International Copyright
Union, by another Order dated 9th August, 1899.

ADDITIONAL SECTION.

THE RIGHTS OF AN ENGLISHMAN ABROAD.

Treaty countries accord the rights of their domestic law—The English author's rights under the Berne Convention and the Vienna Treaty—Fulfilment of English conditions and formalities required by the treaty countries—Conditions exacted by the United States—Possible qualifications of general rule as to author's rights—Translating right—Lawful translations—Performing right—Indirect Appropriation ; Adaptations, etc.—Newspaper and magazine articles—The right of extract for school books, etc.—Mechanical musical instruments—Term given in the countries of the Union ; the country of origin—Term given in Hungary, Austria, and the United States—Simultaneous publication in the British dominions and a foreign country—Remedies and procedure—Retroactivity of treaties.

It will have been seen by this time that the rights accorded to foreign authors in England are by no means inconsiderable. It remains in conclusion to give some account of the rights which an English author[1] enjoys in foreign countries. From the practical point of view the importance of these countries depends on the magnitude of the demand within them for English works in original or in translation. The author of an English work will care little whether or not that work is protected in, say, Russia and Turkey, since his works are not likely to find any appreciable sale in either of these countries. On the other hand, in the great literary countries of the world international protection is exceedingly valuable to an English author.

---

[1] *I.e.* an author who, having first published his work in the British dominions, enjoys the domestic protection of the English law.

In particular this is true of the United States of America, where English works in the original tongue are intelligible to the ordinary native public. But this latter country has not yet come to recognise the principle of international protection, in spite of the Chace Act of 1891 ; that statute does not protect any works except those first published in the United States, or simultaneously published there and in a foreign State, and all these must fulfil in other respects the ordinary conditions of the American law. Hence the English author cannot gain copyright in the United States, unless he independently assumes the additional character of the author of an American work.

Treaty Countries accord the rights of their Domestic Law.— The basis of all international agreements is reciprocity ; and it will be found that the countries to whose authors Great Britain extends her own domestic protection, in return extend their domestic protection to the authors of English works. Thus an English author will gain in each of the countries of the International Copyright Union,—in Belgium, Denmark, France, Germany, Haïti, Italy, Japan, Luxemburg, Monaco, Norway, Spain, Sweden, Switzerland, and Tunis,—and in addition in Austria and Hungary, all the rights which those countries respectively accord to their own native authors. And, since in most foreign States an international treaty *ipso facto* becomes law, without need of any special statutory legislation to carry it into effect, he will usually get these rights without any such exceptions as are created in England, where the International Acts have failed to carry out the full intention of the treaties which they enforce. There is in such countries no room for the discrepancies which exist between the English law and the Berne Convention, as a consequence of the imperfect re-enactment of some of the provisions of the latter agreement in the International Copyright Act of 1886.

The English Author's Rights under the Berne Convention and the Vienna Treaty.—Speaking generally, then, the English author has only to consult the Berne Convention and the Vienna Treaty with Austria-Hungary, in order to ascertain his foreign rights. That is, his foreign *international* rights— for, apart altogether from treaty relations, many States protect an author, if only his work is first published in their territory and the conditions and formalities of the domestic law are fulfilled ; even in the United States, where the author's nationality is still of considerable importance, English authors, as we have seen, are admitted to copyright under such a rule. Here, however, we are mainly concerned with the rights which a work *published in the British dominions* will obtain in foreign countries.[1]

In France, Belgium, and Luxemburg such a work receives under the domestic law the same rights as are accorded to native works, but in other countries its protection depends entirely upon the provisions of treaties which Great Britain may have concluded with them. Of such treaties the Berne Convention of 1886 and the Vienna Treaty of 1893 with Austria-Hungary are the only two now in force. No treaty with the United States exists, and works first published in the British dominions are not protected in that country.

As the treaties relating to copyright which are actually in force between Great Britain and foreign countries all embody the principle of reciprocity, the protection of English works in such countries, considered apart from the details of the various domestic codes, follows the same principles as the protection of foreign works in England ; and of these principles

---

[1] Under the Berne Convention, the right of unpublished works to protection is regulated by the nationality of the author, so that, as long as the work of an Englishman remains unpublished, it is protected throughout the Union. A published work is only protected by the Convention if the first publication took place in one of the countries of the Union.

a general knowledge may be obtained by a perusal of the preceding Sections of this chapter, with the exception, however,
of Sections 1 and 2, which describe matters peculiar to international protection as granted in England.

**Fulfilment of English Conditions and Formalities required by
the Treaty Countries.**—The general rule, as stated above, is
that in each of the treaty countries the author of a work
published in the British dominions[1] gets the same rights as a
native. In order to be eligible for copyright at all, the work
must, of course, be a literary or artistic work. The only
other condition of protection is that it shall have fulfilled
the conditions and formalities of the country of origin, *i.e.*
that it shall have been duly registered in England.[2] Deposit
of copies, though provision is made for it in the English
Copyright Acts, has strictly nothing to do with copyright,
since the question whether it has been carried out can in no
way affect the vesting of protection or the right of action ;
the duty of deposit is in fact an independent obligation,
enforced by a separate penalty. Hence, from the point of view
of international protection, there is no need for the English
author to make the deposit required by the English Copyright
Acts.

No country of the Union now requires the fulfilment of any
formalities beyond those of the country of origin. It is
probable that these alone were contemplated by Art. 2 of the
Convention of 1886, but in imposing the conditions and

---

[1] Or the English author of an unpublished work.

[2] In view of the fact that in England registration is not a condition of the
vesting of copyright, but only a condition precedent to suing, it is doubtful
whether, even if he does not register, the author of an English work is not
entitled to the benefit of the Convention. In practice it would always be safer
to carry out the registration. Moreover, registration would be found useful in the
event of litigation in a foreign country, since an official extract from the register
would doubtless be accepted by the Courts as a certificate of title in the country
of origin under Art. 11 of the Convention.

formalities of the country of origin this Article made no express provision that no others should be imposed. The Interpretative Declaration of 1896,[1] however, made it clear that this inference was drawn by all the countries of the Union except Great Britain.[2] Hence there can be no reasonable doubt that an English author who has duly registered in England is entitled to protection throughout the Union without further formalities.

With regard to protection in Austria a similar rule is expressly laid down by the Treaty of 1893 (Art. 5). For protection in Hungary it is required that both the English conditions and formalities and those prescribed by the law of Hungary shall be fulfilled.[3]

Conditions exacted by the United States.—In the United States the English author receives no special international protection, though since the international arrangement of 1891 his alien nationality no longer debars him from obtaining protection upon satisfying the ordinary domestic conditions and formalities. The American law requires that the work shall be first (or simultaneously) published, and the type set (or the negative or drawing on stone made), within the limits of the United States; while a printed copy of the title-page, and also two copies of the work itself must, on or before the day of publication, be deposited at the office of the Librarian of Congress, and every copy of every edition of the work must bear a notice of the existence and date of copyright. If the work is a work of the fine arts—a painting, drawing, or

---

[1] Clause 1 of the Interpretative Declaration: 'With reference to the terms of Art. 2, § 2 of the Convention, the protection assured by the aforesaid Acts depends solely upon the accomplishment, in the country of origin of the work, of the conditions and formalities prescribed by the law of that country.'

[2] As to Great Britain, the case of *Hanfstaengl v. Holloway* (1893), 2 Q.B. 1, has set up the rule that no further formalities than those of the country of origin are required.

[3] See Art. 5, § 3 of the Treaty.

statue—the type-setting condition cannot, of course, apply ; and, instead of the title-page and copies of the work, the author is required to deliver a description or model of the work (according to its nature), and a photograph thereof, respectively.

Possible Qualifications of general rule as to Author's Rights. —The author of an English work gets in each foreign treaty country all the rights which that country accords to natives, as extended or otherwise modified by the Berne Convention or the Vienna Treaty, subject to such qualifications as may be induced by the failure of any State to give full effect to those agreements.

Translating Right.—Thus, under Art. 5 of the Berne Convention, the English author is entitled to claim from every Union country, whatever its own domestic rules, a translating right equal to the whole duration of his right in the original work, subject to the condition that he shall have produced a translation in the language for which he claims protection within ten years from the publication of the original. But this, the rule of the Additional Act of Paris, does not hold as regards Norway and Sweden ; those countries, following the Convention of 1886, give only a ten years translating right.

In Austria and Hungary, the English author gets a translating right equal to the full duration of his right in the original work, unqualified by any condition of translating within ten years.[1] In the United States when a copyright in a work has once been obtained it will carry with it the

---

[1] See Art. 2 of the Convention with Austria-Hungary : 'The right of translation forming part of the copyright, the protection of the right of translation is assured under the conditions laid down by this Convention.' The Article goes on to make it a condition for the full protection of the translating right in Austrian and Hungarian works that a translation in English shall be produced within ten clear years from publication, but it in no way limits the translating right in English works.

exclusive right to dramatise and to translate the work during the whole duration of the right in the original.[1]

Lawful Translations.—Passing from the author's right to prohibit the translating of the original work to the right of the person who has made a lawful translation[2] to prevent this from being copied, we see that in all the countries of the Union, as well as in Austria and Hungary, the English translator gets protection in his translation as if it were an original work.[3] Examples of the way in which the author's translating right and the translator's copyright often coincide in whole or part are given in Section 6 above.

Performing Right.—Under Art. 9 of the Berne Convention, the English composer may claim protection for his performing right in musical and dramatic works from those countries of the Union which themselves recognise such a right[4] ; but, as to printed music, this is subject to the condition that each copy must be provided with a notice of reservation, if the performing right is to be retained.[5] In the United States the right of representation is included in copyright by a special Act of 1856.

Indirect Appropriation; Adaptations, etc.—Speaking generally, the English author has a right in each country of the Union,

---

[1] See Sec. 4952 of the American Revised Statutes.

[2] A translation is lawful if (*a*) made by the author of the original work, (*b*) made by another with the author's consent, or (*c*) made by anyone after the author's exclusive right of translating the original work has expired.

[3] Art. 6 of the Berne Convention and Art. 3 of the Convention with Austria-Hungary.

[4] He has a similar claim to protection in Austria and Hungary, though no specific mention of performing right is made in the Austro-Hungarian Convention. Cf. Art. 1 of that Convention with Art. 8, which preserves subsisting interests in the performance of dramatic or musical works.

[5] Opinion within the Union, however, is strongly in favour of abolishing the requirement of notice of reservation so soon as this may be practicable. See Recommendation No. 2 of the Paris Conference, 1896.—*Actes de la Conférence de Paris*, p. 229.

in Austria, and in Hungary, to be protected against all forms of literary and artistic appropriation which are deemed to be infringements by the law of the country from which he seeks redress. The Berne Convention, however, deals specifically with certain classes of such appropriations, and the general rule must be modified in the light of its provisions so far as regards protection in the countries of the Union. Art. 10 specially forbids unauthorised indirect appropriations, such as adaptations and arrangements of music.[1] All countries of the Union are bound in principle to protect the English author against these; but there is a proviso to the Article which enables them, in enforcing the general rule, to give effect to any specific reservations which may be made by their respective domestic laws.

Hence in seeking protection from any country of the Union against any particular form of indirect appropriation, it is necessary for the English author first of all to consult the domestic law of the country, in order to ascertain whether the offending work is exempted by that law from treatment as an infringement.

The same applies to an English author who seeks protection from Austria or Hungary.

Among the various forms of indirect appropriation the dramatisation of novels and the novelisation of dramas are prominent. Although, as has already been stated, these processes are not forbidden by the English law, the Interpretative Declaration of Paris, to which all the countries of the Union except Great Britain are parties, especially included them among the indirect appropriations forbidden by Art. 10 of the Berne Convention.

---

[1] *I.e.* works which are ' merely the reproduction of another literary or artistic work, in the same form or in another form, with non-essential alterations, additions, or abridgements, without in other respects presenting the character of a new original work.'

Hence, if the Declaration was, as it professed to be, merely interpretative, or declaratory, of the construction placed by the subscribing countries upon the wording and intention of the Convention, the English author will probably gain protection against these forms of infringement from the various countries of the Union. Even in the absence of reciprocity on the part of Great Britain, these countries may reasonably be expected to follow out their own view of their conventional obligations. If, on the other hand, it were possible to regard the Declaration as being in effect a separate supplementary treaty, then no doubt it would be idle for the author of an English work to expect to share its benefits.

Newspaper and Magazine Articles.—Under the Convention (Art. 7), any foreign periodical may reproduce English newspaper or magazine articles (with the exception of serial novels and short stories) on two conditions. These conditions are : (*a*) that such taking is not expressly forbidden in the newspaper or magazine from which the extract is made, (*b*) that when the borrowed matter is reproduced the source from which it is derived shall be indicated. The former condition, however, is not applicable to articles of political discussion, news of the day, and miscellaneous items (notes and jottings), which cannot be protected even by express notice.

Nothing is said about borrowing from newspapers and magazines in the Austro-Hungarian Convention, so that as regards Austria and Hungary the domestic law of the two countries respectively is the sole criterion.

The Right of Extract for School Books, etc.—The Berne Convention (Art. 8) allows each country to make special provision in favour of borrowings from copyright works made for educational or scientific works, or books of extracts from classical authors. The English author who feels aggrieved

by such forms of appropriation must therefore, before taking
legal proceedings, look carefully to the domestic law of the
country from which he seeks protection.[1]

The Austro-Hungarian Convention makes no mention of
the matter.

Mechanical Musical Instruments.—The Closing Protocol to
the Berne Convention (§ 3) provides that the manufacture and
sale of mechanical instruments serving to reproduce copyright
musical airs shall not be considered as constituting musical
infringement, so that the English composer whose music
is adapted by foreign manufacturers to the mechanism of
musical boxes, or reproduced on discs, rolls, bands, cylinders,
etc., made for use with mechanical musical instruments of more
complicated structure, has no claim to interfere with the trade
in such instruments and parts of instruments.   The Convention, however, says nothing against his right to protection
against the public performance of his music on such instruments, which is obviously a very different matter from his claim
to suppress mechanical adaptations of his sheet music in virtue
of his literary copyright ; and it would seem that every foreign
country of the Union is bound to give to the English composer
—as part of his performing right under Art. 9—redress
against such public performance.

There is no special exemption in the Austro-Hungarian
Convention in favour of the manufacture and sale of
mechanical musical instruments.

---

[1] The German Act of 1901 contains a long list of the various forms of appropriation which are permitted in behalf of education, science, and literature.
Thus Sec. 19 enacts that reproduction is permitted (1) when separate passages are
quoted in an independent literary work ; (2) when separate essays or poems are
inserted in an independent scientific work ; (3) when separate poems are
included in a collection made from a number of writers and intended for use in
the performance of vocal music ; (4) when separate essays, poems, or extracts are
included in a collection made from a number of authors and intended for use in
churches or schools, or in education, or for some special literary purpose.

Term given in the Countries of the Union; the Country of Origin.—The English author is entitled to protection from each country of the Union for the period which is granted to native works; subject to the important qualification that no country is bound to continue its protection after the copyright in the work has expired in the country of origin, *i.e.*, in this case, England.[1] The English period of protection is forty-two years, or author's life *plus* seven years, whichever is the longer; and most of the countries of the Union grant a term of copyright theoretically longer than this, the common period being life *plus* fifty years,[2] though in several cases life *plus* thirty years only is given,[3] and in one country, *i.e.* Spain, the author is entitled to a term of protection equal to life *plus* eighty years.[4]

Foreign term may be shorter than English.—Thus in the majority of cases the English author's rights in the foreign countries of the Union will cease and determine before the end

---

[1] Art. 2, §§ 1 and 2, of the Convention runs as follows : ' Authors belonging to any country of the Union, or their lawful representatives, shall enjoy in the other countries for their works, whether unpublished or published for the first time in one of those countries, the rights that the respective laws do now or may hereafter grant to natives. The enjoyment of these rights is subjected to the accomplishment of the conditions and formalities prescribed by law in the country of origin of the work; *it cannot exceed in the other countries the duration of the protection granted in the said country of origin.*'

[2] Life *plus* fifty years is given by Belgium, Denmark, France, Luxemburg, Monaco, Norway, Sweden, and Tunis.

[3] Life *plus* thirty years is the domestic term of Germany, Japan, and Switzerland.

[4] The most important of the other countries is Italy, which gives an alternative term of author's life *or* forty years, whichever is the longer, with a further period of forty years during which anyone is at liberty to reproduce the work, on payment of a royalty of five per cent. to the author or his representative. The work may be regarded as in the public domain, and the public domain as yielding a certain rent for it. Hence this state of affairs is described in French as the *domaine public payant*. A complete table of the respective terms of protection, including the periods of subsidiary rights, like performing right or translating right, as well as the ordinary periods of copyright, is given in the Appendix.

of the normal domestic term given in those countries, owing to the prior expiration of his copyright in England, the country of origin. But under certain circumstances his rights in those foreign countries which give a term of life *plus* thirty years may expire before the lapse of his copyright in England.[1] This will be so whenever the author dies within twelve years of the date of publication.

Thus if an English work is published in 1900 and the author dies in, say 1910, it is clear that the longer of the two alternative terms of protection offered by the English law is the period of forty-two years. Hence in England the work will be protected until 1942. In Germany, however, in which the ordinary period is life *plus* thirty years, there is no alternative, and so the German rights in the work come to an end in 1940, which is two years before the expiration of the English copyright. The same result will be found to hold good if the English author dies at any time before 1912.

In those countries which grant a domestic term of life *plus* fifty years, or any longer period, it is obvious that the English author's rights can never run their normal course,[2] but must always be determined prematurely by the expiration of the copyright in the country of origin. However long an English author may live, it is plain that the English term of life *plus* seven years must always expire before a foreign term of life *plus* fifty years ; and, however soon he may die, it is equally plain that the foreign term can never become less than the alternative of forty-two years.

---

[1] This would be always so in Italy, as the Italian period of author's life or forty years must in either alternative be shorter than the English period of author's life *plus* seven years or forty-two years.

[2] *I.e.* under the Convention—though of course it is open to any country to exceed its treaty obligations by giving foreign authors protection for the full domestic period. This is actually done by Luxemburg.

Term given in Austria-Hungary and the United States.—The rule of the treaty with Austria-Hungary in respect of duration is the same as that of the Berne Convention.[1] The period of protection given by the Austrian domestic law is life *plus* thirty years; the law of Hungary, however, gives life *plus* fifty years. Hence, following out what has been said above, it is clear that in Hungary the rights of the English author must in every case come to an end before the expiration of the Hungarian domestic period ; whilst in Austria this will only be so when the author dies some time after the lapse of twelve years from the date of publication.

The period of protection given in the United States is twenty-eight years from the time of recording the copyright, with a further extension of fourteen years for the author, or (if he be no longer alive) for his widow or children; provided that the title is again recorded and the other formalities again fulfilled.

Simultaneous publication in the British Dominions and a Foreign Union Country.—When an author publishes his work simultaneously in the British dominions and a foreign country of the Union, the rule both of the Berne Convention and of the English law is that the country which gives the shorter term of protection is to be regarded as the country of origin[2] ; so that, for the purpose both of English and of international law, a work published simultaneously in the

---

[1] See Art. 1 of the Austro-Hungarian Treaty, the material part of which runs as follows : 'These advantages [*i.e.* of international protection] shall only be reciprocally guaranteed to authors and their legal representatives when the work in question is also protected by the laws of the State where the work was first published, and the duration of protection in the other country shall not exceed that which is granted to authors and their legal representatives in the country where the work was first published.'

[2] See Art. 2, § 3, of the Convention, and the English International Copyright Act, 1886, sec. 3 (ii), together with Sec. 5 of the Order in Council of 1887.

British dominions and in Italy (domestic period—author's life or forty years) will be regarded as an Italian work; while a work published simultaneously in the British dominions and a country like France, which gives a domestic period of life *plus* fifty years, will be regarded as an English work.[1]

Remedies and Procedure.—As to remedies and procedure, the English author must follow the rules of the country in which he seeks protection. If he has placed his name on the work he is, however, entitled under Art. 11 of the Berne Convention to the benefit of a presumption that he is the actual author; while if the work is anonymous or pseudonymous, the publisher whose name is placed upon it is entitled to be regarded as the representative of the author. These presumptions may, of course, be rebutted by the production of good evidence to the contrary.

Again, Art. 12 of the Convention enables the author to call for the seizure of offending reprints by the authorities of any country of the Union in which his work has a right to protection; such seizure to be carried out in conformity with the domestic law of the country in question.

On the other hand, if any country of the Union sees fit to suppress the circulation of an English work in its territory for administrative reasons, *e.g.* because it contains doctrines which are considered to be subversive of public order, it is quite at liberty to do this, in accordance with Art. 13 of the Convention, which makes an express provision to this effect.

Retroactivity of Treaties.—Works published in England before 5th December, 1887—the date at which the Berne

---

[1] For a discussion of the difficulties which arise from the competition of the English alternative period of life *plus* seven or forty-two years with the period of life *plus* thirty years granted by Germany, Japan, and Switzerland, the reader is referred to Section 6 above.

Convention came into force—are on general principles[1] entitled to such protection as they would have had if the Convention had in fact been in force at the time of their publication. In enforcing this principle of retroactivity, however, each country is at liberty to make what reservations it pleases by its domestic law.[2]   In England, as we have seen, a reservation has been made for the protection of subsisting rights and interests in copied matter lawfully obtained before 1887 ; and the author of an English work published before the coming into force of the Convention will be well advised if, before seeking protection in any foreign country, he examines the law of that country in order to ascertain whether any reservations are made by it for the same or any other purpose.   The rule is the same with regard to the alterations and extensions in the author's right which are effected by the Additional Act of Paris ; this agreement came into force on the 9th September, 1897, and authors of works published before that date must not assume that in every country they will get the full benefit of the Additional Act.[3]

Retroactivity under the Austrian Treaty.—The treaty with Austria-Hungary, like the Berne Convention, adopts in principle the general rule of retroactivity.   It contains, however, a list of specific exceptions to the rule.   Those which affect English works (published before 24th April, 1894, the date at which the treaty came into force) are as follows :

  (i) Copies lawfully made before that date may still be circulated in the Austro-Hungarian Monarchy ;
  (ii) Lawfully produced appliances for reproduction, *e.g.* stereotypes, wood-blocks, lithographers' stones, may continue to be used for four years

----

[1] See Art. 14 of the Convention.
[2] See § 4 of the Closing Protocol to the Convention.
[3] See § 4 of the Closing Protocol to the Convention.

from the date of coming into force of the Convention;

(iii) Dramatic and dramatico-musical works lawfully
performed before that date may be performed
in the future.[1]

---

[1] See Art. 8 of the treaty.   It is provided that the circulation of the copies
and the use of the appliances referred to in (i) and (ii) above are to be permitted
only if a Government inventory has been made of them within three months
from the coming into force of the Convention, and they have been marked with
a special stamp.

CHAPTER II.

COLONIAL COPYRIGHT.

SECTION I.

THE RELATION BETWEEN THE UNITED KINGDOM AND THE COLONIES.

Colonial laws must not be inconsistent with imperial statutes—The authority of the Crown in colonial legislation—The two sources of law for a colony—Both imperial and local interests are involved in copyright—Every British book protected throughout the Empire—Formalities necessary for imperial copyright—Imperial protection for works of art limited to United Kingdom—Colonial interests need separate consideration—Each colony allowed to regulate protection of its own works within its own territory—Colonies which have their own copyright laws—A work may have copyright throughout the Empire, yet not in the colony of first publication—Where Colony has no law of its own, copyright is wholly regulated by imperial Acts—English books protected throughout the Empire—Summary of results—International position of colonial works— The British colonies belong to the International Union—Is the colony of publication the 'country of origin'?—Special formalities of a colony— Special formalities imposed in colony of publication should be fulfilled.

Colonial Laws must not be inconsistent with Imperial Statutes. —The British Empire is a State composed of a number of separate communities, each with its own constitution enjoying a large amount of actual independence, but all united together by the legal bond of common submission to the Imperial Parliament and by the sentimental bond of patriotism.

Though in theory the powers of the Imperial Parliament are absolute, in practice it seldom intervenes in the strictly internal affairs of a colony, the management of these being usually left to the Crown in Council or the colonial Congress ; but it delegates to none the conduct of the affairs of the Empire at large. No colony can make a valid law which shall conflict or be at variance with any imperial statute,[1] and the British Parliament can override any colonial Act or Ordinance.

This principle will find a full illustration in the course of this Chapter. There is a long-standing dispute between the Canadian Government and the Colonial Office as to the validity of the Canadian Copyright Act of 1889, and in the course of the controversy the Canadian Congress has claimed full powers of copyright legislation ; but, even so, its claim was based solely upon the provisions of an imperial statute, the British North America Act of 1867.

The authority of the Crown in Colonial Legislation.—Moreover in every colony the Crown is a necessary party to legislation ; whether, as in ' Crown colonies,' it is the sole source of law, or, as in ' self-governing colonies,' it has only a right of veto on the Acts of the colonial legislature. Nor is this veto a dead letter in the latter class of colonies ; the general principles of colonial administration call for its exercise as against any statutes which are inconsistent with imperial policy on imperial matters, like merchant shipping or copyright. But where the internal interests of a self-governing colony alone are involved, the colonial legislature will in practice usually

---

[1] Sec. 2 of the Colonial Laws Validity Act, 1865 (28 and 29 Vict. c. 63): ' Any colonial law which is or shall be in any respect repugnant to the provisions of any Act of Parliament extending to the colony to which such law may relate, or repugnant to any order or regulation made under authority of such Act of Parliament, or having in the colony the force and effect of 'such Act, shall be read subject to such Act, order, and regulation, and shall, to the extent of such repugnancy, but not otherwise, be and remain absolutely void and inoperative.' This enactment was merely declaratory of the existing law.

be allowed to do as it likes, and neither Parliament nor the Crown will interfere adversely.

IMPERIAL AND COLONIAL COPYRIGHT.

The two sources of law for a Colony.—In dealing with the law which obtains in any colony, it is necessary to bear in mind that it proceeds from two distinct sources. In the first place, there is the law of England, which includes so much of the old common law as the colony has inherited, and so much of the statute law of the British Parliament as is of imperial scope. And then there is the law of the colony itself, its own in a special sense, whether, as in a self-governing colony, it consists of Acts of the colonial congress, or, as in a Crown colony, of Ordinances made for the colony by the Crown or the Governor.

This latter body of law has force only within the area of the colony itself, and even there is invalid so far as it conflicts, or is at variance, with imperial statutes. The British Parliament, however, beyond its legislation for the affairs of the United Kingdom, deals only with matters of importance to the Empire; for example, it would never interfere with the right of the Canadian Congress to regulate Canadian customs duties, or to make such rules as it might think fit for the enforcement of Canadian contracts.

Both Imperial and Local Interests are involved in Copyright.— Copyright cannot be regarded exclusively either as a colonial or as an imperial matter. Strictly speaking, the right of an author in his work is in essence a right against the public, to prohibit the making of unauthorised copies. The author is invested by law with a monopoly which restricts the liberties of the general public, while, on the other hand, the interests

of the latter are safeguarded by the imposition of certain
conditions and formalities which the author is required to
fulfil.

Now there are obvious reasons in favour of making such a
right available against the whole public of the State in the
territory of which the publication of the work has taken
place, especially when the members of that public speak a
common language.   Every member of a State should be
obliged to respect the rights and privileges of every other
member.   Moreover if the author is protected in one part of
the State and not in another, it is exceedingly difficult to
prevent fraud on the law ; for unauthorised copies which may
be lawfully made and sold in the part to which the copyright
does not extend, may very easily be imported into the part to
which it does extend.

Every British Book protected throughout the Empire.—It is,
then, highly advisable for every nation to grant such a wide
recognition to copyright that, upon the fulfilment of certain
necessary conditions and formalities, every work first published
anywhere within its confines shall gain protection throughout
the whole territory.   And, acordingly, by the joint operation
of the Literary Copyright Act, 1842,[1] and the International
Copyright Act, 1886,[2] a literary work first published in

---

[1] Sec. 29 : ' This Act shall extend to the United Kingdom of Great Britain and
Ireland, and to every part of the British Dominions.'   This was construed to
relate only to the scope of protection, while it was held that publication within
the United Kingdom was a *condition* of protection.   The latter rule, however,
was altered by the International Act of 1886.

[2] Sec. 8 (i) : ' The Copyright Acts shall, subject to the provisions of this
Act, apply to a literary or artistic work first produced in a British possession
in like manner as they apply to a work first produced in the United Kingdom ;
Provided that (*a*) the enactments respecting the registry of the copyright
in such a work shall not apply if the law of such possession provides for the
registration of such copyright ; and (*b*) where such work is a book the
delivery to any persons or body of persons of a copy of any such work shall not
be required.'

the United Kingdom or any other part of the British dominions will be protected against copying throughout the whole Empire.

Formalities necessary for Imperial Copyright.—If the book is first published in the United Kingdom or in a colony which by its domestic law makes no provision for registration, it will gain copyright without registration, though it will have to be registered before any action can be brought in respect of infringements of its copyright. If, on the other hand, it first appears in a colony which has a system of registration of its own, it must fulfil the requirements of the colonial law as to registration.

If the book is first published in the United Kingdom, the author will be obliged to fulfil the rules of the English law as to deposit of copies, though an omission to make such deposit will not affect his copyright but will merely subject him to certain pecuniary penalties. If the work is a colonial work, no deposit of copies whatever will be required for the obtaining of copyright.[1] Apart from these special formalities, the work, whether English or colonial, must, of course, fulfil the fundamental conditions of the English law as to originality, innocence, etc.[2]

[1] The International Act of 1886 is quite clear as to this. But so late as 1894 Sir Edward Maunde Thompson, on behalf of the Trustees of the British Museum, complained to the Colonial Office that, though ' by the Imperial Copyright Act of 1842, Canadian publications ought to be deposited in the British Museum, the obligation was not observed by the Canadian Government, so that the Trustees had to purchase Canadian books.' He went on to point out that the rule of deposit was observed by the Governments of India, of the Cape, and of several Crown colonies. Upon this ill-founded complaint, the Colonial Office made representations to the Canadian Government, with the ultimate result that a Canadian Act of 1895, amongst other things, provided for the deposit of a copy of each new work at the British Museum. But this cannot add to the conditions of *imperial* copyright.—See Blue Book, entitled *Correspondence on Copyright in Canada*, pp. 90, 91, and 113.

[2] The rule as to innocence is that the work must not be libellous, indecent, blasphemous, or seditious.

Imperial Protection for Works of Art limited to United Kingdom.
—The rule that any work published anywhere in the British
dominions will, upon satisfying the necessary conditions, be
protected throughout the Empire, does not hold good in its
entirety for works of art.

The International Copyright Act of 1886, which first
extended imperial protection to colonial works, provided
merely that such works should enjoy the same protection as if
they had been first produced in the United Kingdom. Now,
while the proposition that works first produced in the United
Kingdom are entitled to protection throughout the British
dominions is (in virtue of the Literary Copyright Act, 1842,
sec. 29) true for books, it is not true for works of engraving
or fine art, and probably not for sculptures. Protection in
the Colonies does not seem to have entered into the contemplation of those responsible for Engraving Acts, the Fine
Arts Act, and the Sculptures Act. The conclusion is that
colonial engravings, paintings, drawings, photographs, and
sculptures will under the English law be protected only
against infringements committed in the United Kingdom.[1]

As to paintings, drawings, and photographs, this has now
been expressly decided by the Judicial Committee of the Privy
Council, in the case of *Graves v. Gorrie* (1903).[2] Protection
was claimed in Canada for a picture entitled ' What we have
we'll hold,' as to which plaintiffs had not complied with the
Canadian Copyright Acts. The Canadian Courts held that
copyright under the Fine Arts Copyright Act was limited to
the United Kingdom, and did not extend to confer on the
plaintiffs a copyright in the Dominion of Canada. On appeal
this decision was upheld by the Judicial Committee.[3] This

[1] Cf. *Jefferys v. Boosey* (1854), 4 H.L.C. 815, and *Routledge v. Low* (1868), L.R.
3 H.L. 100.

[2] *Graves v. Gorrie* (1903), A.C. 496.

[3] Cf. *Tuck and Sons v. Priester* (1887), 19 Q.B.D. 629.

case is not, of course, binding on the English Courts; but it represents the view of the law taken by a very eminent tribunal.

Colonial Interests need Separate Consideration.—While, however, in one respect copyright is an imperial matter, it cannot be denied that each colony is a separate area, with a separate public of its own; being in fact for many purposes dealt with on an independent footing by Great Britain itself. It follows that a colony should recognise that its authors have a special claim to its protection, over and above the claim which they have in virtue of their membership of the British Empire. And it may well feel that the conditions and formalities necessary to safeguard the interests of its own public are not precisely the same as those imposed by the Imperial Parliament for the protection of the British public at large.

Thus, owing perhaps to the limited number of its population, it may consider that it is superfluous to demand of its authors anything whatever in the nature of registration; or it may deem some special formality, such as the insertion of the date of copyright on the title-page of each book, to be of utility in giving information to the public at little expense to the author. Such matters as these it should be allowed to regulate for itself, so far as regards the protection of its own works within its own territory.

Each Colony allowed to regulate Protection of its own works within its own territory.—The British Parliament, adopting this view, has left it to the legislature in self-governing colonies, and to the Crown in Crown colonies, to determine the conditions upon which works first produced in the territory shall be protected. The Literary Copyright Act of 1842, it is true, provided that works enjoying its protection should have copyright through the whole of the British dominions; but, as it was made an essential condition of protection that the work

should be first published in the United Kingdom, this Act did
not interfere with the liberty of each Colony to decide for
itself how works first published within its own territory should
be treated.

Again, the International Copyright Act of 1886 (sec. 8),
though it enacted that works first produced in any part of the
British dominions should have the same protection as if first
produced in the United Kingdom, thus obliging every colony
to protect every British work wherever in the Empire it
should have first appeared, expressly reserved to each
colony, by a subsequent proviso, the right to treat works first
published within its own limits in its own way.[1]

Colonies which have their own Copyright Laws.—A number of
colonies—India, Ceylon, Canada, the Australian Colonies,
New Zealand, the Cape of Good Hope, Natal, Hong Kong,
and Newfoundland—have local copyright laws of their own.
Hence the conditions of protection which affect works first
published in any of these must be sought in two bodies of
law—in the Acts of the British Parliament, as regards their
protection throughout all parts of the British dominions except
the Colony of first publication, and in the Acts or Ordinances
of the Colonial legislative authority (the Crown or Colonial
Parliament), as regards their protection within the territory
of that colony itself.

**A Work may have copyright throughout the Empire, yet not
in Colony of first publication.**—Since the requirements of the

---

[1] The International Copyright Act, 1886, sec. 8 (iii) and (iv) : ' Where, before
the passing of this Act, an Act or ordinance has been passed in any British
possession respecting copyright in any literary or artistic works, Her Majesty in
Council may make an Order modifying the Copyright Acts and this Act, so far
as they apply to such British possession, and to literary and artistic works first
produced therein, in such manner as to Her Majesty in Council seems expedient.
Nothing in the Copyright Acts or this Act shall prevent the passing in a British
possession of any Act or Ordinance respecting the copyright within the limits of
such possession of works first produced in that possession.'

two bodies of law may differ, it may well happen that a work will be protected in the colony of first publication without enjoying copyright in any other part of the British dominions, and even that it will be protected throughout the rest of the British dominions and not in the colony of first publication itself.   Thus a work published in New Zealand, the law of which contains no requirement of registration, will be protected in New Zealand and not elsewhere—unless, indeed, it is registered at Stationers' Hall ; while, on the other hand, a work published in Canada and duly registered, but not provided with the requisite notice of the date of copyright on the title-page, will be protected everywhere else in the Empire, but not in Canada.

Where Colony has no Law of its own, copyright is wholly regulated by Imperial Acts.—To the colonies which have no local legislation of their own, these observations necessarily fail to apply.   The protection of works first published within such colonies depends entirely on the Imperial Acts.   When the conditions of those Acts are satisfied, such works are necessarily protected in the colony of first publication, as well as in all other parts of the Empire.[1]

English Books Protected throughout the Empire.—Finally, literary works published within the United Kingdom are protected throughout the British dominions upon satisfying the conditions of the English law.

---

[1] But if they are engravings, works of fine art, or sculptures, it seems that their protection will be limited to the United Kingdom.

Extent of Protection Accorded to English and Colonial Works in the British Empire.

Summary of Results.—The results that have now been reached may be tabulated as follows :

I. **Literary works.**—Protected throughout the Empire, if the conditions and formalities of the English law have been fulfilled,

> *Except* in the colony of first publication—they are protected here only when the conditions and formalities, if any, of the Colonial law itself have been fulfilled.

II. **Artistic works.**—Protected in the United Kingdom, if the conditions of the English Acts have been fulfilled; and also in any colony, including the colony of first publication, if the Colonial law so provides.

International Position of Colonial Works.

The British Colonies belong to the International Union.—In view of the fact that a colonial work may be protected in the colony of first publication and not in the United Kingdom, or *vice versâ*, it is necessary to give some consideration to the international position of such a work under the Berne Convention. By that agreement all the countries of the International Copyright Union—Belgium, Denmark, France, Germany, Great Britain, Haïti, Italy, Japan, Luxemburg, Monaco, Norway, Spain, Sweden, Switzerland, and Tunis—are bound to protect every work first published in any one of them, provided only that the conditions and formalities of the country of origin have been fulfilled.

The Convention allows its parties to bring their colonies into the Union with them, and Great Britain is one of the

States that have availed themselves of this provision, so that the British colonies form part of the system of the International Union. The result is that works first published anywhere within the British dominions will gain international protection throughout the Union, so long as they have satisfied the rule requiring that the conditions and formalities imposed by law in the country of origin of the work shall be fulfilled.

Is the Colony of publication the Country of Origin?—In the case of a British colony, the important question arises, Which is the country of origin of the work—the colony or the Empire as a whole? As we have seen, there are two bodies of law, the imperial and the local, applicable to every work published in a colony which has a copyright law of its own; and the conditions and formalities imposed by the colonial law may differ very considerably from those imposed by the law of England, which is the general law for the Empire.

The *conditions* of the English law relate to matters like the originality and innocence of the work, and are adopted expressly or tacitly into the law of every colony. The *formalities* of the English law relate to the registration of works and the deposit of copies. Registration is not a condition of the acquisition of copyright, but merely 'a condition precedent to suing'; while deposit, being an independent obligation enforced under a separate penalty, in no way affects the acquisition, or even the enforcement, of copyright.

Hence in all probability neither of these is to be regarded as a condition or formality in the sense of the Berne Convention.

Special Formalities of a Colony.—Some of the colonies, however, impose formalities of their own, which, being necessary under the colonial law to the acquisition of copyright, are of the sort contemplated by the Convention. Thus the Canadian

law requires that every work shall bear on its title-page a
notice of copyright in the form 'Entered according to Act
of the Parliament of Canada in the year . . . . by A. B., at
the Department of Agriculture'; and if the notice is omitted
copyright is withheld.

In its practical aspect, then, the question is whether a work
first published in a colony like Canada is or is not bound to
fulfil the requirements of the colonial law, in order to gain
the international protection of the Berne Convention. Such
a work, if the special colonial formalities are omitted, will be
protected in the rest of the British Empire, but not in the
colony of first publication. That a work should have copyright in one part of the State in which it first appeared and
not in another can hardly have been contemplated in the
scheme of the Berne Convention.

**Special Formalities imposed in Colony of Publication should be
fulfilled.**—This being so, it is scarcely fair to expect a foreign
country of the Copyright Union to forbid its subjects to reprint an English work so long as they are able to point to one
part of the British Empire, which, be it remembered, is all one
State—a single unit—for international purposes, and say that
there the work is freely open to reproduction. What is permitted within the bounds of the country of origin cannot well
be made matter of complaint when done in a foreign country.

It must be borne in mind, however, that if this reasoning
were pressed, it would altogether exclude English artistic
works from the protection of the Convention; but here the
difficulty does not spring from the existence of two distinct
sets of formalities.

Where, as in the case of most colonial works, there is a
special set of conditions and formalities, without which the
copyright will not be valid within a certain portion of the
territory to which the general law of the State does not apply,

these should be fulfilled in order to make certain of securing international protection for the work. Unless the special requirements of the colonial law have been satisfied, the English author will have to take the risk that the Courts of foreign Union countries will not give a liberal interpretation to the provisions of the Convention.

SECTION II.

IMPERIAL COPYRIGHT AS IT SUBSISTS IN THE COLONIES.

Colonies may allow importation of foreign reprints on certain conditions —Copyright protection in the Colonies—Importation of foreign reprints absolutely forbidden by Copyright Act, 1842—Difficulty of preventing importation of American reprints into Canada—Under the Foreign Reprints Act, 1847, importation into certain Colonies was allowed—Difficulty of collecting import duties on foreign reprints—The protection of Imperial copyright in Canada—The Canadian Copyright Act, 1875—Under Act of 1875, English authors republishing in Canada protected against foreign reprints—Imperial copyright not diminished—All British copyright works now protected in Canada and Cape Colony against foreign reprints— Canadian reprints of English works may not be imported into England— Arguments for and against free circulation of cheap Colonial reprints—The opinion of the Copyright Commission of 1876—Canadian Act of 1900 conditionally prohibits importation of English editions—Does this conflict with Imperial statutes ?—Present position of English works in the Colonies— The law relating to the importation of foreign reprints into Canada.

Domestic Laws of the Colonies not under Discussion.—The object of this chapter is merely to give an outline of the nature and extent of Imperial copyright, *i.e.* of the protection which, under the English Acts, a work published in any part of the British Empire will receive in every other part. It is not our purpose to give an account of the domestic copyright law of every colony which has a law of its own,[1] upon which law, as has already been indicated, the protection

---

[1] *I.e.* India, Ceylon, Canada, the Australian Colonies, New Zealand, the Cape of Good Hope, Natal, Hong Kong, and Newfoundland.

within the colony itself of all works first appearing in its
territory will depend. We are not concerned with the protection that Indian works get in India, Canadian in Canada,
and so forth, but with the protection which Indian works get
in all the colonies except India, Canadian in all the colonies
except Canada—in short, with the protection that every
British work gets throughout the Empire, except in the
colony of first publication.

Just as we have considered international relations between
separate and independent States, so now we have to consider
the inter-colonial relations existing between the various parts
of the British Empire. These, of course, differ from international relations in that they are created by express statutory
legislation, emanating from a supreme authority, *i.e.* by Acts
of the British Parliament, instead of by separate negotiation
on the part of each colony ; but in other respects the analogy
holds.

Canadian Domestic Law dealt with in next Section.—The
details of the domestic law of each colony must, therefore, be
sought in the Acts or Ordinances of the Colonial Congress, of
the Governor, or of the Crown ; but it has been deemed well
to give at the end of this chapter a brief outline of the main
features of the Canadian law as it affects Canadian works ;
because this, the most highly developed of all colonial systems
of copyright law, will serve both to illustrate what has been
said as to the difference between Imperial and local copyright,
and to show how widely the law of a colony, left to grow in
its own way, may diverge from the law of the mother country.
In so far as, in virtue of special permission given by English
statutes or otherwise, the Canadian domestic law has modified
the scope of *Imperial* protection as it exists in Canada, *i.e.* of
the protection in Canada of works published elsewhere in the
Empire, it will take its place in the course of this Section.

No other colony has ventured to attempt to modify Imperial protection by legislation of its own.

Colonies may allow Importation of Foreign Reprints on certain conditions.—We have hitherto dealt with 'Imperial copyright' as if it involved a uniform protection for British works throughout the whole of the British Empire—as if every such work got in every colony (save in some cases the colony of production) the protection afforded by the English domestic copyright Acts, no more and no less. And this is true thus far—a work which is under the protection of the English law is secured against the making and publication of unauthorised reprints throughout the whole of the British dominions. But under the Foreign Reprints Act of 1847 a large number of colonies have been enabled to permit the *importation* of *foreign* reprints of English copyright works into their territory, on making provision for the collection of an author's royalty. These colonies are Antigua, Bahamas, Barbadoes, Bermuda, British Guiana, Grenada, Jamaica, Mauritius, Natal, Nevis, Newfoundland, St. Christopher, St. Lucia, St. Vincent, and Trinidad. In these colonies, then, though no one within the colony is at liberty to reprint such works on his own account without the consent of the copyright owner, yet anyone may import and sell unauthorised reprints manufactured in foreign countries.

The position of copyright protection in the colonies may briefly be set out thus :—

COPYRIGHT PROTECTION IN THE COLONIES.

WORKS PUBLISHED	ARE DEPENDENT FOR PROTECTION ON
I. Within the Colony in which protection is sought.	(i) If Colony has copyright legislation of its own.—*Copyright depends on Colonial law.* (ii) If Colony has no copyright legislation of its own.—*Copyright depends on ordinary English law.*

II. Outside such Colony, but within the Empire.	(i) If Foreign Reprints Act does not apply to such Colony.—*Copyright depends on ordinary English law and works are protected against :*
	    (*a*) *Reprinting.* (*b*) *Importation of foreign reprints.* (*c*) *Selling, etc., of unlawful copies.*
	(ii) If Foreign Reprints Act applies to such Colony.—*Copyright is modified accordingly and works are protected against only :*
	    (*a*) *Reprinting.* (*b*) *Selling, etc., of unlawful copies.*
	Note.—Artistic works are protected only in the United Kingdom, unless the law of the Colony specially provides for them.

III. In a foreign country of the Copyright Union.	*The rules for these are the same as the rules for works published outside the Colony from which protection is claimed, but inside the Empire.*
IV. In any other treaty countries, *i.e.* Austria or Hungary.	*The same rules apply,* except as to Canada, the Cape of Good Hope, New South Wales, and Tasmania, where such works are not protected.
V. In a foreign non-treaty country.	*No protection in any Colony.*

Importation of Foreign Reprints absolutely forbidden by Copyright Act, 1842.—The protection given by the Literary Copyright Act, 1842, to works first published in the United Kingdom, and subsequently extended by the International Copyright Act, 1886, to works first published anywhere in the British dominions, was expressly declared by Sec. 29 of the Act of 1842 to extend to the United Kingdom and to every part of the British dominions.   The latter statute, which expressly forbade the unauthorised printing and sale of copies, contained a particularly stringent section [1] directed against the importation of foreign reprints of copyright works.

This prohibited the following acts, when done in respect of such reprints :

(*a*) importing, or causing to be imported into any part of the British dominions, for sale or hire ;

(*b*) knowingly selling, publishing, or exposing for sale or hire ;

(*c*) knowingly having in possession for sale or hire ; under pain of forfeiture of the offending copies, together with £10 and twice the value of each book.   And besides this a special action for damages was given (sec. 15) in respect of these infringements.

The author thus acquired a right to have the importation of offending works prevented, but of· course this could be made effective only by the intervention of the customs officers. In 1845 the conditions on which such intervention should take place were laid down by a comprehensive *Act to regulate the trade of British possessions abroad*, which absolutely prohibited the importation into the British possessions abroad of foreign reprints of any works ' first composed or written or printed in the United Kingdom,' provided that due notice of the existence of copyright had been given to the Customs

---

[1] The Literary Copyright Act, 1842, sec. 17.

authorities.[1]   This latter statute was repealed by the Customs Consolidation Act of 1853,[2] but the provisions of Sec. 9 were re-enacted in Sec. 160 of that statute.

Difficulty of preventing Importation of American Reprints into Canada.—These statutes were mainly directed towards protecting British authors and publishers against the wholesale importation of cheap American reprints of their works into the Canadian colonies.   But mere legislation, however stringent, could hardly avail to prevent this.   If the offending works were not seized at the moment of importation from America the opportunity of effective seizure was lost ; for after they had once gained a footing in Canada it became very hard to trace them.   Seizure upon importation itself was exceedingly difficult to carry out efficiently.   All books are not copyright,—it is only a minority that are ; and the burden of distinguishing between copyright and non-copyright works was laid upon the shoulders of the customs officers, in addition to the burden of discovering the books.   In view of the enormous number of books published every year, and of the ever-increasing number in which copyright has expired, it is small wonder that the task often went unperformed.

It is not surprising that, even in the United Kingdom itself at the present day, authors should be found to complain of the inefficiency of the protection afforded by the law against the importation of foreign reprints.   Much more, then, in Canada at this early time was it found almost impracticable to put a stop to the noxious import trade ; for the United States was a great centre of the reproduction of English works, importation thence was easy, and the English author was not on the spot to see that the Customs officials performed their duty rigorously.

---

[1] Stat. 8 and 9 Vict. c. 93, sec. 9.
[2] 16 and 17 Vict. c. 107, sec. 358.

Moreover public opinion in Canada, prompted by self-interest, was ranged against the claims of the English author. In those days of dear books, the people of Canada could not afford to buy the authorised English editions, the publishers of Canada would not undertake their sale, and in Canada there were no lending libraries, as there were in England, to circulate expensive books at a small charge. Canada had no great authors of its own, and if cheap American reprints were shut out from the colony, where, it was asked, were the people to go for their supply of English literature? This was the popular feeling, and so public opinion aided and abetted the customs officials in their neglect of duty.

Under the Foreign Reprints Act, 1847, importation into certain Colonies was allowed.—Hence, in spite of the Act of 1845, the rule forbidding the introduction of foreign reprints into the colonies remained a dead letter. The English Government, making a virtue of necessity, in 1847 passed a statute to render legal a state of things which it had found impossible to prevent.

This statute, the Foreign Reprints Act, 1847, provided that, if the legislature or proper legislative authorities in any British possession should make due provision for securing the rights of British authors in such possession, the Crown, by Order in Council, might suspend as to that colony the prohibitions contained in the Copyright Acts against the importation, etc., of foreign reprints of books 'first composed, written, printed or published' in the United Kingdom.[1] A large number of colonies have, at one time or another, taken advantage of this Act; there are fifteen to which it now applies, but Canada, the Australian Colonies, India, and the

---

[1] Sec. 2 of the Foreign Reprints Act, 1847 (10 and 11 Vict. c. 95, sec. 2), provides that a copy of the Order and of the Colonial Act or Ordinance shall be laid before Parliament within six weeks.

Cape of Good Hope are notable absentees from the list.[1] Canada was amongst the first to apply for an Order in Council under the Act; but, as will be seen later, it has since voluntarily renounced all its benefits.

Difficulty of collecting Import Duties on Foreign Reprints.— The 'due provision for securing or protecting the rights of British authors' in the Colony which is required by the Act is usually made by means of import duties. Lists of English copyright books are furnished to the Colonial customs authorities, and the theory is that the duty is collected by them upon importation.[2]

In point of fact, however, the 'security' for his rights thus offered to the British author is an exceedingly empty thing. All the difficulties in the way of successful dealing with imported reprints which we have pointed out above in regard to the absolute preventing of importation apply, with even greater force, to the levying of import duties. Detection itself remains as precarious, and, since the consequences of neglect are not so serious, the chance of neglect is greater.

Moreover, since the time of the Foreign Reprints Act, the development of postal facilities has vastly increased the difficulties of the work of detection. Even at the present day,

---

[1] The following are the names of the colonies to which the Act does apply, arranged according to the date of the respective Orders in Council: Bermuda, Bahamas, Newfoundland, St. Christopher, Antigua, St. Lucia, British Guiana, Mauritius, Grenada, Nevis, Natal, Jamaica, Trinidad, St. Vincent, Barbadoes.

[2] The whole process is clumsy. As to Canada, 'it was shown that the Canadian Government could not collect the duty until the British copyright owner had entered his work at the English customs house. In course of time the English authorities would transmit this title to the Customs Department at Ottawa, who would in turn send word to the various customs ports throughout the Dominion. All this, of course, took time, and in many cases, most undoubtedly, thousands of copies of the work had been imported from the United States before the Canadian customs officers had any authority to collect the royalty duty.'—R. T. Lancefield, *Notes on Copyright*, § 78.

when importation of foreign reprints into Canada is *absolutely* prohibited, large numbers of American reprints are periodically poured into Canada through the cheap book post. These it is impossible to detect with any certainty—and if detection is not fairly certain, it will usually be considered worth while to run the risk.

Small wonder, then, that the colonies have practically abandoned the work of collecting duties; so that from the point of view of an author seeking remuneration the Foreign Reprints Acts must be pronounced a complete failure. Thus in 1875 Her Majesty's Treasury notified Archbishop Trench that the sum of *elevenpence* lay to his credit in the hands of the Paymaster General: this represented the whole amount collected in Canada (then under the Foreign Reprints Act) for upwards of ten years—although during the period in question the Archbishop's works had had a steady sale in Canada. And during the ten years ending in 1876 the whole amount received on account of all imported reprints from the nineteen colonies which had at that time taken advantage of the Act was only £1,155 13s. 2½d., of which £1,084 13s. 3½d. was contributed by Canada; of these nineteen colonies, seven paid nothing whatever to the authors, while six now and then paid small sums amounting to a few shillings.[1] It was notorious that during this period large numbers of foreign reprints were imported into the colonies.

On the other hand, at the present day seventeen colonies have made due provision for stamping each imported copy in the Customs House upon collecting the royalty thereon, every unstamped copy being liable to seizure. This system, which provides a useful safeguard against smuggling, has

---

[1] See *Report of the Copyright Commission of* 1876, p. xxxi.

been lately proposed for Canada;[1] but would not now be applicable in that colony, since, as will be seen later, Canada has ceased to enjoy the benefits of the Foreign Reprints Act.

THE PROTECTION OF IMPERIAL COPYRIGHT IN CANADA.

Royalty System proposed by Canada.—The failure of the remuneration provided by the Foreign Reprints Act led to complaints from British authors and publishers, and attempts were made to procure the repeal of the Act. The Canadians, who were the chief offenders, alleged in their defence the great extent of their frontier, and the negligence of British publishers in not giving to the proper authorities timely notice of the publication of copyright works. They urged that they were forced to take American reprints, because they were forbidden to republish English copyright works on their own account; and that thus a book trade which might otherwise have been theirs was thrown into the hands of the Americans.

They proposed that they should be allowed to republish English books themselves, under licence from the Governor General, and that, in respect of each licence, publishers should pay an excise duty of $12\frac{1}{2}$ per cent. for the benefit of the author. So the Canadian publishers would be able to undersell the American exporters, and the duty being an excise, not a customs, duty would be less liable to evasion—since the authorities would, in this case, be able to go directly to the source of production, and levy the duty there.

The Canadian Copyright Act, 1875.—While these matters were in debate, the Canadian legislature passed their Copy-

---

[1] See letter dated 20th February, 1890, from Mr. F. R. Daldy to Sir J. S. D. Thompson, reprinted in the Blue Book entitled *Correspondence relating to Copyright in Canada*, p. 11.

right Act of 1875, which provided for the full protection of English works against foreign reprints, on condition that such works were reprinted and republished in Canada. This having been reserved by the Governor General for the Queen's assent, doubts arose as to whether the measure was not repugnant to the Foreign Reprints Act, as applied to Canada ;[1] and so a special Act of the British Parliament was passed to give Her Majesty power to assent to the Canadian Bill, and in virtue of this power the Royal assent was given.

The Canadian statute enacts (secs. 4 and 6) that any author domiciled in Canada or any other part of the British possessions, or being a citizen of any country having an international copyright treaty with the United Kingdom, may gain copyright in Canada for twenty-eight years, by printing and publishing, or reprinting and republishing, his work in Canada, and fulfilling the formalities of the Canadian Law. There is a proviso that nothing in the Act shall be held to prohibit the importation into Canada from the United Kingdom of copies of English copyright works legally printed there ;[2] though a recent Act (of 1900) provides that in certain circumstances this shall be forbidden.

On the other hand, the Imperial Act passed to confirm the Canadian statute expressly enacts (sec. 4) that Canadian copies of an English copyright work shall not be imported into the United Kingdom without the author's consent.[3]

---

[1] By an Order in Council of 12th December, 1850.

[2] In 1889 another Canadian Act (Stat. 52 Vict. c. 29, sec. 2) purported to repeal the whole section (6) of which this proviso formed part. This Act is, however, of no force or effect.—See Section 3 of this Chapter.

[3] 'Where any book in which, at the time when the said reserved Bill comes into operation, there is copyright in the United Kingdom, or any book in which thereafter there shall be such copyright, becomes entitled to copyright in Canada in pursuance of the provisions of the said reserved Bill, it shall be unlawful for any person, not being the owner, in the United Kingdom, of the copyright in such book, or some person authorised by him, to import into the United

Under Act of 1875, English author republishing in Canada protected against Foreign Reprints.—As regards works enjoying Imperial copyright, the net effect of the legislation of 1875 is to enable the copyright-owner to gain protection from foreign reprints by causing his work to be republished in Canada, whether by assigning the Canadian copyright, or by granting a licence for reproduction in Canada, or by publishing in Canada at his own risk.

Imperial Copyright not diminished.—But the two Acts do not—as was thought at the time by Canadian publishers—extend to permit the free reproduction in Canada of British copyright works, without assignment or licence. This was decided in 1876 in the case of *Smiles v. Belford.*[1] Messrs. Belford, a firm of Canadian publishers, had seized upon Smiles's *Thrift* at the moment of its appearance and had ventured to reproduce it in Canada without attempting to obtain the author's or publisher's consent. The case was made a test case upon the question of the rights of Canadian publishers, and judgment in both the Canadian Court of Chancery and the Supreme Court of Canada went in favour of the plaintiff. It was held that it was unnecessary for the author of an English literary copyright work to gain copyright under the Canadian statute in order to be able to restrain *Canadian* reprints; though if he wished to prevent the importation into Canada of *foreign* reprints, as allowed by the Foreign Reprints Act, he must acquire a good Canadian copyright. As to the purpose of the British Act of 1875, Burton, J. A., said : ' I am of opinion . . . that it was intended to preserve intact so much of the Imperial Act [of

Kingdom any copies of such book reprinted or republished in Canada ; and for the purposes of such importation the 17th section of the said Act of 5 and 6 Vict. c. 45 shall apply to all such books in the same manner as if they had been reprinted out of the British dominions.'

[1] *Smiles v. Belford* (1876), 1 Tupp. App. Rep. 436.

1842] as prohibits the printing of a British copyright work in Canada, but giving to the author a further right on certain conditions of securing a Canadian copyright, and thus preventing the importation into Canada of foreign reprints.'

The Canadian Act of 1875 and the Imperial Act which was passed to confirm it do not, then, in any way impair the force of Imperial copyright; on the contrary, they hold out a prospect of increased vigour.

All British Copyright Works now protected in Canada and Cape Colony against Foreign Reprints.—Now, however, it is no longer needful for the British author who wishes to obtain protection against the importation into Canada of foreign reprints to secure the republication of his work within the Dominion; for since 23rd July, 1895, the Canadian Government has ceased to collect the author's royalties on imported foreign reprints. Canada, therefore, no longer satisfies the conditions of the Foreign Reprints Act, and can no longer enjoy its benefits. Hence the importation of foreign reprints of English copyright works into Canada is now absolutely and at all times illegal, whether or not the works in question have themselves been republished in Canada.[1] The same applies to the Cape of Good Hope, which has also ceased to collect the royalty.

Canadian Reprints of English Works may not be imported into England.—When an authorised edition of an English work has been republished in Canada, it is obviously of some importance to determine whether or not regular copies of the English edition may be imported into Canada, and *vice versâ*. Importation from one part of the Empire to another was not included in the prohibition of the Copyright Act of 1842, but, as we have seen, the English Act of 1875, passed to confirm the Canadian statute of that year, expressly prohibits

---

[1] See *Morang v. Publishers* (1900), 32 Ont. Rep. 393.

the importation of Canadian copies into the United Kingdom
without the author's consent.

Argument for Free Circulation of cheap Colonial Reprints.—
This provision gave rise to much discussion, and its repeal
was strongly urged before the Copyright Commission of 1876.
It was contended that as the English author had the benefit of
an extended area in which to sell his books, so also he ought
to be content with a less profit per copy and submit to other
consequent disadvantages. If he chose to arrange for the sale
of copies at a low price in one part of the British dominions,
that was his own business, and he could not expect the law to
intervene in order to protect him from being undersold in his
own proper market by these cheap reprints made with his own
permission. In England at that time the prices of books
were very high,[1] and it was said that, if the introduction of
colonial reprints, which had to be sold at a low price in order
to win the colonial market, was allowed, prices generally would
be greatly reduced. It was urged that it was unfair to the
British public that they should be the only section of the
community to be debarred from participating in the advantages of cheap colonial editions !

Argument against Importation of cheap Colonial Reprints.—On
the other hand, the authors and publishers objected strongly
to the proposed change in the law, thinking that the reduction
of prices which would follow from the free introduction of
colonial reprints would do them much harm. In their view,
the result of abolishing the restraint upon importation would
be that no English author or publisher would consent to the
republication of a cheap edition in the colonies, owing to the

---

[1] In those days novels were usually issued in three volumes at £1 11s. 6d. and
circulated in England by means of lending libraries. In Canada there were no
such libraries. Few novels are now published in England at a higher price
than 6s.

danger of such an edition ousting the principal edition from the home market.

The opinion of the Copyright Commission of 1876.—The Commission of 1876 decided in favour of the authors, saying : 'On the whole we think that the admission of such reprints would probably operate injuriously towards British authors and publishers, and that it is doubtful if it would be attended in many cases with the result anticipated . . . that is to say, the cheapening of books for home consumption. We think the almost certain result would be that it would operate as a preventive to republication in the colonies by authors themselves, so that . . . the colonial reader would be in no better condition than he is now. We therefore think that colonial reprints of copyright works first published in the United Kingdom should not be admitted into the United Kingdom without the consent of the copyright owners ; and, conversely, that reprints in the United Kingdom of copyright works first published in any colony should not be admitted into such colony without the consent of the copyright owner.' No change in the law of England has yet followed from the labour of this Commission.

Canadian Act of 1900 conditionally prohibits importation of English Editions.—In 1900 Canada affected to carry out for itself what it had for many years been beseeching the Imperial Parliament to do on its behalf, by passing a statute which provides that, when the owner of the copyright in a British work first published outside Canada has lawfully granted a licence to reproduce it in Canada, then, 'notwithstanding anything in the Copyright Act,' the Canadian Minister of Agriculture may prohibit the importation into Canada of any copies printed elsewhere.[1] It would seem that no such prohibition can affect the importation of foreign

---

[1] Stat. (Canadian) 63 and 64 Vict. c. 25, sec. 1.

reprints, which is already illegal, as explained above.   Hence apparently the sole effect of the Act of 1900 is to enable the importation of copies of the legitimate English edition to be prevented.

Does this conflict with Imperial Statutes?—The ordinary English law of copyright, as set forth in the Act of 1842, says nothing to prohibit the free circulation of copies lawfully printed between the various parts of the British dominions ; and, in view of this, it has been suggested that the Canadian Act is *ultra vires* of the Canadian legislature, and is therefore void.   Imperial copyright, it is urged, is an Imperial matter, and involves the right to sell copies throughout the Empire ; it is not within the power of any colony to make laws which shall in any way diminish its content.

This view is supported by the fact that Canada at first should have found it necessary to invoke the aid of the Imperial Parliament, and should have ventured to take action on its own account only when the coming of that aid seemed to be indefinitely postponed.   On the other hand, it may be said on behalf of the colony that whilst, according to the rule laid down in *Smiles v. Belford*, every colony is bound to protect the English author against infringements of his copyright, yet the question whether or not the author shall be allowed to import his books into its territory is a question, not of Imperial copyright, but of domestic economy, for each colony concerned.   True that the colonies cannot diminish the scope of imperial copyright ; nevertheless, it is with books as with other commodities, they can lay down the terms upon which importation will be permitted, and even, if need be, forbid it altogether.   There is much to be said for either view ; and the question cannot be settled in the absence of authority.

Present Position of English Works in the Colonies.—Of course, as already explained, the protection of works first published in Canada is regulated entirely by the Canadian law, so that the requirements of this law as to registration, notice of copyright on title-page, etc., must be fulfilled. In a colony which has no law of its own, copyright for domestic works will depend upon the ordinary English law. The Foreign Reprints Act does not now extend to Canada and the Cape of Good Hope, so that English copyright works, whether or not they gain copyright under the local statutes, are protected against the importation of foreign reprints into these colonies. From a colony to which that Act applies the English author cannot demand protection against this form of importation, though he can exact the collection of a royalty on his behalf. For artistic works these rules do not hold. Such works are protected under the Imperial Acts only in the United Kingdom, and if the artist seeks protection in a colony, he must fulfil the requirements of the colonial domestic law.

The Law Relating to the Importation of Foreign Reprints into Canada.

1. **Literary Copyright Act, 1842,** forbids importation of foreign reprints of British copyright works into any part of the British dominions.

2. **Foreign Reprints Act, 1847,** allows importation of such foreign reprints into colonies which collect a customs duty upon such reprints for the author's benefit. An Order in Council of 1850 extended this Act to Canada.

3. **Canadian Copyright Act, 1875** (confirmed by Imperial Act of same year), protects English works, *if reprinted and republished in Canada*, against the importation of foreign reprints.

4. **Canadian Customs Tariff Act, 1894,** abolished the royalty duty on foreign reprints of British copyright works ; hence,

it is submitted, Canada no longer satisfies the conditions of the Foreign Reprints Act, that Act ceases to apply, and foreign reprints may not now be imported into Canada under any circumstances.

5. **Canadian Copyright Act, 1900,** enables the Minister of Agriculture to prohibit the importation of copies of British copyright works, when the British copyright owner has granted a licence for the reproduction of his work in Canada. This presumably affects only the importation of copies of the English edition, unless in the Canadian view the Foreign Reprints Act still applies to Canada ; in such a view, the importation of foreign reprints would be forbidden only in the circumstances contemplated in the Act of 1900.

SECTION III.

THE DOMESTIC LAW OF CANADA.

Influence of the United States on Canadian legislation—Canadian Act of 1875 the main source of present law—The Canadian Act of 1889— Effect of British North America Act, 1867—Republication in Canada required by Act of 1000 English objections to this statute The Canadian argument—The Act not yet in force—Imperial copyright in Canada—No Canadian statute can reduce Imperial copyright—Anomalous state of affairs in Canada—Protection of copyright under Canadian law— The condition of Nationality—Unpublished works—Place of publication— Registration, deposit of copies, etc.—Temporary copyright in magazine articles—Interim copyright—Duration of copyright—Penalty prescribed for infringement—Licence to reproduce—Penalties for importation of foreign reprints—If licence for reproduction granted, importation of English edition may be prohibited.

As has already been pointed out, the protection that a work published in the United Kingdom or in any of the colonies enjoys throughout the rest of the British Empire, being an Imperial matter, depends entirely on the English Copyright Acts. It is true that, under the Foreign Reprints Act, by providing due remuneration for British authors any colony is enabled to permit the importation of foreign reprints of English copyright works into its territory, but no colony can do even this for itself; the Crown must legislate for it by a special Order in Council deriving its force from the Imperial statute.

As to the protection of its own works within its own limits, on the other hand, each colony is left free to make laws for itself.[1] It is now proposed to deal with the domestic law of Canada, and to show how this colony—which of all our possessions has given most careful consideration to the subject of copyright—has availed itself of its liberty of legislation. An account of the Canadian law of copyright, while giving much information which may be of immediate use in connection with this important colony, will at the same time serve generally to illustrate the very extensive scope of colonial law. It will also provide an excellent example of the way in which a colony, if left to itself, may evolve a body of law considerably diverging from the law of the mother country.

Influence of the United States on Canadian Legislation.—In the case of Canada, the law has almost throughout been animated by the spirit of American copyright legislation. A very close connection can be traced between the development of the two systems. The American code of 1831 was followed by the great Canadian statute of 1832 ; while, in a similar way, a Canadian Act of 1875 succeeded the American consolidating statute of 1870, which was revised in 1873 and 1874. And the Chace Act of 1891, securing the protection of the American law to aliens belonging to certain countries upon condition that the type of their works should be set in the States, resulted in a strong movement in Canada, having for its object the introduction of a similar type-setting clause into the law of that country in the interests of native trade.

Turning from the historical to the analytical aspect, the two systems in their existing form present very striking analogies. Thus, to take a broad feature, the Canadian law, like that of the United States, gives great prominence to registration and other formalities, on the fulfilment of which, as in

---

[1] See sec. 8 (iv.) of the International Copyright Act, 1886 : ‘Nothing in the Copyright Acts or this Act shall prevent the passing in a British possession of any Act or Ordinance respecting the copyright within the limits of such possession of works first produced in that possession.’

America, the very existence of the copyright is made to depend ; and further, the formalities required are, in their incidents as well as in their nature, almost exactly the same as those imposed by the American Law. This is not altogether matter for regret ; for, as a mode of securing a clear statement of the person entitled and the date of commencement of copyright, the American system of registration is far superior to our own.

Act of 1875 the main source of present Canadian Law.—The Canadian Copyright Act of 1875 was incorporated as Chap. 62 of the Revised Statutes of 1886 by an Act of that year.[1] In this shape it contains the substance of the Canadian law relating to copyright, though in certain particulars it has been modified by subsequent statutes, notably the recent Act of 18th July, 1900. Another very important Act is that of 1889 ; but this, though it has been regularly passed by Congress and assented to by the Governor, has not yet come into force. Its history is of special interest, and well illustrates the relation between the Canadian Congress and the Imperial authorities at home.

The Canadian Act of 1889.

Effect of British North America Act, 1867.—The British North America Act, passed in 1867 to provide for the union of Canada, Nova Scotia, and New Brunswick, and of the Governments thereof, specifies (sec. 91) copyright among the subjects which are to be within the exclusive legislative authority of the Parliament of Canada as distinct from the legislatures of the several provinces.[2] The rule of the

[1] Stat. (Canadian) 49 Vict. c. 4.
[2] See Sec. 13 of the Report of the Departmental Committee on the Canadian Copyright Act, 1889.—*Correspondence relating to Copyright in Canada*, p. 46.

Imperial Acts as to protection in Canada was then that any work first published in the United Kingdom gained protection in that colony, although a work first published in Canada could not gain protection in the United Kingdom or anywhere else in the British dominions. This state of affairs existed until 1886, when, as we have seen, the International Copyright Act provided that any work published in any part of the British dominions should be protected throughout the British Empire, thus conferring Imperial copyright upon Canadian works.

Republication in Canada required by Act of 1889.—Even after this, the Canadian printers and publishers, dissatisfied with the state of affairs, agitated against the restraints placed upon them, and in 1889 the Canadian Congress, acting on the assumption that the British North America Act conferred upon it unrestricted powers to legislate for copyright within the limits of the colony, passed an Act which purported to remedy their grievance. Under this it was made a condition of copyright that the work should be printed or published or produced in Canada, or reprinted or republished or reproduced in Canada, within one month after publication or production elsewhere. The Act went on to provide that, if a person were entitled to gain copyright in this way,[1] and failed to do so, the Minister of Agriculture might grant to any person domiciled in Canada a licence to issue the work in question upon paying to the author a royalty of ten per cent. on the retail price of each copy.

The whole Act, especially in view of the shortness of the time—one month—fixed for republication in Canada, has the

---

[1] Only authors of certain nationalities were to be eligible for copyright, i.e. persons domiciled in Canada or any part of the British possessions, or citizens of any country having an international copyright treaty in which Canada should be included.

appearance of an attempt to steal a march on the British author.

The Statute not to have Force till Proclaimed.—In spite of its claim to exclusive powers of legislation for Canada, Congress itself seems to have had some doubt as to the independent validity of this statute, and so a section was inserted therein, providing that the Act should not come into force until it should be proclaimed by the Governor-General of the Dominion ; doubtless this was done with the object of giving time for the necessary Imperial and international adjustments to be made, by legislation of the British Parliament or otherwise.

English Objections to the Act.—When the Governor-General of Canada applied to the Colonial Office for permission to proclaim the Act, it was at once seen in England that the statute was inconsistent with the view generally accepted in this country as to the scope of colonial legislation. The Copyright Association and the Society of Authors[1] objected most strongly to the licensing system which it was proposed to establish. The law officers of the Crown reported that in their opinion the legislative powers conferred on the Dominion Parliament by the British North America Act, 1867, did not authorise that Parliament to amend or repeal, so far as related to Canada, an Imperial Act conferring privileges in Canada, and advised the Crown to withhold its assent from the Canadian Act.[2]

In this view, all that the British North America Act did was

---

[1] These Societies are cited merely as representing the opinions of certain influential sections of the public ; it should be noticed that in the Copyright Association the publishing interest is predominant, while the Society of Authors is almost an authors' Trade Union.

In this instance, however, the Societies seem to have had good ground for complaint.

[2] See the decision in *Smiles v. Belford*, 1876, 1 Tupp. A.C. 436.

to confer on the Dominion Parliament in Canada the powers previously enjoyed by the Parliament of the several constituent States.

It was generally recognised, too, that if the recent piece of legislation were allowed to stand, Canada would render itself unable to carry out its international obligations under the Berne Convention, and so impair the solidarity of the Empire in its relations to the Union.

The Canadian Argument.—The Canadian Government, on the other hand, urged that the copyright system previously in force under Imperial and Canadian legislation had been found to be most unsuitable for Canada, while the Berne Convention only increased the causes of complaint.

American authors, who could secure copyright throughout the British Empire by publishing in England (even by publishing a limited edition not sufficient to supply the market[1]), were able to gain control of the Canadian market, whilst a Canadian could not obtain such copyright privileges in the United States.[2]

The Canadians asserted that British authors and publishers had greatly abused their Imperial rights by selling their works to American publishers and refusing to deal with Canadian publishers on the same terms. By this means American publishers were enabled to command the Canadian market under the provisions of legislation intended not for their benefit, but for the benefit of the British author and publisher.

From the Canadian standpoint, these evils were augmented

---

[1] It is doubtful whether such limited publication would satisfy the requirements of the English law.

[2] This, of course, is no longer true since the Chace Act of 1891. Moreover at no time did the law of the United States impose any special disabilities upon Canadians. Before 1891, no Englishman, unless he satisfied a condition of residence—which practically meant domicil—in the United States, could under any circumstances get copyright in the United States.

by the provisions of the Berne Convention, which extended
copyright privileges without publication in Canada to authors
of any country belonging to the International Union. The
Canadian Government demanded that, if any Imperial legislation were necessary to confer upon them the powers they
claimed, such legislation should forthwith be carried out ; and
as to the Berne Convention, they intimated their desire that
Great Britain should denounce that agreement so far as it
related to Canada.

The Act of 1889 not yet in force.—In England, the
various Departments interested, *i.e.* the Colonial Office, the
Foreign Office, the Board of Trade, and the Parliamentary
Counsels' Office, appointed a Committee to consider the
question, and this Committee reported very strongly against
compliance with the claims of Canada, either by Imperial
legislation or by authorising the Governor-General to proclaim
the Act of 1889. No further action has been taken by Great
Britain and no proclamation of the Act made in Canada, so
that at present it stands on the Canadian Statute Book, a
dead letter, a law without any force.

If at any time, however, the Governor-General, having
obtained the necessary authority from the Colonial Office,
shall proclaim it, the statute will actively come into force
without further formality. Indeed it has already, in view of
its position as a valid though ineffectual Act, been amended
by a later Canadian Act of 22nd July, 1895. Still, if it
were proclaimed, it would be *ipso facto* without legal effect so
far as it conflicts with Imperial legislation ; thus, in default of
any change in the English law, an author would continue to
be entitled to protection in Canada for any work of his first
published in Great Britain, or in any one of the countries of
the International Union, without complying with the special
Canadian conditions.

IMPERIAL COPYRIGHT IN CANADA.

No Canadian Statute can reduce Imperial Copyright.—Even as it is, it may be pointed out that the Canadian law now in force, which renders printing and publishing, or reprinting and republishing in Canada, though without any limit of time, a condition of copyright, cannot operate to prevent the author of a British work from gaining protection in Canada without publishing in that country. He gets this right under Imperial legislation, which no Canadian statute can override. It is true that before 1895 by gaining a title to protection in Canada under the Canadian as well as under the Imperial Acts, an author of a British copyright work improved his position, being thus enabled to prevent importation of foreign reprints of his work into Canada. But since the 23rd July, 1895, the Foreign Reprints Act has ceased to apply to Canada, and Canadian copyright offers no special advantages to an author who is already in possession of Imperial copyright under the English Acts.

Anomalous state of affairs in Canada.—The position of affairs in Canada at the present time is highly anomalous. It can only be said that, except for a Canadian work, an author is secure if he has obtained Imperial rights, however the provisions of the Canadian domestic law may appear to affect him. In the account of that law which follows, no attempt has been made to distinguish between that part which is valid and that which, on account of conflict with Imperial legislation, is void. The reader must therefore be on his guard against the assumption that the domestic law of Canada, as outlined here, is the only factor to be taken into account in estimating the nature, extent, and value of copyright protection in that country.

Protection of Copyright under Canadian Law.

The Condition of Nationality.—It is laid down in the domestic law that, in order to be eligible for Canadian copyright, a person must be

(*a*) Domiciled in Canada or some other part of the British possessions ; or

(*b*) A citizen of a country that has an international copyright treaty with the United Kingdom.[1]

Hence in Canada, as in the United States, a national element enters into copyright,—it is not possible for a person who does not belong to one of the prescribed countries to gain Canadian copyright by publishing in Canada.

Unpublished Works.—It is an infringement, rendering the offender liable to an action for damages, to print or publish any manuscript without the author's consent.[2]

Place of publication.—As to published works, the condition for obtaining copyright is that the work shall be either

(*a*) Printed and published, or (if a work of art) produced in Canada ; or

(*b*) Reprinted and republished, or (if a work of art) reproduced in Canada.

The author or his representative can alone gain copyright, but it is important to note that it does not matter whether he makes his publication in Canada before, simultaneously with, or after publication elsewhere.

No immoral, licentious, irreligious, treasonable or seditious work can gain copyright.[3]

---

[1] Sec. 4 of the Copyright Act, 1886. Though, presumably, Austrian and Hungarian citizens are eligible for protection under the Canadian domestic law, it is noteworthy that Canada has refused to accept the Treaty of 1893 concluded between Austria-Hungary and England.

[2] Sec. 20 of the Copyright Act, 1886.

[3] Sec. 5 of the Copyright Act, 1886.

Registration, Deposit of Copies, etc.—The author's claim to the protection of the law depends upon his having fulfilled the formal requirements of the law. It is no infringement on the part of another to print or publish a copy of a work before it has been registered—or even after registration, if notice of copyright has not been given on the work in accordance with the requirements of the law.

In the case of literary works,[1] three copies of the first edition[2] must be deposited at the Department of Agriculture, which, strangely enough, has charge of the copyright business. For works of fine art,[3] it is sufficient that a written description be furnished. Upon the completion of the deposit, the Minister will cause the copyright to be entered in the Register. It is not necessary to deposit any copies of the second, or any subsequent, edition of any book unless the same contains very important alterations or additions.[4] It is a misdemeanour to make, or cause to be made, a false entry in any of the Registry books, or to produce in evidence a paper falsely purporting to be an extract therefrom.[5]

Every copy of every edition must contain on the title-page (or the page immediately following) if it is a volume, or on the front if it is a map, chart, musical composition, print, cut, engraving, or drawing, a notice of registration, in the form 'Entered according to Act of the Parliament of Canada in the year . . . . by A.B. at the Department of Agriculture.'[6] It is an offence, punishable with a penalty of three hundred

---

[1] *I.e.* in the words of Sec. 9 of the Copyright Act, 1886, of 'books, maps, charts, musical compositions, photographs, prints, cuts, or engravings.'

[2] Of these one will be placed in the library of the Parliament of Canada and another sent to the British Museum.

[3] *I.e.* 'paintings, drawings, statuary, or sculpture.'

[4] Sec. 11 of the Copyright Act, 1886.

[5] Sec. 28 of the Copyright Act, 1886.

[6] Sec. 12 of the Copyright Act, 1886. The law of the United States is identical, except that this provides an alternative short form of notice.

dollars, to insert a false notice.[1] Works of fine art need no
notice, the signature of the artist being deemed a sufficient
declaration of proprietorship.

Temporary Copyright in Magazine Articles.—When a work
is first published in separate articles in a periodical, with the
intention of reproducing it subsequently in book form, copyright for the time being may be secured by depositing at the
Department of Agriculture the title of the MS. and a short
analysis of the work. In addition, a notice must be inserted
at the beginning of every article so published, in the
form ' Registered in accordance with the Copyright Act.'
When the publication in book form actually takes place,
the work will be subject to the ordinary requirements of
the Act.[2]

Interim Copyright.—For works first published outside Canada
which it is intended to republish in that country, the author
may secure an interim copyright, by depositing at the Department a copy of the title, *i.e.* title-page, or a designation of
the work, which title or designation is to be registered in
a special register. Such interim copyright is not to last for
more than one month after the work has been first published
outside Canada, within which period the work is to be printed
and published in Canada.[3] It is an offence, punishable with a
penalty of one hundred dollars, to fail to publish a work within
this term of one month after entry.[4]

Duration of Copyright.—Copyright is to endure for the term
of twenty-eight years from the day of recording the copyright

---

[1] Sec. 33 (i) of the Copyright Act, 1886. As is generally the case with penalties
under this Act, one-half of the sum is to go to the Crown for the public uses of
Canada, and the other half to the informer.

[2] Sec. 7 of the Copyright Act, 1886.

[3] Sec. 13 of the Copyright Act, 1886.

[4] Sec. 33 (ii) of the Copyright Act, 1886. One half of the penalty is to go to
the Crown for the public uses of Canada, and the other half to the informer.

by deposit in the manner set out above.[1]   But if at the expiration of this term the author[2] is still living, or if, though he himself be dead, his widow or child survives, then the author, his widow, or his child, as the case may be, may obtain a renewal for the further term of fourteen years.   For this purpose, the work must be re-registered and all other formalities necessary for the acquisition of an original copyright must be complied with again.   Moreover a notice of the renewal must be published in the *Canada Gazette* within two months.[3]   Both in the general rule as to duration and in particular details, the law of Canada here very closely follows that of the United States.

Rectification of the Registers.—Conflicting claims in respect of copyright[4] are to be referred to a court of competent jurisdiction, which will generally be the Exchequer Court of Canada, and upon judgment given the Minister will, if necessary, amend the register.[5]

Penalties for Infringement.—The penalty prescribed for infringement is the forfeiture of every copy of the infringing work, together with a fine of from ten cents to a dollar per copy.[6]   In the case of works of fine art, the plates which have been used in the unlawful reproduction are also forfeited.[7]

Licence to Reproduce.—If a copyright work has become out of print, and upon notification by the Minister[8] the author has

---

[1] Sec. 4 of the Copyright Act, 1886.

[2] Or (in cases of joint authorship) any of the authors.

[3] Secs. 17 and 18 of the Copyright Act, 1886.

[4] Whether arising between a person whose name is on the register and another claiming to be registered in respect of the same work, or between simultaneous applicants whose claims conflict, or between the registered proprietor and a person attempting to get the entry cancelled.

[5] Sec. 19 of the Copyright Act, 1886.

[6] Sec. 30 of the Copyright Act, 1886.

[7] Sec. 31 of the Copyright Act, 1886.

[8] Any person may lodge a complaint with the Minister, who is required to notify the author upon assuring himself that the complaint is well founded.

failed to provide a remedy,[1] then the Minister of Agriculture
may grant to any person domiciled in Canada a licence to
reproduce the work in that country.[2]

Penalties for Importation of Foreign Reprints.—The importation into Canada of foreign reprints of Canadian copyright
works, and of British copyright works[3] which have been also
copyrighted in Canada, is an offence punishable with a penalty
of $200, together with forfeiture of the parcel or package of
goods in which the reprints are found ;[4] and, under the English
Copyright Act of 1842 (sec. 17), which now applies to

---

[1] Sec. 21 of the Copyright Act, 1886. Under the Act of 1889, which is as
yet without legal force, it would be necessary to add the two following cases :

(*a*) if any person entitled to copyright neglects or fails to obtain it, or

(*b*) if any person, when he has obtained copyright, at any time after first
publication fails to meet the demand of the Canadian public for his work.
According to the rule of the 1889 Act the author is to receive a royalty of 10
per cent. on the retail price of each copy issued by the licensee, for the
payment of which royalty the latter must give satisfactory security.

[2] **Proposed Prohibition upon Importation.**—Under the (invalid) Act of 1889,
when such a licence had been granted, the Governor-General in Council, if
satisfied that the licensee had provided for the Canadian demand, might, by
proclamation published in the *Canada Gazette*, prohibit the importation, during
the term of the author's copyright, of any copies or reproductions of the work
to which the licence related. But no such prohibition was to apply to copies
of British copyright works lawfully printed in the United Kingdom. A prohibition might be revoked at any time if it were shown to the Governor-General
in Council that the work was not, under the licence, printed or published in
such manner as to meet the Canadian demand.

The licence itself might be revoked if the Governor-General were satisfied that
the holder of the copyright was prepared, and *bona fide* intended, during the
remaining period of his term of copyright, to print and publish the work himself
in Canada so as to meet the Canadian demand. But no such revocation was
to render unlawful the subsequent sale in Canada of any copies of such work,
then already printed under the authority of the licence.—The Copyright Act,
1895 (sec. 5), amending the Act of 1889. None of these provisions is yet in force.

[3] Apart altogether from the royalty dues formerly levied on foreign reprints
of English copyright works for the benefit of the author, which were abolished
in 1895, an ordinary import duty of 20 per cent *ad valorem* is levied on novels,
etc., in sheets or paper-bound, going into Canada, and a duty of 10 per cent.
ad valorem on bound books. For British manufactured goods, these charges
are reduced by one-third.

[4] Sec. 814, Schedule D, of the Customs Act of 1886.

Canada, owing to the abolition of the author's royalty dues in 1895, the importation into that country of reprints of any British copyright work is unlawful, entailing forfeiture of the offending copies, together with a penalty of £10 *plus* twice the value of the copies imported.

If Licence for Reproduction granted, Importation of English edition may be prohibited.—If a book first published in any other part of the British dominions except Canada has acquired copyright in Canada, and the owner of the copyright has granted a licence for the reproduction (in Canada) of a Canadian edition, then the Minister of Agriculture may prohibit the importation into Canada of any copies of such book printed elsewhere—including, that is, copies lawfully printed in the United Kingdom or any other part of the British dominions.[1] This prohibition may be revoked by the Minister if it is proved to his satisfaction :

> (*a*) that the licence to reproduce in Canada has terminated or expired ;
>
> (*b*) that the reasonable demand for the book in Canada is not sufficiently met without importation ;
>
> (*c*) that the book is not, having regard to the demand in Canada, being suitably printed or published, or
>
> (*d*) that 'any other state of things exists on account of which it is not in the public interest to further prohibit importation.'[2]

There is some doubt, however, as to the validity of these provisions of the Act of 1900, which *primâ facie* are in conflict with the Imperial statutes.[3] They cut off the owners

---

[1] Sec. 3 of the Act of 1900 provides, however, that two such copies may be specially imported, for the *bona fide* use of any public library, or for the library of any duly incorporated institution or society.

[2] Sec. 2 of the Canadian Copyright Act, 1900.

[3] See Section 2 of this Chapter.

of the copyright in English books from the Canadian market, if such owners have granted away the Canadian rights. Of this market the Canadian licensee is to have a monopoly. And, as we have seen, under the Imperial Act of 1875, Canadian copies, lawfully made, of an English copyright work cannot be imported into the United Kingdom. The effect is virtually to sever the Canadian market from the English and to put a check on the circulation of books (lawfully printed) between the various parts of the British dominions.

Prohibition may be withdrawn if Licensee does not satisfy Canadian demand.—At any time after the importation of a book has been prohibited under the Act of 1900, the licensee is bound, upon demand from any member of the Canadian public, to import and sell a copy of any edition of such book then 'reasonably obtainable' in any part of the British dominions [1]; and failure or neglect on his part to do so will be a reason for which the Minister may revoke the prohibition upon importation.[2]

---

[1] The book must be sold at the ordinary selling price in the country of production, with the duty and reasonable forwarding charges added.

[2] Sec. 3 of the Act of 1900.

PART V.

PROTECTION OF FOREIGN AUTHORS IN THE UNITED STATES.

§ 1. Sources of the American Law.
§ 2. The Chace Act, 1891.
§ 3. The Conditions and Formalities of the American Law.
§ 4. The Nature and Extent of Copyright in America.
§ 5. Infringements, Remedies, and Procedure under the American Law.
Additional §. The Rights of an American author in Foreign Countries.

SECTION I.

SOURCES OF THE AMERICAN LAW.

The evolution of Confederation copyright—The question of common law copyright—The Consolidating Act of 1870—Effects of limiting copyright to American authors—Conditional protection now extended to foreign authors.

Copyright in the United States is very important, since that country has a great public with a taste for reading. On this account it offers a ready market both to the English author and to the foreign author intending to publish an English work in England ; it is often found convenient to publish simultaneously in England and America at the same time, double profits being thus secured. An English author, desiring to gain information as to his rights in foreign countries, would naturally look first to the United States, since in that country alone can he obtain a valuable market for his work in its original literary form, without translation or adaptation.

The Evolution of Confederation Copyright.—In the beginning, copyright legislation in America was carried on separately and independently by the different States. In 1783 Connecticut, taking the lead, passed a ' law for the encouragement of literature and genius.' Its example was soon followed by Massachusetts, Maryland, New Jersey, and other States. Meanwhile Congress made a general recommendation to the States at large that they should secure to authors and publishers—being citizens of the United States—copyright

for not less than fourteen years from first publication, with
an extension for fourteen years if the author survived the first
term.

Before 1787, all the American States except Delaware had
responded to the recommendation.   In that year the Federal
Constitution of the United States conferred upon Congress
power ' to promote the progress of science and the useful arts,
by securing for limited times to authors and inventors the
exclusive right to their respective writings and discoveries.'
The result of this was the passing in 1790[1] of a federal
statute, which gave copyright for fourteen years, with a
proviso that protection should be renewed to the author for a
further term of fourteen years, if he should survive the first
term.   The Act protected only citizens of, and residents in,
the United States, and it expressly enacted that nothing it
contained should be construed to prohibit the importation,
sale, reprinting, or publishing within the United States of
any work written, printed or published abroad by any person
not a citizen of that country.

In 1831 the initial period of copyright was increased to
twenty-eight years, the conditional extension for a further
term of fourteen years being still retained.

The Question of Common Law Copyright.—These early
American Copyright Acts gave rise to a question similar to
that which had arisen towards the end of the eighteenth century
under the English Act of Anne, *i.e.* whether, if any common
law copyright ever existed, it was extinguished by the
grant of statutory copyright.   In spite of the American
statutes, an attempt was made in 1834 to assert the existence
and subsistence of a common law right in a certain series of

[1] The United States, though at a considerable distance of time, was thus the
first country to follow England in granting statutory recognition to copyright.
France came next, in 1793.

law reports. This was in the case of *Wheaton v. Peters* (1834)[1] which came to the Supreme Court of the United States on appeal from Pennsylvania. In that case it was contended that the English common law prevailed in the United States, and that its effect had not been diminished by the Act of 1790. The Court held, however, by a majority of three to two, that the English common law of copyright did not obtain ; also that the statute of 1790 created a right, and did not simply serve to secure one already in existence. The Court further decided, although this does not concern us here, that the English common law had not been adopted into the law of Pennsylvania.

In America, then, considered as a Federal State, the English common law does not obtain, and it may be added that the courts are averse to holding that it has been adopted by any of the individual States.

The Consolidating Act of 1870.—In 1870, after a number of statutes had been passed to make alterations in the details of the law, all the previous Acts were repealed, and the whole law relating to copyright was embodied in one Act, entitled ' An Act to revise, consolidate and amend the statutes relating to patents and copyrights.'[2] This Act added paintings, drawings, chromos, statues, statuary, models, and designs intended to be perfected as works of the fine arts to the list of the subjects of copyright ; otherwise it made little change in the substance of the law. In 1873 the Act was embodied in sections 4948 to 4971 of the Revised Statutes (Title 60, c. 3), and, though since considerably amended, this is the shape in which the American law stands at present.

---

[1] *Wheaton v. Peters*, 8 Pet. 591.

[2] It is noteworthy that in American speech the word ' copyright ' is more elastic than in English. In America the word is used as a verb—' to copyright ' is to perform those formalities of registration and deposit of copies which are necessary to the acquisition of copyright in a work. In English this use is not tolerated.

Effect of limiting Copyright to American Authors.—Till this time no law had removed or modified the rule of the original Act of 1790, limiting protection to works published in America by citizens of, or residents in, the United States.

As to the condition of publication within the United States, this afforded little ground for complaint and was generally accepted without question; but the condition of nationality gave rise to much criticism from 1837 onwards, both outside the United States and within. As has already been set forth earlier in this work, English authors in particular were injured by the provisions of a law which, while denying them all opportunity of gaining copyright themselves, allowed their works to be reprinted at will by American publishers. The author was thus deprived of a considerable market, which he might fairly regard as legitimately his.

On the other hand, all sections of the community in America except those second-rate printers who made a business of this reprinting of English works, united in complaining against the provisions of the law. American authors were placed at a disadvantage in their own country, their works suffered an unfair competition with English works, which publishers could reprint without giving any remuneration to their authors. American publishers of the better class, whose reputations stood high, were also injured by the unfair competition of less scrupulous tradesmen; for, while they themselves recognised in some degree the author's claim to remuneration, and had thus to recover the author's remuneration as well as their own outlay on the actual production of the books, their rivals were put to no expense on account of author's charges. Finally, the American public was injured by the debasement of its literature. The publishers who pursued the reprint trade had usually little capital and less standing, so that,

having to seek for quick returns, they did not find it
worth while to appropriate any but the most trashy and
ephemeral of the English publications.   The works that
were reproduced were such as appealed to the worst tastes of
the American public.   They were sensational, low-priced,
badly printed, and badly bound.

As Mr. Putnam,[1] speaking at the time when the Chace Act
was yet before Congress, said : ' The good stories of England
were long since exhausted by the American re-printers, and
as a consequence we are having poured out upon us an
unstinted flood of printed stuff, often nasty, still oftener weak
and silly, and always foreign in tone, sentiment, and description.   In the aggregate these stories constitute a powerful
means of undesirable education, as well as of vitiation of
American taste ; and this force is exerted more largely than
otherwise upon minds and morals which are in the plastic and
formative stage.'[2]

Conditional Protection now Extended to Foreign Authors.—
Hence nearly all classes in the United States whose opinions
on literary questions were worth hearing united in voicing a
desire to bring about the repeal of the law which debarred the
English author from copyright in America.   But this was
in the later stages of the movement for international protection.   In the beginning the agitation was confined to a
Member of Congress here and there, who would move a Bill
which, after passing through a stage or two, would always be
dropped at last.   In 1837 the subject was brought before
Congress for the first time by a petition of British authors,
presented to the Senate by Henry Clay ; a Select Committee
was appointed, and this reported in favour of the passing of
an International Copyright Law.   From that time down

---

[1] Putnam, *The Question of Copyright*, p. 98.

[2] See on the whole question Part II., Chap. i., of this work.

to 1891 Bills were brought forward almost annually for the consideration of the Senate or the House of Representatives.

Ultimately, about the year 1888, the opinion in favour of the amendment of the law became too strong to be resisted. Copyright Associations were formed in many parts of the country, and petitions were presented by authors, colleges, publishers, libraries, and others. The result was the enactment of the Chace Act in 1891, which renders it possible for alien authors to obtain copyright in the United States, though in so doing they are subjected to certain very stringent conditions.

SECTION II.

THE CHACE ACT, 1891.

No special international protection in the United States—Only authors belonging to certain foreign countries protected—The 'type-setting clause'—The Chace Act does not give International Copyright in the true sense—Conditions under which a country can take advantage of the Chace Act—Countries entitled to the benefits of the Chace Act.

No special International Protection in the United States.— In the United States, such protection as foreign authors may obtain does not in any way depend upon special International Acts.   There is no distinction in the American law, as there is in that of England, between domestic and international statutes.   This is mainly because works first published abroad, in whatever country, cannot under any circumstances obtain protection in the United States ; so that it is not necessary to adjust the features of a system of copyright constructed solely for native works to suit the special needs of works published out of the country.   In England, on the other hand, where works first published abroad are, upon certain conditions, capable of obtaining protection, it has been found advisable to modify the domestic law to meet this case.   Thus, to take only one example, it has been found necessary to give special prominence to the subject of translating right in the International Acts.

Only Authors belonging to certain Foreign Countries Protected. —Even for works actually first published in America, it is not by any means every foreign author that is eligible for protection. The law of the United States does not follow the law of England in making a general grant of protection to all works first published within the country which comply with the conditions of the law.[1] The benefits of its copyright law are strictly limited to authors of certain specified nationalities.

As we have seen, the old law required that a protected author should be a citizen of, or a resident in, the United States, and though the Chace Act was passed to extend this rule in favour of foreigners and is said by American authors to introduce the principle of International Copyright into the American law, yet it strictly limits the benefits of copyright to citizens of foreign States which satisfy a pre-scribed condition of reciprocity. The Section (13) which regulates this matter of ' international ' protection simply stands as part of the ordinary domestic code. It states the conditions upon which the American Act shall apply to a citizen or subject of a foreign State or nation, but neither that Section nor any other makes any attempt to adapt the conditions of copyright in America to the special needs of aliens to whom the Act does apply ; except that an Act of 3rd March, 1905, has now enabled authors of foreign works in a *foreign* language to obtain copyright upon complying with the necessary conditions within twelve months.

The Protective ' Type-setting Clause.'—When the Chace Act was under discussion, a special ' Manufacturing Clause,' making copyright dependent upon type-setting within the States, was inserted with the very object of securing the interests of the American printing industry,[2] by preventing the foreign author from following the natural and convenient course of

---

[1] That is, as to England, subject to the legal doubt with reference to the question of residence within the British dominions.

[2] The Bill was originally without this manufacturing clause, which was inserted as a special concession to the Typographical Unions, whose consent and co-operation could only thus be obtained.

T T

having his work set up in type in his own country, and sending
the new work to the United States, in moulds, stereos, electros,
or quires, for first (or simultaneous) publication.   The effect of
the clause is to debar the foreign author from offering for sale
in America any works printed outside the States.   The foreign
author is also required to fulfil all the other conditions of the
American law, such as registration, deposit of copies, and notice
of copyright.   Thus, even if his country has made arrangements for so-called reciprocity under the Chace Act, protection
is not accorded to him, as in England and other countries of
the International Union, upon the mere performance of the
conditions and formalities of the country of origin of his work.

**The Chace Act does not give International Copyright in the true
sense.**—In short, the United States, whatever its own views
and claims as to the nature of the Chace Act, does not recognise the principle of International Copyright.   As Mr. G. H.
Putnam, the well-known American publisher, says :[1] ' The
conditional measure for securing American Copyright for
aliens . . . a measure which is the result of fifty-three years
of effort on the part of individual workers and of successive
Copyright Committees and Leagues, brings the United States
to the point reached by France in 1810 and by Great Britain
and the States of Germany in 1836-1837.'[2]   While in England
every foreign author may probably gain protection merely by
publishing his work within the British dominions, in the
United States it is only certain classes of foreign authors
that can gain protection on any conditions.   The position of

---

[1] Putnam, *The Question of Copyright*, p. xvii.

[2] This opinion carries the more weight as coming from an American publisher.
But, of course, the strongest animadversions on the American law have come from
English authors and other non-Americans who consider themselves unfairly
treated.   In this connection, see the correspondence started in the *Standard* during
the last week of 1904, by Sir Conan Doyle and Messrs. Douglas Sladen and
Rider Haggard.

the foreign author who does get protection in America is very similar to his position under the English domestic law ; it is not in any respect analogous to the position of the foreign author under the English International Acts.

Conditions under which a country can take advantage of the Chace Act.—Under the Chace Act (sec. 13) one of the following conditions must be satisfied before a foreign author can be eligible for copyright in America :

(1) That the State to which he belongs permits to citizens of the United States of America the benefit of copyright on substantially the same basis as to its own citizens, or

(2) That the State to which he belongs is a party to an international agreement for the reciprocal protection of copyright, to which the United States may at will become a party.

When a country satisfies either of these conditions, and the fact has been made known officially by a Proclamation to that effect issued by the American President, the disqualification of its authors for protection in the United States is removed.[1]

As to the condition of admitting American citizens to domestic protection, it is enough that the foreign State in question does not disqualify American authors on the mere ground of their nationality from the protection which they would otherwise obtain. There is no need for it to relax on their behalf any of the conditions, like that of first publication

---

[1] Sec. 13 of the Chace Act provides : ' That this Act shall only apply to a citizen or subject of a foreign State or nation when such foreign State or nation permits to citizens of the United States of America the benefits of copyright on substantially the same basis as its own citizens ; and when such foreign State or nation is a party to an international agreement which provides for reciprocity in the granting of copyright, by the terms of which agreement the United States of America may, at its pleasure, become a party to such agreement. The existence of either of the conditions aforesaid shall be determined by the President of the United States by Proclamation made from time to time as the purposes of this Act may require.'

within the country, exacted in respect of works of native authors. Thus, at least with regard to literary works, England fulfils the condition, since under its ordinary domestic law copyright is (probably) conceded to all such works which are first published within the British dominions, and an American citizen, like a Russian or a German, or a person of any other nationality, may obtain protection for works which satisfy this requirement.[1]

As to the alternative condition—being a party to an international agreement for the reciprocal protection of copyright to which the United States may at will become a party—the American view is that the Berne Convention is not an agreement of the kind here contemplated. The members of the International Copyright Union, as such, are not recognised as coming within the conditions of the Chace Act, though each country individually may gain recognition by granting copyright to American citizens on the same basis as to its own citizens. The Berne Convention, as we have seen, provides that each of its parties shall give to the authors of foreign works published within any country of the International Union the same protection as it gives to its own authors for its own works; and in the United States no work produced outside America, in whatever country, can gain protection. Hence, in the present state of its domestic law, the United States is debarred from joining the International Copyright Union. The obstacle would be removed

---

[1] The English Foreign Secretary gave an assurance to the American President to the effect that American citizens could gain copyright in England by mere publication in the British dominions. In this the Secretary acted on the advice of the Law Officers of the Crown, who, following the doubtful dicta of Lords Cairns and Westbury, in *Routledge v. Low*, 1868, were of opinion that no residence in the British dominions at the time of publication was necessary in order to enable a foreign author to obtain English domestic copyright. The balance of authority may be said to be in favour of this ruling, but, in view of the division of opinion in the case of *Routledge v. Low*, the point can hardly be regarded as settled. Moreover, the statement of the Foreign Secretary is plainly wrong as applied to works of the fine arts.—See Part IV., Chap. i., sec. 1.

by the amendment of the American Copyright Act—a matter which lies wholly within the hands of the United States— but the construction placed by that country upon the words of the Chace Act (sec. 13) referring to an agreement to which the United States may at its pleasure become a party, is that these exclude an agreement to which the United States cannot become a party without altering its domestic law.

Countries entitled to benefits of Chace Act.—Great Britain (with its possessions), Belgium, France, and Switzerland, which granted copyright to Americans on the same basis as their own subjects, were the first countries to receive recognition under Sec. 13 of the Chace Act, and on 1st July, 1891, the day on which that Act came into force, the President of the United States issued a Proclamation admitting subjects of these countries to the benefits of American copyright. Since then Proclamations have been issued in favour of Germany, Italy, Denmark, Portugal, Spain, Mexico, Chili, Costa Rica, Holland (with its possessions), and Cuba, in the order named.[1] Hence any subject of any of these countries can now obtain protection in the United States for works published in that country, upon satisfying the ordinary conditions of the American domestic law. Moreover, on the 8th October, 1903, a treaty was entered into with China which, if ratified, will result in the admission of Chinese subjects to the benefits of American copyright.[2]

[1] The dates of these Proclamations are, respectively: Germany, 15th April, 1892; Italy, 31st October, 1892; Denmark, 8th May, 1893; Portugal, 20th July, 1893; Spain, 10th July, 1895; Mexico, 27th February, 1896; Chili, 25th May, 1896; Costa Rica, 19th October, 1899; Holland, 20th November, 1899; Cuba, 17th November, 1903.

[2] This treaty is of some interest, as it is the first agreement dealing with copyright entered into by China. It is a commercial treaty, and by Art. 11, in return for the admission of its subjects to the benefits of the Chace Act, China agrees to protect for ten years from registration books, charts, etc., prepared specially for the use and education of the Chinese people, if such works emanate from or belong to American citizens.—See *Le Droit d'Auteur*, 1904, p. 6.

SECTION III.

THE CONDITIONS AND FORMALITIES OF THE AMERICAN LAW.

Works capable of copyright—Unpublished works—First publication in United States—Delivery of copies—Type must be set up in United States—Subsequent editions to be delivered—Registration—Notice of copyright on work required.

Works Capable of Copyright.— When a foreign country has satisfied the conditions of the Chace Act, its authors can gain copyright in America for their works, upon satisfying the necessary conditions and formalities. The following classes of works are enumerated in Section 4952 of the American Copyright Code as being subjects of copyright : books, maps, charts, dramatic and musical compositions, engravings, cuts, prints, or photographs or negatives thereof,—paintings, drawings, chromos, statues, statuary, and models or designs intended to be perfected as works of the fine arts.

Unpublished Works.—An unpublished work belonging to any of these classes is protected, on the sole condition that the author or the proprietor of the copyright belongs to a country in favour of which a Proclamation under the Chace Act has been issued. Such an author or proprietor can sue for damages against any person who prints or publishes his manuscript without his consent.[1]

First Publication in United States.—As to published works, on the other hand, there are many conditions and formalities to be fulfilled, even by an author who is personally eligible for American copyright. In the first place, the work must be published in the United States before, or simultaneously with,

---

[1] Sec. 4967 of the American Revised Statutes.

its publication in any other country. It is true that the American Code contains no express condition to this effect, but, as Drone says,[1] 'There can be no doubt that the proper construction of the Act is the same as that given to the English statutes, and that an author forfeits his claim to copyright in this country by a first, but not by a contemporaneous, publication of his work abroad.'

Since the Act of 3rd March, 1905, however, it is possible for the author of a work in a foreign language first published abroad to gain an interim protection for twelve months. This protection applies only to citizens or subjects of countries proclaimed under the Chace Act; and it cannot be secured for English works. The following conditions must be complied with: (1) A notice reserving the American rights must be printed at the beginning of each copy of the work; (2) A copy of the work must be deposited at the Library of Congress within thirty days from first publication. If during the twelve months' interim protection the author duly files the title-page and deposits two copies of the work printed from type set within the United States, he will gain full American copyright.

Delivery of Copies.—Where this interim protection does not apply, it is necessary that, on or before the day of publication, the author shall deliver at the office of the Librarian of Congress, or deposit in the mail within the United States, addressed to the Librarian, a printed copy[2] of the title (*i.e.* title-page) of the work; unless this is a work of the fine arts, when a mere description of it will suffice. Besides this, the author must, on or before publication, deposit with the Librarian of Congress two copies of the work; unless, again, this is a work of the fine arts, when a photograph thereof will be sufficient.[3]

---

[1] Drone, *Treatise on Copyright*, p. 295.
[2] The printing may, however, be done by hand.
[3] Sec. 4956 of the Revised Statutes.

Type must be Set Up in United States.—By themselves these formalities would not be a source of great trouble to the foreign author, but to them is added the onerous condition of type-setting. This makes it necessary that in the case of a book, photograph, chromo or lithograph,[1] the two copies deposited should be printed from type set within the limits of the United States, or plates made therefrom, or from negatives or drawings on stone made within the limits of the United States, or transfers made therefrom.

In order to gain a bare copyright, it will thus be sufficient for the author to have but two copies of his work printed in America.[2] If this be all, however, his copyright will be of little value to him, since the American statutes makes a provision which has the effect of preventing him from offering for sale in the United States any copies of his book, photograph, chromo, or lithograph not printed from type set, or negatives or drawings on stone made, within the United States : during the existence of the American copyright in the work, the importation into the United States of any copies not so printed is prohibited.[3]   To this rule, however, exceptions are made for the cases specified in §§ 512-516 of the Revenue Act, 1890, Sec. 2—*i.e.* for old books, books printed exclusively in foreign languages, books imported

---

[1] The condition is construed strictly. It does not apply to sheet music, lithographs, or to any work capable of copyright except the four classes mentioned in the text.—See *Littleton v. Oliver Ditson & Co.*, 62 Fed. Rep. 597 ; and *Hills & Co. v. Austrich*, 120 Fed. Rep. 862.   The condition does not apply to work copyrighted before 1891.—*Patterson v. Ogilvie*, 119 Fed. Rep. 451.

[2] It is probable that the mere deposit of two copies, as provided by the law, operates as publication and vests the copyright.   This was held, *obiter*, by three of the judges in *The Jewellers' Mercantile Agency v. The Jewellers' Weekly Publishing Co.*, 155 N.Y. 241.   Cf. *Ladd v. Oxnard*, 75 Fed. Rep. 703.

[3] Sec. 4956 of the Revised Statutes. This, again, does not apply to musical compositions, lithographs, maps, etc., which may be imported by the owner of the copyright even if produced abroad.   The unauthorised importation of such works by other persons is, however, prohibited under penalty by Sec. 4965 of the Statutes.   The same rules apply to books copyrighted before 1891.—See U.S. Treasury Decisions, Nos. 21012, 22781, and 23225, cited in Hamlin's *Copyright Cases and Decisions*, pp. 176-179.

for use of the State, etc. The Copyright Act further provides that, subject to the duty thereon, anyone may import two copies of any book for his own use, and makes certain other exemptions. Books in foreign languages of which only translations in English have been copyrighted may be imported, though the translations themselves may not.

Subsequent Editions to be delivered.—When second and subsequent editions of a copyright book are published, one copy of each must be deposited if any substantial changes are made.[1]

Registration.—Upon the completion of the necessary deposit of copies, the Librarian of Congress is required to register the title of the work in a book kept for that purpose ; and to give a copy of the record, under seal, to the proprietor, whenever he shall require it. In return for these services, he is entitled to certain fees, as follows : (*a*) for registration—fifty cents, (*b*) for furnishing a copy of the record—fifty cents. But it is provided that where the author is an alien, the fee for registration shall be one dollar. This is noteworthy, being the only instance throughout the whole Act in which any distinction is made between a protected American author and a protected foreign author.

The distinction, however, in this case is not altogether an arbitrary one ; it is made with the object of compelling the alien author to pay for certain precautions deemed necessary to keep the law from being infringed by the introduction of foreign copies of his work, whether authorised by him or not. In order to prevent the importation of copies of copyright books not printed from type set in the United States, the Librarian of Congress is required to furnish to the Secretary of the Treasury transcripts of all entries made on the register ; while, at intervals of not more than a week, the latter must prepare catalogues of these entries and distribute

---

[1] Sec. 4959 of the American Revised Statutes.

them to the customs' officers and the postmasters of all post offices receiving foreign mails.[1]   The object is, of course, to facilitate the exercise by these persons of their duty of detecting foreign copies of American copyright works.   The fees of one dollar paid by foreign authors upon registration are to be applied for defraying the expenses of these lists.[2]

Notice of Copyright on work required.—The author is required to insert on the title-page of every copy of every edition of his work, or the page immediately following, if it is a book, or upon some visible portion thereof, or of the substance upon which it is mounted, if it belongs to any other class of copyright subjects, a notice in the form[3] 'Entered according to Act of Congress in the year . . . , by A B. in the Office of the Librarian of the Congress at Washington,' or, at his option, in the short form 'Copyright . . . . by A.B.'   Failure to insert this notice in any copy of the work will deprive the author of all protection against infringements, whether the copy actually used in the infringement was itself provided with a notice or not.[4]   It is an offence punishable with a penalty of one hundred dollars[5] to insert a false notice of copyright in or upon a work, or knowingly to sell or to import a work which contains such false notice.   An injunction may be obtained to prevent the issuing, publishing, or selling, of any such work.[6]

[1] Copies of these weekly lists are to be issued to all persons desiring them, at a charge not exceeding five dollars per annum.

[2] Sec. 4958 of the Revised Statutes.

[3] If the work is a moulded decorative article, a tile, a plaque, or an article of pottery or metal subject to copyright, the notice may be put upon the back or bottom, or other customary place.

[4] Sec. 4962 of the Revised Statutes.

[5] As is usual with penalties under the Copyright Code, one half of this sum is to go to the informer and the other half to the State.

[6] Sec. 4963 of the Revised Statutes.

SECTION IV.

THE NATURE AND EXTENT OF COPYRIGHT IN AMERICA.

Enumeration of rights included in copyright—Translating right—Copyright in translations—Author's right of dramatisation—Performing right—Period of protection in the United States—Protection for twenty-eight years, with extension to forty-two years.

Enumeration of rights included in Copyright.—The careful enumeration of the rights included in the general grant of copyright forms a notable feature of the American law, a feature in which it resembles the law of Germany and other foreign countries rather than that of England. Even as to the ordinary right of multiplying copies of the original work in its original form, the American statute gives a list of the means in which this multiplication may take place. It confers on the author the sole liberty 'of printing, reprinting, publishing, completing, copying, executing, finishing, and vending' his work, and, in the case of a dramatic composition, 'of publicly performing or representing it, or causing it to be performed or represented by others.' Besides this, the rights of translation and dramatisation are specifically included in the copyright.[1] No such enumeration finds a place in the existing English law, although something similar is introduced into the recent House of Lords Copyright Bill.

Translating Right.—Since the United States does not protect works first published in foreign countries, the duration of

[1] Sec. 4952 of the American Revised Statutes.

translating right has not engaged very much of its attention. As already indicated, the importance of this right is much diminished where a country does not protect any works first published abroad. A single clause, stating that authors shall have exclusive right to translate any of their works which enjoy copyright in the United States, is all that the American Copyright Code contains on the subject.

There is no suggestion here of any distinction, such as finds a place in the English law and the Berne Convention, between the author's exclusive right to translate a work and the translator's right in a translation lawfully made. There is nothing to indicate that the author is not to enjoy an exclusive right to control or to prevent the translation of his work during the whole period of the copyright therein. The *délai d'usage* of the Berne Convention and the English law—the period within which an author must publish a translation of his work if he is to retain his exclusive right during the whole term—is wholly absent from the American law.

Copyright in Translations.—As to the rights in respect to a translation lawfully made the law is silent, but it is fairly certain that, apart from the exclusive translating right in the original, copyright can be obtained for a translation as a separate work ; it follows that the literary form of the translation may be protected after the copyright in the original has expired, although the translation will then no longer continue to have protection in its substance.

Thus Drone, writing in 1879, says : ' There is no reasonable doubt that valid copyright will vest in a translation, abridgement, or dramatisation made by a citizen or resident from the work of a foreign author. The law recognises such productions as proper subjects of copyright ; and, as the copyright does not extend to the original, it matters not that this is the work of a foreign author. But in such case the law protects each author only in his own production. The original, being common property, may be used by any person without infringing the copyright in a protected abridgement, translation, or dramatisation.'[1] Moreover the Chace Act has made a special rule as to the prohibition of importation ' in the case of books in foreign languages of which only translations in English are copyrighted,'[2] thereby implying that the right in a translation may exist independently of the copyright in the original work.

Although it is not now true, as it was in 1879, that the work of a foreign author is necessarily common property, both these extracts show that under the American law a translation can get protection as such if the original work is not a copyright work. *A fortiori* it follows that the translation will get protection if the original work still enjoys copyright and the translation is made by the author or with his leave.

Every translation lawfully made will thus gain copyright in its literary form, and this for the ordinary term, which will begin and end independently of the period of copyright in the original.

Author's Right of Dramatisation. — A right analagous to translating right, which is reserved to the author by the American law and not by the English law, is the right of dramatisation. In England the law does not forbid the dramatisation of a novel even when made without the author's consent. Nevertheless, as is recognised by the other great literary States of Europe, the author should be enabled to prevent the use of his work in this manner, just as he is able to prevent the unathorised translation of his work. And, accordingly, the law of the United States expressly confers upon him the exclusive right to dramatise his copyright works.[3]

---

[1] Drone, *Treatise on Copyright*, p. 232.

[2] Sec. 4956 of the Revised Statutes, as amended by the Chace Act.

[3] ' Authors or their assigns shall have exclusive right to dramatise or translate any of their works for which copyright shall have been obtained under the laws of the United States.'—Sec. 4952 of the Revised Statutes.

This right, like the translating right, was unconditionally conferred for the first time by the Chace Act of 1891, before which it could only be secured by express notice of reservation.

What has been said as to the distinction between translating right and the right in a translation lawfully made probably applies also to the distinction between the right to dramatise and the right in a dramatised version lawfully made, *i.e.* such a version can no doubt be copyrighted as a separate work, and in that case will have an independent term of its own.

Performing Right is expressly conceded by the American law, which in so many words confers on the author of a dramatic work the right 'of publicly performing or representing it.' This right is simply a part of the copyright in the original work, and will necessarily begin and end with such copyright. The unauthorised public performance of any copyright dramatic or musical composition renders the offender liable to an action for damages, and also, if done wilfully and for profit, to imprisonment. It is noteworthy that, while in England, by a clause in the Literary Copyright Act, 1842, the public performance of a musical or dramatic work is to be deemed to constitute publication, in the United States, as in most of the continental countries of Europe, this is not so.

PERIOD OF PROTECTION IN THE UNITED STATES.

We now come to the question of the duration of copyright. In the United States, for the oft-repeated reason that that country recognises no international copyright, this question is not complicated by any considerations connected with the country of origin. The United States itself is always the country of origin for such works as it protects, and, in these circumstances, there is no room for any limitation of the ordinary period of protection, nor for any other modification of the domestic law. Throughout the whole American law, the only respect in which the position of a protected alien differs from that of an American citizen is in that the former has to pay one dollar instead of fifty cents as a registration fee.

Protection for 28 years, with extension to 42 years. — All copyright works are protected for the same term, *i.e.* for twenty-eight years from the time of recording the title in the manner required by the law. If, however, the author is living at the end of this period, or, being dead, has left a widow or child who still survives, then an extension of the term for a further period of fourteen years may be obtained by such author, widow, or child. For this purpose the title of the work or description of the article must be recorded a second time, and all other regulations with regard to original copyrights observed, within six months of the expiration of the first term. Moreover it is necessary that, within two months from the date of the renewal, a copy of the record thereof should be published for the space of four weeks in one or more newspapers printed in the United States.[1]

[1] Sec. 4954 of the Revised Statutes.

SECTION V.

INFRINGEMENTS, REMEDIES AND PROCEDURE UNDER THE AMERICAN LAW.

Various kinds of infringements—Penalties and damages—Infringement of performing right—Importation of non-American copies—Injunctions.

Various kinds of Infringements.—The American law as to infringements is very much the same as the English domestic law. In the case of a book, after the recording of the title and the deposit of copies have been carried out, it is an infringement[1]

    (i)   to print ;   (iv) to translate ;

    (ii) to publish ;   (v) to import ; or

    (iii) to dramatise ; (vi) knowingly to sell or expose for sale

any copy of such book. In the case of a work of any other kind, after the recording of the title or the description thereof, as the case may be, it is an infringement[1]

    (i)   to engrave, etch, work, copy, or print ;

    (ii) to publish ; (iii) to dramatise ;

    (iv) to translate ; (v) to import ; or

    (vi) knowingly to sell or expose for sale

any copy of such article.[2]

Penalties and Damages.—In the case of a book, when an infringement has been committed, the owner of the copyright may bring an action for damages in any court of competent

---

[1] Without the consent of the owner of the copyright first obtained in writing and signed in the presence of two or more witnesses.

[2] Secs. 4964, 4965 of the American Revised Statutes.

jurisdiction, and may also secure the forfeiture of every offending copy.[1] There is here no pecuniary penalty prescribed for infringement.

In the case of works other than books, however, the statute provides a penalty of one dollar for every sheet found in the defendant's possession, together with the forfeiture of the plates and every sheet of the work ; as to paintings, statues, and statuary, the pecuniary penalty is increased to ten dollars for every copy found in the defendant's possession or by him sold or exposed for sale. It is provided that, where the copyright in a photograph made from an object not a work of the fine arts is infringed, the sum to be recovered by way of penalty shall be not less than one hundred dollars or more than five thousand dollars, and that, where the copyright in an engraving, etching, print, or work of the fine arts is infringed, this sum shall not be less than two hundred and fifty dollars or more than ten thousand dollars.[2] In all these cases the offender also forfeits all the plates used in the process of copying.[3] No action for damages is given by the statute when the copyright in works other than books is infringed; but it is probable that such an action lies at the common law.[4]

Infringement of Performing Right.—With reference to performing right, it is an infringement publicly to perform or to represent any copyright dramatic or musical composition, without the consent of the owner of the copyright. The offender is liable in damages, at the discretion of the Court, to the amount of not less than one hundred dollars for the first, and fifty dollars for every subsequent, performance. Moreover if the unlawful performance or representation be wilful and for profit, the offender is guilty of a misdemeanour and is

---

[1] See 4964 of the Revised Statutes.

[2] One half of the penalty is to go to the owner of the copyright, and the other half for the use of the United States.

[3] Sec. 4965 of the Revised Statutes.

[4] See Drone, *Treatise on Copyright*, p. 494.

liable on conviction to imprisonment for a period of not more than one year.[1]

Importation of non-American Copies.—During the existence of the copyright in a book, photograph, chromo, or lithograph, the importation of any copy thereof not made from type set, or negatives or drawings on stone made, within the limits of the United States is absolutely prohibited;[2] and the Secretary of the Treasury and the Postmaster-General are required to make and enforce such rules and regulations as shall ensure the carrying out of this prohibition.[3]

Injunctions.—The equitable remedies given in the United States are the same as those given by the English Courts, consisting of injunctions and orders for account of profits.

In England, however, since the Judicature Acts, the distinction between Courts of law and equity has been done away with, while in the United States it still remains ; hence, while in England all the higher Courts have power to administer both legal and equitable remedies as may be appropriate to the matter in hand, in the United States the law may be regarded as settled that the penalties and forfeiture imposed by the statute must be sued for in a Court of law.

It is true that the Circuit Courts of the United States, which are Courts of common law, have original jurisdiction over all suits of law and equity arising under the copyright laws, and are expressly authorised to grant injunctions according to the principles of Courts of Equity in order to prevent the violation of any right secured by those laws ; yet no statute confers on any Court of Equity power to decree forfeitures or penalties.[4]

[1] Sec. 4966 of the Revised Statutes,
[2] Subject to certain small exceptions.—See Sec. 3 of this Chapter.
[3] Sec. 4958 of the Revised Statutes
[4] See Drone, *Treatise on Copyright*, pp. 548, 549.

ADDITIONAL SECTION.

THE RIGHTS OF AN AMERICAN AUTHOR IN FOREIGN COUNTRIES.

Countries which grant the protection required by the Chace Act— American law renders treaty-making difficult—Position of American authors in Great Britain—Position in France, Belgium, and Luxemburg— Conditions of nationality waived in favour of American authors—The Copyright Treaty with Germany, 1892 — Important concessions by Germany.

Countries which grant the Protection required by the Chace Act. —The following countries, in the order named, have given to the United States the assurance required by the Chace Act : Belgium, France, Great Britain (and its colonies), Switzerland, Germany, Italy, Denmark, Portugal, Spain, Mexico, Chili, Costa Rica, Holland (and its possessions), and Cuba.[1]

As to the rights of the American author in these countries, the only general rule that can be laid down is that his American nationality will not debar him from obtaining protection. He may be subject to any of the conditions of the domestic law, except that of nationality ; hence he may be required to make first publication within the territory. So much is true also of certain other countries in favour of which no Proclamation under the Chace Act has yet been issued.

There are several countries which, though in them no condition of nationality is attached to domestic copyright, have not

---

[1] The Proclamation in favour of the first four countries was of even date with the coming into force of the Chace Act itself, viz. 1st July, 1891.

sought the benefits of the Chace Act. The most conspicuous example is Luxemburg, which protects all works, wherever they may be published and whatever may be the nationality of their authors.

In order to gain satisfactory information as to the exact extent of his rights in any foreign country, it is thus necessary that the American author should investigate the particular domestic law. For an account of the general principles of domestic protection in the more important countries, reference may be made to Part II., Chap. iv., of this work, entitled 'Alien authors and alien laws.'

American Law renders Treaty-making difficult.—It is a consequence of the peculiar way in which the American law provides for the protection of alien authors, that the United States has but limited opportunities of concluding with foreign countries treaties which involve any relaxation of their domestic law. Since under the Chace Act the United States is not at liberty to protect works published by foreign authors in foreign countries, it is not likely that other States will agree to protect works of American authors published in America. A law which provides for 'diplomatic reciprocity' with reference only to the relaxation of the condition of nationality is not a very valuable aid to international negotiation. Most of the arrangements made under the Chace Act have involved no special concession to American authors by foreign countries. As far as those countries are concerned, such arrangements have as a rule consisted in mere declarations that the existing law did not exclude American authors, as such, from protection—they have rarely involved any promise to alter a previously unfavourable domestic law so as to admit American authors to protection.

Americans entitled to Copyright on same Conditions as Natives.—All that is required of a foreign State by the Chace Act is that it shall permit to citizens of the United States the benefit of copyright on substantially the same basis as to its own citizens.[1]   Hence if under the domestic law first publication within the territory is the only fundamental condition of copyright, the country is already in a position to treat with the United States without making any further concession.   Where the domestic law of a State makes no condition of nationality, it is clear that American citizenship is no disqualification.

Position of American Authors in Great Britain.—This is probably the case in Great Britain, and so, as we have seen, that country has been able to give to the United States the assurance required by the Chace Act.   This made no difference to the position of American authors in England ; it simply stated the existing law.   Its only effect was to enable English authors to obtain protection in America.   The United States gave in return for an advantage it already enjoyed.

As to works of art, indeed, the assurance inadvertently misrepresented the law, since, though it stated that for purposes of copyright residence is not required of an American citizen, the Fine Arts Copyright Act, 1862, restricts artistic copyright to persons who are British subjects or resident within the dominions of the Crown.   This unfortunate mistake cannot alter the law, and so non-resident American authors will not be able to obtain copyright in England for their paintings, drawings, or photographs.

Position in France, Belgium, and Luxemburg.—In France Belgium, and Luxemburg all authors, whatever their nationality, gain copyright for all their works wherever published. Hence in these countries American authors get protection— even for works first published in the United States,—apart altogether from any international intercourse which may have taken place.   Proclamations under the Chace Act have been issued in favour of Belgium and France, but these affect only

---

[1] Or be a party to a treaty providing for the reciprocal protection of copyright which the United States may accept at will.

the international rights of Belgian and French authors, not those of Americans.

Conditions of Nationality waived in favour of American Authors.—On the other hand, in countries where the ordinary condition of domestic copyright is one of nationality, *i.e.* where only subjects or citizens are protected, American authors do distinctly gain by the establishment of international relations. If as a general rule a country only protects its own citizens, it is obviously necessary for it to extend its law before it can declare that it treats citizens of the United States in the same way as its own.

If the only condition made by such a State is that of nationality—if it protects all works of its own subjects wherever they may be published,—it will have to protect all works of American authors wherever these may be published. This, it is clear, is a great advantage to American authors, in that it will enable them to secure copyright in a foreign country for works published in the ordinary way on American soil.

If, again, the foreign country in question imposes a condition of first publication in its territory as well as a condition of nationality, then the American author will at least obtain the privilege of being able to get copyright upon fulfilling the requirement of publication.

Even at the worst, the United States, when it has concluded its international negotiations—whether or not those negotiations themselves bring about any special concession to its authors—will be actually in the enjoyment of better terms for its own authors than those which it gives to authors of the foreign country, for in no other country is the American condition of type-setting attached to the more ordinary conditions of publication within the territory.[1]

---

[1] In Holland, however, "publication by means of printing" on Dutch territory is required.

The Copyright Treaty with Germany, 1892.—America thus usually gets much the better of the bargain. In only one case has that country entered into a formal copyright treaty,[1] and there it sacrificed nothing and gained a great deal. The treaty in question was concluded with Germany on 15th January, 1892. It provides (Art. 1) that ' Citizens of the United States of America shall enjoy in the German Empire the protection of copyright as regards works of literature or art, as well as the protection of photographs against illegal reproduction, on the same basis as that on which such protection is granted to subjects of the Empire.'[2] In return for this, the Government of the United States simply entered into an engagement (Art. 2) that the President would make a proclamation under the Chace Act for the purpose of extending its benefits to German subjects.[3]

Important Concessions by Germany.—This involved a great concession on the part of Germany, for under the domestic law of that country, aliens are protected only for works first published within the German Empire ; while Germans get protection for all their works, wherever published.[4]

Hence in placing the citizens of the United States on a level with its own subjects, Germany confers upon them the special privilege of protection for works published in their own country, *i.e.* in America, or, indeed, anywhere else. All that Germany gets in consideration for this is the protection of its authors for works first (or simultaneously) published in the United States—and that subject to the type-setting clause.

---

[1] A recent treaty with China, dated 8th October, 1903, contains an **Art. 11** relating to copyright, but its main objects are commercial.

[2] The American text reads: ' . . . the protection of copyright as regards literature and art as well as photographs against illegal reproduction. . . .' The difference is not of any material importance.—*Le Droit d'Auteur*, 1892, p. 59.

[3] The only other article of the treaty—Art. 3—related to ratification. For the text of the treaty see *Le Droit d'Auteur*, 1892, p. 61.

[4] See the Act of 19th June, 1901 (secs. 54 and 55).

According to *Le Droit d'Auteur*,[1] at the time when it was made the treaty evoked only one German voice in its favour,—the voice of a publisher who contemplated founding a German agency in New York.[2] The general opinion was that Germany gave with both hands only to receive a very slight return. 'As to the manufacturing clause,' said the *Bœrsenblatt*,[3] 'it imposes upon the publisher a condition which in the majority of cases cannot be fulfilled. The expenses of type-setting are considerably higher in America.[4] The number of works for which a publisher will run the risk of double the expenses will be very limited. The American reprinter will not have to pay royalties or transport dues . . . and so he will always sell his reprints at a lower price than that of the original work . . . The Convention only puts a premium on protection in favour of the printer and publisher ; it will act as a direct encouragement to the more rapid development of the business of reproduction and will render the existing state of things worse.'[5] This is somewhat extravagant language, but no country can consider the American Chace Act as fairly satisfying the condition of reciprocity.

Another concession made by Germany in this treaty relates to the protection of photographs. Under the German domestic law, protection for photographs is restricted to native authors,[6] and in the German treaties with France, Belgium, and Italy[7] a clause is inserted expressly declaring that, owing to the state

---

[1] *Le Droit d'Auteur*, 1892, p. 60.

[2] M. Ackermann, who wrote : 'Whoever knows the enormous injury caused to the publication of industrial and artistic works in America . . . will understand that art publishers have good reason to congratulate themselves upon the obtaining of copyright.'—*Le Droit d'Auteur*, 1892, p. 60.

[3] March 10th, 1892.

[4] Coming from a German, this is doubtless true ; but in England the cost of type-setting is, on the whole, greater than in the United States.

[5] See *Le Droit d'Auteur*, 1892, p. 60.

[6] Act of 10th January, 1886.

[7] Dated 1883, 1883, and 1884 respectively.

of its domestic law, Germany cannot include photographs
in their scope.[1] In the treaty with the United States, on the
other hand, photographs are expressly mentioned. This
indicated a change of attitude on the part of Germany,
which bore further fruit a few years later in the modification
of § 1 of the Closing Protocol to the Berne Convention, which
now makes it obligatory for countries protecting photographs
by their domestic law to confer upon them international protection under the Convention.

[1] These treaties, however, all contain a 'most favoured nation' clause, so that
the inclusion of photographs in the protection of the American treaty will
indirectly benefit France, Belgium, and Italy.

CONVENTION DE BERNE

CONCERNANT LA CRÉATION

D'UNE UNION INTERNATIONALE POUR LA PROTECTION DES ŒUVRES LITTÉRAIRES ET ARTISTIQUES

DU 9 SEPTEMBRE 1886

COMBINÉE AVEC

L'ACTE ADDITIONNEL ET LA DÉCLARATION INTERPRÉTATIVE

DU 4 MAI 1896.

THE BERNE CONVENTION

OF THE 9TH SEPTEMBER 1886

FOR THE CREATION OF

AN INTERNATIONAL UNION FOR THE PROTECTION OF LITERARY AND ARTISTIC WORKS,

COMBINED WITH

THE ADDITIONAL ACT AND THE INTERPRETATIVE DECLARATION

OF THE 4TH MAY 1896.

NOTA.—Les dispositions contenues dans l'Acte additionnel ont été intercalées à leur place respective et imprimées en italiques; le texte des articles de la Convention de 1886 revisés par l'Acte additionnel a été reproduit sous forme de notes.

Les dispositions de la Déclaration interprétative sont placées au bas des articles auxquelles elles se rapportent, et imprimées en petits caractères.

ARTICLE PREMIER.

Les pays contractants sont constitués à l'état d'Union pour la protection des droits des auteurs sur leurs œuvres littéraires et artistiques.

ART. 2.

Les auteurs ressortissant à l'un des pays de l'Union, ou leurs ayants cause, jouissent, dans les autres pays, pour leurs œuvres, soit non publiées, soit publiées pour la première fois dans un de ces pays, des droits que les lois respectives accordent actuellement ou accorderont par la suite aux nationaux.[1]

La jouissance de ces droits est subordonnée à l'accomplissement des conditions et formalités prescrites par la législation du pays d'origine de l'œuvre; elle ne peut excéder, dans les autres pays, la durée de la protection accordée dans ledit pays d'origine.

Est considéré comme pays d'origine de l'œuvre, celui de la première publication, ou, si cette publication a lieu simultanément dans plusieurs pays de l'Union, celui d'entre eux dont la législation accorde la durée de protection la plus courte.

Pour les œuvres non publiées, le pays auquel appartient l'auteur est considéré comme pays d'origine de l'œuvre.

---

[1] *Convention du 9 septembre,* 1886, *article* 2, 1er *alinéa, ancien texte :* 'Les auteurs ressortissant à l'un des pays de l'Union, ou leurs ayants cause, jouissent, dans les autres pays, pour leurs œuvres, soit publiées dans un de ces pays, soit non publiées, des droits que les lois respectives accordent actuellement ou accorderont par la suite aux nationaux.'

N.B.—The provisions of the Additional Act have been inserted in their proper places and printed in italics; the text of the articles of the Convention of 1886, which were modified by the Additional Act, have been placed in footnotes.

The provisions of the Interpretative Declaration are placed underneath the Articles to which they relate and printed in small type.

Art. 1.

The contracting States are formed into a Union for the protection of the rights of authors over their literary and artistic works.

Art. 2.

Authors belonging to any country of the Union, or their lawful representatives, shall enjoy in the other countries for their works, whether unpublished or published for the first time in one of those countries, the rights which the respective laws do now or may hereafter grant to natives.[1]

The enjoyment of these rights is subjected to the accomplishment of the conditions and formalities prescribed by the law of the country of origin of the work: it cannot exceed, in the other countries, the duration of the protection granted in the said country of origin.

The country of first publication, or, if that publication takes place simultaneously in several countries of the Union, that one of them in which the shortest period of protection is granted by law, is considered to be the country of origin of the work.

For unpublished works, the country to which the author belongs is considered to be the country of origin of the work.

---

[1] *Original wording of Article* 2, § 1, *in the* 1886 *Convention :* 'Authors belonging to any country of the Union, or their lawful representatives, shall enjoy in the other countries for their works, whether published in one of those countries or unpublished, the rights which the respective laws do now or may hereafter grant to natives.

Les œuvres posthumes sont comprises parmi les œuvres protégées.[1]

> *Déclaration Interprétative :* ' 1° Aux termes de l'article 2, alinéa
> 2, de la Convention, la protection assurée par les actes précités
> dépend uniquement de l'accomplissement, dans le pays d'origine de
> l'œuvre, des conditions et formalités qui peuvent être prescrites par
> la législation de ce pays. Il en sera de même pour la protection des
> œuvres photographiques mentionnées dans le n° 1, lettre B, du
> Protocole de clôture modifié.'
>
> ' 2° Par œuvres *publiées,* il faut entendre les œuvres *éditées* dans
> un des pays de l'Union. En conséquence, la représentation d'une
> œuvre dramatique ou dramatico-musicale, l'exécution d'une œuvre
> musicale, l'exposition d'une œuvre d'art, ne constituent pas une
> *publication* dans le sens des actes précités.'

Art. 3.

*Les auteurs ne ressortissant pas à l'un des pays de l'Union, mais
qui auront publié ou fait publier, pour la première fois, leurs œuvres
littéraires ou artistiques dans l'un de ces pays, jouiront, pour ces
œuvres, de la protection accordée par la Convention de Berne et par
le présent Acte additionnel.*[2]

Art. 4.

L'expression ' œuvres littéraires et artistiques ' comprend les
livres, brochures ou tous autres écrits ; les œuvres dramatiques
ou dramatico-musicales, les compositions musicales avec ou sans
paroles ; les œuvres de dessin, de peinture, de sculpture, de gravure ;
les lithographies, les illustrations, les cartes géographiques ; les
plans, croquis et ouvrages plastiques, relatifs à la géographie, à la
topographie, à l'architecture ou aux sciences en général ; enfin toute
production quelconque du domaine littéraire, scientifique ou artistique, qui pourrait être publiée par n'importe quel mode d'impression ou de reproduction.

---

[1] *Texte nouveau,* ajouté à la Convention de 1886.

[2] *Convention de 1886, article 3, ancien texte :* ' Les stipulations de la présente
Convention s'appliquent également aux éditeurs d'œuvres littéraires ou artistiques publiées dans un des pays de l'Union, et dont l'auteur appartient à un
pays qui n'en fait pas partie.'

Posthumous works are included among the works protected.[1]

> *Interpretative Declaration :* § 1. 'With reference to the terms of Article 2, § 2, of the Convention, the protection assured by the aforesaid Acts depends solely upon the accomplishment, in the country of origin of the work, of the conditions and formalities which are prescribed by the law of that country. The same shall hold good for the protection of the photographic works mentioned in § 1, B of the revised Closing Protocol.'
>
> § 2. 'By works *published*, is to be understood works *issued to the public* in one of the countries of the Union. Consequently, the representation of a dramatic or dramatico-musical work, the performance of a musical work, and the exhibition of a work of art do not constitute *publication* in the sense of the aforesaid Acts.'

ART. 3.

Authors not belonging to any country of the Union, if they shall have published their literary or artistic works, or caused them to be published, for the first time in one of those countries, shall enjoy for such works the protection granted by the Berne Convention and by the present Additional Act.[2]

ART. 4.

The expression 'literary and artistic works' comprises books, pamphlets, and all other writings; dramatic or dramatico-musical works, and musical compositions, with or without words; works of design, painting, sculpture, and engraving; lithographs, illustrations, geographical charts; plans, sketches, and plastic works relating to geography, topography, architecture, or to the sciences in general; finally, every production whatsoever in the literary, scientific, or artistic domain which can be published by any mode of impression or reproduction whatever.

---

[1] *Fresh words*, added to the 1886 Convention.

[2] *Original wording of Article 3 in the* 1886 *Convention :* 'The stipulations of the present Convention apply equally to the publishers of literary or artistic works published in any country of the Union, though the author belongs to a country which is not a party to the Union.'

Art. 5.

Les auteurs ressortissant à l'un des pays de l'Union, ou leurs ayants cause, jouissent, dans les autres pays, du droit exclusif de faire ou d'autoriser la traduction de leurs œuvres pendant toute la durée du droit sur l'œuvre originale. Toutefois, le droit exclusif de traduction cessera d'exister lorsque l'auteur n'en aura pas fait usage dans un délai de dix ans à partir de la première publication de l'œuvre originale, en publiant ou en faisant publier, dans un des pays de l'Union, une traduction dans la langue pour laquelle la protection sera réclamée.[1]

Pour les ouvrages publiés par livraisons, le délai de dix années ne compte qu'à dater de la publication de la dernière livraison de l'œuvre originale.

Pour les œuvres composées de plusieurs volumes publiés par intervalles, ainsi que pour les bulletins ou cahiers publiés par des sociétés littéraires ou savantes ou par des particuliers, chaque volume, bulletin ou cahier est, en ce qui concerne le délai de dix années, considéré comme ouvrage séparé.

Dans les cas prévus au présent article, est admis comme date de publication, pour les calculs des délais de protection, le 31 décembre de l'année dans laquelle l'ouvrage a été publié.

Art. 6.

Les traductions licites sont protégées comme des ouvrages originaux. Elles jouissent, en conséquence, de la protection stipulée aux articles 2 et 3 en ce qui concerne leur reproduction non autorisée dans les pays de l'Union.

Il est entendu que, s'il s'agit d'une œuvre pour laquelle le droit de traduction est dans le domaine public, le traducteur ne peut pas s'opposer à ce que la même œuvre soit traduite par d'autres écrivains.

---

[1] *Convention de* 1886, *article* 5, *premier alinéa, ancien texte :* ' Les auteurs ressortissant à l'un des pays de l'Union, ou leurs ayants cause, jouissent, dans les autres pays, du droit exclusif de faire ou d'autoriser la traduction de leurs ouvrages jusqu'à l'expiration de dix années à partir de la publication de l'œuvre originale dans l'un des pays de l'Union.'

Art. 5.

Authors belonging to any country of the Union, or their lawful representatives, shall enjoy in the other countries the exclusive right of making or authorising translations of their works during the whole duration of the right in the original work. Nevertheless, the exclusive right of translation shall cease to exist when the author shall not have made use of it within a period of ten years from the time of the first publication of the original work, by publishing or causing to be published, in one of the countries of the Union, a translation in the language for which protection is claimed.[1]

For works published by instalments, the period of ten years does not begin to run until the publication of the last instalment of the original work.

For works composed of several volumes published at intervals, as well as for reports or papers published by literary or learned societies or by individuals, each volume, report, or paper is, with regard to the period of ten years, considered as a separate work.

In the cases provided for by the present Article, the 31st December of the year in which the work was published is to be considered as the date of publication for the purpose of calculating the period of protection.

Art. 6.

Lawful translations are protected as original works. Hence they enjoy the protection stipulated for in Articles 2 and 3 as regards their unauthorised reproduction in the countries of the Union.

It is understood that, in the case of a work for which the translating right has fallen into the public domain, the translator cannot oppose the translation of the same work by other writers.

---

[1] *Original wording of Article 5, § 1, in the* 1886 *Convention :* 'Authors belonging to any country of the Union, or their lawful representatives, shall enjoy in the other countries the exclusive right of making or authorising translations of their works until the expiration of ten years from the publication of the original work in one of the countries of the Union.'

Art. 7.

Les romans-feuilletons, y compris les nouvelles, publiés dans les journaux ou recueils périodiques d'un des pays de l'Union, ne pourront être reproduits, en original ou en traduction, dans les autres pays, sans l'autorisation des auteurs ou de leurs ayants cause.

Il en sera de même pour les autres articles de journaux ou de recueils périodiques, lorsque les auteurs ou éditeurs auront expressément déclaré, dans le journal ou le recueil même où ils les auront fait paraître, qu'ils en interdisent la reproduction. Pour les recueils, il suffit que l'interdiction soit faite d'une manière générale en tête de chaque numéro.

A défaut d'interdiction, la reproduction sera permise à la condition d'indiquer la source.

En aucun cas, l'interdiction ne pourra s'appliquer aux articles de discussion politique, aux nouvelles du jour et aux 'faits divers.' [1]

Art. 8.

En ce qui concerne la faculté de faire licitement des emprunts à des œuvres littéraires ou artistiques pour des publications destinées à l'enseignement ou ayant un caractère scientifique, ou pour des chrestomathies, est réservé l'effet de la législation des pays de l'Union et des arrangements particuliers existants ou à conclure entre eux.

Art. 9.

Les stipulations de l'article 2 s'appliquent à la représentation publique des œuvres dramatiques ou dramatico-musicales, que ces œuvres soient publiées ou non.

---

[1] *Convention de 1886, article 7, ancien texte :* 'Les articles de journaux ou de recueils périodiques publiés dans l'un des pays de l'Union peuvent être reproduits, en original ou en traduction, dans les autres pays de l'Union à moins que les auteurs ou éditeurs ne l'aient expressément interdit. Pour les recueils, il peut suffire que l'interdiction soit faite d'une manière générale en tête de chaque numéro du recueil.

'En aucun cas, cette interdiction ne peut s'appliquer aux articles de discussion politique ou à la reproduction des nouvelles du jour et des *faits divers.*'

ART. 7.

Serial novels (romans-feuilletons), *including short stories, published in the newspapers or magazines of any country of the Union may not be reproduced, in original or in translation, in the other countries, without the authorization of the authors or their lawful representatives.*

This applies equally to other articles in newspapers or magazines, whenever the authors or publishers shall have expressly declared in the newspaper or magazine in which they have published such articles that they forbid the reproduction of these. For magazines, it is sufficient if the prohibition is made in a general way at the beginning of each number.

In the absence of prohibition, reproduction will be permitted on condition of indicating the source.

No prohibition can in any case apply to articles of political discussion, news of the day, or miscellaneous items (notes and jottings).[1]

ART. 8.

As regards the liberty of lawfully making extracts from literary or artistic works for use in publications destined for education, or having a scientific character, or for chrestomathies, this matter is reserved to the law of the countries of the Union and to the particular arrangements existing or to be concluded between them.

ART. 9.

The stipulations of Article 2 apply to the public performance of dramatic or dramatico-musical works, whether such works be published or not.

---

[1] *Original reading of Article 7 in the* 1886 *Convention :* 'Articles in newspapers or magazines published in any country of the Union may be reproduced, in original or in translation, in the other countries of the Union, unless the authors or publishers have expressly forbidden it. For magazines, it is sufficient if the prohibition is made in a general manner at the beginning of each number of the magazine.

'No prohibition can in any case apply to articles of political discussion or to the reproduction of news of the day or miscellaneous items (notes and jottings).'

Les auteurs d'œuvres dramatiques ou dramatico-musicales, ou leurs ayants cause, sont, pendant la durée de leur droit exclusif de traduction, réciproquement protégés contre la représentation publique non autorisée de la traduction de leurs ouvrages.

Les stipulations de l'article 2 s'appliquent également à l'exécution publique des œuvres musicales non publiées, ou de celles qui ont été publiées, mais dont l'auteur a expressément déclaré sur le titre ou en tête de l'ouvrage qu'il en interdit l'exécution publique.

Art. 10.

Sont spécialement comprises parmi les reproductions illicites auxquelles s'applique la présente Convention, les appropriations indirectes non autorisées d'un ouvrage littéraire ou artistique désignées sous des noms divers, tels que : *adaptations, arrangements de musique*, etc., lorsqu'elles ne sont que la reproduction d'un tel ouvrage, dans la même forme ou sous une autre forme, avec des changements, additions ou retranchements, non essentiels, sans présenter d'ailleurs le caractère d'une nouvelle œuvre originale.

Il est entendu que, dans l'application du présent article, les tribunaux des divers pays de l'Union tiendront compte, s'il y a lieu, des réserves de leurs lois respectives.

> *Déclaration interprétative :* ' 3° La transformation d'un roman en pièce de théâtre, ou d'une pièce de théâtre en roman, rentre dans les stipulations de l'article 10. '

Art. 11.

Pour que les auteurs des ouvrages protégés par la présente Convention soient, jusqu'à preuve contraire, considérés comme tels et admis, en conséquence, devant les tribunaux des divers pays de l'Union à exercer des poursuites contre les contrefaçons, il suffit que leur nom soit indiqué sur l'ouvrage en la manière usitée.

Pour les œuvres anonymes ou pseudonymes, l'éditeur dont le nom est indiqué sur l'ouvrage est fondé à sauvegarder les droits

Authors of dramatic or dramatico-musical works, or their lawful representatives, are, during the existence of their exclusive right of translation, in like manner protected against the unauthorised public representation of translations of their works.

The stipulations of Article 2 apply equally to the public performance of unpublished musical works, and of published works as to which the author has expressly declared upon the title-page or at the commencement of the work that he forbids their public performance.

ART. 10.

Unauthorised indirect appropriations of a literary or artistic, work, which are known by various names, such as 'adaptations,' 'arrangements of music,' etc., are specially included among the unlawful reproductions to which the present Convention applies, when they are merely the reproduction of such a work, in the same form or in another form, with non-essential alterations, additions, or abridgements, without in other respects presenting the character of a new original work.

It is understood that, in the application of the present Article, the Courts of the various countries of the Union will, if occasion arises, take into account the reservations of their respective laws.

> *Interpretative Declaration :* § 3. 'The transformation of a novel into a play, or of a play into a novel, comes within the stipulations of Art. 10.'

ART. 11.

In order that the authors of works protected by the present Convention may, in the absence of proof to the contrary, be considered as such, and consequently admitted to institute proceedings against infringements before the courts of the various countries of the Union, it is sufficient for their name to be indicated on the work in the accustomed manner.

For anonymous or pseudonymous works, the publisher whose name is indicated on the work is entitled to safeguard the rights

appartenant à l'auteur. Il est, sans autres preuves, réputé ayant cause de l'auteur anonyme ou pseudonyme.

Il est entendu, toutefois, que les tribunaux peuvent exiger, le cas échéant, la production d'un certificat délivré par l'autorité compétente, constatant que les formalités prescrites, dans le sens de l'article 2, par la législation du pays d'origine ont été remplies.

Art. 12.

Toute œuvre contrefaite peut être saisie par les autorités compétentes des pays de l'Union où l'œuvre originale a droit à la protection légale.[1]

La saisie a lieu conformément à la législation intérieure de chaque pays.

Art. 13.

Il est entendu que les dispositions de la présente Convention ne peuvent porter préjudice, en quoi que ce soit, au droit qui appartient au Gouvernement de chacun des pays de l'Union de permettre, de surveiller, d'interdire, par des mesures de législation ou de police intérieure, la circulation, la représentation, l'exposition de tout ouvrage ou production à l'égard desquels l'autorité compétente aurait à exercer ce droit.

Art. 14.

La présente Convention, sous les réserves et conditions à déterminer d'un commun accord, s'applique à toutes les œuvres qui, au moment de son entrée en vigueur, ne sont pas encore tombées dans le domaine public dans leur pays d'origine.

Art. 15.

Il est entendu que les Gouvernements des pays de l'Union se réservent respectivement le droit de prendre séparément, entre eux, des arrangements particuliers, en tant que ces arrangements conféreraient aux auteurs ou à leurs ayants cause des droits plus

---

[1] *Convention de 1886, article 12, premier alinéa, ancien texte:* ' Toute œuvre contrefaite peut être saisie à l'importation dans ceux des pays de l'Union où l'œuvre originale a droit à la protection légale.'

belonging to the author. He is, without further proof, reputed the lawful representative of the anonymous or pseudonymous author.

It is understood, nevertheless, that the courts may, if necessary, require the production of a certificate from the competent authority, stating that the formalities prescribed, according to Article 2, by the law of the country of origin, have been fulfilled.

ART. 12.

Every infringing work shall be subject to seizure by the competent authorities of the countries of the Union in which the original work has a right to legal protection.[1]

The seizure will take place conformably to the domestic law of each country.

ART. 13.

It is understood that the provisions of the present Convention cannot in any way derogate from the right which belongs to the Government of each of the countries of the Union to permit, to supervise, and to prohibit, by legislative measures or police regulations, the circulation, representation, and exhibition of every work or production in respect of which the competent authority may find it necessary to exercise that right.

ART. 14.

The present Convention, under the reservations and conditions to be determined by a common agreement, applies to all works which, at the time of its coming into force, have not yet fallen into the public domain in their country of origin.

ART. 15.

It is understood that the Governments of the countries of the Union reserve to themselves respectively the right to make separately particular arrangements between themselves, so far as such arrangements confer upon authors or their representatives more

---

[1] *Original reading of Article* 12, § 1, *in the* 1886 *Convention :* 'Every infringing work shall be subject to seizure upon importation into those countries of the Union in which the original work has a right to legal protection.'

étendus que ceux accordés par l'Union, ou qu'ils renfermeraient d'autres stipulations non contraires à la présente Convention.

Art. 16.

Un office international est institué sous le nom de *Bureau de l'Union internationale pour la protection des œuvres littéraires et artistiques.*

Ce Bureau, dont les frais sont supportés par les Administrations de tous les pays de l'Union, est placé sous la haute autorité de l'Administration supérieure de la Confédération Suisse, et fonctionne sous sa surveillance. Les attributions en sont déterminées d'un commun accord entre les pays de l'Union.

Art. 17.

La présente Convention peut être soumise à des revisions en vue d'y introduire les améliorations de nature à perfectionner le système de l'Union.

Les questions de cette nature, ainsi que celles qui intéressent à d'autres points de vue le développement de l'Union, seront traitées dans les Conférences qui auront lieu successivement dans les pays de l'Union entre les délégués desdits pays.

Il est entendu qu'aucun changement à la présente Convention ne sera valable pour l'Union que moyennant l'assentiment unanime des pays qui la composent.

Art. 18.

Les pays qui n'ont point pris part à la présente Convention et qui assurent chez eux la protection légale des droits faisant l'objet de cette Convention, seront admis à y accéder sur leur demande.

Cette accession sera notifiée par écrit au Gouvernement de la Confédération Suisse, et par celui-ci à tous les autres.

Elle emportera, de plein droit, adhésion à toutes les clauses et admission à tous les avantages stipulés dans la présente Convention.

extended rights than those accorded by the Union, or embrace other stipulations not contrary to the present Convention.

Art. 16.

An international office is established under the name of *Office of the International Union for the protection of literary and artistic works.*

This office, the expenses of which will be borne by the Governments of all the countries of the Union, is placed under the high authority of the Superior Administration of the Swiss Confederation, and works under its supervision. Its functions shall be determined by common agreement between the countries of the Union.

Art. 17.

The present Convention may be submitted to revisions with the object of introducing therein amendments calculated to perfect the system of the Union.

Questions of this kind, as well as those which concern the development of the Union from other points of view, shall be considered in Conferences to be held successively in the countries of the Union by delegates of the said countries.

It is understood that no alteration in the present Convention shall be binding for the Union in the absence of the unanimous consent of the countries composing it.

Art. 18.

Countries which have not become parties to the present Convention, if they assure in their own territory legal protection to the rights which form the object of this Convention, shall be permitted to accede thereto upon their request.

This accession shall be notified in writing to the Government of the Swiss Confederation, and by the latter to all the others.

It shall imply, as a necessary consequence, adhesion to all the clauses and admission to all the advantages stipulated in the present Convention.

Art. 19.

Les pays accédant à la présente Convention ont aussi le droit d'y accéder en tout temps pour leurs colonies ou possessions étrangères.

Ils peuvent, à cet effet, soit faire une déclaration générale par laquelle toutes leurs colonies ou possessions sont comprises dans l'accession, soit nommer expressément celles qui y sont comprises, soit se borner à indiquer celles qui en sont exclues.

Art. 20.

La présente Convention sera mise à exécution trois mois après l'échange des ratifications, et demeurera en vigueur pendant un temps indéterminé, jusqu'à l'expiration d'une année à partir du jour où la dénonciation en aura été faite.

Cette dénonciation sera adressée au Gouvernement de la Confédération Suisse. Elle ne produira son effet qu'à l'égard du pays qui l'aura faite, la Convention restant exécutoire pour les autres pays de l'Union.[1]

Art. 21.

La présente Convention sera ratifiée, et les ratifications en seront échangées à Berne, dans le délai d'un an au plus tard.

En foi de quoi, les Plénipotentiaires respectifs l'ont signée et y ont apposé le cachet de leurs armes.

Fait à Berne, le neuvième jour du mois de septembre de l'an mil huit cent quatre-vingt-six.

(*Signatures.*)

---

[1] *Convention de* 1886, *article* 20 , *deuxième alinéa, ancien texte :* ' Cette dénonciation sera adressée au Gouvernement chargé de recevoir les accessions. Elle ne produira son effet qu'à l'égard du pays qui l'aura faite, la Convention restant exécutoire pour les autres pays de l'Union.'

ART. 19.

Countries acceding to the present Convention shall also have the right to accede thereto at any time for their colonies or foreign possessions.

To this end, they may either make a general declaration, by which all their colonies or possessions are comprised in the accession, or expressly name those which are included therein, or limit themselves to indicating those which are excluded therefrom.

ART. 20.

The present Convention shall be put into effect three months after the exchange of the ratifications, and shall remain in force for an indeterminate time, until the expiration of one year from the day on which it may have been denounced.

This denunciation shall be addressed to the Government of the Swiss Confederation. It shall only take effect in respect of the country which shall have made it, the Convention remaining operative for the other countries of the Union.[1]

ART. 21.

The present Convention shall be ratified, and the ratifications thereof shall be exchanged at Berne, within a period of one year at the latest.

In witness whereof, the respective Plenipotentiaries have hereunto set their hands and seals.

Done at Berne, this ninth day of the month of September in the year one thousand eight hundred and eighty-six.

(*Signed.*)

---

[1] *Original reading of Article* 20, § 2, *in the* 1886 *Convention :* ' This denunciation shall be addressed to the Government charged to receive accessions. It shall only take effect in respect of the country which shall have made it, the Convention remaining operative for the other countries of the Union.'

ARTICLE ADDITIONNEL.

Les Plénipotentiaires réunis pour signer la Convention concernant la création d'une Union internationale pour la protection des œuvres littéraires et artistiques, sont convenus de l'article additionnel suivant, qui sera ratifié en même temps que l'acte auquel il se rapporte :

La Convention conclue à la date de ce jour n'affecte en rien le maintien des Conventions actuellement existantes entre les pays contractants, en tant que ces Conventions confèrent aux auteurs ou à leurs ayants cause des droits plus étendus que ceux accordés par l'Union, ou qu'elles renferment d'autres stipulations qui ne sont pas contraires à cette Convention.

En foi de quoi, les Plénipotentiaires respectifs ont signé le présent article additionnel.

Fait à Berne, le neuvième jour du mois de septembre de l'an mil huit cent quatre-vingt-six.

(*Signatures.*)

PROTOCOLE DE CLÔTURE.

Au moment de procéder à la signature de la Convention conclue à la date de ce jour, les Plénipotentiaires soussignés ont déclaré et stipulé ce qui suit :

1. Au sujet de l'article 4, il est convenu ce qui suit :

A.—Dans les pays de l'Union où la protection est accordée non seulement aux plans d'architecture, mais encore aux œuvres d'architecture elles-mêmes, ces œuvres sont admises au bénéfice des dispositions de la Convention de Berne et du présent Acte additionnel.

B.—Les œuvres photographiques et les œuvres obtenues par un procédé analogue sont admises au bénéfice des dispositions de ces actes, en tant que la législation intérieure permet de le faire, et dans la mesure de la protection qu'elle accorde aux œuvres nationales similaires.

Il est entendu que la photographie autorisée d'une œuvre d'art protégée jouit, dans tous les pays de l'Union, de la protection légale, au

ADDITIONAL ARTICLE.

The Plenipotentiaries assembled to sign the Convention relating to the creation of an International Union for the protection of literary and artistic works, are agreed upon the following Additional Article, which will be ratified at the same time as the instrument to which it relates:

The Convention concluded this day does not in any way affect the maintenance of the treaties actually existing between the contracting countries, so far as those treaties confer upon authors or their representatives rights more extended than those accorded by the Union, or embrace other stipulations which are not contrary to this Convention.

In witness whereof the respective Plenipotentiaries have hereunto set their hands.

Done at Berne, this ninth day of the month of September in the year one thousand eight hundred and eighty-six.

(*Signed.*)

CLOSING PROTOCOL.

At the time of proceeding to the signature of the Convention concluded this day, the undersigned Plenipotentiaries have declared and agreed as follows:

1. With reference to Article 4, it is agreed as follows:

A. In the countries of the Union in which protection is accorded not only to architectural plans, but also to works of architecture themselves, those works are admitted to the benefit of the provisions of the Berne Convention and of the present Additional Act.

B. Photographic works, and works obtained by analogous processes, are admitted to the benefit of the provisions of those Acts, in so far as the domestic law of each country allows this to be done, and in the measure of the protection that it accords to similar national works.

It is understood that an authorised photograph of a protected work of art enjoys legal protection, in all the countries of the Union, within

sens de la Convention de Berne et du présent Acte additionnel, aussi longtemps que dure le droit principal de reproduction de cette œuvre même, et dans les limites des conventions privées entre les ayants droit.[1]

> *Déclaration interprétative :* ' 1° Aux termes de l'article 2, alinéa 2, de la Convention, la protection assurée par les actes précités dépend uniquement de l'accomplissement, dans le pays d'origine de l'œuvre, des conditions et formalités qui peuvent être prescrites par la législation de ce pays. Il en sera de même pour la protection des œuvres photographiques mentionnées dans le n° 1, lettre B, du Protocole de clôture modifié.'

2. Au sujet de l'article 9, il est convenu que ceux des pays de l'Union dont la législation comprend implicitement, parmi les œuvres dramatico-musicales, les œuvres chorégraphiques, admettent expressément lesdites œuvres au bénéfice des dispositions de la Convention, conclue en date de ce jour.

Il est d'ailleurs entendu que les contestations qui s'élèveraient sur l'application de cette clause demeurent réservées à l'appréciation des tribunaux respectifs.

3. Il est entendu que la fabrication et la vente des instruments servant à reproduire mécaniquement des airs de musique empruntés au domaine privé ne sont pas considérées comme constituant le fait de contrefaçon musicale.

4. L'accord commun prévu à l'article 14 de la Convention est déterminé ainsi qu'il suit :

L'application de la Convention de Berne et du présent Acte additionnel aux œuvres non tombées dans le domaine public dans leur pays d'origine au moment de la mise en vigueur de ces actes,

---

[1] *Convention de 1886, Protocole de clôture, n° 1, ancien texte :* ' 1. Au sujet de l'article 4, il est convenu que ceux des pays de l'Union où le caractère d'œuvres artistiques n'est pas refusé aux œuvres photographiques s'engagent à les admettre, à partir de la mise en vigueur de la Convention conclue en date de ce jour, au bénéfice de ces dispositions. Ils ne sont, d'ailleurs, tenus de protéger les auteurs desdites œuvres, sauf les arrangements internationaux existants ou à conclure, que dans la mesure où leur législation permet de le faire.

' Il est entendu que la photographie autorisée d'une œuvre d'art protégée jouit, dans tous les pays de l'Union, de la protection légale, au sens de ladite Convention, aussi longtemps que dure le droit principal de reproduction de cette œuvre même, et dans les limites des conventions privées entre les ayants droit.'

the meaning of the Berne Convention and of the present Additional Act, so long as the principal right of reproduction of this work itself lasts, and within the limits of private agreements between the parties entitled. [1]

> *Interpretative Declaration :* ' § 1. With reference to the terms of Article 2, § 2, of the Convention, the protection assured by the aforesaid Acts depends solely upon the accomplishment, in the country of origin of the work, of the conditions and formalities which are prescribed by the law of that country. The same shall hold good for the protection of the photographic works mentioned in § 1 B of the revised Closing Protocol.'

2. With reference to Article 9, it is agreed that those countries of the Union the law of which implicitly includes choregraphic works amongst dramatico-musical works, expressly admit the said works to the benefit of the provisions of the Convention concluded this day.

It is, however, understood that disputes which may arise upon the application of this clause shall be reserved for the decision of the respective Courts.

3. It is understood that the manufacture and sale of instruments serving to reproduce mechanically musical airs in which copyright subsists shall not be considered as constituting musical infringement.

4. The common agreement provided for in Article 14 of the Convention is concluded as follows :

The application of the Berne Convention and of the present Additional Act to works not fallen into the public domain in their country of origin at the time of the coming into force of those Acts,

---

[1] *Original reading of Closing Protocol,* § 1, *in the* 1886 *Convention :* '1. With reference to Article 4, it is agreed that those countries of the Union in which the character of artistic works is not refused to photographic works, bind themselves to admit them, from the coming into force of the Convention concluded this day, to the benefit of its provisions. They are, however, only bound to protect the author of the said works in so far as their law permits, saving the international arrangement at present existing or hereafter to be entered into.

' It is understood that an authorised photograph of a protected work of art enjoys legal protection, in all the countries of the Union, within the meaning of the Berne Convention, so long as the principal right of reproduction of this work itself lasts, and within the limits of private agreements between the parties entitled.'

aura lieu suivant les stipulations y relatives contenues dans les Conventions spéciales existantes ou à conclure à cet effet.

A défaut de semblables stipulations entre pays de l'Union, les pays respectifs régleront, chacun pour ce qui le concerne, par la législation intérieure, les modalités relatives à l'application du principe contenu dans l'article 14.

Les stipulations de l'article 14 de la Convention de Berne et du présent numéro du Protocole de clôture s'appliquent également au droit exclusif de traduction, tel qu'il est assuré par le présent Acte additionnel.

Les dispositions transitoires mentionnées ci-dessus sont applicables en cas de nouvelles accessions à l'Union.[1]

---

5. L'organisation du Bureau international prévu à l'article 16 de la Convention sera fixée par un règlement que le Gouvernement de la Confédération Suisse est chargé d'élaborer.

La langue officielle du Bureau international sera la langue française.

Le Bureau international centralisera les renseignements de toute nature relatifs à la protection des droits des auteurs sur leurs œuvres littéraires et artistiques. Il les coordonnera et les publiera. Il procédera aux études d'utilité commune intéressant l'Union et rédigera, à l'aide des documents qui seront mis à sa disposition par les diverses Administrations, une feuille périodique, en langue française, sur les questions concernant l'objet de l'Union. Les Gouvernements des pays de l'Union se réservent d'autoriser, d'un commun accord, le Bureau à publier une édition dans une ou plusieurs autres langues, pour le cas où l'expérience en aurait démontré le besoin.

---

[1] *Convention de 1886, Protocole de clôture, n° 4, ancien texte:* ' L'application de la Convention aux œuvres non tombées dans le domaine public au moment de sa mise en vigueur aura lieu suivant les stipulations y relatives contenues dans les conventions spéciales existantes ou à conclure à cet effet.

' A défaut de semblables stipulations entre pays de l'Union, les pays respectifs régleront, chacun pour ce qui le concerne, par la législation intérieure, les modalités relatives à l'application du principe contenu à l'article 14.'

shall take effect according to the stipulations relative thereto contained in special Conventions existing or to be concluded for the purpose.

In default of such stipulations between countries of the Union, the respective countries shall regulate, each for itself, by domestic law, the manner in which the principle contained in Article 14 is to be applied.

The stipulations of Article 14 of the Berne Convention and of this paragraph of the Closing Protocol apply equally to the exclusive right of translation, as granted by the present Additional Act.

The above-mentioned temporary provisions are applicable in case of new accessions to the Union.[1]

---

5. The organisation of the International Office provided for by Article 16 of the Convention shall be settled by a code of regulations which the Government of the Swiss Confederation is appointed to draw up.

French shall be the official language of the International Office.

The International Office shall collect information of all kinds relating to the protection of the rights of authors over their literary and artistic works. It shall classify and publish such information. It shall turn its attention to matters of common utility concerning the Union, and shall edit, with the help of the documents placed at its disposal by the various Governments, a periodical paper, in the French language, on questions concerning the object of the Union. The Governments of the countries of the Union reserve to themselves the right to authorise the Office, by common consent, to publish an edition in one or more other languages, in the event of experience showing the need of so doing.

---

[1] *Original reading of Closing Protocol,* § 4, *in the* 1886 *Convention:* 'The application of the Convention to works not fallen into the public domain at the time of its coming into force shall take effect according to the stipulations relative thereto contained in special treaties existing or to be concluded for the purpose.

' In default of such stipulations between countries of the Union, the respective countries shall regulate, each for itself, by domestic law, the manner in which the principle contained in Article 14 is to be applied.'

Le Bureau international devra se tenir en tout temps à la disposition des membres de l'Union pour leur fournir, sur les questions relatives à la protection des œuvres littéraires et artistiques, les renseignements spéciaux dont ils pourraient avoir besoin.

L'Administration du pays où doit siéger une Conférence préparera, avec le concours du Bureau international, les travaux de cette Conférence.

Le Directeur du Bureau international assistera aux séances des Conférences et prendra part aux discussions sans voix délibérative. Il fera sur sa gestion un rapport annuel qui sera communiqué à tous les membres de l'Union.

Les dépenses du Bureau de l'Union internationale seront supportées en commun par les pays contractants. Jusqu'à nouvelle décision, elles ne pourront pas dépasser la somme de soixante mille francs par année. Cette somme pourra être augmentée au besoin par simple décision d'une des Conférences prévues à l'article 17.

Pour déterminer la part contributive de chacun des pays dans cette somme totale des frais, les pays contractants et ceux qui adhéreraient ultérieurement à l'Union seront divisés en six classes contribuant chacune dans la proportion d'un certain nombre d'unités, savoir:

1re classe	... 25 unités,	4re classe	... 10 unités,
2me ,,	... 20 ,,	5me ,,	... 5 ,,
3me ,,	... 15 ,,	6me ,,	... 3 ,,

Ces coefficients seront multipliés par le nombre des pays de chaque classe, et la somme des produits ainsi obtenus fournira le nombre d'unités par lequel la dépense totale doit être divisée. Le quotient donnera le montant de l'unité de dépense.

Chaque pays déclarera, au moment de son accession, dans laquelle des susdites classes il demande à être rangé.

L'Administration suisse préparera le budget du Bureau et en surveillera les dépenses, fera les avances nécessaires et établira le compte annuel qui sera communiqué à toutes les autres Administrations.

The International Office shall at all times hold itself at the disposal of the members of the Union for the purpose of supplying them with any special information which they may require, on questions relating to the protection of literary and artistic works.

The Government of the country in which a Conference is to take place shall prepare the *agenda* for this Conference, with the help of the International Office.

The Director of the International Office shall be present at the sessions of the Conferences and shall take part in the debates, without having the right of voting. He shall draw up an annual report of his administration, which shall be transmitted to all the members of the Union.

The expenses of the Office of the International Union shall be borne in common by the contracting countries. Until further arrangements are made, these shall not be allowed to exceed sixty thousand francs a year. This sum may be increased, if necessary, by the simple decision of one of the Conferences provided for by Article 17.

In order to determine the contributions of each country to this sum total of expenses, the contracting countries and those countries which may subsequently enter the Union shall be divided into six classes, each class contributing a share in the proportion of a certain number of units, as follows :

1st class	...	25 units,	4th class	...	10 units,
2nd ,,	...	20 ,,	5th ,,	...	5 ,,
3rd ,,	...	15 ,,	6th ,,	...	3 ,,

These co-efficients shall be multiplied by the number of countries belonging to each class, and the sum of the products thus obtained will give the number of units by which the total of the expense is to be divided. The quotient of this will give the amount of the unit of expense.

Each country shall declare, on joining, in which of the aforesaid classes it wishes to be enrolled.

The Swiss Government shall prepare the budget of the Office and supervise its expenditure ; it shall make all necessary advances and draw up the annual balance-sheet, which shall be communicated to all the other Governments.

6. La prochaine Conférence aura lieu à Paris, dans le délai de quatre à six ans à partir de l'entrée en vigueur de la Convention.

Le Gouvernement français en fixera la date dans ces limites, après avoir pris l'avis du Bureau international.

7. Il est convenu que, pour l'échange des ratifications prévu à l'article 21, chaque Partie contractante remettra un seul instrument, qui sera déposé, avec ceux des autres pays, aux archives du Gouvernement de la Confédération Suisse. Chaque Partie recevra en retour un exemplaire du procès-verbal d'échange des ratifications, signé par les Plénipotentiaires qui y auront pris part.

Le présent Protocole de clôture, qui sera ratifié en même temps que la Convention conclue à la date de ce jour, sera considéré comme faisant partie intégrante de cette Convention, et aura même force, valeur et durée.

En foi de quoi, les Plénipotentiaires respectifs l'ont revêtu de leur signature.

Fait à Berne, le neuvième jour du mois de septembre de l'an mil huit cent quatre-vingt-six.

(*Signatures.*)

Procès-verbal de signature.

Les Plénipotentiaires soussignés, réunis ce jour à l'effet de procéder à la signature de la Convention concernant la création d'une Union internationale pour la protection des œuvres littéraires et artistiques, ont échangé les Déclarations suivantes :

1. En ce qui concerne l'accession des colonies ou possessions étrangères prévue à l'article 19 de la Convention :

Les Plénipotentiaires de Sa Majesté Catholique le Roi d'Espagne réservent pour leur Gouvernement la faculté de faire connaître sa détermination au moment de l'échange des ratifications.[1]

---

[1] D'après le Protocole du 5 septembre 1887 constatant le dépôt des Actes de Ratification, S. E. M. le Ministre d'Espagne a déclaré que 'l'accession de l'Espagne à la Convention comporte celle de tous les territoires dépendant de la Couronne espagnole.'

6. The next Conference shall take place at Paris within a period of from four to six years from the date of the coming into force of the Convention.

Within these limits the French Government shall fix the date of this Conference, after having consulted the International Office.

7. It is agreed that, for the exchange of ratifications provided for by Article 21, each contracting Party shall hand in a single document, which shall be deposited, together with those of the other countries, in the archives of the Government of the Swiss Confederation. Each Party shall receive in return a copy of the official record of exchange of ratifications, signed by the Plenipotentiaries who have taken part therein.

The present Closing Protocol, which shall be ratified together with the Convention concluded this day, shall be considered as forming an integral part of this Convention, and shall have the same force, effect, and duration.

In witness whereof the respective Plenipotentiaries have hereunto set their hands.

Done at Berne, this ninth day of the month of September in the year one thousand eight hundred and eighty-six.

(*Signed.*)

Procès-Verbal of the Signing.

The undersigned Plenipotentiaries, assembled this day for the purpose of proceeding to the signing of the Convention concerning the creation of an International Union for the protection of literary and artistic works, have exchanged the following declarations:

1. With regard to the accession of colonies or foreign possessions provided for by Article 19 of the Convention:

The Plenipotentiaries of his Catholic Majesty the King of Spain reserve liberty to their Government to make known its determination at the time of the exchange of ratifications.[1]

---

[1] According to the Protocol of September 5th, 1887, evidencing the deposit of the Acts of Ratification, His Excellency the Spanish Minister declared that: ' the accession of Spain to the Convention carries with it that of all the territories dependent on the Spanish Crown.'

Le Plénipotentiaire de la République française déclare que l'accession de son pays emporte celle de toutes les colonies de la France.

Les Plénipotentiaires de Sa Majesté Britannique déclarent que l'accession de la Grande-Bretagne à la Convention pour la protection des œuvres littéraires et artistiques comprend le Royaume-Uni de la Grande-Bretagne et d'Irlande et toutes les colonies et possessions étrangères de Sa Majesté Britannique.

Ils réservent toutefois au Gouvernement de Sa Majesté Britannique la faculté d'en annoncer en tout temps la dénonciation séparément pour une ou plusieurs des colonies ou possessions suivantes, en la manière prévue par l'article 20 de la Convention, savoir : les Indes, le Dominion du Canada, Terre-Neuve, le Cap, Natal, la Nouvelle-Galles du Sud, Victoria, Queensland, la Tasmanie, l'Australie méridionale, l'Australie occidentale et la Nouvelle-Zélande.

2. En ce qui concerne la classification des pays de l'Union au point de vue de leur part contributive aux frais du Bureau international (chiffre 5 du Protocole de clôture) :

Les Plénipotentiaires déclarent que leurs pays respectifs[1] doivent être rangés dans les classes suivantes, savoir :

Allemagne	dans la	1re classe
Belgique	,,	3me ,,
Espagne	,,	2me ,,
France	,,	1re ,,
Grande-Bretagne ...	,,	1re ,,
Haïti	,,	5me ,,
Italie	,,	1re ,,
Suisse	,,	3me ,,
Tunisie...	,,	6me ,,

---

[1] Les pays, qui ont demandé depuis à faire partie de l'Union, ont exprimé le désir d'être placés respectivement dans les classes suivantes :

Le Danemark, dans la cinquième ; Le Japon, dans la deuxième ; le Luxembourg, dans la sixième ; le Monaco, dans la sixième ; la Norvège, dans la quatrième ; la Suède, dans la troisième.

The Plenipotentiary of the French Republic declares that the accession of his country includes that of all the French colonies.

The Plenipotentiaries of Her Britannic Majesty declare that the accession of Great Britain to the Convention for the protection of literary and artistic works comprises the United Kingdom of Great Britain and Ireland and all the colonies and foreign possessions of Her Britannic Majesty.

Nevertheless, they reserve to the Government of Her Britannic Majesty the liberty to make denunciation at any time separately, in the manner provided for by Article 20 of the Convention, for one or more of the following colonies or possessions, to wit:—India, the Dominion of Canada, Newfoundland, the Cape, Natal, New South Wales, Victoria, Queensland, Tasmania, South Australia, West Australia, and New Zealand.

2. With regard to the classification of the countries of the Union as to their respective contributions to the expenses of the International Office (§ 5 of the Closing Protocol) :

The Plenipotentiaries declare that their respective countries[1] shall be placed in the following classes, viz. :

Germany...	in the 1st class
Belgium	„ 3rd „
Spain	„ 2nd „
France	„ 1st „
Great Britain	„ 1st „
Haïti	„ 5th „
Italy	„ 1st „
Switzerland	„ 3rd „
Tunis	„ 6th „

---

[1] The countries which have subsequently entered the Union have declared their wish to be placed respectively in the following classes :

Denmark, in the fifth class ; Japan, in the second class ; Luxemburg, in the sixth class ; Monaco, in the sixth class ; Norway, in the fourth class ; and Sweden, in the third class.

Le Plénipotentiaire de la République de Libéria déclare que les pouvoirs qu'il a reçus de son Gouvernement l'autorisent à signer la Convention, mais qu'il n'a pas reçu d'instructions quant à la classe où ce pays entend se ranger au point de vue de sa part contributive aux frais du Bureau international. En conséquence, il réserve sur cette question la détermination de son Gouvernement, qui la fera connaître lors de l'échange des ratifications.

En foi de quoi les Plénipotentiaires respectifs ont signé le présent Procès-verbal.

Fait à Berne, le neuvième jour du mois de septembre de l'an mil huit cent quatre-vingt-six.

(Signatures.)

The Plenipotentiary of the Republic of Liberia declares that the powers which he has received from his Government authorise him to sign the Convention, but that he has not received instructions with regard to the class in which that country desires to be included respecting its contribution towards the expenses of the International Office. Hence on this point he reserves the decision of his Government, which will announce it at the time of the exchange of ratifications.

In witness whereof the respective Plenipotentiaries have hereunto set their hands.

Done at Berne, this ninth day of the month of September in the year one thousand eight hundred and eighty-six.

(Signed.)

Convention signed	9th September, 1886, at Berne.
Ratifications deposited	5th September, 1887, at Berne.
Coming into force of Convention	5th December, 1887.
Additional Act and Interpretative	
Declaration signed	4th May, 1896, at Paris.
Ratifications deposited	9th September, 1897, at Paris.
Coming into force of Additional	
Act	9th December, 1897.
Coming into force of Interpreta-	
tive Declaration	9th September, 1897.

List of Countries which are Members of the Union.

Belgium	
France (with Algeria and its colonies) ...	
Germany	
Great Britain (with its colonies and posses-	From the date of the
sions)	coming in force of
Haïti	the Convention.
Italy	
Spain (with its colonies)	
Switzerland	
Tunis	
Luxemburg	from 20th June, 1888.
Monaco	from 30th May, 1889.
Norway	from 13th April, 1896.
Japan	from 15th July, 1899.
Denmark (with the Faroë Islands)	from 1st July, 1903.
Sweden ... ...:	from 1st August, 1904.

The Additional Act and the Interpretative Declaration have been accepted and ratified by all these States except Great Britain, which has accepted only the Additional Act, and Norway and Sweden, which have accepted only the Interpretative Declaration. Acceptance of these Acts on the part of the Union States which have hitherto rejected them, or of States which shall hereafter enter the Union, should be made in the form prescribed by Art. 18 of the Convention.

THE MONTEVIDEO CONVENTION [1]

OF THE 11TH JANUARY, 1889.

ART. 1.

The signatory States agree to recognise and to protect the rights of literary and artistic property in conformity with the stipulations of the present treaty.

ART. 2.

The author of every literary or artistic work and his successors shall enjoy, in the signatory States, the rights accorded to him by the law of the State in which the first publication or production of this work shall have taken place.

ART. 3.

The author's right of property in a literary or artistic work includes the liberty to dispose of it, to publish it and to transfer it, to translate it or to authorise its translation, and to reproduce it in any form whatever.

ART. 4.

No State shall be bound to recognise the right of literary or artistic property for a period longer than that fixed for authors in the enjoyment of such a right under the domestic law.

This period may be limited to that accorded in the country of origin, if the latter period be less.

ART. 5.

The expression 'literary or artistic works' comprises books, pamphlets, and all other writings ; dramatic or dramatico-musical works, choregraphic works, and musical compositions, with or

---

[1] Translated from *Le Droit d'Auteur*, 1897, p. 3.

without words; designs, paintings, sculptures, engravings; photographic works, lithographs, geographical charts, plans, sketches and plastic works relating to geography, topography, architecture, or to the sciences in general; finally, every production whatsoever in the literary or artistic domain which can be published by any mode of impression or reproduction whatever.

Art. 6.

The translators of works in which the right of property secured does not exist, or has ceased to exist, shall enjoy in respect of their translations the rights mentioned in Art. 3, but they cannot prevent the publication of other translations of the same work.

Art. 7.

Newspaper articles may be reproduced, provided that the publication from whence they are taken is mentioned; articles treating of art and science of which the reproduction has been expressly prohibited by their authors are excepted.

Art. 8.

Speeches made or read in deliberative assemblies, before courts of justice, or in public meetings may be published in the periodicals without any authorisation being necessary.

Art. 9.

Unauthorised indirect appropriations of a literary or artistic work, which are known by various names such as *adaptations*, *arrangements*, etc., are considered as unlawful reproductions, when they are merely reproductions of such a work, without presenting the character of an original work.

Art. 10.

The rights of authorship shall be recognised, in the absence of proof to the contrary, in favour of the persons whose names or pseudonyms are indicated in the literary or artistic work.

If an author wishes to preserve his anonymity, the publisher must state that the rights of authorship belong to him.

Art. 11.

The liabilities incurred by those who infringe a copyright shall be established before the courts, and regulated by the laws, of the country where the offence has been committed.

Art. 12.

The recognition of the right of property in literary or artistic works does not deprive the signatory States of their right to prohibit, in conformity with their laws, the reproduction, publication, circulation, representation, and exhibition of works which are considered as contrary to morality or to decency.

Art. 13.

It is not indispensable for the putting into force of this treaty that its ratification on the part of the signatory States shall be simultaneous. Every State that approves it shall notify the fact to the Governments of the Argentine Republic and the Republic of Uruguay, in order that they may bring it to the notice of the other contracting nations.

This procedure shall serve as an exchange of ratifications.

Art. 14.

When the exchange has been carried out in the form indicated by the preceding article, the present treaty shall remain in force for an indefinite time.

Art. 15.

If any of the signatory nations thinks fit to free itself from the treaty, or to introduce any modification into it, such nation shall give notice of its intention to the others, but it shall only be freed two years after the denunciation, during which time efforts shall be made to arrive at a fresh agreement.

Art. 16.

Art. 13 may be extended to States not having taken part in the present Congress, which wish to adhere to the present treaty.

ADDITIONAL PROTOCOL (OF THE 12TH FEBRUARY, 1889).

ART. 1.

The laws of the contracting States shall be applied, if occasion should arise, whether the persons interested in the litigation in question are subjects or aliens.

ART. 2.

They shall be applied by the judge of the case as a matter of duty, though it will rest with the parties to uphold and to prove the existence and the provisions of the law invoked.

ART. 3.

All the remedies conferred by the rules of procedure in the place where judgment is given with reference to cases decided in conformity with its domestic law, shall be similarly conceded with reference to cases which are to be decided by the application of the laws of any of the other States.

ART. 4.

The laws of the other States shall never be applied against the political institutions or the rules of public order and decency of the place where the action is brought.

ART. 5.

In conformity with the stipulations of this Protocol, the Governments agree to send to each other two authentic copies of the laws now in force and of those which may be afterwards enacted in their country.

ART. 6.

At the time of the ratification of the treaties which have been concluded, the Governments of the signatory States shall declare whether they accept the accession of nations which have not been invited to take part in the Congress, in the same form as the accession of nations which have given their approval to the principle of the Congress but have not participated in its deliberations.

ART. 7.

The provisions of the preceding articles shall be considered as forming an integral part of the treaties to which they relate and shall have the same duration as those treaties.

CONVENTION BETWEEN GREAT BRITAIN AND AUSTRIA-HUNGARY FOR THE ESTABLISHMENT OF INTERNATIONAL COPYRIGHT.

Signed at Vienna, April 24, 1893.

[*Ratifications exchanged at Vienna, April* 14, 1894.]

ART. 1.

Authors of literary or artistic works and their legal representatives, including publishers, shall enjoy reciprocally, in the dominions of the High Contracting Parties, the advantages which are, or may be, granted by law there for the protection of works of literature or art.

Consequently, authors of literary or artistic works which have been first published in the dominions of one of the High Contracting Parties, as well as their legal representatives, shall have in the dominions of the other High Contracting Party the same protection and the same legal remedy against all infringement of their rights as if the work had been first published in the country where the infringement may have taken place.

In the same manner, the authors of literary or artistic works, and their legal representatives, who are subjects of one of the High Contracting Parties, and who reside within its dominions, shall in the dominions of the other Contracting Party enjoy the same protection and the same legal remedies against all infringements of their rights as though they were subjects of or residents in the State in which the infringement may have taken place.

These advantages shall only be reciprocally guaranteed to authors and their legal representatives when the work in question is also protected by the laws of the State where the work was first published, and the duration of protection in the other country shall not

exceed that which is granted to authors and their legal representatives in the country where the work was first published.

ART. 2.

The right of translation forming part of the copyright, the protection of the right of translation is assured under the conditions
laid down by this Convention. If ten years after the expiry of the
year in which a work to be protected in Her Majesty's dominions
on the basis of this Convention has appeared, no translation in
English has been published, the right of translating the work into
English shall no longer within those dominions exclusively belong
to the author.

In the case of a book published in numbers, the aforesaid period
of ten years shall commence at the end of the year in which each
number is published.

ART. 3.

Authorized translations are protected as original works. They
consequently enjoy the full protection granted by this Convention
against the unauthorized reproduction of original works.

It is understood that in the case of a work for which the translating right has fallen into the public domain, the translator cannot
oppose the translation of the same work by other writers.

ART. 4.

The expression "literary or artistic works" comprehends books,
pamphlets, and all other writings; dramatic or dramatico-musical
works, musical compositions, with or without words; works of
design, painting, sculpture, and engraving, lithographs, illustrations, geographical charts, plans, sketches, and plastic works
relating to geography, topography, architecture, or science, in
general; in fact, every production whatsoever in the literary,
scientific, or artistic domain which can be published by any mode
of impression or reproduction.

ART. 5.

In the British Empire, and in the kingdoms and States represented in the Austrian Reichsrath, the enjoyment of the rights

secured by the present Convention is subject only to the accomplishment of the conditions and formalities prescribed by the law of that State in which the work is first published; and no further formalities or conditions shall be required in the other country.

Consequently, it shall not be necessary that a work which has obtained legal protection in one country should be registered, or copies thereof deposited in the other country, in order that the remedies against infringement may be obtained which are granted in the other country to works first published there.

In the dominions of the Hungarian Crown the enjoyment of these rights is subject, however, to the accomplishment of the conditions and formalities prescribed by the Laws and Regulations both of Great Britain and of Hungary.

Art. 6.

In order that the authors of works protected by the present Convention shall, in the absence of proof to the contrary, be considered as such, and be, consequently, admitted to institute proceedings in respect of the infringement of copyright before the Courts of the other State, it will suffice that their name be indicated on the work in the accustomed manner.

The Tribunals may, however, in cases of doubt, require the production of such further evidence as may be required by the Laws of the respective countries.

For anonymous or pseudonymous works the publisher whose name is indicated on the work is entitled to protect the rights belonging to the author. He is, without other proof, reputed the legal representative of the anonymous or pseudonymous author, until the latter or his legal representative has declared and proved his rights.

Art. 7.

The provisions of the present Convention cannot in any way derogate from the right of each of the High Contracting Parties to control, or to prohibit by measures of domestic legislation or police, the circulation, representation, exhibition, or sale of any work or production.

Z Z

Each of the High Contracting Parties reserves also its right to prohibit the importation into its own territory of works which, according to its internal Laws, or to the stipulations of Treaties with other States, are or may be declared to be illicit reproductions.

Art. 8.

The provisions of the present Convention shall be applied to literature or artistic works produced prior to the date of its coming into effect, subject, however, to the limitations prescribed by the following Regulations:—

(*a*.) In the Austro-Hungarian Monarchy—

Copies completed before the coming into force of the present Convention, the production of which has been hitherto allowed, can also be circulated in future.

In the same manner, appliances for the reproduction of works, such as stereotypes, wood-blocks, and engraved plates of every description, such as lithographers' stones, if their production has not hitherto been prohibited may continue to be used during a period of four years from the coming into force of the present Convention.

The distribution of such copies, and the use of the said appliances, is, however, only permitted if an inventory of the said copies and appliances is taken by the Government in question, in consequence of an application of the interested party, within three months from the coming into force of the present Convention, and if these copies and appliances are marked with a special stamp.

Dramatic and dramatico-musical works or musical compositions legally performed before the coming into force of the present Convention, can also be performed in the future.

(*b*.) In the United Kingdom of Great Britain and Ireland—

The author and publisher of any literary or artistic work first produced before the date at which this Convention comes into effect shall be entitled to all legal remedies against infringement; provided that where any person has, before the date of the publication of the Order in Council putting this Convention into effect, lawfully produced any work in the United Kingdom, any rights or interests arising from or in connection with such production, which are subsisting and valuable at the said date, shall not be diminished or prejudiced.

Art. 9.

The provisions of the present Convention shall apply to all the Colonies and foreign possessions of Her Britannic Majesty, excepting to those hereinafter named, that is to say, except to—

India.	Victoria.
The Dominion of Canada.	Queensland.
Newfoundland.	Tasmania.
The Cape.	South Australia.
Natal.	Western Australia.
New South Wales.	New Zealand.

Provided always that the provisions of the present Convention shall apply to any of the above-named Colonies or foreign possessions on whose behalf notice to that effect shall have been given by Her Britannic Majesty's Representative at the Court of His Imperial and Royal Apostolic Majesty within two years from the date of the exchange of ratifications of the present Convention.

Art. 10.

The present Convention shall remain in force for ten years from the day on which the ratifications are exchanged; and in case neither of the two High Contracting Parties shall have given notice twelve months before the expiration of the said period of ten years of their intention of terminating the present Convention, it shall remain in force until the expiration of one year from the day on which either of the High Contracting Parties shall have given such notice.

Her Britannic Majesty's Government shall also have the right to denounce the Convention in the same manner, on behalf of any of the Colonies or foreign possessions mentioned in Article 9, separately.

Art. 11.

The present Convention shall be ratified, and the ratifications shall be exchanged at Vienna as soon as possible. It shall come into effect ten days after its publication in conformity with the forms prescribed by the Laws of the High Contracting Parties respectively.

In witness whereof, the respective Plenipotentiaries have signed this Convention, and have hereunto affixed their seals.

Done at Vienna, the 24th day of April, in the year of our Lord one thousand eight hundred and ninety-three.

(Signed)

LIST OF BRITISH COLONIES AND POSSESSIONS WHICH HAVE ACCEDED TO THE ABOVE CONVENTION UNDER ARTICLE 9.

NEWFOUNDLAND	September 29, 1894.
INDIA	October 5, 1894.
VICTORIA	October 5, 1894.
QUEENSLAND	October 5, 1894.
NEW ZEALAND	October 26, 1894.
WESTERN AUSTRALIA	November 14, 1894.
NATAL	November 14, 1894.
SOUTH AUSTRALIA	December 10, 1894.

THE FOLLOWING BRITISH COLONIES HAVE NOT ACCEDED TO THE CONVENTION.

THE DOMINION OF CANADA.
THE CAPE.
NEW SOUTH WALES.
TASMANIA.

ENGLISH STATUTES OF IMPORTANCE IN INTERNATIONAL COPYRIGHT.

THE COPYRIGHT ACT, 1842.[1]

5 AND 6 VICT. CAP. XLV.

An Act to amend the Law of Copyright.

[*1st July* 1842.]

*W*HEREAS *it is expedient to amend the Law relating to Copyright, and to afford greater Encouragement to the Production of literary Works of lasting Benefit to the World*[2]*:*

Be it enacted by the Queen's most Excellent Majesty, by and with the Advice and Consent of the Lords Spiritual and Temporal, and Commons, in this present Parliament assembled, and by the Authority of the same, That from the passing of this Act an Act passed in the Eighth Year of the Reign of Her Majesty Queen Anne, intituled 'An Act for the Encouragement of Learning, by vesting the Copies of Printed Books in the Authors or Purchasers of such Copies during the Times therein mentioned'; and also an Act passed in the Forty-first Year of the Reign of His Majesty King George the Third, intituled 'An Act for the further Encouragement of Learning in the United Kingdom of Great Britain and Ireland, by securing the Copies and Copyright of Printed Books to the Authors of such Books, or their Assigns, for the Time therein mentioned'; and also an Act passed in the Fifty-fourth Year of the Reign of His Majesty King George the Third, intituled 'An Act to amend the several Acts for the Encouragement of Learning, by securing the Copies and Copyright of Printed Books to the Authors of such Books or their Assigns,' be and the same are hereby repealed, except so far as the Continuance of either of them may be necessary for carrying on or giving effect to any Proceedings at Law or in Equity pending at the Time of passing this Act, or for enforcing any Cause of Action or Suit, or any Right or Contract, then subsisting.[3]

Marginal notes: Repeal of former Acts; 8 Anne, c. 19. 41 G. 3 c. 107. 54 G. 3 c. 156.

---

[1] Short Titles Act, 1896.
[2] Repealed by Statute Law Revision Act, 1890 (2).
[3] Repealed by Statute Law Revision Act, 1874 (2).

II. *And be it enacted, That*[1] in the Construction of this Act the Interpretation of Act. Word 'Book' shall be construed to mean and include every Volume, Part or Division of a Volume, Pamphlet, Sheet of Letter-press, Sheet of Music, Map, Chart, or Plan separately published; *that*[1] the Words 'Dramatic Piece' shall be construed to mean and include every Tragedy, Comedy, Play, Opera, Farce, or other scenic, musical, or dramatic Entertainment; *that*[1] the Word 'Copyright' shall be construed to mean the sole and exclusive Liberty of printing or otherwise multiplying Copies of any Subject to which the said Word is herein applied; *that*[1] the Words 'personal Representative' shall be construed to mean and include every Executor, Administrator, and next of Kin entitled to Administration; *that*[1] the Word 'Assigns' shall be construed to mean and include every Person in whom the Interest of an Author in Copyright shall be vested, whether derived from such Author before or after the Publication of any Book, and whether acquired by Sale, Gift, Bequest, or by Operation of Law, or otherwise; *that*[1] the Words '*British* Dominions' shall be construed to mean and include all Parts of the United Kingdom of *Great Britain* and *Ireland*, the Islands of *Jersey* and *Guernsey*, all Parts of the *East* and *West Indies*, and all the Colonies, Settlements, and Possessions of the Crown which now are or hereafter may be acquired; and *that*[1] whenever in this Act, in describing any Person, Matter, or Thing, the Word importing the Singular Number or the Masculine Gender only is used, the same shall be understood to include and to be applied to several Persons as well as one Person, and Females as well as Males, and several Matters or Things as well as one Matter or Thing, respectively, unless there shall be something in the Subject or Context repugnant to such Construction.

III. *And be it enacted, That*[1] the Copyright in every Book which Endurance of Term of Copyright in any Book hereafter to be published in the Lifetime of the Author; shall after the passing of this Act be published in the Lifetime of its Author shall endure for the Natural Life of such Author, and for the further Term of Seven Years, commencing at the Time of his Death, and shall be the Property of such Author and his Assigns : Provided always, that if the said Term of Seven Years shall expire before the End of Forty-two Years from the first

---

[1] Repealed by Statute Law Revision Act, 1888 (2).

Publication of such Book, the Copyright shall in that Case endure for such Period of Forty-two Years; and *that*[1] the Copyright in every Book which shall be published after the Death of its Author shall endure for the Term of Forty-two Years from the first Publication thereof, and shall be the Property of the Proprietor of the Author's Manuscript from which such Book shall be first published, and his Assigns.

if published after the Author's Death.

In Cases of subsisting Copyright, the Term to be extended, except when it shall belong to an Assignee for other Consideration than natural Love and Affection, in which Case it shall cease at the Expiration of the present Term, unless its Extension be agreed to between the Proprietor and the Author.

IV. *And whereas it is just to extend the Benefits of this Act to Authors of Books published before the passing thereof, and in which Copyright still subsists; be it enacted, That*[2] the Copyright which at the Time of passing this Act shall subsist in any Book theretofore published (except as herein-after mentioned) shall be extended and endure for the full Term provided by this Act in Cases of Books thereafter published, and shall be the Property of the Person who at the Time of passing of this Act shall be the Proprietor of such Copyright: Provided always, that in all Cases in which such Copyright shall belong in whole or in part to a Publisher or other Person who shall have acquired it for other Consideration than that of natural Love and Affection, such Copyright shall not be extended by this Act, but shall endure for the Term which shall subsist therein at the Time of passing of this Act, and no longer, unless the Author of such Book, if he shall be living, or the personal Representative of such Author, if he shall be dead, and the Proprietor of such Copyright, shall, before the Expiration of such Term, consent and agree to accept the Benefits of this Act in respect of such Book, and shall cause a Minute of such Consent in the Form in that Behalf given in the Schedule to this Act annexed to be entered in the Book of Registry herein-after directed to be kept, in which Case such Copyright shall endure for the full Term by this Act provided in Cases of Books to be published after the passing of this Act, and shall be the Property of such Person or Persons as in such Minute shall be expressed.

Judicial Committee of the Privy Council may license the

V. *And whereas it is expedient to provide against the Suppression of Books of Importance to the Public; be it enacted, That*[2] it shall be lawful for the Judicial Committee of Her Majesty's Privy

---

[1] Repealed by Statute Law Revision Act, 1888 (2).

[2] Repealed by Statute Law Revision Act, 1890 (2).

Council, on Complaint made to them that the Proprietor of the Republication of Books which the Pro-prietor re-fuses to re-publish after Death of the Author.

Copyright in any Book after the Death of its Author has refused to republish or to allow the Republication of the same, and that by reason of such Refusal such Book may be withheld from the Public, to grant a Licence to such Complainant to publish such Book, in such Manner and subject to such Conditions as they may think fit, and *that*[1] it shall be lawful for such Complainant to publish such Book according to such Licence.

VI. *And be it enacted, That*[2] a printed Copy of the whole of every Copies of Books pub-lished after the passing of this Act, and of all subsequent Editions, to be delivered within cer-tain Times at the British Museum. Book which shall be published after the passing of this Act, to-gether with all Maps, Prints, or other Engravings belonging thereto, finished and coloured in the same Manner as the best Copies of the same shall be published, and also of any second or subsequent Edition which shall be so published with any Additions or Altera-tions, whether the same shall be in Letter Press, or in the Maps, Prints, or other Engravings belonging thereto, and whether the first Edition to such Book shall have been published before or after the passing of this Act, and also of any second or subsequent Edition of every Book of which the first or some preceding Edition shall not have been delivered for the Use of the *British Museum*, bound, sewed, or stitched together, and upon the best Paper on which the same shall be printed, shall, within One Calendar Month after the Day on which any such Book shall first be sold, published, or offered for Sale within the Bills of Mortality, or within Three Calendar Months if the same shall first be sold, published, or offered for Sale in any other Part of the United Kingdom, or within Twelve Calendar Months after the same shall first be sold, published, or offered for Sale in any other Part of the *British* Dominions, be delivered, on Behalf of the Publisher thereof, at the *British Museum*.

VII. *And be it enacted, That*[2] every Copy of any Book which Mode of de-livering at the British Museum. under the Provisions of this Act ought to be delivered as aforesaid shall be delivered at the *British Museum* between the Hours of Ten in the Forenoon and Four in the Afternoon on any Day except *Sunday, Ash Wednesday, Good Friday,* and *Christmas Day,* to one of the Officers of the said Museum, or to some Person authorized by the Trustees of the said Museum to receive the same, and such

---

[1] Repealed by Statute Law Revision Act, 1890 (2).
[2] Repealed by Statute Law Revision Act, 1888 (2).

Officer or other Person receiving such Copy is hereby required to give a Receipt in Writing for the Same, and such Delivery shall to all Intents and Purposes be deemed to be good and sufficient Delivery under the Provisions of this Act.

A Copy of every Book to be delivered within a Month after Demand to the Officer of the Stationers Company, for the following Libraries; the Bodleian at Oxford, the Public Library at Cambridge, the Faculty of Advocates at Edinburgh, and that of Trinity College, Dublin.

VIII. *And be it enacted, That*[1] a Copy of the whole of every Book, and of any second or subsequent Edition of every Book containing Additions and Alterations, together with all Maps and Prints belonging thereto, which after the passing of this Act shall be published, shall, on Demand thereof in Writing, left at the Place of Abode of the Publisher thereof at any Time within Twelve Months next after the Publication thereof, under the Hand of the Officer of the Company of Stationers who shall from Time to Time be appointed by the said Company for the Purposes of this Act, or under the Hand of any other Person thereto authorized by the Persons or Bodies Politic and Corporate, Proprietors and Managers of the Libraries following, (*videlicet*), the *Bodleian* Library at *Oxford*, the Public Library at *Cambridge*, the Library of the Faculty of Advocates at *Edinburgh*, the Library of the College of the Holy and Undivided Trinity of Queen *Elizabeth* near *Dublin*, be delivered, upon the Paper on which the largest Number of Copies of such Book or Edition shall be printed for Sale, in the like Condition as the Copies prepared for Sale, by the Publisher thereof respectively, within One Month after Demand made thereof in Writing as aforesaid, to the said Officer of the said Company of Stationers for the Time being, which Copies the said Officer shall and he is hereby required to receive at the Hall of the said Company, for the Use of the Library for which such Demand shall be made within such Twelve Months as aforesaid; and the said Officer is hereby required to give a Receipt in Writing for the same, and within One Month after any such Book shall be so delivered to him as aforesaid to deliver the same for the Use of such Library.

Publishers may deliver the Copies to the Libraries, instead of at the Stationers Company.

IX. Provided also, *and be it enacted,*[1] That if any Publisher shall be desirous of delivering the Copy of such Book as shall be demanded on behalf of any of the said Libraries at such Library, it shall be lawful for him to deliver the same at such Library, free of Expense, to such Librarian or other Person authorized to receive the same (who is hereby required in such Case to receive and give a Receipt

---

[1] Repealed by Statute Law Revision Act, 1888 (2).

in Writing for the same), and such Delivery shall to all Intents and Purposes of this Act be held as equivalent to a Delivery to the said Officers of the Stationers Company.

X. *And be it enacted, That*[1] if any Publisher of any such Book, or of any second or subsequent Edition of any such Book, shall neglect to deliver the same, pursuant to this Act, he shall for every such Default forfeit, besides the Value of such Copy of such Book or Edition which he ought to have delivered, a Sum not exceeding Five Pounds, to be recovered by the Librarian or other Officer (properly authorized) of the Library for the Use whereof such Copy should have been delivered, in a summary Way, on Conviction before Two Justices of the Peace for the County or Place where the Publisher making default shall reside, or by Action of Debt or other Proceeding of the like Nature, at the Suit of such Librarian or other Officer, in any Court of Record in the United Kingdom, in which Action, if the Plaintiff shall obtain a Verdict, he shall recover his Costs reasonably incurred, to be taxed as between Attorney and Client.

Penalty for Default in delivering Copies for the use of the Libraries.

XI. *And be it enacted, That*[1] a Book of Registry, wherein may be registered, as herein-after enacted, the Proprietorship in the Copyright of Books, and Assignments thereof, and in Dramatic and Musical Pieces, whether in Manuscript or otherwise, and Licences affecting such Copyright, shall be kept at the Hall of the Stationers Company, by the Officer appointed by the said Company for the Purposes of this Act, and shall at all convenient Times be open to the Inspection of any Person, on Payment of One Shilling for every Entry which shall be searched for or inspected in the said Book ; and *that*[1] such Officer shall, whenever thereunto reasonably required, give a Copy of any Entry in such Book, certified under his Hand, and impressed with the Stamp of the said Company, to be provided by them for that Purpose, and which they are hereby required to provide, to any Person requiring the same, on payment to him of the Sum of Five Shillings ; and such Copies so certified and impressed shall be received in Evidence in all Courts, and in all summary Proceedings, and shall be *primâ facie* Proof of the Proprietorship or Assignment of Copyright or Licence as therein expressed, but subject to be rebutted by other Evidence, and in the Case of Dramatic or Musical

Book of Registry to be kept at Stationers Hall.

[1] Repealed by Statute Law Revision Act, 1888 (2).

Pieces shall be *primá facie* Proof of the Right of Representation or Performance, subject to be rebutted as aforesaid.

Making false Entry in the Book of Registry, a Misdemeanor.

XII. *And be it enacted, That*[1] if any Person shall wilfully make or cause to be made any false Entry in the Registry Book of the Stationers Company, or shall wilfully produce or cause to be tendered in Evidence any Paper falsely purporting to be a Copy of any Entry in the said Book, he shall be guilty of an indictable Misdemeanor, and shall be punished accordingly.

Entries of Copyright may be made in the Book of Registry.

XIII. *And be it enacted, That after the passing of this Act*[1] it shall be lawful for the Proprietor of Copyright in any Book heretofore published, or in any Book hereafter to be published, to make Entry in the Registry Book of the Stationers Company of the Title of such Book, the Time of the first Publication thereof, the Name and Place of Abode of the Publisher thereof, and the Name and Place of Abode of the Proprietor of the Copyright of the said Book or of any Portion of such Copyright in the Form in that Behalf given in the Schedule to this Act annexed, upon Payment of the Sum of Five Shillings to the Officer of the said Company; and *that*[1] it shall be lawful for every such Registered Proprietor to assign his Interest, or any Portion of his Interest therein, by making Entry in the said Book of Registry of such Assignment, and of the Name and Place of Abode of the Assignee thereof, in the Form given in that Behalf in the said Schedule, on Payment of the like Sum; and such Assignment so entered shall be effectual in Law to all Intents and Purposes whatsoever, without being subject to any Stamp or Duty, and shall be of the same Force and Effect as if such Assignment had been made by Deed.

Persons aggrieved by any Entry in the Book of Registry may apply to a Court of Law in Term, or Judge in Vacation, who may order such Entry to be varied or expunged.

XIV. *And be it enacted, That*[1] if any Person shall deem himself aggrieved by any Entry made under colour of this Act in the said Book of Registry, it shall be lawful for such Person to apply by Motion to the Court of Queen's Bench, *Court of Common Pleas, or Court of Exchequer, in Term Time, or to apply by Summons to any Judge of either of such Courts in Vacation,*[2] for an Order that such Entry may be expunged or varied; and *that*[1] upon any such Application *by Motion or Summons to either of the said Courts, or to a Judge as*

---

[1] Repealed by Statute Law Revision Act, 1888 (2).

[2] Repealed by Statute Law Revision Act, 1893.

aforesaid, such Court *or Judge*[1] shall make such Order for expunging, varying, or confirming such Entry, either with or without Costs, as to such Court *or Judge*[1] shall seem just; and the Officer appointed by the Stationers Company for the Purposes of this Act, shall, on the Production to him of any such Order for expunging or varying any such Entry, expunge or vary the same according to the Requisitions of such Order.

XV. *And be it enacted, That*[2] if any Person shall, in any Part of the *British* Dominions, *after the passing of this Act*,[1] print or cause to be printed, either for Sale or Exportation, any Book in which there shall be subsisting Copyright, without the Consent in Writing of the Proprietor thereof, or shall import for Sale or Hire any such Book so having been unlawfully printed from Parts beyond the Sea, or knowing such Book to have been so unlawfully printed or imported, shall sell, publish, or expose to Sale or Hire, or cause to be sold, published, or exposed to Sale or Hire, or shall have in his Possession, for Sale or Hire, any such Book so unlawfully printed or imported, without such Consent as aforesaid, such Offender shall be liable to a special Action on the Case at the Suit of the Proprietor of such Copyright, to be brought in any Court of Record in that Part of the *British* Dominions in which the Offence shall be committed: Provided always, that in *Scotland* such Offender shall be liable to an Action in the Court of Session in *Scotland*, which shall and may be brought and prosecuted in the same Manner in which any other Action of Damages to the like Amount may be brought and prosecuted there. *(margin: Remedy for the Piracy of Books by Action on the Case.)*

XVI. *And be it enacted, That after the passing of this Act*[2] in any Action brought within the *British* Dominions against any Person for printing any such Book for Sale, Hire, or Exportation, or for importing, selling, publishing, or exposing to Sale or Hire, or causing to be imported, sold, published, or exposed to Sale or Hire, any such Book, the Defendant, on pleading thereto, shall give to the Plaintiff a Notice in Writing of any Objections on which he means to rely on the Trial of such Action; and if the Nature of his Defence be, that the Plaintiff in such Action was not the Author or first Publisher of the Book in which he shall by such *(margin: In Actions for Piracy the Defendant to give Notice of the Objections to the Plaintiff's Title on which he means to rely.)*

---

[1] Repealed by Statute Law Revision Act, 1893.
[2] Repealed by Statute Law Revision Act, 1888 (2).

Action claim Copyright, or is not the Proprietor of the Copyright therein, or that some other Person than the Plaintiff was the Author or first Publisher of such Book, or is the Proprietor of the Copyright therein, then the Defendant shall specify in such Notice the Name of the Person who he alleges to have been the Author or first Publisher of such Book, or the Proprietor of the Copyright therein, together with the Title of such Book, and the Time when and the Place where such Book was first published, otherwise the Defendant in such Action shall not at the Trial or Hearing of such Action be allowed to give any Evidence that the Plaintiff in such Action was not the Author or first Publisher of the Book in which he claims such Copyright as aforesaid, or that he was not the Proprietor of the Copyright therein; and at such Trial or Hearing no other Objection shall be allowed to be made on behalf of such Defendant than the Objections stated in such Notice, or that any other Person was the Author or first Publisher of such Book, or the Proprietor of the Copyright therein, than the Person specified in such Notice, or give in Evidence in support of his Defence any other Book than one substantially corresponding in Title, Time, and Place of Publication with the Title, Time, and Place specified in such Notice.

No Person except the Proprietor, &c. shall import into the British Dominions for Sale or Hire any Book first composed, &c. within the United Kingdom, and reprinted elsewhere under Penalty of Forfeiture thereof, and also of 10l. and Double the Value.

XVII. *And be it enacted, That after the passing of this Act*[1] it shall not be lawful for any Person, not being the Proprietor of the Copyright, or some Person authorized by him, to import into any Part of the United Kingdom, or into any other Part of the *British* Dominions, for Sale or Hire, any printed Book first composed or written or printed and published in any Part of the said United Kingdom, wherein there shall be Copyright, and reprinted in any Country or Place whatsoever out of the *British* Dominions; and if any Person, not being such Proprietor or Person authorized as aforesaid, shall import or bring, or cause to be imported or brought, for Sale or Hire, any such printed Book, into any Part of the *British* Dominions, contrary to the true Intent and Meaning of this Act, or shall knowingly sell, publish, or expose to Sale or let to Hire, or have in his Possession for Sale or Hire, any such Book, then every such Book shall be forfeited, and shall be seized by any Officer of Customs or Excise, and the same shall be

Books may be seized by Officers of

---

[1] Repealed by Statute Law Revision Act, 1888 (2).

destroyed by such Officer; and every Person so offending, being Customs or Excise. duly convicted thereof before Two Justices of the Peace for the County or Place in which such Book shall be found, shall also for every such Offence forfeit the Sum of Ten Pounds, and Double the Value of every Copy of such Book which he shall so import or cause to be imported into any Part of the *British* Dominions, or shall knowingly sell, publish, or expose to Sale or let to Hire, or shall cause to be sold, published, or exposed to Sale or let to Hire, or shall have in his Possession for Sale or Hire, contrary to the true Intent and Meaning of this Act, Five Pounds to the Use of such Officer of Customs or Excise, and the Remainder of the Penalty to the Use of the Proprietor of the Copyright in such Book.

XVIII. *And be it enacted, That*[1] when any Publisher or other As to the Copyright in Person shall, before or at the Time of the passing of this Act, have Encyclo- projected, conducted, and carried on, or shall hereafter project, pædias, Periodicals, conduct, and carry on, or be the Proprietor of any Encyclopædia, and Works published Review, Magazine, Periodical Work, or Work published in a Series in a Series, Reviews, or of Books or Parts, or any Book whatsoever, and shall have employed Magazines. or shall employ any Persons to compose the same, or any Volumes, Parts, Essays, Articles, or Portions thereof, for Publication in or as Part of the same, and such Work, Volumes, Parts, Essays, Articles, or Portions shall have been or shall hereafter be composed under such Employment, on the Terms that the Copyright therein shall belong to such Proprietor, Projector, Publisher, or Conductor, and paid for by such Proprietor, Projector, Publisher, or Conductor, the Copyright in every such Encyclopædia, Review, Magazine, Periodical Work, and Work published in a Series of Books or Parts, and in every Volume, Part, Essay, Article, and Portion so composed, and paid for, shall be the Property of such Proprietor, Projector, Publisher, or other Conductor, who shall enjoy the same Rights as if he were the actual Author thereof, and shall have such Term of Copyright therein as is given to the Authors of Books by this Act; except only that in the case of Essays, Articles, or Portions forming Part of and first published in Reviews, Magazines, or other Periodical Works of a like Nature, after the Term of Twenty-eight Years from the first Publication thereof respectively the Right of publishing the same in a separate Form shall revert to the Author for the Remainder of the Term given by this Act: Provided always, that during the

---

[1] Repealed by Statute Law Revision Act, 1888 (2).

Term of Twenty-eight Years the said Proprietor, Projector, Publisher, or Conductor shall not publish any such Essay, Article, or Portion separately or singly without the Consent previously obtained of the Author thereof, or his Assigns: Provided also, that nothing herein contained shall alter or affect the Right of any Person who shall have been or who shall be so employed as aforesaid to publish any such his Composition in a separate Form, who by any Contract, express or implied, may have reserved or may hereafter reserve to himself such Right; but every Author reserving, retaining, or having such Right shall be entitled to the Copyright in such Composition when published in a separate Form, according to this Act, without prejudice to the Right of such Proprietor, Projector, Publisher, or Conductor as aforesaid.

Proviso for Authors who have reserved the Right of publishing their Articles in a separate Form.

XIX. *And be it enacted, That*[1] the Proprietor of the Copyright in any Encyclopædia, Review, Magazine, Periodical Work, or other Work published in a Series of Books or Parts, shall be entitled to all the Benefits of the Registration at Stationers Hall under this Act, on entering in the said Book of Registry the Title of such Encyclopædia, Review, Periodical Work, or other Work published in a Series of Books or Parts, the Time of the first Publication of the First Volume, Number, or Part thereof, or of the first Number or Volume first published after the passing of this Act in any such work which shall have been published heretofore, and the Name and Place of Abode of the Proprietor thereof, and of the Publisher thereof, when such Publisher shall not also be the Proprietor thereof.

Proprietors of Encyclopædias, Periodicals, and Works published in a Series may enter at once at Stationers Hall, and thereon have the Benefit of the Registration of the whole.

XX. *And whereas an Act was passed in the Third Year of the Reign of His late Majesty, to amend the Law relating to Dramatic Literary Property, and it is expedient to extend the Term of the sole Liberty, of representing Dramatic Pieces given by that Act to the full Time by this Act provided for the Continuance of Copyright: And whereas it is expedient to extend to Musical Compositions the Benefits of that Act and also of this Act; be it therefore enacted, That*[2] the Provisions of the said Act of His late Majesty, and of this Act, shall apply to Musical Compositions, and *that*[2] the sole Liberty of representing or performing, or causing or permitting to be represented or performed, any Dramatic Piece or Musical Composition,

The Provisions of 3 & 4 W. 4. c. 15 extended to Musical Compositions, and the Term of Copyright, as provided by this Act, applied to the Liberty of representing Dramatic Pieces and Musical Compositions.

---

[1] Repealed by Statute Law Revision Act, 1888 (2).

[2] Repealed by Statute Law Revision Act, 1890 (2).

shall endure and be the Property of the Author thereof, and his Assigns, for the Term in this Act provided for the Duration of Copyright in Books ; and the Provisions herein-before enacted in respect of the Property of such Copyright, and of registering the same, shall apply to the Liberty of representing or performing any Dramatic Piece or Musical Composition, as if the same were herein expressly re-enacted and applied thereto, save and except that the first public Representation or Performance of any Dramatic Piece or Musical Composition shall be deemed equivalent, in the Construction of this Act, to the first Publication of any Book : Provided always, that in case of any Dramatic Piece or Musical Composition in Manuscript, it shall be sufficient for the Person having the sole Liberty of representing or performing, or causing to be represented or performed the same, to register only the Title thereof, the Name and Place of Abode of the Author or Composer thereof, the Name and Place of Abode of the Proprietor thereof, and the Time and Place of its first Representation or Performance.

XXI. *And be it enacted, That*[1] the Person who shall at any Time have the sole Liberty of representing such Dramatic Piece or Musical Composition shall have and enjoy the Remedies given and provided in the said Act of the Third and Fourth Years of the Reign of His late Majesty King *William* the Fourth, passed to amend the Laws relating to Dramatic Literary Property, during the whole of his Interest therein, as fully as if the same were re-enacted in this Act.

Proprietors of Right of Dramatic Representations shall have all the Remedies given by 3 & 4 W. 4. c. 15.

XXII. *And be it enacted, That*[1] no Assignment of the Copyright of any Book consisting of or containing a Dramatic Piece or Musical Composition shall be holden to convey to the Assignee the Right of representing or performing such Dramatic Piece or Musical Composition, unless an Entry in the said Registry Book shall be made of such Assignment, wherein shall be expressed the Intention of the Parties that such Right should pass by such Assignment.

Assignment of Copyright of a Dramatic Piece not to convey the Right of Representation.

XXIII. *And be it enacted, That*[1] all Copies of any Book wherein there shall be Copyright, and of which Entry shall have been made in the said Registry Book, and which shall have been unlawfully

Books pirated shall become the Property of

[1] Repealed by Statute Law Revision Act, 1888 (2).

A A A

the Proprietor of the Copyright, and may be recovered by Action. printed or imported without the Consent of the registered Proprietor of such Copyright, in Writing, under his Hand first obtained, shall be deemed to be the Property of the Proprietor of such Copyright, and who shall be registered as such, and such registered Proprietor shall, after Demand thereof in Writing, be entitled to sue for and recover the same, or Damages for the Detention thereof, in an Action of Detinue, from any Party who shall detain the same, or to sue for and recover Damages for the Conversion thereof in an Action of Trover.

No Proprietor of Copyright commencing after this Act shall sue or proceed for any Infringement before making Entry in the Book of Registry. Proviso for Dramatic Pieces.

XXIV. *And be it enacted, That* [1] no Proprietor of Copyright in any Book which shall he first published after the passing of this Act shall maintain any Action or Suit, at Law or in Equity, or any summary Proceeding, in respect of any Infringement of such Copyright, unless he shall, before commencing such Action, Suit, or Proceeding, have caused an Entry to be made, in the Book of Registry of the Stationers Company, of such Book, pursuant to this Act: Provided always, that the Omission to make such Entry shall not affect the Copyright in any Book, but only the Right to sue or proceed in respect of the Infringement thereof as aforesaid: Provided also, that nothing herein contained shall prejudice the Remedies which the Proprietor of the sole Liberty of representing any Dramatic Piece shall have by virtue of the Act passed in the Third Year of the Reign of His late Majesty King *William* the Fourth, to amend the Laws relating to Dramatic Literary Property, or of this Act, although no Entry shall be made in the Book of Registry aforesaid.

Copyright shall be Personal Property.

XXV. *And be it enacted, That* [1] all Copyright shall be deemed Personal Property, and shall be transmissible by Bequest, or, in case of Intestacy, shall be subject to the same Law of Distribution as other Personal Property, and in *Scotland* shall be deemed to be Personal and Moveable Estate.

General Issue.

XXVI. *And be it enacted, That* [1] if any Action or Suit shall be commenced or brought against any Person or Persons whomsoever for doing or causing to be done anything in pursuance of this Act, the Defendant or Defendants in such Action may plead the General Issue, and give the special Matter in Evidence ; and if upon such

[1] Repealed by Statute Law Revision Act, 1888 (2).

Action a Verdict shall be given for the Defendant, or the Plaintiff shall become nonsuited, or discontinue his Action, then the Defendant shall have and recover his full Costs, for which he shall have the same Remedy as a Defendant in any Case by Law hath; and *that*[1] all Actions, Suits, Bills, Indictments, or Informations, for any Offence that shall be committed against this Act shall be brought, sued, and commenced within Twelve Calendar Months next after such Offence committed, or else the same shall be void and of none effect; provided that such Limitation of Time shall not extend or be construed to extend to any Actions, Suits, or other Proceedings which under the Authority of this Act shall or may be brought, sued, or commenced for or in respect of any Copies of Books to be delivered for the Use of the *British Museum*, or of any One of the Four Libraries herein-before mentioned. *[margin: Limitation of Actions; not to extend to Actions, &c., in respect of the Delivery of Books.]*

XXVII. Provided always, *and be it enacted*,[1] That nothing in this Act contained shall affect or alter the Rights of the Two Universities of *Oxford* and *Cambridge*, the Colleges or Houses of Learning within the same, the Four Universities in *Scotland*, the College of the Holy and Undivided Trinity of Queen *Elizabeth* near *Dublin*, and the several Colleges of *Eton*, *Westminster*, and *Winchester*, in any Copyrights heretofore and now vested or hereafter to be vested in such Universities and Colleges respectively, anything to the contrary herein contained notwithstanding. *[margin: Saving the Rights of the Universities and the Colleges of Eton, Westminster, and Winchester.]*

XXVIII. Provided also, *and be it enacted, That*[1] nothing in this Act contained shall affect, alter, or vary any Right subsisting at the Time of passing of this Act, except as herein expressly enacted; and all Contracts, Agreements, and Obligations made and entered into before the passing of this Act, and all Remedies relating thereto, shall remain in full force, any thing herein contained to the contrary notwithstanding. *[margin: Saving all subsisting Rights, Contracts, and Engagements.]*

XXIX. *And be it enacted, That*[1] this Act shall extend to the United Kingdom of *Great Britain* and *Ireland*, and to every Part of the *British* Dominions. *[margin: Extent of the Act.]*

XXX. *And be it enacted, That*[1] this Act may be amended or repealed by any Act to be passed in the present Session of Parliament. *[margin: Act may be amended this Session.]*

[1] Repealed by Statute Law Revision Act, 1888 (2).

SCHEDULE TO WHICH THE PRECEDING ACT REFERS.

No. 1.

FORM of MINUTE of CONSENT to be entered at Stationers Hall.

We, the undersigned, *A.B.* of   the Author of a certain Book, intituled *Y.Z.* [*or* the personal Representative of the Author, *as the case may be*], and *C.D.* of   do hereby certify, That we have consented and agreed to accept the Benefits of the Act passed in the Fifth Year of the Reign of Her Majesty Queen Victoria, Cap.   , for the Extension of the Term of Copyright therein provided by the said Act, and hereby declare that such extended Term of Copyright therein is the Property of the said *A.B.* or *C.D.*

Dated this   Day of   18   .

Witness   (Signed)   *A.B.*
                                                              C.D.

To the Registering Officer appointed by the Stationers Company.

No. 2.

FORM of REQUIRING ENTRY of PROPRIETORSHIP.

I *A.B.* of   do hereby certify, That I am the Proprietor of the Copyright of a Book, intituled *Y.Z.*, and I hereby require you to make Entry in the Register Book of the Stationers Company of my Proprietorship of such Copyright, according to the Particulars underwritten.

Title of Book.	Name of Publisher and Place of Publication.	Name and Place of Abode of the Proprietor of the Copyright.	Date of First Publication.
Y.Z.		*A.B.*	

Dated this   Day of   18

Witness, *C.D.*   (Signed)   *A.B.*

No. 3.

ORIGINAL ENTRY of PROPRIETORSHIP of COPYRIGHT of a BOOK.

Time of making the Entry.	Title of Book.	Name of the Publisher and Place of Publication.	Name and Place of Abode of the Proprietor of the Copyright.	Date of First Publication.
	Y.Z.	A.B.	C.D.	

No. 4.

FORM of CONCURRENCE of the PARTY assigning in any BOOK previously registered.

I *A.B.* of   being the Assigner of the Copyright of the Book hereunder described, do hereby require you to make Entry of the Assignment of the Copyright therein.

Title of Book.	Assigner of the Copyright.	Assignee of Copyright.
Y.Z.	A.B.	C.D.

Dated this   day of   18   .

(Signed)   *A.B.*

No. 5.

FORM of ENTRY of ASSIGNMENT of COPYRIGHT in any BOOK previously registered.

Date of Entry.	Title of Book.	Assigner of the Copyright.	Assignee of Copyright.
	[*Set out the Title of the Book, and refer to the Page of the Registry Book in which the original Entry of the Copyright thereof is made.*]	A.B.	C.D.

THE INTERNATIONAL COPYRIGHT ACT, 1844.[1]

7 VICT. CAP. 12.

An Act to amend the Law relating to International Copyright.

[10th *May* 1844.]

*W*HEREAS *by an Act passed in the Session of Parliament held in the First and Second Years of the Reign of Her present* Majesty, *intituled ' An Act for securing to Authors in certain Cases the Benefit of international Copyright' (and which Act is herein-after, for the sake of Perspicuity, designated as 'the International Copyright Act'), Her Majesty was empowered by Order in Council to direct that the Authors of Books which should after a future Time, to be specified in such Order in Council, be published in any Foreign Country, to be specified in such Order in Council, and their Executors, Administrators, and Assigns, should have the sole Liberty of printing and reprinting such Books within the British Dominions for such Term as Her Majesty should by such Order in Council direct, not exceeding the Term which Authors, being British Subjects, were then, (that is to say) at the Time of passing the said Act, entitled to in respect of Books first published in the United Kingdom; and the said Act contains divers Enactments securing to Authors and their Representatives the Copyright in the Books to which any such Order in Council should extend: And whereas an Act was passed in the Session of Parliament held in the Fifth and Sixth Years of the Reign of Her present* sent Majesty, *intituled 'An Act to amend the Law of Copyright' (and which Act is herein-after, for the sake of Perspicuity, designated as 'the Copyright Amendment Act'), repealing various Acts therein mentioned relating to the Copyright of printed Books, and extending, defining, and securing to Authors and their Representatives the Copyright of Books: And whereas an Act was passed in the Session of Parliament held in the Third and Fourth Years of the Reign of His*

1 & 2 Vict. c. 59.

5 & 6 Vict. c. 45.

---

[1] Short Titles Act, 1896.

late Majesty King William the Fourth, intituled 'An Act to amend 3 & 4 W. 4. *the Laws relating to Dramatic Literary Property' (and which Act* c. 15. *is herein-after, for the sake of Perspicuity, designated as 'the Dramatic Literary Property Act'), whereby the sole Liberty of representing or causing to be represented any Dramatic Piece in any Place of Dramatic Entertainment in any Part of the British Dominions, which should be composed and not printed or published by the Author thereof or his Assignee, was secured to such Author or his Assignee; and by the said Act it was enacted, that the Author of any such Production which should thereafter be printed and published, or his Assignee, should have the like sole Liberty of Representation until the End of Twenty eight Years from the first Publication thereof: And whereas by the said Copyright Amendment Act the Provisions of the said Dramatic Literary Property Act and of the said Copyright Amendment Act were made applicable to Musical Compositions; and it was thereby also enacted, that the sole Liberty of representing or performing, or causing or permitting to be represented or performed, in any Part of the British Dominions, any Dramatic Piece or Musical Composition, should endure and be the Property of the Author thereof and his Assigns for the Term in the said Copyright Amendment Act provided for the Duration of the Copyright in Books, and that the Provisions therein enacted in respect of the Property of such Copyright should apply to the Liberty of representing or performing any Dramatic Piece or Musical Composition: And whereas under or by virtue of the Four several Acts next herein-after mentioned; (that is to say,) an Act passed in the Eighth Year of the Reign of His late Majesty King George the Second, intituled 'An Act for the Encourage-* 8 G. 2. c. 13. *ment of the Arts of designing, engraving, and etching historical and other Prints, by vesting the Properties thereof in the Inventors or Engravers during the Time therein mentioned'; an Act passed in the Seventh Year of His late Majesty King George the Third, intituled 'An Act to amend and render more effectual an Act made in the* 7 G. 3. c. 38. *Eighth Year of the Reign of King George the Second, for Encouragement of the Arts of designing, engraving, and etching historical and other Prints; and for vesting in and securing to Jane Hogarth, Widow, the Property in certain Prints'; an Act passed in the Seventeenth Year of the Reign of His late Majesty King George the Third, intituled 'An Act for more effectually securing the Property of* 17 G. 3. c. 57. *Prints to Inventors and Engravers, by enabling them to sue for and recover Penalties in certain Cases'; and an Act passed in the Session of Parliament held in the Sixth and Seventh Years of the Reign of*

His late Majesty King William the Fourth, intituled ' An Act to extend the Protection of Copyright in Prints and Engravings to Ireland'; (and which said Four several Acts are herein-after, for the sake of Perspicuity, designated as the Engraving Copyright Acts;) every Person who invents or designs, engraves, etches, or works in Mezzotinto or Chiaro-oscuro, or from his own Work, Design, or Invention causes or procures to be designed, engraved, etched, or worked in Mezzotinto or Chiaro-oscuro any historical Print or Prints, or any Print or Prints of any Portrait, Conversation, Landscape, or Architecture, Map, Chart, or Plan, or any other Print or Prints whatsoever, and every Person who engraves, etches, or works in Mezzotinto or Chiaro-oscuro, or causes to be engraved, etched, or worked, any Print taken from any Picture, Drawing, Model, or Sculpture, either ancient or modern, notwithstanding such Print shall not have been graven or drawn from the original Design of such Graver, Etcher, or Draftsman, is entitled to the Copyright of such Print for the Term of Twenty-eight Years from the first publishing thereof; and by the said several Engraving Copyright Acts it is provided that the Name of the Proprietor shall be truly engraved on each Plate, and printed on every such Print, and Remedies are provided for the Infringement of such Copyright: And whereas under and by virtue of an Act passed in the Thirty-eighth Year of the Reign of His late Majesty

King George the Third, intituled 'An Act for encouraging the Art of making new Models and Casts of Busts and other Things therein mentioned,' and of an Act passed in the Fifty-fourth Year of the

Reign of His late Majesty King George the Third, intituled 'An Act to amend and render more effectual an Act of His present Majesty, for encouraging the Art of making new Models and Casts of Busts and other Things therein mentioned, and for giving further Encouragement to such Arts,' (and which said Acts are, for the sake of Perspicuity, herein-after designated as the Sculpture Copyright Acts,) every Person who makes or causes to be made any new and original Sculpture, or Model or Copy or Cast of the Human Figure, any Bust or Part of the Human Figure clothed in Drapery or otherwise, any Animal or Part of any Animal combined with the Human Figure or otherwise, any Subject, being Matter of Invention in Sculpture, any Alto or Basso Relievo, representing any of the Matters aforesaid, or any Cast from Nature of the Human Figure or Part thereof, or of any Animal or Part thereof, or of any such Subject representing any of the Matters aforesaid, whether separate or combined, is entitled to the Copyright in such new and original Sculpture, Model, Copy, and Cast, for Fourteen Years from first putting forth and publishing the same, and for an additional Period of Fourteen Years in case the original Maker is living at the End of the first Period; and by the said Acts it is provided that the Name of the Proprietor, with the Date of the Publication thereof, is to be put on all such Sculptures, Models, Copies, and Casts, and Remedies are provided for the Infringement of such Copyright: And whereas the Powers vested in Her Majesty by the said International Copyright Act are insufficient to enable Her Majesty to confer upon Authors of Books first published in Foreign Countries Copyright of the like Duration, and with the like Remedies for the Infringement thereof, which are conferred and provided by the said Copyright Amendment Act with respect to Authors of Books first published in the British Dominions; and the said International Copyright Act does not empower Her Majesty to confer any exclusive Right of representing or performing Dramatic Pieces or Musical Compositions first published in Foreign Countries upon the Authors thereof, nor to extend the Privilege of Copyright to Prints and Sculpture first published abroad; and it is expedient to vest increased Powers in Her Majesty in this respect, and for that Purpose to repeal the said International Copyright Act, and to give such other Powers to Her Majesty, and to make such further Provisions, as are herein-after contained[1]: *Be it therefore enacted by the Queen's most Excellent Majesty, by and with the Advice and Consent of the Lords Spiritual and Temporal, and Commons, in this present Parliament assembled, and by the Authority of the same, That the said recited Act herein designated as the International Copyright Act shall be and the same is hereby repealed.*[2]

Repeal of International Copyright Act.

II. *And be it enacted, That*[1] it shall be lawful for Her Majesty, by any Order of Her Majesty in Council, to direct that, as respects all or any particular Class or Classes of the following Works, (namely,) Books, Prints, Articles of Sculpture, and other Works of Art, to be defined in such Order, which shall after a future Time, to be specified in such Order, be first published in any Foreign Country to be named in such Order, the Authors, Inventors,

Her Majesty, by Order in Council, may direct that Authors, &c. of Works first published in Foreign Countries shall have

[1] Repealed by Statute Law Revision Act, 1891.
[2] Repealed by Statute Law Revision Act, 1874 (2).

Copyright
therein
within Her
Majesty's
Dominions. Designers, Engravers, and Makers thereof respectively, their respective Executors, Administrators, and Assigns, shall have the Privilege of Copyright therein during such Period or respective Periods as shall be defined in such Order, not exceeding, however, as to any of the above-mentioned Works, the Term of Copyright which Authors, Inventors, Designers, Engravers, and Makers of the like Works respectively first published in the United Kingdom may be then entitled to under the herein-before recited Acts respectively, or under any Acts which may hereafter be passed in that Behalf.

If the Order
applies to
Books, the
Copyright
law as to
books first
published
in this
Country
shall apply
to the Books
to which
the Order
relates, with
certain
Exceptions. III. *And be it enacted, That*[1] in case any such Order shall apply to Books, all and singular the Enactments of the said Copyright Amendment Act, and of any other Act for the Time being in force with relation to the Copyright in Books first published in this Country, shall, from and after the Time so to be specified in that Behalf in such Order, and subject to such Limitation as to the Duration of the Copyright as shall be therein contained, apply to and be in force in respect of the Books to which such Order shall extend, and which shall have been registered as herein-after is provided, in such and the same Manner as if such Books were first published in the United Kingdom, save and except such of the said Enactments, or such Parts thereof, as shall be excepted in such Order, and save and except such of the said Enactments as relate to the Delivery of Copies of Books at the *British Museum*, and to or for the Use of the other Libraries mentioned in the said Copyright Amendment Act.

If the Order
applies to
Prints,
Sculptures,
&c., the
Copyright
Law as to
Prints or
Sculptures
first pub-
lished in
this
Country
shall apply
to the
Prints,
Sculptures,
&c. to
which such
Order re-
lates. IV. *And be it enacted, That*[1] in case any such Order shall apply to Prints, Articles of Sculpture, or to any such other Works of Art as aforesaid, all and singular the Enactments of the said Engraving Copyright Acts and the said Sculpture Copyright Acts, or of any other Act for the Time being in force with relation to the Copyright in Prints or Articles of Sculpture first published in this Country, and of any Act for the Time being in force with relation to the Copyright in any similar Works of Art first published in this Country, shall, from and after the Time so to be specified in that Behalf in such Order, and subject to such Limitation as to the Duration of the Copyright as shall be therein

[1] Repealed by Statute Law Revision Act, 1891.

contained respectively, apply to and be in force in respect of the Prints, Articles of Sculpture, and other Works of Art to which such Order shall extend, and which shall have been registered as herein-after is provided, in such and the same Manner as if such Articles and other Works of Art were first published in the United Kingdom, save and except such of the said Enactments or such Parts thereof as shall be excepted in such Order.

V. *And be it enacted, That*[1] it shall be lawful for Her Majesty, by any Order of Her Majesty in Council, to direct that the Authors of Dramatic Pieces and Musical Compositions which shall after a future Time, to be specified in such Order, be first publicly represented or performed in any Foreign Country to be named in such Order, shall have the sole Liberty of representing or performing in any Part of the *British* Dominions such Dramatic Pieces or Musical Compositions during such Period as shall be defined in such Order, not exceeding the Period during which Authors of Dramatic Pieces and Musical Compositions first publicly represented or performed in the United Kingdom may for the Time be entitled by Law to the sole Liberty of representing and performing the same; and from and after the Time so specified in any such last-mentioned Order the Enactments of the said Dramatic Literary Property Act and of the said Copyright Amendment Act, and of any other Act for the Time being in force with relation to the Liberty of publicly representing and performing Dramatic Pieces or Musical Compositions, shall, subject to such Limitation as to the Duration of the Right conferred by any such Order as shall be therein contained, apply to and be in force in respect of the Dramatic Pieces and Musical Compositions to which such Order shall extend, and which shall have been registered as herein-after is provided, in such and the same Manner as if such Dramatic Pieces and Musical Compositions had been first publicly represented and performed in the *British* Dominions, save and except such of the said Enactments or such Parts thereof as shall be excepted in such Order.

Her Majesty may, by Order in Council, direct that Authors and Composers of Dramatic Pieces and Musical Compositions first publicly represented and performed in Foreign Countries shall have similar Rights in the British Dominions.

VI. Provided always, *and be it enacted*,[1] That no Author of any Book, Dramatic Piece or Musical Composition, or his Executors, Administrators, or Assigns, and no Inventor, Designer, or

Particulars to be observed as to Registry

---

[1] Repealed by Statute Law Revision Act, 1891.

Engraver of any Print, or Maker of any Article of Sculpture, or other
Work of Art, his Executors, Admini.trators, or Assigns, shall be
entitled to the Benefit of this Act, or of any Order in Council to be
issued in pursuance thereof, unless, within a Time or Times to be
in that Behalf prescribed in each such Order in Council, such Book,
Dramatic Piece, Musical Composition, Print, Article of Sculpture,
or other Work of Art, shall have been so registered, and such Copy
thereof shall have been so delivered as herein-after is mentioned;
(that is to say,) as regards such Book, and also such Dramatic
Piece or Musical Composition, (in the event of the same having
been printed,) the Title to the Copy thereof, the Name and Place
of Abode of the Author or Composer thereof, the Name and Place
of Abode of the Proprietor of the Copyright thereof, the Time and
Place of the first Publication, Representation, or Performance
thereof, as the Case may be, in the Foreign Country named in the
Order in Council under which the Benefits of this Act shall be
claimed, shall be entered in the Register Book of the Company of
Stationers in *London*, and One printed Copy of the whole of such
Book, and of such Dramatic Piece or Musical Composition, in the
event of the same having been printed, and of every Volume
thereof, upon the best Paper upon which the largest Number or
Impression of the Book, Dramatic Piece, or Musical Composition
shall have been printed for Sale, together with all Maps and Prints
relating thereto, shall be delivered to the Officer of the Company
of Stationers at the Hall of the said Company; and as regards
Dramatic Pieces and Musical Compositions in Manuscript, the
Title to the same, the Name and Place of Abode of the Author or
Composer thereof, the Name and Place of Abode of the Proprietor
of the Right of representing or performing the same, and the Time
and Place of the first Representation or Performance thereof in the
Country named in the Order in Council under which the Benefit
of the Act shall be claimed, shall be entered in the said Register
Book of the said Company of Stationers in *London*; and as regards
Prints, the Title thereof, the Name and Place of Abode of the
Inventor, Designer, or Engraver thereof, the Name of the Proprietor of the Copyright therein, and the Time and Place of the
first Publication thereof in the Foreign Country named in the
Order in Council under which the Benefits of the Act shall be
claimed, shall be entered in the said Register Book of the said
Company of Stationers in *London*, and a Copy of such Print, upon

the best Paper upon which the largest Number or Impressions of the Print shall have been printed for Sale, shall be delivered to the Officer of the Company of Stationers at the Hall of the said Company; and as regards any such Article of Sculpture, or any such other Work of Art as aforesaid, a descriptive Title thereof, the Name and Place of Abode of the Maker thereof, the Name of the Proprietor of the Copyright therein, and the Time and Place of its first Publication in the Foreign Country named in the Order in Council under which the Benefit of this Act shall be claimed, shall be entered in the said Register Book of the said Company of Stationers in *London*; and the Officer of the said Company of Stationers receiving such Copies so to be delivered as aforesaid shall give a Receipt in Writing for the same, and such Delivery shall to all Intents and Purposes be a sufficient Delivery under the Provisions of this Act.

VII. Provided always, *and be it enacted*,[1] That if a Book be published anonymously it shall be sufficient to insert in the Entry thereof in such Register Book the Name and Place of Abode of the first Publisher thereof, instead of the Name and Place of Abode of the Author thereof, together with a Declaration that such Entry is made either on behalf of the Author or on behalf of such first Publisher, as the Case may require.

In case of Books published anonymously, the Name of the Publisher to be sufficient.

VIII. *And be it enacted, That*[1] the several Enactments in the said Copyright Amendment Act contained with relation to keeping the said Register Book, and the Inspection thereof, the Searches therein, and the Delivery of certified and stamped Copies thereof, the Reception of such Copies in Evidence, the making of false Entries in the said Book, and the Production in Evidence of Papers falsely purporting to be Copies of Entries in the said Book, the Applications to the Courts and Judges by Persons aggrieved by Entries in the said Book, and the expunging and varying such Entries, shall apply to the Books, Dramatic Pieces, and Musical Compositions, Prints, Articles of Sculpture, and other Works of Art, to which any Order in Council issued in pursuance of this Act shall extend, and to the Entries and Assignments of Copyright and Proprietorship therein, in such and the same Manner as if such Enactments were here expressly enacted in relation thereto,

The Provisions of the Copyright Amendment Act as regards Entries in the Register Book of the Company of Stationers, &c. to apply to Entries under this Act.

---

[1] Repealed by Statute Law Revision Act, 1891.

save and except that the Forms of Entry prescribed by the said Copyright Amendment Act may be varied to meet the Circumstances of the Case, and that the Sum to be demanded by the Officer of the said Company of Stationers for making any Entry required by this Act shall be One Shilling only.

As to expunging or varying Entry grounded in wrongful first Publication.

IX. *And be it enacted, That*[1] every Entry made in pursuance of this Act of a first Publication shall be *primâ facie* Proof of a rightful first Publication; but if there be a wrongful first Publication, and any Party have availed himself thereof to obtain an Entry of a spurious Work, no Order for expunging or varying such Entry shall be made unless it be proved to the Satisfaction of the Court or of the Judge taking cognizance of the Application for expunging or varying such Entry, first, with respect to a wrongful Publication in a Country to which the Author or first Publisher does not belong, and in regard to which there does not subsist with this Country any Treaty of International Copyright, that the Party making the Application was the Author or first Publisher, as the Case requires; second, with respect to a wrongful first Publication either in the Country where a rightful first Publication has taken place, or in regard to which there subsists with this Country a Treaty of International Copyright, that a Court of competent Jurisdiction in any such Country where such wrongful first Publication has taken place has given Judgment in favour of the Right of the Party claiming to be the Author or first Publisher.

Copies of Books wherein Copyright is subsisting under this Act printed in Foreign Countries other than those wherein the Book was first published prohibited to be imported.

X. *And be it enacted, That*[1] all Copies of Books wherein there shall be any subsisting Copyright under or by virtue of this Act, or of any Order in Council made in pursuance thereof, printed or reprinted in any Foreign Country except that in which such Books were first published, shall be and the same are hereby absolutely prohibited to be imported into any Part of the *British* Dominions, except by or with the Consent of the registered Proprietor of the Copyright thereof, or his Agent authorized in Writing, and if imported contrary to this Prohibition the same and the Importers thereof shall be subject to the Enactments in force relating to Goods prohibited to be imported by any Act relating to the Customs; and as respects any such Copies so prohibited to

[1] Repealed by Statute Law Revision Act, 1891.

be imported, and also as respects any Copies unlawfully printed in any Place whatsoever of any Books wherein there shall be any such subsisting Copyright as aforesaid, any Person who shall in any Part of the *British* Dominions import such prohibited or unlawfully printed Copies, or who, knowing such Copies to be so unlawfully imported or unlawfully printed, shall sell, publish, or expose to sale or hire, or shall cause to be sold, published, or exposed to sale or hire, or have in his Possession for sale or hire, any such Copies so unlawfully imported or unlawfully printed, such Offender shall be liable to a special Action on the Case at the Suit of the Proprietor of such Copyright, to be brought and prosecuted in the same Courts and in the same Manner, and with the like Restrictions upon the Proceedings of the Defendant, as are respectively prescribed in the said Copyright Amendment Act with relation to Actions thereby authorized to be brought by Proprietors of Copyright against Persons importing or selling Books unlawfully printed in the *British* Dominions.

XI. *And be it enacted, That*[1] the said Officer of the said Company of Stationers shall receive at the Hall of the said Company every Book, Volume, or Print so to be delivered as aforesaid, and within One Calendar Month after receiving such Book, Volume, or Print shall deposit the same in the Library of the *British Museum*. *(Officer of Stationers Company to deposit Books, &c. in the British Museum.)*

XII. Provided always, and *be it enacted, That*[1] it shall not be requisite to deliver to the said Officer of the said Stationers Company any printed Copy of the Second or of any subsequent Edition of any Book or Books so delivered as aforesaid, unless the same shall contain Additions or Alterations. *(Second or subsequent Editions.)*

XIII. *And be it enacted, That*[1] the respective Terms to be specified by such Orders in Council respectively for the Continuance of the Privilege to be granted in respect of Works to be first published in Foreign Countries may be different for Works first published in different Foreign Countries and for different Classes of such Works; and *that*[1] the Times to be prescribed for the Entries to be made in the Register Book of the Stationers Company, and for the Deliveries of the Books and other Articles to the said Officer of the Stationers Company, as herein-before is *(Orders in Council may specify different Periods for different Foreign Countries and for different Classes of Works.)*

[1] Repealed by Statute Law Revision Act, 1891.

mentioned, may be different for different Foreign Countries and for different Classes of Books or other Articles.

No Order in Council to have any Effect unless it states that reciprocal Protection is secured.

XIV. Provided always, and be it enacted, That no such Order in Council shall have any Effect unless it shall be therein stated, as the Ground for issuing the same, that due Protection has been secured by the Foreign Power so named in such Order in Council for the Benefit of Parties interested in Works first published in the Dominions of Her Majesty similar to those comprised in such Order.[1]

Orders in Council to be published in Gazette, and to have same Effect as this Act.

XV. And be it enacted, That[2] every Order in Council to be made under the Authority of this Act shall as soon as may be after the making thereof by Her Majesty in Council be published in the *London Gazette*, and from the Time of such Publication shall have the same Effect as if every Part thereof were included in this Act.

Orders in Council to be laid before Parliament.

XVI. And be it enacted, That[2] a Copy of every Order of Her Majesty in Council made under this Act shall be laid before both Houses of Parliament within Six Weeks after issuing the same, if Parliament be then sitting, and if not, then within Six Weeks after the Commencement of the then next Session of Parliament.

Orders in Council may be revoked.

XVII. And be it enacted, That it shall be lawful for Her Majesty by an Order in Council from Time to Time to revoke or alter any Order in Council previously made under the Authority of this Act, but nevertheless without Prejudice to any Rights acquired previously to such Revocation or Alteration.[1]

Translations.

XVIII. Provided always, and be it enacted, That nothing in this Act contained shall be construed to prevent the printing, Publication, or Sale of any Translation of any Book the Author whereof and his Assigns may be entitled to the Benefit of this Act.[1]

Authors of Works first published in Foreign Countries not entitled to Copyright except under this Act.

XIX. And be it enacted, That[2] neither the Author of any Book, nor the Author or Composer of any Dramatic Piece or Musical Composition, nor the Inventor, Designer, or Engraver of any Print, nor the Maker of any Article of Sculpture, or of such other Work of Art as aforesaid, which shall after the passing of this Act be first published out of Her Majesty's Dominions, shall have any Copyright therein respectively, or any exclusive Right to the public

[1] Repealed by the International Copyright Act, 1886, sec. 12.
[2] Repealed by Statute Law Revision Act, 1891.

Representation or Performance thereof, otherwise than such (if any) as he may become entitled to under this Act.

XX. *And be it enacted, That*[1] in the Construction of this Act the Word 'Book' shall be construed to include 'Volume,' 'Pamphlet,' 'Sheet of Letter-press,' 'Sheet of Music,' 'Map,' 'Chart,' or 'Plan'; and the Expression 'Articles of Sculpture' shall mean all such Sculptures, Models, Copies, and Casts as are described in the said Sculpture Copyright Acts, and in respect of which the Privileges of Copyright are thereby conferred; and the Words 'printing' and 're-printing,' shall include engraving and any other Method of multiplying Copies; *and the Expression 'Her Majesty' shall include the Heirs and Successors of Her Majesty*[1]; and the Expressions 'Order of Her Majesty in Council,' 'Order in Council,' and 'Order,' shall respectively mean Order of Her Majesty acting by and with the Advice of Her Majesty's Most Honourable Privy Council; and the Expression 'Officer of the Company of Stationers' shall mean the Officer appointed by the said Company of Stationers for the Purposes of the said Copyright Amendment Act; and in describing any Persons or Things any Word importing the Plural Number shall mean also One Person or Thing, and any Word importing the Singular Number shall include several Persons or Things, and any Word importing the Masculine shall include also the Feminine Gender; unless in any of such Cases there shall be something in the Subject or Context repugnant to such Construction.

Interpretation Clause.

XXI. *And be it enacted, That this Act may be amended or repealed by any Act to be passed in this present Session of Parliament.*[2]

Act may be repealed this Session.

[1] Repealed by Statute Law Revision Act, 1891.
[2] Repealed by Statute Law Revision Act, 1874 (2).

THE COLONIAL COPYRIGHT ACT, 1847.[1]

10 AND 11 VICT. CAP. 95.

An Act to amend the Law relating to the Protection in the Colonies of Works entitled to Copyright in the United Kingdom.

[*22d July* 1847.]

WHEREAS by an Act passed in the Session of Parliament holden in the Fifth and Sixth Years of Her present Majesty,

5 & 6 Vict. c. 45.

intituled 'An Act to amend the Law of Copyright,' it is amongst other things enacted, that it shall not be lawful for any Person not being the Proprietor of the Copyright, or some Person authorized by him, to import into any Part of the United Kingdom, or into any other Part of the British Dominions, for Sale or Hire, any printed Book first composed or written or printed or published in any Part of the United Kingdom wherein there shall be Copyright, and reprinted in any Country or Place whatsoever out of the British Dominions: And whereas by an Act passed in the Session of Parliament holden in the Eighth and Ninth Years of the Reign of Her present Majesty,

8 & 9 Vict. c. 93.

intituled 'An Act to regulate the Trade of the British Possessions abroad,' Books wherein the Copyright is subsisting, first composed or written or printed in the United Kingdom, and printed or reprinted in any other Country, are absolutely prohibited to be imported into the British Possessions abroad: And whereas by the said last-recited Act it is enacted, that all Laws, Bye Laws, Usages, or Customs in practice, or endeavoured or pretended to be in force or practice in any of the British Possessions in America, which are in anywise repugnant to the said Act or to any Act of Parliament made or to be made in the United Kingdom, so far as such Act shall relate to and mention the said Possessions, are and shall be null and void to all Intents and Purposes whatsoever: Now be it enacted, by the Queen's most Excellent Majesty, by and with the Advice and Consent of the Lords Spiritual and Temporal, and Commons, in this

[1] Short Titles Act, 1896.

*present Parliament assembled, and by the Authority of the same,
That*[1] in case the Legislature or proper legislative Authorities in
any *British* Possession shall be disposed to make due Provision for
securing or protecting the Rights of *British* Authors in such
Possession, and shall pass an Act or make an Ordinance for that
Purpose, and shall transmit the same in the proper Manner to the
Secretary of State, in order that it may be submitted to Her
Majesty, and in case Her Majesty shall be of opinion that such
Act or Ordinance is sufficient for the Purpose of securing to
British Authors reasonable Protection within such Possession, it
shall be lawful for Her Majesty, if She think fit so to do, to
express Her Royal Approval of such Act or Ordinance, and there-
upon to issue an Order in Council declaring that so long as the
Provisions of such Act or Ordinance continue in force within such
Colony the Prohibitions contained in the aforesaid Acts, and
herein-before recited, and any Prohibitions contained in the said
Acts or in any other Acts against the importing, selling, letting
out to hire, exposing for Sale or Hire, or possessing Foreign
Reprints of Books first composed, written, printed, or published in
the United Kingdom, and entitled to Copyright therein, shall be
suspended so far as regards such Colony; and thereupon such
Act or Ordinance shall come into operation, except so far as may
be otherwise provided therein, or as may be otherwise directed by
such Order in Council, any thing in the said last-recited Act or in
any other Act to the contrary notwithstanding.

Her Majesty may suspend in certain Cases the Prohibitions against the Admission of pirated Books into the Colonies in certain Cases.

II. *And be it enacted, That*[1] every such Order in Council shall,
within One Week after the issuing thereof, be published in the
London Gazette, and *that*[1] a Copy thereof, and of every such Colonial Act or Ordinance so approved as aforesaid by Her Majesty,
shall be laid before both Houses of Parliament within Six Weeks
after the issuing of such Order, if Parliament be then sitting, or if
Parliament be not then sitting, then within Six Weeks after the
opening of the next Session of Parliament.

Orders in Council to be published in Gazette.

Orders in Council and the Colonial Acts or Ordinances to be laid before Parliament.

III.   *And be it enacted, This Act may be amended or repealed by
any Act to be passed in the present Session of Parliament.*[2]

Act may be amended, &c.

---

[1] Repealed by Statute Law Revision Act, 1891.
[2] Repealed by Statute Law Revision Act, 1875.

THE INTERNATIONAL COPYRIGHT ACT, 1852.[1]

15 VICT. CAP. 12.

An Act *to enable Her Majesty to carry into effect a Convention with France on the Subject of Copyright ;*[2] *to extend and explain the International Copyright Acts ; and to explain the Acts relating to Copyright in Engravings.*

[*28th May* 1852.]

*W*HEREAS *an Act was passed in the Seventh Year of the Reign of Her present Majesty, intituled ' An Act to amend the Law relating to International Copyright,' herein-after called ' The International Copyright Act ' : And whereas a Convention has lately been concluded between Her Majesty and the French Republic, for extending in each Country the Enjoyment of Copyright in Works of Literature and the Fine Arts first published in the other, and for certain Reductions of Duties now levied on Books, Prints, and Musical Works published in France : And whereas certain of the Stipulations on the Part of Her Majesty contained in the said Treaty require the Authority of Parliament : And whereas it is expedient that such Authority should be given, and that Her Majesty should be enabled to make similar Stipulations in any Treaty on the Subject of Copyright which may hereafter be concluded with any Foreign Power : Be it enacted by the Queen's most Excellent Majesty, by and with the Advice and Consent of the Lords Spiritual and Temporal, and Commons, in this present Parliament assembled, and by the Authority of the same, as follows :*[2]

7 & 8 Vict. c. 12.

Translations.

Partial Repeal of 7 & 8 Vict. c. 12. § 18.

I. *The Eighteenth Section of the said Act of the Seventh Year of Her present Majesty, Chapter Twelve, shall be repealed, so far as the same is inconsistent with the Provisions herein-after contained.*[3]

---

[1] Short Titles Act, 1896.
[2] Repealed by Statute Law Revision Act, 1892.
[3] Repealed by the International Copyright Act, 1886, sec. 12.

II. Her Majesty may, by Order in Council, direct that the Authors of Books which are, after a future Time, to be specified in such Order, published in any Foreign Country, to be named in such Order, their Executors, Administrators, and Assigns, shall, subject to the Provisions herein-after contained or referred to, be empowered to prevent the Publication in the British Dominions of any Translations of such Books not authorized by them, for such Time as may be specified in such Order, not extending beyond the Expiration of Five Years from the Time at which the authorized Translations of such Books herein-after mentioned are respectively first published, and in the Case of Books published in Parts, not extending as to each Part beyond the Expiration of Five Years from the Time at which the authorized Translation of such Part is first published.[1]

III. Subject to any Provisions or Qualifications contained in such Order, and to the Provisions herein contained or referred to, the Laws and Enactments for the Time being in force for the Purpose of preventing the Infringement of Copyright in Books published in the British Dominions shall be applied for the Purpose of preventing the Publication of Translations of the Books to which such Order extends which are not sanctioned by the Authors of such Books, except only such Parts of the said Enactments as relate to the Delivery of Copies of Books for the Use of the British Museum, and for the Use of the other Libraries therein referred to.[1]

IV. Her Majesty may, by Order in Council, direct that Authors of Dramatic Pieces which are, after a future Time, to be specified in such Order, first publicly represented in any Foreign Country, to be named in such Order, their Executors, Administrators, and Assigns, shall, subject to the Provisions herein-after mentioned or referred to, be empowered to prevent the Representation in the British Dominions of any Translation of such Dramatic Pieces not authorized by them, for such Time as may be specified in such Order, not extending beyond the Expiration of Five Years from the Time at which the authorized Translations of such Dramatic Pieces herein-after mentioned are first published or publicly represented.[1]

V. Subject to any Provisions or Qualifications contained in such last-mentioned Order, and to the Provisions herein-after contained or referred to, the Laws and Enactments for the Time being in force for

---

Her Majesty may by Order in Council direct that the Authors of Books published in Foreign Countries may for a limited Time prevent unauthorized Translations.

Thereupon the Law of Copyright shall extend to prevent such Translations.

Her Majesty may by Order in Council direct that the Authors of Dramatic Works represented in Foreign Countries may for a limited Time prevent unauthorized Translations.

Thereupon the Law for protecting the Representation of

[1] Repealed by the International Copyright Act, 1886, sec. 12.

such Pieces shall extend to prevent unauthorized Translations.

ensuring to the Author of any Dramatic Piece first publicly repre-sented in the British Dominions the sole Liberty of representing the same shall be applied for the Purpose of preventing the Representation of any Translations of the Dramatic Pieces to which such last-men-tioned Order extends, which are not sanctioned by the Authors thereof.[1]

Adaptations, &c. of Dramatic Pieces to the English Stage not prevented.

VI. Nothing herein contained shall be so construed as to prevent fair Imitations or Adaptations to the *English* Stage of any Dramatic Piece or Musical Composition published in any Foreign Country.

All Articles in News-papers, &c. relating to Politics may be repub-lished or translated; and also all similar Articles on any Subject, unless the Author has notified his Intention to reserve the Right.

VII. Notwithstanding anything in the said International Copy-right Act or in this Act contained, any Article of political Discussion which has been published in any Newspaper or Periodical in a Foreign Country may, if the Source from which the same is taken be acknowledged, be republished or translated in any Newspaper or Periodical in this Country; and any Article relating to any other Subject which has been so published as afore-said may, if the Source from which the same is taken be acknow-ledged, be republished or translated in like Manner, unless the Author has signified his Intention of preserving the Copyright therein, and the Right of translating the same, in some conspicuous Part of the Newspaper or Periodical in which the same was first published, in which Case the same shall, *without the Formalities required by the next following Section,[2]* receive the same Protection as is by virtue of the International Copyright Act or this Act extended to Books.

No Author to be entitled to Benefit of this Act without complying with the Requisitions herein specified.

VIII. No Author, or his Executors, Administrators, or Assigns, shall be entitled to the Benefit of this Act, or of any Order in Council issued in pursuance thereof, in respect of the Translation of any Book or Dramatic Piece, if the following Requisitions are not com-plied with; (that is to say,)

1. The original Work from which the Translation is to be made must be registered and a Copy thereof deposited in the United Kingdom in the Manner required for original Works by the said International Copyright Act, within Three Calendar Months of its First Publication in the Foreign Country:

[1] Repealed by the International Copyright Act, 1886, sec. 12.
[2] Repealed by Statute Law Revision Act, 1894.

2. *The Author must notify on the Title Page of the original Work, or if it is published in Parts, on the Title Page of the First Part, or if there is no Title Page, on some conspicuous Part of the Work, that it is his Intention to reserve the Right of translating it:*

3. *The Translation sanctioned by the Author, or a Part thereof, must be published either in the Country mentioned in the Order in Council by virtue of which it is to be protected or in the British Dominions, not later than One Year after the Registration and Deposit in the United Kingdom of the original Work, and the whole of such Translation must be published within Three Years of such Registration and Deposit:*

4. *Such Translation must be registered and a Copy thereof deposited in the United Kingdom within a Time to be mentioned in that Behalf in the Order by which it is protected, and in the Manner provided by the said International Copyright Act for the Registration and Deposit of original Works:*

5. *In the Case of Books published in Parts, each Part of the original Work must be registered and deposited in this Country in the Manner required by the said International Copyright within Three Months after the First Publication thereof in the Foreign Country:*

6. *In the Case of Dramatic Pieces the Translation sanctioned by the Author must be published within Three Calendar Months of the Registration of the original Work:*

7. *The above Requisitions shall apply to Articles originally published in Newspapers or Periodicals if the same be afterwards published in a separate Form, but shall not apply to such Articles as originally published.*[1]

IX. All Copies of any Works of Literature or Art wherein there is any subsisting Copyright by virtue of the International Copyright Act and this Act, or of any Order in Council made in pursuance of such Acts or either of them, and which are printed, reprinted, or made in any Foreign Country except that in which such Work shall be first published, and all unauthorized Translations of any Book or Dramatic Piece the Publication or public

Pirated Copies prohibited to be imported, except with Consent of Proprietor;

[1] Repealed by the International Copyright Act, 1886, sec. 12.

Representation in the *British* Dominions of Translations whereof not authorized as in this Act mentioned shall for the Time being be prevented under any Order in Council made in pursuance of this Act, are hereby absolutely prohibited to be imported into any Part of the *British* Dominions, except by or with the Consent of the registered Proprietor of the Copyright of such Work or of such Book or Piece, or his Agent authorized in Writing; and the Provision of the Act of the Sixth Year of Her Majesty 'to amend the Law of Copyright,' for the Forfeiture, Seizure, and Destruction of any printed Book first published in the United Kingdom wherein there shall be Copyright, and reprinted in any Country out of the *British* Dominions, and imported into any Part of the *British* Dominions by any Person not being the Proprietor of the Copyright, or a Person authorized by such Proprietor, shall extend and be applicable to all Copies of any Works of Literature and Art, and to all Translations the Importation whereof into any Part of the *British* Dominions is prohibited under this Act.

Provisions of 5 & 6 Vict. c. 45. as to Forfeiture, &c. of pirated Works, &c. to extend to Works prohibited to be imported under this Act.

Foregoing Provisions and 7 & 8 Vict. c. 12. to be read as One Act.

X. The Provisions herein-before contained shall be incorporated with the International Copyright Act, and shall be read and construed therewith as One Act.

French Translations to be protected as herein-before mentioned, without further Order in Council.

XI. And whereas Her Majesty has already, by Order in Council under the said International Copyright Act, given effect to certain Stipulations contained in the said Convention with the French Republic; and it is expedient that the Remainder of the Stipulations on the Part of Her Majesty in the said Convention contained should take effect from the passing of this Act without any further Order in Council: During the Continuance of the said Convention, and so long as the Order in Council already made under the said International Copyright Act remains in force, the Provisions herein-before contained shall apply to the said Convention, and to Translations of Books and Dramatic Pieces which are, after the passing of this Act, published or represented in France, in the same Manner as if Her Majesty had issued Her Order in Council in pursuance of this Act for giving effect to such Convention, and had therein directed that such Translations should be protected as herein-before mentioned for a Period of Five Years from the Date of the First Publication or public Representation thereof respectively, and as if a Period of Three Months from the Publication of such Translation were the Time mentioned in such Order as the Time within which the same must be registered and a Copy thereof deposited in the United Kingdom.[1]

XII. *And whereas an Act was passed in the Tenth Year of Her present Majesty, intituled 'An Act to amend an Act of the Seventh and Eighth Years of Her present Majesty, for reducing, under certain Circumstances, the Duties payable upon Books and Engravings':* *And whereas by the said Convention with the French Republic it was stipulated that the Duties on Books, Prints, and Drawings published in the Territories of the French Republic should be reduced to the Amounts specified in the Schedule to the said Act of the Tenth Year of Her present Majesty, Chapter Fifty-eight: And whereas Her Majesty has, in pursuance of the said Convention, and in exercise of the Powers given by the said Act, by Order in Council declared that such Duties shall be reduced accordingly: And whereas by the said Convention it was further stipulated that the said Rates of Duty should not be raised during the Continuance of the said Convention; and that if during the Continuance of the said Convention any Reduction of those Rates should be made in favour of Books, Prints, or Drawings published in any other Country, such Reduction should be at the same Time extended to similar Articles published in France: And whereas Doubts are entertained whether such last-mentioned Stipulations can be carried into effect without the Authority of Parliament: Be it enacted, That the said Rates of Duty so reduced as aforesaid shall not be raised during the Continuance of the said Convention; and that if during the Continuance of the said Convention any further Reduction of such Rates is made in favour of Books, Prints, or Drawings published in any other Foreign Country, Her Majesty may, by Order in Council, declare that such Reduction shall be extended to similar Articles published in France, such Order to be made and published in the same Manner and to be subject to the same Provisions as Orders made in pursuance of the said Act of the Tenth Year of Her present Majesty, Chapter Fifty-eight.*[2]

Reduction of Duties.

Recital of 9 & 10 Vict. c. 58.

Rates of Duty not to be raised during Continuance of Treaty, and if further Reduction is made for other Countries it may be extended to France.

XIII. *And whereas Doubts have arisen as to the Construction of the Schedule of the Act of the Tenth Year of Her present Majesty, Chapter Fifty-eight:*

It is hereby declared, That for the Purposes of the said Act every Work published in the Country of Export, of which Part has

For Removal of Doubts as to Construc-

---

[1] Repealed by International Copyright Act, 1886, sec. 12.

[2] Repealed by Statute Law Revision Act, 1875.

tion of
Schedule to
9 & 10 Vict.
c. 58.
*been originally produced in the United Kingdom, shall be deemed
to be and be subject to the Duty payable on ' Works originally produced in the United Kingdom, and republished in the Country of
Export,' although it contains also original Matter not produced in
the United Kingdom, unless it shall be proved to the Satisfaction of
the Commissioners of Her Majesty's Customs by the Importer, Con-
signee, or other Person entering the same that such original Matter
is at least equal to the Part of the Work produced in the United
Kingdom, in which Case the Work shall be subject only to the Duty
on ' Works not originally produced in the United Kingdom.'*[1]

*Litho-
graphs, &c.*

Recital of
8 G. 2. c. 13.
17 G. 3. c. 38.
7 G. 3. c. 57.
6 & 7 W. 4.
c. 59.

XIV. And whereas by the Four several Acts of Parliament fol-
lowing; (that is to say,) an Act of the Eighth Year of the Reign
of King *George* the Second, Chapter Thirteen; an Act of the
Seventh Year of the Reign of King *George* the Third, Chapter
Thirty-eight; an Act of the Seventeenth Year of the Reign of
King *George* the Third, Chapter Fifty-seven; and an Act of the
Seventh Year of King *William* the Fourth, Chapter Fifty-nine,
Provision is made for securing to every Person who invents, or
designs, engraves, etches, or works in Mezzotinto or Chiaro-oscuro,
or, from his own Work, Design, or Invention, causes or procures
to be designed, engraved, etched, or worked in Mezzotinto or
Chiaro-oscuro, any Historical Print or Prints, or any Print or
Prints of any Portrait, Conversation, Landscape, or Architecture,
Map, Chart, or Plan, or any other Print or Prints whatsoever, and
to every Person who engraves, etches, or works in Mezzotinto
or Chiaro-oscuro, or causes to be engraved, etched, or worked any
Print taken from any Picture, Drawing, Model, or Sculpture, notwithstanding such Print has not been graven or drawn from
his own original Design, certain Copyrights therein defined: And
whereas Doubts are entertained whether the Provisions of the said
Acts extend to Lithographs and certain other Impressions, and it
is expedient to remove such Doubts:

For Removal
of Doubts as
to the Pro-
visions of the
said Acts
including
Lithographs,
Prints, &c.

It is hereby declared, That the Provisions of the said Acts are
intended to include Prints taken by Lithography, or any other
mechanical Process by which Prints or Impressions of Drawings
or Designs are capable of being multiplied indefinitely, and the
said Acts shall be construed accordingly.

---

[1] Repealed by Statute Law Revision Act, 1875.

THE INTERNATIONAL COPYRIGHT ACT, 1875.[1]

38 VICT. CAP. 12.

An Act to amend the Law relating to International Copyright.

[*13th May* 1875.]

W̄HEREAS by an Act passed in the fifteenth year of the reign 15 Vict.
of Her present Majesty, chapter twelve, intituled 'An Act c. 12.
*to enable Her Majesty to carry into effect a convention with France
on the subject of copyright; to extend and explain the International
Copyright Acts; and to explain the Acts relating to copyright in
engravings,' it is enacted, that 'Her Majesty may, by Order in
Council, direct that authors of dramatic pieces which are, after a
future time, to be specified in such order, first publicly represented
in any foreign country, to be named in such order, their executors,
administrators, and assigns, shall, subject to the provisions therein-after
mentioned or referred to, be empowered to prevent the representation
in the British dominions of any translation of such dramatic pieces
not authorised by them, for such time as may be specified in such
order, not extending beyond the expiration of five years from the time
at which the authorised translations of such dramatic pieces are first
published and publicly represented:'*

*And whereas by the same Act it is further enacted, 'that, subject
to any provisions or qualifications contained in such order, and to the
provisions in the said Act contained or referred to, the laws and
enactments for the time being in force for ensuring to the author of
any dramatic piece first publicly represented in the British dominions
the sole liberty of representing the same shall be applied for the
purpose of preventing the representation of any translations of the
dramatic pieces to which such order extends, which are not sanctioned
by the authors thereof:'*

---

[1] Short Titles Act, 1896.

And whereas by the sixth section of the said Act it is provided, that 'nothing in the said Act contained shall be so construed as to prevent fair imitations or adaptations to the English stage of any dramatic piece or musical composition published in any foreign country:'

And whereas it is expedient to alter or amend the last-mentioned provision under certain circumstances:

Be it therefore enacted by the Queen's most Excellent Majesty, by and with the advice and consent of the Lords Spiritual and Temporal, and Commons, in this present Parliament assembled, and by the authority of the same, as follows; viz.,[1]

Section 6 of recited Act not to apply to dramatic pieces in certain cases.

1. In any case in which, by virtue of the enactments hereinbefore recited, any Order in Council has been or may hereafter be made for the purpose of extending protection to the translations of dramatic pieces first publicly represented in any foreign country, it shall be lawful for Her Majesty by Order in Council to direct that the sixth section of the said Act shall not apply to the dramatic pieces to which protection is so extended; and thereupon the said recited Act shall take effect with respect to such dramatic pieces and to the translations thereof as if the said sixth section of the said Act were hereby repealed.

[1] Repealed by Statute Law Revision Act, 1893 (2).

THE CANADA COPYRIGHT ACT, 1875.

38 AND 39 VICT. CAP. 53.

An Act to give effect to an Act of the Parliament of the Dominion of Canada respecting Copyright.

[*2d August* 1875.]

WHEREAS by an Order of Her Majesty in Council, dated the 7th day of July 1868, it was ordered that all prohibitions contained in Acts of the Imperial Parliament against the importing into the Province of Canada, or against the selling, letting out to hire, exposing for sale or hire, or possessing therein foreign reprints of books first composed, written, printed, or published in the United Kingdom, and entitled to copyright therein, should be suspended so far as regarded Canada :

And whereas the Senate and House of Commons of Canada did, in the second session of the third Parliament of the Dominion of Canada, held in the thirty-eighth year of Her Majesty's reign, pass a Bill intituled 'An Act respecting Copyrights,' which Bill has been reserved by the Governor-General for the signification of Her Majesty's pleasure thereon :

And whereas by the said reserved Bill provision is made, subject to such conditions as in the said Bill are mentioned, for securing in Canada the rights of authors in respect of matters of copyright, and for prohibiting the importation into Canada of any work for which copyright under the said reserved Bill has been secured ; and whereas doubts have arisen whether the said reserved Bill may not be repugnant to the said Order in Council, and it is expedient to remove such doubts and to confirm the said Bill :

Be it enacted by the Queen's most Excellent Majesty, by and with the advice and consent of the Lords Spiritual and Temporal, and

Commons, in this present Parliament assembled, and by the authority of the same, as follows : [1]

Short title of Act. **1.** This Act may be cited for all purposes as The Canada Copyright Act, 1875.

Definition of terms. **2.** In the construction of this Act the words 'book' and 'copyright' shall have respectively the same meaning as in the Act of the fifth and sixth years of Her Majesty's reign, chapter forty-five, intituled 'An Act to amend the Law of Copyright.'

Her Majesty may assent to the Bill in schedule. **3.** It shall be lawful for Her Majesty in Council to assent to the said reserved Bill, as contained in the schedule to this Act annexed, and if Her Majesty shall be pleased to signify Her assent thereto, the said Bill shall come into operation at such time and in such manner as Her Majesty may by Order in Council direct; anything in the Act of the twenty-eighth and twenty-ninth years of the reign of Her Majesty, chapter ninety-three, or in any other Act to the contrary notwithstanding.

Colonial reprints not to be imported into United Kingdom. **4.** Where any book in which, at the time when the said reserved Bill comes into operation, there is copyright in the United Kingdom, or any book in which thereafter there shall be such copyright, becomes entitled to copyright in Canada in pursuance of the provisions of the said reserved Bill, it shall be unlawful for any person, not being the owner, in the United Kingdom, of the copyright in such book, or some person authorised by him, to import into the United Kingdom any copies of such book reprinted or republished in Canada; and for the purposes of such importation the seventeenth section of the said Act of the fifth and sixth years of the reign of Her Majesty, chapter forty-five, shall apply to all such books in the same manner as if they had been reprinted out of the British dominions.

Order in Council of 7th July 1868 to continue in force subject to this Act. **5.** The said Order in Council, dated the seventh day of July one thousand eight hundred and sixty-eight, shall continue in force so far as relates to books which are not entitled to copyright for the time being, in pursuance of the said reserved Bill.

[1] Repealed by Statute Law Revision Act, 1893 (2).

THE CUSTOMS LAWS CONSOLIDATION ACT, 1876.

39 AND 40 VICT. CAP. 36.

An Act to consolidate the Customs Laws.

[*24th July* 1876.]

42. The goods enumerated and described in the following table of prohibitions and restrictions inwards are hereby prohibited to be imported or brought into the United Kingdom, save as thereby excepted, and if any goods so enumerated and described shall be imported or brought into the United Kingdom contrary to the prohibitions or restrictions contained therein, such goods shall be forfeited, and may be destroyed or otherwise disposed of as the Commissioners of Customs may direct. *Prohibitions and restrictions.*

A TABLE OF PROHIBITIONS AND RESTRICTIONS INWARDS.

Goods prohibited to be imported.

Books wherein the copyright shall be first subsisting, first composed, or written or printed, in the United Kingdom, and, printed or reprinted in any other country, as to which the proprietor of such copyright or his agent shall have given to the Commissioners of Customs a notice in writing, duly declared, that such copyright subsists, such notice also stating when such copyright will expire. *Table of prohibitions and restrictions.*

44. The Commissioners of Customs shall cause to be made, and to be publicly exposed at the Custom Houses in the several ports in the United Kingdom, lists of all books wherein the copyright shall be subsisting, and as to which the proprietor of such copyright, or his agent, shall have given notice in writing to the said *IMPORTATION AND WAREHOUSING. —— Lists of prohibited books to be exposed at*

Custom
Houses.

Commissioners that such copyright exists, stating in such notice when such copyright expires, accompanied by a declaration made and subscribed before a collector of Customs or a justice of the peace, that the contents of such notice are true.

Persons complaining of prohibition of books in copyright lists may appeal to a judge in chambers.

45. If any person shall have cause to complain of the insertion of any book in such lists, it shall be lawful for any judge at chambers, on the application of the person so complaining, to issue a summons, calling upon the person upon whose notice such book shall have been so inserted to appear before any such judge, at a time to be appointed in such summons, to show cause why such book shall not be expunged from such lists, and any such judge shall at the time so appointed proceed to hear and determine upon the matter of such summons, and make his order thereon in writing; and upon service of such order, or a certified copy thereof, upon the Commissioners of Customs or their secretary for the time being, the said Commissioners shall expunge such book from the list, or retain the same therein, according to the tenor of such order; and in case such book shall be expunged from such lists, the importation thereof shall not be deemed to be prohibited. If at the time appointed in any such summons the person so summoned shall not appear before such judge, then upon proof by affidavit that such summons, or a true copy thereof, has been personally served upon the person so summoned, or sent to him by post to or left at his last known place of abode or business, any such judge may proceed ex parte to hear and determine the matter; but if either party be dissatisfied with such order, he may apply to a superior court to review such decision and to make such further order thereon as the court may see fit: Provided always, that nothing herein contained shall affect any proceeding at law or in equity which any party aggrieved by reason of the insertion of any book pursuant to any such notice, or the removal of any book from such list pursuant to any such order, or by reason of any false declaration under this Act, might or would otherwise have against any party giving such notice, or obtaining such order, or making such false declaration.

Nothing to prevent persons aggrieved from proceeding at law, &c.

Foreign reprints of books under copyright prohibited.

152. Any books wherein the copyright shall be subsisting, first composed or written or printed in the United Kingdom, and printed or reprinted in any other country, shall be and are hereby absolutely prohibited to be imported into the British possessions abroad: Provided always, that no such books shall be prohibited to be imported as aforesaid unless the proprietor of such copyright, or his agent, shall have given notice in writing to the Commissioners of Customs that such copyright subsists, and in such notice shall have stated when the copyright will expire; and the said Commissioners shall cause to be made and transmitted to the several ports in the British possessions abroad, from time to time to be publicly exposed there, lists of books respecting which such notice shall have been duly given, and all books imported contrary thereto shall be forfeited; but nothing herein contained shall be taken to prevent Her Majesty from exercising the powers vested in her by the tenth and eleventh Victoria, chapter ninety-five, intituled 'An Act to amend the law relating to the protection in the colonies of works entitled to copyright in the United Kingdom,' to suspend in certain cases such prohibition.

THE INTERNATIONAL COPYRIGHT ACT, 1886.

49 AND 50 VICT. CAP. 33.

An Act to amend the Law respecting International and Colonial Copyright.

[*25th June* 1886.]

*W*HEREAS *by the International Copyright Acts Her Majesty is authorised by Order in Council to direct that as regards literary and artistic works first published in a foreign country the author shall have copyright therein during the period specified in the order, not exceeding the period during which authors of the like works first published in the United Kingdom have copyright :*

And whereas at an international conference held at Berne in the month of September one thousand eight hundred and eighty-five a draft of a convention was agreed to for giving to authors of literary and artistic works first published in one of the countries parties to the convention copyright in such works throughout the other countries parties to the convention :

And whereas, without the authority of Parliament, such convention cannot be carried into effect in Her Majesty's dominions and consequently Her Majesty cannot become a party thereto, and it is expedient to enable Her Majesty to accede to the convention :[1]

Be it therefore enacted by the Queen's most Excellent Majesty, by and with the advice and consent of the Lords Spiritual and Temporal, and Commons, in this present Parliament assembled, and by the authority of the same, as follows :

Short titles and construction.

1.—(1.) This Act may be cited as the International Copyright Act, 1886.

(2.) The Acts specified in the first part of the First Schedule to this Act *are in this Act referred to and may be cited by the short*

---

[1] Repealed by Statute Law Revision Act, 1898.

titles in that schedule mentioned, and those Acts,[1] together with the enactment specified in the second part of the said schedule, are in this Act collectively referred to as the International Copyright Acts.[2]

The Acts specified in the Second Schedule to this Act *may be cited by the short titles in that schedule mentioned, and those Acts*[1] are in this Act referred to, and may be cited collectively as the Copyright Acts.

(3.) This Act and the International Copyright Acts shall be construed together, and may be cited together as the International Copyright Acts, 1844 to 1886.

2. The following provisions shall apply to an Order in Council under the International Copyright Acts :— *Amendment as to extent and effect of order under International Copyright Acts.*

(1.) The order may extend to all the several foreign countries named or described therein :

(2.) The order may exclude or limit the rights conferred by the International Copyright Acts in the case of authors who are not subjects or citizens of the foreign countries named or described in that or any other order, and if the order contains such limitation and the author of a literary or artistic work first produced in one of those foreign countries is not a British subject, nor a subject or citizen of any of the foreign countries so named or described, the publisher of such work, unless the order otherwise provides, shall for the purpose of any legal proceedings in the United Kingdom for protecting any copyright in such work be deemed to be entitled to such copyright as if he were the author, but this enactment shall not prejudice the rights of such author and publisher as between themselves :

(3.) The International Copyright Acts and an order made thereunder shall not confer on any person any greater right or longer term of copyright in any work than that enjoyed in the foreign country in which such work was first produced.

3.—(1.) An Order in Council under the International Copyright Acts may provide for determining the country in which a literary or artistic work first produced simultaneously in two or more *Simultaneous publication.*

---

[1] Repealed by Statute Law Revision Act, 1898.
[2] *Cf.* Short Titles Act, 1896.

countries, is to be deemed, for the purpose of copyright, to have been first produced, and for the purposes of this section 'country' means the United Kingdom and a country to which an order under the said Acts applies.

(2.) Where a work produced simultaneously in the United Kingdom, and in some foreign country or countries is by virtue of an Order in Council under the International Copyright Acts deemed for the purpose of copyright to be first produced in one of the said foreign countries, and not in the United Kingdom, the copyright in the United Kingdom shall be such only as exists by virtue of production in the said foreign country, and shall not be such as would have been acquired if the work had been first produced in the United Kingdom.

Modification of certain provisions of International Copyright Acts.

4.—(1.) Where an order respecting any foreign country is made under the International Copyright Acts the provisions of those Acts with respect to the registry and delivery of copies of works shall not apply to works produced in such country except so far as provided by the order.

(2.) Before making an Order in Council under the International Copyright Acts in respect of any foreign country, Her Majesty in Council shall be satisfied that that foreign country has made such provisions (if any) as it appears to Her Majesty expedient to require for the protection of authors of works first produced in the United Kingdom.

Restriction on translation.

5.—(1.) Where a work being a book or dramatic piece is first produced in a foreign country to which an Order in Council under the International Copyright Acts applies, the author or publisher, as the case may be, shall, unless otherwise directed by the order, have the same right of preventing the production in and importation into the United Kingdom of any translation not authorised by him of the said work as he has of preventing the production and importation of the original work.

(2.) Provided that if after the expiration of ten years, or any other term prescribed by the order, next after the end of the year in which the work, or in the case of a book published in numbers each number of the book, was first produced, an authorised translation in the English language of such work or number has not been produced, the said right to prevent the production in and importation into the United Kingdom of an unauthorised translation of such work shall cease.

(3.) The law relating to copyright, including this Act, shall apply to a lawfully produced translation of a work in like manner as if it were an original work.

(4.) Such of the provisions of the International Copyright Act, 1852, relating to translations as are unrepealed by this Act shall apply in like manner as if they were re-enacted in this section.

6. Where an Order in Council is made under the International Copyright Acts with respect to any foreign country, the author and publisher of any literary or artistic work first produced before the date at which such order comes into operation shall be entitled to the same rights and remedies as if the said Acts and this Act and the said order had applied to the said foreign country at the date of the said production: Provided that where any person has before the date of the publication of an Order in Council lawfully produced any work in the United Kingdom, nothing in this section shall diminish or prejudice any rights or interests arising from or in connection with such production which are subsisting and valuable at the said date. *Application of Act to existing works.*

7. Where it is necessary to prove the existence or proprietorship of the copyright of any work first produced in a foreign country to which an Order in Council under the International Copyright Acts applies, an extract from a register, or a certificate, or other document stating the existence of the copyright, or the person who is the proprietor of such copyright, or is for the purpose of any legal proceedings in the United Kingdom deemed to be entitled to such copyright, if authenticated by the official seal of a Minister of State of the said foreign country, or by the official seal or the signature of a British diplomatic or consular officer acting in such country, shall be admissible as evidence of the facts named therein, and all courts shall take judicial notice of every such official seal and signature as is in this section mentioned, and shall admit in evidence, without proof, the documents authenticated by it. *Evidence of foreign copyright.*

8.—(1.) The Copyright Acts shall, subject to the provisions of this Act, apply to a literary or artistic work first produced in a *Application of Copyright Acts to colonies.*

British possession in like manner as they apply to a work first produced in the United Kingdom:

Provided that—

(a) the enactments respecting the registry of the copyright in such work shall not apply if the law of such possession provides for the registration of such copyright; and

(b) where such work is a book the delivery to any persons or body of persons of a copy of any such work shall not be required.

(2.) Where a register of copyright in books is kept under the authority of the government of a British possession, an extract from that register purporting to be certified as a true copy by the officer keeping it, and authenticated by the public seal of the British possession, or by the official seal or the signature of the governor of a British possession, or of a colonial secretary, or of some secretary or minister administering a department of the government of a British possession, shall be admissible in evidence of the contents of that register, and all courts shall take judicial notice of every such seal and signature, and shall admit in evidence, without further proof, all documents authenticated by it.

(3.) Where before the passing of this Act an Act or ordinance has been passed in any British possession respecting copyright in any literary or artistic works, Her Majesty in Council may make an Order modifying the Copyright Acts and this Act, so far as they apply to such British possession, and to literary and artistic works first produced therein, in such manner as to Her Majesty in Council seems expedient.

(4.) Nothing in the Copyright Acts or this Act shall prevent the passing in a British possession of any Act or ordinance respecting the copyright within the limits of such possession of works first produced in that possession.

Application of International Copyright Acts to colonies.
9. Where it appears to Her Majesty expedient that an Order in Council under the International Copyright Acts made after the passing of this Act as respects any foreign country, should not apply to any British possession, it shall be lawful for Her Majesty by the same or any other Order in Council to declare that such Order and the International Copyright Acts and this Act shall not, and the same shall not, apply to such British possession, except so far as is necessary for preventing any prejudice to any

rights acquired previously to the date of such Order; and the expressions in the said Acts relating to Her Majesty's dominions shall be construed accordingly; but save as provided by such declaration the said Acts and this Act shall apply to every British possession as if it were part of the United Kingdom.

10.—(1.) It shall be lawful for Her Majesty from time to time *Making of* to make Orders in Council for the purposes of the International *Orders in Council.* Copyright Acts and this Act, for revoking or altering any Order in Council previously made in pursuance of the said Acts, or any of them.

(2.) Any such Order in Council shall not affect prejudicially any rights acquired or accrued at the date of such Order coming into operation, and shall provide for the protection of such rights.

11. In this Act, unless the context otherwise requires—   *Definitions.*

The expression 'literary and artistic work' means every book, print, lithograph, article of sculpture, dramatic piece, musical composition, painting, drawing, photograph, and other work of literature and art to which the Copyright Acts or the International Copyright Acts, as the case requires, extend.

The expression 'author' means the author, inventor, designer, engraver, or maker of any literary or artistic work, and includes any person claiming through the author; and in the case of a posthumous work means the proprietor of the manuscript of such work and any person claiming through him; and in the case of an encyclopædia, review, magazine, periodical work, or work published in a series of books or parts, includes the proprietor, projector, publisher, or conductor.

The expressions 'performed' and 'performance' and similar words include representation and similar words.

The expression 'produced' means, as the case requires, published or made, or, performed or represented, and the expression ' production ' is to be construed accordingly.

The expression 'book published in numbers' includes any review, magazine, periodical work, work published in a series of books or parts, transactions of a society or body, and other books of which different volumes or parts are published at different times.

The expression 'treaty' includes any convention or arrangement.

The expression 'British possession' includes any part of Her Majesty's dominions exclusive of the United Kingdom; and where parts of such dominions are under both a central and a local legislature, all parts under one central legislature are for the purposes of this definition deemed to be one British possession.

Repeal of Acts.

12. *The Acts specified in the Third Schedule to this Act are hereby repealed as from the passing of this Act to the extent in the third column of that schedule mentioned:*

Provided as follows :[1]

(*a.*) Where an Order in Council has been made before the passing of this Act under the said Acts as respects any foreign country the enactments hereby repealed shall continue in full force as respects that country until the said Order is revoked.

(*b.*) *The said repeal and revocation shall not prejudice any rights acquired previously to such repeal or revocation, and such rights shall continue and may be enforced in like manner as if the said repeal or revocation had not been enacted or made.*[1]

[1] Repealed by Statute Law Revision Act, 1898.

SCHEDULES.

FIRST SCHEDULE.

INTERNATIONAL COPYRIGHT ACTS.

PART I.

Session and Chapter.	Title.	Short Title.
7 & 8 Vict. c. 12.	An Act to amend the law relating to International Copyright.	The International Copyright Act, 1844
15 & 16 Vict. c. 12.	An Act to enable Her Majesty to carry into effect a convention with France on the subject of copyright, to extend and explain the International Copyright Acts, and to explain the Acts relating to copyright in engravings.	The International Copyright Act, 1852
38 & 39 Vict. c. 12.	An Act to amend the law relating to International Copyright.	The International Copyright Act, 1875

PART II.

Session and Chapter.	Title.	Enactment referred to
25 & 26 Vict. c. 68.	An Act for amending the law relating to copyright in works of the fine arts, and for repressing the commission of fraud in the production and sale of such works.	Section twelve.

SECOND SCHEDULE.

COPYRIGHT ACTS.

Session and Chapter.	Title.	Short Title.
8 Geo. 2. c. 13.	An Act for the encouragement of the arts of designing, engraving, and etching, historical, and other prints by vesting the properties thereof in the inventors and engravers during the time therein-mentioned.	The Engraving Copyright Act, 1734.
7 Geo. 3. c. 38.	An Act to amend and render more effectual an Act made in the eighth year of the reign of King George the Second, for encouragement of the arts of designing, engraving, and etching, historical and other prints, and for vesting in and securing to Jane Hogarth, widow, the property in certain prints.	The Engraving Copyright Act, 1766.
15 Geo. 3. c. 53.	An Act for enabling the two Universities in England, the four Universities in Scotland, and the several Colleges of Eton, Westminster, and Winchester, to hold in perpetuity their copyright in books given or bequeathed to the said universities and colleges for the advancement of useful learning and other purposes of education; and for amending so much of an Act of the eighth year of the reign of Queen Anne, as relates to the delivery of books to the warehouse keeper of the Stationers' Company for the use of the several libraries therein mentioned.	The Copyright Act, 1775.
17 Geo. 3. c. 57.	An Act for more effectually securing the property of prints to inventors and engravers by enabling them to sue for and recover penalties in certain cases.	The Prints Copyright Act, 1777.

Session and Chapter.	Title.	Short Title.
54 Geo. 3. c. 56.	An Act to amend and render more effectual an Act of His present Majesty for encouraging the art of making new models and casts of busts and other things therein mentioned, and for giving further encouragement to such arts.	The Sculpture Copyright Act, 1814.
3 Will. 4. c. 15.	An Act to amend the laws relating to Dramatic Literary Property.	The Dramatic Copyright Act, 1833.
5 & 6 Will. 4. c. 65.	An Act for preventing the publication of Lectures without consent.	The Lectures Copyright Act, 1835.
6 & 7 Will. 4. c. 69.	An Act to extend the protection of copyright in prints and engravings to Ireland.	The Prints and Engravings Copyright Act, 1836.
6 & 7 Will. 4. c. 110.	An Act to repeal so much of an Act of the fifty-fourth year of King George the Third, respecting copyrights, as requires the delivery of a copy of every published book to the libraries of Sion College, the four Universities of Scotland, and of the King's Inns in Dublin.	The Copyright Act, 1836.
5 & 6 Vict. c. 45.	An Act to amend the law of copyright.	The Copyright Act, 1842.
10 & 11 Vict. c. 95.	An Act to amend the law relating to the protection in the Colonies of works entitled to copyright in the United Kingdom.	The Colonial Copyright Act, 1847.
25 & 26 Vict. c. 68.	An Act for amending the law relating to copyright in works of the fine arts, and for repressing the commission of fraud in the production and sale of such works.	The Fine Arts Copyright Act, 1862.

THIRD SCHEDULE.[1]

ACTS REPEALED.

Session and Chapter.	Title.	Extent of Repeal.
7 & 8 Vict. c. 12.	An Act to amend the law relating to international copyright.	Sections fourteen, seventeen, and eighteen.
15 & 16 Vict. c. 12.	An Act to enable Her Majesty to carry into effect a convention with France on the subject of copyright, to extend and explain the International Copyright Acts, and to explain the Acts relating to copyright engravings.	Sections one to five both inclusive, and sections eight and eleven.
25 & 26 Vict. c. 68.	An Act for amending the law relating to copyright in works of the fine arts, and for repressing the commission of fraud in the production and sale of such works.	So much of section twelve as incorporates any enactment repealed by this Act.

[1] Repealed by Statute Law Revision Act, 1898.

THE REVENUE ACT, 1889.

52 AND 53 VICT. CAP. 42.

An Act to amend the Law relating to the Customs and Inland Revenue, and for other purposes connected with the Public Revenue and Expenditure.

[*26th August* 1889.]

1. The following goods shall from and after the passing of this Act, be included amongst the goods enumerated and described on the table of prohibitions and restrictions contained in section forty-two of the Customs Consolidation Act, 1876; namely, *Prohibition of importation of certain books, and compressed tobacco.*

    Books, first published in any country or state other than the United Kingdom, wherein, under the International Copyright Act, 1886, or any other Act, or any Order in Council made under the authority of any Act, there is a subsisting copyright in the United Kingdom, printed or reprinted in any country or state other than the country or state in which they were first published, and as to which the owner of the copyright, or his agent in the United Kingdom, has given to the Commissioners of Customs in the manner prescribed by section forty-four of the Customs Consolidation Act, 1876, a notice in such form and giving such particulars as those Commissioners require, and accompanied by a declaration as provided in that section. *49 & 50 Vict. c. 33.* *39 & 40 Vict. c. 36.*

ORDER IN COUNCIL

(Adopting Berne Convention).

London Gazette, Friday, December 2, 1887.

At the Court at Windsor, the 28th day of November, 1887.

Present :

The Queen's Most Excellent Majesty,

Lord President,

Lord Stanley of Preston,

Secretary Sir Henry Holland, Bart.

Whereas the Convention, of which an English translation is set out in the First Schedule to this Order, has been concluded between Her Majesty the Queen of the United Kingdom of Great Britain and Ireland, and the foreign countries named in this Order, with respect to the protection to be given by way of copyright to the authors of literary and artistic works :

And whereas the ratifications of the said Convention were exchanged on the fifth day of September, One thousand eight hundred and eighty-seven, between Her Majesty the Queen and the Governments of the foreign countries following, that is to say :

Belgium ; France; Germany ; Haïti ; Italy; Spain; Switzerland ; Tunis.

And whereas Her Majesty in Council is satisfied that the foreign countries named in this Order have made such provisions as it appears to Her Majesty expedient to require for the protection of authors of works first produced in Her Majesty's dominions.

Now, therefore, Her Majesty, by and with the advice of Her Privy Council, and by virtue of the authority committed to Her by the International Copyright Acts, 1844 to 1886, doth order; and it is hereby ordered, as follows:

1. The Convention as set forth in the First Schedule of this Order, shall, as from the commencement of this Order, have full effect throughout Her Majesty's dominions, and all persons are enjoined to observe the same.

2. This Order shall extend to the foreign countries following, that is to say:

Belgium; France; Germany; Haïti; Italy; Spain; Switzerland; Tunis.

and the above countries are in this Order referred to as the foreign countries of the Copyright Union, and those foreign countries together with Her Majesty's dominions, are in this Order referred to as the countries of the Copyright Union.

3. The author of a literary or artistic work which, on or after the commencement of this Order, is first produced in one of the foreign countries of the Copyright Union shall, subject as in this Order and in the International Copyright Acts, 1844 to 1886, mentioned, have as respects that work throughout Her Majesty's dominions the same right of copyright, including any right capable of being conferred by an Order in Council under section two or section five of the International Copyright Act, 1844, or under any other enactment, as if the work had been first produced in the United Kingdom, and shall have such right during the same period;

Provided that the author of a literary or artistic work shall not have any greater right or longer term of copyright therein, than that which he enjoys in the country in which the work is first produced.

The author of any literary or artistic work first produced before the commencement of this Order shall have the rights and remedies to which he is entitled under section six of the International Copyright Act, 1886.

4. The rights conferred by the International Copyright Acts, 1844 to 1886, shall, in the case of a literary or artistic work first produced in one of the foreign countries of the Copyright Union by an author who is not a subject or citizen of any of the said foreign countries, be limited as follows, that is to say, the author shall not be entitled to take legal proceedings in Her Majesty's dominions

for protecting any copyright in such work, but the publisher of such work shall, for the purpose of any legal proceedings in Her Majesty's dominions for protecting any copyright in such work, be deemed to be entitled to such copyright as if he were the author, but without prejudice to the rights of such author and publisher as between themselves.

5. A literary or artistic work first produced simultaneously in two or more countries of the Copyright Union shall be deemed for the purpose of copyright to have been first produced in that one of those countries in which the term of copyright in such work is shortest.

6. Section six of the International Copyright Act, 1852, shall not apply to any dramatic piece to which protection is extended by virtue of this Order.

7. The Orders mentioned in the Second Schedule to this Order are hereby revoked;

Provided that neither such revocation, nor anything else in this Order, shall prejudicially affect any right acquired or accrued before the commencement of this Order, by virtue of any Order hereby revoked, and any person entitled to such right shall continue entitled thereto, and to the remedies for the same, in like manner as if this Order had not been made.

8. This Order shall be construed as if it formed part of the International Copyright Act, 1886.

9. This Order shall come into operation on the sixth day of December, One thousand eight hundred and eighty-seven, which day is in this Order referred to as the commencement of this Order.

And the Lords Commissioners of Her Majesty's Treasury are to give the necessary orders accordingly.

C. L. PEEL.

ORDER IN COUNCIL

OF 7TH MARCH, 1898,

PUTTING IN FORCE THE ADDITIONAL ACT OF PARIS.

WHEREAS on the 9th day of September, 1886, a Convention (herein-after called the Berne Convention) with respect to the protection to be given by way of copyright to the authors of literary and artistic works was concluded between Her Majesty the Queen of the United Kingdom of Great Britain and Ireland and the foreign countries following, that is to say :—

Belgium, France, Germany, Hayti, Italy, Spain, Switzerland, and Tunis :

And whereas on the 5th day of September, 1887, the ratifications of the said Convention were duly exchanged between Her Majesty the Queen and the aforesaid countries :

And whereas by an Order in Council dated the 28th day of November, 1887, and made under the authority committed to Her Majesty by the International Copyright Acts, 1844 to 1886, Her Majesty was pleased to make provision for giving rights of copyright throughout Her Majesty's dominions to the authors of literary and artistic works first produced in any of the said foreign countries (therein referred to as the foreign countries of the Copyright Union), and otherwise giving effect throughout Her Majesty's dominions to the terms of the said Berne Convention, and an English translation of the said Convention was set out in the First Schedule to the Order in Council now in recital :

And whereas since the date of the said Order in Council hereinbefore recited, the foreign countries following, namely, Luxembourg, Monaco, Montenegro, and Norway, have acceded to the said Berne Convention, and by Orders in Council dated respectively the 10th day of August, 1888, the 15th day of October, 1889, the 16th day of May, 1893, and the 1st day of August, 1896, and made under the authority aforesaid, the provisions of the herein-before recited Order in Council of the 28th day of November, 1887, have been

D D D

extended to the last-mentioned foreign countries respectively, and the last-mentioned foreign countries, together with the foreign countries comprised in the said Order in Council of the 28th day of November, 1887, now constitute the foreign countries of the Copyright Union within the meaning of the said Order in Council:

And whereas an additional Act to the said Berne Convention, of which additional Act an English translation is set out in the Schedule to this Order, has been agreed upon between Her Majesty and the foreign countries next herein-after mentioned for the purpose of varying the provisions of the herein-before recited Convention of the 9th day of September, 1886:

And whereas on the 9th day of September, 1897, the ratifications of the said additional Act were exchanged between Her Majesty and the foreign countries following, that is to say:—

Germany, Belgium, Spain, France, Italy, Luxembourg, Monaco, Montenegro, Switzerland, and Tunis:

And whereas Her Majesty in Council is satisfied that the foreign countries named in the body of this Order, and parties to the said additional Act, have made such provisions as it appears to Her Majesty expedient to require for the protection of authors of works first produced in Her Majesty's dominions:

Now, THEREFORE, Her Majesty, by and with the advice of Her Privy Council, and by virtue of the authority committed to Her by the International Copyright Acts, 1844 to 1886, doth order, and it is hereby ordered as follows:—

1. The additional Act to the Berne Convention set forth in the Schedule to this Order shall, as from the commencement of this Order, have full effect throughout Her Majesty's dominions, and all persons are enjoined to observe the same.

2. This Order shall extend to the foreign countries following, that is to say:—

Germany, Belgium, Spain, France, Italy, Luxembourg, Monaco, Montenegro, Switzerland, and Tunis.

3. The fourth Article of the herein-before recited Order in Council of the 28th day of November, 1887, shall, as from the commencement of this Order, cease to apply to the foreign countries to which this Order extends.

4. The herein-before recited Order in Council of the 28th day of November, 1887, shall continue to be of full force and effect, save in so far as the same is varied by this Order.

5. Nothing contained in this Order shall prejudicially affect any right acquired or accrued before the commencement of this Order, by virtue of the said Order in Council of the 28th day of November, 1887, or otherwise, and any person entitled to such right shall continue entitled thereto, and to the remedies for the same in like manner as if this Order had not been made.

6. The author of any literary or artistic work first produced before the commencement of this Order shall have the rights and remedies to which he is entitled under section 6 of the International Copyright Act, 1886.

7. This Order shall be construed as if it formed part of the International Copyright Act, 1886.

8. This Order shall come into operation on the date hereof, which day is in this Order referred to as the commencement of this Order.

And the Lords Commissioners of Her Majesty's Treasury are to give the necessary orders herein accordingly.

C. L. PEEL.

SCHEDULE.

[The Schedule contains the Additional Act of Paris done into English. For this Act see the Berne Convention set out at the beginning of the Appendix.]

CANADIAN STATUTES.

THE CANADIAN REVISED STATUTES, 1886,
CHAPTER 62.

As amended by later Acts.

10 VICT. CAP 1.

Rev. Stat.
A.D. 1886.

An Act respecting Copyright.

HER Majesty, by and with the advice and consent of the Senate and House of Commons of Canada, enacts as follows:—

Short title.　　**1.** This Act may be cited as '*The Copyright Act*,' 38 V., c. 88, s. 31.

Interpretation.
'Minister.'　　**2.** In this Act, unless the context otherwise requires,—

(*a.*) The expression 'the Minister' means the Minister of Agriculture;

'Department.'　　(*b.*) The expression 'The Department' means the Department of Agriculture.

'Legal representatives.'　　(*c.*) The expression 'legal representatives' includes heirs, executors, administrators and assigns or other legal representatives.

Minister of Agriculture to keep registers of copyrights.　　**3.** The Minister of Agriculture shall cause to be kept, at the Department of Agriculture, books to be called the 'Registers of copyrights' in which proprietors of literary, scientific and artistic works or compositions, may have the same registered in accordance with the provisions of this Act.　38 V., c. 88, s. 1.

Who may obtain copyrights.　　**4.** Any person domiciled in Canada or in any part of the British possessions, or any citizen of any country which has an International copyright treaty with the United Kingdom, who is the author of any book, map, chart or musical composition, or of any _{Translation} Terms of original painting, drawing, statue, sculpture or photograph, or who copyright. invents, designs, etches, engraves or causes to be engraved, etched or made from his own design, any print or engraving, and the legal representatives of such person or citizen, shall have the sole and exclusive right and liberty of printing, reprinting, publishing, reproducing and vending such literary, scientific or artistic works or compositions, in whole or in part, and of allowing translations to be printed or reprinted and sold, of such literary works from one language into other languages, for the term of twenty-eight years, from the time of recording the copyright thereof in the manner hereinafter directed.[1] 38 V., c. 88, s. 4, *part.*

5. The condition for obtaining such copyright shall be that the said Condition for obtaining copy-literary, scientific or artistic works shall be printed and published ing copy-right. or reprinted and republished in Canada, or in the case of works of art that they shall be produced or reproduced in Canada, whether they are so published or reproduced for the first time, or contemporaneously with or subsequently to publication or production elsewhere ; but in no case shall the said sole and exclusive right and Proviso. liberty in Canada continue to exist after it has expired elsewhere ;

2. No immoral, licentious, irreligious, or treasonable or seditious Exception as to literary, scientific or artistic work, shall be the legitimate subject immoral works, etc. of such registration or copyright.[1] 38 V., c. 88, s. 4, *part.*

6. Every work of which the copyright has been granted and is Copyright in Canada subsisting in the United Kingdom, and copyright of which is not of British copyright secured or subsisting in Canada, under any Act of the Parliament works—on what condi-of Canada, or of the legislature of the late Province of Canada, or tions ob-tainable. of the legislature of any of the Provinces forming part of Canada, shall, when printed, and published, or reprinted and republished in Canada, be entitled to copyright under this Act ; but nothing in this Proviso. Act shall be held to prohibit the importation from the United Kingdom of copies of any such work lawfully printed there :

2. If any such copyright work is reprinted subsequently to its pub-As to foreign re-lication in the United Kingdom, any person who has, previously to prints im-ported the date of entry of such work upon the registers of copyright, im-before copy-ported any foreign reprints, may dispose of such reprints by sale right is

[1] The Canadian Coypright Act of 1889 (52 Vict., Cap. 29) purports to modify these sections, but the Act is at present without legal force.

obtained in Canada. or otherwise ; but the burden of proof of establishing the extent and regularity of the transaction shall, in such case, be upon such person.[1]   38 V., c. 88, s. 15.

Registration of work first published in separate articles in a periodical. **7.** Any literary work intended to be published in pamphlet or book form, but which is first published in separate articles in a newspaper or periodical, may be registered under this Act while it is so preliminarily published, if the title of the manuscript and a short analysis of the work are deposited at the department, and if every separate article so published is preceded by the words 'Registered in accordance with the Copyright Act,' but the work, when published in book or pamphlet form, shall be subject, also, to the other requirements of this Act.   38 V., c. 88, s. 10, *part.*

Anonymous books may be entered in the name of first publisher. **8.** If a book is published anonymously, it shall be sufficient to enter it in the name of the first publisher thereof, either on behalf of the un-named author, or on behalf of such first publisher, as the case may be.   38 V., c. 88, s. 25.

(As amended by Act of 1895.) Deposit of copies, etc., with the department. **9.** No person shall be entitled to the benefit of this Act, unless he has deposited at the department three copies of such book, map, chart, musical composition, photograph, print, cut or engraving, and in the case of paintings, drawings, statuary and sculpture, unless he has furnished a written description of such works of art; Record of copyright. and the Minister shall cause the copyright of the same to be recorded forthwith in a book to be kept for that purpose, in the manner adopted by him, or prescribed by the rules and forms made, from time to time, as herein provided.   38 V., c. 88, s. 7.

Copies to be sent to the Library of Parliament and to the British Museum. **10.**   The Minister shall cause one of such three copies of such book, map, chart, musical composition, photograph, print, cut or engraving, to be deposited in the Library of the Parliament of Canada and one in the British Museum.   38 V., c. 88, s. 8.

As to second and subsequent editions. **11.** It shall not be requisite to deliver any printed copy of the second or of any subsequent edition of any book unless the same contains vere important alterations or additions.   38 V., c. 88, s. 26.

Notice of copyright to appear on the work. **12.** No person shall be entitled to the benefit of this Act unless he gives information of the copyright being secured, by causing to

---

[1] The Canadian Copyright Act of 1889 (52 Vict., Cap. 29) purports to abolish this section, but the Act is at present without legal force.

be inserted in the several copies of every edition published during the term secured, on the title-page, or on the page immediately following, if it is a book,—or if it is a map, chart, musical composition, print, cut, engraving or photograph, by causing to be impressed on the face thereof, or if it is a volume of maps, charts, music, engravings or photographs upon the title-page or frontispiece thereof the following words, that is to say : ' Entered according to Act of the Parliament of Canada, in the year   , by A.B., at the Department of Agriculture ; ' but as regards paintings, drawings, statuary and sculptures, the signature of the artist shall be deemed a sufficient notice of such proprietorship.   38 V., c. 88, s. 9. *Form.*

Exception.

13. The author of any literary, scientific or artistic work or his legal representatives, may, pending the publication or republication thereof in Canada, obtain an interim copyright therefor by depositing at the department a copy of the title or a designation of such work, intended for publication or republication in Canada,—which title or designation shall be registered in an interim copyright register at the said department,—to secure to such author aforesaid or his legal representatives, the exclusive rights recognized by this Act, previous to publication or re-publication in Canada, but such interim registration shall not endure for more than one month from the date of the original publication elsewhere, within which period the work shall be printed or reprinted and published in Canada : *Interim copyright, how obtainable and its effect.*

Duration of interim copyright.

2. In every case of interim registration under this Act the author or his legal representatives shall cause notice of such registration to be inserted once in the *Canada Gazette.*   38 V., c. 88, s. 10, *part.* *Notice to be given.*

14. The application for the registration of an interim copyright, of a temporary copyright and of a copyright, may be made in the name of the author or of his legal representatives, by any person purporting to be the agent of such author or legal representatives ; and any damage caused by a fraudulent or an erroneous assumption of such authority shall be recoverable in any court of competent jurisdiction.   38 V., c. 88, s. 23, *part.* *Application for registration may be made through an agent.*

Punishment of pretended agents.

15. The right of an author of a literary, scientific or artistic work, to obtain a copyright, and the copyright when obtained, shall be assignable in law, either as to the whole interest or any part thereof, by an instrument in writing, made in duplicate, and which shall be *Copyright and right to obtain it to be assignable.*

registered at the department on production of both duplicates and payment of the fee hereinafter mentioned:

Duplicates, how disposed of. 2. One of the duplicates shall be retained at the department, and the other shall be returned, with a certificate of registration, to the person depositing it. 38 V., c. 88, s. 18.

Copyright to assignee of author. **16.** Whenever the author of a literary, scientific or artistic work or composition which may be the subject of copyright, has executed the same for another person, or has sold the same to another person for due consideration, such author shall not be entitled to obtain or to retain the proprietorship of such copyright, which is, by the said transaction, virtually transferred to the purchaser,— and such purchaser may avail himself of such privilege, unless a reserve of the privilege is specially made by the author or artist in a deed duly executed. 38 V., c. 88, s. 16.

Renewal of copyright, for what term and on what conditions. **17.** If, at the expiration of the said term of twenty-eight years, the author, or any of the authors, (when the work has been originally composed and made by more than one person), is still living, or if such author is dead and has left a widow or a child, or children living, the same sole and exclusive right and liberty shall be continued to such author, or to such authors still living, or, if dead, then to such widow and child or children, as the case may **Title to be again registered, &c.** be, for the further term of fourteen years; but in such case, within one year after the expiration of such term of twenty-eight years, the title of the work secured shall be a second time registered, and all other regulations herein required to be observed in regard to original copyrights shall be complied with in respect to such renewed copyright. 38 V., c. 88, s. 5.

Record of renewal to be published. **18.** In all cases of renewal of copyright under this Act, the author or proprietor shall, within two months from the date of such renewal, cause notice of such registration thereof to be published once in the *Canada Gazette*. 38 V., c. 88, s. 6.

Cases of conflicting claims in respect of copyright to be settled before a competent court. **19.** In case of any person making application to register as his own, the copyright of a literary, scientific or artistic work already registered in the name of another person, or in case of simultaneous conflicting applications or of an application made by any person other than the person entered as proprietor of a registered copyright, to cancel the said copyright, the person so applying shall be notified by the Minister that the question is one for the decision of a court of competent jurisdiction, and no further proceedings shall be had or taken by the Minister concerning the application until a judgment is produced maintaining, cancelling or otherwise deciding the matter:

2. Such registration, cancellation or adjustment of the said right shall then be made by the Minister in accordance with such decision. 38 V., c. 88, s. 19. *Action on decision.*

3. The Exchequer Court of Canada shall be a competent court within the meaning of this Act, and shall have jurisdiction to adjudicate upon any question arising under this section, upon information in the name of the Attorney General of Canada, or at the suit of any person interested. 53 V., c. 12; 54-55 V., c. 34. *Jurisdiction of Exchequer Court.*

20. Every person who, without the consent of the author or lawful proprietor thereof first obtained, prints or publishes, or causes to be printed or published, any manuscript not previously printed in Canada or elsewhere, shall be liable to the author or proprietor for all damages occasioned by such publication, and the same shall be recoverable in any court of competent jurisdiction. 38 V., c. 88, s. 3. *Liability of persons printing manuscripts without owner's consent.*

21. If a work copyrighted in Canada becomes out of print, a complaint may be lodged by any person with the Minister, who on the fact being ascertained to his satisfaction, shall notify the owner of the copyright of the complaint and of the fact; and if, within a reasonable time no remedy is applied by such owner, the Minister may grant a license to any person to publish a new edition or to import the work, specifying the number of copies and the royalty to be paid on each to the owner of the copyright. 38 V., c. 88, s. 22. *Provision for the case of a copyrighted work being out of print.*

License to print, &c.

22. The following fees shall be paid to the Minister before an application for any of the purposes herein mentioned is received, that is to say: *Fees payable under this Act.*

On registering a copyright	$1 00
On registering an interim copyright	0 50
On registering a temporary copyright	0 50
On registering an assignment	1 00
For a certified copy of registration	$0 50
On registering any decision of a court of justice, for every folio	0 50

On office
copies.

For office copies of documents not above mentioned, the following charges shall be made :—

> For every single or first folio, certified copy... $0 50
> For every subsequent hundred words, fractions under or not exceeding fifty, not being counted, and over fifty being counted for one hundred.................................... 0 25

Fees to be in
full for all
services.

2. The said fees shall be in full of all services performed under this Act by the Minister or by any person employed by him under this Act :

To form part
of Con.
Rev. Fund.

3. All fees received under this Act shall be paid over to the Minister of Finance and Receiver General, and shall form part of the Consolidated Revenue Fund of Canada :

No exemp-
tion from
payment of
fees.

4. No person shall be exempt from the payment of any fee or charge payable in respect of any services performed under this Act for such person, and no fee paid shall be returned to the person who paid it. 38 V., c. 88, s. 28.

Proviso: as
to scenery,
&c.

23. Nothing herein contained shall prejudice the right of any person to represent any scene or object, notwithstanding that there may be copyright in some other representation of such scene or object. 38 V., c. 88, s. 14.

As to news-
papers, &c.,
containing
portions of
British
copyright
works.

24. Newspapers and magazines published in foreign countries, and which contain, together with foreign original matter, portions of British copyright works republished with the consent of the author or his legal representatives, or under the law of the country where such copyright exists, may be imported into Canada. 38 V., c. 88, s. 10, *part.*

Clerical
errors, how
corrected.

25. Clerical errors which occur in the framing or copying of any instrument drawn by any officer or employee in or of the department shall not be construed as invalidating such instrument but when discovered they may be corrected under the authority of the Minister. 38 V., c. 88, s. 20.

Certified
copies and
extracts,—
their effect.

26. All copies or extracts certified, from the department, shall be received in evidence, without further proof and without production of the originals. 38 V., c. 88, s. 21.

27. The Minister may, from time to time, subject to the approval of the Governor in Council, make such rules and regulations, and prescribe such forms, as appear to him necessary and expedient for the purposes of this Act; and such regulations and forms, circulated in print for the use of the public, shall be deemed to be correct for the purposes of this Act; and all documents, executed and accepted by the Minister shall be held valid, so far as relates to all official proceedings under this Act. 38 V., c. 88, s. 2. *Minister to make rules, forms, &c.* *Their effect.*

28. Every person who wilfully makes or causes to be made any false entry in any of the registry books hereinbefore mentioned of the Minister, or who wilfully produces or causes to be tendered in evidence, any paper which falsely purports to be a copy of an entry in any of the said books, is guilty of a misdemeanour, and shall be punished accordingly. 38 V., c. 88, s. 24. *Making false entries, &c., to be a misdemeanour.*

29. Every person who fraudulently assumes authority to act as agent of the author or of his legal representative for the registration of a temporary copyright, an interim copyright, or a copyright, is guilty of a misdemeanour and shall be punished accordingly. 38 V., c. 88, s. 23, *part.* *Fraudulent assumption of authority, a misdemeanour.*

30. Every person who, after the interim registration of the title of any book according to this Act, and within the term herein limited, or after the copyright is secured and during the term or terms of its duration, prints, publishes, or reprints or republishes, or imports, or causes to be so printed, published or imported, any copy of any translation of such book without the consent of the person lawfully entitled to the copyright thereof, first had and obtained by assignment, or who, knowing the same to be so printed or imported, publishes, sells or exposes for sale, or causes to be published, sold or exposed for sale, any copy of such book without such consent, shall forfeit every copy of such book to the person then lawfully entitled to the copyright thereof; and shall forfeit and pay for every such copy which is found in his possession, either being printed or reprinted, published, imported or exposed for sale, contrary to the provisions of this Act, such sum, not exceeding one dollar and not less than ten cents, as the court determines,—which forfeiture shall be enforceable or recoverable in any court of competent jurisdiction; and moiety of such sum shall *Penalty for the infringement of copyright of a book.* *Recovery and application.*

belong to Her Majesty for the public uses of Canada, and the other moiety shall belong to the lawful owner of such copyright.   38 V., c. 88, s. 11.

Penalty for the infringement of copyright of a painting, &c.

31. Every person who, after the registering of any painting, drawing, statue or work of art, and within the term or terms limited by this Act, reproduces in any manner, or causes to be reproduced, made or sold, in whole or in part, any copy of any such work of art, without the consent of the proprietor, shall forfeit the plate or plates on which such reproduction has been made, and every sheet thereof so reproduced, to the 'proprietor of the copyright thereof; and shall also forfeit for every sheet of such reproduction published or exposed for sale, contrary to this Act, such sum, not exceeding one dollar and not less than ten cents as the court determines,—which forfeiture shall be enforceable or recoverable in any court of competent jurisdiction; and a moiety of such sum shall belong to Her Majesty for the public uses of Canada, and the other moiety shall belong to the lawful owner of such copyright.   38 V., c. 88, s. 12.

Recovery and application.

Penalty for the infringement of a print, chart, music, photograph, &c.

32. Every person who, after the registering of any print, cut or engraving, map, chart, musical composition, or photograph, according to the provisions of this Act, and within the term or terms limited by this Act, engraves, etches or works, sells or copies, or causes to be engraved, etched or copied, made or sold, either as a whole or by varying, adding to or diminishing the main design, with intent to evade the law, or who prints or reprints or imports for sale, or causes to be so printed or reprinted or imported for sale, any such map, chart, musical composition, print, cut or engraving, or any part thereof, without the consent of the proprietor of the copyright thereof first obtained as aforesaid, or who, knowing the same to be so reprinted, printed or imported without such consent, publishes, sells or exposes for sale, or in any manner disposes of any such map, chart, musical composition, engraving, cut, photograph or print, without such consent as aforesaid, shall forfeit the plate or plates on which such map, chart, musical composition, engraving, cut, photograph or print has been copied, and also every sheet thereof, so copied or printed as aforesaid, to the proprietor of the copyright thereof; and shall also forfeit, for every sheet of such map, musical composition, print, cut or engraving found in his possession, printed or published or exposed for sale, contrary to this Act, such sum, not exceeding one dollar and not less than ten cents, as the court determines,—which forfeiture Recovery and application. shall be enforceable or recoverable in any court of competent jurisdiction ; and a moiety of such sum shall belong to Her Majesty for the public uses of Canada, and the other moiety shall belong to the lawful owner of such copyright.   38 V., c. 88, s. 13.

33. Every person who has not lawfully acquired the copyright Penalty for falsely pretending to have copyright. of a literary, scientific or artistic work, and who inserts in any copy thereof printed, produced, reproduced or imported, or who impresses on any such copy, that the same has been entered according to this Act, or words purporting to assert the existence of a Canadian copyright in relation thereto, shall incur a penalty not exceeding three hundred dollars :

2. Every person who causes any work to be inserted in the Penalty for registering interim copyright without publishing. register of interim copyright and fails to print and publish or reprint and republish the same within the time prescribed, shall incur a penalty not exceeding one hundred dollars :

3. Every penalty incurred under this section shall be recoverable Recovery and application of penalties. in any court of competent jurisdiction ; and a moiety thereof shall belong to Her Majesty for the public uses of Canada, and the other moiety shall belong to the person who sues for the same. 38 V., c. 88, s. 17.

34. No action or prosecution for the recovery of any penalty Limitation of actions. under this Act, shall be commenced more than two years after the cause of action arises.   38 V., c. 88, s. 27.

THE CANADIAN COPYRIGHT ACT, 1900.

63 AND 64 VICT. CAP. 25.

An Act to amend the Copyright Act.

[18*th July* 1900.]

H ER Majesty, by and with the advice and consent of the Senate and House of Commons of Canada, enacts as follows :—

In case of license to reprint book copyrighted in U.K. or British possessions, Minister may prohibit importation of other reprints.

1. If a book as to which there is subsisting copyright under *The Copyright Act* has been first lawfully published in any part of Her Majesty's dominions other than Canada, and if it is proved to the satisfaction of the Minister of Agriculture that the owner of the copyright so subsisting and of the copyright acquired by such publication has lawfully granted a license to reproduce in Canada, from movable or other types, or from stereotype plates, or from electro-plates, or from lithograph stones, or by any process for facsimile reproduction, an edition or editions of such book designed for sale only in Canada, the Minister may, notwithstanding anything in *The Copyright Act*, by order under his hand, prohibit the importation, except with the written consent of the licensee, into Canada of any copies of such books printed elsewhere ; provided that two such copies may be specially imported for the *bonâ fide* use of any public free library or any university or college library, or for the library of any duly incorporated institution or society for the use of the members of such institution or society.

Suspension or revocation of prohibition.

2. The Minister of Agriculture may at any time in like manner, by order under his hand, suspend or revoke such prohibition upon importation if it is proved to his satisfaction that—

(*a*) the license to reproduce in Canada has terminated or expired ; or (*b*) the reasonable demand for the book in Canada is not sufficiently met without importation; or

(*c*) the book is not, having regard to the demand therefor in Canada, being suitably printed or published; or

(*d*) any other state of things exists on account of which it is not in the public interest to further prohibit importation.

3. At any time after the importation of a book has been pro- Failure of hibited under section 1 of this Act, any person resident or being licensee to supply book. in Canada may apply, either directly or through a bookseller or other agent, to the person so licensed to reproduce such book, for a copy of any edition of such book then on sale and reasonably obtainable in the United Kingdom or some other part of Her Majesty's dominions, and it shall then be the duty of the person so licensed, as soon as reasonably may be, to import and sell such copy to the person so applying therefor, at the ordinary selling price of such copy in the United Kingdom or such other part of Her Majesty's dominions, with the duty and reasonable forwarding charges added; and the failure or neglect, without lawful excuse, of the person so licensed to supply such copy within a reasonable time, shall be a reason for which the Minister may, if he sees fit, suspend or revoke the prohibition upon importation.

4. The Minister shall forthwith inform the Department of Customs Department Customs of any order made by him under this Act. to be notified.

5. All books imported in contravention of this Act may be seized Penalty for unlawful by any officer of Customs, and shall be forfeited to the Crown and importation. destroyed; and any person importing, or causing or permitting the importation, of any books in contravention of this Act shall, for each offence, be liable, upon summary conviction, to a penalty not exceeding one hundred dollars.

AMERICAN STATUTES.

CONSTITUTION, 1787.

[*17th September* 1787.]

ART. 1, SEC. 8. The Congress shall have power :......To promote the progress of science and useful arts, BY SECURING FOR LIMITED TIMES TO AUTHORS and inventors THE EXCLUSIVE RIGHT TO THEIR respective WRITINGS and discoveries.

AMERICAN REVISED STATUTES, 1873.

TIT. 60, CAP. 3, 1874, AS AMENDED BY ACTS OF 1874, 1882, 1891, 1893, 1895, AND 1897.

Copyright records.

SECTION 4948. All records and other things relating to copyrights and required by law to be preserved, shall be under the control of the Librarian of Congress, and kept and preserved in the Library of Congress.

Register of copyrights.

[The Appropriation Act approved February 19, 1897, provides for the appointment of a '*Register of Copyrights, who shall, on and after July first, eighteen hundred and ninety-seven, under the direction and supervision of the Librarian of Congress, perform all the duties relating to copyrights, and shall make weekly deposits with the Secretary of the Treasury, and make monthly reports to the Secretary of the Treasury and to the Librarian of Congress, and shall, on and after July first, eighteen hundred and ninety-seven, give bond to the Librarian of Congress, in the sum of twenty thousand dollars, with approved sureties, for the faithful discharge of his duties.*']

SEC. 4949. The seal provided for the office of the Librarian of Congress shall be the seal thereof, and by it all records and papers issued from the office and to be used in evidence shall be authenticated. Seal of the copyright office.

SEC. 4950. The Appropriation Act approved February 19, 1897, provides: 'The Librarian of Congress shall on and after July first, eighteen hundred and ninety-seven, give bond, payable to the United States, in the sum of twenty thousand dollars, with sureties approved by the Secretary of the Treasury, for the faithful discharge of his duties according to law.' Bond of Librarian of Congress.

SEC. 4951. The Librarian of Congress shall make an annual report to Congress of the number and description of copyright publications for which entries have been made during the year. Annual report to Congress of copyright publications.

SEC. 4952. The author, inventor, designer, or proprietor of any book, map, chart, dramatic or musical composition, engraving, cut, print, or photograph or negative thereof, or of a painting, drawing, chromo, statue, statuary, and of models or designs intended to be perfected as works of the fine arts, and the executors, administrators, or assigns of any such person shall, upon complying with the provisions of this chapter, have the sole liberty of printing, reprinting, publishing, completing, copying, executing, finishing, and vending the same; and, in the case of a dramatic composition, of publicly performing or representing it, or causing it to be performed or represented by others. And authors or their assigns shall have exclusive right to dramatize or translate any of their works, for which copyright shall have been obtained under the laws of the United States. Author, etc., and his assigns shall have sole liberty of printing and vending. Authors shall have exclusive right to dramatize or translate.

In the construction of this act the words 'engraving,' 'cut,' and 'print,' shall be applied only to pictorial illustrations or works connected with the fine arts, and no prints or labels designed to be used for any other articles of manufacture shall be entered under the copyright law, but may be registered in the Patent Office. And the Commissioner of Patents is hereby charged with the supervision and control of the entry or registry of such prints or labels, in conformity with the regulations provided by law as to copyright of prints, except that there shall be paid for recording the title of any print or label, not a trade-mark, six dollars, which Definition of 'engraving,' 'cut,' and 'print.' Labels.

shall cover the expense of furnishing a copy of the record, under the seal of the Commissioner of Patents, to the party entering the same.   [This Section has now been altered by an Act of 1905.]

Copyright term 28 years.

SEC. 4953. Copyrights shall be granted for the term of twenty-eight years from the time of recording the title thereof, in the manner hereinafter directed.

Renewal for second term of 14 years.

Publication of renewal.

SEC. 4954. The author, inventor, or designer, if he be still living, or his widow or children, if he be dead, shall have the same exclusive right continued for the further term of fourteen years, upon recording the title of the work or description of the article so secured a second time, and complying with all other regulations in regard to original copyrights, within six months before the expiration of the first term.   And such person shall, within two months from the date of said renewal, cause a copy of the record thereof to be published in one or more newspapers, printed in the United States, for the space of four weeks.

Assignment of copyrights.

SEC. 4955. Copyrights shall be assignable in law by any instrument of writing, and such assignment shall be recorded in the office of the Librarian of Congress within sixty days after its execution; in default of which it shall be void as against any subsequent purchaser or mortgagee for a valuable consideration, without notice.

Deposit of title or description.

Deposit of two copies.

SEC. 4956. No person shall be entitled to a copyright unless he shall, on or before the day of publication, in this or any foreign country, deliver at the office of the Librarian of Congress, or deposit in the mail within the United States, addressed to the Librarian of Congress, at Washington, District of Columbia, a printed copy of the title of the book, map, chart, dramatic or musical composition, engraving, cut, print, photograph, or chromo, or a description of the painting, drawing, statue, statuary, or a model or design for a work of the fine arts, for which he desires a copyright; nor unless he shall also, not later than the day of the publication thereof, in this or any foreign country, deliver at the office of the Librarian of Congress, at Washington, District of Columbia, or deposit in the mail, within the United States, addressed to the Librarian of Congress, at Washington, District of Columbia, two copies of such copyright book, map, chart, dramatic or musical composition, engraving, chromo, cut, print, or photograph, or in case of a painting, drawing, statue, statuary, model, or design for a work of the fine arts, a photograph of the same: Provided, That in the case of a book, photograph, chromo, or lithograph, the two copies of the same required to be delivered or deposited as above, shall be printed from type set within the limits of the United States, or from plates made therefrom, or from negatives, or drawings on stone made within the limits of the United States, or from transfers made therefrom. During the existence of such copyright the importation into the United States of any book, chromo, lithograph, or photograph, so copyrighted, or any edition or editions thereof, or any plates of the same not made from type set, negatives, or drawings on stone made within the limits of the United States, shall be, and is hereby prohibited, except in the cases specified in paragraphs 512 to 516, inclusive, in section two of the act entitled, an act to reduce the revenue and equalize the duties on imports and for other purposes, approved October 1, 1890[1]; and except in the case of persons purchasing for use and not for sale, who import subject to the duty thereon, not more than two copies of such book at any one time; and, except in the case of newspapers and magazines, not containing in whole or in part matter copyrighted under the provisions of this act, unauthorized by the author, which are hereby exempted from prohibition of importation:

Provided, nevertheless, That in the case of books in foreign

Printed from type set within the United States.

Prohibition of importation.

Exceptions to prohibition of importation.

Newspapers and magazines may be imported.

Books in foreign

---

[1] The paragraphs cited above are from the list of articles allowed to be imported free of duty, and are as follows:

512. Books, engravings, photographs, bound or unbound etchings, maps and charts, which shall have been printed and bound or manufactured more than twenty years at the date of importation.

513. Books and pamphlets printed exclusively in languages other than English; also books and music, in raised print, used exclusively by the blind.

514. Books, engravings, photographs, etchings, bound or unbound, maps and charts imported by authority or for the use of the United States or for the use of the Library of Congress.

515. Books, maps, lithographic prints, and charts, specially imported, not more than two copies in any one invoice, in good faith, for the use of any society incorporated or established for educational, philosophical, literary, or religious purposes, or for the encouragement of the fine arts, or for the use or by order of any college, academy, school, or seminary of learning in the United States, subject to such regulations as the Secretary of the Treasury may prescribe.

516. Books, or libraries, or parts of libraries, and other household effects of persons or families from foreign countries, if actually used abroad by them not less than one year, and not intended for any other person or persons, nor for sale. (51st Congress, 1st session, chap. 1244: 26 Statutes at Large, p. 604.)

languages, of which only translations in English are copyrighted, the prohibition of importation shall apply only to the translation of the same, and the importation of the books in the original language shall be permitted.

SEC. 4957. The Librarian of Congress shall record the name of such copyright book, or other article, forthwith in a book to be kept for that purpose, in the words following: ' Library of Congress, to wit: Be it remembered that on the   day of A. B., of   hath deposited in this office the title of a book, (map, chart, or otherwise, as the case may be, or description of the article), the title or description of which is in the following words, to wit: (here insert the title or description,) the right whereof he claims as author, (originator, or proprietor, as the case may be,) in conformity with the laws of the United States respecting copyrights. C. D., Librarian of Congress.' And he shall give a copy of the title or description under the seal of the Librarian of Congress, to the proprietor, whenever he shall require it.

SEC. 4958. The Librarian of Congress shall receive from the persons to whom the services designated are rendered, the following fees: 1. For recording the title or description of any copyright book or other article, fifty cents. 2. For every copy under seal of such record actually given to the person claiming the copyright, or his assigns, fifty cents.[1] [3. For recording and certifying any instrument of writing for the assignment of a copyright, one dollar. 4. For every copy of an assignment, one dollar.] All fees so received shall be paid into the treasury of the United States: Provided, That the charge for recording the title or description of any article entered for copyright, the production of a person not a citizen or resident of the United States, shall be one dollar, to be paid as above into the treasury of the United States, to defray the expenses of lists of copyrighted articles as hereinafter provided for.

[1] The clauses in section 4958 inclosed within brackets are made to accord with section 2 of the Amending Act of June 18, 1874, which reads as follows: ' That for recording and certifying any instrument of writing for the assignment of a copyright, the Librarian of Congress shall receive from the persons to whom the service is rendered, one dollar ; and for every copy of an assignment, one dollar ; said fee to cover, in either case, a certificate of the record, under seal of the Librarian of Congress ; and all fees so received shall be paid into the Treasury of the United States.' (43rd Congress, 1st session, chap. 301: 18 Statutes at Large, pp. 78-79.)

And it is hereby made the duty of the Librarian of Congress to *Catalogue of title entries.* furnish to the Secretary of the Treasury copies of the entries of titles of all books and other articles wherein the copyright has been completed by the deposit of two copies of such book printed from type set within the limits of the United States, in accordance with the provisions of this act, and by the deposit of two copies of such other article made or produced in the United States; and the Secretary of the Treasury is hereby directed to prepare and print, at intervals of not more than a week, catalogues of such title-entries for distribution to the collectors of customs of the United States and to the postmasters of all post offices receiving foreign mails, and such weekly lists, as they are issued, shall be furnished *Subscription, 5 dols.* to all parties desiring them, at a sum not exceeding five dollars per *a year.* annum; and the Secretary and the Postmaster General are hereby *Secretary of Treasury* empowered and required to make and enforce such rules and regu- *and Postmaster* lations as shall prevent the importation into the United States, *General to* except upon the conditions above specified, of all articles prohibited *prevent importation.* by this act.

Sec. 4959. The proprietor of every copyright book or other *Deposit of copy of* article shall deliver at the office of the Librarian of Congress, or *subsequent edition.* deposit in the mail, addressed to the Librarian of Congress, at Washington, District of Columbia, a copy of every subsequent edition wherein any substantial changes shall be made: Provided, *New editions of foreign* however, That the alterations, revisions, and additions made to *books may* books by foreign authors, heretofore published, of which new *be copyrighted.* editions shall appear subsequently to the taking effect of this act, shall be held and deemed capable of being copyrighted as above provided for in this act, unless they form a part of the series in course of publication at the time this act shall take effect.

Sec. 4960. For every failure on the part of the proprietor of *Failure to deposit* any copyright to deliver, or deposit in the mail, either of the *copies.* published copies, or description, or photograph, required by sections 4956 and 4959, the proprietor of the copyright shall be liable to a penalty of twenty-five dollars, to be recovered by the Librarian of Congress, in the name of the United States, in an action in the nature of an action of debt, in any district court of the United States within the jurisdiction of which the delinquent may reside or be found.

The following act in relation to the deposit of copies was approved March 3, 1893: 'That any author, inventor, designer, or proprietor of any book, or other article entitled to copyright, who has heretofore failed to deliver in the office of the Librarian of Congress, or in the mail addressed to the Librarian of Congress, two complete copies of such book, or description or photograph of such article, within the time limited by title sixty, chapter three, of the Revised Statutes relating to copyrights, and the acts in amendment thereof, and has complied with all other provisions thereof, who has, before the first day of March, anno Domini eighteen hundred and ninety-three, delivered at the office of the Librarian of Congress, or deposited in the mail addressed to the Librarian of Congress two complete printed copies of such book, or description or photograph of such article, shall be entitled to all the rights and privileges of said title ninty, chapter three, of the Revised Statutes and the acts in amendment thereof.'

SEC. 4961. The postmaster to whom such copyright book, title, or other article is delivered, shall, if requested, give a receipt therefor; and when so delivered he shall mail it to its destination.

SEC. 4962. No person shall maintain an action for the infringement of his copyright unless he shall give notice thereof by inserting in the several copies of every edition published, on the title-page, or the page immediately following, if it be a book; or if a map, chart, musical composition, print, cut, engraving, photograph, painting, drawing, chromo, statue, statuary, or model or design intended to be perfected and completed as a work of the fine arts, by inscribing upon some visible portion thereof, or of the substance on which the same shall be mounted, the following words, viz: 'Entered according to act of Congress, in the year ———, by A. B., in the office of the Librarian of Congress, at Washington'; or, at his option, the word 'Copyright,' together with the year the copyright was entered, and the name of the party by whom it was taken out, thus: 'Copyright, 18—, by A. B.'

That manufacturers of designs for molded decorative articles, tiles, plaques, or articles of pottery or metal subject to copyright may put the copyright mark prescribed by section forty-nine hundred and sixty-two of the Revised Statutes, and acts additional thereto, upon the back or bottom of such articles, or in such other place upon them as it has heretofore been usual for manufacturers of such articles to employ for the placing of manufacturers, merchants, and trade-marks thereon.

SEC. 4963. Every person who shall insert or impress such notice, False claim of copyright or words of the same purport, in or upon any book, map, chart, (penalty for). dramatic or musical composition, print, cut, engraving or photograph, or other article, whether such article be subject to copyright or otherwise, for which he has not obtained a copyright, or shall knowingly issue or sell any article bearing a notice of a United States copyright which has not been copyrighted in this country; or shall import any book, photograph, chromo, or lithograph or other article bearing such notice of copyright or words of the same purport, which is not copyrighted in this country, shall be liable to a penalty of one hundred dollars, recoverable one-half for the Penalty, 100.00 dols. person who shall sue for such penalty and one-half to the use of the United States; and the importation into the United States of any book, chromo, lithograph, or photograph, or other article bearing such notice of copyright, when there is no existing copyright thereon in the United States, is prohibited; and the circuit courts of the United States sitting in equity are hereby authorized to enjoin the issuing, publishing, or selling of any article marked or imported in violation of the United States copyright laws, at the suit of any person complaining of such violation: Provided, That this Act shall not apply to any importation of or sale of such goods or articles brought into the United States prior to the passage hereof.

SEC. 4964. Every person who, after the recording of the title of Printing, or importany book and the depositing of two copies of such book as provided ing, etc., book withby this act, shall, contrary to the provisions of this act, within out perthe term limited, and without the consent of the proprietor of the prohibited. copyright first obtained in writing, signed in presence of two or more witnesses, print, publish, dramatize, translate, or import, or, knowing the same to be so printed, published, dramatized, translated, or imported, shall sell or expose to sale any copy of such book, shall forfeit every copy thereof to such proprietor, and shall also forfeit and pay such damages as may be recovered in a civil action by such proprietor in any court of competent jurisdiction.

Printing,
etc., map,
chart,
dramatic or
musical
composition
or art work
without
permission
prohibited.

SEC. 4965. If any person, after the recording of the title of any map, chart, dramatic or musical composition, print, cut, engraving, or photograph, or chromo, or of the description of any painting, drawing, statue, statuary, or model or design intended to be perfected and executed as a work of the fine arts, as provided by this act, shall, within the term limited, contrary to the provisions of this act, and without the consent of the proprietor of the copyright first obtained in writing, signed in presence of two or more witnesses, engrave, etch, work, copy, print, publish, dramatize, translate, or import, either in whole or in part, or by varying the main design, with intent to evade the law, or, knowing the same to be so printed, published, dramatized, translated, or imported, shall sell or expose to sale any copy of such map or other article, as aforesaid, he shall forfeit to the proprietor all the plates on which the same shall be copied, and every sheet thereof, either copied or printed, and shall further forfeit one dollar for every sheet of the same found in his possession, either printing, printed, copied, published, imported, or exposed for sale ; and in case of a painting, statue, or statuary, he shall forfeit ten dollars for every copy of the same in his possession,

Penalty for
infringe-
ment of
copyright of
photograph.

or by him sold or exposed for sale : Provided, however, That in case of any such infringement of the copyright of a photograph made from any object not a work of fine arts, the sum to be recovered in any action brought under the provisions of this section shall be not less than one hundred dollars, nor more than five thousand dollars,

Penalty for
infringe-
ment of
copyright of
a work of
the fine arts.

and : Provided, further, That in case of any such infringement of the copyright of a painting, drawing, statue, engraving, etching, print, or model or design for a work of the fine arts, or of a photograph of a work of the fine arts, the sum to be recovered in any action brought through the provisions of this section shall be not less than two hundred and fifty dollars, and not more than ten thousand dollars. One-half of all the foregoing penalties shall go to the proprietors of the copyright and the other half to the use of the United States.

Penalty for
performing
or represent-
ing dramatic
or musical
composition
without
consent.

SEC. 4966. Any person publicly performing or representing any dramatic or musical composition for which a copyright has been obtained, without the consent of the proprietor of said dramatic or musical composition, or his heirs or assigns, shall be liable for damages therefor, such damages in all cases to be assessed at such sum, not less than one hundred dollars for the first and fifty dollars for every subsequent performance, as to the court shall appear to be just. If the unlawful performance and representation be willful and for profit, such person or persons shall be guilty of a misdemeanor and upon conviction be imprisoned for a period not exceeding one year. Any injunction that may be granted upon hearing after notice to the defendant by any circuit court in the United States, or by a judge thereof, restraining and enjoining the performance or representation of any such dramatic or musical composition may be served on the parties against whom such injunction may be granted anywhere in the United States, and shall be operative and may be enforced by proceedings to punish for contempt or otherwise by any other circuit court or judge in the United States; but the defendants in said action, or any or either of them, may make a motion in any other circuit in which he or they may be engaged in performing or representing said dramatic or musical composition to dissolve or set aside the said injunction upon such reasonable notice to the plaintiff as the circuit court or the judge before whom said motion shall be made shall deem proper; service of said motion to be made on the plaintiff in person or on his attorneys in the action. The circuit courts or judges thereof shall have jurisdiction to enforce said injunction and to hear and determine a motion to dissolve the same, as herein provided, as fully as if the action were pending or brought in the circuit in which said motion is made. *Injunction.*

Suit for injunction.

The clerk of the court, or judge granting the injunction, shall, when required so to do by the court hearing the application to dissolve or enforce said injunction, transmit without delay to said court a certified copy of all the papers on which the said injunction was granted that are on file in his office. *Certified copy of papers.*

SEC. 4967. Every person who shall print or publish any manuscript whatever, without the consent of the author or proprietor first obtained shall be liable to the author or proprietor for all damages occasioned by such injury. *Penalty for printing MS. without consent.*

SEC. 4968. No action shall be maintained in any case of forfeiture or penalty under the copyright laws, unless the same is commenced within two years after the cause of action has arisen. *No action shall be maintained after two years.*

SEC. 4969. In all actions arising under the laws respecting copyrights the defendant may plead the general issue, and give the special matter in evidence. *Defendant may plead the general issue.*

Circuit and district courts may grant injunctions.

SEC. 4970. The circuit courts, and district courts having the jurisdiction of circuit courts, shall have power, upon bill in equity, filed by any party aggrieved, to grant injunctions to prevent the violation of any right secured by the laws respecting copyrights, according to the course and principles of courts of equity, on such terms as the court may deem reasonable.

Jurisdiction of courts in copyright cases.

[Revised Statutes, title 13, THE JUDICIARY, provides as follows : Chap. 7 (sec. 629). The circuit courts shall have original jurisdiction as follows : . . . Ninth. Of all suits at law or in equity arising under the patent or copyright laws of the United States. (Rev. Stat., 1878, pp. 110, 111.) Chap. 11 (sec. 699). A writ of error may be allowed to review any final judgment at law, and an appeal shall be allowed from any final decree in equity hereinafter mentioned, without regard to the sum or value in dispute : First. Any final judgment at law or final decree in equity of any circuit court, or of any district court acting as a circuit court, or of the supreme court of the District of Columbia, or of any Territory, in any case touching patent-rights or copyrights. (Rev. Stat., 1878, p. 130.) Chap. 12 (sec. 711). The jurisdiction vested in the courts of the United States in the cases and proceedings hereinafter mentioned, shall be exclusive of the courts of the several States : . . . Fifth. Of all cases arising under the patent-right or copyright laws of the United States. (Rev. Stat., 1878, pp. 134, 135.) Chap. 18 (sec. 972). In all recoveries under the copyright laws, either for damages, forfeiture, or penalties, full costs shall be allowed thereon. (Rev. Stat., 1878, p. 183.)]

Act of March 3, 1891. Special provisions.

The Chace Act, approved March 3, 1891 (51st Congress, 1st session, chap. 565 : 26 Statutes at Large, pp. 1106-1110), in addition to amendments of sections 4952, 4954, 4956, 4958, 4959, 4963, 4964, 4965, and 4967 of the Revised Statutes, which have been incorporated into the above text, provides further as follows :

Each volume requires separate entry.

'That for the purpose of this act each volume of a book in two or more volumes, when such volumes are published separately, and the first one shall not have been issued before this act shall take effect, and each number of a periodical shall be considered an independent publication, subject to the form of copyrighting as above.' (Sec. 11.)

'That this act shall go into effect on the first day of July, anno Domini eighteen hundred and ninety-one.' (Sec. 12.)

'That this act shall only apply to a citizen or subject of a foreign state or nation when such foreign state or nation permits to citizens of the United States of America the benefit of copyright on substantially the same basis as its own citizens; or when such foreign state or nation is a party to an international agreement which provides for reciprocity in the granting of copyright, by the terms of which agreement the United States of America may at its pleasure become a party to such agreement. The existence of either of the conditions aforesaid shall be determined by the President of the United States, by proclamation made from time to time as the purposes of this act may require.' (Sec. 13.)[1]

When amendments of March 3, 1891, apply to foreigners.

[An Act providing for the public printing and binding and the distribution of public documents, (January 12, 1895, 53d Congress, 3d session, chap. 23, sec. 52: 28 Statutes at Large, p. 608,) provides as follows: The Public Printer shall sell, under such regulations as the Joint Committee on Printing may prescribe, to any person or persons who may apply additional or duplicate stereotype or electrotype plates from which any Government publication is printed, at a price not to exceed the cost of composition, the metal and making to the Government and ten per centum added: Provided, That the full amount of the price shall be paid when the order is filed: And provided, further, That no publication reprinted from such stereotype or electrotype plates and no other Government publication shall be copyrighted.]

Government publications shall not be copyrighted.

[1] *List of Countries with which the United States have established Copyright relations.*—July 1, 1891—Belgium, France, Great Britain and her possessions, and Switzerland. April 15, 1892—Germany. October 31, 1892.—Italy. May 8, 1893—Denmark. July 20, 1893—Portugal. July 10, 1895—Spain. February 27, 1896—Mexico. May 25, 1896—Chile. Oct. 19, 1899—Costa Rica. Nov. 20, 1899—Netherlands (Holland) and possessions.

AN ACT APPROVED MARCH 3RD, 1905, TO AMEND
SEC. 4952 OF THE REVISED STATUTES.

Be it enacted by the Senate and House of Representatives of the United States of America in Congress assembled, That section forty-nine hundred and fifty-two of the Revised Statutes be, and the same is hereby, amended so as to read as follows:

'SEC. 4952. The author, inventor, designer, or proprietor of any book, map, chart, dramatic or musical composition, engraving, cut, print, or photograph, or negative thereof, or of a painting, drawing, chromo, statue, statuary, and of models or designs intended to be perfected as works of the fine arts, and the executors, administrators, or assigns of any such person shall, upon complying with the provisions of this chapter, have the sole liberty of printing, re-printing, publishing, completing, copying, executing, finishing, and vending the same; and, in the case of a dramatic composition, of publicly performing or representing it, or causing it to be performed or represented by others. And authors or their assigns shall have exclusive right to dramatize or translate any of their works for which copyright shall have been obtained under the laws of the United States.

'Whenever the author or proprietor of a book in a foreign language, which shall be published in a foreign country before the day of publication in this country, or his executors, administrators, or assigns, shall deposit one complete copy of the same, including all maps and other illustrations, in the Library of Congress, Washington, District of Columbia, within thirty days after the first publication of such book in a foreign country, and shall insert in such copy, and in all copies of such book sold or distributed in the United States, on the title page or the page immediately following, a notice of the reservation of copyright in the name of the proprietor, together with the true date of first publication of such book, in the following words: " Published   , nineteen hundred and   . Privilege of copyright in the United States reserved under the Act approved   , nineteen hundred and five, by   ," and shall within twelve months after the first publication of such book in a foreign country, file the title of such

book and deposit two copies of it in the original language or, at
his option, of a translation of it in the English language, printed
from type set within the limits of the United States, or from plates
made therefrom, containing a notice of copyright, as provided by
the copyright laws now in force, he and they shall have during the
term of twenty-eight years from the date of recording the title of
the book or of the English translation of it, as provided for above,
the sole liberty of printing, reprinting, publishing, vending, translating and dramatizing the said book : *Provided*, That this Act
shall only apply to a citizen or subject of a foreign State or nation
when such foreign State or nation permits to citizens of the United
States of America the benefit of copyright on substantially the
same basis as to its own citizens.'

A MODEL LAW.

Drafted by the International Literary and Artistic Association at Paris, 1900.[1]

Art. 1.

The author of an intellectual work has the exclusive right to make it public and to reproduce it by any process, under any form and for any purpose.

Thus all written or oral manifestations of thought, dramatic, musical and choregraphic works, and all works of the graphic and plastic arts are protected whatever their merit, their use and their destination. This applies to works which have appeared in newspapers or periodical magazines.

Official documents of public authorities and judicial decisions cannot be the subjects of an exclusive right.

Art. 2.

The exercise of copyright is not subjected to the accomplishment of any conditions or formalities.

Art. 3.

The exclusive right provided for by Art. 1 continues for eighty years after the death of the author for the benefit of his representatives.

Art. 4.

The right in anonymous works continues for eighty years dating from the first lawful publication of the work. The right shall be exercised by the publisher so long as the true author has not made himself known.

When the author has made himself known before the expiration of the period, the right shall continue for the life of the author and eighty years after his death.

Works published in the name of an artificial person are assimilated to anonymous works.

[1] Translated from *Le Droit d'Auteur*, 1900, pp. 105, 106.

Art. 5.

Collaborators shall have equal rights over the joint work, in the absence of stipulations to the contrary.

The rights of the representatives of a predeceased collaborator shall subsist until the expiration of a period of eighty years from the death of the last surviving collaborator.

In default of representatives of one of the collaborators, his share shall accrue to the other collaborators or to their representatives.

Art. 6.

Whoever causes to be published a posthumous work of which he has the right to dispose enjoys an exclusive right of reproduction during eighty years, dating from such first publication.

Works which, in the lifetime of the author, have not received, with the consent of the author, a reasonable publicity, having regard to their nature, are considered as posthumous works.

Art. 7.

Every reproduction, whole or partial, made without the consent of the author or of his representatives, is illicit.

This applies to translation, and also to public representation and performance.

Reproductions which involve abridgements, additions and alterations—such as adaptations, transformations of dramas into novels, and, *vice versâ*, of novels into dramas, arrangements of music, reproduction by another art, illustration of a work—are also illicit.

The same applies to reproductions of musical works by mechanical musical instruments.

Art. 8.

The author, once his work is published, cannot prohibit analyses and short quotations which, made with a critical, controversial or educational object, bear an indication of the name of the author and of the source.

Speeches delivered in deliberative assemblies or in public meetings may be reproduced for the purpose of giving information or of discussion.

Art. 9.

The right of reproduction is independent of the right of property over the material object (manuscript or original); the assignment of the material object, therefore, does not of itself involve an assignment of the right of reproduction, and *vice versâ*.

The assignment of the rights belonging to the author (right to publish, to represent, to execute, to translate, to illustrate, etc.) is always to be interpreted restrictively.

Art. 10.

The author of every intellectual work has the right to compel recognition of his authorship and to take legal proceedings against anyone who assumes to himself that capacity.

An author who has assigned his rights of reproduction retains the right to sue infringers, to supervise the reproduction of his work, and to oppose all modifications made without his consent.

An author who has assigned the material object constituting his work has the right to prevent any public exhibition of the work if it has been modified without his consent.

Art. 11.

After the death of the author the preservation of the rights provided for by Art. 10 belongs to his heirs, in default of a special agent designed by him.

Art. 12.

No modification is to be made in a work, even by the heirs or representatives of the author, unless this modification is openly brought to the knowledge of the public.

Art. 13.

For every injury done to the right of the author, as defined by the present model law, an action for damages lies; if the injury has been done knowingly it may become the subject of a penal action.

Art. 14.

The same applies to the forgery of the name of an author, as well as to the fraudulent imitation of his signature or of any distinctive sign, whether a monogram or another, adopted by him.

Art. 15.

The author or his representatives may require the police authorities to execute the seizure of objects involved in a charge of infringement and that of plates, moulds or matrices and other utensils, having served or destined to serve specially for the manufacture of the said objects.

If a reproduction or performance is the subject of complaint, the authors can cause proceedings, under the same forms, to be taken for the seizure of the whole of the receipts.

The publisher or the producer (*entrepreneur*) of plays (*spectacles*) must give documentary proof of the previous consent of the author or his representatives.

The confiscation of infringing objects, in the same way as that of plates, moulds, or matrices and other utensils having served or intended to serve specially for the manufacture of the said objects, will be ordered for the benefit of the author or his representatives.

In case of unlawful performance or representation, the receipts seized shall be awarded to the plaintiff.

Art. 16.

The law applies to all authors, whatever may be their nationality and in whatever place the work may have been first published.

F F F

THE PERIODS OF PROTECTION GRANTED IN VARIOUS COUNTRIES.

Country.	Ordinary Period of Copyright.	Period of Translating Right.	Photographs.
Austria.	The life of the author *plus* thirty years.	Five years from publication of a translation with right reserved, upon condition that such publication takes place within three years from the publication of the original.	Ten years from publication or from the making of the negative.
Belgium.	The life of the author *plus* fifty years.	See Column II.	See Column II.
Denmark.	The life of the author *plus* fifty years.	Ordinary period of copyright for the right of translating into a dialect (Danish, Norwegian, or Swedish). If the work has been translated into several languages within a period of ten years, with regard to such languages translating right subsists during the ordinary period of copyright. In any other case, the period is ten years from the end of the year in which the original work was first published.	Five years.

Country.	Ordinary Period of Copyright.	Period of Translating Right.	Photographs.
France.	The life of the author *plus* fifty years.	See Column II.	See Column II.
Germany.	The life of the author *plus* thirty years; but in any case until ten years after the first publication of the literary or musical work.	See Column II.	Five years from publication of the first copies or the making of the negative.
Great Britain.	For literary works, the life of the author *plus* seven years; but in any case until forty-two years from first publication. For works of sculpture, fourteen years from making or from first publication, with a prolongation for a further fourteen years if the artist is still living and has retained his right in his own hands. For paintings, drawings, and photographs, the life of the author *plus* seven years. For engravings, twenty-eight years from first publication.	For British works, probably the ordinary period of copyright. For foreign works admitted to the benefits of the English law: the period of translating right is assimilated to the ordinary period of copyright, provided that, within ten years from the end of the year in which the original work was first published, an authorised English translation thereof has appeared.	The life of the author *plus* seven years.
Haïti.	The life of the author and that of his widow. Twenty years from the death of the author for the benefit of his children, or, if there are no children, for the benefit of his other heirs.	See Column II.	—

Country.	Ordinary Period of Copyright.	Period of Translating Right.	Photographs.
Holland.	Fifty years from first publication, counting from the date of the certificate of deposit; but in any case for the whole period of the author's life, if he has not transferred his right.	For unpublished works and oral lectures, the ordinary period of copyright; for printed works, five years from the date of the certificate of deposit, if a translation has been printed and deposited within three years from the publication of the original.	——
Hungary.	The life of the author *plus* fifty years.	Five years from the first publication of an authorised translation, which must appear within three years from the publication of the original work; or, if the work is intended for the stage, within six months from the publication of the original.	Five years from the expiration of the year in which the original work first appeared, or the original of the edition was obtained.
Italy.	*1st period:* the author's life, or forty years at least from publication. *2nd period:* An additional forty years, during which anyone may publish the work upon paying a royalty of five per cent. of the nominal price.	Ten years from publication.	——
Japan.	The life of the author *plus* thirty years.	The life of the author *plus* thirty years, provided that a translation is published within ten years from the publication of the original work.	Ten years from first publication, or from the making of the negative.

Country.	Ordinary Period of Copyright.	Period of Translating Right.	Photographs.
Luxemburg.	The life of the author *plus* fifty years.	The life of the author *plus* fifty years, provided that a translation is published within ten years from the first publication of the original work.	——
Monaco.	The life of the author *plus* fifty years.	See Column II.	See Column II.
Norway.	The life of the author *plus* fifty years.	Ordinary period of copyright for the right of translating into one of the three Scandinavian languages. If the work is published simultaneously or, at the latest, within one year, in several languages, the ordinary period of copyright, as regards such languages. Ten years from the end of the year of the first publication of the original work, in other cases.	Five years from the end of the year of the first publication of the photographic reproduction, unless the photographer dies first before this period has expired.
Portugal.	The life of the author *plus* fifty years.	Ordinary period of copyright. But if the author is a foreigner, then the period is reduced to ten years, and this only on condition that a translation is begun within three years from publication of the original work.	——

Country.	Ordinary Period of Copyright.	Period of Translating Right.	Photographs.
Russia.	The life of the author *plus* fifty years.	Anyone may translate at will; except in the case of books for which special scientific researches have been necessary, which bear a reservation of the right of translation, and of which a translation has appeared within two years from the authorisation of the publication of the original work.	———
Spain.	The life of the author *plus* eighty years. In case of transfer *inter vivos* and of the existence of heirs at law, the copyright reverts to the latter twenty-five years after the author's death, for a period of twenty-five years.	See Column II.	See Column II.
Sweden.	For ordinary works, the life of the author *plus* fifty years. For works of art, the life of the author *plus* ten years.	The life of the author *plus* fifty years for the right of translation into one of the three Scandinavian languages; for the right of translation into other languages, ten years from the first publication of the original work.	Five years from the year in which the photograph has been first published.
Switzerland.	The life of the author *plus* thirty years.	Ordinary period of copyright, provided that the author publishes a translation within five years from the first publication of the original work.	Five years from registration, which is to be carried out within three months.

Country.	Ordinary Period of Copyright.	Period of Translating Right.	Photographs.
Tunis.	The life of the author *plus* fifty years.	Ordinary period of copyright.	——
United States.	Twenty-eight years from the registration of the title. An additional period of fourteen years is allowed for the benefit of the author, his widow, or his children, if the title is entered afresh and two copies are deposited six months before the expiration of the first period.	See Column II.	See Column II.

INTERNATIONAL PROTECTION OF THE WORKS OF FOREIGN AUTHORS PUBLISHED ABROAD.

i. Countries not granting any International Protection.

Abyssinia.
Afghanistan.
Bulgaria.
Corea.
Liberia.

Morocco.
Oman.
Persia.
Russia.

Servia.
Siam.
Turkey.
Venezuela.

ii. Countries protecting foreign works only through the medium of Treaties.

Argentine Republic.
Austria.
Brazil.
Chili.
China.
Congo.
Cuba.
Dominican Republic.

Ecuador.
Germany.
Guatemala.
Haïti.
Honduras.
Hungary.
Japan.
Montenegro.

Paraguay.
Peru.
Salvador.
San Marino.
The Netherlands.
Tunis.
Uruguay.

iii. Countries protecting foreign works without special Treaty, upon condition of Reciprocity.

Bolivia.
Columbia.
Costa-Rica.
Denmark.
Great Britain.
Greece.

Italy.
Mexico.
Monaco.
Nicaragua.
Norway.
Portugal.

Roumania.
Spain.
Sweden.
Switzerland.
United States.

iv. Countries protecting foreign works without special Treaty, and without condition of Reciprocity.

Belgium.
France.
Luxemburg.
Egypt (under decisions of the mixed tribunals, based upon equity).

SYNOPSES AND TABLES

THE BERNE CONVENTION, 1886,

As Modified by the Additional Act of Paris, 1896,

Creating an International Copyright Union.

Art. i. International Copyright Union formed by contracting States.

ii. Authors of one country of Union shall enjoy in other Union countries same rights as natives, if conditions and formalities of country of origin of work have been fulfilled, but for no longer period than that granted in country of origin.

Posthumous works are protected.

iii. Authors not subjects of any Union country will be protected for works first published in Union country.

iv. 'Literary and artistic works' comprises every production in literature, science, and art which can be published by any mode of reproduction whatever.

v. Exclusive right of translation belongs to author of original work, but ceases if not exercised within 10 clear years.

vi. A lawful translation is protected in its text as an original work, but when translating right has fallen into public domain one translator cannot prevent others translating.

vii. Serial novels in Union newspapers or magazines cannot be reproduced. This applies to other articles in newspapers or magazines where reservation is made ; in magazines a general notice of reservation is sufficient.

In the absence of prohibition such articles may be reproduced on condition that the source is acknowledged.

No prohibition can apply to news, articles of political discussion, etc.

viii. Extent to which extracts may be taken for educational and scientific works is to be decided by each country for itself.

ix. Performing right in dramatic and dramatico-musical works, published or unpublished, is protected.

Exclusive right of translation of dramas carries with it exclusive right of performing translations.

In unpublished music and, if expressly reserved, in published music also, the performing right is protected.

x. Such adaptations, arrangements, etc., as are substantially reproductions and not new original works are unlawful.

xi. Author's name on work or, where the latter is anonymous or pseudonymous, the publisher's, is *primâ facie* proof of title. But the Courts may require a certificate showing that formalities of country of origin have been fulfilled.

xii. Piratical copies may be seized in Union countries where original work is protected.

xiii. The Convention does not take away the domestic rights of each State to regulate and restrain publication, circulation, etc.

xiv. With reservations, the Convention applies to all works not in public domain in country of origin at time of its coming into force (see Final Protocol, par. 4).

xv. Union countries may make special treaties *inter se*, provided that these give to authors rights which are more extended than, or others not repugnant to, those given by Union.

xvi. 'Office of the International Union for the Protection of Literary and Artistic Works' established, and placed under the authority of the Swiss Government.

xvii. Revisions will be considered at Conferences; alterations, to be binding on the Union, require unanimous consent.

xviii. Any country which grants the requisite copyright protection will on request be admitted to the Union.

xix. Union countries may, at any time, accede for any or all of their possessions.

xx. Any country may retire with a year's notice, the Convention remaining in force for the other countries.

[xxi. This Convention shall be ratified within one year at Berne.]

Additional Article. Existing treaties which give to authors rights more extended than, or otherwise not repugnant to, those given by the Convention are not affected.

Final Protocol. i. (*a*) Works of architecture themselves, as well as their plans, and (*b*) photographs, shall be protected in countries where they are deemed respectively works capable of copyright ; authorised photographs of works of art enjoy protection as long as the principal works from which they are taken. (Add to iv.)

ii. Choregraphic works are protected in countries where such works are deemed dramatico-musical. (Add to ix.)

iii. It is no infringement of musical copyright to make or sell mechanical musical instruments which reproduce copyright airs.

iv. The operation of Art. xiv. respecting works which have not fallen into the public domain in the country of origin at the time of the Convention's coming into force is to be regulated by special conventions or, where none, by domestic law.

The stipulations of Art. xiv. apply equally to the exclusive right of translation.

Chief Modifications effected in the Berne Convention by the Act of Paris.

Art. ii. The Convention of 1886 was silent as to posthumous works.

iii. Under the Convention of 1886, where author of work published in Union country was not a subject of Union country, rights were conferred only on the publisher.

v. This Article formerly read : 'Authors belonging to any country of the Union, or their lawful representatives, shall enjoy in the other countries the exclusive right of making or authorizing translations of their works until the expiration of 10 years from the publication of the original work in one of the Union countries.'

vii. In the 1886 Convention no special mention was made of serial novels ; and no acknowledgment of unprohibited takings was required.

Final Protocol. i. Architectural works were not included in the 1886 Convention.

iv. Before the Act of Paris no reference was made in this section to the exclusive right of translation.

INTERNATIONAL COPYRIGHT ACT, 1886 [49 & 50 Vict. c. 33].

ENABLES HER MAJESTY TO ACCEDE TO THE BERNE CONVENTION (DRAFTED SEPTEMBER 1885), AND TO ISSUE ORDERS IN COUNCIL GRANTING PROTECTION TO FOREIGN WORKS.

I. 3. The International Copyright Acts, 1844 to 1886, to be construed together.

II. 2. Where author is ineligible under O.C.* for protection in U.K.† publisher may act in his stead.

   3. No greater rights in U.K. for foreigner than given in country of origin of work.

III. 1. Where simultaneous publication, O.C. may decide which is country of origin.

   2. And this decides rights in U.K.

IV. 1. No registration or delivery required, unless so provided by O.C.

   2. O.C. will be made only where foreign country has made proper provision for protection of our works.

V. 1. Production and importation into U.K. of unauthorised translation are to be prevented, just as of the original work.

   2. But if no authorised translation in English appears within ten clear years, this prohibition ceases.

   3. Lawfully produced translations are protected as if original works.

   4. Re-enacts unrepealed sections of I.C.‖ Act 1852, of which s. 7 allows translation of political articles with acknowledgment of source, and of others with acknowledgment unless copyright specially reserved, and s. 9 extends remedies given by 1842 Act against importation of piratical copies of British works, to importation of unauthorised translations.

VI. O.C. protects existing works, but does not prejudice subsisting and valuable interests in works lawfully produced in U.K.

VII. Foreign copyright may be proved by duly authenticated document.

VIII. 1. The Copyright Acts shall apply to works first produced in a British Possession as if first produced in U.K., except that—
   (a) Registration not required in U.K. if Possession has official register.
   (b) No delivery of copy of book necessary.

   2. Where official register kept in a Possession a duly authenticated extract is to be admitted as proof of contents.
As regards British Possessions and copyright works first produced therein:—

   3. Where there has been local legislation O.C. may modify the Copyright Acts.

   4. Nothing in the Copyright Acts shall prevent enactments respecting copyright within the limits of such Possession of works first produced therein.

IX. The I.C. Acts shall apply to British Possessions as if part of U.K., except that where an O.C. is made respecting a foreign country they may be excluded, if desirable, by the same or some subsequent O.C., existing rights being left unprejudiced.

X. 1. (a) New O.C. may revoke or alter previous O.C., (b) saving existing rights.

XI. Defines:—'literary and artistic works,' 'author,' 'performed,' 'produced' (= 'published or made, performed or represented'), 'book published in numbers,' 'treaty,' 'British Possessions.'

XII. Repeals :—I.C. Act 1844, ss. 14, 17, 18 ; I.C. Act 1852, ss. 1 to 5, 8, 11 ; Fine Arts Copyright Act 1862, s. 12 (part).
   (a) Till revoked, O.C.'s made under repealed Acts continue in force, (b) saving existing rights.

---

* O.C. = Order in Council.　　+ U.K. = United Kingdom.　　‖ I.C. = International Copyright.

LITERARY COPYRIGHT ACT 1842 [5 & 6 Vict. c. 45]

(IN SO FAR AS IT RELATES TO BOOKS).

Gives to authors and their assigns sole and exclusive liberty throughout British Dominions (s. 29) of multiplying copies of any "book" (*i.e.* every "volume, sheet of letterpress, map, chart or plan separately published" (s. 2)). Such copyright being personal property (s. 25).

Duration .	Author's life + 7 years, *or* 42 years from publication. **s. 3.** In periodicals, above term to publisher in his periodical, only if contribution paid for. After 28 years, "the right of publishing in a separate form shall revert to the Author, for the remainder of the term." **s. 18.**
Requirements .	Registration [a condition precedent to suing (**s. 24**)], giving 1. Title, 2. Time of publication, 3. Names and Abodes of Publisher and Proprietor. (Fee 5*s.*) **ss. 11-14.** Delivery of a copy [whether copyright desired or not] to British Museum and on demand to four other Libraries. Penalty in default (£5 + value of copy). **ss. 6-10.**
Assignment .	May be made of whole or part of copyright by Registered Proprietor by an entry giving Name and Abode of Assignee. [Stamp not necessary on assignment by entry, as is required where assignment by mere writing.] **ss. 11, 13.**
Licences .	Must be in writing. **s. 15.** May be entered in Register. **s. 11.**
Infringement .	Without proprietor's written consent— i. To print for sale or exportation. **s. 15.** ii. To import for sale or hire. **ss. 15, 17.** iii. Knowingly to sell or expose to, or possess for, sale or hire books so printed or imported. **ss. 15, 17.**
Remedies .	I. Damages for i., ii., iii., by Special Action on the Case. **s. 15.** II. Forfeiture of unlawful copies to Proprietor and damages for their detention or conversion (in cases i., ii., iii.). **s. 23.** III. Destruction by Customs of copies unlawfully imported and penalty of £10 + twice value of imported copies on conviction before two J.P.'s (ii. and iii. only). **s. 17.** [Injunctions not mentioned in this Act, but practice same as under Fine Arts Copyright Act 1852 s. 9.]
Limitation .	Action to be brought within 12 months of offence. **s. 26.**

In these tables the mark ‡ indicates what is no longer in force.

FINE ARTS COPYRIGHT ACT 1862 [25 & 26 VICT., c. 68].

Gives to authors of paintings, drawings, and photographs wherever made, being British subjects or resident in the Britisl. dominions, sole copyright—which previously they had not ;

Deals with the fraudulent production and sale of such works.

Duration . .	Author's life + 7 years. **s. 1.**
Requirements .	Copyright (and Assignment) must be registered. (Fee 1*s.*) [No action or penalty for "anything done before Registration."] Entry requires : 1. Date of Assignment ; 2. Names of Parties ; 3. Names and Abodes of Assignee and Author ; 4. Short description of work. **s. 4.**
Assignment .	When work first changes hands, copyright is lost unless, by signed agreement, reserved to artist or passed to buyer. In commissions, copyright passes to buyer without writing. **s. 1.** Must be in writing and signed. **s. 3.** Must be registered. **s. 4.**
Licence . .	Must be in writing and signed. **s. 3.**
Infringements .	Without consent— i. To repeat or imitate work or its design, for sale, hire, exhibition, or distribution ; ii. Knowingly to import into United Kingdom, publish, sell, let to hire, exhibit, or distribute such copies. **s. 6.**
Remedies . .	I. Forfeit to Proprietor for each offence £10 (or less), + unlawful copies. **s. 6.** [Penalties and copies recoverable by Action or before two J.P.'s]. **s. 8.** II. Damages by Action on the Case for infringements—even if committed unknowingly—and for retention or conversion of unlawful copies. **s. 11.** III. Injunction, Inspection or Account by order of Superior Court. **s. 9.** IV. Detention by Customs of piratical copies after notice from proprietor. **s. 10.**
Limitation .	*Act silent.*
Fraudulent Productions and Sales.	i. To fraudulently affix any name, initials, etc., upon any work ; ii. To fraudulently dispose of or exhibit work bearing wrong name ; iii. To fraudulently dispose of copy of work (whether copyright or not) as work of author of original ; iv. After author has parted with work, to alter it during his life without his consent and knowingly to sell such altered work or copies of it as unaltered. **s. 7.**
Penalties for above Frauds.	Offender shall forfeit :— i. To person aggrieved—£10 (or less) or double price at which spurious works offered for sale ; ii. To person whose name wrongly used or his representatives, —the spurious works. These penalties are not incurred unless artist whose name is wrongly used was alive within twenty years preceding offence. **s. 7.**

ENGRAVINGS (AND PRINTS) COPYRIGHT ACTS.

1734 (8 Geo. II. c. 13) Protects those who from their *own* works and inventions design and engrave any print.
1766 (7 Geo. III. c. 38) Extends protection to all who engrave prints whether from original designs or not.
1777 (17 Geo. III. c. 57) Secures property by giving Action for Damages in certain cases.
1836 (6 & 7 Will. IV. c. 69) Extends above Acts to Ireland.
1852 (15 & 16 Vict. c. 12, s. 14) Expressly includes lithographs and all prints taken by mechanical processes as engravings.
1862 (25 & 26 Vict. c. 68, s. 8) Makes recovery of penalties and forfeited copies easier.

Duration . .	1734	‡ 14 years from publication. **s. 1.**‡
	1766	28 years from publication. **s. 6.**
Requirements .	1734	Name of Proprietor and Date of publication on each plate and print. **s. 1.**
	1777	To be "engraved, etched, drawn, or designed" in Great Britain. **s. 1.**
	1836	Extends protection of 1777 Act to works "published" in Great Britain or Ireland. **s. 2.**
Assignment .		*Acts silent.*
Licence . .	1734	‡ Requires writing signed and presence of two witnesses. **s. 2.**‡
	1777	Requires writing signed and *attestation* of two witnesses. **s. 1.**
	1836	Re-enacts provisions of 1777. **s. 2.**
Infringement .	1734	Unless plate be purchased or consent obtained as above :— i. To copy and sell ; ii. To print or import for sale ; iii. Knowingly to publish, sell, or dispose of. **s. 1.**
	1777	Defines infringements as 1734, but omits "knowingly." **s. 1.**
	1836	"To engrave, etch, or publish" without consent (not necessarily "for sale"). **s. 2.**
Remedies . .	1734	Forfeit plates and sheets to Proprietor for destruction. **s. 1.** Penalty 5s. for each print found in offender's possession, half to Crown, half to informer. **s. 1.**
	1766	Re-enacts above remedies. **s. 5.**
	1777	Damages, by Action on the Case ‡ with double costs.‡ **s. 1.** [Double costs taken away 1861.]
	1862	Penalties and forfeited copies recoverable by Action or before two J.P.'s. **s. 8.**
Limitation .	1734	‡ Three months from offence discovered. **s. 4.**‡
	1766	Six months from offence committed. **s. 5.**

COPYRIGHT (MUSICAL AND DRAMATIC) ACTS—*PERFORMING RIGHTS.*

1833 (3 Will. IV. c. 15) Protects performing rights at "places of Dramatic entertainment" of Dramatic Property ("Tragedy, Comedy, Play, Opera, Farce, or any other Dramatic piece or entertainment").

1842 (5 & 6 Vict. c. 45) enlarges (s. 20) the protection given to Dramatic pieces, including scenic and musical entertainments (s. 2), and extends it to Music (s. 20).

1882 (45 & 46 Vict. c. 40) } (Music only) protect public and tenants of Halls against vexatious proceedings.
1888 (51 & 52 Vict. c. 17) }

	Year	DRAMA	MUSIC
Duration	1833	‡ Unprinted drama, indefinite protection. **s. 1.**‡ ‡‡ Printed drama, Author's life *or* 28 years. **s. 1.**‡‡	
	1842		Author's life + 7 years, *or* 42 years from first performance. **s. 20.**
Requirements	1842	Same as for books, **s. 20**, except registration not *necessary* **s. 24** [incorporating 1833].	Exactly as for books. **s. 20.**
	1842	Unprinted drama and music may be registered by entry of—1. Title. 2. Name and Abode of Author and Proprietor. 3. Time and Place of first performance. **s. 20.**	
	1882		Notice on title-page to be given if right reserved. **s. 1.**
Assignment	1842	Performing rights do not pass in an assignment of the book unless the intention be expressed "in the Register." **s. 22.**	
Licence	1833	Must be in writing. **s. 2.**	
	1842		Must be in writing. **s. 20.**
	1842	May be registered. **ss. 20, 11.**	
Infringement	1833	‡ Performance at "place of dramatic entertainment" without written consent. **s. 2.**‡	
	1842	Performance at *any* place without written consent, as Proprietor has "*sole* liberty of representing." **ss. 20, 21, 24.**	
Remedies	1833	Fine of not less than 40s., or profits of performance, or loss to proprietor of drama. ‡ and double costs. ‡ **s. 2.**	
	1842	Re-enacts remedies of 1833 for dramas, and extends them to music. **s. 21.** [5 & 6 Vict. c. 97, s. 2, substituted "indemnity" for double costs.]	
	1882	Where plaintiff recovers 40s. or less for performance of music published before this Act, costs in Judge's discretion. **s. 4.**	
	1888	Gives Judge absolute discretion as to penalty, damages, **s. 1**, and costs, **s. 2**, *whenever* music published.	
Limitation	1833	Action to be brought within 12 months of offence. **s. 3.**	
	1842	Re-enacts provisions of 1833 for dramas, and extends them to music. **s. 26.**	

INDEX.

V.

Value, a property feature of copyright, 17.

Vaud, Swiss Canton, 403 *n.*

Venice :
granted first recorded privilege to author, 1491, 28.

Vevey, International Congress at, 1901, 178.

Vienna, Congress of German authors at, 1893, 369, 433 *n.*

Vienna Treaty, 511, 703-708.
English author, rights of, under, 572-586.
English Colonies, how far accepted by, 511, 708.
text, 703-708

Vocabulary, International, the question of, 183.

Vœux : *see* **Recommendations.**

Von Bar :
high Court fees for aliens, 104.
on domicil, 188, 189.
on French Decree of 1852, 106.
on most favoured nation clause, 143.
on protection of trade-interest, 95.
on universal protection, 109.
reciprocity an unsound principle, 123, 133.
theory of potential publication as to unpublished works, 317.

Von Savigny on possession, 14.

W.

Wagner's works and Austrian Act of 1893, 67 *n.*

'Wall Act'—Musical Copyright Act, 1882, 300, 543, 816.
tabular summary of, 816.

War, effect of, on commercial treaties, 144.

Washington, Pan-American Conference at, 1890, 473.

Westbury, Lord, in *Routledge v. Low*, 491.

William of Holland, subsidised piratical reprinting, 36.

Works protected :
under American law, 646.
under Canadian law, 627 *n.*
under English International Copyright Act, 1886, 519-521.
under the Berne Convention, 334-385.
architecture, 383-385.
authorised photographs of protected works of art, 361-363.
choregraphic works, 380-383.
'literary and artistic works,' definition of works protected (Art. 4), 334, 338-354.
five classes, 338.
newspaper and magazine articles, 364-372.
photographs, 373-380.
translations, 357-361.
see also **Architecture, Artistic works, Choregraphic works, Drawings, Engravings, Newspaper and Magazine articles, Paintings, Photographs, Sculpture, Translations, etc., etc.**

'Works published' :
defined by Interpretative Declaration, 313-317, 451, 542 *n.*

Wurtemburg, 28, 66.
protection by privileges, 1836, 28.

Y.

Yates, J., in *Millar v. Taylor*, 16, 19.

Z.

Zola, *l'Assommoir*, 41.

Zollverein, The, 66 *n.*